Religious Traditions of North Carolina

Religious Traditions of North Carolina

Histories, Tenets and Leaders

Edited by W. GLENN JONAS, JR.,
FOR THE NORTH CAROLINIANA SOCIETY

Foreword by James W. Clark, Jr., and Willis P. Whichard

NORTH CAROLINIANA SOCIETY IMPRINTS, NO. 57

McFarland & Company, Inc., Publishers
Jefferson, North Carolina

LIBRARY OF CONGRESS CATALOGUING-IN-PUBLICATION DATA

Names: Jonas, W. Glenn, Jr. (William Glenn), 1959– editor. |
North Caroliniana Society.
Title: Religious traditions of North Carolina : histories, tenets and leaders
/ edited by W. Glenn Jonas, Jr. for the North Caroliniana Society ;
foreword by James W. Clark Jr. and Willis P. Whichard.
Description: Jefferson, North Carolina : McFarland & Company, Inc.,
Publishers, 2018. | Includes bibliographical references and index.
Identifiers: LCCN 2018026966 | ISBN 9781476676463
(illustrated case : alk. paper) ∞
Subjects: LCSH: North Carolina—Religion.
Classification: LCC BL2527.N67 R45 2018 | DDC 200.9756—dc23
LC record available at https://lccn.loc.gov/2018026966

BRITISH LIBRARY CATALOGUING DATA ARE AVAILABLE

ISBN (print) 978-1-4766-7646-3
ISBN (ebook) 978-1-4766-3470-8

Front cover images © 2018 iStock

Printed in the United States of America

*McFarland & Company, Inc., Publishers
Box 611, Jefferson, North Carolina 28640
www.mcfarlandpub.com*

To
H.G. Jones,
former director, North Carolina Division
of Archives and History;
former curator, North Carolina Collection,
University of North Carolina Library, Chapel Hill;
founder and guiding spirit of the North Caroliniana Society

Table of Contents

Foreword

JAMES W. CLARK, JR., *and* WILLIS P. WHICHARD

As stated by its founder, H.G. Jones, to whom this work is dedicated, the North Caroliniana Society is "committed to the understanding and appreciation of the entire sweep of the state's cultural heritage." Jones was one of three incorporators of the Society in 1975. He served as its secretary-treasurer for most of its existence. While formal leadership of the Society has passed to others, Jones remains involved and is the moving spirit behind its endeavors.

That the idea for this publication was his will not surprise those familiar with the Society and its work. The Society has no religious position. Its members and friends represent numerous faith traditions, or perhaps none at all. It is undeniable, however, that religion is an integral part of "the state's cultural heritage." A full-orbed understanding of that heritage thus is impossible apart from at least basic comprehension of major faith traditions and their role in the life of the state. Hence, a North Caroliniana Society publication on the subject fits the Society's express purpose well.

A work of this nature inevitably presents problems of inclusion and exclusion. The Society readily acknowledges the omission of traditions that arguably merited inclusion. It believes, however, that the included groups cover the considerable majority of the state's many faith perspectives. If there are serious omissions, it invites others to address them.

The Society was most fortunate to secure the services of W. Glenn Jonas, Jr.—then chair of the Department of Religion, now Associate Dean of the College of Arts and Sciences at Campbell University—as editor of the project. Jonas is an accomplished teacher and scholar in the field of religion, and his knowledge and experience were essential to the success of the endeavor. We have benefited greatly from a close working relationship with Jonas, and with one another, throughout this endeavor. We are also indebted to our copyeditor, Jane Hobson Snyder.

The Society's H.G. Jones Fund has financed this publication. The contributions to that fund from Jones, and from others in his honor, are gratefully acknowledged.

We welcome this addition to the Society's Imprints Series, and we invite the reader's attention to this significant aspect of the state's cultural heritage.

James W. Clark, Jr., is a professor emeritus of English at North Carolina State University and president of the North Caroliniana Society with degrees from UNC–Chapel Hill and Duke. A literary historian, he has special intersts in North Carolina writers, especially Thomas Wolfe and Paul Green, having served as president of the Thomas Wolfe Society and the Paul Green Foundation.

Willis P. Whichard is the only person who has served in both houses of the North Carolina General Assembly and on the state's Court of Appeals and the Supreme Court. He was dean of the Campbell University School of Law from 1999 to 2006 and from 1994 to 2014 president of the North Caroliniana Society.

Introduction

W. Glenn Jonas, Jr.

The settlers who drifted into the Carolinas in the seventeenth century brought with them their religion. The colony's charter of 1663 granted by Charles II to eight Lords Proprietors provided for the Anglican Church to become the established religion in the colony but allowed toleration of other believers. Quakers, Presbyterians, and Baptists soon joined the Anglicans in developing a diverse mix of faith communities in the various Carolina settlements.[1] By 1775, the population of the colony grew to approximately 200,000 as immigrants from Wales, Scotland, Switzerland, France, and Germany joined the English; and an assortment of other religious traditions began to populate the Carolina settlements.[2] By 1800, the primarily Christian landscape of North Carolina also included Native American and African religions.[3]

Diversity consistently characterized North Carolina religion in the early years, but not all religions received equal treatment. The original state constitution adapted in 1776 provided for the free exercise of religion, prohibited the establishment of a state church, and created a religious test for holding public office. The document also prevented any member of the clergy from holding office and required that all office holders must affirm a belief in God and the truth of the Protestant religion.[4] These mandates were not always strictly enforced. In 1809, Jacob Henry, a Jew from Carteret County, survived a challenge to his state house election after a determination that the constitutional test was not applicable to the legislature. Later, William Gaston, a Roman Catholic from New Bern, enjoyed a long and distinguished career as a public servant in both chambers of the legislature, the United States Congress, and finally as a state supreme court judge.[5]

The state constitution's religious test provision remained in force until the Constitutional Convention of 1835 changed the wording from "Protestant" to "Christian," a change still discriminatory toward non–Christian religious traditions practiced in the state.[6] In 1868, the provision was changed again to require only a belief in God to hold public office. This requirement remains in the North Carolina Constitution to date.[7]

North Carolinians continue to value religion. In 2014, the Pew Research Center conducted a comprehensive, nationwide Religious Landscape Study.[8] The study provides interesting data about North Carolinians: 77 percent identify themselves as Christian in the survey, with 3 percent identifying with other religions; 20 percent profess no religion; 73 percent of North Carolinians indicate an "absolutely certain" belief in God; 62 percent say that religion is important in their lives, although only 39 percent attend weekly religious services; 66 percent reveal that they pray daily. Interestingly, however, when it comes to ethical decisions, only 41 percent of North Carolinians say they look to religion for guidance, whereas another 41 percent respond that "common sense" is their determinative factor. More surprisingly, 36 percent believe "there are clear standards for what is right and wrong," whereas 62 percent believe that "right and wrong depends on the situation."[9]

A study completed in 2000 found that there are 86 religious groups in the state with 3,651,416 participants, about half of the state's population at that time.[10] In the essays that follow, we open a window into the diverse religious traditions in North Carolina. Although a history of each religious tradition in the state is not represented, we believe that the following essays reflect most of the major faith communities present.

Fifteen scholars representing different faith perspectives accepted my invitation to contribute essays to this collection. Two authors joined in a collaborative effort, and the other thirteen produced separate essays. Each of the fourteen essays presents the religious tenets, special locales as well as events, and selected leaders who have sustained particular religious traditons in North Carolina.

Lydia Huffman Hoyle begins this collection with an overview of the Baptist faith in North Carolina. Her essay does an excellent job of capturing the diversity that exists within this tradition. In the second essay, Sandy Dwayne Martin highlights black cultural practices and beliefs within several Christian denominations in the state. Jeff Bach then introduces readers to the tradition of the Brethren. While this Christian group is not nearly as well-known as some of the other faiths, it nevertheless is an important player in the symphony of North Carolina religion. In essay four, N. Brooks Graebner gives a strong account of the Episcopal tradition. North Carolina Episcopalians trace their roots back to colonial days, and his essay provides a helpful chronology of that movement. H. Stanley York writes about North Carolina's Holiness/Pentecostals—a tradition that is both diverse and highly energetic. His essay explores a rich history that extends back more than a century into the Civil War era. Jewish tradition in the Tar Heel state is then meticulously chronicled by James Ingram Martin, Sr., who conveys the richness, strength, and historical roots of this ancient faith. Essay seven, written by Gary R. Freeze, explores the state's Lutherans. This religious community has roots extending back into colonial days, and his essay chronicles that European church culture's growth. Thomas A. Lehman writes about North Carolina's Mennonites. While not a large community of believers, its witness to issues related to peace and justice is an important voice in the state's religious history. Michael Perdue then presents the venerable history of Methodism, a statewide religious community with deep roots in our state's past as well as present times. In the tenth essay, C. Riddick Weber describes the Moravian tradition, most often associated with Old Salem, that has been successfully integrated into this state's culture. Robert J. Cain then provides an outstanding survey of Presbyterianism, one of North Carolina's oldest and most popular religious communities. Max L. Carter writes about Quaker roots and their growth in North Carolina. His fine essay surveys the history and values of one of the first religious voices to oppose slavery in the state. Daniel Hutchinson describes the gradual spread of Roman Catholicism across North Carolina, a development that continues today as our population increases in ethnic and geographical diversity. George W. Braswell, Jr., and Lisa Stover Grissom round out the collection with a rich discussion of several non–Christian religious traditions still evolving in our changing state, exploring how diversity of faith deepens our culture.

NOTES

1. William S. Powell, *North Carolina Through Four Centuries* (Chapel Hill: University of North Carolina Press, 1989), 73–74. In the early years of the colony, establishment of the Anglican Church enjoyed varying degrees of success due to a lack of bishops, thereby opening the door for other religious traditions to enjoy freedom of expression.

2. Donald Keyser, "Christianity in North Carolina: Its Roots and Its Fruits," unpublished manuscript (Keyser Collection, Archives of Campbell University, Wiggins Library, n.d.), 4.

3. Powell, 326. Powell indicates that by 1860, Christian groups present in North Carolina included Baptists, Methodists, Presbyterians, Lutherans, Episcopalians, Disciples, Moravians, Quakers, German Reformed, and Roman Catholics.

4. David W. Owens, "Additional Information on the North Carolina Constitutional Provisions Regarding Religion," located at: https://www.sog.unc.edu/resources/legal-summaries/additional-information-north-carolina-constitutional-provisions-regarding-religion, last accessed December 20, 2017.

5. *Ibid.*

6. See *Journal of the Convention, Called by the Freemen of North-Carolina, to Amend the Constitution of the State, Which Assembled in the City of Raleigh, on the 4th of June, 1835, and Continued in Session Until the 11th Day of July Thereafter.* North Carolina Constitutional Convention (Raleigh, NC: Joseph Gales & Son, 1835), 47, http://docsouth.unc.edu/nc/conv1835/conv1835.html, last accessed December 20, 2017.

7. Owens, 2.

8. http://www.pewforum.org/religious-landscape-study/state/north-carolina/ last accessed December 21, 2017. The survey was based on telephone interviews with 35,000 respondents in all 50 states, 1,022 of whom were North Carolinians. The reader is able to view the data from each state and compare with the national trend.

9. *Ibid.*

10. Alfred W. Stuart, "Overview of Religion in NC," located at: https://www.ncpedia.org/religion/overview, last accessed December 21, 2017.

Baptists

Lydia Huffman Hoyle

Although other Southern states boast a greater preponderance of Baptists, North Carolina may be home to a wider assortment of Baptists than any other state. As a tradition known to divide over seemingly small differences in theology or practice, Baptists in America have created nearly sixty Baptist denominations.[1] The majority of these have had adherents in North Carolina. Some of these individual Baptist denominations have even found their genesis amidst the pines and hills of the Old North State. North Carolina, it seems, has long provided an environment that is conducive to Baptist expansion and creativity. The story of Baptists in North Carolina thus unfolds as a multifaceted tale with an abundance of characters, and many fascinating plot twists and turns.[2]

Beginnings

Although Baptists grew to be the largest denominational family in North Carolina, claiming 43 percent of all churchgoers in 1890,[3] they had an undeniably slow start. The first permanent white settlers of the state migrated south from Virginia between 1655 and 1660 and settled in colonies along the northern shore of the Albemarle Sound.[4] By the turn of the century, a few of these colonists were likely Baptists, though a clear record of religious affiliation cannot be found before 1714. In that year, an Anglican minister in the Chowan Precinct complained that two of his vestrymen were "professed Anabaptists."[5] Baptists may have been drawn out of Virginia and Puritan colonies further north by the promise of religious freedom. Beginning in 1663, the eight Lords Proprietors to whom King Charles granted the land that became North Carolina declared that they would give "liberty of conscience in all religious and spiritual things" to those who would settle there.[6] Given that most American colonies had established a particular denomination immediately upon settlement, North Carolina must have initially been an inviting location for dissenters of all sorts—including Baptists.[7]

Whatever the number of scattered Baptists in the first seventy years of the colony, they were not gathered into a church. The first church was formed in 1727 by an enterprising minister, Paul Palmer, who had arrived in North Carolina some seven years earlier.[8] An early historian of Baptists in America, David Benedict, reported that Palmer was a native of Maryland, baptized (presumably as a Baptist) in Delaware, ordained in Connecticut, and a resident of New Jersey and Maryland before coming to North Carolina no later than 1720.[9] Upon arrival, Palmer married a wealthy widow, Johanna Laker Peterson, and came to own a substantial amount of land in Perquimans Precinct in the northeast corner of the colony.

At some point after his arrival in North Carolina, Paul Palmer began promoting Baptist ideas. He appealed to the governor of the colony, Sir Richard Everard, for the right to preach and convert under the English Toleration Act. Everard granted the license and Palmer went to work,[10] forming a congregation of like-minded souls in Chowan Precinct, an area that shared a border with Perquimans. By 1729, this church boasted thirty-two members, apparently meeting in the homes of members.[11] Little more is known of this first Baptist church in North Carolina. It seemed to disappear a year or two later when its first and only pastor, Joseph Parker, moved from Chowan. Parker, however, would go on to gather and pastor at least five additional Baptist churches in eastern North Carolina.[12]

Meanwhile, Paul Palmer continued his efforts to spread the "Baptist Way" and found Baptist congregations in North Carolina. No later than 1729, he helped start a second church closer to the border with Virginia that came to be known as Shiloh.[13] This congregation initially met in the home of William Burges, who also served as its pastor for over twenty years. Unlike the church at Chowan, this congregation continued (even to the present), producing many of the early ministers that spread the Baptist understanding of Christianity across the region.[14]

Soon, the evangelistic work of Palmer and others was noted by colonial and local leaders. Late in 1729, Governor Richard Everard, in a letter to the Bishop of London, complained of the great religious enthusiasm engendered by Palmer's preaching.[15] He worried that he would be unable to stem the tide. Indeed, in a region that was otherwise known for its "great religious destitution,"[16] Baptists were beginning to make inroads. By 1754, seventeen churches had been founded—primarily in the eastern part of the colony.[17]

The Baptists in North Carolina were a part of a growing Baptist movement in the colonies. By 1750, at least eleven different Baptist "denominations" had formed.[18] The seventeen churches in North Carolina were all a specific kind of Baptist that had come to be known as General Six Principle Baptists. General Baptists, a group named for their Arminian commitment to Christ's general atonement for all people, were one of the two earliest forms of Baptists in England. In addition to their Arminian theology, most General Baptists in America embraced six principles they found in Hebrews 6: repentance, believer's baptism, laying on of hands, resurrection of the dead, and final judgment. One of these principles set them apart from other Baptists—the laying on of hands. They believed that church members should place their hands on newly baptized believers as a sign of their receipt of the Holy Spirit. Unlike in other denominations, this ritual was not to be offered exclusively to ministers being set apart for ordination.

General Baptist hegemony in North Carolina did not last long. Beginning in 1750, a Baptist named Robert Williams, recently from South Carolina, returned to visit his North Carolina home, and used the opportunity to spread his Calvinist theology. A number of General Baptist ministers soon came under his sway.[19] Williams then apparently alerted the Philadelphia Association, the earliest association of Calvinist Baptist churches in the colonies, to the need for its help.[20] In the mid–1750s, it sent an emissary, John Gano, south to preach Calvinism to the General Baptists—especially to the leaders. His trip included a stop in Reedy Creek where, though uninvited, he spoke passionately to an assembly of ministers. Upon his return to Philadelphia, the Association sent out two more men. One, Benjamin Miller, traveled to North Carolina where he helped establish the Particular Baptist Jersey Church. This was the first Baptist church established west of Granville County.[21] In short order, the majority of the small cadre of Baptist ministers in North Carolina became Calvinists. With the support of a minority within their congregations, the young churches led by these ministers also became Calvinist, or Particular Baptist, in name and ownership. (The four ministers who desisted and refused to participate in the Calvinist transition became the seedbed for the Free Will Baptist denomination.)[22]

The Baptist shake-up in the mid-eighteenth century did not end with the almost wholesale takeover of the General Baptist churches by the Calvinist Particular Baptists. Soon, the tiny North Carolina Baptist world felt the impact of the First Great Awakening. This came at the hands of two recently "converted" couples. Martha Stearns Marshall, along with her husband Daniel, brother Shubal, and sister-in-law Sarah, moved south from Connecticut into the piedmont section of North Carolina in 1755, preaching with a previously unknown evangelistic zeal. They were part of a new Separate Baptist movement. Driven by revivalistic fervor, the Marshalls and Stearns brought emotional worship and fervent preaching to central North Carolina, particularly the area known as Sandy Creek. Surprising to many, no doubt, was the effective preaching not only of Shubal Stearns and Daniel Marshall, but also of Martha Stearns Marshall, whose "zeal and eloquence" in preaching were noteworthy.[23] By 1772, the work of the Marshalls and Stearns had produced forty-two Separate Baptist churches in North Carolina and beyond.[24]

Although Baptists were congregational in their polity, they began to come together in associations early in their history in England and America. Thus, it is no surprise to find like-minded churches come together in central North Carolina as the Separate Baptist movement spread. The Sandy Creek Association formed in 1758. For twelve years, the ever-growing number of Separate churches in North Carolina, South Carolina, and Virginia were a part of this organization.

Shubal Stearns stood at the helm of the Sandy Creek Association, establishing it "as an ecclesiastical council, with members chosen by its component churches, yet greater in power than the churches themselves and with authority to impose rule over them."[25] This made the Sandy Creek Association more influential than most Baptist associations would be. Ultimately, though, Stearns struggled to maintain control of the burgeoning organization, and in 1769 it divided into three parts by state.

The Separate Baptists brought new religious practices to North Carolina. Unlike the Particular Baptists, they opposed paying their ministers and actively sought to convert others to the Baptist way. Although all Baptists at the time held to a congregational polity of some sort, the Separates were fervently democratic and egalitarian.[26] Women played notable roles in the congregations. Not only did they preach, as noted above, they "led public prayers, presided over mass meetings, served as deaconesses and elderesses, organized care for the sick and poor, conducted separate women's meetings, and counseled."[27] Black church members were also given a voice in the Separate gatherings.[28]

The egalitarian and democratic qualities of the Separates, combined with their religious intensity, fed a newly developing political radicalism in the region—the Regulator movement. Most Separate Baptists, including at least five preachers, became a part of this backcountry movement that sought, among other things, to curtail the dishonesty of local officials.[29] In 1769, just before the Sandy Creek Association divided, it issued an order promising excommunication to any Baptist who took up arms against the legal authority. Regulator leaders immediately faced down Shubal Stearns, functionally negating this promised action.[30]

By the beginnings of the Revolution in 1775, there were more Baptists than adherents of any other religious group in the colony.[31] Their growing numbers, in combination with the involvement of many Baptists in the Regulator movement, made the Baptists a scary lot to the government. Governor William Tryon (1765–71) actively promoted the Anglican Church and suppressed the Baptists, describing them as "an avowed enemy to the mother church."[32] In the short term, Tryon was successful in driving out the Baptists. Indeed, when the Regulators failed, many Separate Baptists left North Carolina for Tennessee and South Carolina, pursued and harassed by Tryon's army. According to Morgan Edwards, the earliest historian of Baptists in North Carolina, the Sandy Creek Association was reduced from 606 to fourteen souls after the Battle of Alamance. Other churches in the area were likewise decimated.[33] Still, the Baptists marched on.

Although "unifying" is generally not the Baptist modus operandi, Baptists in the eastern part of the State began to come together in the late eighteenth century to form a second association. In 1769, several of the newly Calvinist churches of the East drew together as the Kehukee Association and adopted the Philadelphia Confession of Faith, a confession issued in 1742 by the Philadelphia Association, the first Baptist association in America.[34] The new Kehukee Association grew relatively quickly and came to include both Separate and "Regular" Baptists.[35] A young minister, Lemuel Burkitt, became the clerk of the organization.

Within a year, the young association found itself in turmoil. The Separate and Regular Baptists struggled to come to a consensus regarding the requirements for church membership. The Separates were quite concerned that candidates for church membership give evidence of "true conversion" prior to baptism. There was grave concern that the Regular churches continued to include members who had been baptized without testifying to an experience of conversion.[36] Burkitt, who was increasingly becoming "the most influential man among the Baptists of North Carolina,"[37] fought for reform in the Association. Apparently, he had experienced a dream when he was a young boy that he understood to be a call to preach the Gospel to eastern North Carolina. This dream seemed to impel him. Upon his conversion at the age of twenty-two, Burkitt became a passionate preacher, spreading the Good News as well as the need for a "pure" church membership. Ultimately, Burkitt and those that joined him formed a new Kehukee Association called "The United Baptist Association, formerly called the Kehukee Association." This new association came to include the great majority of Baptists in Eastern North Carolina, even those who had originally remained in the old Kehukee Association.[38] It adopted a Calvinistic "Abstract of Principles" as its guide.[39]

Perhaps the Baptists of Eastern North Carolina were able to unite, in part, because they were engaged together in a greater fight. As the Revolutionary War began, Baptists were, almost uniformly, supporters of the Revolution.[40] Religious liberty had been a clarion cry of Baptists since their inception early in the seventeenth century and this commitment meshed well with the spirit of independence that drove the Revolution forward. A number of prominent Baptists outside of North Carolina, like John Leland and Isaac Backus, worked tirelessly to ensure others realized that religious freedom would be good for both the new country and the churches. Baptist leaders in North Carolina, though less influential, joined the cause of religious liberty.

Even before the war began, the writing was on the wall for the Established Church as such in North Carolina. As early as 1774, only two or three Anglican clergy remained in the state.[41] The departure of the Anglican leadership, in combination with the commitment of Baptists to democratic decision-making and religious liberty, made the revolutionary era a time of expansion for Baptists in North Carolina and beyond.

Baptists Move West

North Carolina saw a large growth in its population in the fifty years prior to the Revolutionary War, and some of these immigrants began to settle the foothills and "backcountry." Large numbers of Irish Protestants and Germans traveled south from Pennsylvania, Virginia, and other colonies on the Great Wagon Road to North Carolina. Among these were six Dunker, or German Baptist, congregations.[42] This tiny Baptist sect that began in Germany earlier in the century was known for its commitment to simplicity in life and worship, total abstinence from alcohol, and pacifism. This group was also noted for its method of baptism. Baptismal candidates were baptized facedown and were dipped into the water three times. This practice was unique in these two ways, though as was the case with other Baptists, it was reserved for believers. Although few of the earliest Dunker communities survived in western North Carolina, they paved the way for other settlers in the area. Ultimately, in the late nineteenth century, the Dunkers saw a degree of growth.[43]

Around 1770, additional Baptist churches began to form west of the Yadkin River, as the North Carolina legislature established counties to the west. These churches were most often named for prominent geographical features in their vicinity. So we find churches with names like Timber Ridge, Forks of Yadkin, Deep Creek, Dutchman's Creek, Flat Rock, and Grassy Knob.[44] (In 1790, these churches formed the Yadkin Association.) Generally, these churches met one Sunday a month with a business meeting the day before. Members were expected to be present for both events.[45]

Church records reveal many wonderful glimpses into these early Baptist churches that dotted the foothills and mountain areas of the state. At a time when few institutions existed to bring order or encourage civility among settlers, churches gave attention to disciplining their members. In particular, members took to heart their covenant "not to suffer sin in our brother or sister as far as it shall please God to discover it unto us."[46] Church record books were filled with such discoveries and complaints. Apparently, many of the grievances were brought by women regarding other women in the congregation, but the disputes included courtship and marital issues between men and women as well as physical altercations between men in the congregation. Sometimes, even disputes between people in neighboring churches were settled in Saturday church business meetings.[47]

Churches also dealt with individual behaviors of church members that were deemed sinful. These included activities like fiddling, dancing, frolicking, drunkenness, fraud, and sexual encounters outside of marriage.[48] "Bastardy" was a particular concern, and women who bore children outside of wedlock faced this charge.[49] Apparently, their male partners were rarely held responsible. At this point, trafficking slaves was also considered dishonorable and potentially worthy of disciplinary action.[50]

The discipline most often meted out by churches was exclusion from the congregation.

Given the paucity of opportunities for social discourse outside of the churches, this punishment seemed to have its desired end in most circumstances. Within a few months, disciplined members were often back, apparently repentant. Of course, in some situations, the matter of concern was not so easily rectified. Flat Rock Church, for example, recorded an issue that resulted in a long-term dismissal. Apparently Sister Mary J. left her husband and refused to return. In 1800 at Cove Creek Church, a couple was excluded for "dubble marredg [sic]."[51] Presumably, bigamy was also not an easily resolved issue.

By the beginning of the nineteenth century, General, Regular (or Particular) and Separate Baptists had spread across the state of North Carolina. According to early Baptist historian David Benedict, there were eleven associations, two hundred churches and about thirteen thousand church members by 1812.[52] Although the total population of North Carolina exceeded half a million by this point, Baptists were a large enough group to have an impact if they worked together.

The Beginnings of a Baptist State Convention

At the beginning of the nineteenth century, a series of religious revivals spread across Kentucky, Tennessee, and beyond. The revivals began in North Carolina in 1801. A leading minister, Lemuel Burkitt, had traveled north to observe the multi-denominational revival gatherings. Upon his return, he reported to the Kehukee annual associational meeting where many apparently were drawn to some of the new revivalistic measures being discussed. Soon, churches in the association began to report large numbers of conversions and baptisms. According to the records of the Association, 872 new members were added to the churches of the Association in 1802, a number that was nearly ten times the figure reported in each of the previous three years.[53]

Driven, in part, by the energy unleashed by the series of religious awakenings, Protestant Christians across the country began to talk and think about the need to communicate the message of Christ to those who had not heard. Up to this point, Protestants had only shown minimal interest in the whole idea. However, a British Baptist named William Carey had brought the topic to the fore in 1792 when he published a book entitled *An Enquiry into the Obligations of Christians to Use Means for the Conversion of the Heathens.* Revival enthusiasm across the colonies was soon combined with the new missionary spirit, propelling women and men to raise money and, in some cases, commit their lives to the mission endeavor.

A pastor named Martin Ross came before the Kehukee Association in 1803, seeking to pass a resolution calling for the association to take up the cause of missions. The following year, the resolution was adopted. Soon, the first missionary organization among Baptists in North Carolina formed—the Baptist Philanthropic Missionary Society.[54] For the first several years of its existence, the missionary society did little more than collect a little money and talk about the plight of the "unhappy savages" in other lands.[55] In 1809, Martin Ross determined to pursue a different tack. This time he went before the Chowan Association in the northeast corner of the state and called for the organization of the North Carolina General Meeting of Correspondence that would draw Baptists together across multiple associations. The Chowan Association supported the idea and issued invitations to nine other associations in the eastern half of the state. Six of them agreed; delegates from the Kehukee, Chowan, Sandy Creek and three other associations met in 1811 and organized with these named goals: "to extend religious acquaintance; to encourage the preaching of the gospel, and to diffuse useful knowledge."[56] Although the mission cause may have been implied by "the preaching of the Gospel," it was not explicitly stated at this point. By the next year, the General Meeting determined to draw more North Carolina Baptists into the fold. Across the next seven years, further invitations went out, with some additional associations joining but other original participants leaving. Preaching remained central to the annual gathering throughout this period. In 1816, however, Luther Rice, the leading fundraiser for the newly pursued missionary cause, spoke at the meeting, raising $126 for the effort.[57]

Energy and zeal for the missionary enterprise had been growing across the country, and Protestant Christians were forming organizations to fund and promote the endeavor. Baptists were soon motivated to join the movement. In some ways, they had little choice. Congregationalists Adoniram and Ann Hasseltine Judson, along with Luther Rice, had been among the first Americans who, in 1812, made up their minds "to preach the Gospel to the heathen."[58] Before they reached their destination in Burma, however, the three had embraced the Baptist way. This meant that the mostly Congregationalist sending-agency that had financed their travel would no longer support their work. Rice determined to return to the United States to draw together Baptists in a society that would support the newly Baptist missionaries and those who would join them. He returned to the United States on the next ship and began traversing the East Coast, preaching and helping to form mission societies. Soon, Rice was driven by the vision of forming one national Baptist mission society with delegates from societies in each state. In 1814, his dream began to be realized when the General Missionary Convention of the Baptist Denomination in the United States of America for Foreign Missions (or Triennial Convention) formed.[59]

By the time this occurred, many states had already formed mission societies, North Carolina among them. The North Carolina Baptist Society for Foreign Missions formed in March 1814, two months before the national organization began. Unlike in the General Meeting of Correspondence, "missions" was a clear focus. According to their constitution, "the avowed and determined object of this Society" was "to aid in sending forth and supporting Missionaries for the purpose of translating the Scripture, preaching the Gospel, and gathering Churches in Heathen and Idolatrous parts of the world."[60] Across the next decade, local mission societies also formed across the state, bringing monies raised to the annual North Carolina Society gathering. By 1824, three hundred contributing organizations and individuals were listed in the minutes of this group.[61]

Two years later, Martin Ross, the pastor who had worked for many years to organize like-minded Baptists in North Carolina, began to call publicly for a state convention that would unite the multiple organizations of Baptists already in existence. Although Ross passed away before the work could be accomplished, Thomas Meredith, a Baptist pastor who had studied at Columbian College, an institution founded by Luther Rice, stepped up to continue the effort. In 1829, Meredith and other supporters of the mission cause met in Greenville and formed the North Carolina Baptist Benevolent Society. The purpose of the group was to raise money and support itinerant ministers in the state, "being concerned for the condition of the multitudes within the borders of our State, who are unhappily destitute of the preaching of the Word of God...."[62] When the group met the following year, Meredith came prepared to see the organization transform itself into a state convention with broader goals. He offered an impassioned message and a constitution ready for adoption.[63] The constitution laid out the "primary objects" of the Convention as being "the education of young men called of God to the ministry, and approved of by the churches to which they respectively belong; the employment of missionaries within the bounds of the State and cooperation with the Baptist General Convention of the United States in the promotion of Missions in general."[64] The fourteen white men gathered in Greenville adopted the constitution, and Meredith then wrote a circular letter, the common form of mass communication among Baptists at the time, and sent it out, hoping that many of the fourteen associations, 272 churches and over fifteen thousand Baptists in the state would join the cause. The letter described the proceedings of the meeting and offered a print version of his own address.[65] By 1833, forty-one churches, associations, and societies were present at the annual meeting, and a Board of Trustees was elected for the Wake Forest Institute to be opened the following year. Samuel Wait, who would ultimately become the first president of Wake Forest College, was named Agent of the Convention for the third year, continuing his work of preaching across the state and starting local mission societies.[66]

According to one early historian, the response of Baptists around the state to the new convention was an "indifference well-nigh appalling."[67] Nonetheless, the new Baptist State Convention would come to have a significant impact, not only on the Baptists of North Carolina, but on the rest of the state as well.

Baptists of Other Stripes

Although the majority of Baptists in North Carolina came to join associations that in turn became a part of the State Convention, that was certainly not the case for all Baptists. Two groups should be mentioned here. A significant reaction to the growing involvement of Baptists in the missionary cause produced one such group. Five years after North Carolinians gathered to form the Society for Foreign Missions, a movement began to form in opposition. Baptists who held strong Calvinist leanings and independent spirits began to voice their concerns. They noted that there were no mission societies in the Bible and that missionaries should not be paid for preaching the Gospel. They also believed God would save those God chose without human assistance. These ideas came to hold sway particularly in frontier areas like Tennessee and Kentucky. Although the anti-mission movement was less intense in North Carolina, it nonetheless worked to weaken the mission commitment and to divide Baptists further.

In 1826, Joshua Lawrence, a leader of anti-missionism in eastern North Carolina, presented a declaration to the Kehukee Association seeking to "discard all Missionary societies" as "inventions of men." A year later, a majority of the churches represented at the Association voted to endorse Lawrence's declaration.[68] In subsequent years, many associations deliberated the mission endeavor as well as other newfangled practices like Sunday schools and a paid ministry. Several additional associations joined the anti-mission movement. In some, like the Yadkin, the association voted to support the new Baptist State Convention, causing at least one congregation to "schismatically rent" from them to join like-minded souls in other anti-mission associations.[69] Several new associations of either pro-mission or anti-mission congregations formed when a significant number of churches disagreed with the vote of their association.

One of the most significant of the anti-mission associations was the Mountain Association, which became anti-mission in 1838. This group became quite hostile toward associations that did not share their opinions, dissolving fellowship with any such body.[70] In the hills of North Carolina, the anti-mission movement found many kindred spirits, and the group saw early but slow growth. They spread their message through both ministers and circular letters across several decades. Their practices, maintained to the present day, were perhaps common among many Baptists in the late eighteenth century: celebrating foot washing after communion, utilizing untrained ministers, and singing without musical accompaniment.[71]

Over time, the anti-mission associations and churches adopted the name of Old School or Primitive Baptists. Like most Baptists, soon after they came together they found reasons to divide. The Regular Primitives emphasize that salvation is determined before birth; the Absolutes are committed to the foreordination of all things by God; the Progressives have opened the door to innovations like Sunday school; and the Universalists proclaim that ultimately God will save all people.[72] Today, Primitive Baptists are small in number in North Carolina and elsewhere, with the Universalist group being the smallest of the four groups.

Another significant group of North Carolina Baptists held a theology that was strongly opposed to the strict Calvinism of the Primitive Baptists. In the mid-eighteenth century, when many General Baptist congregations in North Carolina were "converted" to Calvinism by emissaries from the Philadelphia Baptist Association, four or five General Baptist churches refused to give up their Arminian theology (as noted earlier). These churches ultimately formed the foundation of what would become the Free Will Baptist movement. After fifty years of little growth, these churches began to multiply as they adopted the techniques utilized during the revivals in the early nineteenth century. In 1828, they adopted the name Free Will Baptists. Soon, with twenty-five participating churches, they established two conferences, Shiloh and Bethel. Both were made up of churches in eastern North Carolina. After uniting with a national freewill Baptist organization for a few decades in the twentieth century, the North Carolina Free Will Baptists reestablished themselves as an independent organization and became the Original Free Will Baptist denomination. This group came to support a number of strong institutions: a press, a college (Mount Olive), a children's home, and an assembly ground.[73] Throughout their history, almost all Original Free Will Baptists have resided in North Carolina.

True to their heritage, the Original Free Will denomination maintains a strong Arminian theology. Like a few other Baptist groups, they practice the "washing of the saint's feet" as one of the three ordinances of the church (along with baptism and the Lord's Supper). Uniquely, they also uphold a strong connectional form of church government like that of Methodists. They have strong conferences that are responsible for licensing, ordaining, and disciplining ministers. These conferences also investigate and settle church disputes. Few Baptists have ceded this much authority to any institution beyond the local congregation.[74]

An Expanding State Convention

Although the Baptist State Convention had an inauspicious beginning, in part due to the strong backlash from the anti-mission contingent, it soon began to expand its reach. In 1833 and 1834, two major steps were taken. First, as mentioned earlier, the convention worked to make an educated ministry possible for white Baptists. In February of 1834, the Wake Forest Manual Labour Institute opened in Wake County with Samuel Wait serving as principal of the sixteen students. Soon after it opened, the country faced an economic crisis, leading the school to near bankruptcy. In 1834, the school dropped the commitment to manual labor and requested a new charter as Wake Forest College. After struggling with debt for over a decade, the college stabilized financially.[75] The school was the first of what would become a strong and extensive array of denominational colleges in the state, preparing ministers and other professionals for meaningful vocations.

The year 1833 also saw the beginning of a regular Baptist publication in the state. Early Baptist historian Charles Williams referred to this paper as "the first child of the Baptist State Convention."[76] Thomas Meredith, then pastor of the Baptist church of Edenton, stepped forward to edit this new monthly newspaper called the *North Carolina Baptist Interpreter*. According to its extended title, the paper was "devoted to Sacred Criticism, Moral and Religious Essays, Miscellaneous Selections and General Intelligence."[77] Meredith, who had graduated from the University of Pennsylvania, was well suited to this work. He seemed to excel as both a writer and an editor. Success bred expansion, and in 1835 the *Interpreter* was replaced with a weekly newspaper called the *Biblical Recorder*. Soon, Meredith, who had since moved to New Bern, recognized the need for the paper to be published in a more central location and moved to Raleigh, giving up his work as pastor to commit his full-time efforts to the paper.[78] The paper proved to be an efficient way for Baptists to communicate and draw together. Through the paper, the mission cause was celebrated, and Baptists from across the state were brought together to pursue common causes. Every subsequent work of the convention was publicized and pushed forward by the *Biblical Recorder*.[79]

The Baptist State Convention expanded across the next three decades, with 326 new churches established between 1830 and 1859.[80] According to their charters, the churches included both white and black members.[81] In addition to its early work starting a college and a weekly paper, the convention enthusiastically took up a number of other causes. Prominent among them was the establishment of Sunday schools. This movement, first begun in England in 1780, had reached the United States quickly. As early as 1805, a few associations had begun to gather children to form Sunday schools.[82] The new convention charged its missionaries with organizing new Sunday schools, and the number quickly mushroomed.[83] Gradually, Sunday school became a staple of Baptist life for many children and adults, bringing many into churches throughout the nineteenth and twentieth centuries.

Fifteen years after the formation of the Baptist State Convention, a portion of the convention separated from it to form an auxiliary convention.[84] This organization, called the Western Convention, formed in 1845 and drew together churches that were generally located west of the Blue Ridge Mountains. These churches had had difficulty sending representatives to Annual Convention meetings that were held east of the mountains. Thus, the Western Convention decided to establish its own Sunday School Board, Mission Board, and Education Board as well as its own publications. Sharing the eastern commitment to education, the Western Convention founded several schools, including French Broad Baptist Institute (1856), which later became Mars Hill College, and Judson College (1879–1892), which seemed to have served more as an academy.[85] When the railroad system was completed and the west was no longer isolated from the east, associations in the west began to rejoin the east. In 1898, the Western conference was dissolved.[86]

By the time the Western Convention rejoined the State Convention, a lot had changed. Around the same time the Western Convention separated from its eastern sisters and brothers, the Triennial Convention of Baptists was also dividing. As sentiments regarding slavery began to divide the nation, Baptists also struggled to maintain the peace. After years of compromises and affirmations of neutrality on the subject of slavery, Southern leaders became convinced (with good cause) that neither the Home Mission Society nor the Board of Foreign Missions would appoint a slave-owner. Such a stand did not constitute neutrality in their view. For many, the division over slavery had become quite personal. As early as 1841, a North Carolinian wrote the *Biblical Recorder* declaring that North Carolina delegates to the Triennial Convention "were unwilling to sit in council with certain abolitionists ... (who) had virtually expelled southerners from their pulpits, their communion tables, and their fellowship."[87] On May 8, 1845, a group of Baptists from the South met in Augusta, Georgia, to form the Southern Baptist Convention (SBC). Representatives from North Carolina were present. In October of the same year, the Baptist State Convention voted to approve the SBC. Apparently, most white Baptists in North Carolina were happy to designate slavery a political issue, not a moral or religious one. As the disagreement over slavery that divided Baptists and others increased across the next decades, North Carolina Baptist pastors, like other Southern Christian leaders, used their pulpits to develop "moral" arguments for slavery and to encourage "religious" support for the Southern armies. This support came to include the distribution of tracts and Bibles to Confederate soldiers by *colporteurs*, or traveling missionaries.[88] In 1864, thirty-six colporteurs in North Carolina distributed twenty-five thousand Bibles, seventeen thousand hymnbooks, and thousands of tracts.[89]

Of course, the Southern Baptist Convention, once formed, was not primarily focused on slavery; the organization was composed of numerous societies committed to mission outreach, education, and other endeavors. "Foreign and domestic" mission efforts figured prominently in their work, and these became well supported in the state of North Carolina. Indeed, a North Carolinian was one of the first international missionaries appointed by the new board. Matthew Tyson Yates (1819–1885), a native of Wake County and an early graduate of Wake Forest, traveled to China in 1847 with his new wife, Eliza Moring of Chatham County. Yates' letters, describing the couple's forty years of evangelism and translation were published in the *Biblical Recorder*, no doubt expanding the interest of North Carolina Baptists in the mission endeavor.[90] By the end of the nineteenth century, twenty-two missionaries from the state were working outside the country under the auspices of the SBC.[91]

An auxiliary to the SBC also came to have a great influence on Baptist life in North Carolina. In 1888, the Woman's Missionary Union formed and proclaimed the dual commitments of "stimulating the missionary spirit" and "aiding in collecting funds" for missions.[92] It was notably successful at doing both. This occurred in part through the strong state and local WMU groups that formed before and after the national organization began. North Carolina had one of the earliest and strongest of these groups. A Raleigh woman named Mattie Heck had begun traveling about the state in 1877, starting mission societies and raising money. "Concerned" men shut down her efforts, but nine years later Heck's daughter Fannie agreed to restart the work. She became the President of the state WMU in 1886, two years before the national group formed. Heck went on to serve as the President of the State WMU for twenty-nine years and the National WMU for fifteen years.[93] The WMU had a major impact on churches, as it brought the cause of missions to the forefront. In addition, the WMU began a hugely successful program in which children from the ages of three to eighteen, and women of all ages, participated in weekly mission education. This weekly reminder of both the importance of missions and the potential call of God into this work came to have a significant impact on Baptist churches in North Carolina—especially on the girls and young women.[94]

Even with the establishment of the Southern Baptist Convention, North Carolina Baptists continued some relationships with Baptists in the North. In 1845, five months after the formation of the SBC, a group organized the North Carolina Baptist Sunday School and Publication Society. It began as an auxiliary to the American Baptist Publication and Sunday School Society (a northern Baptist organization). For the next decade, the state organization purchased materials published by the American Society. As sectional hostilities grew, however, this relationship became untenable.[95]

For a time, accessing Sunday school literature may have been a moot point for North Carolina Baptists. In the 1860s and 1870s, Baptists, like everyone else, were primarily engaged in the problems and challenges that accompanied Civil War and Reconstruction. Nonetheless, even during this devastating period, the Baptist State Convention established 296 new churches and twelve new associations.

The Growth of Black Churches

Although a few black churches began prior to the Civil War, one of the results of the war was the extensive growth of Baptist churches among those North Carolinians who had once been enslaved.[96] As North Carolina historian Milton Ready notes: After the war "the invisible churches and congregations of African Americans emerged, phoenix-like, to become the unhidden rock on which an entire, separate society had existed for centuries."[97] Some of these now visible churches quickly began to join together to promote missions and other causes, meeting for the first time in October 1867. They were assisted by a committee from the mostly white Baptist State Convention. The new organization took the name "The General Association of the Colored Baptists of North Carolina" and adopted a constitution using the State Convention's constitution as a model. The limited funds they were able to collect in the early years were used to support missionaries who traveled across the state starting Sunday schools and churches. By 1875, participants were also encouraged to support an institution recently formed by Southern Baptist leader H.M. Tupper: Shaw Collegiate Institute in Raleigh. This school would become Shaw University, the first black institution of higher learning in the South.

At this point, the vast majority of black churches did not participate in the new convention.[98] Great growth, however, was coming. In 1881, Caesar Johnson, the President of the General Association, reported that as of that year the association included "more than 800 well-equipped churches with more than 90,000 members."[99] Minutes also indicated that the convention was supporting a missionary in Africa, a man named James O. Hayes.[100]

Soon after the National Baptist Convention formed in 1895, the General Association (that ultimately came to be called the General Baptist State Convention of North Carolina, Inc.) joined. When the National Convention faced division early in its history, the General State Convention likewise struggled and divided. Nonetheless, even with these divisions and frequent issues with financial resources, it actively worked to start churches and support education in the state. Like the predominantly white convention, it has long published a state paper called the *Baptist Informer*. Many black Baptists in North Carolina today have a strong commitment to the General Baptist Convention that sometimes exceeds their involvement or interest in any national body.

Like white Baptists, black Baptists have formed a number of separate denominations that reflect their commitments. In 1867, the first black Free Will Baptist church formed. An association followed in 1887. Today, this denomination, called the United American Free Will Baptist Church, is composed of churches primarily in North Carolina where it maintains its headquarters. It shares similar commitments with the white Original Free Will Baptist denomination.[101] On the opposite side of the theological spectrum is the National Primitive Baptist Convention, USA, Inc. This group, headquartered in Pensacola, Florida, holds to Calvinist ideas regarding election and utilizes foot washing along with baptism and the Lord's Supper as rites of the church. The National Primitive Baptist Church differs from most Primitive Baptists in that it offers ministerial training and Sunday schools and is engaged in evangelism and mission efforts.[102]

Twentieth-Century Denominational Heyday

In the last two decades of the nineteenth century and for much of the twentieth century, Baptists, especially those with a strong mission impulse, expanded their ministries in many directions. The Baptist foray into building academies and colleges that began with Wake Forest, Shaw, and Mars Hill continued. By 1930, Baptists had established over forty academies. In the early twentieth century, seven academies and high schools founded between 1848 and 1905 became colleges and junior colleges affiliated with the Baptist State Convention. These included Meredith (1904), Chowan (1910), Wingate (1923), Campbell (1925) and Gardner Webb (1942).[103] The Original Free Will Baptists likewise opened Mount Olive College in 1952.

Baptists also made a significant commitment to establishing Christian schools in the mountain regions of eight states for students who lacked opportunity for basic education. The effort in North Carolina was a joint venture of the Home Mission Board of the Southern Baptist Convention and the Baptist State Convention and was led by a North Carolinian named Albert E. Brown. Ten of the forty-seven schools supported between 1900 and 1930 by the Mountain Mission School program were in North Carolina. As public school systems developed, the mission schools were discontinued but not before they played a role in opening up opportunities to many mountain children.[104]

A third area of ministry for Baptists was in the establishment of orphanages and children's homes. In 1884, the Baptist State Convention considered the possibility of supporting an orphanage already begun by John Haymes Mills. The idea was rejected initially, but when individual Baptists began supporting the orphanage, the convention had a change of heart. In 1892, it began encouraging churches to take up a special annual offering for the orphanage. By 1904, the convention was ready to establish an "organic connection" with the orphanage.[105] Over time, the single orphanage multiplied and came to be called "Baptist Children's Homes." Today it includes twelve facilities across the state.[106] In 1920, the Original Free Will Baptists also opened a children's home. This facility in Middlesex has grown and expanded and has now provided a home or emergency shelter to over 2100 children.[107]

As the twentieth century moved forward, the Baptist State Convention added other ministries. Some were short-lived while others became a part of the warp and weave of the North Carolina Baptist cloth. Five endeavors are worthy of mention here. Between 1919 and 1926, a Baptist hospital was started in Winston-Salem. When Wake Forest College moved to Winston-Salem in 1956, students at its Bowman Gray School of Medicine would train at this hospital. Baptists also began student work during this period in both state and denominational colleges. This work even included assistance with building churches near universities in Chapel Hill and Raleigh. A third work began in 1949 when the State Convention purchased an old fort that became its Assembly Ground. Youth and adults have visited the North Carolina Baptist Assembly known as "Caswell" ever since. Finally, Homes for the Aging were established in 1951 with locations in Winston-Salem and Albemarle. The convention has since changed the name to Baptist Retirement Homes of North Carolina and expanded to include facilities in Concord and Asheville. Today, Baptist Retirement Homes operates independently from the State Convention.[108]

The Southern Baptist Convention also contributed to twentieth-century Baptist life in North Carolina in multiple ways. Three new ministries with an extensive impact were all in the area of education. In 1895, the Baptist Young People's Union organized as an auxiliary to the SBC. It brought youth and young adults (and later children) together to promote Christian growth using materials produced by the Sunday School Board. In 1934, the program expanded to include all age groups and took the name Training Union.[109] From this point forward, many North Carolina Baptists would start their Sundays with Sunday school and worship and end them with Training Union and a second worship service.

The SBC also contributed in ministry to college students. The Sunday School Board, building on work that had begun earlier in the century, formed Baptist Student Unions beginning in 1928 that connected college students with churches but also provided opportunities for students to build community, participate in mission projects, and grow in the life of faith. In North Carolina, Baptist Student Unions were often headquartered in actual buildings near college campuses. Today, these organizations are called Baptist Collegiate Ministries and are often a joint effort between churches, colleges, and State Conventions. Most colleges in North Carolina have a Baptist Campus Ministry organization and are served by a Campus Minister.

A third important contribution of the SBC to Baptist life in North Carolina in the twentieth century was the opening of a denominational seminary in the state. Prior to the opening of the seminary, the closest Baptist seminary was located in Louisville, Kentucky. In 1951, the SBC opened Southeastern Baptist Theological Seminary in the Music-Religion building on the Wake Forest College campus. When the college moved to Winston-Salem in 1956, the old college facilities were renovated and the student body of the seminary significantly increased in size.[110] The school developed a strong faculty and was widely respected across the state.

Baptists Today

Twenty-first century Baptists in North Carolina continue to be diverse and divided. Theological differences, idiosyncratic practices, and unique histories ensure that those involved in the multiple Baptist denominations that formed across the centuries will continue to practice their faith separate from their similarly named sisters and brothers. In addition, although many Baptist options exist throughout the state, new Baptist groups may form. This has happened in recent decades. At least two new Baptist organizations formed in the 1980s. These denomination-like groups were born out of a conflict in the Southern Baptist Convention that occurred at that time. After the denomination came to be controlled by fundamentalists, many theologically moderate Baptists, particularly those who supported women in ministry, left the SBC and formed the Cooperative Baptist Fellowship (CBF). Today, the Cooperative Baptist Fellowship of North Carolina (CBF–NC) lists over 300 congregations that partner with the national or state CBF.[11] In addition to CBF, a smaller group known as the Alliance of Baptists formed out of the SBC denominational conflict. This group has a small presence in the state with approximately sixteen partnering congregations.

Baptists in North Carolina also continue to be ethnically diverse and divided. Although most churches remain dominated by one race or ethnic group, Baptist churches do come together on occasion for shared worship or mission involvement. Today, in addition to predominantly black and white churches, many Latino churches take part in either the Baptist State Convention or the Cooperative Baptist Fellowship. In addition, the Burnt Swamp Baptist Association (now affiliated with the Baptist State Convention) serves approximately seventy churches whose members are primarily Native American.

As the largest denominational family in North Carolina, Baptists, by intention or accident, have had a significant impact on the state. They have stood both on the side of progress and compassion and on the side of bigotry and indifference. At times, they have held tight to their traditions. At times, they have opened themselves to change. Hopefully, on balance, Baptists have made North Carolina a better place for all its citizens.

NOTES

1. See Lydia Huffman Hoyle, "Baptist Americanus" in *The Baptist River: Essays on Many Tributaries of a Diverse Tradition*, ed. by W. Glenn Jonas, Jr. (Macon, GA: Mercer University Press, 2008). Not all of these Baptist groups would use "denomination" to describe their connection.

2. You will not find the story of all Baptists in North Carolina in any volume, but many have worked to tell the story of the larger Baptist groups. The most extensive of these is George Washington Paschal's two-volume *History of North Carolina Baptists* published in 1930. Others can be seen in the notes that follow.

3. Rebecca Tippett, "Religion in North Carolina: Southern Baptists Dominate, Catholicism and Non-Denominational Affiliation Rising," last modified June 2, 2014, accessed June 6, 2017, demography.cpc.unc.edu. The earliest official data on religious affiliation was collected in 1890. Baptists continue to be the largest denominational family in North Carolina today.

4. Henry Smith Stroupe, "Baptist State Convention of North Carolina: Baptist Beginnings," in *Encyclopedia of Southern Baptists* v. II (Nashville, TN: Broadman, 1958), 988; and Charles B. Williams, *A History of the Baptists in North Carolina* (Raleigh, NC: Edwards and Broughton, 1901), 6.

5. Samuel S. Hill, *Religion in the Southern States* (Macon, GA: Mercer University Press, 1983), 220. Baptists, from their earliest days in England, were mistakenly referred to as "Anabaptists."

6. George Washington Paschal, *History of North Carolina Baptists* v.1 (Raleigh: NC Baptist State Convention, 1930), 49.

7. Early twentieth-century historian Charles B. Williams was convinced that many Baptists from New England must have headed to the Albemarle Sound region to escape persecution but notes that "history is apparently silent on this point," 3.

8. M.A. Huggins, *A History of North Carolina Baptists 1727–1932* (Raleigh, NC: General Board Baptist State Convention of North Carolina, 1967), 32.

9. David Benedict, *A General History of the Baptist Denomination in America, and Other Parts of the World* (London: Lincoln and Edmands, 1813).

10. Milton Ready, *The Tar Heel State: A History of North Carolina* (Columbia: University of South Carolina Press, 2005), 62.

11. Paschal, v.1, 139.

12. Huggins, 40.

13. Henry Sheets, in his history of the Liberty Association of Baptists, seems to claim that the Shiloh Church and the Chowan Church were the same church and it was begun in 1727. See Henry Sheets, *A History of the Liberty Baptist Association from its Organization in 1832 to 1906* (Raleigh, NC: Edwards and Broughton, 1907) xiii.

14. Paschal, v.1, 144–48.

15. *Ibid.*, 155.

16. Huggins, 42.

17. Stroupe, 989. Apparently, there were only twenty-five churches of any kind in North Carolina in 1750.

18. Pam R. Durso and Keith E. Durso, *The Story of Baptists in the United States* (Brentwood, TN: Baptist History and Heritage Society, 2006) 41.

19. Paschal, v.1, 204–06.

20. The Particular Baptists emphasized the doctrine of election and believed that God chose before creation who would be saved.

21. Huggins, 44.

22. Stroupe, 989–90; and Michael R. Pelt, *A History of Original Free Will Baptists* (Mount Olive, NC: Mount Olive College Press, 1996) 68.

23. A.H. Newman in Durso, 53.

24. Morgan Edwards, *Materials Towards a History of the Baptists in the Province of North Carolina* (Philadelphia: Joseph Crukshank and Isaac Collins, 1772), 17–18.

25. Elder John Sparks, *The Roots of Appalachian Christianity: The Life and Legacy of Elder Shubal Stearns* (Lexington: University of Kentucky Press, 2001), 88.

26. William A. Link, *North Carolina: Change and Tradition in a Southern State* (Wheeling, IL: Harlan Davidson, Inc., 2009), 88.

27. Ready, 63.

28. *Ibid.*

29. *Ibid.*, 90.

30. Sparks, 151.

31. Hugh Talmage Lefler and Albert Ray Newsome, *The History of a Southern State: North Carolina* 3rd ed. (Chapel Hill: University of North Carolina Press, 1973), 140.

32. Tryon in Stroupe, 992.

33. Morgan in Huggins, 62.

34. Paschal, v.1, 417f.

35. The Particular Baptists had come to be known as "Regular Baptists" as a way of distinguishing themselves from the Separate Baptists.

36. Huggins, 75.

37. Paschal, v.1, 432.

38. Paschal, v.1, 432–34; and Stroupe, 992.

39. William L. Lumpkin, *Baptist Foundations in the South* (Nashville, TN: Broadman Press, 1961) 139.

40. Huggins, 93.

41. Huggins, 95.

42. Lefler and Newsome, 86.

43. See Roger E. Sappington, *The Brethren in the Carolinas: The History of the Church of the Brethren in the District of North and South Carolina* (Kingsport, TN: Church of the Brethren, 1971) for a detailed history of the group.

44. Huggins, 133–37.

45. Paschal, v. II, 218.

46. *Ibid.*

47. *Ibid.*, 218–28.

48. Paschal, v. II., 232–38.

49. *Ibid.*, 230.

50. Huggins, 141.

51. Paschal, v. II., 228–29.

52. Benedict, 141.

53. Huggins, 82.

54. Stroupe, 994.

55. See a description of an address prepared by the society in George Bullard, "Baptist State Convention of North Carolina: History of Convention," in *Encyclopedia of Southern Baptists* v. II (Nashville, TN: Broadman, 1958), 994.

56. *Ibid.*, 995.

57. *Ibid.* Notably, this collection included five dollars "contributed by the Black People."

58. Rice in H. Leon McBeth, *The Baptist Heritage* (Nashville, TN: Broadman, 1987) 345.

59. *Ibid.*, 346.

60. Bullard, 995.

61. *Ibid.*, 996.

62. Williams, 1901.

63. Bullard, 997.

64. The document is quoted in full in Huggins, 231.

65. Huggins, 224. These were the numbers recounted by Judge Pittman, an early twentieth-century historian. According to Huggins, there were a total of nineteen associations at the time, but some had become or were becoming anti-missionary. Huggins was only able to discover a total of 256 churches established between 1729 and 1830.

66. Huggins, 235.

67. B.F. Riley, *A History of the Baptists in the Southern States East of the Mississippi* (Philadelphia: American Baptist Publication Society, 1898), 186.

68. Bullard, 996.

69. Daniel Merritt, *Faith Flowing Freely: History of the Yadkin Baptist Association, 1790–1990* (Elkin, NC: Nu-line Printing, 1990), 67.

70. Paschal, v II., 274.

71. Sparks, 250.

72. *Ibid.*, 249.

73. Lydia Huffman Hoyle, "Original Free Will Baptists" in Mark A. Lamport and George Thomas Kurian, ed. *Encyclopedia of Christianity in the United States* (Lanham, MD: Rowman and Littlefield, 2016).

74. *Ibid.* For an extensive history of the denomination, see Michael R. Pelt's *A History of Original Free Will Baptists.*

75. Bill J. Leonard, ed. *Dictionary of Baptists in America* (Downers Grove, IL: Intervarsity Press, 1994) 281.

76. Williams, 78.

77. Williams, 85–90 and Bullard, 998.

78. Williams, 80.

79. Except for two brief suspensions, the paper has been published weekly to the present time.

80. A table listing all churches established during this period can be found in Huggins, 417–34.

81. Ready, 189. By 1860, 12 percent of Christians in North Carolina were black.

82. Williams, 139–40, and Bullard, 1000.

83. Williams, 140.

84. From 1857 to 1898, the Western Convention was independent from the state convention. See Huggins, 246.

85. Tom Orr, "Ridge Lines: Judson College, a Lost Landmark" (June 14, 2015). www.blueridgenow.com/article/NC/20150614/News/606016440/HT/ Accessed 6/27/2017.

86. Bullard, 999.

87. Quoted in Bullard, 999.

88. John R. Woodard, "North Carolina," in *Religion in the Southern States* ed. Samuel S. Hill (Macon, GA: Mercer University Press, 1983), 222.

89. Bullard, 1000.

90. John R. Woodard, "Matthew Tyson Yates," *NCPedia.org,* www.ncpedia.org/biography/yates-matthew-tyson (accessed June 28, 2017).

91. Huggins, 301.

92. "Preamble to the WMU Constitution, 1888," in Catherine Allen, *A Century to Celebrate: History of the Woman's Missionary Union* (Birmingham, AL: Woman's Missionary Union, 1987), 47.

93. Bea McRae, "Our Glorious Heritage," *Woman's Missionary Union of North Carolina*, http://docs.wixstatic.com/ugd/4f59ca_f26a4b9f356e45d7955f5f17e421d955.pdf (accessed June 24, 2017.)

94. See Lydia Huffman Hoyle, "The Subversive Power of Calling: The Girls' Auxiliary and Baptist Women in Ministry," in *Reimagining Baptist History*, ed. Karen Seat and Elizabeth Flowers (unpublished manuscript).

95. Bullard, 1000.

96. The first known black church in the South was Silver Bluff in South Carolina. Several churches formed in North Carolina during the war when the Black members withdrew from mixed congregations to form separate churches.

97. Ready, 190.

98. Claude R. Trotter, Sr., John W. Fleming, and W. B. Lewis, *A Splendid Enterprise* (Raleigh, NC: General Baptist State Convention of North Carolina, 1999), 9–29.

99. Trotter, Fleming, and Lewis, 34.

100. *Ibid.*

101. L.H. Williams, "United American Free Will Baptist Church," in *Dictionary of Baptists in America*, ed. Bill J Leonard (Downers Grove, IL: Intervarsity Press, 1994), 273.

102. National Primitive Baptist Convention, USA, Inc., www.npbcconvention.org/, accessed June 27, 2017.

103. The years listed indicate the year the institution became a junior college or college.

104. A.B. Cash, "Mountain Mission Schools," in *Encyclopedia of Southern Baptists*, v.II (Nashville, TN: Broadman, 1958), 926–28. See also Charles W. Deweese, *Baptist Mountain Mission Schools* (Mars Hill, NC: Mars Hill University Press, 2016).

105. Bullard, 1001–1002.

106. Glenn Jonas, "Baptist Children's Homes," *NCPedia.org*, www.ncpedia.org/baptist-childrens-homes (accessed 6/20/2017).

107. Michael Pelt, "Free Will Baptist Children's Home," *NCPedia.org*, www.ncpedia.org/free-will-baptist-childrens-home (accessed 6/20/2017). The General Baptist Convention also serves as a major sponsor of a children's home called the Central Children's Home in Oxford, NC. The home, however, is nondenominational and independent.

108. Bullard, 380–88.

109. J.E. Lambdin, "Baptist Training Union," in *Encyclopedia of Southern Baptists*, v. I (Nashville, TN: Broadman, 1958), 123–24.

110. Pope A. Duncan, "Southeastern Baptist Theological Seminary," in *Encyclopedia of Southern Baptists*, v. II (Nashville, TN: Broadman, 1958), 1239–42.

111. You can see the list at http://www.cbfnc.org/about/partner-churches. CBF-NC offers extensive opportunities for churches in the area of missions, leadership development and faith development. Support for women in ministry is also provided by an organization called Baptist Women in Ministry of North Carolina.

Black Religion

SANDY DWAYNE MARTIN

This essay provides a historical outline of African American religion in North Carolina from colonial times to the present, focusing for the most part on the two largest groups of black religious adherents in the state, the Baptists and the Methodists (especially the African Methodist Episcopal Zion Church). A more comprehensive treatment of all African American religious groups is beyond the scope of this study, considering the bounty of resources over a period of three centuries or more. However limited this overview may be in terms of inclusiveness, the reader will gain a deep and appreciable understanding of religion among blacks in the state.

The study of black religion in North Carolina is of immense importance. First, a significant percentage of the state's inhabitants are black.[1] According to a 2010 estimate, more than one-fifth (about 22.1 percent) of the population of the state is black; the white population represents more than two-thirds (about 71.2 percent), with the remainder Native American (1.6 percent), Asian (2.8 percent), and Hispanic not broken down by race (9.1 percent).

Second, religion plays a considerable role in the lives of black and nonblack people in the state. A 2014 Pew Research Survey of adult North Carolinians reveals helpful information.[2] Yet the survey is problematic as it relates to nomenclature used for religious categories. For example, while only 10 percent of blacks identify as "evangelical Protestants," the fact remains that many people in the "historically black denominations" (57 percent) are members of groups, such as Baptists and Methodists, that are greatly if not mainly evangelical Protestants. In other words, some blacks identifying as mainline Protestant could conceivably place themselves in two Pew categories: "evangelical Protestants" and members of "historically black denominations." Also notable, the survey's sample size is relatively small, with 712 white respondents and 183 black respondents.

Acknowledging the above cautions, the survey provides some useful insights. First, in North Carolina as in other places, blacks and whites tend to affiliate and worship with members of their own race or ethnicities rather than in racially mixed denominations or congregations. Second, the vast majority of black and white adults in North Carolina, according to the 2014 Pew Research Survey, are Protestants. The second-largest group identifies as unaffiliated with any church; the third-largest is Catholic. Given the fact that some of Pew's categories overlap, it would be reasonable to estimate that *at least* 50 percent of religious whites are evangelicals, whether they are listed as members of groups generally identified as evangelical Protestants or as members of those classified as mainline Protestants. Likewise, it would be reasonable to estimate that *at least* 50 to 60 percent of religious black adults are evangelical, whether they identify as evangelical Protestants, members of historically black Protestant groups, or as mainline Protestants. But perhaps the most surprising statistic is the large percentage of blacks (21 percent) and whites (20 percent) identifying as "None," not affiliated with any religious community, though evidence indicates that most citing "None" are simply opting out of organized religion but still see themselves as "spiritual." This could very well be the majority of people in the None category, yet there is also evidence of a growth in agnosticism and atheism in American society.

The following statistics are perhaps even more revealing of the continuing importance of religion in the lives of blacks and non-blacks in the state: Among North Carolinian black adults, 77 percent are Christians (57 percent of whom belong to historically black Protestant groups); 1 percent are atheist; less than 1 percent agnostic; 20 percent "nothing in particular." Among white adults, 78 percent are Christian; 3 percent are atheists; 4 percent are agnostics; 13 percent "nothing in particular." In a more significant percentage difference between the races, the survey reports 79 percent of blacks stating that religion is *very* important to them, compared to 57 percent of whites; 11 percent of blacks and 24 percent of whites stating religion is *somewhat* important.[3]

Colonial Period to 1783

While persons of African descent were among the early explorers of the Americas, it was the African-European slave trade that introduced the great body of Africans to the Western Hemisphere.[4] Africans sold by other Africans to representatives of European nations came from various ethnic or tribal groups in Africa, but especially from west and west central portions of the continent. While a scarce number of Christians were, perhaps, among them, most Africans entering the Americas practiced traditional African ethnic-based religions. A reasonable and moderate-to-conservative estimate is that 10 to 20 percent of Africans came from areas heavily populated by practitioners of Islam. Another interesting factor is that less than 10 percent of all Africans were imported into what we know as the United States of America.

Much more academic research, including archaeological explorations, must be done before we have a more complete picture of the lives of colonial Africans in North America, including their religious practices. There are some general points, however, that we can make regarding colonial North America, including North Carolina. First, Africans, within decades, became virtually the only racial/ethnic group confined to lifelong, hereditary, chattel slavery in the Americas. Second, it is true that throughout colonial America, among both the English and non–English, there were Africans who converted to Christianity during the period from 1619 to the 1730s. Yet African people were largely non–Christians, practicing either African traditional religions or Islam. Third and more specific to North Carolina, thus far there is no documented congregation in North Carolina considered among the very earliest of independent black congregations. Fourth, though scholars might still debate the degree of impact that traditional African culture and religion had on black American culture and religion, it is generally acknowledged in academic circles that a significant degree of African influence existed in colonial days and continues to exist in African American cultural life. While North Carolina does not have the same degree of African traditional religious and African Islamic influence as do coastal areas of Georgia and South Carolina, it is correct to say that throughout the United States, including North Carolina, some significant strands of African culture and religion have persisted.

Yet to remain in the Americas meant that these original Africans would eventually become more and more American. As Africans achieved greater facility in English and continued to develop their own African American world, many of the impassable cultural barriers between the two groups were reduced and sometimes eliminated. Therefore, groundwork was laid in North Carolina and other places for Africans to embrace Christianity on a broader scale. In addition to the diminution of linguistic and other cultural barriers separating Africans and Europeans, the Great Awakening (a series of revivals between the 1720s and 1760s, and especially in the 1730s through the 1750s) attracted large numbers of people, including African Americans, to the churches. Evangelical Christianity's many appeals included an emphasis on the immediacy of God's presence and power that attracted many people of all backgrounds.[5] It was also similar to the African traditional approach to religion. For instance, the assertiveness of preachers and teachers, black and white, in evangelizing among the enslaved and the poor, as well as the strong belief that God calls people to be leaders in Christianizing and in worship regardless of their educational background, social standing, or even the color of their skin. And, finally, a strong contingent of evangelicals, black and white, saw slavery as inconsistent with the will of God and advocated vigorously for its demise. This is not to say that white evangelicals by and large were antislavery or that they were devoid of racial bias. But with the exception of the Quakers, it would be among the evangelicals that one was most likely to find a large Christian group with bold antislavery positions.

Evangelical Christianity was an approach to the faith that allowed converts, including black slaves, to claim greater ownership of their religion and to adapt it to their needs and wants. Black men could not in many circumstances be formally ordained as pastors or even preachers, but the evangelical faith shared by blacks and whites alike declared that God calls all people to service and uses them to bring the news of salvation to others, even to members of the racially dominant group. The greatest fear of whites when they learned that black enslaved Christians might be holding secret worship services was not that they were acting in contradiction to the rules of the church. Of course, Christians can freely assemble and hear from those called by God words of exhortation and instruction. The greatest fear, rather, was that black slaves were meeting without the presence of whites and might plan an insurrection or antislavery revolt. Hence—and this is the point—in a society and in a social station that very much denied them freedom, blacks could find a liberty in evangelical Christianity not found in most non-evangelical churches. No wonder then that most black Christians, like many white and Native American Christians, were evangelical Baptists, evangelical Presbyterians, and evangelical Anglicans (who mostly would later become Methodists).

National and Antebellum Period, 1783–1860

Most black Christians would become Baptists and Methodists, though many would be members of Congregationalist, Presbyterian, and other churches, including Roman

Catholic.[6] By 1790, it is quite possible that at least one-fourth or more of all Baptists and Methodists were African Americans. Most blacks, like most whites, however, were not official members of any Christian church. Many enslaved blacks had not really been exposed to Christianity. At least three major movements would work in tandem to increase the number of black Christians during the early national and antebellum periods: (a) the Second Great Awakening, ca. 1790s to 1830s; (b) the Mission to the Slaves and corresponding activities by predominantly white churches to evangelize among the enslaved; and (c) the continued efforts of black Christians, clergy and lay, to share the faith with fellow African Americans.

The Second Great Awakening, like the First Great Awakening, was a series of revivals that called people particularly to an evangelical Christianity. This Awakening, like the first, also gained many converts from all backgrounds, including those who were African American. A "Mission to the Slaves" began around 1830; it was an organized, systematic attempt to carry the gospel to those enslaved persons, especially on the plantations and farms, who were not Christians. Some of the motivation for plantation missions, or the Mission to the Slaves, was the desire to prove to their white northern Baptist counterparts that slavery was consistent with Christianity. For, although most white southern slaveholders had clearly rejected the antislavery appeal, they cared for the souls of the enslaved and their physical well-being in this life. Overall, the mission did not reach its goal in numbers of converts or its objective in reforming the system of slavery to eliminate its harsher aspects such as the separation of families when individuals were sold away from their kin. Nor did a universal relationship between slaves and slaveholders come about, one in which the enslaved willingly carried out their duties and the masters and the mistresses genuinely cared about the slaves. Nonetheless, the mission did succeed in introducing Christianity to many slaves and directing the services of enslaved preachers and leaders to missionize among the slaves, thereby helping to create a ministerial and church culture that would play an instrumental role in church organization with the coming of freedom.[7] This notation leads us to the larger point about black leadership. It is important to note that Christianity largely passed from blacks to other blacks. Overall, blacks were the largest contingent of religious leadership, instruction, and evangelizing among blacks. To be sure, when we speak of Christianization during the antebellum era, Christianity did pass from whites to blacks and the reverse. But largely the faith passed from whites to whites and from blacks to blacks. This general pattern of Christianization applied to North Carolina as it did to the rest of the nation.

A Focus on the Baptists

Baptists are the largest religious group among African Americans in North Carolina and therefore serve as a good case study for black religion before the Civil War. In his 1908 history of black Baptists, J.A. Whitted stresses the difficulty of writing a full, accurate account of black Baptists in that era because so much information went unrecorded. He notes a total of 400,000 documented African American Baptists in the entire United States by the end of the Civil War and says that all were connected to white-controlled churches.[8] Whitted's account of black Baptist life in the antebellum period matches contemporary historians' and scholars' findings about African American Christians in general. His description of antebellum church life notes that white Baptists made some efforts to evangelize African Americans. But he points out that this extension of Christian fellowship operated within the bounds of race and servitude. In the visible, institutional churches, African Americans were often leaders among their people but always under the supervision of whites or certainly subject to their supervision. Church life was segregated, with separate seating for whites and blacks and separate reception of Holy Communion or the Lord's Supper, with blacks receiving the elements after whites had been served. Governance of the church, including regulating the behavior of members, was solidly in the hands of the white membership, though as Whitted adds, occasionally black members did receive some fair treatment.[9]

Demonstrating the evangelical connection between whites and blacks, Whitted notes that at an early point of Baptist faith, whites in the South were quite expressive in their feelings, exclaiming "hallelujah!" and showing clear signs of joy. Therefore, it was not surprising to whites that African American fellow worshippers would likewise be expressive. Whitted also points out how differences over slavery caused difficulties between northern and southern whites. White northern and southern Baptists agreed on the necessity of extending the gospel to the African American population, though perhaps they differed over aspects of that effort. They increasingly divided over the morality of slavery, leading to the separation of the two groups in 1845. North Carolinian white Baptists, like Baptists elsewhere, continued to labor among the enslaved African American population even after this North–South ecclesiastical division.

Whitted proceeds to discuss the spread of the gospel among the enslaved. White ministers and revivals were significant means by which many people embraced Christianity. One such congregation that arose from a revival conducted by two white ministers was the Pleasant Plains Baptist Church located in Hertford County. Significantly, these white clergypersons—a white Methodist and a white Baptist—cooperated in conducting the revival. With the Baptist and Methodist ministers standing on opposite sides, the newly professed believers selected their own denominational affiliation. Practically all of the new black Christians selected the Baptist side, and this was the genesis of the Pleasant Plains Baptist congregation. It would not be until well after the Civil War that the congregation was led by a black minister, the Reverend Calvin Scott Brown, who played a pivotal role in the North Carolina Baptist organization, particularly among African Americans.

Black ministers also played a major role in spreading the gospel among the enslaved. There were relatively few formally ordained and/or licensed black ministers according to the regular order of the Baptist denomination, but records indicate that many black preachers effectively served as pastors of their people even without official ordination from local churches or associations. At any rate, Whitted mentions one early influential black Baptist minister, "Uncle Harry" Cowan, a slave of Thomas Cowan. Master Cowan apparently became immensely impressed with Harry Cowan's gift for preaching when he first heard the latter during a funeral. Evidently Thomas Cowan had a lawyer draw up what were known as "privilege" papers for Harry Cowan, documents that granted him the right to preach freely, to perform marriages, and to baptize on all four plantations that the Cowan family owned. While Whitted does not point out this fact, such an authorization to minister did not follow regular Baptist rules and polity. It should have been a local church that selected Cowan to preach. Even so, it is noteworthy that the influence of the slave master was so significant in regard to a person's ministry. Harry Cowan's ministerial success was such that his right to preach the gospel extended beyond Thomas

Cowan's plantation to encompass any place where it would be safe for him to preach. Harry Cowan's ministry continued through the Civil War, during which he served as General Joseph Johnston's body servant. After the Civil War, his great service continued in the age of freedom. During the seventy years he preached the gospel, Cowan baptized eight thousand people.[10]

Whitted correctly points out that "Uncle Harry" Cowan was but one example of black leaders, both deacons and preachers, who had great leadership ability and fine character, though very few had the freedom or privileges of Cowan. Another well-known antebellum black minister was "Dr. Lewis Perry," a name by which both blacks and whites often addressed him.[11] A slave of Dr. Willie Perry, he ministered around Louisburg, North Carolina. Like Cowan, Perry also carried papers in connection with his ministry, papers that granted him the right to conduct prayer meetings and exhort. Also like Cowan, his preaching audience included whites as well as blacks. In the local white-controlled church, the pastor upon completing his sermon would almost always ask Perry to lead congregational prayer. We might say he was a type of associate pastor with oversight of the African American members since any African American candidate for membership could only join with Perry's approval. Interestingly, Perry conducted revivals in the basements of Louisburg's Baptist and Methodist congregations, through which many people embraced the faith. Ministers were not the only religious leaders among the enslaved and free blacks. In the city of Raleigh, there were lay leaders such as Henry Jett, Jim Adkins, Sandy Pinkin, Richard Jett, and Todd Palmer.[12] These early black leaders, lay and ministerial, helped establish the foundation of a strong Baptist presence among blacks prior to and following the war.

Black Methodists in Antebellum North Carolina

Given that Methodists have constituted the second largest religious group of African Americans since the antebellum period, it would be useful to provide at least a brief overview of black Methodism in North Carolina.[13] The Methodists in the new nation largely emerged out of the evangelicals of the former Church of England, or Anglican Church, whereas the largely non-evangelical portion became what is now known as the Episcopal Church. It appears that North Carolina Methodists became a separate conference in 1836 after having been, first, a part of the Virginia Conference and, later, the Virginia and the South Carolina Annual Conferences. According to the 1844 North Carolina conference statistics, the membership of the conference was 19,495 whites and 3,190 "colored," or blacks. Like white Baptists, southern white Methodists organizationally withdrew from their white northern counterparts, but a year earlier in 1844, formed the Methodist Episcopal Church, South, and, again like their Baptists counterparts, did so without consulting with their black co-members. The North Carolina Annual Conference did not assemble between 1845 and 1865. During and following the Civil War the black membership in the MEC, South, joined the African Methodist Episcopal Zion Church (AMEZ). The African Methodist Episcopal Church (AME) became the founding membership of the Colored (later Christian) Methodist Episcopal Church (CME) in 1870. Black Baptists and some other churches joined the Methodist Episcopal Church (AME), based mainly in the North.

Civil War and Post–Civil War, 1860–1880

While Whitted's work focuses on North Carolina black Baptists, many of his general comments are equally applicable to other black Christians.[14] Many antebellum blacks deeply valued Christianity, making great sacrifices to worship, generously contributing to the church from the paucity of their means, and some walking up to twenty miles for prayer meetings held as late as midnight. As Whitted points out, sometimes these meetings were secret, with the attendees liable to be treated as lawbreakers. Later scholars, such as Albert Raboteau, also discuss the "invisible institution," the secret practices and beliefs of African Americans often concealed from whites.

Whitted, like other scholars, points to the sincerity of these worshippers, remarking how even whites sometimes would call for black Christians to have prayer with them as they faced death. This discussion regarding black Christianity during the antebellum period is immensely important. Many northern Christians, black and white, during the antebellum period often questioned the depth and doctrinally accurate nature of the religion of the enslaved because they did not trust that southern slave owners and their supporters correctly conveyed true Christianity to the enslaved. What many of these northern Christians missed, however, was the agency of black Christians themselves in spreading the gospel in their communities. Furthermore, even when blacks received preaching and teaching from white missionary slaveholders or their supporters, the fact remains that black recipients of the Good News had their own interpretations of the faith that often contradicted that of white missionaries. As we can see from written accounts of missionaries and teachers among the enslaved and freed people, generally the respect for black southern Christians rose greatly upon sustained contact with these people of faith.

Whitted is correct to note that the devotion of Christians across racial lines was, in certain cases, so strong that even after the war blacks chose to remain with the white-controlled churches rather than leave for their own separate churches. But it seems that another pattern more often prevailed. It is clear even from Whitted's account that with the coming of freedom, most African Americans did in fact pursue separate ecclesiastical paths and that both whites and blacks were comfortable with that parting of the ways. Of course, many people in the South in the aftermath of the war were quite poor. Certainly that was the case with enslaved and formerly enslaved people, who brought no real assets with them as they embarked on the road of freedom. Facing the challenge of survival, they had few resources to build church structures or to compensate ministers who labored among them. Often, the newly freed people constructed rather crude structures, sometimes brush arbors—that is, tree limbs and other things affixed together to make a building or makeshift shelter—or sometimes it meant simply worshipping beneath trees. Whitted notes how worship houses for many former slaves progressed over time from these crude structures to log churches and on to framed churches and to brick constructions.

For this progression from crude structures to brick edifices, one could say, represents what was happening regarding the educational and professional changes in the churches. In some instances, ministers and other leaders who had labored so tirelessly and sacrificially during antebellum and even postwar years to advance the gospel found themselves struggling to deal with the increasingly new order, with some of them being gradually and painfully removed from positions of leadership as ministers and laypeople and replaced by ministers and laity with greater education. Whitted observes that "Only a few of these old ministers survived in the midst of these changes. Most of them outlived their generation."[15] Generally these older leaders "would yield with extreme reluctance." How ironic that persons who had labored so hard at what amounted to laying the foundations of the church of the freedom era would find themselves in many instances pushed aside.

There were those leaders who continued to make great contributions to the church, such as the Reverend G.W. Holland of Winston-Salem, who in his lifetime established twenty-eight Baptist congregations. In later life, he not only commanded the respect of older people but also won the great admiration of younger church people. Likewise, the Reverend Thomas Parker continued to be very effective in the new era of freedom. In his lifetime he baptized perhaps four thousand people, pastored four churches with the greatest membership in the Kenansville Association, and served as that association's moderator for thirty years.[16]

The Growth of Black Baptists in North Carolina

Having examined briefly local black religious leaders and congregations among Baptists, let us turn to the activities of regional associations and state conventions. One of the most important parts of Baptist polity or governance is the local association, composed of a number of churches within a given area within a state or sometimes given areas in adjoining states. From the end of the Civil War to the year 1940, more than fifty black Baptist associations appeared in North Carolina.[17] The following overview is not comprehensive, but should provide a sketch of the earliest organized associations with attention to those in the eastern portion of the state, where black people and black Baptists mainly resided, and the central and western portions, where fewer blacks live and Baptists are significant but fewer in numbers compared to the eastern section.

The Old Eastern Missionary Baptist Association is one of the first associations organized, having formed in James River in 1865 with the presence of Thad Wilson, John Washington, and Thomas Erkett. Two other associations formed from the Old Eastern group: the Neuse River Association in 1866; and, in 1875, the New Bern Eastern Association. By 1904, it had purchased land and built the Tar River Institute in Greenville. The Gray Creek Baptist Association, one of the earliest associations organized in the state, emerged in Bladen County in the eastern portion of the state right after the Civil War, perhaps in 1865 or 1866. It organized with three participating congregations—New Light, Gray's Creek, and New Hope—and its founding leadership included the presence of elders J.M. Whitted, S.H. McCoy, H.S. McNeil, and Gilbert Monroe. By 1940, five other associations had been formed from this original group: Lumber River, Kinston Lake, Union, Lake Waccamaw, and Hammond's Creek. The Reverend Ananias Buck and C. Johnson were among the organizers of the Neuse River Baptist Association formed in Halifax in 1866. By 1940, it was one of the leading state associations with over ninety churches, actively supporting domestic endeavors and foreign missions. The Cedar Grove Baptist Association (founded as Pleasant Grove, and later renamed Oak Grove) organized in Person County in 1868. Noteworthy regarding this association is the affiliation of a white minister, the Reverend L.C. Ragland, around 1870, and his continued membership with the group until he passed away after having given active service. Differences led to the formation of another association from this one, the East Grove Baptist Association in the eastern part of the former district.

Shifting westward, the Reverend Samuel Fox in 1867 was the main organizer of the Shiloh Baptist Association in Waco, near Charlotte. Two years later, this association separated into Mecklenburg and Shiloh Baptist Associations. Also in the western and central portion of the state, the Mountain and Catawba Baptist Association formed in 1875. Black Baptists were fewer in numbers in the western area of North Carolina, but the association succeeded at an early date in establishing a school in Claremont. Initially the Mountain and Catawba Association did not affiliate with the State Baptist Educational and Missionary Convention but did so in later years.

Returning to the eastern portion of North Carolina, the Kenansville Baptist Association, formed in Kenansville in 1870, was the home association of James O. Hayes, who for a number of years served as a missionary in Africa. The Wake Baptist Association was known for its support of education, including Shaw University in Raleigh as well as an orphanage for blacks in Oxford. New Hope Baptist Association, formed in 1870 in Chatham County, was an active supporter of foreign missions. The Middle District Association organized in 1872 in Wilmington, North Carolina. This association appointed three missionaries to form and strengthen churches in five counties, including the county of its founding, New Hanover. It started Burgaw High School, which as late as 1940 was still operating and still owned by the association. Major laborers in this association around 1940 included persons who were also quite active at the state level of Baptist work, among them Dr. and Mrs. W.H. Moore, the Reverend J.D. McRae, Mrs. Lillian Shaw, and Mrs. Irene Mandy.

In the central-to-western portion of the state, the Rowan Baptist Association organized in Salisbury in 1877 and had in its presence there the venerable Harry Cowan. The association did not secure ownership and support associational schools as much as other groups. It did, however, provide great support to Shaw University and foreign missions. By 1940, it encompassed ninety churches with twenty-five thousand congregants in rural areas as well as in the larger urban areas such as Charlotte, Winston-Salem, and Greensboro.

State Baptist Conventions in the Postwar Period

Throughout the South, separate black Baptist conventions were established soon after the Civil War.[18] The Baptist Educational and Missionary Convention appears to be the first black convention established in North Carolina, founded in 1867 by ten ministers with the assistance of some white Baptists. Those ministers meeting in Goldsboro to establish this organization were L.W. Boone, Charles Bryant, Sutton Davis, Edward Eagles, H. Grimes, R.H. Harper, C. Johnson, B.B. Spicer, William Warwich, and John Warwich. They started with but few resources: brush arbors and log huts generally sufficed for church edifices; little formal education or money supported the work. Yet the organization and Baptist work grew tremendously and extended to every section of the state, and they pursued the acquisition of books and the advancement of an educated ministry. White Baptists[19] in their formal meetings stressed the need to support "the religious and educational development of the Negro" and provided tangible means of support. Of course, the northern-based white Baptists contributed even more in terms of personnel and resources to the building of black church life in the South. Yet we must recall that whites in the postwar South also had pressing economic concerns in and outside the church, and white northern Baptists had obligations in addition to the southern field.

These black Baptists in North Carolina and other portions of the South, therefore, had to carry most of the financial burden themselves. Indeed, many, while greatly appreciative of white support, were delighted that they themselves were able to labor and sacrifice on behalf of their black brothers and sisters. And, of course, regardless of money and other resources available, the work of evangelizing and establishing new churches required zeal and hard work that was provided by determined and committed early ministers and laypeople. The early missionaries of the newly founded convention included John Washington, E.E. Eagles (supported by the northern-based American Baptist Publication Society), F.R. Howell, and P.F. Malloy. These early pioneering ministers literally walked great distances as they evangelized, sold Bibles and other religious materials, and established Sunday schools and congregations.[20]

The interest expressed by white southern and northern Baptists in spreading the gospel and furthering education among blacks following the Civil War points to the cooperative plans that emerged. Soon after the conflict, black and white Baptists worked alongside each other in the pursuit of missions, mainly in the United States but also in Africa, cooperative attempts that lasted into the 1900s.[21] These interracial cooperative agreements involved one or more black conventions collaborating with one or more white conventions, among them the Baptist Education and Missionary Convention (black), the Southern Baptist Convention (white), the Baptist State Convention of North Carolina (white), and the American Baptist Home Mission Society and American Baptist Missionary Union (mainly white northern groups). In 1895, a new national organization of black Baptists formed in Atlanta, Georgia—the National Baptist Convention (NBC)—which would become the most successful, enduring unification of black Baptists in that era. A couple of years following the formation of the NBC, strong tensions emerged between "cooperationists" and "independents."[22] The real issue was not so much whether black and white Baptists should work together. Both cooperationists and independents favored such interracial solidarity. The main question was to what extent should black Baptists yield control to white Baptists in these arrangements. Cooperationists were much more willing to permit a strong white voice in the management of unified enterprises, whereas independents firmly believed that blacks should take the lead and exercise greater control in decision making. Cooperationists believed that blacks were not ready to go it alone without strong financial backing from whites. Independents believed that it was a matter of racial pride that blacks do for themselves.

In North Carolina and Virginia, the debate between cooperationists and independents was most intense; hence, they were in the forefront of establishing a new national or regional group, the Lott Carey Baptist Convention in 1897. Divisions also occurred within state conventions, including the Baptist Educational and Missionary Convention in North Carolina. The North Carolina independent group, whose support appears to have been strongest in the eastern portion of the state, formed a new convention, the Union Baptist Convention of North Carolina. In 1908 the two sides reunited, merging the two conventions to form the Union Baptist Convention of North Carolina but later renamed the General Baptist State Convention of North Carolina.[23] In a sense, the cooperation debate reflected much regarding how black North Carolinians sought to survive and progress in an increasingly racially restrictive environment. With the fastening of rigid and legal racial segregation, the disfranchisement of the great majority of black voters, and the growth of racial terrorist groups such as the Ku Klux Klan, cooperation was one effort to maintain positive connection with whites and to secure the assistance of sympathetic whites. Whereas many independents might have seen racial survival and progress most aided by group solidarity and pride, cooperationists could point to the "better class of white people" with whom they maintained interaction. Perhaps we see an example of this use of the cooperationist approach in Williams and Watkins' references to John E. White, who served as the corresponding secretary of the white state convention. The authors describe White as "a powerful force in maintaining good will and the spirit of brotherhood in Christ among Negro and white people of the State, during a political upheaval which discouraged many Negroes and caused them to leave the State."[24]

Apparently the authors refer to what has historically been termed the "Wilmington Riot of 1898" but more accurately could be referenced as the "Wilmington Insurrection of 1898." In that year, a group of conservative and/or reactionary whites in what was then the largest city in North Carolina literally took arms and overthrew the city government controlled by moderate whites and blacks. Many blacks were literally chased out of town, and a leading black newspaper was destroyed. Neither the state nor the federal government took any steps to restore the properly elected government or to secure protection for the black citizens of the town. For many decades, the trauma of this event stymied the growth of Wilmington and left a sense of intimidation over the black population there. Speaking to the black Baptist state convention as he departed the state for a pastorate in Atlanta, Georgia, White's text, "Strengthen the Things that Remain," might have had a particularly encouraging and hopeful political and economic message for African Americans.

But most likely no white Baptist earned higher esteem among African American Baptists in North Carolina or elsewhere in the South than Mrs. Joanna P. Moore, who came from the North and settled in Nashville, Tennessee, to labor among the enslaved in the postwar South. Whitted's high opinion of Moore is made clear in the notes from the meeting of the 1899 Educational and Missionary Convention of North Carolina: "The saintly Miss Joanna P. Moore, of Nashville, Tenn., was also present [;] and since she had done more than they all in behalf of the colored people, not only in one respect, but in all that pertained to their general uplift, like her blessed Savior, who gave His very life for humanity, the Convention heard her with breathless silence and appreciation."[25]

Baptist associations and conventions, with the support of blacks and whites, established a great number of secondary schools in the state. Like schools founded by other denominations, such as the Methodists, and in other states, the great majority of these institutions no longer operate. In many instances the properties are still held by Baptist entities; others were awarded to the counties and the state for operation as public schools. Other facilities by agreement were on loan to the state for use in the education of African American children. Since the Civil War, these schools, such as Burgaw High School and Lumberton's Thompson Institute, have played a crucial role in the education of African Americans.[26]

Black Methodists in North Carolina During the Civil War and Postwar Years

During the Civil War and postwar period, we see some black Methodists[27] leaving congregations affiliated with the white-controlled Methodist Episcopal Church, South, and aligning themselves with the largely white Methodist Episcopal Church, based in the North. But in far greater numbers, we see African American North Carolinian

Methodists, as in other southern states, entering black denominations when freedom arrived: the African Methodist Episcopal Church (AME, which organized in 1816 in Philadelphia) and the African Methodist Episcopal Zion Church (AMEZ, which organized in the 1820 to 1822 period in New York City). By 1870, the remaining blacks in the Methodist Episcopal Church, South, in cooperation with and having the support of their white denominational counterparts, form a separate group, the Christian [originally, Colored] Methodist Episcopal Church (CME).

North Carolina would become perhaps the strongest base for the AMEZ Church, especially in the South. Whereas the AME would predominate among Methodists in states such as South Carolina and Virginia, the AMEZ would constitute the largest Methodist group in North Carolina and Alabama. The Baptists' primary college would be Shaw University in Raleigh; the AMEZ's major college would be Livingstone College in Salisbury. The AMEZ Church had an antebellum connection with North Carolina, given that one of its earliest bishops and church historians, Christopher Rush, formerly enslaved, was a native of New Bern in the northeastern portion of the state. During the Civil War when many northern-based denominations, white and black, began sending missionaries and teachers to the South, the AMEZ commissioned Bishop John J. Clinton and future AME Zion church leader Bishop James Walker Hood for the southern work. In the winter of 1864, Hood entered New Bern and by 1865 was serving as the president of the first Freedmen Convention in Raleigh.

The 1865 annual session of the North Carolina Annual Conference of the African Methodist Episcopal Zion Church, an annual conference that organized in 1864, assembled in Purvis Chapel in Beaufort, North Carolina, on December 26, 1865, with Bishop J.J. Clinton presiding as Superintendent of the Fourth Episcopal District.[28] (At this point in history, the AMEZ Church was still employing the terms "bishop" and "superintendent" interchangeably.) In attendance were two secretaries, thirteen elders, seventeen deacons, and three preachers. At least two elders, James Walker Hood and William J. Moore, and at least one deacon, William H. [Hillery], would in the coming years be elevated to the office of bishop. Indeed, Deacon Hillery would be elevated to elder in this conference session. Another deacon, Andrew Cartwright, would eventually become a missionary to Africa. Among the North Carolina churches with the largest memberships (that included full members, probationers, local preachers, and exhorters) were these six: Andrew Chapel in New Bern, 771; Blockhouse, 403; Pineville, 401; Fayetteville, 391; Wilmington with a total of 391; and Charlotte, 201.

A survey of the committees appointed provides a look at the priorities of the AMEZ in the state. With each composed of usually three but sometimes two members, the committees were those dealing with Public Worship, Missions, the State of the Country, Education, Sabbath Schools, Finance, Rules, Holy Orders, Temperance, Credentials of Lay Delegates, Circuits and Stations, Complaints, and Post Office. In the churches of this era, a great deal of emphasis was placed on the moral character of the membership, and especially the leadership. Accordingly and interestingly, the minutes read that the Chairman, Bishop J.J. Clinton, at the beginning of the session after the devotion, "proceeded to examine the character of the members," that is, the members of the annual conference who were likely all ministers at this historical time. After four elders gave accounts of their work during the past year, their characters "passed." In addition to making an annual report of activities, there appears to have been time for anyone to express anything negative about the character of the individual making the report. The conference approved a report from the Committee On Complaints, which included the recommendation that one deacon be suspended for a year; but regarding a complaint against a second member, the committee did not find any basis for sustaining that complaint. No one had been dropped from membership. True to Methodist fashion and evangelical practice, these Methodists often fellowshipped across denominational lines, for there is some indication that at least two session members were scheduled to participate in a worship service at a local Baptist church.

The committee on The State of the Country perhaps gives us a good sense of what most African Americans in 1865 were thinking regarding civil affairs. The committee recalled that, a year previous, the astute could tell how the war would ultimately end, but no one was certain about just when that termination would occur. Now with the war ended, America had a great future ahead of it and had the opportunity to commence with an unprecedented "era of liberty" in human history. The committee laments the assassination of President Abraham Lincoln, a great friend of republicanism and oppressed people throughout the world, but expresses confidence in the current President Andrew Johnson. The committee sees the necessity of preserving peace, obeying "just laws," and calls upon "our people," presumably African Americans, to be honest, industrious, to work to cultivate, repair, and build up the land. There was no question that the United States was the home of black people and that they will endeavor to have full rights as American citizens. "That as this is our native land, here we design to stay, acting our part as patriotic citizens, engaging in every thing that will conduce to the well being of the entire people of this our beloved country."

The Committee on Business recommended that the conference take care with ordination of clergy, that people be duly qualified to serve the people, that ministers be encouraged to secure money due the superintendent or bishop, and endorsed *The Anglo-African* newspaper.

The Committee on Temperance stood firmly against the use of alcoholic beverages, urged ministers not to use tobacco in the church and to teach the same to youth, and to set up temperance societies in Sunday or Sabbath schools.

The Committee on Education spoke about the wonderful opportunity to gain education, something that had long been denied people. The committee urged the establishment of "day schools," thanked white benefactors for their assistance in this regard but indicated the importance of blacks taking responsibility as soon as feasible, encouraged the location of black teachers, praised the work of the American and British Freedmen's Commission under the presidential leadership of Bishop J.J. Clinton for its work to improve the "temporal, moral and intellectual" condition of African Americans, and urged support of the Reverend B.T. Roberts' plans to establish a state manual labor school. Indeed, the conference not only adopted this report but proceeded to establish a North Carolina Annual Conference literary *society*.

The Committee on Missions—with a membership of John Williams, J.W. Hood, and R.B. Hampton—stated that mission work was active and fruitful; that since last annual conference, missions have expanded from a small part of the eastern section of the state to the western, southern, and northern portions. The major challenge for conducting mission work was the lack of personnel and, even more, the lack of resources. They expressed dismay that older conferences in Zion had not supported the North Carolina Conference as they should have, in particular noting that the New England Annual Conference really had provided only a small portion of the large amount of funding that that conference had collected for southern mission work. The committee declared that the North Carolina conference membership itself must play a great role in promoting missions. Therefore, it resolved to organize a conference mission board, encouraged the establishment of missionary societies, required pastors to deliver four sermons on missions annually and collect and report funds to support the missions, and commended Bishop Clinton's tireless work of expanding missions into states in the deep South. It also gratefully acknowledged the support that Methodist Episcopal Church, South, ministers had extended to Zion in the South, including ministers in Wilmington, Fayetteville, and New Bern, and urged abstention from the use of harsh language regarding others in both public and private spheres. The New England Annual Conference sent out a public appeal for new and used books and money to be donated for the education of the freed people in the South. A copy of that appeal is in the minutes of the NC Annual Conference.

Urbanization Period, 1900–1950

The urbanization period as characterized in this chapter covers a number of major events in American and African American general and religious history.[29] These events include the final disfranchisement of the great mass of black voters in all the states of the former Confederacy; the continued pressures of segregation and racial terrorism, exemplified by the renewal and political strength of the Ku Klux Klan; a massive movement of African Americans (and others) from the rural and small-town areas of the South to larger cities of both the South and the North; two world wars; a worldwide depression; and continuing religious diversity in the U.S. This section focuses on African American religion, the Great Migration, and continuing religious diversity.

Scholars differ on the dating of the Great Migration, the movement of blacks from rural and smaller urban areas of the South to larger urban areas in and outside the South. Possibly the height of this migration of millions of people over a number of decades varied from state to state. In general, we might say the Great Migration occurred from around 1900 to the 1940s. On one hand, circumstances drove blacks out of North Carolina and other southern states. As Reconstruction came to a close—marked by the withdrawal of federal troops from the South in 1877 as a result of the compromise arising out of the resolution of the presidential election of the previous year—life gradually became politically, socially, and economically tougher for blacks in all the southern states. North Carolina in the Upper South experienced less intense racism than states in the deep South such as Mississippi or Louisiana. Nonetheless, the same patterns of discrimination and oppression characterized the entire South, even those regarded as more moderate in race interactions. Included were the passing of laws establishing racial segregation in all areas of life; an increase in lynching and other forms of racial terrorism by groups such as the Ku Klux Klan; continued economic proscriptions and inequalities; and, perhaps most devastating of all, the disfranchisement of black voters through poll taxes, literacy tests, grandfather clauses, economic pressures, and plain physical intimidation. In North Carolina the Wilmington Insurrection of 1898 began a strong exodus of African Americans from the port city to other portions of the state and outside the state.

Just as there were conditions and events that pushed blacks out of the South, there were opportunities that drew blacks to the urbanized North—or to the non-southern areas with fewer racial restrictions in social and political life—namely greater job opportunities, especially with the beginning of World War I and the need for factory workers. The impact of the Great Migration on the availability of labor was felt keenly by the early 1920s. White southerners in power tended toward two responses: First, efforts to shut down the emigration included commissioning law officials literally to remove migrants from trains headed to non-southern locations, placing northern work agents under arrest, and prohibiting the placement of advertisements in newspapers for northern employment. A second and more positive approach was the encouragement of efforts to improve the lives of blacks in the state. Of course the basic principles and system of white supremacy, disfranchisement, and racial segregation were not renounced, but certain persons and entities, such as the North Carolina Division of Negro Economics, urged an improvement in areas such as employment conditions, better homes, availability of electricity, and better schools. It must also be noted that African American migrants often found that the North, or the non-southern portion of the country, while offering a much better living environment than many had known in the South, had its share of racial discrimination, lack of job opportunities, and uncomfortable living conditions. Furthermore, it is noteworthy that while many black North Carolinians and other southerners moved outside the South, a great number of them never surrendered their memories and even fondness for the positive aspects of southern life and culture. Much of northern black church life shows clear foundations in southern religiosity.

Black Church and Society During the Urbanization Period

As World War I drew to a close, black Methodists in North Carolina had experienced a tremendous increase in their membership. In 1864, North Carolina had only one annual conference, which it perhaps shared with South Carolina Methodists. By 1919, however, multiple annual conferences had convened in the state, with one having been formed less than a decade before in the Wilmington area. The Eighth Annual Conference of the Cape Fear Conference was held at St. John's AMEZ Church in Wilson, North Carolina, December 3, 1919. In attendance at this conference were one bishop, the Reverend Andrew J. Warner, three presiding elders, fifty-nine elders, fourteen deacons, thirteen students in their first year of seminary, perhaps three elders to be elevated to that office during the conference, and four elders retired because of old age or physical incapacity. Ten female representatives from Woman's Home and Foreign Missionary Societies were present along with eight from the Daughters of Conference, six from the Widows and Orphans department, twenty-two General Officers, and eight lay delegates. There is clear evidence that women played much more prominent roles in the 1919 Cape Fear Conference than in the 1865 North Carolina Annual Conference.

The Report of the Committee on the State of the Country did not paint a rosy picture of American life at the time, but does provide a good look at how the majority of black Christians in North Carolina viewed the era. The committee referred to labor conflicts, the peace treaty that remained unratified by Congress, immigration, problems with Mexico, and continuing racial problems resulting in "race riots, lynchings, burnings, assaults, electrocutions." The committee lamented: "Never in the history of the world has the spirit of unrest been more marked than it is today." The joint actions of the federal and state governments to restore prewar normality have apparently not worked. Reporting good news, the committee mentions that the country appears to have reached the apex of prosperity, which means that churches have been quite active in securing a large amount of funds for missions and education. Academic institutions have benefited in their enrollments, illiteracy has been reduced, and schools have a higher quality of teachers thanks to higher educational standards. Yet the committee does not rejoice regarding the overall state of the country: "We pray and we hope that this awful state of the country as briefly described by our committee, may in the near future be changed for the better by the wise ruling of Divine Providence."[30]

Four years later, in 1923, this same Cape Fear Annual Conference received a report from the Prohibition and Good Morals Committee focusing on the progress of the effort in the United States to enforce Prohibition, which in 1919 had been ratified as the Eighteenth Amendment to the Constitution of the United States.[31] The sentiments of this committee and the Annual Conference likely mirror those of most traditionally evangelical Christians in North Carolina, black or white, at the time. According to the committee, Prohibition in the land was well on its way to being triumphant. It contended that the traffic in alcohol had taken its toll on society, pointing particularly to the damage it had done to "the manhood of the race," that is, to African Americans. Alcohol was responsible for growth in prison population and hospital cases. Interestingly, the committee did present both sides of the argument, between the opponents of legal Prohibition—"the wets"—and the proponents of Prohibition—"the drys." The committee noted the opponents' arguments: (a) People have the constitutional right to decide what they will or will not consume; (b) It is futility to employ the law to change people's morals; (c) Prohibition raises the level of unemployment because it compels a reduction in revenue from the sale of alcohol. The Prohibitionists, on the other hand, emphasized the impact of alcohol use on society: (a) It damages the moral, intellectual, and social character of the nation; (b) Making alcoholic beverages is not the most effective use of resources; (c) Alcohol use harms the community because it contributes to divorce and family dissolution; and (d) Alcohol use leads to other illnesses. The committee had a realistic understanding of the limits of the law to change the actual behavior of people. They noted that people, even some church people, were still becoming intoxicated because of the illegal making of alcohol and smuggling. Hence, the strict enforcement of Prohibition had not removed alcohol's danger to people's lives or property. The committee appealed to God for improved conditions.

Blacks in Other Denominations: Methodist, Holiness/Pentecostal, Mennonite

Thus far, this chapter has focused attention on the two largest Christian denominations among black North Carolinians: the Baptists and the AMEZ. Yet to reflect the reality of religious activity, this article will devote some brief attention to a few other groups, including black Methodists who continued to affiliate with the mainly white Methodist Episcopal Church and its successors, The Methodist Church (1939) and The United Methodist Church (since 1968). We also find blacks well represented in Holiness/Pentecostal denominations, such as the Church of God in Christ and the Pentecostal Holiness Church; and the presence of blacks in a distinctly minority tradition among both blacks and nonblacks, the Mennonite tradition. Let us take a brief look at these: the North Carolina Central Jurisdiction of The Methodist Church (successor to the Methodist Episcopal Church), the United Holy Church, and black Mennonites.

BLACKS IN PREDOMINANTLY WHITE DENOMINATIONS:
NORTH CAROLINA'S CENTRAL JURISDICTION
OF THE METHODIST EPISCOPAL CHURCH, AN EXAMPLE

There remained in 1939 blacks in North Carolina who were affiliated with a predominantly white Methodist body,[32] which had represented the main body of Methodists in the United States at the beginning of the nineteenth century: the Methodist Episcopal Church. Around 1830, the Methodist Protestant Church seceded from the mother body—as the AME Church and the AME Zion Church had done over the previous fourteen years. One major concern for Methodist Protestants was a belief that the episcopacy was gaining too much power in the church. In 1844, the Methodist Episcopal Church, South, and the largely non-southern portion of the Methodist Episcopal Church parted ways over the issue of slavery. For some time, especially after the Civil War, there were efforts to unite these three bodies—Methodist Episcopal Church, the Methodist Protestant Church, and the Methodist Episcopal Church, South—into one Methodism. We must also note that there were overtures especially from the largely white northern-based Methodist Episcopal Church to merge with the AME and the AMEZ, as there were efforts among the three black groups to form one Methodist union.

Finally, in May 1939, the three largely white Methodist groups agreed to merge as The Methodist Church (which was subsequently succeeded by The United Methodist Church when The Methodist Church merged with the United Brethren Church in 1968). Along with that merger was a decision to place all African American members or churches of the newly merged denomination, regardless of where they lived, into one episcopal district known as the Central Jurisdiction. This racial separation was perhaps nationalizing what had been the de facto case in parts of the South where there were significant numbers of whites and blacks affiliated with the former Methodist Episcopal Church. Black Methodists were of two opinions regarding this racially separate arrangement. Some regarded it as segregation, the mandatory separation of blacks and whites. Others viewed it as an opportunity for African American Methodists to exercise some degree of autonomy under the leadership of a black bishop while remaining in communion with the larger church.

The year 1939 was one in which some black districts transitioned to the new system, as was the case in North Carolina. Listing the assembly as their 81st Annual Session, the North Carolina Annual Conference of the Methodist Episcopal Church, Central Jurisdiction, met in West Raleigh, North Carolina, in October 1939, five months after the merger meeting that formed The Methodist Church. The group assembled with the black presiding bishop, Matthew W. Clair of Kentucky, present in Raleigh at the Wilson Temple Methodist Church on October 25, 1939, a Wednesday evening. They officially closed the Methodist Episcopal Church North Carolina Annual Conference with a unanimously received resolution. Four delegates received the conference privilege to address in strong terms the meaning that the Methodist Episcopal Church had "and of the opportunities and responsibilities of the place that we now occupy in the Methodist Church, Central Jurisdiction." The minutes did express dissatisfaction or complaints about the new arrangement. After these remarks, the annual conference adjourned in order to reassemble as the annual conference of the Central Jurisdiction. On the following day, Thursday, October 26, a number of resolutions were advanced and adopted whereby the boards of the former annual conferences were for the most part made the boards of the new conference of the Central Jurisdiction with the same responsibilities and membership. The conference responded to the Uniting Conference establishing the new The Methodist Church in May 1939 in Kansas City with the District Superintendents' Report pleased that the three Methodist bodies had healed their separation. The newly merged and united church, said the superintendents, will now garner greater respect from other religious groups.

In terms of the ongoing work of the North Carolina group, the report on education extolled the conference's continued commitment to and support of Bennett College in Greensboro and the Allen School in Asheville. Both institutions operated for the education of black women. The report noted that the Allen School was organized soon after enslavement ended and that it was "well known for the training in home making and aesthetic culture." The school deserved the continued support of the conference. The conference set as its goal making a contribution of $2500 for Bennett College. Pointing to the active role of women in the conference, the report spoke strongly about the great work of the Woman's Home Missionary Societies and the Ladies' Aids groups that had contributed immensely and critically to the needs of the church. The district superintendents noted the needs of the churches in North Carolina, the indebtedness and disrepair of church edifices and parsonages. There appear to have been more than twelve thousand blacks affiliated with the Methodist Episcopal Church in North Carolina in 1939, located in four major districts: Greensboro District with a membership of 3498 in eighteen charges or churches; Laurinburg District, 3301, in eighteen churches; Western District, 3278, in twenty-six churches; and Winston District, 3522, in twenty-one churches. The superintendents note that many poor, struggling, and some unemployed church members had contributed sacrificially out of their few resources to support the work of the church in other parts of the world, often to the financial detriment of the work of their own local congregations. These churches also required assistance so that they might continue this benevolent service.

HOLINESS AND PENTECOSTAL GROUPS

African Americans in North Carolina are members of various Holiness and Pentecostal Churches,[33] among them the Church of God in Christ, the International Holiness Pentecostal Church, and the United Holy Church of America. Indeed, blacks were involved with the Holiness and Pentecostal denominations in the earliest days of their origins in North Carolina and elsewhere, including the Church of God in Christ, which arose out of a Holiness group in Mississippi and is now headquartered in Memphis, Tennessee; and the International Pentecostal Holiness Church, which originated with primarily white leadership but during its early years and more recently has had blacks among its members.

The United Holy Church of America was black in its original membership, and it arose in North Carolina, more specifically in Method, North Carolina, just outside of Raleigh. Its organizational beginnings in 1886 are closely connected to revivals conducted by Isaac Cheshier. Known previously as the Holy Church of North Carolina, the Holy Church of North Carolina and Virginia, and finally in 1918 as the United Holy Church, this denomination grew from a regional, to a national, then to an international group. It is noteworthy for being one of the first Pentecostal denominations to ordain women in ministerial leadership positions, such as pastors in local congregations, and as bishops. The United Holy Church is if not the oldest then certainly one of the oldest black

Holiness-Pentecostal denominations. With less than sixty thousand members, the United Holy Church of America has more than five hundred congregations in eighteen districts in various parts of the U.S. and in Bermuda, Barbados, and St. Lucia in the Caribbean, and Ghana. Even with this geographical expansion, North Carolina remains one of the main areas for denominational membership, and the church's international headquarters is based in Greensboro.

MENNONITES: AN EXAMPLE OF A "MINORITY" GROUP
WITHIN BLACK CHRISTIANITY

Mennonites, like other denominations such as the Church of the Brethren, are members of the Anabaptist tradition that emerged during the Protestant Reformation in the 1500s. Anabaptists emphasize that only conscious believers, not infants, should be baptized and that true baptism is by immersion. They interpret the Sermon on the Mount (chapters 5 through 7 of the Gospel of Matthew) more literally than most other Christians, reject taking oaths, affirm pacifism, and in general stress an approach to Christianity that places the faithful in tension with the values of societal approval, comfort, and quest for power. More specifically for this chapter, Conrad Ostwalt has provided very important information regarding the Mennonites in the United States and, especially for our purposes, black Mennonites in North Carolina. Mennonite history in the state dates back to mission efforts around the turn of the twentieth century. Peter and Elizabeth Wiebe were teachers who in 1901 began the Salem Mennonite Mission Church and Orphanage in 1901 in Elk Park, North Carolina. When the facility closed in 1912, the mission work was redirected to establishing churches for blacks in the mountains.

Joseph W. Tschetter established a Mennonite church in Boone in 1918. Peter and Katherine Siemens were strong laborers who came to this section in 1925, worked for three decades, and set up a number of churches, all members of the North Carolina District of the Mennonites, one of five American Mennonite districts. The North Carolina District as of the 1990s was home to churches found in the following towns: Beech Bottom, Boone, Laytown, Darby, and Lenoir. Mainly black, these congregations are the only mainly African American churches among American Mennonites. Furthermore, these churches and some in Chicago are the only ones not found west of the Mississippi River. One of the major leaders among these Mennonites was Ronda Horton, an African American from the city of Boone, who served as moderator of the district conference from his election in 1955 until 1986, the year of his death. The congregation at Boone "is the largest and most active church in the North Carolina District of Mennonite Brethren Churches."[34]

Professor Ostwalt discusses how the mainly African American congregations in this area of North Carolina have combined their fidelity to the Mennonite tradition with their black religious and cultural background. Seven congregations comprise the Mennonite Brethren North Carolina District, and it is unique among Mennonite Brethren conferences in that most of its membership is African American. Located in the hilly and mountainous areas of the state, six of these seven congregations have combined black cultural ways with traditional Mennonite theology. In looking particularly at the Boone, North Carolina, congregation, Professor Conrad Ostwalt focused on this black–historically Mennonite combination that he saw as illustrative of the possibilities of meaning for intercultural and multicultural exchange. Ostwalt notes the black Mennonite churches follow a style that is characteristic of many evangelical black Baptist, Methodist and—one might add—Pentecostal/Holiness churches: expressive worship that includes shouts, "holy dancing," movement and clapping, "call-and-response preaching," singing of gospel songs with musical accompaniment more than singing traditional Mennonite hymns, and the extended time of worship services. According to Ostwalt, the earliest missionaries in the area seemed to have welcomed the sincerity, spirituality, and enthusiasm of black worship.

While there is a culturally specific approach to black Mennonite worship, there is also a strong sense of connection with the historic Mennonite tradition, particularly as it applies to the Mennonites' experience of persecution. Having faced racial discrimination and mistreatment, these black faithful in Boone easily relate their particular racial experiences with the worldwide Mennonites' struggle with persecution, finding it easy, for example, to identify with the past struggles of Russian Mennonites in their homeland. While the Mennonite teachings on love and compassion are quite congruent with efforts to help the less fortunate and the general community, those teachings as they relate to the requirements regarding pacifism and separating the civil from the religious spheres did not lend themselves to involvement of the black Mennonite community in the Civil Rights Movement of the 1960s or current involvement in political matters. The Boone Mennonites have steered clear of active social protests, including the 1960s Civil Rights Movement, as well as civil rights organizations, such as the National Association for the Advancement of Colored People (NAACP). In the past there has been the strong conviction that race relations among the mountain people fared better than among other southern people. While there has been a lack of participation of churches in protests and activism, black Mennonites have stressed the need for education and community betterment.[35]

Civil Rights and Contemporary Period, 1950–Present

The Civil Rights Movement of the 1950s and the 1960s led by groups such as the Southern Christian Leadership Conference, the NAACP, the Congress of Racial Equality, and individuals such as Roy Wilkins and Martin Luther King, Jr., both encouraged and was encouraged by local, grassroots leaders across the South, including North Carolina.[36] Indeed, sometimes such local civil rights leaders pushed national leaders to take up struggles about which the latter often were convinced were premature battles. Furthermore, it is not enough to secure positive judicial rulings, passage of effective legislation, or to reach an agreement with business or governmental leaders. Local people must exercise the determination and courage to take advantage of those rights. Accordingly, North Carolina civil rights leaders have labored to dismantle the system of racial inequality in that state. Two examples reflect these efforts: one in Greensboro at the beginning of the 1960s focused on the integrationist approach; and the second in Wilmington during the 1970s, when many blacks had grown frustrated with the integrationist approach and were advocating more nationalistic philosophies and methods.

Greensboro Four: Integrationism

The "Greensboro Four"—David Richmond, Franklin McCain, Ezell Blair, Jr. (Jibril Khazan), and Joe McNeil—are examples of local leaders. These four seventeen-year-olds walked into a local Woolworth store, bought supplies, and insisted that they also had the right to have meals at the whites-only lunch counter. By doing so, they paved the way for the integrationist movement in North Carolina and set a strong example for students elsewhere, such as the young John Lewis in Nashville, Tennessee, to apply the methods of nonviolence and civil disobedience in challenging Jim Crow laws.[37]

The Wilmington Ten

Just as the Greensboro Four represent an earlier nonviolent approach based on commitment to the U.S. Constitution and the equal-justice possibilities of American democracy, the Wilmington Ten[38] represent a later movement emerging in the middle 1960s and extending into the 1970s: the Black Power or Black Nationalist strand, which questioned whether the basic political and economic structure of the country would permit success for those struggling against racial and economic domination. Ten years after the protest of the Greensboro Four, in 1971, many African Americans distrusted the sincerity and commitment of the federal government regarding the enforcement of the 1964 and 1965 civil rights legislation and the 1968 open housing law. Nearly twenty years after the Supreme Court had judged that racial segregation in public education was unconstitutional, progress toward a desegregated or racially integrated educational system seemed elusive in many places.

In Wilmington, black protests and business boycotts were met by armed Klansmen and other antagonists patrolling the downtown area and expressing hostility toward the boycotters. Early in February 1971, violence broke out; there were fires, a firebombing, and sniper shots at firefighters. Benjamin Chavis and some students barricaded themselves inside the Gregory Congregational Church. An ensuing gunfight left two persons dead. When the National Guard finally succeeded in taking the church, they found no one inside. Two black men who claimed to have been inside Gregory Church gave testimony that was taken as pointing to The Wilmington Ten, nine black men and a white woman. The ten individuals were convicted and given sentences collectively totaling 282 years. Some local people and increasingly a national and international cadre of folks believed that the real reason for the stiff sentences had less to do with their supposed participation in violence and more to do with their racial beliefs. In 1978, Governor Jim Hunt reduced but did not invalidate the sentences. In 1980, a federal court invalidated the convictions on due process grounds, but the charges against the now-freed people still stood. It was in 2012 that another governor, Beverly Perdue, pardoned the group based on what she believed was the racist means of selecting the jury. By that time four had died and a number of others were in poor health.

The Reverend Dr. William Barber
and the Moral Mondays Movement, 2000s

The commitment to racial justice and equality in the African American religious tradition preceded the Civil Rights Movement of the 1950s and 1960s and has persisted into the 2000s. An example is the "Moral Mondays" movement that began in North Carolina and has spread to other states. The Reverend William Barber II, immediate past president of the North Carolina chapter of the National Association for the Advancement of Colored People, has led the movement. Many in the African American religious community view it as a current manifestation of the Old Testament prophetic tradition of Jeremiah, Isaiah, and Amos, reflected more recently by religious leaders such as the Reverend Martin Luther King, Jr. The movement is an effort to counter—through peaceful, nonviolent protests and advocacy—state and national policies deemed harmful to those whom Jesus called "the least of these" (Matthew 25: 40).[39]

Conclusion

In the preceding pages we have outlined black religion in North Carolina from colonial times to the present. To reiterate, this is by no means an exhaustive study of black religion in the state. We have focused mainly on Baptists and Methodists, the two largest groups of religious adherents in the state, because of the author's manageability of such a voluminous amount of material and not for reasons of excluding or minimizing the significance of other groups. We should say that religion in North Carolina among blacks is very diverse. It is hoped that this brief survey, despite any methodological shortcomings, has provided for many readers an increased understanding and appreciation of black (and non-black) religion in North Carolina.

NOTES

1. United States Census, 2010; population estimate, vintage year July 1, 2016. https://www.census.gov/quickfacts/fact/table/NC/PST045216.

2. Pew Research Center, "Religious Tradition among Adults in North Carolina by Race/Ethnicity," *Religious Landscape Study,* 2014. http://www.pewforum.org/religious-landscape-study/compare/religious-tradition/by/racial-and-ethnic-composition/among/state/north-carolina/.

3. Pew Research Center, *Religious Landscape Study,* 2014.

4. For a study of blacks in colonial North Carolina, see Marvin L. Michael Kay and Lorin Lee Cary, *Slavery in North Carolina, 1748–1775* (Chapel Hill: University of North Carolina Press, 1995). See especially the chapter on "Slave Religiosity," 173–217. See also Albert J. Raboteau, *Slave Religion: The "Invisible Institution" in the Antebellum South,* Updated Edition (New York: Oxford University Press, 2004), particularly 3–94.

5. Regarding evangelical Christianity among blacks and whites in the colonial and antebellum periods, see Raboteau, *Slave Religion,* and Donald G. Mathews, *Religion in the Old South* (Chicago: University of Chicago Press, 1977).

6. For black and white religion in the South during the national and antebellum periods dealing with topics such as the Second Great Awakening and the Mission to the Slaves, see Raboteau, *Slave Religion,* particularly 95–322; Mathews, *Old South,* pp. 39–250. In addition, this article draws heavily upon J. A. Whitted's *A History of the Negro Baptists of North Carolina* (Raleigh, NC: Presses of Edwards & Broughton Printing Co., 1908), especially 7–15. Digitized by the Internet Archive in 2012 with funding from University of North Carolina at Chapel Hill. http://archive.org/details/historyofnegrobaOOwhit.

7. Whitted, *History of Negro Baptists,* 7–9.

8. Whitted, *History of Negro Baptists,* 7.

9. Whitted, *History of Negro Baptists,* 12.

10. Whitted, *History of Negro Baptists,* 9–11.

11. Whitted, *History of Negro Baptists,* 12–13.

12. Whitted, *History of Negro Baptists,* 11–12.

13. In addition to the works by Raboteau and Mathews cited above, see the historical sketch of black Methodists in the *Minutes, North Carolina Annual Conference of the Methodist Episcopal Church, Central Jurisdiction,* 1939, p. 67. https://ia802709.us.archive.org/21/items/minutesofnorthca811939/minutesofnorthca811939.pdf.

14. For Whitted's general comments about black Christians in the antebellum and Civil War and postwar periods and his references to local churches and leaders, see his *History,* especially 14–17.

15. Whitted, *History of Negro Baptists,* 16.

16. Whitted, *History of Negro Baptists,* 15–17.

17. For an account of these associations, see M.W. Williams and George W. Watkins, *Who's Who Among North Carolina Negro Baptists: With a Brief History of Negro Baptist Organizations* (N. P, Authors: 1940), 45–68.

18. See Williams and Watkins, *Who's Who,* 11–22, for information regarding black Baptists in the Civil War and postwar periods, including the North Carolina conventions. In addition to movement toward state organizations, black Baptists in the Civil War and postwar period also made important strides in the formation of national organizations. See James M. Washington, *Frustrated Fellowship: Baptist Quest for Social Power* (Macon, GA: Mercer University Press, 1982). The most chronologically complete history of the denomination(s) is Leroy Fitts' *A History of Black Baptists* (Nashville, TN: Broadman Press, 1985).

19. Williams and Watkins, *Who's Who,* 16–17.

20. Williams and Watkins, *Who's Who,* 17.

21. Williams and Watkins, *Who's Who,* 17.

22. For a look at the cooperationist issue among black Baptists, particularly as it related to African Missions, see Sandy D. Martin, *Black Baptists and African Missions: The Origins of a Movement, 1880–1915* (Macon, GA: Mercer University Press, 1989), 147–64.

23. Williams and Watkins, *Who's Who,* 19–22.

24. Williams and Watkins, *Who's Who,* 19.

25. Whitted, *History of Negro Baptists,* 44.

26. Williams and Watkins, *Who's Who,* 20–21.

27. The reader will find the most comprehensive historical account of the AMEZ Church, including North Carolina history, to be Williams J. Walls, *The African Methodist Episcopal Zion Church: Reality of the Black Church* (Charlotte, NC: The AME Zion Publishing House, 1974). Sandy D. Martin's *For God and Race: The Religious and Political Leadership of AMEZ Bishop James Walker Hood* (Columbia: University of South Carolina Press, 1999), 45–79, offers important information regarding the entry of the Zion Church in North Carolina during the 1864–72 period.

28. AMEZ NC, *Minutes,* 1865, pp. 5–8, 12–16, 18. https://archive.org/details/minutesofnorthca1865afri.

29. For general information regarding the urbanization era, especially the Great Migration and the Wilmington Riot or Insurrection of 1898, see "The Great Migration and North Carolina," by Shepherd W. McKinley and Cynthia Risser McKinley, a reprint from *Tar Heel Junior Historian* 45, No. 2 (Spring 2006) with copyright by North Carolina Museum of History. http://www.learnnc.org/lp/editions/nchist-newcentury/5996. Regarding the Wilmington Riot/Insurrection of 1898, see a newspaper article, "Thousands Gone," at http://gtts.oasis.unc.edu/content/2423/. Also, see http://www.learnnc.org/lp/editions/nchist-newsouth/4360.

30. The quotes in this section are from page 64 of the Cape Fear Annual Conference, AMEZ Church, *Minutes,* 1919. See also pp. 2–4 for other matters discussed in the article. https://archive.org/details/minutesofannuals1919afri.

31. Cape Fear Annual Conference, AMEZ Church, *Minutes,* 1923, 66, https://archive.org/details/minutesofannuals1923afri&autoplay=1&playset=1. For information on the 18th Amendment, see https://www.archives.gov/education/lessons/volstead-act#documents.

32. See *Minutes, Central Jurisdiction in North Carolina/North Carolina Annual Conference, of The Methodist Church,* 1939, particularly pages 5–9, 26–28, 33, 41–44. https://ia802709.us.archive.org/21/items/minutesofnorthca811939/minutesofnorthca811939.pdf.

33. See these references for Holiness/Pentecostals: Karin Lorene Zipf, "Pentecostal Holiness Church," 2006: http://www.ncpedia.org/pentecostal-holiness-church; "The United Holy Church of America": https://www.ncpedia.org/united-holy-church-america. Also, http://uhcainc.org/uhcahistory.html; "Pentecostal Holiness Church": http://pctii.org/arc/synan.html.

34. Conrad E. Ostwalt, Jr., "Crossing of Cultures: The Mennonite Brethren of Boone, North Carolina," in *The Journal of the Appalachian Studies Association*, vol. 4. https://www.jstor.org/stable/41445627?seq=1#page_scan_tab_contents; *Environmental Voices: Cultural, Social, Physical, and Natural* (Johnson City, TN: Center for Appalachian Studies and Services/East Tennessee State University, 1992), 105–12, especially 106–08.

35. See Conrad Ostwalt, "African-Americans in North Carolina: A Symbiotic Relationship," http://www.directionjournal.org/23/2/african-americans-in-north-carolina.html. Also Ostwalt, "Crossing of Cultures," 110.

36. See Akshay Gupta, "Annotated Timeline of the Civil Rights Movement in North Carolina," http://ervin062.web.unc.edu/timelines/annotated-timeline-civil-rights-movement-north-carolina/.

37. Jaime Huaman, "Greensboro Four," http://www.ncpedia.org/history/20th-Century/greensboro-four.

38. Nicholas Graham, "Wilmington Ten," http://www.ncpedia.org/history/20th-century/wilmington-ten.

39. Dani McClain, "The Rev. William Barber Is Bringing MLK's Poor People's Campaign Back to Life," *The Nation,* May 19, 2017, https://www.thenation.com/article/rev-william-barber-is-bringing-mlks-poor-peoples-campaign-back-to-life/.

Brethren

Jeff Bach

The Brethren, also known informally as Dunkers (or Dunkards) for their manner of baptizing adult believers by threefold immersion under water, were a small religious group who settled in North Carolina in the second half of the eighteenth century and continue into the present. The Church of the Brethren has about 1,783 members in North Carolina,[1] a state of about 10.3 million people in 2017. This is the only group of Brethren in North Carolina except for one Grace Brethren congregation in Durham. The Church of the Brethren, the largest group of Brethren in North America, had about 110,000 members in 2015.

The Brethren story in North Carolina has been varied. After settling in the mid-eighteenth century, they lost nearly all of their members by 1800. During a slow recovery in the nineteenth century, they generated four main centers of activity. In the twentieth century, the Brethren experienced both growth and loss. While the Brethren are statistically insignificant in numbers in North Carolina, their story is distinctive.

The Brethren story in North Carolina falls into roughly five time periods. The first period begins with their migration into North Carolina in the mid-eighteenth century and ends in 1800. The second period, a time of stabilizing, extends from 1800 to about 1860. The third period, roughly from about 1860 to about 1900, evidenced growth and the start of daughter congregations. The fourth period comprises all of the twentieth century, marked at first by a flurry of church planting and then later decline. North Carolina Brethren moved toward mainline Protestant patterns such as professional ministry, church programming, and administrative regional structures. The twenty-first century marks a fifth period, as Brethren start some new churches and experience both growth and loss. This essay will follow a chronological framework.

Introduction to the Brethren

The Brethren (or Dunkers) originated in Schwarzenau, Germany, in 1708, when eight adults received baptism by threefold immersion in the names of the Trinity in the Eder River. Choosing no denominational name, they called each other "sister" and "brother." Their opponents called them "New Anabaptists" (*Neu-Täufer*) to distinguish them from the Mennonites who began in the Reformation era.[2] Alexander Mack, Sr. (1679–1735) was the first leader of the Brethren. He was a one-time miller from Schriesheim near Heidelberg, who separated from the Reformed Church in 1706 and moved with his family to Schwarzenau in the county of Wittgenstein,[3] where they found some religious tolerance. Most of the early Brethren were influenced by the Radical Pietist and the Anabaptist movements. Pietism was a renewal movement in Protestantism traced to the Lutheran minister Philipp Jakob Spener in Frankfurt around 1670. Spener developed small group meetings for edification and Bible study. Radical Pietism was a branch of Pietism that tended to separate from the established churches, deeming them too corrupt to reform. Radicals also tended to expect Christ's imminent return in judgment. Mack and the early Brethren were also influenced by writings by Menno Simons and Dirk Philips, two Anabaptist reformers in the sixteenth century, as well as by some Mennonite devotional books.[4] Anabaptism was a third path in the Reformation that practiced adult baptism upon confession of faith, was largely pacifist, practiced church discipline, and emphasized the teachings of Jesus along with his saving grace.

From these influences and their study of scripture, the Brethren formed a church patterned on their understanding of the New Testament. They adopted pacifism, refused oaths, and lived simply.[5] They practiced the ban on members who strayed from New Testament teachings. A banned member could not participate in communion, not receive the holy kiss, and not participate in congregational decision making. Only in rare cases did the Brethren practice shunning, or avoidance, like the Amish. In addition to immersion baptism, the Brethren observed communion by holding a Lovefeast, which included footwashing, and a simple meal (the love meal, or *agape* of ancient Christianity), ending with the bread and cup.[6] They also practiced anointing for healing. Brethren greeted one another with a holy kiss, exchanged only among members of the same gender. In Europe, the Brethren supported celibacy for those called to it. They also upheld the sanctity of marriage, insisting on lifelong monogamy and fidelity, as well as marriage within the church membership. Brethren chose ministers from within their congregations. A congregation typically had multiple ministers; they had no formal training and received no remuneration.

The Brethren were suppressed in Europe because of adult baptism, and refusing military service and oaths. In 1719, some members emigrated to Pennsylvania. They organized their first congregation on Christmas Day, 1723, in Germantown (now part of Philadelphia). By 1750, virtually all of the Brethren had left Europe for the British colonies.[7]

In America, the Brethren expanded westward in Pennsylvania and southward into Maryland in the 1730s and 1740s. Traveling down the Great Wagon Road with other migrants, they reached North Carolina and South Carolina around 1750. At least seven congregations of Brethren formed primarily in the North Carolina Piedmont.[8]

The Brethren stories in colonial North and South Carolina are linked because of a doctrinal conflict in the 1790s. One factor in the dispute was the legacy of an internal schism of the Brethren in 1728 in Pennsylvania. Conrad Beissel broke away from the congregation in Lancaster County that year. He taught that celibacy is superior to marriage and that Saturday is the true Sabbath.[9] By 1732, he organized a community named Ephrata with celibate women and men and married families. He attracted many Brethren to join him.[10] A dispute within Ephrata over leadership led to the expulsion of three brothers, Samuel, Israel, and Gabriel Eckerlin in 1745. They moved that year to the New River in southern Virginia, near present-day Dublin. Other disgruntled Ephrata members followed them.[11] They abandoned the settlement in 1750 due to Indian hostilities. Some

Ephrata members scattered to North and South Carolina, and some regular Brethren joined them to create small congregations worshipping on both Saturdays and Sundays.[12] The Ephrata influence among South Carolina Brethren contributed in part to the development of Universalism there. A popular belief at Ephrata, Universalism held that a loving God would never punish sinners in eternity, so there is no hell. More details of Universalism among the Brethren will be explained below.

Brethren Settlement in Colonial North Carolina

Initial Settlements

The earliest reports of Brethren settlements in North Carolina were written around 1772 by the Baptist historian Morgan Edwards in his account of Baptist-type groups in colonial America.[13] Although Edwards was not well informed about Brethren in North Carolina, his account is helpful because of its date. He described three congregations that he called Catawba, Yadkin on the Atkin, and Ewarrie (Uwharrie), all in the Piedmont. In addition to these three settlements, at least three other congregations formed about which Edwards was uninformed.

Catawba was located west of the Catawba River around Killian's Creek, in present-day Catawba and Lincoln counties. Although Edwards reported that Brethren had moved into North Carolina around 1742, no other records confirm that date. Brethren historian Roger Sappington and John Scott Davenport researched deeds and land records to find more details about the Carolina Brethren. They noted that Christopher Guice (or Guss) purchased land along Middle Creek, west of the Catawba River, in 1756.[14] However, Edwards listed Guice as a Brethren minister in Virginia in 1756.[15] Guice sold his land in 1768. Edwards reported that Samuel Saunder, not Guice, was the minister at Catawba, so Guice must have moved away. Samuel Saunder (or Saunders) appeared in land records in 1767. Thereafter he appears as Lemuel Saunders, who was named in land transactions in the same area in 1772 and in the 1790 census.[16] Land records in this area show several Brethren family names such as Miller, Zimmerman, Saylor, Hoover, Rhodes, Moyer, Ulrich, Yoder, Hendricks, and Keller. Edwards reported that Catawba had about forty families, with thirty baptized members by 1772. Little more is known about this group that seems to have disbanded in the 1790s. In 1794 Lemuel Saunders was listed as the pastor of Long Creek Baptist Church.[17]

The second congregation that Edwards mentioned was Yadkin on the Atkin.[18] He reported that Hans (or John) and Conrad Kearn (or Kern, sometimes Kerns) were the ministers for this group, which numbered about twenty-nine families, from whom forty persons were baptized. Sappington found that most of these Brethren settled around Crane Creek near the Yadkin River in Rowan County around 1755.[19] Conrad and Hans Kearn (or Kerns) were brothers. Conrad first appeared in land records in 1762. Nothing more is known about these two ministers. The wills for Conrad and Hans Kearn were probated in 1812 and 1823, respectively.

The Hendricks family was a prominent extended family in the Brethren settlement on Crane Creek. They were also important among Brethren in York County, Pennsylvania.[20] James Hendricks was a minister there, and his family had long ties to the Mennonite, Quaker, and Brethren traditions in colonial America. Some members of the

Hendricks family had sparked the Universalism crisis in North Carolina in the 1790s, which probably led to the demise of the Yadkin congregation.

The third group of Dunkers settled along the Uwharrie River.[21] Their minister was Jacob Stutzman, of Swiss Mennonite background. He had also lived in York County, Pennsylvania, before coming to North Carolina. Stutzman considered Daniel Leatherman, a minister from York County living in Maryland, as the overseer of the Brethren on the Uwharrie. Stutzman purchased land in 1764. In 1772, a Moravian minister, George Soelle, visited Stutzman at his home on Abbots Creek, close to the Uwharrie.[22] This congregation numbered about nineteen families with about thirty baptized members. They seem to have broken up by 1795.

At least three other Brethren settlements formed during the eighteenth century. In the 1770s, Brethren from York County, Pennsylvania, and Carroll County, Maryland, moved to Dutchman's Creek at the fork of the Yadkin River in Rowan County. Among them were many members of the Hendricks and Rowland families. Gaspar Rowland, a minister, appeared in land records in the 1780s and 1790s.[23] The 1790 census listed several Rowland and Hendricks families near Dutchman's Creek.[24]

A John Hendricks bought land along Dutchman's Creek in 1783, and in 1793 he began to sell some of his land.[25] One land record in North Carolina lists him as a resident of Montgomery County, Kentucky, in 1798. Like Hendricks, Gasper Rowland and his son, Joseph, sold much of their land in Rowan County in 1796.[26] Gasper also purchased some land in Wilkes County in the northwestern corner of North Carolina. This corner of North Carolina was divided from Wilkes County in 1799 to form Ashe County. By 1809, Joseph Rowland was recorded as a landowner in Warren County, Kentucky. Apparently a large migration of Brethren to Kentucky from Dutchman's Creek was underway at the end of the eighteenth century, probably related to the Universalism crisis.

Another settlement formed in the early 1770s as some Brethren settled along Muddy Creek on the southern side of the Moravians' Wachovia Tract, where Salem was located. A report in the Salem diary in 1772 noted that two men, a Tanner and a Schütz (Danner and Sheets) who were Brethren men from Uwharrie, wanted to buy land.[27] This settlement began with Brethren migrating from other parts of North Carolina and expanded with new members arriving from Maryland and Pennsylvania. Jehu Burkhart (or Burket), a Brethren elder from Pennsylvania of Swiss Mennonite background, bought land along Reedy Creek in this area in 1778.[28] The Jacob Pfau (Faw) family arrived around 1780. One of Jacob's sons, Isaac Faw, married Magdalena Burkhart, the daughter of Elder Jehu Burkhart.[29] Isaac Faw succeeded his father-in-law as minister at this congregation, known as Fraternity. It was the only Brethren church in North Carolina begun in colonial times that survived into the nineteenth century.

A third center of Brethren activity formed in the early 1790s along the New River in the part of Wilkes County that became Ashe County after 1799, bordering both Tennessee and Virginia. Gasper Rowland, who had owned land near Dutchman's Creek in Rowan County, bought land in this area of Wilkes County in 1796. However, Gaspar soon moved to Kentucky and provided little if any ministerial service in Wilkes County.

Another minister in this settlement in northwestern Carolina was a Mr. Bauer. In 1804, a Moravian minister named Abraham Steiner visited this area and wrote in his journal that Mr. Bauer was the minister, or "exhorter," for these Brethren.[30] An exhorter was a Brethren minister in the trial phase of his ministry. After faithful service, a congregation would advance the exhorter to become a minister or an elder. The consecration of an elder was called "ordination," even though the person was technically already a minister, as an exhorter.

A more important minister in the Ashe County settlement was Jonathan Miller. He grew up in the Fraternity congregation, and his name appeared in Ashe County land records starting in 1801.[31] Family tradition recounts that Jonathan's wife, Margaret Carpenter (the English form of the German surname Zimmerman) Miller, never joined the church because she owned slaves. However, Jonathan did not have slaves and was a minister for many years.[32] Slaveholding was prohibited to all Brethren members from the time of their arrival in North America. Any prospective member with slaves had to free them in order to join the church.

One additional Brethren congregation in colonial North Carolina was located in Anson County and extended partially into present-day Chester County and Lancaster County, South Carolina. The border between the two colonies was not formally fixed until 1764. Little is known about this group; a fire at the Anson County courthouse destroyed many of the eighteenth-century records. However, the Ephrata community's internal history, the *Chronicon Ephratense* (*Ephrata Chronicle*) mentions this congregation in North Carolina.[33] Its leading minister was Emmanuel Eckerlin, a brother of the three Eckerlins who were expelled from Ephrata in 1745. Emmanuel left Ephrata, joined the Brethren, and then moved to Anson County, where many Brethren had settled. This congregation must have formed by the early 1760s because Emmanuel died in 1767. One surviving record from Anson County pertaining to Eckerlin is a list of items from an estate belonging to "Manuel Eackles" (Emmanuel Eckerlin), sold at a public sale after his death.[34] Some of the buyers are listed. They represent Brethren names such as Frey (or Free), Miller, and Sheets (Sheetz, or Schütz). Little more information is known about this congregation beyond Eckerlin's leadership. The church seems to have dissolved after his death.

During the American Revolution, Brethren (cited as "Dunkers") were treated much like the Quakers and Moravians. The General Assembly in North Carolina allowed for objection to military service but imposed an exemption fee (initially twenty-five pounds). In 1778, they also required an oath of allegiance to the new government.[35] Moravians, Quakers, Dunkers, and Mennonites were permitted to affirm rather than to swear, but a threefold tax was imposed on them. In 1779, they were required to submit a list of taxable property for this tax. In Randolph County both Jacob Stutzman I and his son, Jacob Stutzman II, refused to swear the Oath of Allegiance and to submit a property list.[36] In some places a special tax was imposed on pacifist families. Often this was three times higher than regular taxes, but in some cases tax collectors attempted to extract much more. A court record from Rowan County ordered that Brethren Nicholas Leatherman, John Sears, and Christian Leatherman be relieved from a twelvefold tax and be required to pay only a threefold tax.[37] This limited anecdotal evidence suggests that Brethren were pacifists during the American Revolution in North Carolina, consistent with their avoidance of the Regulator Movement in 1771.

Universalism and the Loss of Brethren Congregations

The controversy over Universalism ruptured the congregations of the Brethren in North and South Carolina during the 1790s. The result was the loss of all Brethren in

South Carolina and all of the congregations in North Carolina except for Fraternity and Ashe County by 1800. The disappearance of Brethren at Catawba, Uwharrie, Crane Creek, and Dutchman's Creek—and perhaps the group in Anson County—is most likely linked to this conflict.

In 1794, a "Brother Stutzman" reported to the Brethren Annual Meeting that "strange doctrines" were surfacing in North Carolina.[38] At the 1798 Annual Meeting the preacher was named as "John H." The Annual Meeting was a practice dating to at least 1742 whereby representatives from all Brethren congregations came together to discuss questions of faith or practice of importance to the entire church. Ministers constituted the largest percentage of attendees, although any person was permitted to speak. Decisions at Annual Meeting were made by consensus in the eighteenth and first part of the nineteenth century. These decisions were considered binding for all congregations.

The strange doctrines from North Carolina reported to the 1794 Annual Meeting included preaching that there is no heaven and no hell, that God would not punish sinners, and that there is no resurrection of the dead. In 1798, Jacob Keller and Samuel van Etten in North Carolina wrote to the Annual Meeting that they heard John H. claim that it would be more a sin for him to stand "on the top of the barn" and swear and blaspheme against God than it would be to "pray to God to forgive him his sins, or to bless him in any respect.[39] John H. reportedly said that he "had not served such a God that required the prayer of human creatures to forgive them their sins," and that he never would serve such a God.

The identity of John H. was long a mystery. Some Brethren in the nineteenth century identified him as John Ham. The noted historian of the Universalist Church, Richard Eddy, included this identification of John H. in Eddy's account of Universalism among the North Carolina Dunkers. Brethren historian Roger Sappington agreed with the identification.[40] Unfortunately, there is no evidence of a John Ham as a Brethren preacher at this time. Brethren historians David B. Eller and John Scott Davenport used land deeds and wills in order to identify John H. as John Hendricks, a Brethren man from York County, Pennsylvania. He belonged to the Hendricks family that moved to Dutchman's Creek in the fork of the Yadkin River in Rowan County, later Davie County. There is a John Hendricks in this area who sold land in the 1790s and surfaced in Kentucky. He is almost certainly the "John H." in question.[41]

The Annual Meeting of 1794 condemned six doctrinal errors attributed to John H.:

1. There is no other heaven but that in man.
2. There is no other hell but that in man.
3. That God has no form or shape; and if a person would worship God, and would conceive in his mind God as in the human form; would imagine or believe that God had an appearance like a man, such person would do the same as one who would worship a horse or any other beast.
4. That God is not wrathful, and would punish no person on account of his sins.
5. That the dead rise not; for out of the grave nothing would come forth.
6. That they will have nothing to do with the ban (or excommunication).[42]

The rejection of heaven and hell other than personal experience and the rejection of God's judgment and punishment of unrepentant sinners are characteristic of Universalist teachings. Alexander Mack, Sr., held a doctrinal opinion known as Universal Restoration, common among many Radical Pietists in Germany. Universal Restoration is quite different from Universalism. According to universal restoration, God judges and punishes sinners in hell. However, after a long period of time in the future, God will restore sinners into fellowship with God.[43] According to Universalism, as John Hendricks taught, there is no hell or heaven, and a loving God would never punish sinners.

The Annual Meeting minutes of 1794 contained refutations of each of the six errors charged to John H. The 1798 Annual Meeting reaffirmed these condemnations and concluded that "we cannot hold said John H. and all who are of his mind as brethren" as long as they held these views. In sum, John H. and his followers were excommunicated. The Annual Meeting of 1800 reiterated the excommunication of John H. and his followers for his "unscriptural doctrines and expressions."[44] The decision in 1800 finalized the break between Universalist Brethren and the larger body of Brethren.

The excommunication of John H. sealed the loss of most of the Brethren in North Carolina by 1800. Many of the Universalist Brethren moved away to Kentucky with John Hendricks and Gaspar Rowland. Universalist Brethren who did not move to Kentucky probably were absorbed into other denominations. The few Universalist congregations formed from the Brethren in South Carolina had disappeared by 1826.[45] The loss of all but two of the Brethren congregations in North Carolina by 1800 marked basically a complete break with the beginnings of Brethren here. In Kentucky, Gasper Rowland continued to minister among former Brethren, along with his son, Joseph. John Hendricks still served as a minister. A James Hendricks, son-in-law to Gasper Rowland, also became a minister. Evidence for the separated ministers from North Carolina preaching in Kentucky is found in an affidavit known as "Ancient Documents," recorded by Joseph Roland (youngest son of Gasper) in 1830 in southern Illinois.[46] In land records in Kentucky, the family name "Rowland" appears as "Roland," and was the form that Joseph used. Joseph Roland wrote that Gasper Rowland and John Hendricks were the founders of the Drake's Creek Church in Warren County (later Simpson County), Kentucky, where many Brethren from North Carolina had moved. Joseph Roland reported some of their beliefs, including "the restitution of all things, upon which gospel faith, the church on Drake's Creek, Warren County, Kentucky, was constituted."[47] This document also stated that John Hendricks was ordained as an elder by Gasper Rowland in 1800,[48] a date that Davenport and Eller suggest is a decade late. The "Ancient Documents" from southern Illinois confirm the role of Gasper Rowland and John Hendricks as leaders of the Universalist controversy in North Carolina, and their continuing ministries after separation from the rest of the Brethren.

Transition in North Carolina: 1800–1860

The two surviving Brethren congregations in North Carolina after 1800 were Fraternity and the Church in Ashe County, which would be known as Flat Rock after 1888. They remained in fellowship with the rest of the Brethren primarily for two reasons: internal leadership and assistance from Brethren leaders outside their areas.

At Fraternity, Elder Jehu Burkhart and his son-in-law, Isaac Faw (Pfau) guided the church. In Ashe County, Jonathan Miller and Andrew Sheets, both originally from Fraternity, maintained a commitment to Brethren faith. After Miller's death in 1854, Sheets was one of the leading ministers there.[49]

The second factor that was equally important for the Brethren in North Carolina was help from visiting Brethren ministers from eastern Tennessee and around Roanoke, Virginia. Universalism made no serious inroads in these areas. The Moravian diary for Salem in 1800 included one of several examples of the bond between Fraternity and the Virginia Brethren. The writer reported that a large Brethren worship service was held in the home of Elder Jehu Burkhart where "two or three preachers from Virginia were present" and preached "much about the sufferings of Jesus."[50] In Ashe County, ministers from Tennessee and Virginia who visited in the early nineteenth century included D.B. Bowman, Joseph Bowman, Abraham and Isaac Naff, and Peter Crumpacker.[51]

Isaac Faw, the son-in-law of Elder Jehu Burkhart at Fraternity, became the leading minister when Burkhart moved to Montgomery County, Ohio, around 1809.[52] Faw's death in 1835 precipitated another case in which support from Virginia made the difference in the survival of a North Carolina church. Faw's death left no minister at Fraternity. In 1838, his youngest son, Jacob (1810–1887), wrote to John Bowman, a Brethren minister in Rocky Mount, near Roanoke. Jacob reported that only a few members remained at Fraternity. He expressed a sense of calling, but wanted to talk with Bowman in order to know more about the Brethren. Jacob was unbaptized, so he could not yet become a minister. There was no Brethren minister at Fraternity to baptize him, nor an elder to lead the election and install him into ministry. Faw traveled to Bowman's home. After a weekend of conversation, Faw was baptized.[53] Brethren from Franklin County, Virginia, began to travel to Fraternity to preach. In 1839, Jacob Faw was elected as the minister for Fraternity.[54]

Jacob Faw enjoyed a reputation as a man of the greatest integrity in his business dealings.[55] He rejected slavery, even though his neighbors were slaveholders. Family tradition also tells of an event when he caught two men stealing from his smokehouse. The man outside the smokehouse ran away when Jacob approached. Jacob continued receiving and stacking the meat from the man inside the building who handed the goods outside. Reportedly the thief asked if they should leave something for the owner and Faw replied "yes." Faw let the men go on a promise that they would not steal again. He gave the men some of the meat as they left.[56]

Upon Jacob Faw's death, Dr. F.P. Tucker, who knew Faw, wrote a remembrance of the elder, published in a Winston-Salem newspaper, *The Union Republican*. Tucker gave a glimpse into the lives of the Brethren. The Brethren maintained "their distinctive individuality as a church by their piety and plainness of life."[57] Tucker noted some "cardinal principles of his [Faw's] church, viz: Opposition to war, to going to law, to slavery and to compensation for ministerial services." The remembrance of Jacob Faw illustrates well the importance of local Brethren ministers' upholding church teachings and the significance of ministers in Virginia and Tennessee to help them.

Stability for Brethren in western North Carolina increased with the emergence of a new center of activity in what is now Mitchell County, which was formed in 1861 from portions of several adjoining counties along the Tennessee border. A Bowman family from Tennessee had already moved here already around 1797. Located near the town of Relief, the fellowship grew slowly. They organized formally in 1844 as the Brummetts Creek congregation, with Peter Peterson and Henry Masters as ministers.

The congregation built a meetinghouse in 1852. Soon afterward they built another meetinghouse at Yellow Poplar to serve the growing congregation. Yellow Poplar soon became known as Hollow Poplar. Several men from the extended Peterson family served as ministers. A third meeting point developed at Elk Shoals but soon dissolved with no further trace.[58] Strong internal leadership and strong family ties helped Brummetts Creek and Hollow Poplar take root in the shelter of the mountains.

By 1860 Brethren had established three significant settlements with multiple local ministers. The ministry of Jehu Burket, Jacob Faw, and Jonathan Miller stabilized their congregations. With the committed efforts of local ministers and continued assistance from eastern Tennessee and southern Virginia these churches began to grow.

Challenges, Stability and Growth: 1860–1900

The impact of the War Between the States is difficult to assess for the Brethren in North Carolina. In 1861, as a part of the Confederate States of America, North Carolina allowed exemption from military service on the grounds of conscience. In 1862, the state added a fee of one hundred dollars for exemption.[59] There are no exact records of how many Brethren men who were members and were eligible for military claimed conscientious objection. Overall among the Brethren, most eligible men who were members refused to fight during the war.

Some cases surfaced during the Civil War in which men from Brethren families fought before they were baptized. In a few cases, the men were later baptized and joined the church, adopted its peace teaching and were later elected to ministry. Because men who were not baptized were not members, they were not subject to the church's discipline. Such men could be warmly welcomed to baptism after military service if they repented of their acts and promised to observe the church's teachings. In North Carolina were two such cases.

Henry Sheets (1842–1918), part of the extensive Sheets family in the Flat Rock congregation, enlisted in the Confederate Army in 1861 and served through 1863, attaining the rank of sergeant before he was mustered out. After the war, Henry (whose mother was a Wyatt) married Emily Wyatt, a relative. William Wilson Wyatt (1834–1917), known as Wilson Wyatt, was from Ashe County. He also fought in the Confederate army. His mother was a Sheets, and he and Henry Sheets were related.

After his military service, which must have ended by 1863, Wyatt married and was baptized. The members of the Flat Creek congregation elected him to ministry in 1863. The elders who presided at his installation included Elder John Lewis (presumably from Flat Rock), Elder Harden P. Hylton from Floyd County, Virginia, and Elder Henry Garst from the Knob Creek congregation in Tennessee.[60] Wyatt's military service prior to his baptism was not an impediment. By 1866, he moved to Miami County, Ohio. In 1870, he moved to western Missouri where he served the Mineral Creek church.

Henry Sheets was called to ministry in 1880 by the Flat Rock congregation and advanced to the eldership in 1888. He served there faithfully until he resigned his position in 1898 due to poor health. He died in 1918. Sheets and Wyatt are examples of a very small, unusual trend among the Brethren of men fighting in the Civil War prior to being baptized, then later coming into the church, adopting its peace teaching, and entering ministry.

In the 1860s, the Church of Ashe County continued to stabilize by developing local leadership and occasionally practicing church discipline. In 1866, Adam Sheets and H. M Prather were elected to ministry.[61] In 1872, D.C. Davis was elected to the ministry. In 1873, he was advanced to the so-called second degree of the Brethren's three-tiered system of ministry. The first degree was a time of apprenticeship and practice, similar to the older office of exhorter. After faithful service, the minister could be advanced to the second degree by the congregation. He would preach and be permitted to baptize, officiate at Lovefeasts, and solemnize marriages. The third degree was the eldership. Many congregations had more than one elder.

Church discipline was applied to ministers and members alike, with no distinction. In 1867 Isaac Miller, a regular member, was disciplined for "immorality and falsehood."[62] The congregation decided to excommunicate him "until satisfaction is made to the church." Brethren typically left open the possibility of reconciliation if offenders admitted their errors and asked for forgiveness. There is no record that Isaac Miller was restored. In January 1891, the congregation voted to silence one of their ministers, D.C. Davis, for unspecified charges.[63] In August of 1891, Davis apologized to the congregation and was restored to ministry.

While the War between the States did not divide the Brethren, conflicting attitudes about how quickly to accommodate to the wider culture split the church into three parties in the 1880s. An equally important question was whether the individual conscience, the congregation, or the Annual Meeting served as arbiter of accommodation. Conflict simmered in the 1870s as some Brethren, such as Henry R. Holsinger, a minister from Pennsylvania, called for Sunday schools, revival meetings, financially supported foreign missions, colleges and formal schooling, and financial support for ministers.[64] Holsinger also wanted to abolish the plain dress as a requirement of church members. Some Brethren saw him as an abrasive critic of the older elders while others supported him as a prophetic leader. Holsinger was expelled from the church in 1882. Within a year, his group, known as the Progressives, formed a Brethren Church centered in Ashland, Ohio.

The second group in the division were traditionalist Brethren seeking to preserve plain ways and the authority of Annual Meeting. They objected to innovations that were emerging, such as normal schools in Huntingdon, Pennsylvania, in 1876,[65] sending missionaries to Denmark in 1876, and the introduction of Sunday schools in some congregations. This group withdrew in 1880 and formed the Old German Baptist Brethren, sometimes informally called Old Order Brethren.

The third group was numerically the largest and claimed to be both conservative and progressive. They embraced some innovation, but only slowly. They were willing to accept colleges, foreign missions, and Sunday schools if they were operated in a humble, Brethren manner. They wanted to retain plain dress and endorsed the authority of the Annual Meeting. This group was known as the German Baptist Brethren. They changed their name to the Church of the Brethren in 1908.

In North Carolina, the three-way division of 1880–1882 had only a small impact. While no Brethren Church (Progressive Brethren) congregation formed in the 1880s, the most conservative branch of the division drew the support of Elder Jacob Faw at Fraternity.[66] He and twelve other members, about one third of the church, formed the Fraternity Old German Baptist Brethren Church a few weeks before his death in 1887.[67] Both Fraternity groups shared the same meetinghouse until 1900, when the Church of the Brethren built their own structure. After the departure of the Old German Baptist Brethren faction from Fraternity in 1887, the remainder of the congregation was served by J.F. Robertson and C.F. Faw, both of whom were elected to ministry in 1883 at the age of twenty-one.

The Fraternity congregation formed a meeting point, Maple Grove, located near Lexington, where ministers had been preaching already in the 1860s. Jacob Faw, Amos

Faw, Levi Spach and William Sides served both Fraternity and Maple Grove until these four men sided with the Old German Baptist Brethren in 1887. After 1887, J.F. Robertson and C.F. Faw served the Maple Grove congregation.[68]

There are some possible explanations for the minimal impact of the divisions in North Carolina. The strong networks of ministers across the various congregations reinforced unity. The Progressives' agenda for higher education and trained, salaried ministry offered no advantages in North Carolina. Non-salaried ministry was an essential ingredient for success in North Carolina in the nineteenth century. The Brethren there already had preaching meetings with visiting ministers, a step toward their home-grown revivalism. The Old Order Brethren offered little attraction for most of the North Carolina Brethren, who still dressed plainly, rejected musical instruments until the twentieth century, practiced church discipline, and upheld the authority of their elders. In short, neither the Progressives nor the Old Orders offered strong incentives to leave the wider body of the church. Brethren in North Carolina negotiated some limited innovation while retaining some traditional elements. Their geographical distance from the main conflict zone in Ohio probably also shielded them from the tensions of the divisions.

Instead of dividing in the 1880s, the Brethren in North Carolina embarked vigorously on forming new, small congregations. By 1888, the Church in Ashe County formed about four congregations. The mother church became Flat Rock, while some members transferred to form a daughter congregation, Peak Creek. Another offshoot from Flat Rock was Pleasant Valley, which organized also around 1890.[69] By 1890, Mt. Carmel was organized as a separate congregation from Flat Rock. Located about twelve miles east of Sparta, it was one of the more successful daughter congregations. Henry Sheets was the founding elder. The extended Reed family provided many members and some ministers for Mt. Carmel.[70]

Two short-lived congregations also developed from Flat Rock. Long Hope was organized around 1890, but ceased to exist around 1906. Bowlin Creek Church (known as Three Top) had begun by the early 1880s when their elder, Hendrik Prather, died. Henry Sheets assisted at this congregation as did Prather's son, Marion. However, this church disbanded in the early twentieth century.[71]

An outgrowth from the Brummetts Creek church in Mitchell County formed slowly as members moved to an area north of Red Hill in the 1850s. Although Brummets Creek ministers preached at Red Hill prior to 1860, the group did not organize as a congregation until 1894.[72] The Herrell, Masters, and Griffiths families comprised much of the membership and served as leaders.

An entirely new center of Brethren activity formed in the 1870s in Polk County, along the border with South Carolina. George A. Branscom, Sr., a Brethren man born in 1855 in Washington County, Tennessee, and baptized there in the Knob Creek, Tennessee, congregation,[73] moved to Polk County around 1876. He was invited by Jim Taylor, a teacher who had come to Tennessee to teach, but intended to return to North Carolina to start a school. Branscom went with Taylor to Polk County, North Carolina, where the new school was organized. Branscom spoke openly about his faith with his neighbors in North Carolina. He invited Brethren ministers from Tennessee to come to Polk County and preach. Frederick Washington Dove and Andy Vines from Tennessee answered the call, and in 1878 they organized the new congregation called Mill Creek. Branscom was the first minister. They numbered thirty-eight members by 1882 and built a meetinghouse in 1893.

Before the end of the nineteenth century, Mill Creek gave birth to two more congregations. Green River Cove was organized near Saluda in 1880.[74] Always quite small, this congregation dissolved by the late 1920s. Another congregation, Brooklyn, was formed in 1893 in South Carolina and ceased activity in 1924.[75]

By the turn of the twentieth century, four centers of Brethren activity had found firm footing in North Carolina and experienced growth. They weathered the storms of war and denominational division thanks to strong, committed local leaders, support from Brethren centers in Virginia and Tennessee, and energetic attempts to launch new congregations.

Growth, Decline and New Challenges Since 1900

Marking a new period for the Brethren in North Carolina at the turn of the twentieth century is somewhat arbitrary because the flurry of revivals and the formation of new congregations began before 1900 and continued in the first two decades immediately afterward. Nevertheless, after 1900 new institutional structures formed, signaling new patterns for church life.

After 1900, the pace of starting new churches increased. Some thrived, some soon disbanded. Economic and social changes brought employment in textile mills and populations shifts. In turn, the loss of manufacturing jobs in the last quarter of the twentieth century in the old centers of Brethren activity brought declining populations and economic contraction. Additionally, brisk changes in transportation and communication spawned both new opportunities and losses for Brethren congregations. The Church of the Brethren experienced denominational change as it adopted more modern attitudes and structures, including professionalized ministry by the 1920s and greater engagement with ecumenical relations after the 1940s.

One important denominational change was the formation of administrative regions called districts. Brethren in Virginia started the process of grouping congregations that were geographically close after the War between the States. The elders formed a leadership body in the districts, and a yearly District Meeting or District Conference was held to handle questions that might be sent on to Annual Meeting. In the 1890s, North Carolina congregations were grouped with Tennessee, and some were aligned with First Virginia District. By 1903, North and South Carolina and Georgia constituted a district. During the twentieth century, district alignments changed considerably, especially after World War II, with the establishment of salaried, full-time executives as mid-level judicatory heads. The office of elder was abolished in 1963.[76] Since 1973, five congregations in the Piedmont plus Shelton in the northwestern part of the state belong to the Virlina District, a combination of southern Virginia, parts of West Virginia, and North Carolina. The remaining thirteen North Carolina congregations, plus Travelers Rest in South Carolina, belong to the Southeastern District, which combines Tennessee, the Carolinas, Alabama, and a few churches in Virginia.

Brethren in North Carolina navigated these changes with some strategies that had served them well in the past, such as revivalism and a network of ministers. Sunday schools, congregational subgroups such as women's fellowships, youth fellowships, and camps for Brethren youth all strengthened the churches. These changes and continuities can be traced through the four main clusters of Brethren, namely Flat Rock and Ashe County, Fraternity, Brummetts Creek and Mitchell County, and finally Mill Creek and Polk County.

Flat Rock and the Ashe County Area

While choosing local men for lifelong ministry was often an asset, sometimes it was a liability. One minister at Flat Rock, George Miller, led a large group of members out of the church to join the Union Baptist Church around 1908.[77] Clayton B. Miller led Flat Rock during the first half of the twentieth century. The congregation held Bible schools and periodic revivals. A women's fellowship and a youth fellowship were created. Still, Flat Rock did not recover its earlier vigor. Flat Rock gave birth to a new outpost in Ashe County, the White Rock congregation, organized around 1901. Unnamed difficulties troubled the church, and it closed by 1911.[78]

Peak Creek lost several members in the 1920s. George A. Branscom, Jr., came from Melvin Hill to aid the congregation, and in 1925 they constructed their first church building.[79] D.M. Glick and the family of S.F. Flory moved to Peak Creek to shore up the membership. Fred Dancy, a North Carolina minister, gave strong leadership in the 1930s. Peak Creek started a new preaching point at Harmon in the 1930s. By 1960, this group had declined and was consolidated back into Peak Creek. Meanwhile Dancy started a small congregation, Lowman Valley, across the state line near Marion, Virginia. Peak Creek reached its highest membership in 1950 with 150 members before changing economic conditions led to outmigration. Peak Creek and Lowman Valley survived despite these changes.

The story of the Pleasant Valley congregation in Ashe County after 1900 was one of decline. Having been formed in Ashe County from Flat Rock around 1890, Pleasant Valley rarely had a local minister.[80] Always a small church, they disbanded late in the twentieth century.

Mount Carmel flourished after 1900 for several decades. A.J. Reed became elder after 1900 and three of his sons were preachers there.[81] W.H. Handy served as elder from the 1920s to 1951. In the 1960s and 1970s, Mary Girtman served the church. She was an ordained minister, quite unusual for Brethren who only began to ordain women ministers in 1958.[82] Mount Carmel's membership declined after the 1950s as members moved to urban areas but continues at present.

Peak Creek birthed a daughter congregation, Blue Ridge, whose main story unfolded after 1900, even though it was organized in 1897 in Wilkes County. Blue Ridge had a start-and-stop existence. Several members of the Sheets and Wingler families comprised the membership when the church was founded. However, the congregation was inactive by 1902.[83] In 1911, they resumed worship services but again became inactive after 1925. In 1931, George A. Branscom, Jr., revived the church, and Clayton B. Miller was elected to serve as minister.[84] Blue Ridge endured for decades but finally closed.

New Bethel and its more successful daughter congregation, New Haven, both located near Sparta in Alleghany County, started after 1900. W.H. Handy and W.A. Reed launched New Bethel, located about seven miles northwest of Sparta, around 1903. By 1942, the congregation disbanded. New Haven, located about four miles north of Sparta, formed in 1926 when several members left New Bethel and formed the new church. All thirty of the charter members belonged to the Sexton family.[85] A strong Sunday School and periodic revival meetings led by the brothers W.A. Reed and N.C. Reed nourished New Haven through much of the twentieth century.[86]

Flat Rock also gave birth to the Little Pine congregation in the early twentieth century, and it in turn produced a daughter congregation. Little Pine, located twelve miles east of Sparta in Alleghany County, started from revival preaching by W.A. Reed in 1905.[87] The church was organized in 1906. Reed served as pastor and elder. Later, Coy Anders was pastor from 1945 to the 1960s. Both Connie Cleary, an ordained minister, and her husband, David Cleary, also a minister, served Little Pine at different times. Like Mary Girtman at Mt. Carmel, Connie Cleary was one of the pioneer women ministers among the Brethren in North Carolina.

Two offshoots from Little Pine, both in Virginia, did not fare so well. Mountain View grew out of Little Pine and was organized in 1906 near Volney, Virginia, just across the state line. N.C. Reed and W.H. Handy started the church, which belonged to the North Carolina district in spite of its location in Virginia.[88] The church closed by the early 1940s. The Rowland Creek congregation grew out of Mountain View and was organized in 1911 in Smyth County, Virginia.[89] W.H. Handy was the first pastor. Clayton B. Miller, David Cleary, and Connie Cleary also served here. Although several members withdrew in the 1950s to form a separate congregation, the Independent Brethren, Rowland Creek persevered as a small group.

In the early twentieth century, a Virginia congregation helped to start a new fellowship in North Carolina. Ministers from the Saint Paul congregation, near Cana, Virginia, started a preaching point known as Christian Chapel around 1900 just outside of Mount Airy in Surry County, North Carolina.[90] One of those ministers was Joseph A. Easter. In a tragedy that shook the members of Saint Paul church and the community, Easter was shot and killed at his home in the night of May 23, 1907. The killing was probably in retaliation for testimony he gave that day about illegal distilling operations in the area.[91] He was fifty at the time of his death and left behind a widow and six children.

The preaching point known as Christian Chapel that Easter helped to start in Surry County, North Carolina, organized formally as the Shelton Church of the Brethren in 1917 with forty-one charter members. S. Cubbage, H.J. Woodie and N.C. Reed served as early ministers. Shelton grew into an active congregation. Internal conflict at Shelton came to a happy ending with the establishment of a new congregation. Around 1960, some Shelton members stopped attending. W.H. Hawks invited them to meet in Mount Airy to form a new Church of the Brethren congregation.[92] Twenty-six people started a fellowship in 1963, with D.B. Osborne as their minister. In 1965, they became the Mount Airy First Church of the Brethren, a vital congregation. In this case, two congregations grew within the denomination, rather than one being lost.

A small cluster of congregations in Wilkes County showed how Brethren could move successfully from the countryside into town. Two small Brethren fellowships, Burke and Mount Olive, existed in the Reddies River area about fifteen miles north of North Wilkesboro in the early twentieth century.[93] Neither one became a lasting church. George A. Branscom made a third attempt in 1929, starting the Riverside congregation. It reached seventy-five members in 1952, but closed by 1966.

However, some Brethren from Riverside moved into the town of North Wilkesboro by the 1940s, probably to follow jobs.[94] David Cleary organized the Friendship Church of the Brethren just outside North Wilkesboro in 1954 with twenty-five members. The church grew slowly, making a successful transition to town.

Fraternity and Maple Grove

In 1904, J.P. Robertson was elected to ministry at Fraternity. In 1912, another minister, H.J. Woodie, moved into the area, thus increasing the local ministerial leadership. The preaching point at Maple Grove was formally organized as a separate congregation in 1921. In 1927, Russel and Bertha (Cecil) Robertson, members from Fraternity, went as medical missionaries to Nigeria and started a leprosarium. He died of yellow fever in 1931 as they prepared to come home on furlough.[95] In the 1940s, both Fraternity and Maple Grove moved toward professional, salaried ministry, sometimes sharing one salaried pastor.[96]

Brummetts Creek

After 1900, the Brummetts Creek church in Mitchell County strengthened the daughter congregation that they launched in 1894, Pleasant Grove, and launched several new churches. The Pleasant Grove members completed a church building in 1907.[97] Revival meetings, Sunday school, and an active youth group strengthened the church in the 1940s and 1950s, in spite of losing thirty-five members in 1933. After 1964, membership declined. Etta Bryant, a member, observed in 1967 that the young adults moved away for education and jobs,[98] a trend affecting the whole region in western North Carolina.

A very short-lived congregation, Bethel, was formed from Brummetts Creek in neighboring Yancey County from 1902 to 1924. More successful was an outgrowth from the Hollow Poplar congregation known as Petersons Chapel, which was also located in Yancey County, a few miles south of Relief.[99] J.R. Jackson organized Petersons Chapel in 1923. With about fifty members in the 1950s, the congregation declined after 1970.

Two other offshoots from Brummetts Creek formed about 1911 and two more around 1930. Bailey was organized around 1911, although Brummetts Creek ministers had been preaching in the Bailey Schoolhouse three miles west of Relief since the 1890s.[100] Membership reached seventy-five in 1956. Pigeon River, located two and half miles north of Relief, was organized in 1912 by Matison Griffith as presiding minister. In 1914, the members built a church building. The church numbered eighty-five members in 1955. Upper Brummetts Creek became a separate congregation in 1930 and had seventy-six members in 1945.[101] Berea was organized near Bakersville in 1932 with twenty members, led by H.H. Masters.[102] The church had fourteen members in 1962.

These four congregations, Bailey, Pigeon River, Upper Brummetts Creek, and Berea, left the Church of the Brethren in 1962. Calvin Barnett, the minister at Pigeon River and Upper Brummetts Creek, attacked the denomination's participation in the World Council of Churches. He upheld the King James Version of the Bible as the only acceptable version.

Unrest in the church had been growing since at least 1957 when nearly two dozen members from Upper Brummetts Creek moved their membership back to Brummetts Creek to reaffirm their identity with the Church of the Brethren. The district adopted a statement of Brethren beliefs that included an endorsement of the denomination's peace position. However, the statement claimed that individual conscience should be the final authority as to whether a member should practice this teaching.[103] The emphasis on individual conscience reflected the drift and weakening of the Brethren peace witness since World War II.

Calvin Barnett finalized the break in 1962 and led Bailey, Pigeon River, Upper Brummetts Creek and Berea to form a separate group, the Fundamental Brethren. Berea, the smallest of the four, did not survive and disbanded by 1970. The separation in 1962 illustrated the continuing influence of Fundamentalism and its challenge to denominational identities. The break also showed some of the tensions as some Brethren leaders moved more publicly toward mainline Protestantism with an openness to more liberal agendas. Only three of the original eight congregations formed in Mitchell and Yancey counties still existed in the Church of the Brethren in 1968.

Mill Creek and Polk County

Mill Creek grew to one hundred forty members by 1902, holding services every Sunday morning and evening. At this time, Brethren rarely held worship every week because the services rotated among the multiple preaching points of a congregation. Mill Creek established a preaching point at Huntley in Rutherford County by 1903, but no church formed there.[104]

Brethren preaching began near Columbus, North Carolina, around 1900, leading to the formation of Melvin Hill in 1906. George A. Branscom and Will Reed were ministers.[105] Melvin Hill had over two hundred members in 1931. Melvin Hill illustrated a growing trend among Brethren to adopt some mainline Protestant denominational patterns such as musical instruments and professional ministry. From 1921 to 1928 members debated whether to allow the use of an organ. It was repeatedly voted down, consistent with the Brethren rejection of musical instruments. In 1928, an organ was brought into the church and a vote was taken on whether to keep it. The organ stayed.[106] Melvin Hill hired their first professional salaried minister, S. Loren Bowman, in 1934. After his departure in 1937 the church sometimes had non-salaried ministers and sometimes salaried ministers.

Melvin Hill and S. Loren Bowmen played vital roles in pressing the Brethren in North Carolina to establish a church camp for the district. The trend of creating church camps has spread among Brethren since the 1920s. In 1933, Melvin Hill members requested that the district form a church camp for youth. The next year, Bowman, the young salaried minister at Melvin Hill, organized a one-week youth camp on a private farm near Scottville.[107] In 1935, Bowman directed another week of camp under the name of Camp Carmel. This arrangement continued through 1938. In the 1940s the weeklong camping experiences became annual weekend retreats at various churches. In 1950, another week of youth camp was held at the Mt. Carmel congregation.

In 1952, the district purchased forty-three acres south of Linville, North Carolina. A week of youth camp was held in August.[108] The new camp was named Camp Carolina, and renamed Camp Carmel in 1961. Enthusiastic Brethren youth and dedicated parents made camping successful. Like other Brethren church camps, Camp Carolina has struggled with decreasing camper participation since the 1980s as church membership decreased and nationally the interest in institutional camps sagged. Camp Carmel is an important touchstone for denominational identity for these churches.

During World War II, Melvin Hill had three young men who were conscientious objectors and went into Civilian Public Service (CPS). Melvin Hill also supported CPS financially, as did other North Carolina churches.[109] The three historic peace churches—the Mennonites, the Quakers, or Friends, and the Brethren—together created the program of alternative service for conscientious objectors during World War II, and they paid for it.

At the time of the war, about 85 to 90 percent of eligible Brethren men chose to enter the armed forces rather than alternative service.[110] That Melvin Hill had three conscientious objectors during the war was noteworthy. Four Brethren men from Sparta—Floyd, Ford, Jay, and Norman Sexton—also served in CPS, as did some other men from North Carolina.[111] Exact figures on the number of Brethren conscientious objectors in North Carolina during World War II are not available, but overall the churches probably reflected the trends for Brethren across the country.

The Brethren in Polk County started other churches in the early twentieth century, but none was as successful as Melvin Hill. A small fellowship near Gaston County formed around 1908 but soon disbanded. In 1907, the Golden congregation was created under the leadership of W.A. Reed.[112] Averaging a few dozen participants, Golden declined after World War II and was disbanded after 1965.[113]

Two more congregations, Laurens and Travelers Rest, grew out of the Polk County Brethren. Laurens was organized in 1907 under the leadership of Marion Prather, but disbanded by 1912. Travelers Rest in South Carolina grew out of W.A. Reed's evangelizing in the 1930s and was organized in 1938.[114] One member, Lynell Peterson, was a conscientious objector during wartime. After his time in CPS he returned as a pastor in the 1950s and 1960s. Travelers Rest continued as a Church of the Brethren congregation in South Carolina after Laurens disbanded and Brooklyn withdrew from the denomination in 1962.[115]

In Spindale, North Carolina, the Brethren made a successful transition into a town setting. The Mountain Creek congregation had formed in 1909 near Hollins in Rutherford County, about fifteen miles northwest of Spindale.[116] Some members moved into Spindale as the town was created with the surge of textile mills in the area after World War I.[117] In 1924, the Mountain Creek congregation moved into the town and became the Spindale Church of the Brethren.[118] As the membership increased, they built a new church building in 1953 and switched to professional, salaried ministry.

Two other short-lived congregations formed in North Carolina in the twentieth century. Around 1896, Louis Foss, a dissatisfied Church of God minister near La Grange, North Carolina, read some publications about the Brethren and decided to join.[119] Elders came from Virginia to organize the Oak Grove congregation around 1904, but it soon disbanded. In 1962, Brethren started a new congregation in Statesville, North Carolina, with twenty-five members.[120] Internal difficulties led to the church's dissolution in 1968.

One other branch of the Brethren family of traditions had a short-lived congregation in Hickory, North Carolina. The Brethren Church, with headquarters in Ashland, Ohio, started a church there in 1982.[121] Robert Payne, Jr., served as pastor, starting in 1984. The congregation closed in 1990.

Into the Twenty-first Century

The Church of the Brethren's Virlina District planted a few new churches around the turn of the twenty-first century, with varying success. Multiple attempts failed to start a lasting congregation in Greensboro since the late twentieth. Flowing Faith was the most recent project there, existing only from 2004 to 2009.[122]

Brethren turned to the tech industry and university population by starting a congregation in Durham. The Peace Covenant Church had begun in 1996 as a fellowship. The membership numbered about fifty in 2015. The Church of the Brethren focused on the North Carolina coastal tourist population with a project at Sunset Beach in 2002. This was the only effort to form a church on the coast. The congregation disbanded in 2007. Another project in Concord, North Carolina, was more successful. The Living Faith congregation started in 1996; by 2015 they reported fifty-five members.

The Southeastern District of the Church of the Brethren attempted to tap into the changing ethnic demographics of North Carolina. Iglesia Jesuscristo El Camino / HIS Way congregation started in Hendersonville and reported fifty-seven members in 2015.

The Grace Brethren, a group that split from the Brethren Church in 1939, started a Hispanic congregation in Durham in 2012.[123] Oscar Chavez served as the organizing pastor, beginning with Bible Study meetings in his home in 2011. Between forty and sixty participants attended in the first year of the project.

Conclusion

While the number of Brethren in North Carolina is minuscule, their story is unique. Never settled in the coastal area, they took root in two small centers in the Appalachian Mountains on the borders with northeastern Tennessee and southwestern Virginia, in one small outpost in the Piedmont, and another on the border with South Carolina. The Brethren were the only historic peace church with a presence in colonial North Carolina that was consistently opposed to slavery from their beginnings. The pacifist and non-swearing Brethren survived the challenges of the Revolutionary War in North Carolina, only to lose almost all of their members due to a doctrinal controversy over Universalism. From that colossal reverse, they stabilized and grew somewhat with the help of ministers from southern Virginia and northeastern Tennessee. The strong connections with Brethren in these two centers still contribute to the endurance of Brethren in North Carolina.

The other major factor in the perseverance of Brethren in North Carolina is the historic strong connection among their ministers, within and across congregations, frequently drawing on the model of self-supporting ministers. From the movement of Brethren leaders from Uwharrie to Fraternity, and from Fraternity to Ashe County at the end of the eighteenth century, to the work of ministers to start and support new churches in the twentieth century, North Carolina Brethren have helped each other. Even as the Church of the Brethren moved toward professional, salaried ministry in the twentieth century, Brethren in North Carolina have taken advantage of training programs for bi-vocational ministers to develop internal leadership alongside the model of salaried ministry.

The Brethren survived the War between the States in unity, and endured relatively minimal effects from a major division within their denomination in the 1880s. However, a gradual shift to emphasizing individual conscience in the twentieth century led to a dramatic decrease in the rate of conscientious objection during World War II. In the 1960s, the influence of Fundamentalism led to the loss of some congregations.

While Brethren distinctiveness in simplicity, their peace witness, and percentage of participation in Lovefeasts has decreased since the latter twentieth century, Brethren identity has by no means disappeared. The North Carolina Brethren continue to support a variety of service activities, including disaster relief. In recent years Brethren have made small moves in new directions with outreach in cities, such as Concord and Durham. A few efforts to reach culturally diverse populations are evidenced in the Church of the Brethren Hispanic congregation in Hendersonville and the Grace Brethren congregation in Durham. For the most part, however, Brethren in North Carolina in recent years have not engaged extensively with the shifting economic and demographic patterns of the state.

The Brethren in North Carolina cannot be judged by numerical growth or by the count of denominational institutions that they created. Their success is best measured by creative ways of mobilizing committed leadership to nurture churches and start new ones in their centers of strength. Their ability to draw from strong ties to Brethren centers in Virginia and Tennessee has augmented internal leadership. The Brethren in North Carolina have faced serious challenges, but they survive. They have been a distinct minority yet have contributed to the complex diversity of Christianity in North Carolina.

NOTES

1. The Church of the Brethren statistics are based on the 2016 denominational report and reflect statistics from 2015. Some congregations had not reported for two years or more, so the numbers are not precise. In addition to the North Carolina members, the Church of the Brethren has one congregation in Travelers Rest, South Carolina, reporting seventy-eight members. The Grace Brethren congregation in Durham had about forty to sixty participants. In addition to the Church of the Brethren and Grace Brethren, the other groups in the family of Brethren traditions include Old Order German Baptist Brethren (New Conference), Old German Baptist Brethren (Old Conference), Dunkard Brethren, Brethren Church, and Conservative Grace Brethren. The largest number of Brethren is in Africa.

2. Donald F. Durnbaugh, *Fruit of the Vine: A History of the Brethren 1708–1995* (Elgin, IL: Brethren Press, 1997), 1–70. See also Marcus Meier, *The Origin of the Schwarzenau Brethren* (Philadelphia: Brethren Encyclopedia, Inc., 2008), 1–22.

3. William G. Willoughby, *Counting the Cost: The Life of Alexander Mack 1679–1735* (Elgin, IL: Brethren Press, 1979) 37–53.

4. Dale R. Stoffer, *Background and Development of Brethren Doctrines (1650–1987)* (Philadelphia: Brethren Encyclopedia, Inc., 1986), 65–86 for sources influencing the formation of the Brethren. See also Meier, *Schwarzenau Brethren*.

5. Alexander Mack, Sr., "A Brief and Simple Exposition of the Outward but Yet Sacred Rights and Ordinances of the House of God," in Alexander Mack, Sr., *The Complete Writings of Alexander Mack*, edited by William R. Eberly (Winona Lake, IN: BMH Books, 1991), 48–75, 92–99.

6. Mack, "Rights and Ordinances," 78–80, 88–92. There are no references to Brethren anointing before 1741.

7. Durnbaugh, *Fruit of the Vine*, 51–70.

8. Roger E. Sappington, *The Brethren in the Carolinas* (Kingsport, TN: Watson's Lithographing Co., 1971), 4–6. Sappington's book is the only monograph about Brethren in North and South Carolina. See also Durnbaugh, *Fruit of the Vine*, 85–86.

9. Jeff Bach, *Voices of the Turtledoves: The Sacred World of Ephrata* (University Park, PA: Penn State Press, 2003), 18–24.

10. Bach, *Voices of the Turtledoves*, 141–69.

11. Klaus Wust, *The Saint-Adventurers of the Virginia Frontier* (Edinburg, VA: Shenandoah History, 1977), 15–28.

12. Sappington, *Carolinas*, 26–39.

13. Morgan Edwards, "Materials Toward a History of the Baptists in the Province of North Carolina," quoted in total in Donald F. Durnbaugh, translator and editor, *The Brethren in Colonial America* (Elgin, IL: Brethren Press, 1963), 189. The portion of Edwards' manuscript relating to North Carolina was published in 1930. See G. W. Paschal, ed., "Materials Toward a History of the Baptists in the Province of North Carolina," *The North Carolina Historical Review* vol. 7, issue 3 (1930): 365–89; also see Brethren material, 393.

14. Roger E. Sappington, *Carolinas*, 6.

15. Durnbaugh, *Colonial America*, 189.

16. Sappington, *Carolinas*, 7.

17. Sappington, *Carolinas*, 7.

18. Durnbaugh, *Colonial America*, 189.

19. Sappington, *Carolinas*, 19–20.

20. Sappington, *Carolinas*, 21; and Durnbaugh, *Colonial America*, 189.

21. Durnbaugh, *Colonial America*, 189. Morgan Edwards gave Stutzman's surname as "Studeman."

22. Sappington, *Carolinas*, 11–13. Sappington quoted Fries' record of Moravians in North Carolina.

23. Sappington, *Carolinas*, 45.

24. Sappington, *Carolinas*, 46.

25. Sappington, *Carolinas*, 44.

26. Sappington, *Carolinas*, 46.

27. Sappington, *Carolinas* 48, 50. Sappington quoted Adelaide Fries and others, *Records of the Moravians in North Carolina* 2: 670 and 729.

28. Sappington, *Carolinas*, 53. A genealogical account by Burkett descendants states that Jehu Burkhart was in North Carolina already in 1775. The Fraternity congregation probably dates to this time.

29. Sappington, *Carolinas*, 83.

30. Jonathan Miller, Clayton B. Miller, "The Flat Rock Church of the Brethren," undated, unpaginated manuscript. This manuscript compiles minutes and memories of the Brethren in Ashe County, who later formed the Flat Rock congregation, dating from its founding to the late nineteenth century. Sappington quotes from this manuscript. See also Sappington, *Carolinas*, 88. Copies of the manuscript are available at the Brethren Historical Library and Archives in Elgin, Illinois, and in the Sappington Papers in the Hess Archives of Elizabethtown College.

31. Clayton B. Miller, "Flat Rock."

32. Clayton B. Miller, "Flat Rock," also quoted in Sappington, *Carolinas*, 91–92.

33. Lamech and Agrippa, *Chronicon Ephratense* (Ephrata, PA: Typis Societatis, 1786), translated by J. Max Hark (Lancaster, PA: S.H. Zahm, 1889) 124–25.

34. "A True List of the Sale of the Estate of manuel [*sic*] Eakles Deceased," Anson County, North Carolina, Record of Wills, Book I, 1751–1795, pp. 288–91.

35. Durnbaugh, *Colonial America*, 371–74. Durnbaugh quotes the specific laws in North Carolina.

36. Sappington, *Carolinas*, 16.

37. Sappington, *Carolinas*, 18 and 14–15 for non-participation in the Regulator movement.

38. Durnbaugh, *Colonial America*, 327–31. See also Sappington, *Carolinas*, 61–68.

39. Durnbaugh, *Colonial America*, 332.

40. Sappington, *Brethren in the Carolinas*, 61–64.

41. John Scott Davenport and David B. Eller, "John H. and the Spread of Universalism West," *Brethren Life and Thought*, 28, 4: 216–17. See also Sappington, *Carolinas*, 44. Sappington held to the older identification, supported by Universalist historian Richard Eddy, that John H. was John Ham. See Durnbaugh, *Colonial America*, 327, for the pertinent passages from Eddy.

42. Durnbaugh, *Colonial America*, 327–30. Durnbaugh quotes the Annual Meeting minutes verbatim.

43. Mack, "Rights and Ordinances," 97–98.

44. Durnbaugh, *Colonial America*, 333.

45. Sappington, *Carolinas*, 57–61, 73–75. David Martin, a Brethren minister in South Carolina, had been preaching Universalism since 1780.

46. John Scott Davenport, "Joseph Roland," in Donald F. Durnbaugh, ed., *The Brethren Encyclopedia* (Philadelphia: Brethren Encyclopedia, Inc., 1983).

47. Joseph Roland, ["Ancient Documents"], June 20, 1830, in Daniel B. Gibson, ed. *Compiled Minutes and History of the Church of the Brethren of the Southern District of Illinois* (Elgin, IL: Brethren Publishing House, 1907), 4. Note Joseph Roland's change of the family name from Rowland to Roland.

48. See Gibson, *Compiled Minutes*, 4, and Davenport and Eller, "John H.," 217.

49. Sappington, *Carolinas*, 102. Sappington cited Miller, "Flat Rock," pp. 2–3.

50. Sappington, *Carolinas*, quoting from Fries, *Records of the Moravians*, 5: 2324.

51. Clayton B. Miller, "Flat Rock." See also Sappington, *Carolinas*, 102.

52. Sappington, *Carolinas*, 80, 95. See also Jess O. Garst, ed., *History of the Church of the Brethren of the Southern District of Ohio* (Dayton, OH: Otterbein Press, 1920), 94.

53. Daniel Peters, "The Brethren Church in Franklin County, Virginia," *Brethren Family Almanac* (Mount Morris, IL: Brethren Publishing House, 1909), 32–33. See also Ethel R. Jamison, "Virgin Timber," *Old Order Notes* 2 (1979): 9–15. The account of the letter is on p. 15. See also Sappington, *Carolinas*, 97.

54. See "Faw, Jacob," in Donald F. Durnbaugh, ed., *Brethren Encyclopedia*, vol. 1, 1838. See also Peters, "Brethren Church in Franklin County," 33.

55. Sappington, *Carolinas*, 99. Sappington quoted from Amy Faw and Linda Faw, *The Faw Family Record* (Chillicothe, IL: privately printed 1955, revised 1964).

56. Sappington, *Carolinas*, 99, quoting from Faw, *Faw Family Record*. A slightly different version of the story is told in Jamison, "Virgin Timber," 14. Jamison was Jacob Faw's great-granddaughter.

57. F.P. Tucker, "Elder Jacob Faw," in the *Union Republican* (June 16, 1887), p. 1.

58. Sappington, *Carolinas*, 109.

59. "Conscientious objection," NCpedia.org. Accessed July 11, 2017.

60. For the ministerial status and location of Hylton and Garst, see Durnbaugh, ed., *Brethren Encyclopedia*, 3: 1667, 1630.

61. Clayton B. Miller, "Flat Rock."

62. Clayton B. Miller, "Flat Rock."

63. Clayton B. Miller, "Flat Rock."

64. Stoffer, *Brethren Doctrines*, 133–56 for a thorough analysis of the divisions and issues related to them.

65. Durnbaugh, *Fruit of the Vine*, 255–57, 354–57 for early Brethren schools and missions. The normal school in Huntingdon eventually became Juniata College.

66. Ethel R. Jamison, "Faw, Jacob," in Donald F. Durnbaugh, ed. *Brethren Encyclopedia*.

67. Jamison, "Virgin Timber," 14.

68. Sappington, *Brethren in Virginia*, 365–66.

69. Clayton B. Miller, "Flat Rock." See also Sappington, *Carolinas*, 131–34.

70. Sappington, *Carolinas*, 133–34.

71. Sappington, *Carolinas*, 105. Due to gaps in congregational records, exact dates of closure are uncertain.

72. Sappington, *Carolinas*, 110, 169.

73. Sappington, *Carolinas*, 113–15.

74. Sappington, *Carolinas*, 188.

75. Brooklyn members resumed worship in 1943. They absorbed influences from Fundamentalism, and in 1962 they withdrew from the denomination and became an independent congregation. See Sappington, *Carolinas*, 189–90.

76. Sappington, *Carolinas*, 211–16.

77. Sappington, *Carolinas*, 122.

78. Sappington, *Carolinas*, 137–38, 140–41.

79. Sappington, *Carolinas*, 126–27.

80. Sappington, *Carolinas*, 131–32.

81. Sappington, *Carolinas*, 133–34.

82. Sappington, *Carolinas*, 136.

83. Sappington, *Carolinas*, 138.

84. Sappington, *Carolinas*, 138–39.

85. Sappington, *Carolinas*, 149–51.

86. Sappington, *Carolinas*, 153.

87. Sappington, *Carolinas*, 142–46.

88. Sappington, *Carolinas*, 147.

89. Sappington, *Carolinas*, 148.

90. Roger Sappington, *The Brethren in Virginia* (Harrisonburg, VA: The Committee on Brethren History in Virginia, 1973), 257.

91. "Foully Assassinated," *Daily Press*, Newport News, VA, vol. 12, no. 122 (May 25, 1907): 1. See also "Minister Called Out and Killed," *The Commonwealth*, Scotland Neck, VA (May 30, 1907): 1. Mary Case Summerlin, *The Legacy of Ada, a Mountain Woman* (Mt. Airy, NC: Hickory Hill Publications, 2007). Roger E. Sappington, *The Brethren in Virginia* (Harrisonburg, VA: The Committee for Brethren History in Virginia, 1973), 356.

92. Sappington, *Carolinas*, 159–60.

93. Sappington, *Carolinas*, 155.

94. Sappington, *Carolinas*, 157–58.

95. Sappington, *Brethren in Virginia*, 365.

96. Sappington, *Brethren in Virginia*, 365–66.

97. Sappington, *Carolinas*, 171.

98. Sappington, *Carolinas*, 175–76.

99. Sappington, *Carolinas*, 168.

100. Sappington, *Carolinas*, 177–78.

101. Sappington, *Carolinas*, 180–81.

102. Sappington, *Carolinas*, 181.

103. Sappington, *Carolinas*, 178–79.

104. Sappington, *Carolinas*, 183.

105. Sappington, *Carolinas*, 184–85.

106. Sappington, *Carolinas*, 193.

107. Sappington, *Carolinas*, 217–18.

108. Sappington, *Carolinas*, 219.

109. Sappington, *Carolinas*, 198.

110. Durnbaugh, *Fruit of the Vine*, 474–75. For comments on the shift to individual conscience regarding

peace, See Carl F. Bowman, *Brethren Society: The Cultural Transformation of a "Peculiar People"* (Baltimore: Johns Hopkins University Press, 1995), 350–53.

111. NISBCO, *Directory of Civilian Public Service. Revised 1996* (Scottdale, PA: Mennonite Publishing House, 1996), 357.

112. Sappington, *Carolinas*, 201.

113. Sappington, *Carolinas*, 202.

114. Sappington, *Carolinas*, 206–07.

115. Sappington, *Carolinas*, 190.

116. Sappington, *Carolinas*, 203.

117. Stephen Franklin, "North Carolina Becoming Threadbare Textile Center," *Chicago Tribune,* June 1, 2004. Articles.chicagotribune.com/2004–06–01/business/0406010099_1_textile-organizations-textile-worker-textile-related.

118. Sappington, *Carolinas*, 205.

119. Sappington, *Carolinas*, 210.

120. Sappington, *Carolinas*, 207–08.

121. History.brethrenchurch.org/details. Accessed July 20, 2017.

122. All of the information about Brethren projects since 1996 was gathered in private correspondence with the Rev. David K. Shumate, district executive of Virlina District, Church of the Brethren, June 24, 2017.

123. Liz Cutler Gates, "Spanish Speaking Church Begun in North Carolina." Graceconnect.us/Spanish-speaking-church-begun-in-north-carolina, May 1, 2012, accessed July 20, 2017.

Episcopalians

N. Brooks Graebner

The story of the Episcopal Church in North Carolina can be traced back to the very first English efforts at colonization during the reign of Elizabeth I. In August 1587, at what is now called "the Lost Colony" on Roanoke Island, the Native American Manteo and the English infant Virginia Dare were baptized. Permanent English settlement did not occur until the mid-seventeenth century, however, and it wasn't until 1701 that the colonial assembly passed its first Vestry Act, thereby making the Church of England the officially sanctioned faith in North Carolina. This act provided for the creation of precincts—or parishes—administered by local vestries, and the precincts of Chowan, Pasquotank, Perquimans, and Currituck along Albemarle Sound and Pamlico Precinct in Bath County date to this time. Principally through levying taxes and fines, colonial vestries in each parish were called upon to make provision for church buildings and ministers, setting aside glebe lands for the minister's use, overseeing the parish poor, and serving other delegated political functions.[1] Thus, the Church of England enjoyed a privileged status and legal advantages not enjoyed by other religious groups in eighteenth-century North Carolina.

But these legal provisions by no means guaranteed a strong and vibrant church, and the history of Colonial Anglicanism in North Carolina is largely a study in frustration. From the outset, many inhabitants were at best indifferent—and often opposed—to the establishment of the Church of England. Already in the late seventeenth century, the region around Albemarle Sound had become a haven for Quakers who launched a campaign to have the Vestry Act repealed.[2] And in the subsequent course of the eighteenth century, piedmont North Carolina would become home to sizable numbers of Presbyterians, Baptists, and Methodists who shared Quaker antipathy to Anglican establishment.

Also daunting were the organizational challenges of erecting houses of worship. Colonial parishes were geographically large, sparsely settled, and difficult to traverse. For example, Chowan Precinct ran from the present Virginia state line south through present-day Chowan County to include Washington and Tyrell Counties on the south side of Albemarle Sound and west to include present-day Bertie County. This led the vestry to give greater priority to the construction of simple wooden chapels throughout the parish than upon the erection of a substantial parish church. In Chowan Precinct, at least six such chapels are known to have been built in the early 1700s. Here services could be held on Sundays, and if no ordained minister were present, a local lay reader could be paid a small stipend to read the service instead.[3] By contrast, St. Paul's, Edenton, the parish church, was not completed until 1760. Many parishes, when faced with the difficulty of raising funds for church construction, simply did without substantial church buildings altogether.[4]

The greatest barrier to the growth and development of the church was the chronic shortage of qualified ministers. One complicating factor was the nature of ministry in the Church of England, which required all clergy to receive ordination at the hands of a bishop. Since there was no resident bishop in any of the colonies, all clergy had to be ordained in England and then authorized to serve abroad by the Bishop of London. Moreover, North Carolina quickly developed a reputation for being a highly undesirable and inhospitable place to serve. Disease was rampant, especially along the coastal plain. Parish size meant arduous travel. Factor in poor wages and living conditions, along with an unreceptive populace, and one can readily understand why most colonial parishes in North Carolina had trouble attracting and retaining ministers.[5]

The established church in North Carolina might well have continued to languish had it not been for the efforts of Governor William Tryon, who was determined to make the Anglican Church a living reality in the colony. As Tryon saw it, the key to vitalizing the established church was to attract and retain good clergy to supply North Carolina parishes and thereby to create an effective ecclesiastical presence. To that end, Tryon began an active campaign to solicit clergy through the Society for the Propagation of the Gospel (S.P.G.), the quasi-official missionary arm of the Church of England. Founded in 1701, the S.P.G. was a voluntary society formed to supply Anglican clergy for colonial service and to counter the growing influence of dissenting religious groups. In some instances, the S.P.G. recruited and paid for clergy to work as missionaries where the church was not established, but in places like North Carolina, they customarily provided salary supplements to make colonial service more attractive. Governor Tryon was himself a member of the S.P.G., and soon after his arrival in North Carolina in 1765, he began a vigorous letter-writing campaign to lobby the Society on behalf of North Carolina.[6] Although the Society had been active in North Carolina from the outset, it generally limited its support to one or two ministers at a time. Through Tryon's personal efforts, thirteen Anglican ministers served North Carolina by 1767 and eighteen by the time of his departure for New York in 1771.[7]

Tryon's efforts on behalf of the established church went hand in hand with his efforts to strengthen and extend Royal Government into the North Carolina backcountry through the county court system. By the late 1760s, growing unhappiness with the policies and practices of the government led to armed clashes with local militias called Regulators. The Regulator uprisings were quickly suppressed, but the triumph of Tryon's forces did nothing to endear the established church to the populace. Instead, it merely reinforced the association of Anglicanism with the imposition of English rule.[8]

To be sure, there were highly commendable clergy among those who served in the colonial period, men who dedicated themselves to serving their parishes and to providing ministrations regardless of Anglican affinity. Particularly noteworthy were Clement Hall in Edenton, Alexander Stewart in Bath, and James Reed in New Bern, all of whose missionary and pastoral efforts embraced enslaved and Native American populations, along with attending to far-flung English settlers.[9] But Tryon's expectation that exemplary and orthodox clergy would win over the adherents of other groups was at best wishful thinking, and such strength as the colonial Church of England did achieve was concentrated in a handful of coastal parishes.

In any event, Royal Government ended with the American Revolution, and the citizens of North Carolina acted quickly to terminate the religious establishment. Article 34 of the 1776 Constitution declared that no one church should be established nor any person compelled to support a church or minister.[10] Although ordinances provided for existing buildings and property to remain in denominational hands, legislatures and local governments were not zealous to enforce these provisions, and former Anglicans did not press their claims vigorously. The fate of the parish church in Hillsborough, St. Matthew's, is emblematic: During the war it was commandeered for housing troops and suffered extensive damage; afterwards, it was briefly used for a school, then pulled down entirely some time before 1800. The lot stood empty until the Presbyterians used it to erect a new church building in 1816.[11]

The coming of the American Revolution also placed Anglican ministers in a precarious position, morally and financially. Clergy with loyalist convictions had to decide whether to flee the colony altogether or reach some accommodation with patriotic vestries. The vestry in New Bern suspended James Reed and withheld his salary for a year over his failure to pray at the behest of the Continental Congress. He was allowed to resume his ministrations, but forced to endure the sound of boys drumming and shouting every time he offered the customary prayers for the king.[12] Even clergy with patriotic sympathies still had to wrestle with matters of conscience over their solemn ordination oaths to uphold royal supremacy and liturgical uniformity. And once the war was over and independence won, the S.P.G. terminated all financial support in the former American colonies.

But the institutional crisis that imperiled the very life of the church in the new American nation was the two-fold lack of any organizational structure beyond the parish and any bishops to ordain new clergy. By 1782, it was evident that the patriots had won the War for Independence, and colonial ties to the English crown and church were irrevocably severed. But what would replace them? The rector of Christ Church, Philadelphia, William White, provided one possible answer in his treatise *The Case of the Episcopal Churches in the United States Considered.* White encouraged his readers to accept the fact that henceforth the only bonds available for uniting the former members of the Church of England in the United States would be "voluntary associations for union and good government."[13] To forge those bonds, White proposed that the churches on this continent develop a system of representative government, beginning at the local level and proceeding to state and regional bodies. These representative bodies would be formed equally of clergy and laity and would exist to make only such decisions as are "judged necessary for their continuing one religious communion," namely, to set forth the doctrine, discipline, and worship of the church. White also brought a moderate, pragmatic bent to the subject of episcopacy. Although he desired to retain a church with bishops (as reflected in his employing the name 'Episcopalian'), he regarded it impracticable to count on having bishops in apostolic succession any time soon, since English bishops were bound by the terms of their own ordinal to require loyalty to the King and Church of England from those they ordained and consecrated. And so White proceeded to advocate for a provisional authority to ordain ministers and organize the church until such time as the episcopacy could be secured.[14]

White's view of the needs and prospects for the new Episcopal Church was not universally shared. His willingness to organize the church without first securing bishops, coupled with his willingness to grant powers of church governance to laity and clergy alike, put him at odds with the clergy in Connecticut, predominantly composed of former S.P.G. missionaries who were unprepared to accept even a temporary suspension of Episcopal government and disinclined to allow laity to sit in the councils of the church. In March of 1783, the Connecticut clergy met to identify suitable candidates for bishop, and one of those candidates, Samuel Seabury, went to England seeking consecration. When rebuffed by English bishops, Seabury had recourse to consecration at the hands of bishops of the nonjuring Episcopal Church of Scotland. On his return to Connecticut in 1785, Seabury quickly began to fulfill his role as bishop. Within six months he had presided over two convocations of clergy, made parochial visitations, issued a pastoral charge, and ordained twelve priests.[15]

At the same time, a call had gone out to Episcopalians in every state to send delegates to an organizing convention in Philadelphia along the lines set forth in White's 1782 proposal. When the convention did meet in Philadelphia in September 1785, there were sixteen clergy and twenty-six laymen representing seven states—but not the state of Connecticut. The two groups continued to walk apart until 1789, by which time England had made special provision for consecrating three bishops for the American church (including White himself), and White's original proposal had been modified along lines agreeable to Bishop Seabury.[16] The hybrid body drew strength from both sources. Thanks to William White, the Episcopal Church met directly the need to adapt itself to the character of its new national context. Without recourse to establishment, the church had no realistic alternative but to embrace denominationalism and voluntarism. That is, the Episcopal Church could expect no privileged position vis-à-vis other religious groups, and it would have to rely on the voluntary support of its members for its continued existence. White took these new realities as his starting point and offered Episcopal churches a way of organizing and making decisions consistent with the prevailing sentiments of post–Revolutionary America. Thanks to Samuel Seabury, the Episcopal Church safeguarded its distinctive and traditional forms of doctrine, discipline, and worship. The result was a solid basis for a national church of sufficient breadth and adaptability to last to the present day.

Yet the 1789 Protestant Episcopal Church was a national church in name only. Although the two competing versions of the church were now unified, the Carolinas and Georgia remained moribund as far as participation was concerned. Bishop White sent letters to North Carolina, urging the clergy to organize and send delegates to General Convention. Charles Pettigrew of Edenton, one of the few remaining clergymen in the state, did call for a meeting in Tarboro in May 1790 that four persons attended. They agreed to accept the 1789 constitution of the church and called for another meeting in Tarboro later in the year. This second meeting was better attended and took the first steps toward a formal statewide organization. Even more promising was the convention of May 1794, when sixteen persons met in Tarboro to adopt a state constitution and elect a bishop. Charles Pettigrew was chosen, and papers to that effect were sent to Bishop White in anticipation of Pettigrew's consecration at the General Convention of 1795. But at that point, all organizing efforts in North Carolina ceased for the next twenty years. Bishop-elect Pettigrew set out for Philadelphia but had turned back at the news of a yellow fever epidemic in Norfolk, Virginia, and he never again made the attempt. Nor did he take steps to hold another statewide meeting after 1794. The most straightforward explanation for his behavior is discouragement. Pettigrew had been ordained in England before the War of Independence; he had endured the revolution and disestablishment;

he had seen the church he served in ruin and held out little prospect for its revival. He therefore contented himself in old age with preaching at a chapel of his own construction near his plantation home in Scuppernong.[17]

New life for the Episcopal Church, in North Carolina and elsewhere, would instead come from a post–Revolutionary generation of leaders, who brought fresh energy and commitment to the task of reviving the church. One path for a renewed and revitalized church followed the High Church vision set forth by Bishop John Henry Hobart of New York. Hobart, who served from 1811 to 1830, sought to forge a distinctive place for the Episcopal Church within American Protestantism as the one true visible church within Reformed Christianity—that is to say, the only church of the Reformation to retain apostolic succession, adherence to faith and practices of the primitive church, and to have a valid sacramental life. He insisted that Episcopalians walk apart from other Protestant denominations; he refused to lend support to the nascent American Bible Society (formed in 1816) or other pan-denominational efforts to join forces to reform American life and make it more overtly reflective of Christian values.

At the same time Hobart was launching his effort to define the Episcopal Church over against other Protestants, an alternative vision for the Episcopal Church was being put forth in the Diocese of Massachusetts by its new Bishop, Alexander Griswold, who also took office in 1811. Unlike Hobart, Griswold wanted to renew the Episcopal Church principally through effective evangelical preaching. Episcopalians might worship in the distinctive voice of the Book of Common Prayer, but their message would contribute to the overall harmony of American evangelical Protestantism. These two views define the High Church/Low Church split in the Episcopal Church in the second and third decades of the nineteenth century.[18]

The pivotal action leading to the revival of the church in North Carolina also occurred in 1811: the calling of a twenty-five-year-old New Yorker, Adam Empie, to serve the parish of St. James', Wilmington. Soon the parish began to flourish. Empie initiated correspondence with other Episcopalians in the state in hopes that an organization could be formed, but his efforts were put on hold in 1814, when he left Wilmington to become the first chaplain at West Point. Empie returned to Wilmington in late 1816 and soon thereafter resumed his statewide organizing efforts. Prospects for taking a definitive step were by then considerably improved. During Empie's absence, the congregation in Wilmington had called another priest, Bethel Judd, but Judd was now preparing to take charge of a newly forming congregation in Fayetteville. Moreover, in January 1817, New Bern called a young minister, Jehu Curtis Clay, as rector and schoolmaster. These three clergymen—Empie, Judd, and Clay—along with lay representatives from their three congregations and St. Paul's, Edenton (nine people in all), gathered on April 24, 1817, in New Bern and proceeded to create a statewide organization that has continued to the present.[19]

Organizing was just the first step. Of these four founding congregations of the Diocese of North Carolina, only St. James', Wilmington, had substantial communicant strength and a full-time rector. The diocesan journal of 1819 provides the first solid evidence for gauging the relative communicant strength of the organizing churches: Wilmington, 151 communicants; Fayetteville, 56 (up 28 from the year before); New Bern, 32, and Edenton, 11.[20] Where, then, was new growth to come from? Who was expected to come forth to bring the church in North Carolina to life? And what path would the new diocese follow?

One principal strategy adopted in these early days of the diocese was to identify families and individuals with some demonstrable connection to the church and to try and elicit their help. Once again Adam Empie played a major role and used the occasion of the founding of the diocese to write letters to prominent men across the state whom he thought might be enlisted in this cause. Empie's letter-writing campaign bears witness to something Bishop Joseph Blount Cheshire, then Historiographer of the Diocese of North Carolina, noted in an 1890 essay: The revival of the church in this early period drew on the work of colonial-era clergy who continued their ministrations after the American Revolution but who often functioned more like private family chaplains than public ministers.[21] Cheshire's point was that even with a paucity of active congregations by 1817, there was still scattered personal and familial affinity upon which to build. One place where Empie's letter-writing campaign evidently bore fruit was in Orange County, where Duncan Cameron, after receiving Empie's letter, took the lead in reopening the colonial-era St. Mary's Chapel and securing the services of a lay reader.[22] St. Mary's subsequently entered into union with convention in 1819.

The new diocese also sought Episcopal oversight and to that end appealed to Bishop Richard Channing Moore of Virginia to serve as Bishop of North Carolina as well. Moore agreed, and for four years—from 1819 to 1822—he presided over the North Carolina Annual Convention, conducting parish visitations and ordinations on his way to and from his Virginia home. Before arriving as Bishop in 1814, Moore had repeatedly demonstrated success in reviving parishes in New York, and he quickly brought new energy and increased visibility for the church throughout Virginia. He made diocesan conventions a multi-day affair with evangelical preaching services open to the public at large. Scholars have characterized this innovation as "the Episcopal answer to the camp meeting."[23]

Moore brought the same kind of effort to his work in North Carolina, if on a more modest scale. With his enthusiastic support, North Carolina held its 1820 and 1821 conventions in the fledgling state capital of Raleigh, even though the Episcopalians did not yet have a church building there and had to hold their convention in the Supreme Court Room. But on Sunday morning they joined with the Methodists in their church building, where the Bishop administered Communion to over one hundred persons, including both the Presbyterian and Methodist ministers. At the conclusion of the 1821 convention, Bishop Moore could say that "the different societies of Christians have received us with open arms, and have wished us success in the name of the Lord."[24]

Also in 1821 an intriguing prospect for ecumenical cooperation arose: a proposal to enter into a close working relationship with the Lutherans of North Carolina. Behind this proposal was the remarkable ministry of Robert Johnston Miller—a Methodist turned Episcopalian—who had sought ordination from the Lutherans in western North Carolina back in the 1790s when it became clear that North Carolina wasn't going to be able to follow through on procuring a bishop. Miller finally received his long-deferred ordination at the hands of Bishop Moore by becoming both deacon and priest during the 1821 convention in Raleigh. And he brought with him an invitation from the Lutheran Synod to establish mutual recognition, including seat and voice at each other's conventions.

Bishop Moore was suitably enthusiastic in his response to this initiative, declaring, "the proposition which has been made to this Convention, by a portion of the Lutheran Church in this State, is calculated to excite our warmest gratitude to God: it proclaims in language which cannot be misunderstood, the confidence they place in our integrity, and the preference they give to our religious institutions." Moore could foresee a complete union of the two churches, gathered around the same altar.[25]

Moore's genial approach to interdenominational cooperation was shared by his gifted nephew, the Rev. Gregory T. Bedell, who had come to North Carolina in late 1818 to succeed Bethel Judd as Rector of St. John's, Fayetteville. In less than six months, Bedell had doubled the communicant strength of the parish. Bedell also fostered interdenominational cooperation, bringing Episcopalians and Presbyterians into a close working relationship. One tribute to Bedell's ministry in Fayetteville reads as follows:

> Mr. Bedell drew many worldlings and careless lives to his Church by the animated and impressive style of his oratory, and made them regular attendants by the earnest appeals to the heart, by his own obvious piety, and by the forbearance and Christian charity, and the manner with which he treated the peculiar doctrines of his Church, which was inoffensive to the casual hearers of a different persuasion.[26]

To outward appearances, then, one might have assumed that North Carolina was well on the way to emulating Virginia and adopting an Evangelical (Low Church) mission strategy, one in which Episcopalians would make common cause with other Protestants. The church in Fayetteville was flourishing under G.T. Bedell's leadership; Bishop Moore clearly welcomed the approbation of other Protestants and saw it as a mark of progress and growing respect for the Episcopal Church.

But North Carolina was instead about to make a decisive shift in sensibility and strategy. In April 1823, the Diocesan Convention met in Salisbury, without Bishop Moore present, and proceeded to elect a bishop of its own. The man chosen unanimously to head the young diocese was John Stark Ravenscroft, a fifty-year-old Virginia planter turned priest. Ravenscroft was already in his forties before his personal study of scripture and tradition led him to embrace the Episcopal Church "for that deposit of apostolic succession, in which alone verifiable power to minister in sacred things was to be found in these United States."[27] He had then presented himself for ordination to Bishop Moore, who received him as a candidate for Holy Orders in 1816 and ordained him a priest the following year.

For Ravenscroft, belonging to the Episcopal Church was not to be likened to membership in another Protestant denomination. He made his views unmistakable in May of 1824 at his first convention after becoming Bishop. He lamented the long absence of the ministrations of the church in North Carolina following the American Revolution. A pernicious notion of "equal safety in all religious denominations" had taken root. He proposed to counter it by calling the clergy to "a steadfast and uniform adherence to the liturgy and offices of the Church, as set forth in the book of Common Prayer and Administration of the Sacraments"[28] and by calling the laity both to restore family use of the Prayer Book and to reserve their financial support exclusively "for the wants of our own communion." The Bishop anticipated that his views would arouse resistance: "Much will be said against this my advice to you, my brethren, and I doubt not it will be called illiberal, uncharitable, perhaps unchristian." But Ravenscroft was resolute in his conviction that only "as the distinctive character of the Church is understood in its principles, applied in its use, and regarded in the hearts of its members, will it be cherished and will flourish."[29]

Ravenscroft was also prepared to proclaim his position publicly in the state at large. He did so in December 1824 when he was invited to address the annual gathering of the North Carolina Bible Society. Once again, the Bishop did not mince words as he attacked the very premises upon which the Bible Society was based. By his lights, promoting Bible reading without at the same time providing the ministrations of the church was to suggest that individuals could come to salvation without authoritative guidance. So Ravenscroft announced that he could not in good conscience approve of this enterprise that otherwise enjoyed broad-based interdenominational support. Needless to say, his position was an affront to Bible Society members, and a number of prominent Presbyterian ministers rushed to offer rejoinders in print.[30]

Here as elsewhere, Ravenscroft was following in the footsteps of John Henry Hobart, who had launched a similar critique of the Bible Society in New York with similar results. Ravenscroft said as much in a candid letter to Hobart written at the height of the Bible Society controversy, in which he justified his actions:

> The situation of this southern country, surrendered for the last forty or fifty years to the exclusive influence of the Dissenters, left me no alternative, but to increase that influence by adopting half-way measures, or, by a decided course, to call into action what was left of predilection for the church to rally her real friends around her standard, and to strike fear into her enemies by the unqualified assertion of her distinctive character; and I have cause of thankfulness beyond expression, that it has pleased God to give success so far to the little I have been enabled to do…. [B]ut I did not anticipate that the wily Presbyterians would have swallowed the bait so readily…. Their opposition has done more for the cause in a year, than without it could have been done in ten.[31]

Ravenscroft had made a calculated determination that the most pressing need in North Carolina was to gain the exclusive loyalty of Episcopalians to their own church. Other strategies might add numerical growth or produce quicker results, but the Bishop noted that "the numerical is not always the real strength, either of the Church or of an army."[32] What was paramount, in Ravenscroft's estimation, was exclusive and faithful commitment to the Episcopal Church. In his view, if the Presbyterians were offended by this attitude, so much the better. Predictably, Ravenscroft also put an end to the proposal to unite with the Lutherans, reporting to the convention in 1825 that "in the immediate neighborhood of the Rev. Mr. Miller" Episcopalians "have commenced retracing their steps, and will in time, I trust, recover from the paralyzing effect of the attempt to amalgamate with the Lutheran body…."[33]

To implement his mission strategy, Ravenscroft required clergy who would enthusiastically embrace his views. This, he understood, was critically important in the North Carolina Piedmont, where Presbyterians and Baptists had long predominated, and where mission work was already underway. The crisis came in Fayetteville, where the church was experiencing growth by following the very different path of interdenominational cooperation. In 1823, Bedell had been succeeded by an equally Evangelical minister, William Hooper. Hooper, the stepson of UNC President and Presbyterian Joseph Caldwell, could not countenance Ravenscroft's insistence upon Episcopalian exclusivity and abandoned the ministry of the Episcopal Church entirely rather than serve under the bishop.[34]

By contrast, two young Wilmington natives serving in the Piedmont, Thomas Wright and William Mercer Green, eagerly embraced Ravenscroft's agenda and made it their own. Ravenscroft's approbation of these two acolytes is clear from his 1825 address to convention, where he said of the church in Wadesboro that "under the direction of the Rev. Mr. Wright, it is second to none in soundness in the Faith and exemplary holiness." The Bishop likewise noted that the church in Hillsborough is organized "under the most flattering prospects and the Rev. Mr. Green called to take charge there."[35] In ensuing years, James Hervey Otey, George Washington Freeman, and Francis Lister Hawks all entered the ordained ministry of the Episcopal Church under the stamp of Ravenscroft's churchmanship and helped to extend it through much of the Old South: Otey as Bishop of Tennessee, Green as Bishop of Mississippi, and Freeman as Bishop of Arkansas and Texas.

Ravenscroft died in 1830, after only seven years in office. During his tenure, the church in North Carolina had grown to a communicant strength of about eight hundred members, with ten clergy serving twenty-one active congregations. As a percentage increase, the Episcopal Church had more than doubled in size; as a statewide body, however, it remained quite small and still regionally concentrated in the eastern part of the state. Where new congregations had been added, they were largely in communities adjacent to an established congregation; almost all clergy served more than one congregation, and some three or four. But Ravenscroft's impact cannot be measured in statistics. More than numerical strength, Ravenscroft had set out to bolster conviction. In the words of one historian, "Bishop Ravenscroft welded his North Carolina flock into an intimate Christian minority fervently devoted to the Episcopal Church."[36] And North Carolina was now the leading High Church diocese in the South.

In searching for Ravenscroft's successor, the diocese turned to someone of the same mold: John Henry Hobart's own son-in-law, Levi Silliman Ives, then serving as a priest in New York City. Ives's personal religious pilgrimage was very similar to that of Hobart and Ravenscroft. He was raised in a Protestant household in Connecticut and became convinced of the truth of High Church claims to retain continuity with apostolic Christianity in faith and practice. He gravitated to New York and received tutelage and support from Hobart, eventually marrying the Bishop's daughter.

As Bishop of North Carolina, Ives initially set out to continue the work begun by Ravenscroft. His first major initiative was to push for the creation of an Episcopal Boys' School in Raleigh, built on the premise that Episcopalians in North Carolina needed an alternative to schools run by other Protestants. That particular enterprise ultimately foundered in the late 1830s, but it led to the creation of a far more successful girls' school, St. Mary's in Raleigh, which continues to this day.[37]

Also successful was the effort to create a separate house of worship for Episcopalians at the University of North Carolina, the Chapel of the Cross. Up until 1838, Chapel Hill had no churches, and compulsory worship for all students was held on campus. But when William Mercer Green became University Chaplain in 1838, he began to lobby for an Episcopal alternative. He was joined in that effort by Bishop Ives, who asked the diocese to support Green's initiative because the sons of churchmen "are comparatively without the means of instruction in the Gospel as held by their fathers; all distinctive views being sedulously precluded from the teachings of the [University] Chapel."[38]

Ives was not simply championing causes that would have warmed the heart of Bishop Ravenscroft. By the 1840s, he was also moving with the leading edge of High Church thought and practice. One outward sign of this transformation was the embrace of Gothic Revival architecture. The push for building Episcopal Churches on a medieval model began in England in the late 1830s, but it soon made its way across the Atlantic. Ives became an early advocate and encouraged the building of Gothic Revival churches in Wilmington, Raleigh, and Chapel Hill.[39]

More significant, Ives looked favorably on the series of tracts published by leaders of the Oxford Movement, starting in 1833. Initially the Oxford Movement was simply a call to remind England that the church had divine origins and was not reducible to a department of state. Thus, initial efforts were little different from what Hobart and his followers had been teaching for several decades. But Oxford Movement leaders pushed further, to a fundamental rethinking of the relationship between the Church of England and the English Reformation. By the beginning of the 1840s, John Henry Newman and a few other Oxford theologians began to look at the English Reformation itself as a mistake and urged the Church of England to reclaim its medieval roots and reform its doctrine and practice in ways that would bring it into closer conformity with medieval (if not modern) Roman Catholicism. A firestorm erupted over Newman's *Tract 90* in 1841, which argued for a thoroughgoing Catholic reading of the Church of England's doctrinal standards, the Thirty-Nine Articles of Religion, to which all English clergy must subscribe. Newman, embittered by the depth of criticism, including from some of his fellow Oxford Movement leaders, left for Roman Catholicism in 1845.[40]

Ives was following something of the same path. In 1847, he established at Valle Crucis, a remote mission outpost in the mountains, a semi-monastic community he called the Order of the Holy Cross, and there he instituted an advanced program in Catholic worship, doctrine, and devotion, including systematic private confession and the Reservation of the Sacrament. Predictably, it opened him up to concern from those in the diocese who thought it too Roman. What ensued was a five-year period of turmoil that put bishop and diocese increasingly at odds—but was compounded by Ives's unhappy tendency to change his own position and to threaten his own clergy with deposition. Perhaps he genuinely didn't know his own mind; perhaps he was ill and unable to withstand the buffeting. In any case, he made himself a solitary figure and lost the respect of clergy and laity alike—who viewed him as at best weak and at worst devious and untrustworthy. The result was a measure of relief at his ultimate departure for Rome—literally and spiritually—in December of 1852.[41]

The controversy embroiling the diocese during the final years of Ives's episcopate should not, however, obscure the signal achievements of his twenty-one-year tenure. Under Ives's leadership, the diocese extended its mission work into the western section of the state, establishing congregations in Charlotte, Lincolnton, Morganton, and Asheville, along with continued development in the east. In total, the number of clergy in the diocese increased from fifteen in 1832 to forty in 1852, and the number of communicants increased from eight hundred to over two thousand.[42] Ives encouraged the founding of Episcopal schools, and he made a point of promoting the church's ministrations to the enslaved population of the state.[43]

The diocese gathered in convention in the spring of 1853 to elect Ives's successor. Clearly the choice would be of great interest and importance in setting the direction of the diocese with respect to party affiliation. Some had assumed that the diocese wanted nothing more to do with High Church attitudes after Ives's departure and would now follow the course of neighboring Virginia.[44] This was a plausible conjecture, but mistaken. A.F. Olmsted, rector of St. Bartholomew's, Pittsboro, spoke for the clergy of the diocese in a sermon delivered at the 1853 convention, immediately preceding the voting for a new bishop. Olmsted spoke in positive terms about the benefits that had flowed into the church from the Oxford Movement—in worship, in devotional tone, in attention to buildings and Christian art, in scholarship, and in missionary activity. He also carefully distinguished between the "excesses" of some individuals running to Rome (read: Newman and Ives) and the legitimate fruit of the Oxford Movement as based on "our Church principles," noting that one of the unhappy consequences of defections to Rome was the "false view that high views of the Church, of her ministry and Sacraments have a natural affinity with, and almost inevitable tendency to Romanism." Olmsted closed with these words:

> Let us not then lose our hold upon those principles which, as Churchmen, we have hitherto cherished. This Diocese has occupied heretofore, in the American Church, an elevated position for true, sound, and high-toned Churchmanship.... Let us hope that the impress stamped upon it by its first Bishop, the lamented Ravenscroft, will remain ineffaceable. Ever blessed be the memory of that true-hearted man and noble Bishop! And may God raise up to sit in his See, one worthy to be his successor; one who shall be to us "the repairer of the breach, the restorer of paths to dwell in."[45]

This they found in the person of Thomas Atkinson, a native Virginian, who had served several Baltimore parishes in the 1840s and early 1850s. Atkinson's commitment to what Olmsted called "church principles" was clearly on display in his 1855 Charge to the Diocese. He spoke of the blessings of a church that is at once comprehensive, creedal, sacramental, dignified, scriptural, and ancient.[46]

Yet Atkinson was not a carbon copy of Ravenscroft. Rather, he mirrored the outlook and agenda of William Augustus Muhlenberg, founding Rector of the Church of the Holy Communion in New York City and a man called "the most influential priest in the 19th-century Episcopal Church."[47] Muhlenberg was deeply concerned for what he saw as the elite cultural captivity of the Episcopal Church. And to counter the notion that the Episcopal Church only catered to the wealthy, Muhlenberg became an outspoken critic of the practice of paying for churches through pew rents. Indeed, the rationale for founding the Church of the Holy Communion was to have a church that would from its beginning have only free pews. Muhlenberg wanted to cultivate clergy from all classes, and he wanted to add flexibility to Sunday morning liturgy. Muhlenberg was also interested in many of the Oxford Movement reforms: gothic architecture, better music, better liturgy, better ornaments and furnishings. He had the first vested boys choir in America. And he also took the lead in introducing women's orders in the Episcopal Church. Muhlenberg adopted the label "Evangelical Catholic" to describe his somewhat eclectic form of churchmanship, as he sought both to heighten and broaden the church. He also broke from the High Church exclusivity characteristic of Hobart to embrace broad-based social outreach and devoted the last decades of his life—and his own financial resources—to the building of St. Luke's Hospital in New York.[48]

Atkinson pursued much the same line as Muhlenberg. In his 1855 charge to the clergy, Atkinson pivoted from his praise for the church to a call for reform. Like Muhlenberg, he lamented the identification of the church with ruling elites. To be truly Catholic, he contended, meant to embrace all sorts and conditions of society. True to Muhlenberg's agenda, Atkinson called for the abolition of pew rents, for flexibility in the use of the prayer book, and for drawing clergy from all ranks of society and not making a shibboleth of an "educated clergy."[49] When Atkinson, who resided in Wilmington, couldn't convince the local parish, St. James, to forsake pew rents, he followed Muhlenberg's lead and formed a new congregation there in 1858 on a "free church" basis, St. Paul's, which became a model for biracial cooperation in the city. The composition of the congregation was two-thirds white and one-third black, and the music was provided by a black choir.[50] Prominent black political leader Abraham Galloway was a member of St. Paul's, and when he died in 1870, he was buried from the church, with white Episcopal priest George Patterson officiating.[51]

From 1861 to 1865, the Civil War consumed the state and dominated the concerns of the church. Atkinson distinguished himself for the calm and principled way he dealt with the creation of the Confederacy and its implications for the church. He took the position that he remained a bishop of the Episcopal Church until such time as a separate Episcopal Church of the Confederacy came into existence, a position that put him at variance with his fellow Southern bishops and in tension with the prevailing southern sentiments. The value of Atkinson's position was clearly evident, however, when he led the way to the reunification of the Church North and South within months of the end of the war.[52]

But the Episcopal Church reunited after the Civil War only to nearly divide itself over matters of ritual. The period from 1866 to 1874 marked the height of this controversy in the Episcopal Church, and Atkinson's position within that controversy is worth noting. Atkinson initially took a moderate stance; in 1866, he refused to join twenty-eight of his fellow bishops in condemning certain contested practices such as the use of altar candles, reverences to the altar, and Eucharistic vestments.[53] But as the controversy wore on, Atkinson made clear his anti–Roman bias and took a firm stance against adopting private confession to a priest as anything more than an occasional practice.[54] Thus, in surveying the roughly fifty-year period from 1823 to 1874, one sees how the diocese of North Carolina had been strongly identified with the High Church movement during the first half of the nineteenth century, but as High Church shifted to mean increasing openness to beliefs and practices previously considered "Roman" (often termed Anglo-Catholicism), Atkinson remained wedded to an earlier stage of High Church development that continued to value the Reformation and maintain separation between Rome and Canterbury.

Where Atkinson chiefly distinguished himself was in drawing out the moral and social implications of his High Church leanings. The Bishop spoke unambiguously about the need for the church to remain catholic, by which he meant that the church could never permit itself to rest content with embracing only one segment or class of society. And this in turn became the bedrock of his insistence that the church seek to minister to and incorporate African Americans. Atkinson, like his predecessors Ravenscroft and Ives, had been a strong proponent of slave evangelization in the years before the war and frequently made a special point of ministering to blacks when he made his visitations. In the aftermath of the war, Atkinson called on North Carolina Episcopalians to help establish black churches and schools and to cultivate black leadership. Atkinson also helped to found the Freedman's Commission of the national Episcopal Church in 1865 and was quick to utilize its resources to start schools for the newly emancipated in New Bern and Wilmington.[55]

At the 1867 convention, Bishop Atkinson reiterated his conviction that the church must take steps to educate the black population and admit black men into ordained ministry. He went on to elaborate the underlying principle for that conviction:

> A man who regards our Church from the point of view in which some of its enemies affect to look at it, that is, as a voluntary society of decided aristocratic spirit and sympathies, may very consistently think that its ministers, and indeed its members, should be confined to a certain class in society, and a certain race among the people; but it is difficult to understand how he reasons who sets out with affirming that our Church is Catholic and Apostolic, and concludes with maintaining that it ought not to receive ministers, and by necessary consequence members, of a different race from his own, although that race may be, as with us, one-third, or with others, half of the entire population.[56]

The signal achievement of Atkinson's commitment to the inclusion of black congregations and clergy was the 1867 founding of St. Augustine's Normal School in Raleigh, which became the signal achievement of the Church's Freedman's Commission as well. Although St. Augustine's was not officially a diocesan institution, its incorporators were Bishop Atkinson and ten other North Carolina Episcopalians, along with the school's first principal, the Rev. Brinton Smith. Also worth noting is the fact that North Carolina, alone among southern dioceses in the nineteenth century, recognized black clergy and congregations as fully participating members of diocesan convention. This, too, can be traced to Atkinson's principled insistence upon the catholicity of the church.[57]

Besides extending the church's ministry to the newly emancipated, Atkinson and the diocese also faced the ongoing challenge of how to minister effectively across the state as a whole. In part, the challenge was geographic: As the church extended its reach into western North Carolina, the physical and practical challenge of arranging for the visitations of the Bishop became increasingly daunting. Moreover, at age sixty Atkinson felt that he no longer had the stamina to maintain the requisite schedule of visits. So for reasons of personal health and practicality, Atkinson proposed the division of the state into two dioceses. But the Episcopal Church, for all the strides it had taken between 1817 and 1860, still represented a small fraction of the overall population of North Carolina, with about three thousand communicants of the church in the entire state. For comparative purposes, Presbyterians counted about five times that many, and Baptists and Methodists about twenty times as many.[58] Indeed, there were an insufficient number of self-supporting congregations in the state to meet the Episcopal Church's own criteria for creating a new diocese. So Atkinson recommended as the "next expedient" the appointment of an assistant bishop.[59]

But a special 1867 committee on diocesan missions put the matter in a different light. The committee believed that the Episcopal Church in North Carolina was suffering from a lack of attention to the distinctive needs for and challenges of missionary activity in different parts of the state. Therefore, the committee saw the division of the diocese as an important step in effective missionary strategy, and they placed the following resolution before the convention: "Resolved, that for a full performance of the Church's work, as a Missionary Church in the State of North Carolina, a division of the Diocese is absolutely essential."[60] The Committee, however, recognized the same constitutional impediments the Bishop had, and so they made a further resolve: to create six regional convocations for missionary purposes. At the convention of 1869, this led to a joint proposal from the Bishop and the committee that each of the six convocations "take into serious consideration the importance and necessity of itinerant missionary labor, and to provide for the same within their bounds, as may seem to them, under the direction of the Bishop, to be wisest and best."[61]

What followed in the 1870s was the adoption of a number of steps designed to meet this mission imperative. One was the establishment of the Ravenscroft School in Asheville to provide clergy training for young men unable to attend seminary out of state. Another was the election of Theodore Lyman as Assistant Bishop in 1873.[62] At the time of his election, Lyman was serving in San Francisco, but he and Atkinson had previously worked together in Maryland and shared a common outlook. They forged a strong working relationship, and when Atkinson died in January 1881, Lyman retained his predecessor's mission principles and priorities.

Equally, if not more important, was the cultivation of a cohort of young, energetic clergy who, coming of age after the Civil War, were inspired by Bishop Atkinson's vision for the church and committed to extending the ministrations of the church into hitherto unserved (or underserved) areas. In 1877, three of these young men—Francis Murdoch, Charles Curtis, and William Shipp Bynum—banded together as the Evangelical Brotherhood, and with Atkinson's blessing, undertook to conduct protracted preaching missions throughout the Piedmont, asking no compensation and taking no collection. They pledged to preach extemporaneously, keep their references to other denominations positive, and encourage their listeners to repent and return to the Lord.[63] Along with their friend and colleague Joseph Blount Cheshire, Jr., these men were responsible for establishing or expanding congregations from Durham to Charlotte, founding a new diocesan newspaper, and embracing innovative strategies to extend the church's ministries. One such strategy was the forming of Associate Missions, where the church would deploy a team of ministers in a central location to serve outlying towns and communities. This was tried with some success in both Asheville and Greensboro. The Greensboro Mission was intentionally designed to utilize the railroad lines linking Greensboro with Winston, Burlington, and High Point.[64]

Another innovation was the creation of the position of diocesan evangelist. Edward Wootten, a priest in Bertie County, proposed this action in the pages of the diocesan newspaper, *The Church Messenger*, in November 1880, having noted that none of the six convocations had yet carried through with the 1869 call for itinerant missionaries, though the need was as urgent as ever. R.S. Bronson, Rector in Wilson and Rocky Mount, seconded the proposal two months later.[65] By the time of the 1881 convention, there was a groundswell of support, and when Wootten introduced it, it passed.[66]

Atkinson had died earlier that year, and Lyman had taken his place. Lyman appointed two men: William Shipp Bynum and a Virginian, George Dame. Both began work in late 1881, but within a matter of months, Dame determined to accept a call to parochial ministry. Bynum continued, and reported to the 1882 convention on his missionary strategy and preliminary results, explaining that it was his practice to preach two or three times a day, sometimes at points ten, twenty, or thirty miles apart. Lyman was effusive in his praise of Bynum and declared his hope that the new missionary spirit would pervade all parishes.[67]

But the Bishop's call to diocese-wide mission consciousness was not the centerpiece of convention action in 1882. Rather, it was the convention's determination to proceed in principle to effect a division of the diocese. The ensuing year became one of the most fascinating and critical in the life of the church in North Carolina. Lyman and Bynum outdid themselves in holding missions and visitations throughout the state. Bynum traveled to forty-five counties, from Cherokee to Currituck. He logged over four thousand miles on railway and steamship lines and nearly fifteen hundred by horse and on foot. Lyman did more visitations than ever before—getting to nearly every parish and missionary station in the state and visiting twenty of them twice.[68]

Why all this effort? In part it was to justify continuation of the current arrangement. Lyman contended that division was premature: the diocese was still numerically and financially weak, and evangelists were a greater priority than another bishop. With the extension of rail lines, one didn't need another bishop to do visitations because travel had become so much easier. Thus he reasoned: "If you can only have two or more active and efficient Evangelists, occasional visits from them, with continued services for two or three days, in each missionary station which is visited, will accomplish far more for the Church than simply an annual visit from the Bishop."[69]

But the funding for the current arrangement of bishop and evangelists was contingent upon keeping the diocese united, since both positions were paid for from the Permanent Episcopal Fund. Bynum himself saw the problem immediately and offered to resign his position, effective at the diocesan convention 1883.[70] Some viewed the loss of the evangelist position with relative equanimity.[71] Others were less sanguine, contending: "This Evangelist scheme has never yet been fully put to work. At one Convention it was started, one most competent Evangelist secured, and the next Convention virtually knocks the whole scheme in the head.... We [the writer] stand to-day where the convention apparently stood two years ago, in the full conviction that two or three Evangelists can achieve a work in this Diocese which no one Bishop can do."[72] It would be a decided understatement to say the letters to the editor in the *Church Messenger* had become quite heated. Editor Edmund Joyner felt it necessary to remind his letter writers that they all followed a gentle savior.[73]

With all this passion flowing through diocesan veins, the 1883 convention was destined to be memorable and momentous. The delegates proceeded with the division of the diocese over the Bishop's dispassionate dissent, albeit not his veto. And however much delegates appreciated Bynum's work, the inevitable elimination of his position proceeded. The thornier issue was precisely where to draw the line. Several proposals were put forward, including one that would have drawn an east-west line through the middle of the state, creating an upper and lower diocese. Ultimately, the line favored by the majority of delegates followed the eastern border of Northampton County and proceeded southwest to the eastern border of Scotland County. Because Bishop Lyman chose to remain in Raleigh, the portion of the state for which he retained jurisdiction was called the Diocese of North Carolina. The newly created diocese was given the name the Diocese of East Carolina, and in December of 1883, it held its first convention and proceeded to elect the Rev. Alfred A. Watson, Rector of St. James', Wilmington, as its first bishop.[74]

At the time of division, there was a rough parity between the two dioceses in terms of communicant strength and financial resources, but not in terms of geographical extent. This reflected the fact that historically the Episcopal Church in North Carolina was strongest along the coastal plain and weakest in the mountains.[75] Indeed, even with the division of the diocese, it was still challenging to give the western part of the state the kind of focused attention that it merited. As a result, a further division of the diocese was effected in 1895, with the creation of the Missionary District of Asheville along the eastern boundary of the counties of Alleghany, Wilkes, Alexander, Catawba, Lincoln, and Gaston. The designation of the western region as a Missionary District meant that it would be entitled to have its own bishop but that it was not yet ready to support itself financially as a diocese. Junius Moore Horner of Oxford, North Carolina, was chosen bishop in 1898, but it would not be until 1922 that the General Convention of the Episcopal Church approved the creation of the Diocese of Western North Carolina.[76]

The tripartite division of the state into separate dioceses would remain a source of contention and controversy into the 1940s. In 1898, East Carolina lobbied to have the Missionary District abolished and the diocesan boundary redrawn to give more territory to East Carolina. This proposal was rejected by both the Diocese of North Carolina and the newly formed Missionary District. By the 1930s, it was the Diocese of Western Carolina initiating the requests. Bishop Horner had died in the spring of 1933, and in anticipation of calling his successor, Western North Carolina reached out to the other two dioceses, inviting them to send representatives to a conference in the summer of 1933 to consider the question of whether the current tripartite division should stand. The conference once again rejected all consideration of a new bipartite division, but it did call on the Diocese of North Carolina to consider ceding portions of its territory to the other two. When the Diocese of North Carolina failed to act on that broad recommendation, Western North Carolina made a targeted request that the counties surrounding Winston-Salem be ceded. This overture met with inaction, as did a 1948 campaign for realignment spearheaded by East Carolina. The boundaries set in the 1880s and 1890s have remained fixed.[77]

Thus the Diocese of North Carolina became much the largest and most urban of the three—roughly twice the size of the others—and embracing the two great population centers of Raleigh and Charlotte, plus all the metropolitan areas in the piedmont crescent. Because dioceses are autonomous governing units, once the division was made there was no longer any way to impel cooperative ventures. But shared heritage and common outlook brought the dioceses together to support a number of institutions and initiatives. One of these was St. Mary's School in Raleigh, which by the 1890s was deeply in debt and in danger of closing. The Diocese of North Carolina arranged purchase and transfer of ownership into the church's hands and was joined in this highly successful effort by East Carolina.[78] St. Augustine's School in Raleigh and the Thompson Orphanage in Charlotte have also enjoyed support from Episcopalians across the state (and beyond).

Helping to forge these bonds across diocesan boundaries into the early decades of the twentieth century were the common background and shared experiences of the leaders of both dioceses. A.A. Watson had served in North Carolina for almost forty years before becoming the first bishop of East Carolina, so he had long and deep associations across the state, even though his ministry had been spent in churches near the coast: Plymouth, Washington, New Bern, and Wilmington. Lyman had been Assistant Bishop of the entire state for a decade before the division, and when he died in 1893, he was succeeded by Tarboro native Joseph Blount Cheshire, Jr., then serving as Rector of St. Peter's, Charlotte. All these men had imbibed Atkinson's convictions about mission and ministry, and collectively they oversaw a period of unprecedented growth and expansion for the church. In the 1880s and 1890s alone, fifty-eight new church buildings were erected, a testimony to enterprising and devoted parish clergy who extended their ministrations beyond the membership of their own congregation. Cheshire himself was one of those, greatly expanding the reach of the church in Charlotte through new congregations and institutions during his decade as Rector of St. Peter's from 1882 to 1893.[79]

Of invaluable assistance to Cheshire in several of these outreach efforts was Jane Wilkes, who also was one of the early leaders of the North Carolina Branch of the Woman's Auxiliary of the Board of Missions. The role of women as supporters of parish projects was long-established, and informal networks of women existed throughout the church. Many clergy, in their parochial reports, would credit "the Ladies" for their assistance as teachers and fundraisers. But the Woman's Auxiliary, organized in North Carolina in 1882, formalized and extended this work and directed it wholly towards mission and social outreach. In Charlotte, Mrs. Wilkes is best remembered for her contributions to the establishment of two church-supported hospitals: St. Peter's and Good Samaritan. She was also executive secretary and "permanent president" in the Woman's Auxiliary, serving from the early 1880s until 1909. Because women were not allowed to take positions of leadership within the convention until the 1960s and 1970s, the Auxiliary became a parallel institution, whose governance and organization mirrored that of the Diocese. Besides hospitals, ministries in mill villages (then called "industrial work") and among the deaf were two areas where women were critical to staffing and financial support of mission initiatives.[80]

Prevailing racial attitudes also led to the creation of a parallel organization for African Americans in the church. In the aftermath of the Civil War, Atkinson had called for the creation of black congregations and schools and for the cultivation of black leadership as ministers and teachers. But in keeping with his "catholic principles" he had also insisted upon having these congregations and clergy as full members of diocesan convention. Starting in 1891, however, all the black congregations of the Diocese of North Carolina were placed within a separate "colored convocation" under the administrative leadership of an Archdeacon for Work among the Colored People. The first Archdeacon was a white priest, William Walker, but in 1898 Bishop Cheshire replaced him with a black priest from South Carolina named John H.M. Pollard. And when Pollard died in 1908, Cheshire appointed another black priest, Henry B. Delany, to the post. At the time, Delany was serving as a teacher and Vice Principal of St. Augustine's School, where he had first entered as a student. After ten years as Archdeacon, Delany's field of service expanded as he became a Suffragan, or Assistant Bishop, working exclusively with the African American congregations throughout the Carolinas, though officially attached to the Diocese of North Carolina. Delany served as bishop for ten years and died in office in 1928. At the same time, the diocese decided to abolish its convocation system and reorganize all mission work through diocesan departments. So the separate convocation for black congregations likewise disbanded, and Delany's position was discontinued.[81]

In addition to broadly shared missions, each of the three dioceses developed its own institutions and specialized ministries that reflected the specific context in which they found themselves. The Diocese of North Carolina, for example, became strongly committed to college work, a reflection of the large number of prominent colleges and universities in the Piedmont. The Diocese of Western North Carolina encouraged craft and parochial schools, and the Diocese of East Carolina strongly supported ministry to the members of the Armed Forces stationed there.[82]

The 1950s saw the Episcopal Church throughout the state expand into the suburbs and start new congregations in large metropolitan areas, a trend that was broadly shared with other religious bodies. Between 1953 and 1963, communicant membership in the Diocese of North Carolina grew from 25,000 to 35,000 members, and thirteen new parishes were formed.[83] Soon, however, pressing social issues came to the forefront, bringing controversy and dissension in their wake. First and foremost was the call in church and society for an end to racial segregation. One ardent segregationist, James Dees, rector of Trinity Church, Statesville, was so disturbed by the church's support for civil rights that in 1963 he renounced his priesthood and organized a new body, the Anglican Orthodox Church, but his was not a widely shared response.[84]

More broadly divisive were the Episcopal Church's efforts to respond to the urban rioting that began in 1965. Deeply shaken by what he saw in American cities, Presiding Bishop for the national church, John Hines, asked the 1967 General Convention to authorize an ambitious fund of nine million dollars (the General Convention Special Program or GCSP) to address social inequities by awarding grants to organizations and programs outside the customary channels. Whatever misgivings North Carolina Episcopalians might have had about this initiative were fanned into active dissent when fund administrators in New York awarded two grants totaling forty-five thousand dollars to the Malcolm X Liberation University in Durham in 1969. At the diocesan convention in 1970,

North Carolina Bishop Thomas Fraser announced that thirty-eight congregations had withheld contributions from the diocese and national church totaling almost one hundred sixty-four thousand dollars. North Carolina weathered the controversy, and by 1973 the Episcopal Church had retreated from the agenda of the GCSP.[85]

But the 1970s did not provide respite from controversial and contentious issues in the church. One was the issue of the ordination of women; the other, the issue of revising the liturgy of the church as expressed in the Book of Common Prayer. Both changes were enacted at the General Convention of 1976, after which some traditionalists left the church.[86] The ordination of women also led to a remarkable event early in 1977 at the Chapel of the Cross in Chapel Hill, when the first African American woman ordained to the priesthood of the Episcopal Church, the Rev. Dr. Pauli Murray, celebrated Holy Communion for the first time in the very building where her grandmother, Cornelia Fitzgerald, had worshipped in the 1850s as an enslaved child.[87] Women's ordination was gradually embraced throughout the church in North Carolina, and by the second decade of the twenty-first century, the clergy of the church were as likely to be women as men. Indeed, North Carolina elected its first woman bishop in 2013, the Rt. Rev. Anne E. Hodges-Copple.[88]

North Carolina was home to another landmark event in the life of the Episcopal Church in 2000, when the Diocese of North Carolina elected the Rt. Rev. Michael B. Curry as the first African American Bishop to lead a southern diocese. In his first convention address after becoming bishop, Curry recalled the diocese to its missionary vocation.[89] His leadership was sorely tested in 2003, however, after he and the other bishops of North Carolina voted with the majority of their colleagues to consent to the election of the Rt. Rev. V. Gene Robinson, an openly gay priest living in a non-celibate relationship, as Bishop of New Hampshire. Some of those unhappy with Robinson's consecration left the Episcopal Church and formed new congregations under a new national organization called the Anglican Church in North America (ACNA; established in 2009) that sees itself as a more traditional alternative to the Episcopal Church within the worldwide Anglican Communion. As of 2015, ACNA reported on its website thirty-four congregations across North Carolina.

Bishop Curry, however, retained the enthusiastic support of the vast majority of Episcopalians in his diocese. He continued to make mission work a priority and called on the church to broaden and deepen its appeal, even invoking the "Primary Charge" of his nineteenth-century predecessor, Thomas Atkinson.[90] In any event, North Carolina was one of only four dioceses of the Episcopal Church to report an increase in membership between 2003 and 2013. And on November 1, 2015, Bishop Curry was installed as the twenty-seventh Presiding Bishop for the national Episcopal Church, the first North Carolina bishop and the first African American bishop to hold the position.[91]

NOTES

1. Robert J. Cain, introduction to *The Church of England in North Carolina: Documents, 1699–1741*, edited by Robert J. Cain. The Colonial Records of North Carolina, Second Series Volume X (Raleigh: North Carolina Office of Archives and History, 1999), xxiv.

2. Cain, introduction to *The Church of England in North Carolina: Documents, 1699–1741*, xxv.

3. Anne Rouse Edwards, *A Celebration of Faith: 300 Years in the Life of St. Paul's* (Edenton, NC: Sweet Bay Tree Books, 2003), 24.

4. Hugh Talmage Lefler, "The Anglican Church in North Carolina: The Royal Period," in *The Episcopal Church in North Carolina, 1701–1959*, ed. Lawrence Foushee London and Sarah McCulloh Lemmon (Raleigh: The Episcopal Diocese of North Carolina, 1987), 24.

5. Cain, introduction to *The Church of England in North Carolina: Documents, 1699–1741*, xiv.

6. In a letter to the S.P.G. in August of 1765, the Governor reported that Presbyterians and a "Sect who call themselves New Lights" were the largest religious groups in the colony, followed by the Church of England, but the Governor expressed his conviction that: "when a sufficient Number of Clergy as exemplary in their Lives, as orthodox in their Doctrine, can persuade themselves to come into This Country, I doubt not but the larger Number of every Sect would come over to the Established Religion." William S. Powell, ed., *The Correspondence of William Tryon, Volume I, 1758–1767* (Raleigh: North Carolina Office of Archives and History, 1980): 144.

7. Paul Conkin, "The Church Establishment in North Carolina, 1765–1776," *The North Carolina Historical Review* 32 (1955): 9, 10.

8. Marjoleine Kars, *Breaking Loose Together: The Regulator Rebellion in Pre-Revolutionary North Carolina* (Chapel Hill and London: University of North Carolina Press, 2002), 108, 109, 184.

9. Lefler, "The Royal Period," 34–43.

10. Sarah McCulloh Lemmon, "The Decline of the Church, 1776–1816," in *The Episcopal Church in North Carolina, 1701–1959*, ed. Lawrence Foushee London and Sarah McCulloh Lemmon (Raleigh: The Episcopal Diocese of North Carolina, 1987), 61.

11. Joseph Blount Cheshire, *An Historical Address Delivered in St. Matthew's Church, Hillsboro, N.C. on Sunday, August 24, 1924: Being the One Hundredth Anniversary of the Parish* (Durham, NC: Christian and King Publishing Company, 1925), 18–20.

12. Lemmon, "The Decline of the Church, 1776–1816," 63.

13. William White, "The Case of the Episcopal Churches in the United States Considered, 1782," in ed. Don A. Armentrout and Robert B. Slocum, *Documents of Witness: A History of the Episcopal Church 1782–1985* (New York: Church Hymnal Corporation, 1994), 4.

14. White, "The Case of the Episcopal Churches Considered," 13.

15. Frederick V. Mills, Sr., *Bishops by Ballot: An Eighteenth-Century Ecclesiastical Revolution* (New York: Oxford University Press, 1978), 233–34.

16. Mills, *Bishops by Ballot*, 240–81.

17. An account of the Tarboro conventions of the 1790s and their aftermath appears in Lemmon, "The Decline of the Church, 1776–1816," 78–86.

18. Robert Prichard, *A History of the Episcopal Church*, revised edition (New York and Harrisburg: Morehouse Publishing Co., 1999), 118–23. On Hobart, see R. Bruce Mullin, *Episcopal Vision/American Reality: High Church Theology and Social thought in Evangelical America* (New Haven: Yale University Press, 1986).

19. Henry S. Lewis, "The Formation of the Diocese of North Carolina, 1817–1830," in *The Episcopal Church in North Carolina, 1701–1959*, ed. Lawrence Foushee London and Sarah McCulloh Lemmon (Raleigh: The Episcopal Diocese of North Carolina, 1987), 95–97.

20. *Journal of the Third Annual Convention of the Protestant Episcopal Church in the State of North Carolina* (1819): 6. Hereinafter abbreviated *NCDJ*.

21. Joseph Blount Cheshire, Jr., ed. *Sketches of Church History in North Carolina: Addresses and Papers by Clergymen and Laymen of the Dioceses of North and East Carolina* (Wilmington, NC: Wm. L. DeRosset, Jr., 1892), 269.

22. Adam Empie to Duncan Cameron, 5 February 1818. Cameron Family Papers, Wilson Library, Chapel Hill.

23. Edward L. Bond and Joan R. Gundersen, "The Episcopal Church in Virginia, 1607–2007," *The Virginia Magazine of History and Biography*, 115 (2007): 222–24.

24. *NCDJ*, 5th (1821): 21.

25. *NCDJ*, 5th (1821): 22. In the 1990s, an agreement between the Episcopal Church and the Evangelical Lutheran Church in America (ELCA) would bring about the very thing Moore envisioned.

26. Stephen H. Tyng, *Memoirs of the Rev. G.T. Bedell, D.D.* (London: R.B. Seeley and W. Burnside, 1835), 39.

27. Walker Anderson, "Memoir" prefaced to John Stark Ravenscroft, *The Works of the Right Reverend John Stark Ravenscroft, D.D.*, vol. I (New York: Protestant Episcopal Press, 1830), 19.

28. John Stark Ravenscroft, "A Sermon on the Church: Delivered Before the Annual Convention of the Protestant Episcopal Church of North-Carolina," in *The Works of the Right Reverend John Stark Ravenscroft*, vol. I, 110.

29. Ravenscroft, "A Sermon on the Church," in *Works* vol. 1, 116.

30. Ravenscroft, "A Sermon preached before the Bible Society of North-Carolina, on Sunday, December 12, 1824," in *Works*, vol. I, 163–78. On the controversy, see Lewis, "The Formation of the Diocese," 130–33.

31. Bishop Ravenscroft to Bishop Hobart March 18, 1826, in John Henry Hobart, *The Posthumous Works of the Late Right Reverend John Hobart, D.D., Bishop of the Protestant Episcopal Church in the State of New York, with a Memoir of His Life*, vol. I (New York: Stanford and Swords, 1833), 365, 366.

32. *NCDJ* 9th (1825): 22.

33. *NCDJ* 9th (1825): 10.

34. Lewis, "The Formation of the Diocese," 127–30.

35. *NCDJ* 9th (1825): 10, 11.

36. Lewis, "The Formation of the Diocese," 169.

37. Blackwell P. Robinson, "The Episcopate of Levi Silliman Ives," in *The Episcopal Church in North Carolina, 1701–1959,* ed. Lawrence Foushee London and Sarah McCulloh Lemmon (Raleigh: The Episcopal Diocese of North Carolina, 1987), 178–85.

38. Robinson, "The Episcopate of Levi Silliman Ives," 194.

39. Robinson, "The Episcopate of Levi Silliman Ives," 194, 196; George E. DeMille, *The Catholic Movement in the American Episcopal Church,* 2nd edition (Philadelphia: Church Historical Society, 1950), 83.

40. DeMille, *The Catholic Movement,* 40–73.

41. Robinson, "The Episcopate of Levi Silliman Ives," 199–219.

42. Matthias M. Marshall, "The Church in North Carolina: Its Present Condition and Prospects," in ed. Joseph Blount Cheshire, Jr., *Sketches of Church History in North Carolina: Addresses and Papers by Clergymen and Laymen of the Dioceses of North and East Carolina* (Wilmington, NC: Wm. L. DeRosset, Jr., 1892), 342.

43. Robinson, "The Episcopate of Levi Silliman Ives," 189–93.

44. Richard Rankin, *Ambivalent Churchmen and Evangelical Churchwomen: The Religion of the Episcopal Elite in North Carolina, 1800–1860* (Columbia, SC: University of South Carolina Press, 1993), 166, 167.

45. *NCDJ* 37th (1853): 69–79.

46. Thomas Atkinson, *Primary Charge of the Rt. Rev. Thomas Atkinson, Bishop of North Carolina, to the Clergy. Delivered at the Convention at Warrenton May 1855* (Fayetteville, NC: Edward J. Hale and Son, 1855), 3–5.

47. David Hein and Gardiner H. Shattuck, Jr., *The Episcopalians* (Westport, CT: Praeger, 2004), 255.

48. Hein and Shattuck, *The Episcopalians,* 255–57.

49. Atkinson, *Primary Charge,* 9–14.

50. Daniel Morrelle, "Extract from the History of St. Mark's Church, Wilmington, N.C." incorporated in *The Parish Register of St. Paul's Episcopal Church, Wilmington, North Carolina 1872–1912:* 7, 8. Special Collections Library of the University of North Carolina at Wilmington. *NCDJ* 45th (1861): 42.

51. David S. Cecelski, *The Fire of Freedom: Abraham Galloway and the Slaves' Civil War* (Chapel Hill: University of North Carolina Press, 2012), 217–18.

52. The subject of the reunification of the Episcopal Church in the aftermath of the Civil War has received extensive scholarly treatment. Journal articles devoted to the subject include: Mark Mohler, "The Episcopal Church and National Reconciliation, 1865," *Political Science Quarterly,* Vol. 41, No. 4 (Dec., 1926), 567–95; Henry T. Shanks, "The Reunion of the Episcopal Church, 1865," *Church History,* Vol. 9, No. 2 (June, 1940), 120–40; Lockert B. Mason, "Separation and Reunion of the Episcopal Church 1861–1865: The Role of Bishop Thomas Atkinson," *Anglican and Episcopal History,* Vol. LIX, No. 3 (September, 1990), 345–65.

53. DeMille, *The Catholic Movement,* 113.

54. Atkinson, "Bishop's Charge," published as "Appendix C" and separately paginated, *NCDJ 58th* (1874): 1–11.

55. *NCDJ, 49th* (1865): 22–24; *Protestant Episcopal Freedman's Commission: Occasional Paper, January, 1866* (Boston, 1866), transcribed by Wayne Kempton and posted to Project Canterbury, 2010. 1, 2.

56. *NCDJ,* 51st (1867): 24.

57. *The Spirit of Missions,* vol. 32 (1867), 817, 818. See also Thelma Johnson Roundtree, *Strengthening Ties that Bind: A History of Saint Augustine's College* (Raleigh, NC: Spirit Press, 2002), 3–8. George Freeman Bragg numbered Bishop Atkinson among the "militant minority" of white men and women who "lost no opportunity to work for the best interest of all, black and white, and such have co-operated in preserving to the Church 'an open door' to the colored race." Of Atkinson, he wrote: "Bishop Atkinson. … ere the smoke of Civil War had cleared came bravely forward in North Carolina, battling in the face of hard, bitter and unrelenting prejudice, established St. Augustine's College for the education of the colored race, organized colored parishes and had them admitted into union with his diocesan convention. And when the Standing Committee refused to pass the papers of a colored candidate for holy orders, invited two 'Yankee' Negro priests from the North to come into his diocese and admitted them to full privileges in his convention. Other Southern Bishops labored earnestly to do the same thing, but could not." George Freeman Bragg, Jr. "The Episcopal Church and the Negro Race," *Historical Magazine of the Protestant Episcopal Church,* Vol. IV, No. 1 (March 1935), 50, 51. A favorable comparison of the Episcopal Church in North Carolina with the efforts of Presbyterians, Baptists, and Methodists is made by Roberta Sue Alexander, *North Carolina Faces the Freedmen: Race Relations During Presidential Reconstruction, 1865–1867* (Durham, NC: Duke University Press, 1985), 67–75.

58. William S. Powell, *North Carolina Through Four Centuries* (Chapel Hill and London: University of North Carolina Press, 1989), 326.

59. *NCDJ,* 51st (1867): 24, 25.

60. *NCDJ,* 51st (1867): 34.

61. *NCDJ,* 53rd (1869): 38, 39.

62. James W. Patton, "The Diocese of North Carolina, 1861–1883," in *The Episcopal Church in North Carolina, 1701–1959,* ed. Lawrence Foushee London and Sarah McCulloh Lemmon (Raleigh: The Episcopal Diocese of North Carolina, 1987), 258; 264–67.

63. This notice appeared in advance of a preaching mission in Winston: "A Mission begins (D.V.) in St. Paul's Church [Winston] on Sunday, June 20th. The clergy conducting it will be members of the Evangelical Brotherhood—a Society whose constitution, rules, and books are submitted to and sanctioned by Bishop Atkinson. The Rev. Frank J. Murdoch of Salisbury is Warden of this Society, and will therefore direct details of the proposed Mission." *The Church Messenger* 2, no. 5 (June 15, 1880). Following the event, there was another piece in the *Messenger*, describing the Evangelical Brothers as a society formed at St. Barnabas, Greensboro, several years ago whose preaching is extemporaneous, the teaching positive, and the practical appeal for repentance. "Together with the Rev. Charles J. Curtis, Mr. Murdoch has held not a few missions and in no instance have they failed to leave permanent impressions for good upon the life and work of Parishes at various points in Central and Northwestern North Carolina. ... The order to which these faithful Priests belong accepts no compensation for what it does. The missions are held literally 'without money and without price.' St. Paul's Parish has had a great refreshment and felt as if an answer were indeed made to the Prophet's prayer: 'Revive thy work O Lord!'" *Church Messenger* 2, no. 8 (July 9, 1880).

64. *NCDJ* 63rd (1879): 196, 197.

65. *Church Messenger* 2 no. 25 (November 11, 1880) and 2 no. 35 (January 20, 1881).

66. *NCDJ* 65th (1881): 38, 44.

67. *NCDJ* 66th (1882): 168–70; 96.

68. For the Bishop's Address, see *NCDJ* 67th (1883): 45–79; for the Evangelist's Report, see *NCDJ* 67th (1883): 151–57.

69. *NCDJ* 66th (1882): 99.

70. *Church Messenger* 4, no. 2 (May 25, 1882).

71. *Church Messenger* 4, no. 46 (April 19,1883).

72. *Church Messenger* 4, no. 47 (April 26, 1883).

73. *Church Messenger* 4, no. 48 (May 3, 1883).

74. Patton, "The Diocese of North Carolina, 1861–1883," 269; Lawrence Fay Brewster, "The Diocese of East Carolina, 1883–1963," in *The Episcopal Church in North Carolina, 1701–1959,* ed. Lawrence Foushee London and Sarah McCulloh Lemmon (Raleigh: The Episcopal Diocese of North Carolina, 1987), 426–28.

75. Patton, "The Diocese of North Carolina, 1861–1883," 269, 270.

76. Elizabeth N. Thomson, "The Episcopal Church in Western North Carolina, 1894–1948," in *The Episcopal Church in North Carolina, 1701–1959,* ed. Lawrence Foushee London and Sarah McCulloh Lemmon (Raleigh: The Episcopal Diocese of North Carolina, 1987), 465–67; 492–96.

77. Thomson, "The Episcopal Church in Western North Carolina," 469; 509, 510; 513; Brewster, "The Diocese of East Carolina," 452, 453.

78. H. G. Jones with David Southern, *Miss Mary's Money: Fortune and Misfortune in a North Carolina Plantation Family, 1760–1924* (Jefferson, NC: McFarland, 2015), 163–67. Jones notes that the Mary Ruffin Smith bequest to the Diocese of North Carolina became a source of protracted litigation between the two dioceses, and that the shared effort to contribute to the saving of St. Mary's School facilitated rapprochement.

79. James S. Brawley, "The Episcopal Church in North Carolina, 1883–1900," in *The Episcopal Church in North Carolina, 1701–1959,* ed. Lawrence Foushee London and Sarah McCulloh Lemmon (Raleigh: The Episcopal Diocese of North Carolina, 1987), 296, 297; Lawrence Foushee London, *Bishop Joseph Blount Cheshire* (Chapel Hill: University of North Carolina Press, 1941), 27–45.

80. London, *Bishop Joseph Blount Cheshire,* 42, 43; Eva Burbank Murphy, "Wilkes, Jane Renwick Smedberg," in ed. William S. Powell, *Dictionary of North Carolina Biography, 6 volumes* (Chapel Hill: University of North Carolina Press, 1979–1996); Lawrence Foushee London, "The Diocese in the First Decades of the Twentieth Century, 1901–1922," in *The Episcopal Church in North Carolina, 1701–1959,* ed. Lawrence Foushee London and Sarah McCulloh Lemmon (Raleigh: The Episcopal Diocese of North Carolina, 1987), 330–34.

81. *NCDJ 75th* (1891): 140–41. Annual reports continued to appear in the Journal of Convention through 1928. See also London, "The Diocese in the First Decades of the Twentieth Century, 1901–1922," 309; 317–28, and George H. Esser, "Rapid Growth and Financial Crisis, 1923–1941," in *The Episcopal Church in North Carolina, 1701–1959,* ed. Lawrence Foushee London and Sarah McCulloh Lemmon (Raleigh: The Episcopal Diocese of North Carolina, 1987), 364–66.

82. For the significance of college work, see the Address of Bishop Thomas A. Fraser, *NCDJ 146th* (1962): 83; on Penland and other Appalachian schools, see Thomson, "The Episcopal Church in Western North Carolina," 472–85; on ministry to the Armed Forces, see Brewster, "The Diocese of East Carolina," 452.

83. *NCDJ 149th* (1965): 69.

84. Gardiner H. Shattuck, Jr., *Episcopalians & Race: Civil War to Civil Rights* (Lexington: University Press of Kentucky, 2000), 118.

85. *NCDJ 154th* (1970), 73–77; Shattuck, *Episcopalians & Race,* 199, 200; Prichard, *A History of the Episcopal Church,* 261–64.

86. Prichard, *A History of the Episcopal Church,* 251–57.

87. Pauli Murray, *Song in a Weary Throat: An American Pilgrimage* (New York: Harper and Row, 1987), 432–35.

88. *NCDJ 197th* (2013): 1, 112–14.

89. *NCDJ 185th* (2001): 116–24.

90. *NCDJ 192nd* (2008): 123–31.

91. G. Jeffrey MacDonald, "Go to Galilee," *The Living Church,* October 18, 2015, 8–14.

Holiness/Pentecostal Traditions

H. Stanley York

The introduction of Holiness sentiments into nineteenth-century North Carolina reveals a tangled web of politics in the church and government. Kurt O. Berends writes, "Over the course of the war, Confederate clergy proclaimed their message of death and redemption in a manner that professing faith in the country became tantamount to professing faith in God.... To put it another way, ministers had so convincingly described the Confederate cause in religious language that many soldiers found salvation in the cause."[1] Thus, Biblical interpretation, application, and government support united to develop an unbalanced religious mindset and heart for North Carolinians. The theological terms of "salvation," "sacrifice," "atonement," "heaven," "hell," and "sin" were mired in nationalism. North Carolina was not unique in this matter; the problem raised its ugliness throughout the South from the 1840s through the early 1900s. Neither was the North spared in this religious struggle.

A post–Reconstruction survey of North Carolina finds a state in the depth of a depression, psychological and economic, with great resentment toward occupying Union troops. During the Civil War, the Tar Heel State had sent a total of 155,000 troops into battle and lost approximately 40,000 of them. The carpetbaggers and scalawags created distrust of the North, and anything considered "Northern" or "Yankee" was an intrusion into southern daily life. These intrusions came to be feared as northern strategies to subvert the renewal of society in the South. Economic and religious culture suffered greatly under Radical Republicans' Reconstruction policies.

The Holiness movement posed another issue for the South. At the General Conference in 1844, the Methodist Episcopal Church split over the issue of slavery into the Methodist Episcopal Church, North, and Methodist Episcopal Church, South,[2] in Louisville, Kentucky. The plantation owners accumulated great wealth from cotton and the value of their slaves. This new wealth enabled southern churches to build larger edifices, rent pews, and reword the message of salvation and obedience to appease their members who owned slaves. This situation led to the formation of the Free Methodist Church and the Wesleyan Methodist Church in the North. The Free Methodist formation was led by the Reverend B.T. Roberts in the Genesee Conference over the issue of the "New School" Methodists, who interpreted sanctification as justification, with "sanctification" and "holiness" being synonyms. The Rev. Roberts aligned with Phoebe Palmer and her teachings on Wesleyan perfection.[3] The Free Methodist Church was the first organized church in history to specifically identify itself with the doctrine of Christian perfection at its founding.[4] The Wesleyan Methodist Church had left the mainstream Methodist Episcopal Church in 1843 over the issues of Wesleyan perfectionism doctrines and the campaign to extirpate slavery as a moral evil. Orange Scott and others called a convention in Utica, New York, to separate as "True Wesleyans" from the main church.[5] This fracture among Methodists gradually led to questions and reinterpretation of John Wesley's theology.

The Methodist Episcopal Church, South, had strayed from the "holiness"/"sanctification" message of John Wesley beginning in the 1840s. A major disagreement arose in defining "sanctification"; the North's instantaneous act, or crisis moment, differed from the gradual progression of "holiness" embraced in the South. At question was the place of John Wesley's *A Plain Account of Christian Perfection* in Methodism. Also, the revivalist methods and the teachings of Phoebe Palmer and others created a theological tension. Yet the Methodist church was not the only denomination affected by the slavery issue.

The Presbyterians and Baptists also split over the ethics of slave ownership. The teaching of Holiness, moreover, conflicted with the Calvinist theology of the Baptist and Presbyterian churches in the South. Within the Presbyterian Church, the battle raged between New and Old School teachings. Adam's guilt, argued the New School camp, was not imputed to all humanity. Guilt was personal and relative to each individual's sins. The New School also emphasized activism and a faith in the ability of humankind to alter history for the better.[6] The Old School conservatives held to the teaching of Calvin's position of total depravity, that the fall of Adam infected humanity's mind, will, and emotions completely. This position of the Old School allowed for the institution of slavery as long as the government upheld the orderliness of society. Randall J. Stephens has written, "Perhaps the starkest example of the role Calvinism played in the prewar South is evident in the region's justice system and in the rigid honor code that was so fundamental to the culture.... Control and order were paramount in the slaveholding states."[7] The Baptists, for their part, struggled with the question of missionaries owning slaves. This struggle led to a split and the formation of the Southern Baptist Convention.[8] Across both North and South, a question repeatedly pondered by the skeptics of Holiness was, "How can one live a sinless life?"

The printing press became an instrument of influence to spread the message of Holiness. Publications such as *The Guide to Christian Perfection* by Timothy Merritt, *The Higher Christian Life* by William E. Broadman, *Guide to Holiness* by Phoebe Palmer, the *Christian Standard and Home Journal* by the Camp Meeting Association, and others generated a revival of Wesleyan Holiness in the North and led folks in a recovery of Holiness life. During the Civil War, on the other hand, the South had cut off Palmer's *Guide to Holiness* in the mail and considered northern ideas advocated by avowed abolitionists as hostile and subversive.[9]

In July 1867, popular Holiness advocates organized a revival camp meeting for the growing movement in Vineland, New Jersey. This revival led to the formation of the National Camp Meeting Association for the Promotion of Holiness (NCMAPH). This development provided the impetus to preach, teach, and publish the Holiness message after the Civil War. William Baker was one of the earliest carpetbag Holiness evangelists to spread perfectionism among southerners. In 1871, he established the South's first Holiness journal, *The Home Altar,* and later renamed it *The Way of Holiness.* He united with R.C. Oliver to establish a southern tract society in Spartanburg, South Carolina.[10] This advance led to the First Holiness Meeting in Knoxville, Tennessee, in 1872 with John Inskip and other Holiness ministers of NCMAPH.

As the northern Holiness evangelists expanded their teachings, writings, and appearances at camp meetings, the traditional strongholds of the South's religious past began to crumble. Quaker women came from Charleston to the Savannah-area islands and began schools for freed slaves. Orphanages and homes for girls arose to help in the proper raising of these children. Southern evangelists led the way. H.C. Morrison, L.L. Pickett, Beverly Carradine, George Douglas Watson, William Baxter Godbey, and others crisscrossed the borders of southern states preaching the message of "holiness" and "sanctification." Their theological foundation was built upon Wesley and his teachings. A major passage of Wesley's message arose from Ezekiel 36:26–27: "And I will give you a new heart, and new spirit, I will put within you. And I will remove your heart of stone from your flesh, and give you a heart of flesh. And I will put my Spirit with you and cause you to walk in my statutes and be careful to obey my rules."[11] Wesley's sermon, *The Circumcision of the Heart,* addressed this issue, "Here is the sum of the perfect law, the circumcision of the heart. Let the spirit return to God that gave it, with the whole train of its affections."[12] This insight from Wesley involved a deeper personal effort to rid oneself of thoughts, habits, and actions established prior to one's conversion experience or renewal of the mind. This second work of grace may be experienced as cutting sin off at its roots.

North Carolina's Role

This message was instrumental in the founding of several Holiness churches and their eventual progress into the Pentecostal denomination. The South was influenced by the following individuals who defied southern societal norms in order to advance this message. A.B. Crumpler, B.H. Irwin, G.B. Cashwell, I.R. Lowery, and the Christian and Missionary Alliance Church traversed North Carolina to plant Holiness/Pentecostal churches. The railroad system in the South aided these evangelists as they traveled from city to city. Dr. Dan Woods has written an excellent paper titled "Spiritual Railroading." He studied the various rail lines in the South and discovered that most tent meetings and the related establishment of churches took place near railroads. An example of this work is in Star, North Carolina, where G.W. Stanley established a Pentecostal Holiness Church.[13] Also, these evangelists blended railroad terminology to describe biblical principles.[14] Each of these individuals taught the "Full Gospel" including salvation, sanctification, healing in the atonement, and "soon-coming king." These ideas were new to members of the Methodists, Baptists, Presbyterians, and the unchurched, yet these earliest seeds developed into Pentecostalism, the fastest growing movement of the religious world.

Biographical Sketches of Early Holiness Leaders in North Carolina

Leaders of any movement need a great sense of resolve and unction. The early Holiness ministers preached and taught with strong conviction of the rightness of their sanctification experience. These men were eccentric, stubborn, creative, and very knowledgeable of Wesleyan theology. Their goal was to plant "Scriptural Holiness" wherever they traveled. They confronted the biblical understanding of southerners with their own deep convictions. George Floyd Taylor's introduction to this new message came at the

Holiness Convention in Magnolia, North Carolina, in 1897. He said, "The full salvation doctrine taught by the holiness folk presented problems for the folks in Magnolia. Doctrine in Magnolia usually meant water baptism, so people had no experience of salvation, leaving the churches cold and lifeless."[15] Little did Taylor realize that the future of his life as an educator, minister, and denominational leader was being transformed in these services. Taylor's inquisitiveness and caution served him well, as acceptance of these new ways began a testing phase prior to his commitment to these Holiness preachers.[16] The testimony of Taylor became normative for new converts to the Holiness way.

A.B. Crumpler

A.B. Crumpler became the Father of the Holiness Movement in North Carolina.[17] Crumpler was born in Honeycutt Township, North Carolina, on June 9, 1864.[18] He studied law at Trinity College in Randolph County and graduated at the age of twenty-four. His Methodist affiliation grew out of his relationship with the Reverend J.T. Kendall. At Kendall's revival in Keener, North Carolina, Crumpler experienced salvation and by 1888 was an ordained minister of the Methodist Episcopal Church, South.[19] In addition to practicing law and preaching, Crumpler suddenly moved to the Midwest. In 1890, he attended a service in Bismarck, Missouri, led by Beverly Carradine, a leading Holiness preacher of this period. During one service, Crumpler received the experience of sanctification. Soon he became convicted to return to the region around Sampson County in North Carolina. His goal was to preach the Holiness message there. On May 15, 1897, Crumpler convened a Holiness meeting in Magnolia, North Carolina. Magnolia Methodist Church hosted the meeting with the blessing of its pastor, L.S. Etheridge.[20] This was the beginning of the modern Holiness Movement in the Old North State.[21]

The Magnolia Holiness meeting led to the founding of the Holiness Church of North Carolina. Prior to this meeting, Crumpler had preached tent revivals in Sampson, Wayne, and Duplin counties. These regional revivals began to build a stronger interest in the Holiness message among southerners. Crumpler continued to maintain his minister's license in the MECS during this time. His preaching was powerful. When he preached, the "power would fall" within the tent and even upon those listening at a distance. Healing, salvation, and sanctification occurred regularly in his meetings. His sermons began with an exhortation for the lost to experience regeneration and justification and then moved on to sanctification.[22] The language of Holiness initiated a new religious terminology with terms such as "holiness, a pure heart, perfect love, moving into Canaan, the double cure, and the baptism with the Holy Spirit."[23] The news of Crumpler's message spread quickly. He conducted the revival meetings in a tent with the capacity of a thousand people. The unique feature of Crumpler's revivals was the interracial character. Jim Crow laws meant nothing to him, and his rule about race became a common practice of Holiness meetings in eastern North Carolina.[24] The Holiness ministers and denominational groups, in fact, approached the work of sanctification as a means to remove the "color line."

With success came opposition; the MECS passed the famous anti–Holiness rule, Article 301, at the 1898 General Conference. This rule attempted to ban preachers and laymen from holding public meetings within the locale of a church or circuit. Anyone found guilty faced punishment from the local Methodist authority. Crumpler scheduled a revival in Elizabeth City, North Carolina, in the summer of 1898, and John H. Hall of the Methodist Church in this town filed a complaint. Again in July 1899, Crumpler scheduled a meeting for Cedar Creek, North Carolina, and the local minister requested him to suspend the revival. This led to Crumpler's trial in Clinton, North Carolina, for violation of Rule 301; the final verdict was guilty, for holding a revival not of church laws.[25] After the trial, Crumpler withdrew his name from the Methodist Church. This separation led to the formation of the first Pentecostal Holiness congregation in Goldsboro, North Carolina.[26] His action placed Crumpler in the "come-outers" group of ministers of the new Holiness denominations. The "come-outers" saw no hope or future with the established denominations to accept their Holiness message and ministry.

Early 1900 found Crumpler issuing a call among several Holiness groups to meet in Fayetteville, North Carolina, for the purpose of organizing an official church and writing a Discipline. Several new churches were organized at this meeting: Antioch, Magnolia, and Goldsboro. Goldsboro called Crumpler as its minister.[27] The annual convention of 1901 conducted business in Magnolia. Two important decisions presented a new direction for the young church, a name change to "The Holiness Church" and a newspaper, *The Holiness Advocate*, to be printed on a bi-monthly basis. Preaching and newspaper articles attacked regularly the issues of tobacco, alcohol, ice cream socials, dances, improper dress, and divorce. The Discipline declared the church government as "congregational" in relation to the "autocracy" of the Methodist organization. This position did not last long due to the Methodist influence in the lives of its ministers and members.[28] As the message and ministry of the Holiness church grew, two men who would be important to its future became members, A.H. Butler and G.F. Taylor.

Benjamin Hardin (B.H.) Irwin

Every movement in the religious sphere gives rise to an eccentric and radical personality, who develops unusual teachings and sometimes lives a peculiar life. Such was B.H. Irwin. Vinson Synan states in his Preface for *Fire Baptized: The Many Lives and Works of Benjamin Hardin Irwin*, "I even pondered naming the book, *B.H. Irwin: 'The Sanctified Rascal.'*"[29] Why was this title considered? In a letter to *Signs of the Time: Devoted to the Old School Baptist Cause* (April 15, 1880), Irwin wrote, "My years have been years of sadness, and my path has been one of thorns; yet I feel that God, in the midst of his wrath against me, has remembered mercy. I trust that he has not forsaken me altogether, nor entirely removed the covenant of his peace."[30] Irwin provided another glimpse into his early theological understanding of God and salvation, as he revealed that his father had been "a firm believer in the doctrine and practice of the Predestinarian Baptists and had experience dating back over fifty years."[31] Irwin sought a position for forgiveness of his sins through this relationship with predestination.

Benjamin Hardin Irwin was born in Mercer County, Missouri, on January 23, 1854, and grew up in Tecumseh, Nebraska, though his family's roots are in Northern Ireland. He was raised in five-point Calvinism, and his family belonged to a very small Baptist group, the Two-Seed-in-the-Spirit Predestinarian Baptists, founded by Daniel Parker.[32] Irwin studied law and practiced in Tecumseh. In 1876, he married Anna M. Stewart. They had two children, a daughter, Maud, and a son, Stewart. Then his life changed. After many years of wicked living, he was converted on April 21, 1879. In 1888, Irwin felt and answered the call to preach. On April 6, 1889, he received his ordination in the Baptist church.[33]

His early years of ministry revealed little fruit, until a minister from the Iowa Holiness Association preached the sanctification message at the First Baptist Church in Tecumseh. The Holiness message permeated Irwin's soul with a deep conviction of his many sinful exploits. The Holiness message led Irwin to seek the second blessing of sanctification of perfect love and Christian perfection as taught by John Wesley. On May 16, 1891, Irwin received this second work of grace.[34] Irwin's experience led him to blaze a Holiness trail of preaching and teaching from the Midwest to the South and northward into Toronto, Canada.

The experience so overwhelmed Irwin that he began an intense study of Wesley's and John Fletcher's works. Accompanying this new experience was Irwin's choice to leave the Baptist Church and join the Wesleyan Methodist Church. The Wesleyan Methodist Church was a perfectionist group, theologically. Within the bounds of this experience, Irwin discovered John Fletcher's *Checks to Antinomianism*. This work taught him of a further experience beyond sanctification. Fletcher called this experience the "baptism of burning love," or "the baptism of the Holy Ghost and fire." The fire experience moved Irwin's theology and preaching beyond most Holiness groups.[35] It is important to remember that Holiness ministers taught that the Baptism of the Holy Spirit occupied one's sanctification. This issue arises later with the introduction of Azusa Street theology of the Baptism of the Holy Spirit with speaking in tongues. Eventually Irwin developed further baptisms of "dynamite, lyddite, and oxidite." Each fire took a person deeper in his or her Holiness experience by completely removing any vestige of sin.

The blending of mystical readings such as Thomas Upton's *Life of Madame Guyon* and George D. Watson's *Live Coals* merged in Irwin's search for deeper experiences.[36] The "fire baptisms" served to remove all dross from the seeker. These baptisms may be seen as a witness to Irwin's salvation, as all sinful emotions, thoughts, and actions dissipated like a vapor. As Wesleyan as Irwin became after his reading of Wesley and Fletcher, the witness of the Spirit appeared to be working hand in hand with his early Predestinarian raising.

As Irwin gained support for his "fire baptisms" teachings, the Wesleyan Methodist Church and J.M. Pikes' *Way of Faith* provided avenues for revivals. Three key events occurred to influence his work: rejection by Isaiah Reid and the Iowa Holiness Association; the favor of the Wesleyan Methodists; and his personal rejection of denominational affiliation.[37] Irwin held meetings from Kansas eastward and became more radical in his ministry. Divine healing soon became a part of his ministry, though it was not viewed as radical due to the work of the Christian and Missionary Alliance Church.

The popularity of Irwin's fire baptisms led to the formation of a national association. He chose to promote his national meeting in Anderson, South Carolina, from July 28 to August 8, 1899. Four important men attended these meetings: R.B. Hayes of Georgia; Samuel D. Page of North Carolina; Joseph H. King, the future General Superintendent of the Pentecostal Holiness Church; and William E. Fuller, a black minister of the Fire-Baptized Holiness Church for African Americans from South Carolina.[38] Irwin brought forth a Discipline based on autocratic leadership vesting him as the General Overseer.[39] Among radical groups, there is a tendency towards "a super Holiness appearance" in contrast to other Holiness groups. The General Rules of the adopted Constitution required that members have no oath-bound membership in secret societies; no use of tobacco, alcohol, morphine, or intoxicants; no filthy speech, no jesting; and no outward adornment of jewelry, gold, or costly apparel.[40] Members observed Old Testament dietary laws concerning pork, catfish, and oysters. The FBHC continued its interracial ministry.

This newly organized association soon began a massive nationwide outreach. News of meetings came from its publication, *Live Coals of Fire*. By a stroke of genius, Irwin chose to mail a weekly copy of the publication to the Library of Congress in Washington, D.C. As the association grew, Irwin's vision expanded in 1899, conceiving of a national headquarters with a school for ministers and missionary training and a school for prophets. Soon Beniah, Tennessee, became the chosen site.[41]

The issue of *hubris* always follows charismatic leaders of organizations. The ministry seems to suffer from misappropriation of money, or sexual sins. In June 1900, Irwin was caught by acquaintances while coming out of a saloon in Omaha, Nebraska. He was smoking a cigar and was drunk.[42] This discovery rattled the association. J.H. King called a meeting in 1901, and Irwin was removed from leadership for open and gross sins.[43] Joseph H. King was elected the new General Overseer of the FBHC.[44] Immediately, he began to remove all excessive teachings on the "fire baptisms" and reorient the association towards a Wesleyan/Arminian theological position. The remnants of the FBHC eventually united with the Pentecostal Holiness Church.

Irwin's life ended with bouts of visitations to the pulpit. It is known that he was at the Azusa Street Mission in Los Angeles, California, in 1907. His legacy ended in shock and horror, as his three sons served prison time. Irwin never divorced his first wife, and became a bigamist. (It appears that he never ceased his habit of visiting houses of prostitution.) His life ended as a Two-Seed-in-the-Spirit Predestinarian Baptist. It is believed that he died on January 22, 1926, in Palestine, Texas, after traveling in his last years over most of the United States.[45] Was his restlessness in daily and theological life a search for a place of rest? Did B.H. Irwin find solace in Predestination? Among the Two-Seeders, the "good" seed was predestined for heaven.[46] His positive impact on the Holiness Church in North Carolina is not clear.

Gaston Barnabas (G.B.) Cashwell

Crumpler and Irwin labored in the South to overcome the refusal of southern folks to hear and accept the Holiness message. This labor prepared the ground for the next important theological position of the Baptism of the Holy Spirit, evidence of speaking in tongues. The Azusa Street revival began in Los Angeles on April 9, 1906, and was led by William J. Seymour, an African American child of former slaves in Louisiana. People traveled from all points of the earth to witness this new spiritual visitation and baptism. Many early people saw this visitation as a fulfillment of the Old Testament prophet Joel 2:23–29 and the New Testament story of Acts 2:1–12. *The Way of Faith* from Columbia, South Carolina, and *The Apostolic Faith* from the Azusa Street Mission carried stories of this revival throughout the United States. News of the revival drew G.B. Cashwell from Dunn, North Carolina, to Los Angeles. His return earned him the title "the apostle of Pentecost to the South."[47] He eventually touched thousands of lives from his Dunn Revival through his ministry to all points in the South.

Cashwell was born on April 5, 1862, in Halls Township, North Carolina. He grew up working on the family farm as the South struggled in the throes of Reconstruction.[48] His early life was very difficult as his family labored under the depressing agricultural conditions. Cashwell was known for being a jovial and daring young man. By 1893, he was working as a demonstrator in Georgia for a North Carolina tobacco company. He taught farmers in non-tobacco growing areas of Georgia the steps of growing tobacco.[49]

Cashwell experienced salvation at the Reverend J.T. Kendall's Cotton Gin Revival in Keener, North Carolina, in August 1885. The time and place of Cashwell's sanctification experience is not known. Cashwell became a member of The Holiness Church of North Carolina in 1903 at The Holiness Convention in Dunn.[50] He also served a Holiness church in Ayden. In 1906, Cashwell's absence from The Holiness Convention in Lumberton brought a stir among the delegates. He left a letter to the convention: "Dear Brethren: If I have offended anyone of you, forgive me. I realize that my life has fallen short of the standard of holiness we preach: but I have been restored in my home in Dunn, N.C. ... I am now leaving for Los Angeles, Calif., where I shall seek for the Baptism of the Holy Ghost."[51]

Cashwell took the six-day trip across the country and fasted and prayed continually to the Lord.[52] Upon arriving, he went immediately to the Azusa Street Mission and discovered that "A new crucifiction [*sic*] began in my life and I had to die to many things, but God gave me victory."[53] The African American leadership of this revival challenged Cashwell's prejudices. He was so shocked when his initial experience for prayer led to his rejecting the laying on of hands by colored folk. For five days, he sought the Baptism of the Holy Spirit; then he released his "color line" feelings and received this baptism. On November 28, Cashwell preached at the Mission for thirty minutes on justification, sanctification, and the Baptism of the Holy Spirit. After this sermon, Cashwell planned his return home to Dunn. The people at the Azusa Street Mission raised funds for his trip.[54]

Upon Cashwell's return, he organized a meeting after Christmas 1906. He extended invitations to The Holiness Church, the Fire-Baptized Holiness Church, and the Holiness group of the Free Will Baptist Church.[55] Vinson Synan wrote, "The meeting opened on December 31, 1906, and immediately it became evident that the Azusa Street pentecost had come to the East. Preachers listened in awe as Cashwell spoke with other tongues and encouraged others to seek the experience."[56] This meeting began a new phase in Holiness theology in North Carolina as the future Pentecostal Holiness Church and Free Will Pentecostal Baptist Church became new denominations to meet the needs of their ministers and members. From Dunn, Cashwell received an invitation to minister in High Point, North Carolina. His ministry moved across North Carolina and into other states. Two future leaders of newly formed Pentecostal denominations received the Baptism of the Holy Spirit under Cashwell, J.H. King of the Pentecostal Holiness Church[57] and A.J. Tomlinson of the Church of God in Cleveland, Tennessee.

In 1907, Cashwell began publishing *The Bridegroom's Messenger* out of Atlanta, Georgia. It became the Pentecostal newspaper for the South. Within three years, Cashwell virtually disappeared from the revival circuit. Many suggestions circulated; they ranged from not becoming the General Superintendent of the Pentecostal Holiness Church to his frustration that the "color lines" were not fading in the face of the Jim Crow laws.

G.B. Cashwell died on March 5, 1916, in Dunn. The cause of his death was congestive heart failure. His health had begun a decline in 1914, and he was treated for mitral valve problems. This large, temperamental man left the movement that he brought to the South after roughly ten years.[58] Cashwell's legacy remains as a contributor to the formation of the Pentecostal Holiness Church and the Cleveland, Tennessee, Church of God. His greatest contribution was bringing the Pentecostal message to the South from Los Angeles.

Other Contributors

The birth of the United Holy Church of America, Inc. (UHCA) and the Christian Missionary Alliance (CMA)[59] contributed to the birth of Holiness in North Carolina, including a removal of the "color line" in the Holiness history of the state. The Reverend A.B. Simpson toured throughout North Carolina and presented the message of the Four-fold Gospel of "Saved, Sanctified, Healing in the Atonement, and the Soon-Coming Return of Jesus Christ." The ministry of the CMA rejected Jim Crow laws. The CMA helped to found an educational institution for freed slaves in Boydton, Virginia. This education ministry also reached out to Mill Spring and Rutherfordton, North Carolina, among the mountain children. Textile mills recruited mountain farmers to move into the Piedmont to work in cotton mills; the children generally received no education and became future workers themselves. The CMA seized an opportunity to elevate these children through basic education for better jobs in the future.

The birth of the UHCA is associated with the ministry of the Reverends C.C. Craig, L.M. Mason, Elijah Lowney and G.A. Mials. These men preached and taught Holiness to the blacks in the areas from Method to Wilmington in eastern North Carolina. The Falcon Camp Meeting in Falcon, for example, served as a conduit for Holiness throughout that part of the state. One person critical to Falcon is J.A. Culbreth. The CMA was instrumental in the formation of the initial camp meeting there in 1900.

Culbreth and his wife, Venie, accepted the sanctification message in May 1896 in Dunn under the preaching of the Reverend A.B. Crumpler. The Culbreth family were people of means with ownership of large plots of land, a general store in Falcon, and investments in Dunn. Eventually, Culbreth moved to Falcon. He built the Octagon Tabernacle for worship, organized the Falcon Holiness School, an orphanage, and the Camp Meeting grounds.[60] These formed a "Holiness quadrilateral" for ministry. Falcon established the example of a Holiness town with its ministries touching every area of a person's life for other camp meeting locations.

Holiness and Pentecostal Development in North Carolina

A question that often arises in denominational studies is, "Why did we need another denomination to serve this theological position?" Close evaluation of the Holiness/sanctification message produces an answer. The denomination provided unique meetings with exuberant music, shouts of praise, people falling in the Spirit, hearers weeping as the message convicted or reveals their sins, and demonic deliverance as a norm. These new Holiness folks sought enthusiastic manifestations that earned a label among established churches of being uncouth and disorderly. So these inspired groups left their places of worship and sought experiences that could not be found in established churches. These "come-outers" saw little possibility for reform of other denominations. So Holiness associations arose in North Carolina and nationwide as the sanctification message won converts to this newfound freedom of religious expression.

In North Carolina, three denominations grew from the Holiness movement after G.B. Cashwell's introduction of the Azusa Street message beginning in late 1906. They were the Pentecostal Holiness Church from The Holiness Church of North Carolina, the

Pentecostal Free Will Baptist from the Free Will Baptist Church, Cape Fear District, and the Cleveland, Tennessee, from the Church at Camp Creek. Holiness churches of The Church of the Nazarene and the Christian Missionary Alliance did not accept the Pentecostal message, yet remained true to the Holiness/sanctification Message. These groups continued in the Wesleyan theological tradition. For the Holiness supporters nationwide, salvation and sanctification were understood as two crisis moments or "two-steps." When a person received sanctification, the Holiness ministers taught that the Baptism of the Holy Spirit took place at the same moment. Azusa Street teaching added the Baptism of the Holy Spirit with evidence of speaking in tongues as a third experience or now "three-steps." B.H. Irwin and George D. Watson had taught a three-experience *ordo salutis* (order of salvation) prior to Azusa Street. In 1906, Holiness Associations nationwide strived to understand this new work of God. Holiness ministers questioned this outpouring of the Holy Spirit by rewriting their books and adjusting their teaching and preaching. In a related effort, the Assembly of God and Foursquare Church supported the "Finished Work" of Christ on Calvary doctrine developed by William H. Durham. This position taught sanctification as a gradual process over a believer's lifetime obtained in salvation rather than an instantaneous work. This teaching aligned with Durham's Baptist roots, and influences by Calvinism.

Between 1906 and 1913, the Azusa Street movement experienced three theological challenges, the first two being Wesleyanism and Durham's Finished Work theology. The third challenge came from R.E. McAlister's sermon on "In Jesus' Name" at the Arroyo Seco Camp Meeting in 1913. McAlister taught that the reason for the apostles baptizing in the Name of the Lord Jesus Christ was that it was commanded by Jesus in Matthew 28:19. Lord Jesus Christ became the christological equivalent of "Father–Son–Holy Spirit." Another name for this theological position was the New Issue; its denomination is the United Pentecostal Church International.

North Carolina Pentecostal Denominations

Four denominations grew out of Cashwell's Dunn Revival. The International Pentecostal Holiness Church, United Holy Church of America, Inc., Pentecostal Free Will Baptist Church, and Church of God in Cleveland, Tennessee, became influential Pentecostal churches throughout the world. These denominations are Wesleyan theologically. These four continue an influence in world missions, homeland missions, disaster support, and providing educational institutions for training their ministers and missionaries.

The International Pentecostal Holiness Church

As the revival continued in Dunn under G.B. Cashwell, trouble began to arise within The Holiness Church. Troubled by Cashwell's meetings, immediately Crumpler began to draw lines in the sand over the issue of tongues as a witness of the Baptism of the Holy Spirit versus sanctification containing the Spirit's fullness. Resisting Cashwell's message, Crumpler traveled to Florida for a series of revival meetings. Unrest settled upon the Holiness Church for the remainder of 1907 as doctrinal differences separated the ministers. The divisions were between the followers of Crumpler and Cashwell, but the Pentecostal fire spread quickly over North Carolina as Cashwell continued revival meetings in many cities. George Floyd Taylor wrote *The Spirit and The Bride* as the first theological statement to address the issues between the Holiness groups and the new Pentecostal groups.

The annual conference of 1907 was held in LaGrange, North Carolina. The sermons of this conference revealed both sides' positions. The Pentecostals reelected Crumpler as the president of the HCNC and A.H. Butler as his assistant. Crumpler continued his attacks on the speaking-in-tongues believers, which eventually led to a battle at the 1908 Annual Conference in Dunn. Both factions attended the conference. Crumpler once again was elected president by acclamation and Butler as his vice president. The meeting remained in tension until Crumpler renounced his presidency and left with five preachers and a few members. Crumpler returned to the Methodist Church for the rest of his life. The convention reconvened the next day and elected C.B. Strickland as president and Butler as vice president. On November 28, the previous day's elections were rescinded and Butler became president and G.F. Taylor vice president.[61]

The next convention gathered in Falcon in November 1909. Two significant business items changed the church forever. The name was returned to The Pentecostal Holiness Church, and a committee was formed to investigate the merger with the Fire-Baptized Holiness Church and the Free Will Baptist Church. Taylor, Culbreth, and Butler served on the merger committee.[62]

J.H. King supported a merger of the two denominations prior to leaving on a world-wide missionary tour. Both churches ministered in an "organic union" during these early days by preaching and teaching in each other's churches. In 1910, the FBHC met in Chadbourn for their General Council. Samuel D. Page, A.E. Robinson, F.M. Britton, M.D. Sellers, and E.D. Cannon served as merger delegates for the BFHC.[63]

In November 1910, the Pentecostal Holiness Church held its Annual Convention in Winston-Salem, North Carolina. G.F. Taylor read a report on the merger, and the preachers voted to approve this union. Taylor worked with the FBHC representative on writing a *Discipline*. This work was drawn up in Taylor's house in Falcon, and a meeting was called for in January 1911.

The delegates assembled on January 30 for prayer and work on the merger at the Falcon Holiness School. The *Discipline* required a close reading, raising questions on rules and regulations, and close examination of grammar and punctuation. This work appeared troublesome, so the delegates chose to work on January 31 in the Octagon Tabernacle. The FBHC had more pastors than the PHC. The merger nearly collapsed due to the urging to accept the FBHC Discipline. Taylor and others agreed to accept the Discipline *verba et ad literatim*. The vote of the delegates approved this merger. Elections were held for the new officers, with S.D. Page as general superintendent, A.H. Butler as assistant general superintendent, and A.E. Robinson as general secretary. The new denomination counted about 2,000 members, and seven districts.[64]

The Pentecostal Holiness Church began to grow throughout the Carolinas, Georgia, and Virginia. This young denomination had to address two more critical issues: snake handling and the "gift movement" in Roanoke, Virginia. The snake issue became critical in Western North Carolina as new churches assembled. The Cleveland Church of God in Tennessee approved snake handling under the leadership of A.J. Tomlinson. In early 1916, churches around Roanoke, Virginia, broke out in revival. Pastor J.B. Daugherty was a leader in this movement. The gifts of the Spirit, he felt, had begun to wane after flourishing at Azusa Street in California a decade earlier. The Reverend E.D. Reeves pronounced the movement to be "of God." At issue was the renaming of people, destroying artifacts, naming sins openly about people, and the China missionary movement. Taylor and F.M. Britton traveled to Roanoke to reinstate order and calm. Sixteen ministers were excommunicated. The revival died. The reason for the excesses was due to little pastoral care and teaching on the gifts of the Spirit.[65]

Annual conventions served an important role in shaping and redefining the needs of the denomination both theologically and operationally. The conventions of 1913, 1917, 1925, and 1941 became critical for the growth of The Pentecostal Holiness Church.

The 1913 Annual Convention met in Toccoa Falls, Georgia. This convention made four critical decisions. The Colored Convention was dropped by the convention. There was no reason given for this decision. The Black Pentecostal Holiness Church joined the Black Fire-Baptized Holiness Church under the leadership of W.E. Fuller. Next, the delegates voted to change from two years to four years for the Annual Convention. Thirdly, the floor debated the issue of marriage and divorce. The imposition of stronger prohibitions was dropped for the present time. Lastly, church government was changed from congregational to an episcopal form.[66] Today the denomination operates with a modified congregational/episcopal government.

The decision was made to divide North Carolina into two Conferences in 1914. The new Western Conference ran from Hamlet to the westernmost part of the state. This decision enabled the Western North Carolina churches to travel shorter distances for their conventions. F.A. Dail became the first superintendent of the Western North Carolina Conference. The first convention was held in Eden in November 1915. (The Western Conference changed its name to the Cornerstone Conference in 1998 under Bishop Tommy McGhee.)

The 1917 Annual Convention met in Abbeville, South Carolina. This meeting became very important to the growth of the denomination. Seven key changes became operational for the next four years:

1. Renaming the conventions to "conferences." The polity book was renamed the "Discipline."

2. The church adopted quarterly conferences for fellowship and teaching.

3. The General Superintendent presided over General Conference and Annual Conferences of each state conference. The General Superintendent had the power to ordain ministers.

4. The General Board was reduced to one from two with foreign and home missions of the church under one umbrella.

5. The delegates approved requirements for licensing and ordaining ministers.

6. The delegates approved the publishing of a weekly periodical known as *The Pentecostal Holiness Advocate*. G.F. Taylor was appointed the first editor of the paper. Now the church had a communication tool to inform its membership for theological purposes, update the work of foreign missions, and circulate letters of testimony from its members.

7. The Bible Conference was instituted for the purpose of continuing Christian education for pastors and laypersons.

J.H. King was elected the General Superintendent, S.D. Page, Assistant Superintendent, A.E. Robinson, General Secretary, and G.F. Taylor, General Treasurer. The church united behind the strong leadership of these individuals. The last important announcement of

1917 was of the move to Franklin Springs, Georgia, as a central location for church government. The church would establish The Franklin Springs Institute as its school, an orphanage, and build a printing office. The church launched into a strong program to spread the Pentecostal message from the eastern Atlantic shores to Oklahoma.[67]

In 1941, J.H. King turned seventy-two years old. His service as General Superintendent had positively shaped the PHC for the previous twenty-three years. The Ninth General Conference assembled in Franklin Springs. The denomination received new leadership to advance the church in the post–World War II years: Joseph Alexander Synan was elected the General Assistant Superintendent. The PHC was changing from the old guard to a new guard in leadership. The membership recorded roughly 22,000 members. King maintained a busy schedule between his travels, leadership at state conferences, and teaching Bible conferences. The program of the church focused on home evangelism and education.[68]

Synan served faithfully in this new position, and in 1950, he became the General Superintendent. Under his leadership, the church moved its headquarters to Memphis, Tennessee. This move was meant to centrally localize, to serve the entire nation. Circumstances arose, however, concerning the title to the land for the Memphis offices. That and smaller issues precipitated a return to the Franklin Springs campus.

The PHC continued to grow worldwide through missions and home growth. Two final major events occurred. In 1973, the PHC moved to Oklahoma City as its central headquarters. This positioned the leadership in the center of the country. In 1975, the word *International* was added to the name of the church, providing a distinction between the PHC and other pentecostal groups with a similar name. The celebration of the church's Centennial took place back in Falcon under the leadership of General Bishop Ronald Carpenter.

The current leadership on the General Level is General Bishop A.D. (Doug) Beacham, Jr.; Bishop of Evangelism USA Gary Bryant; Bishop of Disciple Tommy McGhee; and Bishop of World Missions Talmadge Gardner. The IPHC has over 100 countries with missionary presence and a membership of 1.6 million members in these countries. In North Carolina, Bishop Doyle Marley serves the Cornerstone Conference, and Bishop Danny Nelson serves the North Carolina Conference. The Falcon Children's Home is an orphanage for the surrounding counties, and in 2015, an orphanage was opened in Turbeville, South Carolina. These orphanages receive support from churches throughout the IPHC. Every November the Falcon Children's Home celebrates 'The Harvest Train' as churches of the Carolinas and Virginia bring supplies for the home.

The International Pentecostal Holiness Church has four educational institutions: Emmanuel College in Franklin Springs; Southwestern Christian University in Oklahoma City; Advantage College in Modesto, California; and Holmes Bible College in Greenville, South Carolina.

The Cornerstone Conference has 152 churches and over 16,000 members. The North Carolina Conference has 215 churches and 31,557 members. These statistics include the Hispanic churches and other outreach ministries in each conference.

The current program for the International Pentecostal Holiness Church is to prayerfully value Scripture, Pentecost, Holiness, Christ's Kingdom, All Generations, Justice, and Generosity. The IPHC declares itself to be "A Place of Refuge, A People of Hope" to all people.

Pentecostal Free Will Baptist Church

The Free Will Baptist Church traces its roots to Benjamin Randall and the Free Will Baptist movement in New Hampshire. The first instance of this group in North Carolina gained attention in Chowan County. The original churches were known as Particular Baptists.[69]

Free Will Baptist Church in eastern North Carolina came under the "holiness"/"sanctification" preaching of A.B. Crumpler in 1897. As Crumpler barnstormed the eastern counties, many Free Will Baptists experienced sanctification. These encounters created a problem for the Free Will Baptists due to their original position of sanctification occurring during salvation. The 1883 Discipline stated that sanctification "commences at regeneration" and continues with one "constantly growing in grace." This statement revealed evidence of Finney's Oberlin Views of Holiness.[70] In 1889, the Cape Fear Conference of the Free Will Baptist Church added Article 13 to state sanctification as "an instantaneous work of God's grace in a believer's heart, whereby the heart is cleansed from all sin and made pure by the blood of Christ."[71] This began a major change in the preaching and teaching of eastern North Carolina Free Will Baptists.

When Cashwell began his Dunn Revival on December 31, 1906, a well-known minister, H.H. Goff of the Dunn Free Will Baptist Church, experienced the Baptism of the Holy Spirit with evidence of speaking in tongues. Soon his wife experienced this manifestation of God. The Goffs, who lived in Falcon, led the Children's Ministry during the Falcon Camp Meeting. The children knew them as "Ma and Pa Goff." During the merger of the Pentecostal Holiness Church and the Fire-Baptized Holiness Church, the Pentecostal Free Will Baptists were invited to join this new denomination.

In 1911, the Cape Fear Conference met at Long Branch Church near Dunn. Discovering that some of its ministers refused to accept the new Article 13 on sanctification, the meeting was unable to proceed due to a resolution forbidding these ministers and churches from being seated as delegates due to their doctrinal irregularities.[72]

On January 12, 1912, the unseated delegates left the conference. A meeting was held at the Shady Grove Free Will Baptist Church, also near Dunn. A letter was sent to churches and ministers about the planned departure from the Cape Fear Conference to form a new conference. This division occurred solely over the positions on sanctification and the Holy Spirit from the revivals of Crumpler and Cashwell.[73]

The church has remained basically a local denomination in North Carolina, Florida, and Hawaii; North Carolina has forty-one of these churches. The Foreign Missions serve in nine countries, and short-term missions are supported by the church.[74] In 1959, The Cape Fear Conference merged with the Wilmington and New River Conferences to form the Pentecostal Free Will Baptist Church, the original group organized at the Stoney Run Church in 1855. This conference adheres to the 1907 doctrine of sanctification and the Holy Spirit.[75]

The headquarters are based in Dunn. Heritage Bible College is the denominational school, established in 1971 under the guidance of the Reverend O.T. Spence.[76]

United Holy Church of America, Inc.

The emergence of the Holiness message among the Black Church finds its roots in the African Methodist Episcopal Church and Holiness preachers with little concern for the Jim Crow laws. The theological imprint upon the Black Church was Wesleyan and Perfectionistic. During the Post–Civil War period, the southern churches became segregated. Missionaries from the North brought the Holiness message. The Christian and Missionary Alliance saw the teaching of Holiness as a mission to provide education for poor blacks. The enthusiastic worship of slaves continued in the new outpouring of the Holy Spirit. Holiness associations appeared in most states. The Black Church developed its new identity as the Holiness message spread in the South.

Henry L. Fisher records the first meeting of the Holy Church of America, Inc. in Method outside Raleigh. A group of persons confessing Holiness met on the first Sunday in May 1886.[77] This date is among the earliest given by a modern Holiness-Pentecostal denomination.[78] Immediately after the first meeting, the leaders began organizing churches, conventions, organizations, and revival campaigns to spread the message of Holiness and a black Holiness association. The first church was built in Durham in 1889. It was known as the Durham Tabernacle and became a center for other holiness groups to use. In 1894, the Holy People in North Carolina held their first convocation.[79] L.H. Mason became the first president along with other strong leaders including G.A. Mials and H.C. Snipes.[80] This meeting served to unite other "Holy People" in North Carolina.[81]

The Method revival continued in Wilmington under the ministry of the Reverend Elijah Lowney. This revival stirred the heart of H.L. Fisher to move into a leadership role for the "Holy People."[82] The revival also stirred the population of Wilmington, as folks both black and white embraced Holiness. Indeed Wilmington became a hotbed for this Holiness revival as churches appeared throughout the city. Several African Methodist Episcopal ministers left their pulpits to align themselves with the Holy People. New churches such as Holy Temple Church and New Covenant Church arose. Ministers began to leave the African Methodist Episcopal Zion Church.

The various black holiness groups met in Durham in 1900 for the main purpose of uniting the Holy People of North Carolina as an independent organization. Groups came from Durham, Wilmington, and Sampson County. The new organization took the name of "Holy Church of North Carolina and Virginia."[83] In 1910, the convention adopted a comprehensive manual prepared by H.L. Fisher,[84] one feature of which stated that members of established denominations remain in their churches for reform purposes. These folks became known as "In-Church-People." This was a unique request as most Holiness associations demanded "come-outism."[85] Holiness became a standard of protection from the apostasy of formal denominations as taught in the Scriptures. Also, the Fisher years provided a study course for ministers.

In 1916, the church elected visionary leaders for its future: Henry Lee Fisher became the new president and G.J. Branch vice president. The church changed its name to the United Holy Church of America. The UHCA sought the ability to educate its people in the absence of public educational facilities. In 1919, the UHCA and CMA joined together to fulfill this dream of education with a joint operation in Boydtown, Virginia. The school's name was Boydtown Institute.[86] As the CMA moved across North Carolina with conventions in the largest cities, they remained alert to the plight of the countryside. The educational emphasis fulfilled the Social Holiness ethic within Wesley's understanding of Holiness. By 1920, the church expanded its boundaries into the northern United States. As the church grew, the convocations became the tool to create, expand, and implement new ministries. The titles of president and vice president were renamed Bishop in 1924.

The Right Reverend Harry L. Cohen is the current President Prelate of the UHCA;

the church in North Carolina is led by Bishop Greg K. Hargrave. The International Headquarters is located in Greensboro, and the Triad Christian Academy is located on the headquarters campus. The UHCA has mission projects in Bermuda, Barbados, and Haiti. North Carolina has 32 churches on the UHCA roll.[87]

Church of God

The inclusion of the Church of God in Cleveland, Tennessee, provides an important insight into early Holiness/Pentecostal groups with the emphasis on restorationism and primitivism. R.G. Spurling wrote in *The Lost Link*, "What has been the greatest hindrance to the cause of Christ? … It is because every church or denomination's internal laws are contrary to Christ's law."[88] Church reform leaders or groups are driven to reclaim lost truths in Scripture. Spurling devoted two years of Bible study and reading church history to formulate his positions in *The Lost Link*. He placed the great apostasy upon Constantine and the legalization of Christianity, church councils, and creeds similar to the Anabaptists. He summarized the positions of the Christian Union by two statements: First, the New Testament is the only infallible rule of faith and practice, so we reject all other articles of faith and manmade creeds, and for the basis of union we accept the law of love and faith required in the Gospel; second, the New Testament contains all things necessary for salvation and church government.[89]

Spurling's study led him to form the Christian Union on August 19, 1886, in Monroe County, Tennessee.[90] Eight people joined with Spurling to form this new group. As Spurling preached his new message to churches throughout the mountains of Tennessee and North Carolina, a revival began. In 1899, B.H. Irwin's message of "fire baptisms" spread through the mountains of Tennessee and North Carolina. A fire-baptized revival broke out in Camp Creek, North Carolina, in 1898, at Shearer Schoolhouse under the leadership of Will Bryant, Billy Martin, Joe Tipton, Milt McNabb, and Frank Porter.[91] This work eventually brought Spurling into the fold. On May 15, 1902, Bryant and others established the Holiness Church at Camp Creek. Spurling was ordained in this church on the same day.

The future of this group suddenly entered a new phase of ministry. In 1899, Ambrose Jessup (A.J.) Tomlinson moved to Culberson, North Carolina. He was a salesman for the American Tract Society. During his travels he came into contact with Bryant and the church at Camp Creek. On June 12–13, 1903, Tomlinson united with Bryant and others and soon became convinced of Spurling's vision of a New Testament church.[92] In 1906, Tomlinson and other leaders moved the headquarters to Cleveland, Tennessee. At the Second Assembly in 1907, the church adopted the name Church of God.

The church continued its growth into new states and established its first mission in the Bahamas. In 1914, Tomlinson was named General Overseer for life. With denominational growth, the monies needed to support the various ministries increased. The years 1920 through 1923 became a challenge to the vision of the church as charges of impropriety in use of funds were leveled against Tomlinson. The Assemblies began to remove Tomlinson's oversight and power over the church. Tomlinson realized his need to resign. After his church trial, Tomlinson was dismissed as General Overseer on July 26, 1923, after the Court of Justice upheld the Council of Twelve's decision. (This chapter in the Church of God history is called "The Disruption of 1923.") Tomlinson proceeded to establish the Church of God of Prophecy, which divided families throughout the original denomination over allegiance to Tomlinson and the new leaders in the Church of God.[93] Both groups attempted to reestablish their positions with churches, missions, and ministers. Flavius Lee became the new general overseer at the 1923 Assembly. He restored leadership for the church and established a new vision and purpose for the Church of God.[94] These critical years strengthened the leadership to advance the church's mission as witnessed today with its position in the Pentecostal world.

Tomlinson, infuriated over the actions of the Church of God, advanced toward a new vision and ministry. In November 1923, his Church of God of Prophecy erected a new tabernacle on Central Avenue in Cleveland. The church initiated a new official publication, the *White Wing Messenger*.[95] For Tomlinson, he returned to the original positions for the Church of God concerning manmade creeds, church councils, and establishing a proper church government. When Ambrose Jessup Tomlinson died on October 2, 1943, the Church of God of Prophecy membership stood under 23,000. His death created serious concerns about the new general overseer to follow him. Several groups under the Church of God banner split during the following years.

In 1953, the Reverend Grady Kent left the Church of God of Prophecy to form the Church of God Jerusalem Acres, believing that a new reformation was needed. This group operated as a theocratic government with a Chief Bishop. Grady Kent led this break and served as the first Chief Bishop. They implemented Judaic worship and festivals in the church. This denomination currently has no churches in North Carolina and maintains a stronger presence in the mission field than in the United States.

On April 20, 2004, a group of Church of God of Prophecy ministers and members split to form the Zion Assembly Church of God, with Wade H. Phillips as Presiding Bishop. Zion Assembly returned to Tomlinson's original vision of the church in Cleveland, Tennessee. As with Church of God Jerusalem Acres, the church membership is stronger in its missions than in the United States. Zion Assembly Church of God has one church in North Carolina.

The Church of God (Cleveland) maintains a strong presence in both the United States and foreign missions. The current leadership includes Dr. Tim Hill as General Overseer of the Church of God. North Carolina is divided into the Western and Eastern Districts, with Dr. Ken Bell as the Bishop of Western North Carolina, overseeing 463 churches; and the Reverend Dennis Page as the Bishop of the Eastern North Carolina District, overseeing 220 churches. The educational arms for the denomination are Lee University, located in Cleveland, Tennessee, along with Pentecostal Theological Seminary for graduate studies.

Conclusion

The health of Holiness/Pentecostal denominations remains steady. North Carolina is also the home for Foursquare Church founded by Aimee Semple McPherson; the Church of God in Christ founded by the Reverend C.H. Mason; and numerous other independent Pentecostal groups.[96] The Wesleyan Church, the Church of the Nazarene, and the Christian and Missionary Alliance are three strong Holiness denominations in North Carolina.

What is the future of all these churches? Pentecostals must not lose their theological distinction or succumb to the "seeker church mentality." Each denomination needs to contextualize the "Old Time Religion messages" to provide a message of hope and deliverance in the current cynical society. Their histories reveal that living "in the world but not of the world" is critical for the future. Pentecostal denominations need to push beyond positions of judgment of appearance towards becoming refuges of freedom and deliverance.

Notes

1. Kurt O. Berends, "Confederate Sacrifice and the 'Redemption' of the South," in *Religion in the American South: Protestants and Others in History and Culture*, editors Beth Barton Schweiger and Donald G. Mathews (Chapel Hill: The University of North Carolina Press, 2004).

2. The Methodist Episcopal Church, South, will be referred to as MECS.

3. Melvin Easterday Dieter, *The Holiness Revival of the Nineteenth Century, Second Edition* (Lanham, MD: Scarecrow Press, Inc., 1996), 45–46.

4. *Ibid.*, 105.

5. *Ibid.*, 21.

6. Randall J. Stephens, *The Fire Spreads: Holiness and Pentecostalism in the American South* (Cambridge, MA: Harvard University Press, 2008), 27.

7. *Ibid.*, 28.

8. Grant Wacker, "Warriors for God and Religion," in *Religion in American Life: A Short History*, editors Jon Butler, Grant Wacker, and Randall Balmer (New York: Oxford University Press, 2008).

9. Stephens, 35.

10. Stephens, 44.

11. Ezekiel 36:26–27. English Standard Version (ESV).

12. John Wesley, *Plain Account of Christian Perfection as believed and taught by Mr. John Wesley from the year 1725 to the year 1777* (Franklin, TN: Seedbed Publishing, 2014), 6.

13. G.W. Stanley was the grandfather of Dr. Charles Stanley of the First Baptist Church in Atlanta, Georgia. His grandfather planted sixteen churches in the Western Conference of the Pentecostal Holiness Church.

14. Daniel Woods, "Spiritual Railroading," a paper presented to the Joint Session of the Society of Pentecostal Studies and the Wesleyan Theological Society, Lexington, KY, March 2003.

15. G.F. Taylor, "Our Church History: Chapter III," *PHA*, February 3, 1921, 8.

16. H. Stanley York, *George Floyd Taylor: The Life of an Early Southern Pentecostal Leader* (Maitland, FL: Xulon Press, 2013), 40.

17. G.F. Taylor, "Our Church History: Part I," *PHA*, January 20, 1921. See, Vinson Synan, *The Old-Time Power: A History of the Pentecostal Holiness Church,* revised 1986 (Franklin Springs, GA: Advocate Press, 1986), 56–79; A.D. Beacham, Jr., *A Brief History of the Pentecostal Holiness Church*, revised 1990 (Franklin Springs, GA: Advocate Press, 1983), 33–38; A.D. Beacham, Jr., *Azusa East: The Life and Times of G.B. Cashwell* (Franklin Springs, GA: LifeSprings Resources, 2006), 24–29.

18. Michael Thornton, *Fire in the Carolinas: The Revival Legacy of G.B. Cashwell and A.B. Crumpler* (Lake Mary, FL: Creation House, 2014), 16. I am using this work as Michael Thornton has done very good research work on these men. His thesis is difficult to affirm.

19. *Ibid.*, 24–25.

20. G.F. Taylor, "Our Church History: Chapter II," *PHA*, January 27, 1921,8; Daniel Rollins, *Forward, Ever Forward: A History of the North Carolina Conference of the Pentecostal Holiness Church* (North Carolina Conference of The International Pentecostal Holiness Church, 2011), 22.

21. Synan, *The Old-Time Power*, 69.

22. *Ibid.*, 69–70.

23. *Ibid.*, 71.

24. Thornton, 41.

25. Rollins, *Forward, Ever Forward*, 25; Synan, *The Old-Time Power*, 75; Beacham, *A Brief History of the Pentecostal Holiness Church*, 36.

26. Synan, *The Old-Time Power*, 74. Crumpler used the name Pentecostal Holiness Church at the time; he later changed the name to the Holiness Church of North Carolina (HCNC).

27. Rollins, *Forward, Ever Forward*, 27; Synan, *The Old-Time Power*, 74–75; Beacham, *A Brief History of the Pentecostal Holiness Church* 37.

28. Synan, *The Old-Time Power*, 83–84.

29. Vinson Synan and Dan Woods, *Fire Baptized: The Many Lives of Benjamin Hardin Irwin: A Biography and A Reader* (Lexington, KY: Emeth Press, 2017). xvi.

30. *Ibid.*, 115–16.

31. *Ibid.*, 116. Emphasis is mine.

32. Synan and Woods, 5–7; Beacham, *A Brief History of the Pentecostal Holiness Church*, 43; Rollins, *Forward, Ever Forward*, 43; Synan, *The Old-Time Power*, 45.

33. Synan and Woods, 9–10.

34. Synan and Woods, 15–16; Beacham, *A Brief History of the Pentecostal Holiness Church,* 43; Rollins, *Forward, Ever Forward,* 43; Synan, *Old-Time* Power, 45.

35. Synan and Woods, 24–26; Beacham, *A Brief History of the Pentecostal Holiness Church,* 44; Rollins, *Forward, Ever* Forward, 44–45; Synan, *Old-Time* Power, 45–46.

36. Synan and Woods, 25.

37. *Ibid.,* 36–37.

38. *Ibid.,* 47.

39. *Ibid.,* 48. The Fire-Baptized Holiness Church will be referred to as FBHC.

40. Synan and Woods, 49–50, Beacham, *A Brief History of the Pentecostal Holiness Church,* 45–46, Rollins, *Forward, Ever Forward,* 46–47; Synan, *Old Time* Power, 53–54.

41. Synan and Woods, 65–70.

42. Synan and Woods, 79.

43. Synan and Woods, 80, Beacham, *A Brief History of the Pentecostal Holiness Church,* 46; Rollins, *Forward, Ever Forward,* 49; Synan, *Old-Time Power,* 56.

44. Tony G. Moon, *From Plowboy to Pentecostal Bishop: The Life of J.H. King* (Lexington, KY: Emeth Press, 2017), 94–95.

45. Synan and Woods, 93.

46. *Ibid.,* 91.

47. Doug Beacham, *Azusa East: The Life and Times of G.B. Cashwell* (Franklin Springs, GA: Lifesprings Publications, 2006), 13.

48. Beacham, *The Life and Times of G.B. Cashwell,* 13–14; Thornton, *Fire in the Carolinas: The Revival Legacy of G.B. Cashwell and A. B. Crumpler,* 14.

49. Beacham, *The Life and Times of G.B.* Cashwell, 16–20; Thornton, *Fire in the Carolinas: The Revival Legacy of G.B. Cashwell and A. B. Crumpler,* 13–16.

50. Beacham, *The Life and Times of G.B. Cashwell,* 24–29; Rollins, *Forward, Ever Forward,* 59–61; Synan, *Old-Time* Power, 85.

51. Taylor, *The Pentecostal Holiness Advocate,* May 29, 1930, 1; Rollins, *Forward, Ever Forward,* 61; Synan, *Old-Time* Power, 97; Thornton, *Fire in the Carolinas: The Revival Legacy of G.B. Cashwell and A.B.* Crumpler, 148–51.

52. Cashwell's published account in *The Apostolic Faith,* December 1906, 3.

53. *Ibid.,* 3.

54. Beacham, *The Life and Times of G.B. Cashwell,* 52–55; Rollins, *Forward, Ever Forward,* 61–64; Synan, *Old-Time* Power, 97–98; Thornton, *Fire in the Carolinas: The Revival Legacy of G.B. Cashwell and A.B. Crumpler,* 151–152.

55. Beacham, *The Life and Times of G.B. Cashwell,* 62–65; Rollins, *Forward, Ever Forward,* 65–67; Synan, *Old-Time* Power, 99–101.

56. Synan, *Old-Time Power,* 99.

57. Moon, *From Plowboy to Pentecostal Bishop: The Life of J.H. King,* 147–53.

58. Thornton, *Fire in the Carolinas: The Revival Legacy of G.B. Cashwell and A. B. Crumpler,* 207. See also *The Bridegroom's Messenger* (Atlanta, GA), 1907–1918.

59. The United Holy Church of America, Inc. will be referred to as UHCA and the Christian Missionary Alliance as CMA.

60. Rollins, *Forever, Ever Forward,* 20–22; Synan, *Old-Time Power,* 56–57.

61. Rollins, *Forward, Ever Forward,* 88–89; Synan, *Old-Time Power,* 107–09. See also George Floyd Taylor, *The Spirit and the Bride: A Scriptural Presentation of the Operation, Manifestation, Gifts, and Fruit of the Holy Spirit in His Relation to the Bride* (Dunn, NC: By the Author, 1907).

62. Rollins, *Forward, Ever Forward,* 109–11; Synan, *Old-Time Power,* 93–97.

63. Rollins, *Forward, Ever Forward,* 116–19, Synan, *Old-Time Power,* 104–06.

64. Rollins, *Forward, Ever Forward,* 104–09; Synan, *Old-Time Power,* 120–24; York, *G.F. Taylor: The Life of a Southern Pentecostal Leader,* 63–65.

65. Daniel Woods, "The Gift Movement Controversy of 1916," a paper presented at the Society of Pentecostal Studies (Cleveland, TN: March 1998). An in-depth coverage is Dr. Woods' dissertation, "*Living in the Presence of God: Enthusiasm, Authority, and Negotiation in the Practice of Pentecostal Holiness.*" Ph.D. diss., The University of Mississippi, 1997.

66. W. Eddie Morris, *The Vines and Branches John 15:5: Historic Events, Holiness, and Pentecostal Movements* (Franklin Springs, GA: Advocate Press, 1981), 70–71. Rollins, *Forward, Ever Forward,* 113–14; Synan, *Old-Time Power,* 147–50; Beacham, *A Brief History of the Pentecostal Holiness Church,* 64–67.

67. Morris, *The Vine and The Branches John 15:5,* 71; Synan, *The Old-Time Power,* 150–58; Beacham, *A Brief History of The Pentecostal Holiness Church,* 72–73.

68. Morris, *The Vine and The Branches John 15:5,* 72–73; Synan, *The Old-Time Power,* 205–25; Beacham, *A Brief History of The Pentecostal Holiness Church,* 87–100.

69. http://pfwb.org/history

70. Author unknown, *Pentecost Comes to the Free Will Baptist Church in North Carolina* (location of publication, press, date unknown), 28.

71. *Ibid.*, 28.

72. http://pfwb.org/history.

73. *Ibid.*, 2.

74. pfbc.org.

75. Op. cit., 2.

76. *Ibid.*, 3.

77. Henry L. Fisher, *The History of the United Holy Church of America, Inc.* (Durham, NC: 1945), 11.

78. William C. Turner, Jr., *The United Holy Church of America: A Study in Black Holiness-Pentecostalism* (Piscataway, NJ: Gorgias Press LLC, 2014), 20.

79. *Ibid.*, 21.

80. *Ibid.*, 21.

81. Fisher, *The History of the United Holy Church of America, Inc.*, 11.

82. *Ibid.*, 11.

83. *Ibid.*, 8.

84. *Ibid.*, 8–9.

85. *Ibid.*, 12–13.

86. Turner, *The United Holy Church of America: A Study of Black Holiness-Pentecostalism*, 51.

87. uhcainc.org.

88. Spurling, *The Lost Link* (Cleveland, TN: White Wing Publishing House, 1920), 36–37.

89. *Ibid.*, 45.

90. Wade H. Phillips, *Quest to Restore God's House: A Theological History of the Church of God, Volume 1* (Cleveland, TN: CPT Press, 2014), 64; Charles W. Conn, *Like A Mighty Army: A History of the Church of God 1886–1996* (Cleveland, TN: Pathway Press, 2008), 12–14; C.T. Davidson, *Upon This Rock* (Cleveland, TN: White Wing Publishing House and Press, 1973), 292–94.

91. Phillips, *Quest to Restore God's House*, 152–56; Conn, *Like A Mighty Army*, 53–54; Davidson, *Upon This Rock*, 294–98.

92. Phillips, *Quest to Restore God's House*, 210–12; Conn, *Like A Mighty Army*, 59–62; Davidson, *Upon This Rock*, 312–16.

93. Phillips, *Quest to Restore God's House*, 578–612; Conn, *Like A Mighty Army*, 211–24.

94. Conn, *Like A Mighty Army*, 221–31.

95. Davidson, *Upon This Rock*, 638–43.

96. 96. Stanley M. Burgess, et al., *Dictionary of Pentecostal and Charismatic Movements* (Grand Rapids, MI: Zondervan, 1988 and 2002).

Judaism

JAMES INGRAM MARTIN, SR.

Branches of Judaism

The majority of North Carolina congregations identify as Reform, the most inclusive branch of Judaism. Reform was frequently associated with German-speaking immigrants of the nineteenth century; its leading rabbis included Isaac Mayer Wise (1819–1900) and Stephen Wise (1874–1949). During the nineteenth century, Reform Jews began creating an Americanized form of religion, one that included some "church-like" elements, such as pews with mixed seating, Sunday school, and organ music. Contemporary Reform congregations embrace interfaith couples and some Reform rabbis will perform interfaith marriages.

Social justice and minority rights receive much attention in Reform circles. Most female rabbis adhere to the Reform persuasion, and one's Jewish identity can be derived from the matrilineal line, patrilineal line, or conversion from other faiths. In part because of the "pork infested" south, Reform Jews often do not maintain a kosher household.

Conservative Jews, despite the appellation, occupy the "middle ground." Formal Conservative Judaism traces its origins to Solomon Schechter (1847–1915), who sought to bring order to what he considered to be the increasingly secular and amorphous nature of the Reform movement. Adherents of Conservative Judaism consider the *Torah* and *Talmud* "divinely inspired" but believe that there is a human undercurrent contained in the Scriptures, one that lends itself to "biblical criticism." Conservative rabbis must refrain from performing interfaith marriage. One's matrilineal line provides for the Jewish identity. Conservative Jews frequently embrace kosher dietary law (e.g., prohibiting the mixing of meat and milk).

Orthodox Judaism represents the original faith, one bound by the inerrant *Torah* and its contents. Only a few Orthodox women have been able to obtain ordination. The Lubavitcher movement is a visible branch of Orthodox Judaism, with Chabad centers in Asheville, Cary, Charlotte, Chapel Hill, Elon, Greensboro, Raleigh and Wilmington.

Reconstructionist Judaism traces its origins to Mordecai Kaplan (1881–1983), who de-emphasized the religious components of Judaism and focused more on the integration of the individual into the more secular components of the Jewish community (according to the Jewish Virtual Library, www.jewishvirtuallibrary.org).

Beginnings

New Hanover County—North Carolina's First Jewish Community

The history of Jews in North Carolina can be traced back to Joachim Gans of Prague, a mining and smelting expert who participated in Ralph Lane's 1585 voyage to Roanoke Island. Some historians also contend that Jewish settlers may have migrated to the lower Cape Fear region during the seventeenth century.[1] For all intents and purposes, however, significant numbers of Jews did not reside in the state until the eighteenth century, and then, as now, their most substantial Eastern North Carolina community was the port city, and thus mercantile center, of Wilmington. Records from the 1730s cite Philip David, a carpenter who apparently converted to Christianity before his death. His son David, a member of Wilmington's Merrick Militia, apparently followed his father's example, worshipping at St. James Anglican (now Episcopal) Church and marrying his two daughters to Gentiles.[2] Other Jews included Moses and Esther Gomez, relatives of the Newport, Rhode Island, shipping magnate Aaron Lopez, and like most eighteenth-century American Jews, of Sephardic extraction. Moses' son A.L. served as one of the initiators of the Bank of the Cape Fear while his contemporaries Jacob Levy (an auctioneer) and Abraham Isaacs were active members of Wilmington's St. John's Masonic Lodge. Philip Benjamin, Aaron Gomez, Abraham Isaacs, Aaron Lazarus and J.M. Levy claimed membership in the St. Tammany Lodge.[3] This propensity for civic involvement would characterize the Jewish community down to the present day, as contributing to one's community proved economically and socially beneficial for all the parties involved.

A prominent Wilmington Jewish family of the nineteenth century was that of Philip Benjamin, whose son, Judah Benjamin (1811–1884), served as a U.S. Senator and Secretary of State for the Confederacy. Born in St. Croix, West Indies, Judah Benjamin lived in both Wilmington and Fayetteville as a youngster; his itinerant father, though ostensibly a merchant, was a frustrated musician whose wanderings took the family to a variety of locations.[4] Other Wilmington Jews from the early nineteenth century included Aaron Rivera, who expanded the facilities of the Bank of the Cape Fear in Wilmington and Raleigh, and his contemporary Aaron Lazarus, who was associated with the same financial institution, plus the Wilmington and Weldon Railroad.[5]

Jews worshipped at St. James Episcopal Church on a regular basis; special occasions, however, led them to travel to Charleston, South Carolina, or Northern locations.[6] Given this situation, Wilmington Jews took steps during the years 1867 through 1875 to establish a *bona fide* synagogue. The first synagogue in Wilmington, Orthodox in inclination, was a rented red brick building with Nathaniel Jacobi as president.[7] This initial congregation disintegrated and in 1872, Conservative Rabbi Maurice Jastrow initiated the Mishkan Israel (Temple of Israel) congregation.[8] Thanks to the fundraising efforts of Jastrow and the [Jewish] Ladies Concordia Society, Temple of Israel was finally completed at the corner of Fourth and Market Streets during the period of 1875 through 1876, and Lithuanian-born, German-speaking Samuel Mendelsohn of Norfolk, Virginia, served as the first rabbi from 1875 through 1921.[9] Temple Israel, with its German Jewish members, eventually embraced the nascent Reform movement in 1878 and today continues its affiliation with the Union for Reform Judaism.[10] Once again illustrating the ambivalent position of North Carolina Jews, Rabbi Mendelssohn, who in 1883 received an honorary doctor of laws degree, encouraged interfaith cooperation and even, after the Front Street Methodist Church experienced a fire in 1886, for two years accommodated its congregation in the Temple.[11] Commensurate with the Temple's creation were the Harmony Circle (1867) and B'nai B'rith Lodge (1875); social interaction also entailed intermingling and, it was hoped, marriage between Wilmington Jews and their Northern counterparts.[12]

After 1880, Wilmington, like many parts of the South, experienced some influx of Eastern European Jews from northern climes.[13] From the beginning, tensions existed between the "Americanized" German Jews and the "traditionalist" and often impoverished newcomers. Given this situation, Eastern European Jews opened their shops north of the downtown centers of German Jewish commerce. Fourth Street, for example, constituted a popular Eastern European venue.[14] Eastern European merchants catered to a blue-collar white and African American clientele that was denied entrance to more established stores; names of significant owners include the Lithuanian Abe and Jake D'Lugin (clothing) and Leonard Schwartz (furniture).[15] The Eastern European Jews, more traditional than their Americanized German Reform counterparts, established the B'nai Israel society in 1898; the group convened in members' stores, and in 1914 constructed, with the encouragement of their Reform brethren, the Orthodox (later Conservative) B'nai Israel synagogue.[16] In 1954, under the leadership of Rabbi Samuel Friedman, B'nai Israel moved from downtown Wilmington to its present Chestnut Street location.[17] In 1958, Friedman was active in the integrationist Wilmington and New Hanover Community Council. His involvement could be related to a bombing B'nai Israel experienced in that year.[18]

Both Temple of Israel and B'nai Israel, it should be mentioned, included congregants from outside Wilmington; individuals from such locations as Burgaw, Elizabethtown, Jacksonville, Tabor City, Wallace, Warsaw, and Whiteville retained memberships at one of the two houses of worship.[19]

Reflective also of Jewish civic concern was Temple of Israel's Rabbi Mordecai Thurman, who for nine years preached at African American churches during the last Sunday of January and helped foster a "pulpit exchange program" that included the First Baptist, Grace Methodist, St. James Episcopal and Temple of Israel congregations.[20] B'nai Israel's Robert Waxman was the first rabbi to serve as head of the Wilmington Ministerium.[21] Presently Wilmington's Market Street is home to a Chabad Center administered by Rabbi Moshe Lieblich and his wife Chana.[22]

Buncombe County

The history of the mountain Jewish community is largely that of Asheville and its environs. Asheville at one time possessed the largest Jewish community in the state, and the Jewish population (at approximately 2000 families out of a population of 70,000[23]) remains vibrant with two synagogues (Beth Ha-Tephila [Reform] and Congregation Beth Israel [formerly Bikur Cholim, Conservative]), and a Jewish Community Center. In 1982, the University of North Carolina at Asheville also introduced the Center for Jewish Studies.

In 1891, Congregation Beth Ha-Tephila, initially Conservative, was established. Included in the ranks were Solomon Lipinsky, G.H. Mayer, E. Sternberger, and Abraham Whitlock.[24] Beth Ha-Tephila affiliated with the Reform Union of American Hebrew Congregations in 1908.[25] In 1899, an Orthodox temple, Congregation Bikur Cholim (Visitation of the Sick), was created under the guidance of Solomon Harris Michalove, A. Shenbaum, J.B. Swartzberg, R.B. *Zageir*, and M. Zuglier. The first rabbi, a man named Louis Londow, operated a grocery store on the side. In 1949, Bikur Cholim affiliated with the United Synagogue of America (Conservatives) and changed its name to Beth Israel in 1950. This congregation occupied its present facility in 1969.[26]

Asheville is the smallest city in the nation to possess a Jewish Community Center. Frank Silverman and Julius Levitch founded the center in 1940 (ironically situated opposite William Dudley Pelley's anti–Semitic Silver Shirts League), and throughout its history the Center has served as a military canteen, Red Cross center, a day camp venue (complete with an outdoor swimming pool), Sunday School facility, ballroom, Boy Scouts meeting place, and music school.[27] Similar in purpose to the Jewish Community Center is the Chabad House of Asheville, which provides educational and recreational opportunities for Jews across the spectrum.[28]

Cabarrus County

In Concord, two Jewish merchants operated Koopman, Phelps and Company around 1860; in 1870, Julius Israel inaugurated a short-lived general store. Over a century later, under the leadership of Chicago native Dr. Barbara Shapiro Thiede, who taught religious studies at UNC–Charlotte, from 2003 onward Jews gathered informally as Havurat Olam, which eventually grew into Temple Or-Olam. Of particular note, perhaps reflective of the migration of younger Jews from the rural coastal plain to the more urban Piedmont, was the deeding of one of its *Torah* scrolls to Or-Olam by Temple Emanu-El of Weldon in Halifax County.[29]

Catawba County

Temple Beth Shalom, Hickory's congregation, traces its origins to a Sunday School conducted by Fannie Winters in the 1930s; Jewish children from Burke (Morganton), Caldwell (Lenoir), Catawba (Hickory, Newton), and McDowell (Marion) counties attended.[30] The Temple initially embraced Conservative Judaism but later migrated to Reform (1998).[31] Prior to 1959, Hickory Jews met in a number of venues, including the Old Moose Hall and Lenoir–Rhyne College, affiliated with the Lutherans; circuit-riding rabbi Harold Friedman also conducted services.[32] In 1959, ground was broken for the Hickory Jewish Center; among the founders were Mr. and Mrs. Kurt Berndt, Mr. and Mrs. Phil Datnoff, Mrs. Esther Greene, Mr. and Mrs. David Kraus, Mr. and Mrs. Sam Lavitt, Sigbert Loeb, David Witten, Mr. and Mrs. Marvin Zerden, and Mrs. Sayde B. Zerden.[33] During the 1960s, under the direction of Phil Datnoff, president of the North Carolina Association of Jewish Men, the congregation sponsored a Jewish Book Week at the Elbert Ivey Library; William Furie was one of the speakers.[34] The community dedicated its new Hickory Jewish Center in 1989.[35] It is noteworthy that Temple Beth Shalom has been served in its history by two student rabbis, Ellen Weinberg (1976) and Randy Fleisher (1998), who flew in from New York twice or once a month to conduct services.[36] The present bivocational rabbi, Dennis Jones, is a high school mathematics teacher pursuing rabbinical studies.[37]

Columbus County

The benevolence of Charlotte industrialist I.D. Blumenthal's circuit-riding rabbi program paved the way for the establishment of Beth Israel congregation in Whiteville. Inspired by Rabbi Harold Friedman, who conducted services from a bus, Jews from Elizabethtown, Loris, South Carolina, Tabor City, and Whiteville met in 1958 to formally establish the congregation.[38] Until 1959, Whiteville Jews had worshipped at Wilmington's B'nai Israel (Conservative) synagogue; in that year, the local Beth Israel Center was completed, eventually affiliating with the United Synagogue of America (Conservative).[39] Unlike so many small-town congregations, this one in Whiteville remained in existence, in part because of the concerted efforts of resident Jewish families to pass down religious traditions to their children. Sunday mornings have still found parents taking their sons and daughters to Wilmington for Sunday School instruction at B'nai Israel; when a rabbi was not available on the Sabbath at Beth Israel, the president of the congregation would conduct services.[40] As younger Jews in Whiteville, as in other locations, have migrated to urban areas, the numbers attending the Beth Israel have dwindled, but the congregation does retain its active status.[41]

Craven County

After the War between the States, the Jewish community of New Bern expanded significantly. Initially congregants met at the O. Marks Building on Middle Street.[42] The city witnessed the informal establishment of Temple Chester (named for twelve-year-old Chester Reizenstein[43]) B'nai Sholom in 1881; and in 1894, H. Dannenberg, Meyer Hahn, Oscar Marks, Charles Reizenstein, and Morris Sultan, along with Rabbi I. Kaiser, purchased land on Middle Street to build a synagogue. The edifice became a reality in 1908, and Harry Merfeld came as Rabbi in 1911. He would be Chester B'nai Sholom's only full-time rabbi in its history; student rabbis and later Kinston rabbis such as David Rose, Robert Shafran, and Jerome Tolochko filled the pulpit).[44] From its founding, B'nal Sholem identified with the Reform movement.[45]

New Bern's Jewish community dwindled considerably in the twentieth century, but an influx of Northerners revitalized the congregation in the 1980s.[46] Evidences of this revitalization included the inception of a Temple Constitution (1991), the establishment of the *Shofar* newsletter (1991), reopening of the religious school (1995), and the inauguration of a men's club (2003).[47]

Cumberland County

Fayetteville's Beth Israel synagogue traces its origins to 1910 when local Jewish families organized a congregation. It met in the McKeithan Building adjacent to the Market House. With major assistance from the Stein and Fleishman families, Beth Israel's Cool Spring Street synagogue was constructed in 1922. Initially Orthodox, Beth Israel did not hire its first full-time rabbi until 1943, when Charles Shoulson was called. Although a graduate of an Orthodox seminary, Rabbi Shoulson stressed modernity, broadening the community outreach of Beth Israel and delivering radio addresses on behalf of the Jewish community.[48]

World War II expanded Fort Bragg and thus Fayetteville's Jewish presence. The postwar boom brought additional Jews to the city, and in 1950 Beth Israel established a community center on Morganton Road, an edifice that eventually morphed into a new home for the synagogue and parsonage. With expansion came religious diversity, and in 1972 the formerly Orthodox Beth Israel became Conservative. However, it is not affiliated with the United Synagogue of Conservative Judaism and has members reflecting a broad spectrum of theological inclinations.[49] This change enhanced the role of women, and in 2014 Beth Israel hired Eve Eichenholtz, a Barnard College graduate, New York native, and former "American Bible Challenge" participant, as its first female rabbi.[50]

This present Fayetteville congregation includes a significant military component that fosters a geographically diverse population; outside of some senior members, most of the congregants hail from outside the South. The synagogue holds two services; Friday night's tend to be less formal than Saturday morning's. On Sunday mornings, Beth Israel conducts a religious school. The synagogue also engages in cooperative activities with the Jewish chaplaincy at Fort Bragg. In keeping with its Conservative tradition, Beth Israel maintains separate kitchens for meat and milk products. During 2016 and 2017, the congregation commemorated one hundred years of service to the Fayetteville community.[51]

Durham/Orange Counties

The history of Durham's Jewish community is intertwined with the Duke family's tobacco business. Pivotal in this regard was Ukrainian Jew Mose Gladstein, who brought Jewish cigarette rollers from New York to Durham in the early 1880s. The workers' involvement with labor organizing activity, however, led the Dukes to terminate the association by 1884. While most of Gladstein's compatriots returned to New York, he remained, joining the handful of Jewish merchants who already had opened stores in Durham.[52]

Durham's Conservative congregation Beth-El traces its origins to a Hebrew Burial Society which in 1884 secured part of what is now Maplewood Cemetery. In 1886, the city's Hebrew congregation, with Rabbi Myer Summerfield, came into being, occupying a building at 102 West Main Street. During the 1890s, the congregation established a Jewish Sunday school and in 1910 both a Hebrew school and English-language Sunday school. By 1904, the Jewish community had occupied a Christian church on Liberty Street; this edifice served the Jewish community until 1921. In that year, the congregation built a synagogue on Holloway Street with the new "Beth-El" appellative. In 1957, largely because of an influx of newcomers seeking employment at Duke, UNC, and Triangle manufacturers, Beth-El moved to its present location at Watts and Markham Streets, adjacent to Duke's East Campus. With this expansion, divisions occurred; Congregation Beth-El actually housed Conservative and Orthodox services, but each on separate floors. This diversity of belief also led to the creation of the Judea Reform congregation in 1961.[53]

The Judea Reform congregants, frequently "outsiders" from either the North or Europe, initially met in private homes; under the leadership of Rabbi Efraim Rosenzweig, members also convened at the Chapel Hill Friends Meeting House, Temple Baptist Church, Chapel Hill Community Church, and Duke University's York Chapel. The congregation erected its initial building on West Cornwallis Road in 1971. New additions came in 1977, and Judea Reform is now part of a complex that includes the Lerner Jewish

Day School (1995) and Levin Jewish Community Center (2009). The latter houses the Durham–Chapel Hill Jewish Federation founded in 1977.[54]

In 1996, the Reconstructionist Chapel Hill *Kehillah* (community) was established, and in 2001 the Kehillah opened a synagogue on Mason Farm Road. There is also a Kehillah cemetery at Markham Gardens on Farrington Road near the Durham/Chapel Hill border. Beginning in 1998, the Lubavitcher branch of Judaism established Chabads in Durham and Chapel Hill.[55]

Ironically, while James B. Duke expelled some of Durham's first Jews, his university, along with UNC, brought Jews back. UNC established its Reform-oriented Hillel chapter in 1936, and Hillel acquired its own house in 1951. Duke constructed its Freeman Center for Jewish Life (1999), and in 2003, UNC established the Carolina Center for Jewish Studies. Further evidence of the Jewish community's increased prominence includes the election of Emanuel J. (Mutt) Evans, who served as Durham's mayor from 1951 to 1963. Kenneth Broun, a UNC law professor, was Chapel Hill's mayor from 1991 to 1995.[56]

Edgecombe County

Part of Tarboro's Main Street became known in the 1870s as "Little Jerusalem" because of the proliferation of Jewish shops and residences owned by German-Jewish families with names like Abrams, Arnheim, Feldenheimer, Florsheim, Heilbroner, Jacobs, Kreslowski, Lipinsky, Morris, Rosenthal, and Zander.[57] Later, in the 1880s and 1890s, Eastern European Jewish families with names like Adler, Cohen, Kaufman, Liechtenstein, Levy, Meyers, Rosenbaum, Rosenbloom, and Shugar came to Tarboro. They intermingled with the already established population and contributed to the organization in 1877— and construction in 1895—of the B'nai Israel synagogue (now a Christian Church).[58] By 1900, some Tarboro Jews occupied mansions along Main Street.[59] After World War I, many Jewish families moved to larger towns, and others converted to Christianity.[60]

Forsyth County

Winston-Salem's Jews organized Beth Jacob in 1888; Beth Jacob proved ephemeral, however, and it was not until 1912 that the Winston-Salem Hebrew Congregation came into existence. After meeting in makeshift quarters, the Hebrew Congregation purchased the former First Christian Church at 660 Fourth Street and employed Rabbi P. Berlin.[61]

As Winston-Salem Jews achieved social mobility, they sought to modify Orthodox traditions; in 1932 a Reform contingent, under Meyer Simon, in tandem with the Orthodox faction, began holding services at the Fourth Street synagogue. This arrangement lasted only two years; in 1934, the Reform adherents began meeting in a store and eventually created Temple Emanuel. After meeting in various facilities including the First National Bank at 219 W. Fifth Street, Odd Fellows Hall, and a Greek Orthodox Temple, in May 1952 Temple Emanuel obtained its own building in southwest Winston-Salem on Oakwood Drive. In response to the postwar expansion of Forsyth County's Jewish community, in 1972 Temple Emanuel added an education wing. In 2002, under the leadership of Rabbi Mark Strauss-Cohn, Temple Emanuel completed a new synagogue building, but continues to employ the 1952 and 1972 structure for administrative and educational purposes.[62]

In contrast to Temple Emanuel, Beth Jacob, the original congregation that eventually became part of the Conservative United Synagogue of America, saw its numbers decline. It occupied its Fourth Street location until 1961 when the congregants moved to a house that had been owned by the United Church of Christ at 1833 W. Academy Street.[63] By the 1980s, Beth Jacob was ceasing to exist and formally closed in 1990.[64]

Gaston County

Before the inception of Gastonia's Temple Emanuel, the city's Jews would either attend service in Charlotte, gather in each other's homes, or occupy a variety of buildings.[65] In 1913, the Hebrew Congregation of Gastonia (Orthodox) came into being, but with no permanent facility.[66] It would be David and Lena Lebovitz, along with Harry Schneider, who proved instrumental in the founding of Gastonia's Temple Emanuel, a Greek revival facility designed by Hugh White. It first held services on January 1, 1929. After closing because of the ravages of the Great Depression, the Temple, under the leadership of Clarence Ross, re-opened in 1933, but with an increasingly Reform tendency.[67] The Temple's fortunes have waxed and waned. In 1958 for example, police intercepted thirty sticks of ignited dynamite on the congregation's front steps, but as of 2010, Temple Emanuel enrolled seventy-two families, some of whom traveled from as far away as Huntersville to attend services.[68] In the absence of a full-time rabbi, psychologist Dr. Charles Brown served as cantor.[69]

Guilford County

Greensboro, the "gate city," textile capital, and center of higher education, has embraced its Jewish community from the nineteenth century onward. Two vibrant congregations, Temple Emanuel (Reform) and Beth David (Conservative), claim substantial memberships. There is also a Chabad in the city. The congregations trace their origins to gatherings on South Elm Street, with families like the Cones, Schiffmans, and Sternbergers playing an active role in religious education. It was these families, along with those of Max Block and Isaac Isaacson, who in 1908 purchased a Quaker meetinghouse at 115 Lee Street, and named it the Greensboro Hebrew Congregation. In 1910, the Jewish community purchased a 9.5-acre cemetery tract on what had been the "Gorell Property" on High Point Road, and by 1914 the Greensboro Hebrew Congregation had claimed affiliation with the Union of American Hebrew Congregations (Reform). The identification with the Reform movement created fissures, but both Reform and Orthodox Jews simply worshipped at the Hebrew Congregation at different times. In 1925, the Greensboro Hebrew Congregation, which counted among its founders Woman's College Professor Etta Spier, dedicated a newly constructed facility on Greene Street.[70]

With his arrival in 1931, Rabbi Frederick Rypins and his North Carolina–born wife Ruth Roth brought tremendous vitality to the Greensboro Hebrew Congregation. Greensboro's non–Jewish elite embraced this Nebraska native and World War I Marine; he even received an invitation to join the Greensboro Country Club. Rabbi Rypins also served as president of the Greensboro Ministerium. He promoted social justice, whether it involved sheltering and educating refugees from Hitler, buying war bonds, Zionism, or standing up for African Americans in the Jim Crow South.[71] Of particular note was his inaugurating religious schools for Jews in Albemarle, High Point, Henderson, and Tarboro.[72]

During the early 1940s, some members of the Greensboro Hebrew Congregation left to form the Beth David Synagogue (Conservative); this house of worship derived its name from Meyer David Stadiem. Initially meeting at the Market Street Masonic Temple, the congregants in 1947 constructed a new synagogue on East Lake Drive in the Lake Daniel neighborhood and in 1969 established a religious school at the Kagan Building on Winview Drive in Hamilton Forest. Eventually Beth David would open a new sanctuary building in 1982 at the same location.[73]

In 1949, the Hebrew Congregation, now exclusively Reform in membership, changed its appellative to Temple Emanuel, namesake of industrialist Emanuel Sternberger. By 2003, Temple Emanuel had relocated to Jefferson Road in northwest Greensboro.[74]

Beth David also constructed a new facility on the north side of town on Winview Drive and Jewish families organized the B'nai Shalom Day School there. Thanks largely to the efforts of Zmira and Maurice Sabbah, the American Hebrew Academy came into being in 2001.[75]

High Point, "furniture capital of the world," also embraced a number of Jewish families. Peddlers Louis and Henry Harris came from Russia to High Point around 1888; they operated a men's clothing store, and Louis was a member of the first fire department.[76] In 1927, at a cost of twenty thousand dollars, High Point Jews constructed the original B'nai Israel synagogue on Hamilton Street with the venerable Rev. Elias B. Ershler as rabbi.[77] Under the leadership of Rabbi William Gold, an education center was built in 1952.[78] The congregation, shifting from Orthodox to Conservatism with Conservative and Reconstructionist interludes, moved to a location on Kensington Road in 1965[79] but has experienced a declining membership in recent years. It now identifies with the Union for Reform Judaism.[80] High Point was also North Carolina's site of the first Jewish Debutante Cotillion, a social alternative to the more prominent "Christian only" affairs.[81] Today there is a Chabad Jewish Center in Greensboro and a Chabad chapter at nearby Elon University.[82]

Halifax County

Roanoke Rapids/Weldon, in Halifax County, might have seemed an incongruous place to have a Jewish community, until one considers its location at the intersection of U.S. Highways 158 and 301 as well as that of the Seaboard Airline and Atlantic Coastline Railroads.[83] Weldon's congregation owes much to Henry Farber, a Lithuanian emigrant who like so many came to North Carolina by way of Baltimore.[84] Weldon's Jews organized an Orthodox congregation in 1912; after meeting in private homes and Silvester's Department Store as the Jewish Community Center, the congregation, which by 1939 had begun to invite Conservative rabbis, bought a house on Eighth Street and converted it to a synagogue in 1954 at the cost of thirty-three thousand dollars.[85] The synagogue adopted the name Emanu-El and affiliated with the United Synagogue of America (Conservative).[86] Members included the Halifax County families of Freid, Greenberg, Josephson, Kittner, Liverman, Marks, Samet, and Silvester (Fannye Marks, Marcella Liverman, and Robert Liverman ran an upscale boutique in Roanoke Rapids) as well as the Blooms of Emporia, Virginia.[87] Congregants from Enfield, Scotland Neck, Warrenton, and Lawrenceville, Virginia, also participated in services.[88] Marilyn Levy of Roanoke Rapids held the distinction of being the first female confirmed Bat Mitzvah at Emanu-El; she was confirmed by Dr. William Lurie.[89] In 1976, Emanu-El joined the Union of American Hebrew Congregations

(Reform).[90] Reform rabbinical students, including Rabbi Amy Scheinerman, served the Weldon congregation on a monthly basis during the 1970s and 1980s, but after 1993, no more came; leadership fell to the laity.[91] With the deaths and migration of many of its established members, in 2000 the congregation decided to disband, in the process distributing its Judaica to North Carolina congregations in Chapel Hill and Concord as well as ones in Norfolk and Virginia Beach.[92] In 2006, an African American congregation purchased Emanu-El.[93]

Henderson County

Hendersonville's Agudas Israel Congregation traces its origins to 1922, when twenty-seven members of the Jewish community met to form a synagogue. The first building, occupied in 1925 on King Street, had been an electric company facility that was remodeled in 1964.[94] Early rabbis included Orthodox Chaim Williamowsky (1925–1930) and Beryl Cohen (1930–1964).[95] Some rabbis and laity summering in Hendersonville conducted services from time to time. These included civil rights activist Charles Mantinband of Hattiesburg, Mississippi, who spent three summers in Hendersonville, and Mordecai Kaplan. Author Sholom Ash led prayers at Agudas Israel during the High Holidays. During the 1950s, Harold Friedman, the "circuit-riding rabbi," included Agudas Israel in his route, and Rabbi Samuel Friedman of the Congregation Beth Israel in Asheville held services at the Hendersonville synagogue. For one year, Rabbi David Zalonka of Gastonia, North Carolina, commuted to Agudas Israel to administer High Holiday services.[96]

The late 1950s and 1960s marked the high point of youth involvement in the Agudas Israel synagogue. In 1954, the Congregation bought a residence with 3.5 acres at the intersection of Sixth Avenue and Oak Street, and in 1964 sold the plot to the YMCA, garnering enough resources to expand and modernize the King Street synagogue. The congregation, which had moved increasingly from Orthodox to Conservative to Reform since its founding, affiliated with the Union of American Hebrew Congregations in 1996.[97]

Since the 1960s the number of young people in Agudas Israel has declined substantially, a phenomenon characteristic of practically all small towns in North Carolina—and to some degree a sacrifice reflective of the children's upward mobility. In recent years, the Jewish community of Hendersonville has increased largely because of the influx of baby-boomers and retirees from a variety of locations; Agudas Israel now ministers to 150 members.[98]

In 2000, the congregation decided to construct a new facility at 505 Glasgow Lane in Laurel Park, immediately west of Hendersonville. Burton Greenberg, a New York native who came to Hendersonville by way of Florida, headed the Building Committee and arranged to have five acres purchased. The process of construction took fifteen months. The synagogue now consists of 9000 square feet, including a 180-person sanctuary, rabbi's office, business office, 200-person fellowship hall, kitchen, pantry, storage room, boardroom, two restrooms, a foyer, and a parking lot.[99] The library contains a substantial collection of books, Judaica, a display cabinet of memorabilia, a computer, artwork, magazines, and furniture. The synagogue also contains a *yahrzeit,* or memorial hall, a parlor, air-conditioning/heating units, and a mechanical room.[100] A serpentine wall that can also be used as a bench graces the outside with the names of donors to the building project. Plans call for a terraced back area and a place for a Succoth.[101] In 2005, Philip Bentley became Agudas Israel's first full-time rabbi since 1930.[102]

A substantial number of Christians donated to this new facility's construction, and both the Rev. Alexander Viola of St. James Episcopal Church and the Rev. David Kelly of the First Congregational Church participated in the Temple's dedication on May 17, 2002, when, in Morris Kaplan's words, "the sacred dream of a new synagogue was met."[103]

Iredell County

Isaac Wallace, a herbologist, proved instrumental in the establishment of a States-ville's Reform Congregation Emanuel. At his home in 1883, fifteen families, mostly of German extraction, organized the congregation, and in 1892 a permanent building at Kelly Street and West End Avenue, valued between four and five thousand dollars, was completed. It was closed around 1920, but in 1954 was renewed as a Conservative body; this revitalization came in response to industrial expansion, which brought in a small number of Jews from other locations.[104] These included new residents Joseph and Sally Jay (blouse manufacturing), Max and Florence Lerner (haberdashery in Taylorsville) and Isadore and Albert Schneider (Taylorsville textile plant).[105] I.D. Blumenthal of the circuit-riding rabbi program provided funding.[106] From the 1950s through the 1980s the congregation functioned well but declined after this period due to Jewish outmigration and the establishment of congregations at nearby Lake Norman.[107]

Lenoir County

Kinston's Jewish community in 1903 founded Congregation Tifereth Israel, which was served by Rabbi Hyman Goodkowitz, father of Rabbi Alexander Goode of the ill-fated World War II *Dorchester* battleship.[108] In 1924, the congregation acquired the Second Methodist Church building.[109] Under Rabbi Jerome Tolochoko, Tilfereth Israel would morph into the Temple Israel Reform congregation, affiliating with Union of American Hebrew Congregations in 1952 and constructing a Vernon Avenue facility in 1954. The rabbi also ministered at Cherry Point Marine Air Station, modernized the temple's sound system, and had a "Chanakuh man" deliver presents to the congregants.[110] The synagogue employed a full-time rabbi until 2002.[111]

Macon County

Franklin's Mountain Synagogue is located approximately sixty miles southwest of Asheville; its 1979 beginnings can be traced to retirees, many from the North, who were seeking Jewish fellowship in the mountains of western North Carolina.[112] The congregation, unaffiliated with any formal branch of Judaism, does not possess a formal building but meets at St. Cyprian's Episcopal Church.[113]

Mecklenburg County

Early Jews who settled in Charlotte were frequently of German extraction and thus of the Reform persuasion; it was they who established the first Hebrew Congregation. After the organization of the Cemetery Society (1867), Hebrew Benevolent Society (1870) and Ladies Benevolent Society (1874), these individuals established Temple Israel in 1895. Orthodox Eastern European Jews established Shaarey Israel in 1916.[114] The Jewish Federation of Greater Charlotte came into being in 1939, largely in order to provide assistance to Jewish refugees from Nazism.[115] From Temple Israel in 1942 came Temple Beth El; the new congregation, under the direction of Rabbi Philip Frankel, met initially above a grocery store but in 1949 relocated to 1272 Providence Road.[116] In 1970, approximately twenty Beth El families created Congregation Beth Shalom, but its existence proved short-lived; the two congregations reunited in 1987.[117] Orthodox Shaarey Israel, for its part, became Conservative and occupied a new facility in 1949.[118] The Amity Club, created in part because some Charlotte Country Clubs did not accept Jews, became a community center that same year.[119]

Shalom Park, created in 1986, represents a unique phenomenon of inclusion in the American South. The Providence Road location features Temple Beth El (Reform—constructed in 1992), Temple Israel (Conservative), the Levine-Sklut Judaic Library, and the Jewish Community Center.[120]

Orthodox Charlotteans meet at a Lubavitch congregation, Ohr HaTorah, founded in 1980. Lubavitch Rabbi Yossi Groner came to Charlotte in that year, and Charlotte remains the state headquarters for the Lubavitch movement.[121]

Moore County

Reform Temple Beth Shalom (2002) is located in Foxfire Village and traces its roots to the Sandhills Jewish Cultural Group (1981).[122] In 2001, the congregation called Rabbi Floyd Herman and in 2011 Rabbi Kenneth Brickman to lead monthly Shabbat services.[123]

Nash County

Rocky Mount at one time possessed an influential Jewish population. During the 1920s, the Jewish families included the Bakers, Breens, Epsteins, Hoffmans, Levins, Levys, *Shermans, and* Silvermans; these individuals had formed their own Reform congregation, Beth-El.[124] After occupying space in the Kyser Drug Store, Bulluck Auto Sales, and the Masonic Temple, Beth-El acquired its own facility in 1949, peaked in membership with full-time rabbi Israel Sarasohn during the 1960s, and then descended to a period of decline. The congregation does, however, continue to hold services.[125]

Onslow County

Jacksonville, North Carolina, had a Jewish community tied in with Camp Lejeune Marine Base. While a Jewish chapel was established on post in 1948, it was not until 1955, largely through the influence of circuit-riding rabbi Harold Friedman, that the Jacksonville Hebrew Congregation called Temple B'nai Mordecai came into existence. Names of the original congregants included Adler, Feldstein, Fleishman, Gould, Kalet, Katzin, Leder, Margolis, Messenger, Peck, Popkin, Schwartz, Segerman, Suls, Trachtenberg, and Turem. Jack Peck, who served as the first president, was involved in the bakery and restaurant business as well as a variety of civic organizations; the congregation met initially at his bakery and later at Leder Department Store and the Katzin Building. B'nai Mordecai constructed its own building around 1957.[126] One of the congregants, Trenton, New Jersey, native Jerry Popkin engaged in furniture stores, battery sales and radio (WLAS). He served in the North Carolina State Senate during the mid–1970s and is the namesake of the New River's Jerry Popkin Bridge.[127] In 1950, Julius and Rosalind Leder Segerman came to Jacksonville where they established the Jacksonville Department Store; the Segerman Health Center stands as their legacy.[128]

Pitt County

During the early years of the twentieth century, Greenville's Jewish community included Eli Bloom, a lawyer and later district attorney, his wife, Etta, a dressmaker, and the Brody mercantile family.[129] Charles Baker ran a shoe-repair business.[130] In 1936, Morris Brody of Kinston established a women's store in Kinston; his sister Ruth kept it afloat during World War II.[131] Eventually the Brodys would own stores in Greenville, Kinston, Rocky Mount, Goldsboro and New Bern.[132]

World War II, and more significantly, the growth of East Carolina Teachers College into East Carolina University, added more Jews to Greenville's population. Bayt Shalom, a Conservative synagogue with some Reform leanings, has been in existence since 1976 and had a membership drawn largely from Northern transplants such as industrialist Joe Gantz and his wife, artist Paula Blumenfeld, who were lured south by Greenville's industrial, educational, and medical facilities.[133] The congregation met informally in homes and the First Presbyterian Church until 1993 when the members converted a large residence on Tenth Street east of the city into a formal synagogue.[134] From 1989 to 2007, Rabbi Michael Cain served the congregation, and in 2009 Bayt Shalom had the distinction of having employed Judaism's first female African American rabbi, Alysa Stanton.[135] As of 2015, Virginia native Rabbi Nicole Luna serves Bayt Shalom; outside of Wilmington, she is the only full-time rabbi in eastern North Carolina.[136] Given the opportunities presented by the augmentation of the East Carolina Medical School, largely underwritten by millions from the Brodys, the Jewish community of Pitt County will undoubtedly continue to expand.[137]

Of particular note was Greenville resident Albert Silverman. A rabbi with twenty-two years of experience at a thousand-family congregation in New York, Silverman also graduated from Hofstra University School of Law and came to Greenville when his spouse took a position at the Brody School of Medicine. His desire was to teach law, but when ECU did not present that opportunity, Silverman took on a three-point rabbinate of Rocky Mount, Weldon, and Wilson. Amalgamating the roles of attorney and clergyman, he proved a vocal proponent of social justice.[138]

Robeson County

The Jewish community of Robeson County proved influential. The Moses Fine family, from Poland, resided in Maxton around 1900.[139] In Lumberton, the Weinsteins were probably the most prominent Jews. Aaron Weinstein, originally Dizin, born in 1872 in Keidan, Lithuania, came to the United States in 1893.[140] He originally settled in Baltimore, Maryland, and reached North Carolina after peddling his wares in New York, Louisiana, Maryland, Kentucky, Mississippi, Tennessee, and West Virginia.[141] Following stints in Gastonia and Gibsonville, Aaron arrived in Lumberton in 1897, opened a store, and, reflecting his family's agricultural heritage as cattle dealers, acquired tobacco and vegetable farms[142]; he joined other Jewish families with names like Blacker, Dunie, Fleishman, Levinson, Margolis, Schwartzenberg, Shain, Shocket and Sugar, in establishing a worship center that evolved into the Conservative Beth-El synagogue, now Trinity Baptist Church on Water Street, in 1955.[143] Harry Levinson came from Manning, South Carolina, and established a store in Fairmont.

It is interesting to note that the Jewish community's progressive contribution to Robeson County was exemplified when on October 17, 2003, Temple Beth-El, which had ceased holding services, willed its remaining funds to the University of North Carolina at Pembroke for the purpose of setting up an annual speaker series "to promote racial and cultural harmony."[144] Similarly, the congregation donated its *bimah* chairs, *menorahs,* and reading desk to the Chapel Hill Kehillah in 2001.[145]

Rowan County

During the 1940s, the growing Salisbury Jewish community sought a permanent meeting place. Phil Levenson, a shoe entrepreneur, inaugurated a Sunday School. In 1944, thirteen of the area's families inaugurated Temple Israel Congregation. Reform Rabbi Philip Frankel led the first services, succeeded by Conservative Rabbi Harry Feit. Temple Israel's permanent home was dedicated in 1953, and it remains a Conservative congregation. The keynote speaker was Judge Hubert Olive, a Southern Baptist. Other speakers included Charlotte Jewish leaders Morris Speizman and Harry Golden.[146] In 1972 the Temple added an education wing.[147] During the 1970s, through the cooperative efforts of the Hickory, Salisbury, and Statesville congregations, a chapter of the B'nai B'rith Youth Organization came into being. Temple Israel offered instruction in Hebrew to Salisbury's Jewish children, and merchant Ben Shapiro bar mitzvahed and bat mitzvahed 39 individuals. Unfortunately, Salisbury's Jewish business community declined after the 1970s; by 1990 the Jewish stores had largely disappeared. The resulting decline in membership has led the Temple to offer its space to a Baptist church.[148] Since 1990, Dr. Andrew Ettin, a Wake Forest University English professor, has served as a part-time rabbi for Temple Israel.[149]

Salisbury was the residence of William B. Furie, a Conservative "circuit-riding rabbi" who had served as a military chaplain at Fort Devens, Massachusetts, and as an educational administrator in Massachusetts, Ohio, and Wisconsin. He held three degrees from Boston University, including a Ph.D., and had been employed as a Hebrew instructor at the University of Wisconsin. Rabbi Furie also coordinated the Milwaukee Bureau of Jewish Education.[150] During the mid–1960s in North Carolina, he was traveling via station wagon an average of 1,500 miles weekly to minister to Conservative congregations, which at the time formed a minority of this state's synagogues. Dr. Furie's duties even included teaching Hebrew at Catawba (United Church of Christ), Lenior–Rhyne (Lutheran), and Wake Forest (Baptist) Colleges.[151] He also conducted Passover services at Methodist Pfeiffer College, where his son attended.[152] He later relocated to Baltimore, from whence he had come to North Carolina, where he died in 1969.[153]

Transylvania County

Outside of industrialist Joseph Silversteen,[154] Brevard did not have any Jewish organization of substance until 2001 when Yankees Norman and Shelley Bossert arrived and advertised for a meeting of local Jews for *Torah* study. Initially, the group met in private homes, then on Friday nights in the social hall of Sacred Heart Catholic Church. In 2006, the group obtained a *Torah* from Atlanta and constructed an Ark to house it. Despite the congregation's eclectic Judaic backgrounds, the inclination of the Brevard study group, under the tutelage of Marvin Barg and Norman Bossert, has been Reform with some accommodation to Conservative members.[155]

Wake County

Raleigh's Jewish community had its origins in Warren County, where Jacob Mordecai established a school. His sons Moses and George Washington Mordecai emigrated to Raleigh, and eventually their progeny joined the Episcopal church. Around 1862, Warrenton residents Michael, a tailor, and Regina Grausman, immigrants from Bavaria, migrated to Raleigh. The Grausman residence served as the first house of worship for Raleigh's small Jewish populace. Then came Rosenbaum's Millinery Store on Fayetteville Street. The small congregation eventually disbanded after Michael Grausman's death in 1891, but the twentieth century, with its influx of Eastern European Jews, brought opportunities for revitalization. In 1912, the Hebrew Sunday School Association, later Raleigh Hebrew Congregation, came into being. The Raleigh Hebrew Cemetery was also established in 1912. It derived from a portion of Oakwood Cemetery owned by George Washington Mordecai. Bivocational rabbis ministered to the Raleigh Hebrew Congregation, which, divided by the ethnicity of German vs. Eastern European and religious beliefs of Reform vs. Orthodox, fractured in 1913. From this schism derived Temple Beth Or (Reform) and the House of Jacob (Orthodox).[156]

Temple Beth Or called Harry Nerfeld as its first rabbi, and in 1923 the congregation moved into its own building on Hillsborough Street; among the Gentiles contributing to the facility's construction were Episcopal bishop Joseph Cheshire and Governor O. Max Garner.[157] In 1948, Beth Or constructed a religious-school annex. Three decades later the congregation relocated to Creedmoor Road in northwest Raleigh, where Rabbi Lucy Dinner, a New Orleans native with degrees from UNC–Chapel Hill and Cincinnati's Hebrew Union College, has served the congregation since 1993. Beth Or retains an active religious school and counts in its membership a substantial number of interfaith families.[158]

In regard to the House of Jacob, the congregation originally identified with the Young Men's Hebrew Association. In 1923, the members secured a building on South East Street. The House of Jacob constructed a synagogue on West Johnson Street in 1951; also in that year, the congregation moved into the Conservative ranks and, in commemoration of member Meyer Dworsky, took on the "Beth Meyer" appellative. In 1985, Beth Meyer relocated to its Newton Road facility in North Raleigh. Rabbi Eric Solomon has served the congregation since 2005. He is a Columbia, Maryland, native with degrees from the University of Maryland and Hebrew Union College of New York, plus advanced studies at the Hebrew University of Jerusalem, Pardes Institute for Jewish Studies, and the Shalom Hartman Institute. The *News & Observer* in 2010 recognized him as a *Tar Heel of the Week,* largely because of his involvement with social justice movements. Beth Meyer includes the Kramer Religious School, the synagogue and a daycare and is affiliated with the United Synagogue of Conservative Judaism.[159]

Raleigh's Orthodox Jewish community gathers at Sha'arei Israel (founded in 1979) located on Falls of Neuse Road in North Raleigh. The congregation, which is affiliated with the Lubavitch Hasidim, sponsors a preschool open to children of all faiths and a religious school. Rabbi Pinchas Herman, a Pittsburgh native who completed his religious training at the Rabbinical College of America, has ministered to the congregation since 1989. He is also responsible for certifying kosher foods. The O-U *hechsher* is printed on many food containers; this symbol conveys the New York–based Orthodox Union approval. Adjacent to Sha'arei Israel is the Raleigh Chabad Center, which seeks to connect Jews of various convictions to the intensive study of the sacred texts.[160]

Since October 1983, Cary has hosted Beth Shalom Reform Congregation. Initially the group was known as the Cary Jewish Community Center and held services in a variety of churches. The congregation obtained an Ark in 1988 plus a *Torah* from Charlotte's Temple Israel. Eventually the congregation affiliated with the Union of American Hebrew Congregations and employed a student rabbi. In 2000, Beth Shalom occupied its present southern Wake facility on Yates Mill Road and in 2004 called Rabbi Ariel Edery, a native of Argentina with degrees from the Hebrew University of Jerusalem and the Hebrew Union College in Cincinnati, to be its spiritual leader. Rabbi Edery had previously conducted ministries in Mexico and Spain. Under his direction, the congregation opened a new sanctuary in 2014.[161] There is also a Chabad Center on Cary's Reedy Creek Road.[162]

Watauga County

Due to the appeal of mountains and of Appalachian State University, retirees and native New Yorkers (called "halfbacks" for leaving Florida and returning "halfway back" to the North Carolina mountains) have made Boone, North Carolina, a Jewish community of note in recent years. Thanks to the efforts of circuit-riding rabbis David Kraus, Sheldon Hanft, and Beryl Hanft, a Reform congregation was inaugurated in Boone in 1978; soon after, the congregation obtained a Czech *Torah* cradled in an ark constructed by Dr. Victor Hirsch. The congregation initially met at the Appalachian Wesley Foundation; then, until 2010, its domicile was St. Luke's Episcopal Church and St. Elizabeth Catholic Church.[163]

Also, at present, Appalachian has an active Hillel. The seminal event in the history of the Boone Jewish community has been the construction, through the generosity of Bonnie and Jamie Schaefer and Marvin Hamlisch, of the "Temple of the High Country."[164] One of the most active members is Chuck Lieberman, at one time president of the Association of Jewish Christmas Tree Growers.[165] Saul Chase, a teacher and principal, has served on the Boone Town Council.[166]

Wayne County

Jewish religious organizations in Goldsboro include an 1875 burial society, with members of the Ballenberger, Cohn, and Schultz families as trustees. Temple Oheb Sholom, or Lovers of Peace, was derived from a congregation in Baltimore with the same name and was completed in 1886. It was the second synagogue in North Carolina, with the Rev. Max Moses as rabbi and Adolph Lehman as president.[167] In 1890, Oheb Sholom affiliated with the Reform-based Union of American Hebrew Congregations.[168] Willowdale Cemetery in Goldsboro had a Jewish section by 1875, and there one finds such names as Blume, Levy, Pearl, Spier, and Mayerberg. Rabbi Julius Mayerberg served Oheb Sholom for thirty-four years and was instrumental in its move toward Reform.[169] Goldsboro Jewish veterans of World War I included Leonard Epstein, Edwin Joseph, Isaac Kadis, Morton Rosencower, Emil Rosenthal, Louis Sherman, Harry Shrago, and Jake Shrago.[170]

The Heilig and Meyers families, furniture magnates, were members of Oheb Sholom.[171] The Shrago family owned the land on which the Civil War Battle of Bentonville was fought in 1865.[172]

Wilson County

It was the Eastern European Jews in Wilson who founded the Orthodox Hebrew Mt. Zion congregation, which eventually morphed into Temple Beth-El. Included was Russian-born Morris Barker, a dry goods merchant who came to Wilson in 1907; he eventually established a dime store. Other Jewish entrepreneurs included Joe Barshay, a merchant of female apparel; Irving Mink, owner of Star Credit Store; Joe Strauss of the Jewel Box; and Minnie and Sidney Switzer, who sold women's and men's clothing. In 1953, Temple Beth-El obtained a permanent structure on Kenan Street and moved in a Reform direction. It closed in 1997 and now serves as a private residence.[173]

The Circuit-Riding Rabbi

Before closing this essay, it is fitting to discuss the phenomenon of the circuit-riding rabbi. As previously mentioned, Jewish communities outside of major cities were small and scattered; few congregations could support a full-time spiritual leader. During the 1890s, Rabbi Edward Calisch had traveled throughout North Carolina.[174] The 1920s saw Rabbi F.I. Rypins create religious schools in Albemarle, Henderson, High Point, and Tarboro.[175] Some precedent for the circuit-riding rabbi can be seen in the creation of "Jewish Circles" for Burgaw, Clinton, Wallace, and Warsaw by 1938 and in Fairmont, Tabor City, and Whiteville.[176] During the 1950s, industrialist I.D. Blumenthal of Charlotte, who made a fortune in "GUNK" radiator sealant, provided funding for mobile rabbis who, traveling either by bus or car, could minister to needs of residents in rural communities.[177] On March 27, 1955, a refurbished bus (the original plans had called for a car and trailer) was dedicated at Charlotte's Amity Country Club.[178] Initially the circuit included ten cities— Jacksonville, Wallace, Whiteville, Weldon–Roanoke Rapids, Lumberton, Mt. Gilead– Albemarle, Rock Hill (SC), Statesville, Hickory, and Hendersonville.[179] In terms of residents, additional North Carolina localities served during the period 1954–1971 included Ahoskie, Burgaw, Camp Lejeune/New River, Canton, Dunn, Elizabethtown, Enfield, Fairmont, Farmville, Goldsboro, Hamlet, Henderson, Jackson, Laurinburg, Lenoir, Lincolnton, Morganton, Pembroke, Pinetops, Raeford, Rockingham, Rutherfordton, Salisbury, St. Pauls, Scotland Neck, Sylva, Tabor City, Tarboro, Taylorsville, Valdese, Wadesboro, Warsaw, and Willard.[180] During the period April 24–28, 1955, Rabbi Friedman took the bus on a "goodwill tour" to Jacksonville, Wilmington, Fayetteville, Raleigh, Durham, Greensboro, High Point, Burlington, Salisbury, Statesville, Hendersonville, and Asheville.[181]

Rabbi Friedman, a Scranton, Pennsylvania, native based in Statesville, conducted the circuit from 1954 through 1956; Rabbi Eli Gottesman took Friedman's place from 1956 until 1958. Ralph Weisberger conducted services during the period September 1958 through August 1959. After a three-year hiatus (1959–1961), when the bus was parked in I.D. Blumenthal's lot, William Furie took up the mantle from 1962 to 1968; during this time the ministry was divided into North East, Piedmont, and South East circuits. The

North East and Piedmont circuits foundered, but Rabbi Reuben Kesner, based in Whiteville, continued his ministry in the South East circuit from 1964 through 1985, although his promotion of integration engendered controversy in his adopted town.[182]

Given the short tenures and modest compensation of most circuit-riding rabbis, the demands of the "bus ministry" must have proved daunting.[183] Rabbi Friedman at one time drove the fourteen-thousand-dollar bus a total of twelve hundred miles every two weeks to minister to three hundred families in ten communities, putting in eighteen-hour days.[184] In the words of Rabbi Israel Gerber :

> The bus was literally a synagogue and school on wheels. The carpeted and curtained chapel held ten upholstered chairs to accommodate a *minyan*. If a larger congregation was expected, however, the portable ark and prayerbooks could be carried to a home or other suitable accommodation. The classroom across the back of the bus was as compact as the cabin of a boat and just as complete. It held blackboards, maps, projector and screen, record player and a lending library. Equipped with heating and air-conditioning systems, the facility was operable year-round.[185]

The bus received national attention in *Life* on September 19, 1955; in *Congress Weekly* December 19, 1955; and in the *Jewish Times-Outlook*. It was the topic of an NBC radio broadcast called "Eternal Light" on September 30, 1956; and a CBS-TV program, "The American Jew," on December 7, 1958.[186]

Five years after its inception, the circuit-riding rabbi project was credited in part with the revitalization of Statesville's Temple Emanuel as well as initiating, in 1954 and 1960, the Hickory Jewish Center, Jacksonville's B'nai Mordecai, Lumberton's Temple Beth-El, Weldon's Temple Emanu-El, and Whiteville's Beth Israel.[187] While other factors entered into the picture, such that the 1950s marked the halcyon days of American religion, certainly the bus contributed to a resurgence of Jewish awareness on the part of its patrons.

Whiteville was the "home base" of Morris Reuben Kesner, the circuit-riding rabbi in the South East region for over two decades. A native of Worcester, Massachusetts, Kesner earned degrees from Clark University and the Jewish Theological Seminary of New York.[188] His practical experience included liturgical music, social work, religious education in Cleveland, Detroit, and Los Angeles as well as camp administration in Michigan.[189] He came to Whiteville by way of Chicago and was greatly appreciated during his tenure.[190] Rabbi Kesner became a fixture there, officiating at some Protestant weddings, producing a newspaper column, giving radio addresses, and serving as police chaplain with a Mogen David on his badge. He inaugurated, with a grant of five thousand dollars, the Columbus County Community Center for the area's youth.[191] His charge in 1964 was initially Wallace, Jacksonville, Lumberton, and Wallace; later he served Myrtle Beach, Greenville, and Goldsboro.[192] Concurrent with his circuit-riding capacity, Kesner assumed the position of rabbi at Temple Emanuel in Myrtle Beach; he remained in that position thirty-five years.[193]

A sample itinerary from an August 21, 1977, meeting of the South East Circuit Council of the North Carolina Association of Jewish Men shows Rabbi Reuben Kesner traveling to Wallace, Goldsboro, Whiteville, Lumberton, and Myrtle Beach; communities in the circuit would be assessed for the Rabbi's services.[194] Rabbi Kesner reportedly clocked one thousand miles per week in his Oldsmobile and served as President of the Whiteville Ministerium on two occasions.[195] Today, the circuits no longer exist; moreover, many small-town synagogues are having a difficult time surviving as a substantial number of their congregants have emigrated to larger climes or chosen to practice their faith in Raleigh, Wilmington, or Fayetteville.[196]

In the 1950s, Jewish organizations had included the following: North Carolina Association of Jewish Women, North Carolina Association of Jewish Men, North Carolina Association of Rabbis, North Carolina Association of Jewish Youth, and North Carolina Association of Young Adults. All are now defunct.[197]

Conclusion

From this study of the Jewish community of North Carolina, one can draw a number of conclusions. First, Jewish emigration to North Carolina reflected immigration to the United States as a whole, with the Sephardic, German, and Eastern European Jews coming in succession. Second, Jews initially settled in small towns and large cities, where they frequently engaged in mercantile pursuits. Thirdly, the 1950s and 1960s marked the apogee of American religious life, and this was reflected in the founding and expansion of Jewish congregations, urban and rural, immobile and mobile.

Since the 1960s, however, the small towns have seen their Jewish populations dissipate as the baby boomers, in many cases not content with the retail business, have sought opportunities in the Piedmont crescent and beyond. On the other hand, Northern emigration to the Sunbelt has augmented the Jewish communities of North Carolina's urban areas. It appears that this trend will continue. An oft-neglected group, North Carolina Jews have proved influential and accomplished in proportion to their numbers, and it is the hope of the author that this point has been conveyed.

REFERENCES

Maps Relating to the North Carolina Jewish Community

List of North Carolina Jewish communities (Encyclopedia of Southern Jewish Communities) http://www.isjl.org/north-carolina-encyclopedia.html

North Carolina Counties Map (NC Maps at UNC–Chapel Hill) C:\Users\martin\Pictures\North-Carolina-State-Capitol-Counties-Map.gif

North Carolina Highway Map (North Carolina Department of Transportation) https://www.ncdot.gov/travel/mappubs/statetransportationmap/

Chronology of North Carolina Jewish Congregational History

1876—Construction of North Carolina's first synagogue, Temple of Israel in Wilmington.

1883—Organization of Congregation Emanuel in Statesville. This Reform congregation closed in 1920 and reopened in 1954 as Conservative.

1884—Inauguration of Hebrew Burial Society in Durham. This led to the organization of Beth El synagogue (Orthodox, later Conservative) in 1886. Beth El's facilities were constructed in 1921 and 1957.

1886—Dedication of Oheb Sholom (Reform) congregation in Goldsboro.

1888—Organization of Beth Jacob (Orthodox) in Winston-Salem.

1891—Inauguration of Temple Beth Ha'Tephila (Reform) in Asheville. The present facility was opened in 1949.

1895—B'nai Israel synagogue constructed in Tarboro.

1895—Organization of Temple Israel in Charlotte. Its offspring was Temple Beth El (Reform), organized in 1942.

1899—Inauguration of Congregation Bikur Cholim (Orthodox) in Asheville. In 1950, the congregation changed its name to Beth Israel and identified as Conservative.

1903—Founding of Tilfereth Israel in Kinston. The congregation, as Temple Israel (Reform), moved to a new facility in 1954.

1908—Construction of Temple Chester B'nai Sholom (Reform) on Middle Street in New Bern.

1908—Organization of Greensboro Hebrew Congregation, which divided into Reform Temple Emanuel (1949) and Beth David (Conservative—separated in 1943).

1910—Organization of Congregation Beth Israel in Fayetteville (originally Orthodox with a 1922 facility on

Cool Spring Street). Since 1950, Beth Israel has been located on Morganton Road and is "unofficially" Conservative.

1912—Organization of Winston Salem Hebrew Congregation. In 1934, the Reform Jews created Temple Emanuel, while Conservative Beth Jacob remained active through the 1960s.

1912—Organization of Weldon's Temple Emanuel. The congregation purchased a new facility in 1954. The congregation's affiliation through its history included Orthodox to Conservative to Reform.

1912—Creation of the Hebrew Sunday School Association (Raleigh Hebrew Congregation). A 1913 schism produced Temple Beth Or (Reform) and the Conservative House of Jacob (later Beth Meyer).

1914—Construction of Wilmington's B'nai Israel synagogue (originally Orthodox, today Conservative). B'nai Israel occupied its present facility in 1954.

1916—Organization of Shaarey Israel (Orthodox) in Charlotte (morphed into Conservative Temple Israel).

1922—Organization of Agudas Israel congregation in Hendersonville (Orthodox to Conservative to Reform). Agudas Israel is presently located in Laurel Park, west of Hendersonville, in a 2002 facility.

1927—Dedication of B'nai Israel synagogue in High Point (Orthodox to Conservative to Reconstructionist to Reform). The present Kensington Road facility was constructed in 1965.

1929—Opening of Temple Emanuel in Gastonia.

1936—UNC establishes Hillel chapter.

1944—Creation of Temple Israel congregation (Conservative) in Salisbury. The present building dates from 1953.

1949—Beth-El congregation in Rocky Mount obtains its own facility.

1953—Construction of Temple Beth-El in Wilson.

1954—I.D. Blumenthal initiates the "circuit-riding rabbi" project. Rabbis will include William Furie, Harold Friedman, and Reuben Kesner.

1955—Opening of Temple B'nai Mordecai in Jacksonville, North Carolina.

1955—Completion of Beth-El Synagogue in Lumberton (now Trinity Baptist Church)

1959—Construction of Temple Beth Shalom in Hickory (originally Conservative, now Reform). The present Temple Beth Shalom and the Hickory Jewish Center were completed in 1989.

1959—Completion of Whiteville's Beth Israel Center (Conservative).

1961—Organization of Judea Reform congregation in Durham. The present facility was completed in 1971.

1976—Organization of Bayt Shalom synagogue in Greenville. The present building was occupied in 2003.

1978—Sheldon and Beryl Hanft organized a Reform congregation in Boone. The Temple of the High Country was constructed in 2012.

1979—Organization of Franklin's Mountain Synagogue.

1979—Organization of Sha'arei Israel (Lubavitch) in Raleigh.

1980—Lubavitch congregation Ohr HaTorah created in Charlotte.

1981—Organization of Sandhills Jewish Cultural Group in Foxfire Village (Moore County). Reform Beth Shalom was constructed in 2002.

1983—Organization of Cary's Beth Shalom Reform Congregation.

1996—Organization of Chapel Hill Kehillah (Reconstructionist).

2001—Norman and Shelley Bossert organize a *Torah* study in Brevard.

2003—Dr. Barbara Shapiro Thiede organizes Temple Or-Olam in Concord.

NOTES

1. Gary C. Grassl, "Joachim Gans," in William S. Powell, ed., *Dictionary of North Carolina Biography* (Chapel Hill: University of North Carolina Press, 1982), 2: 272–73; William S. Powell, *North Carolina Through Four Centuries* (Chapel Hill and London: University of North Carolina Press, 1989), 126–27. Harry Golden (1902–1981), noted Charlotte journalist and chronicler of Southern Judaism, contended that Jews came from Barbados in 1665. See the following: Harry Golden, "North Carolina and the New South: Its Jewish Citizens Helped Bring it Prosperity," *World Over* 13 (May 16, 1952): 8; Harry Golden, *Jewish Roots in the Carolinas: A Pattern of American Philosemitism* (Charlotte, NC: Carolina Israelite, 1955), 17; and Leon Huhner, "The Jews of North Carolina Prior to 1800," *Publications of the American Jewish Historical Society* 29 (1925): 138, hereinafter cited as Huhner, "Jews of North Carolina"; Leonard Rogoff, *Down Home: Jewish Life in North Carolina* (Chapel Hill: University of North Carolina Press, 2010), 9, hereinafter cited as Rogoff, *Down Home*.

2. John Henry Gerdes, "The Early Jews of Wilmington," *Lower Cape Fear Historical Society, Inc, Bulletin* (October 1984), 1, hereinafter cited as Gerdes, "Early Jews"; Martin Weitz, ed., *Bibilog* (Wilmington, NC: Temple of Israel, 1976), 4, hereinafter cited as Weitz, *Bibilog*; Huhner, "Jews of North Carolina," 141; Golden, *Our Southern Landsman* (New York: G.P. Putnam's Sons, 1974), 173, hereinafter cited as Golden, *Southern Landsman*; David J. Goldberg, "An Historical Community Study of Wilmington Jewry, 1738–1925" (Unpublished seminar paper, University of North Carolina at Chapel Hill, 1976), 9, hereinafter cited as Goldberg, "Wilmington Jewry."

3. Gerdes, "Early Jews," 3; Huhner, "Jews of North Carolina," 145; Goldberg, "Wilmington Jewry," 9; Rogoff, *Down Home*, 14, 26–27; Walter Conser, Jr., *A Coat of Many Colors: Religion and Society Along the Cape*

Fear River of North Carolina (Lexington: University Press of Kentucky, 2006), 175, hereinafter cited as Conser, *A Coat of Many Colors.*

4. Gerdes, "Early Jews," 3–4; Eli Evans, *Judah P. Benjamin: The Jewish Confederate* (New York: Free Press, 1988), 5–7; Rogoff, *Down Home*, 25, 39. Contemporaneous (1809) with Judah Benjamin's birth was the successful attempt by Jacob Henry, a Jew from Carteret County, to maintain his seat in the North Carolina House of Commons after some of his colleagues, because he was not of the Christian persuasion, attempted to remove him. Notable works that discuss Henry's struggle include Leonard Dinnerstein and Mary Dale Palson, eds., *Jews in the South* (Baton Rouge: Louisiana State University Press, 1973); Morton Borden, *Jews, Turks, and Infidels* (Chapel Hill: University of North Carolina Press, 1984); and Leon Huhner, "The Struggle for Religious Liberty in North Carolina with Special Reference to the Jews," *Publications of the American Jewish Historical Society*, 16 (1907).

5. Gerdes, "Early Jews," 4; Elizabeth Francenia McKoy, *Early Wilmington Block by Block, from 1733 On* (Wilmington, NC: n.p., 1967), 107, hereinafter cited as McKoy, *Early Wilmington*; Huhner, "Jews of North Carolina," 147; Goldberg, "Wilmington Jewry," 10.

6. Reaves, "Wilmington's Jewish Heritage," 4; Leonard Rogoff, "Synagogue and Jewish Church: A Congregational History of North Carolina," *Southern Jewish History* (1998), 47, hereinafter cited as Rogoff, "Synagogue and Jewish Church."

7. "Wilmington, North Carolina," *Encyclopedia of Southern Jewish Communities.* Goldring/Woldenberg Institute of Southern Jewish Life, hereinafter cited as "Wilmington," *ESJC*, accessed 9 January 2016, http://www.isjl.org/north-carolina-wilmington-encyclopedia.html.

8. *Ibid.*

9. Reaves, "Wilmington's Jewish Heritage," 4–5; Weitz, *Bibilog*, 19; *Seventy Fifth Anniversary: Temple of Israel* (Wilmington, NC: n.p., 1951), 8–9, hereinafter cited as *Seventy Fifth Anniversary*; "Wilmington, *ESJC*; Rogoff, *Down Home*, 94, 96; Rogoff, "Synagogue and Jewish Church," 48, 49.

10. Rabbi Harold Friedman of Wilmington, NC, telephone communication with author, 6 March 1996, hereinafter cited as Harold Friedman, telephone communication, 6 March 1996; Leonard Rogoff of Chapel Hill, NC, personal communications, 14 March 1996, 18 July 1996; *Seventy Fifth Anniversary*, 10; Conser, *A Coat of Many Colors*, 181; Temple of Israel Website, accessed 25 July 2016, www.temple-of-israel.org.

11. "Wilmington," *ESJC*; Conser, *A Coat of Many Colors*, 182; Rogoff, *Down Home*, 147.

12. "Wilmington," *ESJC*, Conser, *A Coat of Many Colors*, 177–78.

13. "Wilmington," *ESJC*, Conser, *A Coat of Many Colors*, 177–78.

14. Reaves, "Wilmington's Jewish Heritage," 5: Robert B. Toplin, ed., *A History of B'nai Israel Synagogue* (Wilmington, NC: B'nai Israel, 1984), hereinafter cited as Toplin, *History of B'nai Israel*; Goldberg, "Wilmington Jewry," 38–39; "Wilmington," *ESJC*.

15. "Wilmington," *ESJC*; Rogoff, *Down Home*, 100, 144.

16. "Wilmington," *ESJC*; Conser, *A Coat of Many Colors*, 184–85; Rogoff, "Synagogue and Jewish Church," 59.

17. "Wilmington," *ESJC*; Conser, *A Coat of Many Colors*, 185.

18. Rogoff, *Down Home*, 290–91.

19. Toplin, *History of B'nai Israel; Temple of Israel Directories, 1983–1995.*

20. *Wilmington Morning Star*, 31 December 1985, 3C; *Wilmington Star News*, 16 May 1985, 1D.

21. Toplin, *History of B'nai Israel.*

22. Chabad of Wilmington Website, accessed 11 December 2015, www.chabadofwilmington.org.

23. Congregation Beth Israel Synagogue Website hereinafter cited as Beth Israel Website, accessed 14 December 2015, http://www.bethisraelnc.org/index.php?submenu=Our Community&src=gendocs &ref=JewishAshevillle &category=OurCommunity.

24. "Congregation Beth Ha-Tephila, 100th Anniversary" (Asheville, NC: Unpublished, 1991), 8; "Asheville, North Carolina," *Encyclopedia of Southern Jewish Communities.* Goldring/Woldenberg Institute of Southern Jewish Life hereinafter cited as "Asheville," *ESJC*, accessed January 9, 2016, http://www.isjl.org/north-carolina-asheville-encyclopedia.html; Beth Ha-Tephila Website, hereinafter cited as Beth Ha-Tephila Website, accessed December 15, 2015, http://bethhatephila.org/NewTempleSite/about/index.php.

25. "Asheville," *ESJC*; Beth Ha-Tephila Website; Rogoff, "Synagogue and Jewish Church," 61.

26. Nick Seminoff, "Congregation Bikur Cholim Was Founded 50 Years Ago," *Asheville Citizen-Times*, 12 February 1949; Patricia Beaver, *Leo Finkelstein and the Poor Man's Bank* (Boone, NC: Center for Appalachian Studies, 1998), 7, hereinafter cited as Beaver, "Finkelstein; Beth Israel Synagogue Centennial" (Asheville, NC: Unpublished, 1999), 6–7; "Asheville," *ESJC*; Beth Israel Website.

27. "Center Notes 25 Years of Service," *Asheville Citizen-Times*, 21 February 1965; "Asheville," *ESJC*. New Englander Pelley was situated in Asheville during 1932–1940. A stock fraud arrest triggered his departure from the city (Rogoff, *Down Home*, 240). For a recent account of Pelley's role in Asheville, see Seth Epstein, "The Arrival of a Provocateur: Responses to William Dudley Perry in Asheville, 1930 to 1934," *Southern Jewish History* (2013) 16: 89–125.

28. The Chabad House Asheville Website, accessed December 11, 2015, www.chabadasheville.org.

29. Rogoff, *Down Home*, 331; Stuart Rockoff, "The Rise and Fall of the Jewish South," in Marcie Cohen

Ferris, Mark I. Greenberg and Eli N. Evans, eds., *Jewish Roots in Southern Soil: A New History* (Waltham, MA: Brandeis University Press, 2006), 288–89; Havurat Olam Website. Accessed 1 February 2006. www.havuratolam .org/welcome.htm; Temple Or Olam Website, accessed December 15, 2015, http://www.or-olam.org/?page_ id=1369; Ralf Thiede Website, accessed December 29, 2015, https://clas-pages.uncc.edu/ralf-thiede/; Yonat Shimron "Faithful Give Torah a New Home" *News & Observer*, 24 September 2004, 1A, 10A.

30. "Hickory, North Carolina," *Encyclopedia of Southern Jewish Communities.* Goldring/Woldenberg Institute of Southern Jewish Life, hereinafter cited as "Hickory," *ESJC*, accessed 29 December 2015, http://isjl. org/north-carolina-hickory-encyclopedia.html.

31. Hickory Jewish Center Website, hereinafter cited as Hickory Jewish Center Website, accessed 29 December 2015, http://hickoryjewishcenter.com/about.html; "Hickory," *ESJC*.

32. "Hickory," *ESJC*.

33. "Jews Form Center Here For Culture," *Hickory Daily Record,* 11 September 1965, 15E.; "Hickory," *ESJC*; Circular from Philip Datnoff, 13 November 1964, Blumenthal Family Papers. J. Murrey Atkins Library Special Collections, University of North Carolina at Charlotte, hereinafter cited as Blumenthal Family Papers, Series III, 7:1.

34. Circular from Philip Datnoff, 13 November 1964, Blumenthal Family Papers, Series III, 7:1: 'Hickory" *ESJC*.

35. "Sunday Dedication at Synagogue," *The Hickory News*, 24 August 1989, 9A; "Hickory," *ESJC*.

36. Gayle McCracken, "1st Woman Rabbi to Lead City Services," *Hickory Daily Record*, 23 September 1976; Andie Leatherman, "Congregation Finds Creative Solution to Rabbi Shortage" *Hickory Daily Record*, 5 November 1998, A1, A7.

37. Hickory Jewish Center Website.

38. "Whiteville, North Carolina," *Encyclopedia of Southern Jewish Communities.* Goldring/Woldenberg Institute of Southern Jewish Life, hereinafter cited as "Whiteville," *ESJC*, accessed 30 December 2015, http:// www.isjl.org/ north-carolina-whiteville-encyclopedia.html.

39. *Columbus County Recollections*, 70; Harold Friedman, telephone communication, 6 March 1996; Terry Mann of Whiteville, NC, personal communication with author, 7 March 1997, 4 January 2016, 5 January 2016; "Dedication of Beth Israel Center, 10 April 1960," Blumenthal Family Papers, Series III, 6:50; "Whiteville," *ESJC*.

40. Jacob (Jack) Steinberg, telephone communication, 18 March 1996; "Whiteville," *ESJC*.

41. "Whiteville," *ESJC*.

42. B'nai Sholem Website, hereinafter cited as B'nai Sholem Website, accessed 15 December 2015, www. bnai-sholem.org/about-us/our-history.

43. Rogoff, *Down Home*, 183.

44. Rogoff, "Synagogue and Jewish Church," 48, 62; Mary Baker "Temple B'Nai Sholom," *Journal of the New Bern Historical Society* (May 1990), 3:22, hereinafter cited as Baker, "Temple B'Nai Sholom"; "New Bern, North Carolina," *Encyclopedia of Southern Jewish Communities*, Goldring/Woldenberg Institute of Southern Jewish Life, accessed 9 January 2016, http://www.isjl.org/north-carolina-new-bern-encyclopedia.html; Louis Josephson, responses to a questionnaire sent out by Jacob Rader Marcus of Hebrew Union College, Cincinnati, Ohio, American Jewish Archives, Cincinnati, Ohio; B'nai Sholem Website.

45. B'nai Sholem Website.

46. Rogoff, "Synagogue and Jewish Church," 72; Rogoff, *Down Home*, 330.

47. B'nai Sholem Website.

48. "Fayetteville, North Carolina," Encyclopedia of Jewish Communities, Goldring/Woldenberg Institute of Southern Jewish Life, hereinafter cited as "Fayetteville," *ESJC*, accessed 31 December 2016, http://www.isjl. org/ north-carolina-fayetteville-encyclopedia.html,.

49. "Fayetteville," *ESJC*; United Synagogue of Conservative Judaism Website, accessed 16 January 2016, www.uscj.org; Rabbi Eve Eichenholtz of Fayetteville, NC, interview by author, 6 January 2016, hereinafter cited as Rabbi Eichenholtz interview, 6 January 2016. Rogoff, "Synagogue and Jewish Church," 68, 70, 73.

50. "Fayetteville," *ESJC*; Chick Jacobs, "New Female Rabbi, a First for Fayetteville Synagogue. Eager to Get Started," *Fayetteville Observer*, 7 August 2014, accessed 31 December 2015, http://www.fayobserver.com/ living/new-female-rabbi-a-first-for-fayetteville-synagogue-eager-to/article_3b25bee4–0bac-588f-af10- a68b74ddf4a2.html, "Our Rabbi," Beth Israel Fayetteville Website, accessed 31 December 2015, http://www. bethi.org/#!rabbi-eichenholtz/npaj7; Rabbi Eichenholtz interview, 6 January 2016.

51. Rabbi Eichenholtz interview, 6 January 2016; Rabbi Yossi Levanon of Fayetteville, NC, interview by author, 6 January 2011.

52. "Durham," *Jewish Virtual Library*, hereinafter cited as "Durham," *JVL*, accessed 6 August 2015 www. jewishvirtuallibrary.org/ jsource/judaica/ejud_0002_0006_0_05486.html; "Durham/Chapel Hill, North Carolina," *Encyclopedia of Southern Jewish Communities.* Goldring/Woldenberg Institute of Southern Jewish Life, hereinafter cited as "Durham," *ESJC*, accessed 12 August 2015 http://www.isjl.org/north-carolina-durham-encyclopedia.html; Steven Litt, "A Southern Jewish Community: Durham group celebrates 100 years of tradition, change," *News & Observer*, 20 July 1987, 6C, hereinafter cited as Litt, "A Southern Jewish Community"; "Our History," Beth El Congregation website, hereinafter cited as "Our History" Beth El, accessed 6 August

2015, http://www. betheldurham .org/synagogue /history.html; Liora Moriel, "Two-Tiered Temple: Innovative Synagogue Celebrates Centennial," *Spectator*, 24 September 1987, 35 hereinafter cited as Moriel "Two-Tiered Temple"; Ven Carver, "100 Years of Jewish Tradition: Founding of Durham Synagogue Celebrated," *Durham Morning Herald*, 27 September 1987, 1D, hereinafter cited as Carver, "100 Years of Jewish Tradition." Two excellent sources concerning the Durham–Chapel Hill Jewish community are Leonard Rogoff, *Homelands: Southern Jewish Identity in Durham and Chapel Hill* (Tuscaloosa: University of Alabama Press, 2001) and Eli Evans, *The Provincials: A Personal History of Jews in the South* (Chapel Hill: University of North Carolina Press, 2005).

53. Sigmund Meyer, "Synagogue History" (Unpublished manuscript, 1951); *Report of the Building Committee of the Beth-El Congregation Upon the Completion of the Beth-El Synagogue* (Durham, NC, 1921), 3–7; Robin Gruber, "From Pine Street to Watts Street: An Oral History of the Jews of Durham, North Carolina" (unpublished Honors Thesis, Duke University, 1986), 9, 14, 18, 21, 33, 80; "Durham," *JVL*; "Durham," *ESJC*; "Our History," Beth El; Litt, "A Southern Jewish Community," 6–7C; Moriel "Two-Tiered Temple," 35–36; Carver, "100 Years of Jewish Tradition," 1–2D; Rogoff, "Synagogue and Jewish Church," 48, 62–63, 75.

54. Phil Seib (Program Director of Durham–Chapel Hill Jewish Federation), interview by author, 10 August 2015; Yonat Shimron, "Triangle Jews Build a Center," *The Durham News*, 5 December 2010, 3A; Roger Carp, "History of Judea Reform (pamphlet, 1984); "Our History" Judea Reform Congregation Website, accessed 9 January 2016, www.judeareform .org/60-cbe/about-us/our-history; "Durham," *JVL*; "Durham," *ESJC*; Rogoff, "Synagogue and Jewish Church," 69, 76.

55. Rohr Chabad at UNC–Chapel Hill Website, accessed 9 January 2016, http://www.chabaddch.com; Keillah Synagogue Website, accessed 9 January 2016, http://kehillahsynagogue.org; Freeman Center for Jewish Life Website, hereinafter cited as Freeman Center Website, accessed 9 January 2016, https://studentaffairs.duke. edu/jewishlife/about-us/freeman-center-jewish-life, hereinafter cited "Durham," *JVL*; "Durham," *ESJC*.

56. Freeman Center Website; Kenneth Broun Website, accessed 9 January 2016, http://www.law.unc. edu/ faculty/directory/ brounkenneths, "Durham," *JVL*; "Durham," *ESJC*.

57. Fleming, 17 September 2000; "Tarboro Museum Remembers Jewish Community" *R-C News Herald*, 10 August 2000; "Tarboro, North Carolina," *Encyclopedia of Southern Jewish Communities*. Goldring/Woldenberg Institute of Southern Jewish Life, hereinafter cited as "Tarboro," *ESJC*, accessed 19 March 2016, http:// www.isjl. org/north-carolina-tarboro-encyclopedia.html. For a firsthand account of Jewish life in Tarboro, see the excerpt by "Dancinger" in *Jewish South* (1878) cited in Rogoff, *Down Home*, 90–91.

58. Fleming, 17 September 2000; Robert Raskin, address at "Migrations: Jewish Settlers in Eastern North Carolina," Tarboro, NC, 17 September 2000; Tom Mayer, "Once-Thriving Jewish Society Is Chronicled," *News & Observer*, 24 August 2000, 3A; "Tarboro" *ESJC*; Rogoff, *Down Home*, 93.

59. "Tarboro," *ESJC*.

60. Rogoff, "Synagogue and Jewish Church," 70; "Tarboro," *ESJC*.

61. "Winston-Salem, North Carolina," *Encyclopedia of Southern Jewish Communities*. Goldring/Woldenberg Institute of Southern Jewish Life hereinafter cited as "Winston-Salem," ESJC, accessed 12 August 2015, www.isjl.org/north-carolina-winston-salem-encyclopedia.html; "Beth Jacob, Society Plan Anniversaries," *Twin City Sentinel*, 1 June 1963, 6, hereinafter cited as "Beth Jacob, Society"; "Roman Catholics, Jews Round Out City's Religious Life," *Winston Salem Journal and Sentinel*, 10 April 1966, I-3, I-12, hereinafter cited as "Roman Catholics, Jews." Rabbi Mark Strauss-Cohn of Temple Emanuel, Winston-Salem, NC, interview by author, 11 August 2015, hereinafter cited as "Strauss-Cohn Interview"; Rogoff, "Synagogue and Jewish Church," 48.

62. "Winston-Salem," *ESJC*; "Roman Catholics, Jews," I-3, I-12; "75 Years Temple Emanuel Winston-Salem, NC" (pamphlet, 2007), 14, 17–21, 27–29; "Strauss-Cohn Interview"; Rogoff, "Synagogue and Jewish Church," 67, 76; Rogoff, *Down Home*, 213.

63. "Winston-Salem," *ESJC*; "Beth Jacob, Society," 6; "Roman Catholics, Jews," I-3.

64. "Winston Salem," *ESJC*; "Strauss-Cohn Interview."

65. Temple Emanuel Gastonia Website, hereinafter cited as Temple Emanuel Gastonia Website, accessed 15 December 2015, http://templeemanuelgastonia.org/our-history.

66. Temple Emanuel Gastonia Website.

67. Barry Brodsky, "Temple Emanuel: A History of the First Seventy Five Years of Judaism in Gastonia," (unpublished manuscript, 2004), hereinafter cited as "Temple Emanuel"; "Gastonia, North Carolina," *Encyclopedia of Southern Jewish Communities*. Goldring/Woldenberg Institute of Southern Jewish Life, hereinafter cited as "Gastonia," *ESJC*, accessed 9 January 2016, http://www.isjl.org/north-carolina-gastonia-encyclopedia. html; Temple Emanuel Gastonia Website.

68. "Anti-Defamation League of B'nai B'rith, *Facts: Anti-Semitism in the South: The Bombings* (pamphlet) October-November 1958, 131, Harry Golden Papers. J. Murrey Atkins Library Special Collections, University of North Carolina at Charlotte, hereinafter cited as Harry Golden Papers, 34:7; Rogoff, *Down Home*, 290; Clive Webb, "A Tangled Web: Black-Jewish Relations in the Twentieth Century South," in *Jewish Roots in Southern Soil*, 198; Ira M. Sheskin, "Dixie Diaspora: The 'Loss' of the Small Southern Jewish Community " in Mark Bauman, ed., *Dixie Diaspora: An Anthology of Southern Jewish History* (Tuscaloosa: University of Alabama Press, 2006), 178; Joseph H. Separk, *Gastonia and Gaston County North Carolina, 1846–1949* (Gastonia,

NC: Joseph Separk, 1949), 55–56, hereinafter cited as Separk, *Gastonia; Gastonia: Gastonia Centennial Commemorative Book, 1877–1977* (Gastonia, NC: Gastonia Centennial, 1977), hereinafter cited as *Gastonia Centennial*, 34; "Gastonia," *ESJC;* Temple Emanuel Gastonia Website.

69. "Gastonia," *ESJC;* Temple Emanuel Gastonia Website.

70. Kurt Lauenstein, *Temple Emanuel Greensboro 1907–2007: One Hundred Years of a Unique Jewish Experience in the South* (Greensboro, n.p., 2007), hereinafter cited as Lauenstein, *Temple Emanuel Greensboro*, 16–21, 26; "Hebrew Temple of Worship Formally Opened Tonight," *Greensboro Daily News*, 5 June 1925, 3: "Greensboro, North Carolina," *Encyclopedia of Southern Jewish Communities*. Goldring/Woldenberg Institute of Southern Jewish Life, hereinafter cited as "Greensboro," *ESJC*, accessed 9 January 2016, http://www.isjl.org/north-carolina-greensboro-encyclopedia.html; Rogoff, "Synagogue and Jewish Church," 61, 76; Rogoff, *Down Home*, 216.

71. Eleanor Dare Kennedy, "They Define The Human Venture: Couple Serves Gate City," *Greensboro Daily News*, E1–2"; "Rabbi Rypins Dies at 77," *Greensboro Record*, 11 January 1971, 1B; "Rabbi Rypins Is Dead: Funeral Slated Today," *Greensboro Daily News*, 12 January 1971, 1B; "Jewish Communities in the South: Greensboro, N.C.," *American Jewish Times* (December 1943), 6; Lauenstein, *Temple Emanuel Greensboro*, 24, 28–30, 33–35, 38–44, 48–49, 51–53, 70; "Greensboro," *ESJC;* Rogoff, *Down Home, 219.*

72. Rogoff, "Synagogue and Jewish Church," 60.

73. "Celebrating Fifty Years at Beth David Synagogue: The Vision and Dedication of 50 Years," (pamphlet, June 1, 1997); Lauenstein, *Temple Emanuel Greensboro*, 42; "Greensboro," *ESJC;* Rogoff, "Synagogue and Jewish Church," 68.

74. Rabbi Fred Guttman, interview by author, 4 August 2015; "Greensboro," *ESJC.*

75. "Beth David Synagogue Plans to Move to New Quarters Soon," *Greensboro Daily News*, 19 April 1969; "Synagogue to Open New School," *Greensboro Record*, 11 October 1969, "Greensboro," *ESJC;* Rabbi Fred Guttman, electronic correspondence, 4 June 2016.

76. Mrs. Henry Jacobs, "History of the High Point Jewish Community" (Unpublished document), hereinafter cited as Jacobs, "History"; Staley Cook "Lewis Harris Chopped Wood…. Chips Flew as the Result," *High Point Enterprise*, 13 November 1932; "Lewis Harris Is Taken by Death: Pioneer Retailer," *High Point Enterprise*, 20 May 1936, 1, 2; "Former Local Man Dies in Raleigh: Henry Harris, One of the Pioneer Merchants in This City, Dead—Funeral Services This Afternoon" *High Point Enterprise*, 22 June 1930, B1; "High Point Beginning," *Carolina Israelite*, 1 April 1954, 8, Harry Golden Papers 3:1.

77. Jacobs, "History"; "B'nai Synagogue Is Dedicated in Formal Services," *High Point Enterprise*, 19 September 1927; "New Jewish Synagogue to Be Dedicated in Services at Temple This Afternoon," *High Point Enterprise*, 17 September 1927; "High Point, North Carolina," *Encyclopedia of Southern Jewish Communities*. Goldring/Woldenberg Institute of Southern Jewish Life, hereinafter cited as "High Point," *ESJC*, accessed 9 January 2016, http://www.isjl.org/north-carolina-high-point-encyclopedia.html., Rogoff, *Down Home*, 214; Ronnie Taylor, et al., "Sixty Years of Progress: A History of the High Point Jewish Community" (unpublished document, 1960), hereinafter cited as "Sixty Years of Progress."

78. "Pastor of the Week, Rabbi William Gold," *High Point Enterprise*, 21 October 1954; "Sixty Years of Progress"; "High Point Hebrew Congregation," *High Point Enterprise,* 31 December 1949, 3.

79. Jacobs, "History"; "Jewish Community Began Before 1900," *High Point Enterprise*, 25 January 1985, VI, 14; See also "High Point Hebrew Congregation," *High Point Enterprise*, 31 December 1949, 3; Leon Burnett, "New Jewish Educational Building to Be Dedicated," *High Point Enterprise*, 23 November 1952, D1; "Synagogue Ceremony Conducted," *High Point Enterprise,* 10 February 1964; "Dedication Observed," *High Point Enterprise*, 8 November 1965; "High Point," *ESJC;* "Sixty Years of Progress"; Rogoff, "Synagogue and Jewish Church," 69.

80. "High Point," *ESJC.* Union for Reform Judaism Website, accessed 25 July 2016, http://www.urj.org/find-a-congregation/keywords?keyword=&=&location=North+Carolina.

81. Rogoff, *Down Home*, 272–73.

82. Chabad Jewish Center Greensboro Website, accessed 11 December 2015, www.chabadgreensboro.com. Chabad Jewish Center at Elon University Website, accessed 11 December 2015, www.chabadelon.com.

83. Harry Freid of Weldon, NC, interview by author, 1 April 2000, hereinafter cited as Harry Fried interview, 1 April 2000.

84. Ellis Farber, "The Beginning of the Weldon Jewish Community" (unpublished paper, 1996), hereinafter cited as Farber, "The Beginning of the Weldon Jewish Community"; Ellis Farber of Weldon, NC, personal correspondence, 6 March 1996; Harry Freid, interview, 1 April 2000. Harry Freid, who ran a men's store in Roanoke Rapids, was a prisoner of war during World War II; his B-24 flyer was shot down in Romania.

85. "Circuit Riding Rabbi," unpublished newsletter, 14 January 1955, Blumenthal Family Papers, Series III, 6:50; "Weldon, North Carolina," *Encyclopedia of Southern Jewish Communities*. Goldring/Woldenberg Institute of Southern Jewish Life, hereinafter cited as "Weldon," *ESJC*, accessed 9 January 2016, http://www.isjl.org/north-carolina-weldon-encyclopedia.html.

86. "Weldon," *ESJC.*

87. Farber, "The Beginning of the Weldon Jewish Community"; "75th Anniversary of Temple Emanu-El," *American Jewish Times Outlook* (December 1987): 7, hereinafter cited as "75th Anniversary"; William Kittner of Weldon, NC, address at "Migrations Jewish Settlers in Eastern North Carolina" Exhibit, Tarboro, NC,

17 September 2000; "Weldon," *ESJC;* Robert Liverman of Roanoke Rapids to Herman Blumenthal, 4 December 1980, Blumenthal Family Papers, Series II, 1:51; Rogoff, *Down Home,* 263; "Keeping the Faith," ID, 5D.

88. Farber, "The Beginning of the Weldon Jewish Community"; "75th Anniversary," 7; "Fried Kept Jewish Spirit Going in Small Town," *News & Observer,* 27 August 2006, 3B, hereinafter cited as "Fried Kept Jewish Spirit"; Harry Kittner of Chapel Hill, NC, questionnaire responses of 4 October 2005, hereinafter cited as Harry Kittner, 4 October 2005.

89. "Bas Mitzvah Makes History," *Roanoke Rapids Daily Herald,* 7 June 1964, 8, Blumenthal Family Papers, Series III, 7:1.

90. "Weldon," *ESJC.*

91. Rogoff, *Down Home,* 347; "Weldon," *ESJC.*

92. "Weldon," ESJC.

93. Rogoff, *Down Home,* 354; "Weldon," *ESJC.*

94. Agudas Israel Website, hereinafter cited as Agudas Israel Website, accessed 15 December 2015, http://agudasisraelsynagogue.org/about-us/our-history.

95. Agudas Israel Website.

96. Morris Kaplan, "History of Agudas Israel Congregation" (unpublished manuscript), hereinafter cited as Kaplan, "History of Agudas Israel Congregation"; Morris Kaplan and Sammy Williams, Agudas Israel Congregation, interview by author, 7 September 2003; Morris Kaplan and Sammy Williams, Agudas Israel Congregation, interview by author, 9 November 2003, hereinafter cited as Kaplan/Williams interview, 9 November 2003; Morris Kaplan, personal communication, 20 November 2003; Rogoff, *Down Home,* 272.

97. Kaplan, "History of Agudas Israel Congregation"; "Hendersonville, North Carolina," *Encyclopedia of Southern Jewish Communities.* Goldring/Woldenberg Institute of Southern Jewish Life, hereinafter cited as "Hendersonville," *ESJC,* accessed 9 January 2016, http://www.isjl.org/north-carolina-hendersonville-encyclopedia.html.

98. Kaplan, "History of Agudas Israel Congregation; "Hendersonville," *ESJC.* Longtime members of Agudas Israel Congregation included: Morris and Anne Kaplan, Sammy and Flossie Williams, Max and Janet Provda, Donald and Ellie Michalove, Ann Mottsman Michalove Kolotkin, and Kalman and Frances Sherman (Kaplan/Williams interviews, 9 November 2003); "Hendersonville," *ESJC.*

99. Kaplan "History of Agudas Israel Congregation"; "Hendersonville," *ESJC;* Agudas Israel Website.

100. Morris Kaplan, personal correspondence, 20 November 2003.

101. Kaplan "History of Agudas Israel Congregation"; Burton Greenberg, Agudas Israel Congregation, interview by author, 9 November 2003.

102. "Hendersonville," *ESJC.*

103. "Service of Dedication of a House of God," 17 May 2002; Kaplan/Williams interview, 9 November 2003.

104. "Congregation Emanuel Centennial" (Statesville, NC: unpublished document, 1983), 26, hereinafter cited as "Congregation Emanuel Centennial"; "Statesville, North Carolina," *Encyclopedia of Southern Jewish Communities.* Goldring/Woldenberg Institute of Southern Jewish Life, hereinafter cited as "Statesville," *ESJC,* accessed 9 January 2016, http://www.isjl.org/north-carolina-statesville-encyclopedia.html; Henrietta Wallace, "The History of the Jewish Community of Statesville, N.C.," *Carolina Israelite,* December 1952, 3, Harry Golden Papers, Part Two, 3:1, hereinafter cited as Wallace, "The History," 3. A testimony to the ecumenical outlook of the congregation occurred in 1899, when the Congregation Emanuel allowed the communicants of a decimated Reformed Presbyterian Church to use its facility. The decline of the congregation after 1920 can be attributed in part to prohibition; North Carolina was "dry" during the period 1907–1933, and many Jews, as they had in Russia, engaged in the liquor trade ("Statesville," *ESJC*); Mac Lackey, Jr., "Congregation Emanuel Took in Presbyterians," *Iredell Neighbors,* 7 February 1988, hereinafter cited as Lackey, "Presbyterians"; Jeannie Krider, "History Reflected by Temple," *Statesville Record & Landmark,* 16 October 1971, hereinafter cited as Krider, "History." Hannah Adler, "Congregation Emanuel Celebrates Centennial," *Record & Landmark,* 7 June 1992; Homer Keever, *Iredell: Piedmont County* (Statesville, NC: Brady Printing Company, 1976), 336, hereinafter cited as Keever, *Iredell;* Congregation Emanuel Statesville Website, hereinafter cited as Congregation Emanuel Website, accessed 9 January 2016, http://www.congregation emanuel.us/history _congregation_emanuel.html.

105. "Statesville," *ESJC;* Congregation Emanuel Statesville Website.

106. "Statesville," *ESJC;* Congregation Emanuel Statesville Website.

107. "Statesville," *ESJC;* Congregation Emanuel Statesville Website.

108. On February 3, 1943, the *Dorchester* was torpedoed by a German submarine. Four chaplains, including Rabbi Alexander Goode, sacrificed their life jackets and went down with the vessel. "Hyman Goodkowitz," Geni Website, accessed 31 December 2015, http://www.geni.com/people/ Hyman-Goodkowitz/60000000139 07558953; "Kinston," *Encyclopedia of Southern Jewish Communities.* Goldring/Woldenberg Institute of Southern Jewish Life, hereinafter cited as "Kinston" *ESJC,* accessed 31 December 2015, http://www.isjl.org/north-carolina-kinston-encyclopedia.html ; Rogoff, *Down Home,* 255; "Temple Israel," *The Heritage of Lenoir County 1981* (Winston-Salem, NC: Hunter Publishing Company, 1981) 116, hereinafter cited as "Temple Israel," *Heritage of Lenoir County.*

109. "Kinston," *ESJC;* Rogoff, *Down Home,* 255; "Temple Israel," *Heritage of Lenoir County,* 116.

110. "Rabbi Tolochko of Kinston and 100 Percent Attendance," *Carolina Israelite*, September 1952, 8, Harry Golden Papers, Part Two, 3:1; "Kinston," *ESJC*.

111. "Kinston," *ESJC*; Rogoff, *Down Home*, 255; "Temple Israel" in *Heritage of Lenoir County*, 116.

112. Rogoff, "Synagogue and Jewish Church," 72; Rogoff, *Down Home*, 330; Mountain Synagogue Website, hereinafter cited a Mountain Synagogue Website, accessed 15 December 2015, http://www.mountainsyna gogue.org.

113. Mountain Synagogue Website.

114. Kathryn Bolick Wells, "Building Community and Identity in a New South City: The Jews of Charlotte, North Carolina" (unpublished MA thesis, University of North Carolina at Charlotte, 2005), 19–20, hereinafter cited as Wells, "Building Community"; Rosalie Citron Ashendorf, "The First 75 Years" in *Temple Israel: 100th Anniversary Journal, 1895–1995* (Charlotte, NC: Shalom Park, 1995); Rogoff, "Synagogue and Jewish Church," 48, 75.

115. "Celebrating 75 Years of Living Generously!" (pamphlet, Jewish Federation of Greater Charlotte, 2015).

116. Wells, "Building Community," 31; Morris Speizman, *The Jews of Charlotte: A Chronicle with Commentary and Conjectures* (Charlotte, NC: McNally and Loftin, 1978), 31, hereinafter cited as Speizman, *The Jews of Charlotte*; Temple Beth El Charlotte Website, hereinafter cited as Temple Beth El Charlotte Website, accessed 31 December 2015, http://templebethel.org/about-us/history; Rogoff, "Synagogue and Jewish Church," 69, 76. During the Civil Rights era (1957), Beth-El was a site where thirty sticks of dynamite were situated. Fortunately, the police discovered the explosives before they could do harm (Rogoff, *Down Home*, 290).

117. Speizman, *The Jews of Charlotte*, 34; Temple Beth El Charlotte Website; Rogoff, "Synagogue and Jewish Church," 77; Rogoff, *Down Home*, 353.

118. Speizman, *The Jews of Charlotte*, 23.

119. Wells, "Building Community," 96.

120. Wells, "Building Community," 36; Rogoff, *Down Home*, 338; Temple Beth-El Membership Directory (Charlotte, 2013), 11.

121. Rogoff, "Synagogue and Jewish Church," 72, 77; Rogoff, *Down Home*, 351; Chabad North Carolina Website accessed 11 December 2015, http://www.chabadnc.org; Rabbi Yossi Groner of Charlotte, NC, telephone communication with author, 28 July 2015.

122. Rogoff, *Down Home*, 330, 351–52; "Pinehurst, North Carolina," *Encyclopedia of Southern Jewish Communities*. Goldring/Woldenberg Institute of Southern Jewish Life, hereinafter cited as "Pinehurst," *ESJC*, accessed 31 December 2015, http://isjl.org/north-carolina-pinehurst-encyclopedia.html; Sandhills Jewish Congregation Website, hereinafter cited as Sandhills Jewish Congregation Website, accessed 15 December 2015, http://sandhillsjewish.org/about-us/our-history.

123. Sandhills Jewish Congregation Website.

124. "Rocky Mount, North Carolina," *Encyclopedia of Southern Jewish Communities*. Goldring/Woldenberg Institute of Southern Jewish Life hereinafter cited as "Rocky Mount," *ESJC*, accessed 31 December 2015, http://www.isjl.org/north-carolina-rocky-mount-encyclopedia.html; Rogoff, *Down Home*, 59; Dale Fuerst, untitled history of Beth-El, Blumenthal Family Papers, Series III, 6:49.

125. "Rocky Mount," *ESJC*.

126. "Jacksonville, North Carolina," *Encyclopedia of Southern Jewish Communities*. Goldring/Woldenberg Institute of Southern Jewish Life hereinafter cited as "Jacksonville," *ESJC*, accessed 31 December 2015, http://www.isjl.org/north-carolina-jacksonville-encyclopedia.html .

127. "Jacksonville," *ESJC*; Rogoff, *Down Home*, 317.

128. Obituary of Rosalind "Rozzie" Segerman, *News & Observer*, 20 March 2003.

129. Rabbi Michael Cain, Dr. Todd Savitt, Paula Blumenfeld of Greenville, NC, telephone communications with author, 10 June 1996, hereinafter cited as Cain, Savitt, Blumenfeld, personal communications, 10 June 1996; Leo Brody of Kinston, NC, telephone communication with author, 11 June 1996 hereinafter cited as Brody, telephone communication, 11 June 1996.

130. "Greenville," *ESJC*.

131. "Greenville, North Carolina," *Encyclopedia of Southern Jewish Communities*. Goldring/Woldenberg Institute of Southern Jewish Life, hereinafter cited as "Greenville," *ESJC*, accessed 4 January 2015, http://isjl.org/north-carolina-greenville-encyclopedia.html.

132. Rogoff, *Down Home*, 196.

133. "Greenville," *ESJC*; Rogoff, "Synagogue and Jewish Church," 71.

134. "Greenville," *ESJC*.

135. "Greenville," *ESJC*; Rogoff, *Down Home*, 347.

136. Congregation Bayt Shalom Website, hereinafter cited as Congregation Bayt Shalom Website, accessed 4 January 2016, http://new.baytshalom.org.

137. Cain, Savitt, Blumenfeld, telephone communications, 10 June 1996; Brody, telephone communication, 11 June 1996; Rogoff, "Synagogue and Jewish Church, 71–72; Congregation Bayt Shalom Website; Cain, interview, Greenville, NC, 25 May 2004; "Greenville," *ESJC*; Rogoff, *Down Home*, 369.

138. Diane Winston, "Rabbi on Wheels Carries Message to Jewish 'Tribe,'" *News & Observer* (Raleigh, NC), 23 April 1984, 1C, 3C, Blumenthal Family Papers, Series III, 7:1.

139. "Lumberton, North Carolina," *Encyclopedia of Southern Jewish Communities*. Goldring/Woldenberg Institute of Southern Jewish Life, hereinafter cited as "Lumberton," *ESJC*; accessed 29 March 2016, http:// www.isjl.org/ north-carolina-lumberton-encyclopedia.html.

140. Robert Lawrence, *The State of Robeson* (New York: J.J. Little and Ives, 1939), 265, hereinafter cited as Lawrence, *Robeson*; Melinda Weinstein of Southfield, MI, questionnaire responses, 10 April 2006, hereinafter cited as *Weinstein Questionnaire*; Rogoff, *Down Home*, 137.

141. Lawrence, *Robeson*, 266; *Weinstein Questionnaire*.

142. Lawrence, *Robeson*, 266; Maud Thomas, *Away Down Home: A History of Robeson County, North Carolina* (Charlotte, NC: Delmar, 1982), 209, hereinafter cited as Thomas, *Away Down Home*; *Weinstein Questionnaire*.

143. Thomas, *Away Down Home*, 242–43; "Lumberton," *ESJC*; Rogoff, *Down Home*, 353.

144. "Jewish temple's parting gift is to promote tolerance in its community," *UNCP Today*, Winter 2003, 10.

145. "Lumberton," *ESJC*.

146. "Salisbury, North Carolina," *Encyclopedia of Southern Jewish Communities*. Goldring/Woldenberg Institute of Southern Jewish Life, hereinafter cited as "Salisbury," *ESJC*, accessed 5 January 2016, http://isjl. org/north-carolina-salisbury-encyclopedia.html; Harry Golden, "My Speech at the Dedication of Temple Israel: First Jewish Congregation in Salisbury, N.C., March 15, 1953," *Carolina Israelite*, February 1953, 3, Harry Golden Papers, Part Two, 3:1; Temple Israel Salisbury Website, hereinafter cited as Temple Israel Salisbury Website, accessed 15 December 2015, http://templeisraelsalisbury.org.

147. "Salisbury," *ESJC*; Temple Israel Salisbury Website.

148. Rose Post of Salisbury, NC, telephone communication, 6 September 2001; Rose Post, electronic communication, 5 January 2002; "Salisbury," *ESJC*.

149. "Salisbury," *ESJC*; Temple Israel Salisbury Website.

150. Sue Titcomb, "Dr. Furie Fills In Gap As 'Circuit Riding Rabbi,'" *The Charlotte News*, 27 September 1962, 26A, Harry Golden Papers, 12:9, hereinafter cited as "Dr. Furie Fills."

151. Lewis Green, "Rabbi Rides Circuit At A 'Furious' Pace," *Asheville Citizen-Times*, 13 December 1964; Letter of Catawba College Dean Donald Dearborn to Pastors, 18 January 1963, Blumenthal Family Papers, Series III, 7:1; Letter of Pfeiffer College President J. Lem Stokes II to Dr. William Furie, 15 April 1963, Blumenthal Family Papers, Series III, 7:1.

152. "The Best Antidote for Anti-Semitism," *American Jewish Times Outlook* (no date), Blumenthal Family Papers, Series III, 6:49; Hannah Miller, "Passover at Pfeiffer: Feast Was Kosher, But Students Weren't," *The Charlotte Observer*, 11 April 1963, 1B, Blumenthal Family Papers, Series III, 8:24.

153. Memo from I.D. Blumenthal to All Circuit Communities, 6 January 1969, Blumenthal Family Papers, Series II, 1:51; Dr. Furie was the recipient of various accolades from Jews and non-Jews. See Dr. Sol Singer of Salisbury to William Furie, 28 November 1962, Blumenthal Family Papers, Series III, 7:1; Marvin and Elaine Zerden of Hickory to I.D. Blumenthal, 10 December 1962, Blumenthal Family Papers, Series III, 7:1; Abram Weil of Goldsboro to I.D. Blumenthal, 4 April 1963, Blumenthal Family Papers, Series III, 7:1; Donald J. Selby, Professor of Religion at Catawba College, to I.D. Blumenthal, 8 April 1963, Blumenthal Family Papers, Series III, 7:1; Letter from Mrs. A.H. Moskow of Whiteville, NC, to I.D. Blumenthal, 17 October 1963, Blumenthal Family Papers, Series III 6:49; I.D. Blumenthal to Mrs. A.H. Moskow, 21 November 1963, Blumenthal Family Papers, Series III, 7:1; B. Paul Hammack, Superintendent of Weldon City Schools, to I.D. Blumenthal, 6 December 1963, Blumenthal Family Papers, Series III, 7:1 (eulogy for John F. Kennedy on 24 November 1963); B.W. Shapiro of Salisbury, NC, to I.D. Blumenthal, 14 February 1964, Blumenthal Family Papers, Series III, 7:1; Robert Liverman of Weldon, NC, to I.D. Blumenthal, 14 April 1964, Blumenthal Family Papers, Series III, 7:1; Ellis Farber of Weldon, NC, to I.D. Blumenthal, 26 April 1964, Blumenthal Family Papers, Series III, 7:1; Max Offerman of Wallace, NC, to I.D. Blumenthal, 29 May 1964, Blumenthal Family Papers, Series III, 7:1; Hy and Ruth Diamond of Warrenton, NC, to I.D. Blumenthal, 14 September 1964, Blumenthal Family Papers, Series III, 7. (When the Diamonds' daughter Helen was Bat Mizvahed, her Christian friends attended the ceremony.)

154. Nancy Robinson, "Joseph and Elizabeth Silversteen" in Transylvania Heritage Book Committee, *The Heritage of Transylvania County North Carolina* (Waynesville, NC: Don Mills, Inc., 1995), 187–88.

155. "Brevard, North Carolina," *Encyclopedia of Southern Jewish Communities*. Goldring/Woldenberg Institute of Southern Jewish Life, hereinafter cited as "Brevard," *ESJC*, accessed 5 January 2016, http://www. isjl.org/north-carolina-brevard-encyclopedia.html; Rogoff, *Down Home*, 330, 351; Brevard Jewish Community Website, accessed 5 January 2016, http://www.thebrevardjewishcommunity.org/home.html.

156. "Raleigh, North Carolina," *Encyclopedia of Southern Jewish Communities*. Goldring/Woldenberg Institute of Southern Jewish Life, hereinafter cited as "Raleigh," *ESJC*, accessed 14 December 2015. http:// www.isjl.org/ north-carolina-raleigh-encyclopedia.html; Barbara Freedman, "History in Detail," Temple Beth Or website, hereinafter cited as "Beth Or History," accessed 14 December 2015, http://www.tboraleigh.org/ about/ history/history-by-barbara-freedman; "History of Beth Meyer," Beth Meyer Synagogue Website, here-

inafter cited as "History of Beth Meyer," accessed 14 December 2015, https://bethmeyer.org/ content/ history-beth-meyer); Rogoff, "Synagogue and Jewish Church" 48–49, 61; Rabbi Lucy Dinner and Mrs. Barbara Freedman of Temple Beth Or, Raleigh, NC, interview by author on 7 January 2016, hereinafter cited as Rabbi Dinner and Mrs. Freedman, interview, 7 January 2016. Mrs. Freedman (2016) serves as assistant treasurer of the Raleigh Hebrew Cemetery Society; Rogoff, "Synagogue and Jewish Church," 48, 64, 75–76; Rogoff, *Down Home*, 93. See Henry Gargan, "Walking tour uncovers origins of Raleigh's Jewish history," *News & Observer*, 9 April 2016, accessed 12 April 2016, http://www.newsobserver.com/news/local/counties/wake-county/article 70920842.html.

157. "Raleigh," *ESJC;* "Beth Or History"; Rabbi Dinner and Mrs. Freedman, interview, 7 January 2016; Rogoff, "Synagogue and Jewish Church," 50.

158. "Raleigh," *ESJC;* "Beth Or History"; Rabbi Dinner and Mrs. Freedman, interview, 7 January 2016.

159. "Raleigh," *ESJC;* "Beth Meyer History"; Rabbi Eric Solomon of Beth Meyer Synagogue, Raleigh, NC, interview by author, 16 December 2015.

160. Rabbi Pinchas Herman of Sha'arei Israel, Raleigh, NC, interview by author,7 January 2016; Chabad Center and Sha'arei Israel Synagogues Website, accessed 8 January 2016, http://www.jewishraleigh.org; Rogoff, "Synagogue and Jewish Church," 72.

161. "Raleigh," *ESJC;* Beth Shalom Cary Website, accessed 5 January 2016, http://bethshalomnc.org; Rogoff, *Down Home*, 331; Rogoff, "Synagogue and Jewish Church," 71.

162. Chabad of Cary Website, accessed 11 December 2015, http://www.chabadofcary.org/templates/article cco_cdo/aid/1172409/jewish/Our-History.htm.

163. Sheldon Hanft, "The Boone Jewish Community," in Sanna Gaffney, *The Heritage of Watauga County* (Winston-Salem, NC: Hunter Publishing Company, 1984), 1:36–37, hereinafter cited as Hanft, "Boone Jewish Community"; Sheldon Hanft of Boone, NC, telephone communication, 6 March 2001; Rogoff, "Synagogue and Jewish Church," 70; Temple of the High Country Website, hereinafter cited as Temple of the High Country Website, accessed 5 January 2016, http://www.templeof thehighcountry.org/; Rogoff, *Down Home*, 283; "Boone, North Carolina," *Encyclopedia of Southern Jewish Communities*. Goldring/Woldenberg Institute of Southern Jewish Life hereinafter cited as "Boone," *ESJC*, accessed 5 January 2016.

164. "Boone," *ESJC;* Temple of the High Country Website.

165. Rogoff, *Down Home*, 308; Hanft, "Boone Jewish Community."

166. Rogoff, *Down Home*, 316.

167. Emily Weil, *Temple Oheb Sholom* (Durham, NC: B. Williams and Associates, 2000), 8, hereinafter cited as Weil, *Oheb Sholom*, 8; "Goldsboro, North Carolina," *Encyclopedia of Southern Jewish Communities*. Goldring/Woldenberg Institute of Southern Jewish Life hereinafter cited as "Goldsboro," *ESJC*, accessed 29 March 2016, http://www.isjl.org/north-carolina-goldsboro-encyclopedia.html; Rogoff, *Down Home*, 172–73.

168. Rogoff, "Synagogue and Jewish Church," 54.

169. Weil, *Oheb Sholom*, 8; "Goldsboro," *ESJC;* Rogoff, *Down Home*, 93.

170. Weil, *Oheb Sholom*, 9.

171. Weil, *Oheb Sholom,* 12.

172. William Shrago of Goldsboro, NC, address at "Migrations: Jewish Settlers in Eastern North Carolina," Tarboro, NC, 17 September 2000.

173. "Wilson, North Carolina," Encyclopedia of Southern Jewish Communities. Goldring/Woldenberg Institute of Southern Jewish Life, hereinafter cited as "Wilson," *ESJC*, accessed 29 March 2016, http://www. isjl. org/north-carolina-wilson-encyclopedia.html.

174. Rogoff, "Synagogue and Jewish Church," 57.

175. Rogoff, "Synagogue and Jewish Church," 60.

176. Rogoff, *Down Home*, 245.

177. Harold Friedman, telephone communication, 6 March 1996.

178. North Carolina Association of Jewish Men, "Circuit Riding Rabbi" (pamphlet), Blumenthal Family Papers, Series III (6:49); "Dedication Service of the Circuit Riding Rabbi Bus," 27 March 1955 (program), Blumenthal Family Papers, Series III, 6:49; Rogoff, *Down Home*, 283.

179. "Federation Talk," unpublished newsletter, Blumenthal Family Papers, Series III, 6:49.

180. "Circuit Riding Rabbi Project: Communities served from 1954–1971," typewritten manuscript, Blumenthal Family Papers, Series III, 6:50.

181. Harold Friedman, "Report of Side Visits Week of April 24 to, and including April 28," typewritten manuscript, Blumenthal Family Papers, Series II, 6:50. At the time of his appointment, the "liberal-conservative" Rabbi Friedman was thirty-six years old and ministering to a congregation in Jamestown, NY. He was a graduate of Mesifta Talmudic Seminary in Brooklyn, married to an Israeli, Miriam Reichman, and had chaplained at the Mayo Clinic (Rochester, MN) and then Fairmont, WV (Harold Friedman to I.D. Blumenthal, 13 December, 1953, Blumenthal Family Papers, Series III, 6:52; Harold Friedman to I.D. Blumenthal, 29 December 1953, Blumenthal Family Papers, Series III, 6:52; "Rabbi Friedman Accepts New Post," *Jamestown* [N.Y.] *Sun,* 5 June 1954, Blumenthal Family Papers, Series III, 6:52; Harold Friedman, "Release on Circuit Rabbi Project," Blumenthal Family Papers, Series III, 6:52). Friedman's ministering to "small-town" congregations

in West Virginia and upstate New York, coupled with his civic involvement (Boy Scouts, Kiwanis, Fairmont Library board and Community Chest), undoubtedly helped his candidacy.

182. Harold Friedman, telephone communication, 6 March 1996; "Congregation Emanuel," 27: Rabbi Reuben Kesner of Myrtle Beach, SC, telephone communication, 18 March 1996; David Weil, personal correspondence, 17 June 1996. See Murray Polner, "Small-Town Rabbis: Is Anyone Listening Out There?" *National Jewish Monthly* 92 (September 1977): 20–22, for a citation of Rabbi Kesner; "Whiteville," *ESJC*; Israel J. Gerber, "The Circuit-Riding Rabbi Project," Unpublished Manuscript (1972?), Blumenthal Family Papers Series II, 1:51, 4–8, hereinafter cited as Gerber, "Circuit-Riding Rabbi"; "Circuit Riding Rabbi Project History—March 24, 1971," Blumenthal Family Papers, Series III, 6:50. Rabbi Friedman went on to serve congregations in Mobile, Alabama, Waco, Texas and Galveston, Texas. His son, Dr. Daniel Friedman, born during his North Carolina ministry, went on to earn engineering degrees from Rice University and MIT (Harold Friedman to I.D. Blumenthal, 9 May 1978, Blumenthal Family Papers, Series III, 6:50). Rabbi Friedman also completed a doctorate in ancient languages (Hebrew University of Jerusalem) and taught ancient history at a variety of colleges. He retired to Wilmington, where he ministered to Whiteville's Beth Israel synagogue until his death in July 1997. "Circuit Riding Rabbi Brought Faith to Rural Areas of Carolinas," *Wilmington Star-News*, 21 July 1996; Blumenthal Family Papers, Series III, 6:52; "Rabbi Harold Friedman dies at 79," *Wilmington Star-News*, 25 July 1997; Blumenthal Family Papers, Series III, 6:52; Rogoff, *Down Home*, 284.

183. Some congregations expressed concerns about "revolving door" rabbis and their ability to relate to children. See Wallace Leinwand of Elizabethtown, NC, to I.D. Blumenthal, 9 April 1964, Blumenthal Family Papers, Series III, 7:1; Noah Ginsberg of Wallace, NC, to I.D. Blumenthal, 29 April 1964, Blumenthal Family Papers, Series III, 7:1.

184. "Traveling Synagogue: North Carolina Rabbi Holds Service in Bus," *Life*, 19 September 1955, Blumenthal Family Papers, Series III 6:49; Gerber, "Circuit-Riding Rabbi," 5; Harold Friedman to I.D. Blumenthal, 9 May 1978, Blumenthal Family Papers, Series III, 6:50.

185. Gerber, "Circuit-Riding Rabbi," 4.

186. Information Sheet on Circuit Riding Rabbi Project" (1959?) Blumenthal Family Papers, Series III, 6:49; "Brief History of the Circuit Riding Rabbi Project," unpublished manuscript (1960?), Blumenthal Family Papers Series III, 6:49.

187. *Ibid.*

188. "Rabbi Morris Reuben Kesner" obituary, *Telegram and Gazette* (Worcester, MA), 12 October 2002, A5, hereinafter cited as "Rabbi Morris Reuben Kesner" obituary.

189. "New Circuit Riding Rabbi Serving Wallace Jewish Congregation…," *The Wallace Enterprise*, 5 November 1964, Blumenthal Family Papers, Series III, 7:2.

190. A.H. Moskow to I.D. Blumenthal, 26 October 1964, Blumenthal Family Papers, Series III, 7:1; Noah Ginsburg of Wallace, NC, to I.D. Blumenthal, 26 April 1965, Blumenthal Family Papers, Series III, 7:1; I.D. Blumenthal to Reuben Kesner, 5 March 1968, Blumenthal Family Papers, Series III, 7:1.

191. Reuben Kesner, "Short Circuit," *Women's League Outlook*, Fall 1970, 12, 4, 24, 25, Blumenthal Family Papers, Series III, 7:2; Jon Nordheimer, "A Circuit Riding 'Rabbi' in Bible Belt Helps Jews to Retain Identity," *New York Times*, 28 April 1970, Blumenthal Family Papers, Series III, 7:2; "A Rabbi's Dream for Carolina Youth Is Shattered," *New York Times*, 28 April 1974, Blumenthal Family Papers, Series III, 7:1; Rogoff, *Down Home*, 312.

192. I.D. Blumenthal to Morris Kesner, 31 July 1964, Blumenthal Family Papers, Series III, 7:2.

193. "Rabbi Morris Reuben Kesner" obituary, *Telegram and Gazette* (Worcester, MA), 12 October 2002, A5.

194. North Carolina Association of Jewish Men, meeting minutes of 21 August 1977, 29 August 1977, Blumenthal Family Papers, Series II, 1:51.

195. Jon Nordheimer, "Circuit Rider in the Carolinas: He's a Jew Who Travels 1,000 Miles A Week 'Tending His Flock," *The* [Columbia, SC] *State*, 3 May 1970, Blumenthal Family Papers, Series III, 6:50.

196. Reuben Kesner, telephone communication, 18 March 1996.

197. Mel Baer, personal communication, 9 March 2000; Simcha Kling, "North Carolina: The State Where Jews Are Organized," *The Reconstructionist*, 16 December 1955, 16–18, Blumenthal Family Papers, Series III (6:50).

Lutherans

GARY R. FREEZE

In 1772, with their North Carolina communities in turmoil, two faithful Lutheran laymen trekked back to their native Europe to find authority and acceptance for their denomination. At the instigation of their neighbors and with the full support of provincial officials, Christopher Lyerly and Christopher Rendleman rode to Charles Town, sold their horses to pay for their passage, and made it to London's Court of St. James. There, they hoped that their connection to Mecklenburg, where both the county and the seat had been named for Queen Charlotte, would beg favor from the Crown. It did—George III supported the venture—and soon they were at Germany's University of Halle to enlist the "ripe and thorough scholar" Adolph Nussmann as pastor and the eager and earnest Johann Gottfried Arends as teacher to come to Carolina to uphold the true spirit and order of the Reformation. The two graduates of a sophisticated educational system brought with them, in addition to personal Bibles and catechisms, additional "means of grace"—Lutheran parlance for the baptismal bowl, wine tankard, communal goblet, and wafer box provided them by their continental patrons.[1]

And that, North Carolina Lutherans have said ever since, set the tone for their history, that faith-based actions linearly lead to providentially sound consequences. However, this standard approach in denominational chronicles only superficially explains the wide and divergent ways Lutherans have been simultaneously people of a universal faith and a particular perspective. In the case of the Lutheran creation myth, there was more going on than just a faith journey. British officials, challenged by the terms of the Regulation, had agreed to the quest for a pastor as a means of gaining an ally in the taming of a fractious backcountry. Good pastors, officially sponsored, would mean good people in the pews, putting a damp to "roaming fanatics" in the woods who led "sectarians" to "affront common sense." It turned out, however, that the local laity, conditioned by sectional conflict, was of two minds about what kind of pastor it would accept. The subsequent schisms revealed Lutherans to be in multiple camps in 1773, and they have been of many minds since, often embroiled in frank, sincere disagreement as to how the means of grace should be delivered, how it should be received, and what one does after leaving the altar. This essay, then, respects the traditional pietistic paradigm, but scrutinizes division in order to better place this disparate liturgical tradition within the broad spectrum of the Old North State's denominational history. The Lutheran cultural contribution to North Carolina, it will be argued, follows closely the religious historian Sydney Ahlstrom's observation that "democracy, pluralism, independence of government,

141

[and] deep-reaching social transformations" inform the directions that denominations take.[2]

Lutheran people had resided in North Carolina for decades before the arrival of the first pastors, but the history is fuzzy as to time and place. Presumably, the Palatinate immigrants who helped establish New Bern in 1711 included Lutherans, but no parish resulted, and attempts on the Neuse in the 1730s to "read common prayers in High German" were not denominationally specific. Similarly, the so-called founding dates in the 1740s for the oldest congregations in the western half of the state fall prey to the same sort of speculation. It could be true that gatherings in new barns for devotional purposes might have occurred in places like Friedens, Alamance, by 1745, as folks there have said ever since, but these were not congregations in the literal, organized sense. St. John's, Salisbury, says it was "organized" in 1747, referencing documented migration to the Yadkin River basin, but it could not have been an actual *Stadtkirche*, since Salisbury did not physically exist until 1753. Furthermore, it is hard to figure out even who to call Lutheran among the first immigrants who came down the Great Wagon Road. The wheelwright Michael Braun, whose 1766 stone house still stands near Salisbury, was. In turn, the long hunter Heinrich Weidner wasn't, though his family brought logs to help erect a union church, now St. Paul's, Newton, in 1759, then intermarried into the faith in subsequent generations. By 1773, it *is* known, hundreds of families who identified as Lutheran lived on the tributaries of the three principal back country rivers: along the creeks that fed into the Yadkin in what became Rowan, Davidson, Davie, and Cabarrus counties; on the South Fork of the Catawba; and along branches of the Haw to the southwest of Hillsborough. In those places, Nussmann and Arends found pews and pulpits awaiting their ministries.[3]

The first ministers, their immediate successors, and the original parishioners—one newly arrived pastor in 1794 called them "the dwellers of the forest"—underwent a season of seasoning. From ticks to snakes to the relative irrelevance of vestments to the substitution of brandy for wine, it was a time of adjustment. Arends, it was noted, "even when walking in the fields would wear his high hat, gloves, and carry his cane." At a time when science among the laity was often confined to pickling and distilling, a subsequent pastor was known to be "a man of science" who could "converse in five or six languages." Another was "very correct and exemplary" in "the habits of life," as "dignified" as he was "affable" to "approach by the humblest member of his flock." The same pastor was said to have had "little knowledge of, and great indifference to, mere worldly matters." Yet, he was astute and agile enough to end some of the more backwoods customs of the original worshippers, particularly "episodes of public penance" that shamed individuals for sins like fornication and drunkenness. All the half dozen original pastors also helped in the acculturation of their parishioners, preaching in German and English by the early 1800s.[4]

The initial issues of ministry testified to this period of adjustment. Lutherans proved to be contentious about what went on inside their sanctuaries when it came to denominational matters of doctrine and devotion. From the first, they argued over foundational ideas. The debate began within months of the arrival of the German authority figures in 1774. Some laity on Dutch Second Creek in Rowan decided that Nussmann, raised a Catholic, retained too much of his former Franciscan faith. In what became the first of many schismatic events in the history of Lutheranism in the state, he was dispatched almost immediately to the more accommodating Dutch Buffalo Creek neighborhood in Cabarrus. To fill their pulpit, the pro–Regulator founders of Zion Church took the unprecedented step of having an "inspector"—no such office existed on the nascent frontier—ordain "the catechist" Arends. The two European emigrants then split duties the best they could. Nussmann generally took care of the area to the east of the Yadkin, and Arends moved to Lincolnton in 1785 to be the resident minister on the South Fork.[5]

The parishioners served by these sophisticated emigrants were distinctive residents in their parts of western North Carolina, noted for their "industrious, economical, and thrifty" husbandry. "A traveler [as late as the 1820s] might have believed himself [to be] in some part of Pennsylvania," observed a historian of the day. Hardworking Germans had "four-horse wagons," "fine and well-fed" stock, and used "heavy iron plates" as firebacks forged in Reading. They were "slow to make changes," observed an early pastor, and "tenaciously adhere[d] for a long time to the practices and conduct of their forefathers." They planted by the signs, almost religiously. "The old Dutch prophets were almost never wrong," claimed one Lutheran layman who grew up in the 1830s and who was still keeping to the habit during the First World War. These "Dutch" used Belsnickeling to prepare their youth for "double Christmas," and observed a similar two-day holiday at Easter, with Monday devoted to picnics at places like the foot of Baker's Mountain on the South Fork of the Catawba River. Many took off Ascension Day to fish, a habit that persisted in some places till the Second World War. Many used both languages at home and at services until after the Civil War. (The last recorded bilingual sermon was in 1886, for an old Dutch lady who had never lost her patois.) They held sacred the Christian call to be good neighbors. Women, who almost always made up the majority of communicants, particularly remained forces of stability and cohesion within rural, moderately reclusive German neighborhoods. Rebecca Moser Woodring of St. Peter's, Catawba County—daughter of one Lutheran minister and sister of another—tended the communal needs of her fellow believers, from helping "make 2 shirts 2 dresses and a coat" at a neighbor's, worked hard at quiltings and barn raising, and helped in the dressing of the dead.[6]

In the first hundred years of settlement, almost all the North Carolina Lutherans remained husbanded to the kind of small-scale diversified farming that reflected their Rhinelander backgrounds (and their Jeffersonian dispositions, for most voted for Democrats). They grew cotton once the gin was perfected, but they never gave in willingly to the singularity of staple production. In 1850, for example, households near Mt. Pleasant were almost twice as likely to herd significant flocks of sheep as were the Scots Irish planters across Cabarrus County at Poplar Tent, and three times as unlikely to own slaves or plant cotton. The few large-scale German slaveholders mostly lived on the South Fork and tended to be aligned to the Reformed congregations. Few Lutherans matched their wealth or their intrinsic Calvinist approach to accomplishment, and those that did often switched over to the Calvinist camp. The most materially successful Lutheran in the colony had been John Paul Barringer on Dutch Buffalo Creek in Cabarrus County, but his politically prominent progeny often ended up married to Presbyterians or Episcopalians. The richest Lutheran of the Jacksonian era, the Alamance planter-artisan-merchant-industrialist Michael E. Holt, became a Presbyterian in middle age.[7]

These persnickety yeomen cared as greatly about where, in what, and with whom they worshipped as they did about who loaded up their barns. As soon as prosperity could be stabilized after the Revolution, they were among the first North Carolinians to erect substantial houses of worship. The Dutch Buffalo Church—which evolved into St. John's, Mt. Pleasant—was "the most promising" in the beginning, exhibiting "an interior with rather fine cabinetwork." Zion in eastern Rowan, which had been founded in 1774, became the "so-called Organ church" after a member family built and installed one in the balcony of its 1795 stone sanctuary, both the instrument and the building the first such indigenous demonstrations of faith in the state. St. John's, Salisbury, had a brick sanctuary on the edge of town after 1783, and St. John's in Catawba County ceiled and weatherboarded a log house of worship about 1798. It was "the most magnificent building," said one 1803 visitor, "that I have seen in this land." Almost all the earliest churches were union ventures, a frugal habit these Germans brought down from Pennsylvania that mimicked, a bit, the notion of a parish back in Europe. Most often, the union was with German Reformed families, often known then as "Dutch Presbyterians." The idea of sharing sanctuary space was sometimes extended to English Presbyterians and Episcopalians, particularly right after the American Revolution, when social structures were fluid and inchoate. The generally generous Germans, however, drew a social line in the sand around the parabolic rock of their sanctuaries. They made sure to separate their pulpits from the different approach to conversion taken by Methodists and Baptists. "Saut Fork" Dutch called the Methodists down the road "cougars" because of their tendency to snatch away the young from the heritage ways of their hearths. The writers of the 1789 congregational constitution at Organ in Salisbury forbade just any man from taking the pulpit, or for that matter, just anyone showing up and asking for a child to be baptized. They had to be checked out by the elders beforehand. One reason the original generation of Lutheran pastors held their first synodical meeting in 1803 was to counter two intertwined and inseparable trends: first, the "party spirit [that] has risen to a frightful height" in the wake of the election of Thomas Jefferson; and second, the emotional excesses of the Great Revival then sweeping the southern backcountry. These manifestations of spirit and polity had roiled congregations everywhere the first generation of Lutherans lived.[8]

Efforts to give denominational stability to the ministry among the forest dwellers were only modestly successful in the early years. The first meetings of the European-dominated pastorate sought alliance with roteful Episcopalians and others of similar habit. About a dozen congregations participated in a sort of "Synod of Lutheran and Protestant Episcopalian Church" that evolved into the North Carolina Synod being established in 1803. Toward the goal of ministerial dignity and cooperation, the Lutheran pastorate remained cordial to German Reformed colleagues, provided they were of the old school, and sought outside help, particularly among Methodists and Moravians. For example, the Rev. Robert Johnson Miller, once a Methodist, served both Lutherans and Episcopalians for sixteen years before joining the latter church. Some years Miller and Lutheran laymen like Jacob Troutman and Henry Bustle from St. Michael's, Iredell, attended the meeting of diocese. More significantly, the Rev. Gottlieb Shober, a Moravian, joined the North Carolina Synod in 1811, and soon pushed a stronger emphasis on personal pietism, of inward searching and feeling, to the congregations he served. Shober's focus on "a communion of [like-feeling] saints" meshed well with the Europeanists' tendency to be "liberal toward other denominations." Shober began to rewrite with a pietistic slant the devotional materials distributed to laymen. He also led the effort to have local Lutherans be part of a General Synod with their northern counterparts after the War of 1812, the aim being "living blissfully as one flock."[9]

North Carolina's early national efforts at Lutheran unity were soon sundered by pastors and their particular lay followers who opposed such "new measures." In contrast to the European dandies who were the main cogs of pastoral authority, the multiple pastors of the Henkel family were rustic frontiersmen of the faith, as able to slap away vermin with their bare hands as shake their snake sticks at those with too extreme a Calvinist or Arminian propensity. One constant of their ministry—going back to 1717 to a pioneering parish in Pennsylvania—seems to have been a devotion to a "high German" attitude in worship, transmitted in a Jeffersonian vernacular. This sacerdotal attitude, stridently expressed in opposition to what opponents called a "latitudinarian" response to "the perfect Babel" of revivalism, rifted the North Carolina body of faith. When David Henkel, a third-generation exhorter, was denied ordination by the Shoberites, a significant faction walked out on the new synod. Dissenters demanded a more "primitive Lutheranism," one that disdained what they called the "puffed-up" vanities of emotional evangelicalism, as well as greater parity between the interests of the pastors and the people in the pews. Consequently, hands were laid on Henkel and another aspirant pastor under an oak tree, and—in an atmosphere of Teutonic mythology—the acorn sprouted into the Tennessee Synod in 1821.[10]

North Carolina would have two principal Lutheran synods for the next 100 years. Each synod generally averaged more than thirty congregations, and at various times the jurisdiction of each extended into the mountainous areas of Virginia and Tennessee and into the Dutch Fork of South Carolina. After 1845, there would be a tiny third one. When a Henkelite pastor was accused of adultery, several of his congregations—citing clerical oversight and overreach—refused the results of the synodical inquiry, and renamed themselves the Tennessee Synod, Reorganized. Some church buildings were unhappily shared by as many as four congregations, at least in cases where the Reformed contingent, as at St. Paul's and St. John's, Catawba County, had not fled the premises.[11]

The two principal synods were found in all German neighborhoods, but each had areas of geographical concentration. The self-described "primitive Lutheranism" of the Tennessee Synod tended to appeal most to those who farmed the tributaries of the Catawba. The more Americanized North Carolina Synod (read Methodist, for Lutherans continued to have little truck with Baptists) continued to deepen its roots on the streams that fed into the Yadkin. The congregations on the Haw were similarly divided. The schism, however, roiled neighborhoods and separated families in every watershed. For example, at St. Michael's, Iredell (originally an 1815 union effort with Episcopalians), Henkelites founded St. Martin's in 1833. Within the Lippard family, the older brother who lived in the older house on the hill stayed with the older synod and continued to name his sons John, William, and Peter, as good German yeoman did. The younger brother, whose front yard was across from the new sanctuary, took up the sacerdotal naming practices of the Henkels themselves, and for multiple generations his Lippard descendants included Aaron, Levi, Augustus, Eusebius, Irenius (there were three of those), Polycarp, Jesse, and Cephas.[12]

The doctrinal strife mimicked the partisan rhetoric of the Jackson Era. Henkelites, claimed an opponent, believed a baby received an almost magical "regeneration" through sprinkling and that the grace within and around the sacraments had literally been passed down through the apostolic succession that had been reconstituted in Augsburg. The Henkelites, in turn, claimed theirs was a more dignified "means of the administration of grace," and they were just as truly American, since they, like their Primitive Baptist counterparts, gave congregations more power in choosing a pastor, distrusted funds turned over to denominational administration—some even spoke out against a common fund for the widows of a deceased pastor—and remained skeptical, sometimes downright hostile, to the new idea of an erudite denominational seminary being built in Gettysburg,

Pennsylvania. It could get as rambunctious as a frontier camp meeting. When the Henke-lite minority at Organ Church attempted a Trojan Horse maneuver, Lutherans resorted to fisticuffs. The primitivists hid out behind the pews after a communion preparation sermon on a Friday, hoping to commandeer the "ancient relics" that Nussmann and Arends had brought from London. The moderate majority, tipped off to the scheme, stormed the sanctuary the next morning and tossed the conspirators out the windows.[13]

In contrast, the North Carolina Synod successfully maintained its more moderate evangelical course through pastoral ties to northern denominational trends. The "new measures," as they were called, included public prayer for souls, protracted meetings that imitated the Methodists, and less rigor in catechismal instruction. The Marylander John Reck's focus upon the feelings of belief, harvested with special summer services, was so popular that Salisbury's *Stadtkirche* was revived from dormancy and took to calling itself "John's church." Gettysburg Seminary graduate Samuel Rothrock, who had been raised a Moravian near Salem, presided over four peaceful sessions of the synod in the 1840s and 1850s. His principal pastorate, Organ, continued to have sizeable confirmation classes and significant turnout for its scheduled communion weekends, even when outmigration resulted from downturns in the economy. By the 1850s, Rothrock helped consolidate support for a stronger institutional presence in the synod. After frustrated efforts at supporting a seminary in South Carolina, North Carolinians elected to start a school of their own. North Carolina College was opened in 1859 in Mt. Pleasant, not far from the old Nussmann base at St. John's. Soon after, it was followed by the opening of a female seminary for young women, just down the street.[14]

Tennessee Synod adherents, after the failure of a remote log college in the Holston Valley, stayed devoted to a personal, generational direction of theological readings by respected pastors. Per the charismatic sacerdotalism of David Henkel, the key was to have the right man train the right men in the right place. John Melanchthon Smith completed "the long-desired study of theology" with David Henkel's son, Polycarp ("the best on Baptism," said Smith), in 1852. Smith preached his first sermon in 1856.[15]

The focus on the pastor was, in part, a response to confusion about the proper means of the service that led to the sacraments. The North Carolina Synod had attempted under the leadership of Gottlieb Shober to influence the reinstitution of a common service recognizable over time and space. One resource was a German language hymnal printed in Salisbury in 1797. David Henkel set the tone for the Tennessee faction with his own liturgy, one used until 1872. However, neither the Shober approach nor the Henkelite response quite provided the regularity of liturgical worship long associated with Lutheranism. As one South Carolina pastor noted, "The character of services has varied according to the tastes of her ministers and the prejudices of her people." One minister from the more evangelical North Carolina Synod wryly observed, "We sing a little, and pray a little, and then preach like thunder for two hours."[16]

The variability of Lutheran traditions underwent its next strain at mid-century. For the most part, area Lutherans were reluctant, but dutiful, Confederates with the advent of the Civil War. In their principal counties, they were far more likely to enlist or be conscripted in 1862 than was the case in 1861 for their more eager Scots Irish and English neighbors. How reluctant, however, seems to have been related to how assimilated to an evangelized South their synod had made them. The students at North Carolina College came close to enlisting and serving as a group, but the young Lutheran lads in central Iredell County held back, often concerned about what manpower shortages would do to their extended family larders. Conscription agents targeted them as a peaceful example of dutiful citizenship and successfully rounded them up without incident in July 1862. The cost could be heavy in some communities. The Old Mountain Road Lutherans lost a significant proportion of their young men in a single hour in front of the Dunker Church at Sharpsburg in 1862.[17]

The Civil War delayed but did not break the linear trend toward greater denominational organization. The North Carolinians hosted the organizational meeting of the General Synod of the South at Salisbury in 1862. (Tennessee Synod leaders would have nothing to do with it, since the Synod was dominated by the un-"primitive" South Carolinians.) The Rev. Rothrock and others worked tirelessly throughout the war, trying to keep church and culture alive by holding services on both the home front and the battlefront, as well as attending to the needs of surviving dependents. Both denominational schools and most congregations were reorganized right after Appomattox.[18]

Lutherans more and more moved to town with the advent of an industrial economy, but like their forebears, they were slow to adjust to the new environment. The Rhyne family of Gaston County was the only example of industrial leadership in the Gilded Age. A truce between the two synods, where one would not move into town if the other was already there, did not hold. In the early days of the North Carolina Synod, the only town churches were in Lincolnton and Salisbury, later Concord. (The Tennessee Synod remained decidedly rural.) The first urban congregations were established in 1859 in Charlotte and Wilmington (the latter an anomaly, in that it was made up of a large contingent of recent German emigrants). During the Gilded Age, churches were founded in Hickory, Winston, and Statesville. With the urban transition came a more urbane and broader approach to ministry. Lutheran women advanced to a more inclusive presence in denominational activities. With the advent of collegiate education and missionary auxiliaries, women began to take a more systemic approach to their common faith journey. Missionary society work, first organized at St. John's, Concord, in 1885, worked outward from the towns in the same way that rural free delivery of the mail reoriented people to their tasks and duties. In 1905, for example, the women of St. Enoch in Rowan County began to meet regularly in quarterly afternoon gatherings rather than rapidly and erratically after Sunday services. Missionary enthusiasm at home included support of the effort of the Southern Synod to establish congregations in Japan, beginning in 1892. One of the longtime missionaries in that field was the Rev. Cephas Lippard, of the Henkelite side of that family.[19]

The deliberative way Lutherans were moving from crossroads to village to town dominated their direction in higher education. This had schismatic consequences for the more volatile Tennessee Synod. The leftover leadership of the Henkelites, concerned over the entrainment of their youth in changing times, started Concordia College in the new railroad junction of Conover, in 1877. Despite competition from Gaston College, in the village of Dallas, the coeducational Concordia was made an official institution of the synod in 1885. That, however, did not last, for six years later, dissident Concordia professors, led by N.C. College graduate Robert A. Yoder, took the school up the railroad to faster-growing Hickory, to a defunct high school campus that quickly grew into Lenoir College. The denominational wheeling and dealing resembled short-selling on Wall Street, and words flew like sensationalized headlines in New York tabloids. One observer of the debates expressed shock that his pastors had such an unchristian vocabulary. So rancorous was the separation that Yoder moved his house, trees, and bushes from Conover to the new Hickory campus. Sticks and stones notwithstanding, the college was opened in 1891, and quickly developed an industrialized approach to Lutheran ways. From the beginning, it put as much emphasis on mechanical skills as on theology and included women in classes that prepared them for commercial careers as well as domestic duties.[20]

The creation of a Tennessee Synod college proved both chaotic and catalytic to the future fortunes of all North Carolina Lutherans. Though the schools in Mt. Pleasant carried on into the twentieth century, they were no longer the chief campuses of the faith. Mt. Amoena, in particular, suffered from the establishment of Elizabeth College for Women in Charlotte. In addition, a foundering Tennessee Synod, Reorganized, had absorbed into the Ohio Synod in the 1880s, and that body established a seminary in Hickory. It would never grow beyond a small high school. Back in Conover, angry villagers, mostly Lutheran, determined that they would keep their school going and turned to pastors from the English Branch of the Missouri Synod, whose founders, right after the Civil War, had included the Rev. Polycarp Henkel. By 1900, a half dozen Henkelite congregations in Catawba and Alexander counties had joined in the new jurisdiction, and began to send their youth to be taught by men and women with German names unfamiliar to most North Carolinians. Consequently, Catawba County became ground zero for the next round of competing Lutheran affiliations, highlighted by the alignment of three different congregations, each affiliated to one of the three different synods, on Springs Road northeast of Hickory. All were within sight of one another.[21]

Comparably, Lutheran involvement in postbellum racial issues lacked the same stridency. Antebellum Lutherans had seldom expressed concerns about slavery, though they actively baptized the slaves of their congregants. Some efforts were made in the period after Reconstruction to provide what was at best a detached ministry to Lutheran freedmen. The Tennessee Synod resolved that it was "our imperative duty to assist them," and ordained Tom Frye, who had been baptized a Henkelite at St. John's, Catawba, but did little to follow up on that effort as the nineteenth century waned. Most of the North Carolina Synod support was concentrated in the Quaker-rich area around Greensboro. In 1880, David Koonts, mistakenly said at the time to be "the only colored Lutheran minister in the world," joined with his successors, "the preachers Phifer, Holt, and Clapp," to form the Alpha Synod, which struggled to maintain congregations for decades in spite of the general condition of poverty among many of its members. What white help there was after the white supremacy campaign of 1900 came mostly from the Missouri Synod. That body attempted to make inroads into the North Carolina Synod territory with the establishment of Immanuel College in Concord in 1903. Five years later, an LCMS missionary reported that more than a score of black congregations were active across the state. The one in Salisbury had the help of local white patrons. In the racially tense year of 1899, members of St. John's, Salisbury, helped established a congregation of African Americans, and under the leadership of the Rev. Wiley Lash, members started a school for children in the western end of town. True to the trend among whites, four small missions in rural Rowan were absorbed into the town congregation. Whites, however, had little association with the congregation once it was established. Immanuel would be moved to Greensboro and operated well into the first half of the twentieth century.[22]

North Carolina Lutherans continued to be more industrially oriented, but they had difficulties with the acceleration of assimilation with American entry into the First World War. Both synods were officially supportive and effectively mute about their German heritage. The North Carolina Synod held Luther League conventions that made no mention of worldwide strife, and the Lenoir College chaplain's sermon on faith and Americanism was widely distributed. Lay Lutherans often made sure that area newspapers announced the fact that Kaiser Wilhelm belonged to the Reformed Church. But there was an undercurrent of the old reclusive tendencies. One representative of the American Protective League, a quasi-vigilante organization looking for signs of disloyalty, noted that in Salisbury his only encounters "were" with "Lutherans." In fact, the only disloyalty accusation was lodged against one. In some rural areas where the old-style farming still survived—"Why do you need banks when you have the Clodfelters?" said one old farmer near Troutman—the majority of farmers refused to buy war bonds. Dissent was most demonstrative in the old Henkelite sections—suggesting that there may have been something very indelible about the German quality of "primitive Lutheranism"—particularly in Iredell and Davidson counties. In Catawba County, Maud Yoder Robinson, daughter of the Lenoir College founder, took the banking families to task for leaving their rural counterparts behind in the march of industrial prosperity. Lenoir College nearly failed in the postwar recession, and only remained in Hickory with a singular gift from a layman, industrialist Daniel E. Rhyne. The name was changed to Lenoir–Rhyne College in 1923.[23]

Corporate-like denomination trends helped assimilate local Lutherans in the interwar years. In 1921, the North Carolina Synod and the Tennessee Synods finally joined hands and hearts to form one body. The reconfigured North Carolina Synod became geographically accurate when the remaining South Carolina and Virginia congregations under its jurisdiction were made their own synod by 1924. A century after the Henkelite schism, the majority of Lutherans in the state were for the first time nationally affiliated, the youngest members of the United Lutheran Church in America. (At the same time, St. Michael's and St. Martin's in Troutman, each a product of that long dispute, purposefully merged into Holy Trinity.)

The new synod then enjoyed three decades of steady, standardizing leadership under the Rev. Jacob L. Morgan, who had been its very successful domestic mission developer. Morgan continued to promote expansion into the new suburbs of the growing industrial cities. He helped consolidate support for coeducation at Lenoir-Rhyne College, which led to the closing of the two small academies in Mt. Pleasant during the Great Depression. Morgan encouraged standardization within all congregations; one example was the Summer School for Church Workers, a weeklong series that helped prepare teachers and facilitators of the new non-worship activities. It was held at the Blue Ridge Assembly grounds near Black Mountain. A typical attendee, Sudie Rumple of Holy Trinity, Troutman, who sewed on yokes in the town's work-shirt factory, taught her newly united congregation's first-grade class. Under Morgan, the denomination loosened its regional bounds. Congregations were established in Durham and Rocky Mount in 1923. By the end of the Great Depression, Lutherans, in general, seemed completely caught up into the industrializing, progressively urbanizing culture of the Piedmont. The Lutz family of New Jerusalem, near Hickory, were regarded as exemplars of the new demonstration dairying methods taught by the extension division at N.C. State College. No voices of disaffection arose during the Second World War. This time Lenoir–Rhyne coeds were dispatched into the cotton fields south of Hickory to pick the crop, as a show of patriotism. In the postwar period, one of Morgan's last mission efforts was the acquisition of property south of Asheville for a synodical mountain retreat, as Lutherans once again got around to doing what the Methodists, Baptists, and others had done a generation before. The grounds for Lutheridge, south of Asheville, were acquired in 1946 and fully operational five years later.[24]

During postwar North Carolina's flush industrial times, some Lutherans gained greater social and economic prominence than had their often reclusive agrarian ancestors. In Hickory, besides the Lutzes, the best known Lutheran success story was Dr. Glenn S. Frye. The Holy Trinity stalwart ran his community's Baker Hospital for decades. As much shop steward as skilled surgeon, Frye was known to push a utility cart around to fix toilets and change light bulbs as he made rounds after service on Sunday. That same close sense of proprietorship was well known in Salisbury's Clifford Peeler family, who began to bottle the soft drink Cheerwine in 1917. Two blocks from the bottling plant, Ketner's Supermarket provided a testing ground for what would evolve into the Food Lion grocery chain. Brothers Glenn and Ralph whetted their mastery of inventory control with much the same dedication that their Dutch Side ancestors had given to their granaries and cribs. Peeler and Ketner benevolence helped maintain the largest sanctuary in the unified synod: St. John's, Salisbury, built in 1927 and remodeled in 1948, continued to be the denomination's *Stadtkirche* because the president of synod was nominally in attendance.[25]

In the half century after the synodical mergers, North Carolinians distinguished themselves as servants within the national denomination. Mrs. John M. Cook, of St. James, Concord, helped reorganize the Women's Missionary Society and served as a national officer during the Great Depression. In the same years, Harry E. Isenhour of St. John's, Salisbury, served as president of the ULCA Brotherhood—a mutual benefits and insurance group with Lutherans as the primary customer group. Catharine Stirewalt, descendent of Organ Church's organ builder, served in the mission field to China in the interwar period, endured internment, then returned until the Maoist revolution ended that presence. "Sister Stirewalt" would then become one of the denomination's official deaconesses at the national level. Hickory's Dr. Frye served on the World Missions Board, and Cabarrus farm boy Ray A. Cline, confirmed at St. John's, Mt. Pleasant, was president of the Luther League of America during the Korean War. The most unusual service came in the form of a Lutheran-oriented business, Rufty's Chrismon Shop in Salisbury, where Harold and Barbara Rufty served as middlemen between manufacturers and congregations who had begun to adopt that symbolic form of holiday decorations during the 1950s and 1960s.[26]

Churches in the smaller synods—the Ohio (which became part of the American Lutheran Church in 1930) and Missouri (made part of a new Southeastern District in 1939)—were caught up in the new industrial ways of employment and organization, though at a slower rate of change. They had, as an example, more of a tendency to cling to the union church tradition. At the end of the First World War, the old sanctuary site at St. Paul's, Newton, had a different congregation hold a service each Sunday of the month, including the remnants of a Reformed group. At St. John's, near Conover, the Reformed and Ohio groups were merged into town congregations. What became the ALC congregation in nearby Claremont was barely a stone's throw away from the LCA church, resulting in hymn-singing duels when the sanctuary windows were open in the summer. Bethel, north of Claremont at Catfish crossroads, continued a harvest festival that featured an old-fashioned chicken-pie supper, where yeast dough was layered between shredded meat and gravy. At old St. John's itself, the Missouri Synod adherents remodeled and expanded their Gilded Age sanctuary, only to lose it to fire in 1950. The congregation immediately turned to its agrarian roots to solve both a financial and facility crisis: Members scoured the wood stands of nearby farms, assigned footage to thirty-five different families, and a traditional church raising was the result (though, in tune with the times, the flooring and framing were planed at a nearby lumber yard). The new sanctuary was finished during laying-by time in 1951.[27]

In contrast came the startling decision in 1957 to erect an ultra-modernist sanctuary for Concordia Church on the old campus where the college had been. Designed by A.G. Odell, Jr., who gave the state the first Charlotte Coliseum and the BlueCross headquarters in Chapel Hill, the gleaming edifice became regionally famous for a sweeping roof and pastel windows, and its educational wing came complete with lockers and cubbies. Even the old-timers who had vociferously doubted the Lutheranness of its design began to take pride in it. However, these same-said Lutherans actively supported a parochial school at a time when the state's Baby Boomers were generally all enrolled in the public-school systems. Concordia's most notable layman in the postwar period was Stine Isenhower, who carried the two surnames of prominent defenders of David Henkel. The insurance agent served as national president of the Lutheran Laymen's League.[28]

Lenoir-Rhyne had its ranks swelled by two groups: Cold War veterans who came for the professional advancements offered by its business and science programs and the legacy Lutherans often there as a stepping stone to service. The best example of the former was Albert M. Allran, from Hickory's "wrong side of the tracks," who became a serial entrepreneur of note. His "legacy" counterpart, himself no less an Horatio Alger-esque figure, was Raymond M. Bost, from the mill village at Maiden, who became a serial chief executive at three LCA institutions of higher education.[29]

In contrast to developments within their own traditional bases, the college and the denomination were slow—compared to the more Northern-oriented synods—to embrace racial change. The 1954 effort by Lenoir-Rhyne professor Martin L. Stirewalt, Jr.—a brother of Deaconess Catharine—to have the synod acknowledge the need for integration in anticipation of the *Brown* decision resulted in a lot of "push back" by trustees and affiliated ministers, and little was done until the upheavals of the sixties forced the hand of the denomination. Only gradually did Lutheran congregations begin the process of integration of their ranks, the first African Americans being called in 1979. (The Rev. Earlean Miller also became the first black female pastor in the nation's history.) The majority of churches were still totally white, and defensive about the issue of race, into the 1980s. Even in the Missouri Synod, where interracial efforts were often within segregated congregations, there would be traditional forms of pushback. One denominational official in the 1970s observed that a Charlotte LCMS congregation was actually running with "a Baptist motor on a Lutheran chassis."[30]

Mainline North Carolina Lutherans went through the denominational equivalent of corporate mergers twice during the second half of the twentieth century, into the Lutheran Church in America in 1963 and the Evangelical Lutheran Church in America in 1988. These mergers in part helped the church cope with the swelling ranks of baby-boomer confirmation classes (followed by slower growth with the decline in birth rates among those boomers), remodeling and expansion of educational facilities, the presence (and presidencies) of women on church councils, the hippie-era experiment with team ministries, the updating of church liturgy in 1977, and the regularity of youth retreats to Lutheridge.

The traditionally moderate side of the North Carolina Synod began to move in an ecumenical direction. One of its first bishops—a title created in the gestation of the ELCA—had worked with social missions in the national denominational headquarters, then taught at LRC. The Rev. Michael C.D. McDaniel led conversations about common understandings with the Southeastern District of the Missouri Synod, which led to an unprecedented covenant in 1991 that promoted agreeability among people who had long disagreed. Overtures were also made to Roman Catholics and Episcopalians, as discussions initiated in the Hendersonville area became denomination-wide policy, resulting in joint participation in services and sacraments. It was, in some ways, a return to the "High German" approach that had been part of the colonial experience. As the Rev. Edgar R. Trexler, a denominational journalist, observed, "Being churchy and [having] a sense of churchmanship was highly praised."[31]

The ecumenical impulse resulted in greater efforts to ameliorate the suffering and needs of the marginal, both within and without the church. The ELCA synod erected its first home for the elderly in Hickory in 1962; ten years later it had facilities in Salisbury and Albemarle as well. A decade later, Lutheran Services for the Aging included coordination of home-care help. Retirement communities were started in Salisbury and Asheville in the 1990s. Under the new umbrella of Lutheran Family Services of the Carolinas, established in 1997, the church moved into a broad array of helping ministries for the infirm and handicapped, bolstered by the faith journeys of many baby boomers who saw such efforts as essential to ministry in the new century. One example was the completion in 2016 of a facility for developmentally disabled adults in Raleigh, outside the traditional territory. The denomination also developed conference and recreational centers, at Camp Agape in Kure Beach and Lutherock at Sugar Mountain.[32]

However, the calm sea of the postwar period was no more permanent than the short-lived Era of Good Feeling after the War of 1812. Lutherans became as divided over the nation's culture wars of the late twentieth century as they had with any other period of social change. In 1971, the LCA accepted the ordination of women as part of church policy and polity. The North Carolina Synod soon ordained the Rev. Christine L. Bohr, who served a Kannapolis congregation for just a few years before returning north. The number of women pastors grew slowly in North Carolina until the late 1990s, then the number doubled to forty within the synod after the turn of the twenty-first century. More roiling was the issue of same-sex relations. The national ELCA assembly first made a statement on the issue in 1996, yielding consternation among many North Carolina congregations. In 2009, the same national assembly took action, giving individual congregations the right "to recognize and bless" same-sex marriages, and any congregation could, by will of the majority, call to the pulpit LBGT pastors who were in monogamous relationships. The North Carolina Synod asked congregations to meet and discuss the option, which resulted in heated arguments that sometimes resembled the Henkelite debates in the 1820s. Eventually, about thirty congregations—mostly in the remaining rural enclaves of the Piedmont—left the North Carolina Synod and joined with conservative Midwesterners to establish the North American Lutheran Church (NALC). In the same period, the more conservative Missouri Synod congregations followed their synod's dictum, first announced in 2006, then reaffirmed in 2010, that countenance of same-sex relations was "contrary" to scriptural directives. By 2017, a few churches in North Carolina cities had openly embraced the same-sex orientation, most prominently Holy Trinity in the progressive, multicultural Midwood section of Charlotte, where more than a score of same-sex couples pledged vows in the period after the Supreme Court ruling recognized their right to marry. (A further cultural contrast: only two of the thirty NALC congregations had a female pastor.[33])

The latest round of schisms perhaps heralded, most of all, the inevitable end of the rural character of Lutheranism in the state. The LCMS had several prospering churches in the Triangle with more than a thousand members and operated parochial schools in the Asheville, Hickory, Charlotte, and Greensboro metropolitan areas. In addition, the very conservative Wisconsin Synod had moved into the military base areas of Fayetteville and Jacksonville as well as immigration meccas like Asheville, Charlotte, and Cary. Lenoir-Rhyne, too, looked less like its original self, as it underwent changes in the same direction, becoming a university (in line with the trends of other denominational colleges in the state), and enrolling more Catholics some semesters than Lutherans. Perhaps as a reminder of its roots, in the early 2010s it erected a gleaming chapel dedicated to the reinterpretation of its neo–Gothic roots. Nearby stood a larger-than-life statue of Martin Luther. At the edge of campus, LRU established Lutheran Christian High School as a third means of announcing, per se, a kind of Piedmont "Here I Stand" on doctrine and distinction in the twenty-first century.[34]

So, five centuries after Luther headed for Wittenberg's church door, North Carolina Lutherans are still taking hammer in hand to forge divergent futures. Three centuries after the thwarted attempt to bring the Palatinate to the Neuse, NALC traditionalists are still counted among the faithful in New Bern. Two centuries after the Teutonic oak ordinations of the Henkelites, their Missouri Synod descendants remain resolute on the particulars of closed communion and blended worship. A century after adopting uniformity in synodical attitudes and activities, some North Carolinians accept the erection of digital screen backdrops, and others do not. Whatever their position or past, all have had to acknowledge that they are like their spiritual ancestors, "the dwellers of the forest," adjusting to change all around. Half the new pastors out of denominational seminaries are women, and many recipients of their witness are not as white as the original Dutch who came down the Great Wagon Road. The Hmong in Mt. Airy, Hispanics in Raleigh, and Ethiopians in Charlotte have altered the approach to the altar, as Lutherans in pew and pulpit carry on the next faithful step of their exodus into the postmodern era.

NOTES

1. The story, told in the guise of providential fulfillment, is to be found in every narrative of Lutheranism in North Carolina. Carl Hammer, Jr., *Rhinelanders on the Yadkin* (Salisbury, NC: Rowan Printing, 1940), 38–41, tells it best, but see also Bernard W. Cruse, Ruth Blackwelder, and George W. Shuford, eds., "Foundations of Lutheranism in North Carolina," 1988 pamphlet of the North Carolina Synod, 19–22. The communion vessels brought by Nussmann are stored in the archives of Organ Lutheran Church, located south of Salisbury.

2. For the best treatment of the underlying issues, see Robert M. Calhoon, *Evangelicals and Conservatives in the Early South, 1740–1861* (Columbia: University of South Carolina Press, 1988), 59–64. The thesis-setting quotation is from Sydney E. Ahlstrom, "The Lutheran Church and American Culture: A Tercentenary Retrospect," *The Lutheran Quarterly* 9 (November 1957), 323.

3. These dates in the 1740s for churches west of the Haw River are artifacts of heritage sketches done for newspapers in the 1920s, and once the first script was written, the subsequent histories took them as literal. See the loose *Salisbury Post* clippings in the files for Organ and Lowerstone Churches, McCubbins Collection, History Room, Rowan Public Library. In contrast, St. John's has in its archives an old cornerstone dated 1768, the year a deed was issued for what appears to be a newly organized congregation. For the Haw Fields area, see Walter Whitaker, *Centennial History of Alamance County, 1849–1949* (Charlotte, NC: Dowd Press, 1949), 28–32. The early history told in G.D. Bernheim and George H. Cox, *The History of the Evangelical Lutheran Synod and Ministerium of North Carolina* (Philadelphia: Lutheran Publication Society, 1898), is largely copied from Bernheim's earlier *History of the German Settlements and the Lutheran Church in North and South Carolina* (Philadelphia: Lutheran Publication Society, 1872).

4. The impressions of the first German pastors are drawn from letters published by William K. Boyd and Charles A. Krummel in "German Tracts Concerning the Lutheran Church in North Carolina during the Eighteenth Century," *North Carolina Historical Review* 1 (January and April 1930), 79–147 and 225–82, and Jo White Linn, ed., *Diary of Johann Gottfried Arends, 1740–1807* (Salisbury, NC: privately published, 1999), 4.

5. Gary R. Freeze, "Reading the Handwriting on the Backcountry Church Walls: Rowan's Stone Sanctuaries, 1754–1815," *The Journal of Backcountry Studies*, no. 1. Until this essay, no one since Adolph Nussmann had ever challenged the authenticity of Arends' ordination by "Joachim Buelow, missionary and inspector over South and North Carolina." The incredulous Nussmann told his German patrons that "they had this man ordained ... by a former clerk in a store." See Boyd and Krimmel, "Tracts," 144.

6. The best descriptions of German customs and culture are found in Joseph R. Nixon, "The German Settlers in Lincoln County and Western North Carolina," *James Sprunt Studies in History and Political Science* (vol. 11, 1912). The quotation from Yoder is expounded upon in Gary R. Freeze, "Family, Faith, and Farm in Old Lincoln County, 1789–1889" in Raymond M. Bost, ed., *Lutheranism with a Southern Accent* (St. Louis, MO: Lutheran Historical Conference, Essays and Reports, 1994), 73–84.

7. The data were collected from Betty L. Krimminger and James R. Wilson, "Eighth Census of Cabarrus County, NC, 1987," typescript in the Lore History Collection, Charles Cannon Public Library, Concord. The Barringers are best surveyed in Paul B. Barringer, *The Natural Bent: The Memoirs of Dr. Paul B. Barringer* (Chapel Hill: University of North Carolina Press, 2011). Bess Beatty, *Alamance: The Holt Family and Industrialization in a North Carolina County* (Baton Rouge: Louisiana State University, 1999), 49–51, sees the Holts as cultural capitalists shopping for the best spiritual advantage.

8. Mark Smith, *Lifting High the Cross: St. John's Lutheran Church* (Baltimore, MD: Gateway Press, 1998), 21–56, covers this phase of denominational history with the most thorough documentation. This is also the best example of the providential quality of local Lutheran historiography, albeit a staunchly Missouri Synod perspective.

9. Raymond M. Bost and Jeff L. Norris, *All One Body: The Story of the North Carolina Lutheran Synod, 1803–1993* (Charlotte, NC: Delmar Printing, 1994), 31–58, provides the most balanced narrative of these organizational matters.

10. Socrates Henkel, *History of the Evangelical Lutheran Tennessee Synod, Embracing an Account of the Causes Which Gave Rise to Its Organization; Its Organization and Name; Its Position and Confessional Basis; Objects of Its Work, Development and Various Sessions; Its Policy and Its Future* (New Market, VA: Henkel & Co., 1890), was, as suggested, a defense of family tradition and an apology for the Henkelite perspective. The quotations are from pages 94–101. The literature by and on David Henkel is voluminous; it is aptly summarized and cited in L. DeAne Lagerquist, "The Henkels: A Family and a Church through Six Decades and More," *Lutheranism with a Southern Accent*, 1–22.

11. Smith, *Lifting High the Cross*, 156–178, provides the most thorough documentary-based analysis. Bost and Norris, *All One Body*, 70–72, uses skillfully the Lutheranism that there was "a dissatisfaction existing in the matter."

12. Notes on the Lippard family, including the naming practices, come from the genealogical charts developed by Harriet R. Schroeder, Lippard family file, Homer Keever Collection, Iredell Public Library, Statesville, NC.

13. Carl Hammer, Jr., "Organ Church and the Broken Key" and "Later German Documents from Organ Church," *American–German Review* (June–August 1947 and April 1951), 33–36 and 14–18. Hammer said he based his research on "old scraps of paper," now lost. The likely Odysseus, in this case, was John N. Stirewalt, one of the builders of the organ; his sons and grandsons became Henkelite ministers. The moderates later sued the Henkelites, and the case ended up in the state supreme court.

14. Martha Agner and Martha Morehead, eds., *The Heritage and History of St. John's Evangelical Lutheran Church, Salisbury, North Carolina, through 1983* (Salisbury, NC: Rowan Printing, 1984), is the best source for the congregational activities of the period in the core area of the synod. For a broader perspective on the context of German pietistic evangelism, see Steve Longenecker, *Gettysburg Religion: Refinement, Diversity, and Race in the Antebellum and Civil War Border North* (New York: Fordham University Press, 2014), 80–92.

15. Mark Smith, ed., "Journal of Rev. John Melanchton Smith: Lutheran Minister of the Gospel, 1852–1908," typescript in the Rhodes Local History Room, Catawba County Public Library, Newton. See also H. George Anderson and Robert M. Calhoon, "Lutheranism in Early Southern Culture" in "*A Truly Efficient School of Theology*": *The Lutheran Theological Southern Seminary in Historical Context, 1830–1980* (Columbia: University of South Carolina Press, 1981), H. George Anderson, ed.

16. See the discussion in Bost and Norris, *All One Body*, 200–01. Also see Mark Oldenburg, "Southern Lutherans and the Common Service," in Bost, *Lutheranism with a Southern Accent*, 177–82.

17. There is little scholarship about the role Lutherans played in the Civil War, aside from Bost and Norris, *All One Body*, 11–128. The characterization of Iredell County Germans in the war is lifted from documents in the Abner Sharpe Papers and the William A. Collins Papers, both at the Southern Historical Collection, University of North Carolina at Chapel Hill. For the more proactive attitudes of the Mt. Pleasant German community, see Beverly B. Troxler and Billy D. Barrier, *Dear Father: Confederate Letters Never Before Published* (Margate, FL: Auciello Publishers, 1989).

18. Paul Hess, *History of St. Paul's Evangelical Lutheran Church, Wilmington, N.C., 1858–1958* (Wilmington, NC: Jackson and Bell, 1958), 1–20. The congregation continued to hold services in German until the early part of the twentieth century.

19. Raymond M. Bost, Robert M. Calhoon, Carl Ficken, Jr., Gary R. Freeze, and Susan W. McArver, "North Carolina Lutherans and the Tests of Time," *Concordia Historical Institute Quarterly* 77 (Fall 2004), 146–48.

20. Smith, *Lifting High the Cross*, 218–51, provides the most comprehensive and colorful account.

21. Bost and Norris, *All One Body*, 211–17; and Smith, *Lifting High the Cross*, 249–71.

22. Bost and Norris, *All One Body*, 190–93; Agner and Morehead, *Heritage and History of St. John's*, 187–90; and Bost et al., "Tests of Time," 148–49.

23. The research suggesting that Progressive Era Lutherans were less assimilated than is traditionally thought is included in Gary R. Freeze, "There May Be Some Obstructionists About: Pro-German Sentiment in Western North Carolina, 1917–1918," in an anthology on North Carolina's role in the First World War, to be published by the University of Tennessee Press in 2018.

24. Jacob L. Morgan, Bachman S. Brown, and John Hall, ed., *History of the North Carolina Church in North Carolina, 1803–1953* (Salisbury, NC: North Carolina Synod, 1953), 23–29, and H. George Anderson, *The North Carolina Synod through 175 Years, 1803–1978* (Salisbury, NC: Historical Work Committee, North Carolina Synod, 1978), 43–58.

25. Gary R. Freeze, *The Catawbans: Boomers and Bypasses* (Newton, NC: Catawba County Historical Association, 2016), 90 and 211; Agner and Morehead, *Heritage and History of St. John's*, 263–95.

26. Bost and Norris, *All One Body*, 278–79; and Agner and Morehead, *Heritage and History of St. John's*, 244–45, 260–61, and 349–57.

27. Freeze, *Boomers and Bypasses*, 148–52; and Smith, *Lifting High the Cross*, 346–67.

28. Freeze, *Boomers and Bypasses*, 86–88.

29. Ibid., 90–94; and Jeff L. Norris and Ellis G. Boatman, Jr., *Fair Star: A Centennial History of Lenoir-Rhyne College* (Virginia Beach: Donning Company, 1990), 145–57.

30. Bost et al., *Tests of Time*, 150–52.

31. Recent developments in the denomination's history in the state are best conceptualized in oral histories compiled since the start of the twenty-first century. See, in particular, interviews with Michael C.B. McDaniel, Mark Menees, Bachman Brown, Brady Faggart, Raymond Bost, Leonard Bolick, and Edgar Trexler in "Histories of Pastors" File, Historical Works Committee, North Carolina Evangelical Lutheran Synod, accessed May 10, 2017 at nclutheran.org. Also see *North Carolina Synod, Lutheran Church in America Historical Supplement, 1953–1963* (Columbia SC: The State Printing Company, 1963), n.p.

32. "History Timeline," Lutheran Family Services of the Carolinas, at lscarolinas.net, accessed May 23, 2017.

33. Mary C. Curtis, "In North Carolina, Same-Sex Marriage Goes to Church," *Washington Post*, Oct. 16, 2014, accessed May 20, 2018, at www.washingtonpost.com. The number of female pastors in the new North American Synod was computed by hand count, done May 20, 2018, using data from the synodical directory at thenalc.org.

34. Southeastern District (Lutheran Church–Missouri Synod), en.wikipedia.org, and "Find a Church," wels.net, the national website of the Wisconsin Synod, both accessed May 22, 2017.

Mennonites

Thomas A. Lehman

This essay employs a broad definition of "Mennonite" inasmuch as major or some-times minor differences in church practices have produced numerous branches, most of which still claim the name "Mennonite." The section on origins describes as briefly as possible the early history and nature of the Anabaptist/Mennonite movement and reports only the formation of those Mennonite branches that have appeared in North Carolina. It is thus not a balanced historical account.[1]

The record of early Mennonites in North Carolina starts with the settlement of New Bern in 1710. The history thereafter is sporadic for many years; no congregation in the state can claim any continuity with Mennonites before the year 1900.

North Carolina today is home to about thirty Mennonite congregations, scattered from Pantego, in Beaufort County, to Asheville, ranging in members' lifestyles from tra-ditional to modern. Each congregation is listed along with some of its characteristics. The order is at first chronological, but after the first few congregations, the dates of origin are of little significance; and the order is by groups of churches belonging to the same conference.

The essay ends with a review and assessment of the characteristics of these congre-gations and their impact on the life of North Carolinians.

Origins[2]

The Protestant Reformation is usually dated from the publication of Martin Luther's Ninety-Five Theses in Wittenberg in 1517, although there were earlier stirrings. Moravians claim Jan Hus of Prague as their original reformer. A Catholic scholar, Hus was active a century before Luther, and was burned at the stake for heresy in 1415.

In 1519, Ulrich Zwingli, pastor of the leading church in Zurich, began to call for reform, and soon a few of his young followers challenged him to push for more extensive changes. He was not persuaded, so in January of 1525, a few young men gathered in a house in Zurich, not far from Zwingli's Grossmünster church, and after careful discussion, baptized each other, a defiant, heretical act.[3]

This rebaptism or believers' baptism of adults who had received infant baptism in the Roman Catholic Church marked the end of their membership in the Catholic Church and the beginning of the Anabaptist (baptizing-again) movement. Because both Luther and Zwingli initially sought to reform the church rather than to leave it, the Anabaptists can be considered the first Protestants of the Reformation era. They were quickly recognized as a threat to the established church; in 1526, the Zurich city council, working closely with Zwingli's church, pronounced a death sentence on Anabaptists. Some Swiss cantons followed Zwingli's preaching, while others remained loyal to Rome. Hippolytus "Bolt" Eberle, the first Anabaptist martyr, was put to death in 1525 by Swiss Catholics as a Protestant; Felix Manz became the first person executed as an Anabaptist, drowned in Zurich in 1527 by the city authorities. Church and municipal government worked hand in hand.

Martyrdom continued for decades in the sixteenth century, and Mennonites had to flee their country in order to remain strong in their faith. As a result, they came to be called "the quiet in the land," having learned that it was best not to attract the attention of the civil authorities. This self-imposed separation from "the world" lasted for centuries and is still prominent among some Mennonites.

Anabaptism spread to the North and East. In 1524, Menno Simons was ordained a priest in the Catholic Church of his homeland, the Netherlands. Disappointed by his experience in the church, he studied the scriptures, and in 1536 publicly left the church, taking refuge with Anabaptists. His extensive writing and principled leadership of the cluster of Dutch Anabaptists lifted him to such prominence that his name was in time adopted by his followers, hence Mennonites. Ironically, the name or its Dutch equivalent is not used in the Netherlands.

In 1693, Jakob Ammann led a group out of the primary Mennonite stream in order to establish stricter discipline. His followers exist today as Amish, historical cousins of the Mennonites. Within both groups are various divisions, so that the range of beliefs and practices over the two bodies is quite wide.

In addition to believers' baptism, the Anabaptists felt called to lead lives of Christian discipleship—the intention to follow the teachings of Christ from day to day. Ethics were and still are as important as doctrine. They also insisted on pacifism as necessary for followers of the New Testament. This added to their uniqueness as a small Christian body and caused them much trouble with the secular authorities who often needed soldiers. After some migrations within Western Europe, many accepted the 1786 invitation of Catherine the Great of Russia, herself German by birth, to leave Prussia and settle in southern Ukraine on her promise of farmland, the rights of citizens, and especially freedom from military service.

In Ukraine some prospered, but others did not. In 1860, some of them decided that the Mennonites had fallen away from important matters of Christian conduct; the result was the formation of a new group, Mennonite Brethren, more pious and under some influence of an itinerant Baptist minister.[4] A further separation over a few issues occurred in the late 1860s in Ukraine, and by 1870 the Krimmer Mennonite Brethren (KMB) Church came into existence, *Krimmer* being the German word for *Crimean*. Many of this group soon immigrated to North America, especially to the prairie states, where the agricultural prospects were similar to those in their homeland in Ukraine. The Krimmer Mennonite Brethren did not officially merge with Mennonite Brethren until 1960.

The mid-nineteenth century had brought unrest among some Mennonites in the United States. Among those who contended for the historic faith was John Holdeman (1832–1900), of Wayne County, Ohio. He increasingly felt that the Mennonite Church no longer was practicing true doctrine in many areas. He appealed to church leaders for spiritual revival. Although some agreed with his evaluation, little action was taken to bring about reform. In 1859, he and others began worshipping separately. This small group eventually organized as the Church of God in Christ, Mennonite. John Holdeman also traveled widely as an evangelist, and many who listened to his preaching experienced spiritual rebirth and were baptized.[5] Congregations were established in the United States and Canada, and are often referred to as Holdemans instead of by the much longer official name.

A minority of Baptist historians acknowledge an early Anabaptist influence.[6] The Baptists have been far more successful than the Mennonites in attracting followers in the United States, especially in North Carolina.

Early North Carolina History

Emigration from the Palatinate and Switzerland to North Carolina was organized by Christoph (later: Baron and Landgrave) von Graffenried, eldest son of a noble family in Bern, Switzerland. He had from youth an adventurous spirit and worked through many difficulties over a period of several years to make his dream of a settlement in North America a reality. He was willing to leave his homeland, in part because he was disgusted by Swiss persecution of Anabaptists. More than six hundred of his followers left England for North Carolina early in 1710. Graffenried mapped out the new settlement and called it New Bern, a name that joins the Neuse River and the capital of Switzerland.

The group included an unspecified number of Anabaptists, one of whom wrote, "If one would present me with the whole lowland, in order that I should go back again to Switzerland and take up the former service I would not do it on account of the freedom of conscience."[7] Some names in the settlement are familiar to Mennonites today: Aeshbacher, Albrecht, Habegger, Jantz, and Janzen. Along with supply problems, the settlement faced heavy skirmishes with Native Americans and did not long survive.

It appears that the New Bern experience is the only time when Mennonites emigrated directly from abroad to North Carolina. Several factors suggest the reason: Mennonite immigrants from Europe generally came from colder climates than North Carolina's, and therefore went to more northern states and later Canada. Some came expecting to raise crops; immigrants from Ukraine, for instance, brought trunks of hard winter wheat to Kansas so as to resume the farming they knew well before leaving their homeland. That worked in the Kansas prairie but would have been impossible in the heavily wooded, rolling hills of North Carolina. Before the Civil War, slavery would have been a cultural barrier, as well; after the war, segregation and Jim Crow would have made conscientious Mennonites feel out of place. The Elk Park experience of the Krimmer Mennonite Brethren illustrates this problem, detailed below in "Salem School."

The little that is known about Mennonites in North Carolina in the later years of the eighteenth century comes from an extensive collection of documents compiled by the Moravians. Especially in legal matters and military service, Mennonites are frequently mentioned alongside the Moravians.[8] "In 1778, the Colonial Assembly of North Carolina adopted a resolution stating that 'all Quakers, Moravians, Dunkards and Mennonists ... shall be admitted to the rights of citizens.' Again in 1779 a resolution was adopted that the same categories of persons be exempted from the draft."[9]

In 1777, the Cherokee Indians were given a large tract of land in what is now western

North Carolina and Tennessee. Five years later, the state of North Carolina moved the eastern boundary further to the west, over the objections of the Cherokees. A 1785 treaty tried to appease the Indians by declaring that any citizens of the United States or persons other than Indians who settle the land forfeit the protection of the United States. Nonetheless, in 1797, North Carolina Governor Samuel Ashe disregarded the treaty and offered to sell 200,960 acres of Cherokee land to two men from Lancaster County, Pennsylvania. They in turn sold off most of it to forty prosperous buyers, many of whom were Mennonites; but the purchase was not upheld in the courts, and the buyers lost their money.[10] Had this transaction not been fraudulent, the far western part of the state could have become home to Mennonite settlers.

Mennonite Churches in North Carolina

Salem School[11]

During the 1890s, church work and community development began in the village of Elk Park, North Carolina, west of Boone and slightly south, next to the Tennessee line. From today's perspective Elk Park could hardly be more remote, but from 1882 to 1950 the town of fewer than five hundred people was served by a railroad line.[12]

A school for white children was established, and soon the Elk Park Academy was serving more than three hundred boys and girls. The principal of the school saw that the African American children needed far more help than the white children and resolved to begin educating them. Opposition from the mainly white community was severe, so that it proved nearly impossible to staff the school. Teachers from afar were sought, and in 1900 Elizabeth and Henry Wiebe, a missionary couple from Kansas, moved to Elk Park as the first Mennonite mission workers among African Americans. They were sponsored by the Krimmer Mennonite Brethren (KMB) Church.

After one year, the Wiebes returned to Kansas, intending to enter into mission work elsewhere. However, a petition from the African American citizens whom they had been serving caused them to return to Elk Park. During the second year, their efforts expanded to include an orphanage for African American children after a homeless boy in great need appealed to them to take him in. This effort created more hostility in the community, but after a few years the Wiebes added worship services, Sunday School, and youth work. The KMB Foreign Mission Board and Kansas churches sent clothing, fuel, a stove, corn, and flour by train.

During their third year, they were joined by Mr. and Mrs. Jacob Tschetter and children, also from Kansas. The Wiebes returned to Kansas in 1908, but the Tschetters continued for a few more years. Together they made an exception to the prevailing pattern of white missionaries helping poor Appalachian whites. Their work planted seeds that produced a cluster of Mennonite Brethren churches that are today centered in Lenoir.[13]

Mennonite Brethren Churches, Present and Past[14]

Boone Mennonite Brethren Church, 1918

The congregation began to form in 1912 when worship services were first held. A small church was constructed on a hilltop in 1918. The congregation has provided gifted leaders to the Mennonite Brethren of the area for many years. In the 1930s, its members, mainly African American, would meet with other churches in the community for regular fellowship in spite of the prevailing segregation.[15]

BEECH BOTTOM MENNONITE BRETHREN CHURCH, 1926; NEWLAND

The church is located in a valley surrounded by high mountains, mostly covered with Christmas trees. The scenery around this small white church building is exceptional, especially in the fall.

THE LIFE CENTER, FORMERLY BUSHTOWN MENNONITE BRETHREN CHURCH, 1932; LENOIR

Peter Siemens, a Mennonite Brethren pastor, came to Bushtown, then known as Bushill, and attracted some fifteen large families to an initial meeting. The promise of a church was enthusiastically received, and meetings began soon thereafter in a private home under the leadership of a local pastor. Today The Life Center is a thriving multi-cultural church, always "Doing Life Through Christ."

LAYTOWN MENNONITE BRETHREN CHURCH, 1940; LENOIR

The startup of this congregation was a church planter's dream because an eager body of believers existed before there was any site for worship. Land was acquired in 1940, and the church today has an average attendance of 45 people.

WEST END MENNONITE BRETHREN CHURCH, FORMERLY LENOIR CHURCH, 1945

A pastor was living in Elk Park, enduring very cold winters, and mindful of too few jobs, no opportunity for higher education, and a shrinking population. Young people were leaving. The Krimmer Mennonite Brethren Conference asked the pastor to move to a more promising location. Lenoir, with booming furniture factories, was an obvious choice; a church and a home for the pastor were built, and a congregation developed. Recently a congregational split occurred, but the remaining members show promise of a growing church.

DARBY MENNONITE BRETHREN CHURCH, 1949; FERGUSON

A nucleus of a pastor's family members gathered around him in 1940 for leadership in the Christian life. By 1949, a church building was completed and paid off in full. The building site was donated by a family who wanted their children to be drawn to Christian living. Family life is very important to the people of Darby. The town is in the western part of Wilkes County, north and slightly east of Lenoir, and near Ferguson.

BETHEL MENNONITE BRETHREN CHURCH, 2012; LENOIR

A Spanish-speaking congregation, the group was drawn into the Mennonite Brethren orbit when they needed a place of worship. Two brothers came to a Bible study at The Life Center, after which they lingered to discuss their need for a building in which to worship. They felt that the denomination to which they belonged did not care to be of much help. A pastor-to-pastor relationship developed, and the New Life Center moved ahead to lease their old building to this young group of committed Christian believers, who responded by joining the Mennonite Brethren Conference.

In a long history in the state, the Krimmer Mennonite Brethren have had other congregations that once served small communities but have had to close their doors because of population shifts in a weak economy. They and their starting dates are Cranberry KMB Church, 1913; Heaton KMB Church, 1913; Shell Creek KMB Church (Tennessee), 1932; Cove Creek KMB Church, 1939.

CRESTON: BIG LAUREL MENNONITE CHURCH AND LANSING:
MEADOW VIEW MENNONITE CHURCH

These two Ashe County churches have so much in common that they will be treated together. Ashe is the state's only county that borders both Virginia and Tennessee. It is mountainous and very rural, and the population is declining. Young people leave for lack of jobs. The county was once known as "the lost province" because neither North Carolina nor Tennessee could make a convincing legal claim to it. In the 1940s and 1950s, jobs were nonexistent; a few animals, a garden and a burley tobacco allotment were the basis of a frugal life. Some families emigrated to southeastern Pennsylvania and told stories of the poverty they had left behind in Ashe County. The Maple Grove and Conestoga Mennonite Churches took up the cause and selected two families by lot to move to Ashe County in the late 1940s. By 1951, the Big Laurel Mennonite Church was erected on the road of the same name near Creston. In 1953, the church offered Bible school and some Sunday school in nearby Lansing. Little Horse Creek Mennonite Church, later named Meadow View Mennonite Church, was constructed near Lansing in 1956 on land donated the previous year.[16] A full-time pastoral couple arrived in April of 1956. Considering the Mennonite Brethren mission and church development that started in 1900 in Elk Park as a single unit, the Ashe County Mennonite development can be considered the second Mennonite site in the state.

Members of both churches care about each other and about the well-being of the rural community. Responding to the Christian call to service is more important than doctrinal details. They are active in fire and rescue work and in providing Bibles for the schools. They host achievement breakfasts for primary and middle-school students and hold fundraising suppers for people dealing with large medical bills or loss of property. Among their members are school teachers, contractors and construction workers, farmers, engineers, a mail carrier, nurses, and a beautician. They have found their way in a weak economy.

In the beginning both churches belonged to the Ohio and Eastern Amish Mennonite Conference, which became the Atlantic Coast Conference of the Mennonite Church. The two congregations dropped out when that Conference joined Mennonite Church USA and have been independent ever since. They sing from "Great Hymns of the Faith." Both congregations have established some degree of relationship to Mennonite Disaster Service and Mennonite Central Committee.

To cite one singular success, Big Laurel Mennonite Church brought about the creation of Rainbow Mennonite Church about five miles west of the Tennessee line. Today it is the strongest of these three churches.

Hickory

That rural Hickory became the home of the first North Carolina congregation now in Mennonite Church USA is a unique story. Hickory is far from the state capital and other major cities, and was not chosen as a site for church development by any Mennonite agency. However, four men from the Franconia Mennonite Conference in Pennsylvania felt called to evangelize in the South. They distributed tracts and held street meetings in several states. In Tennessee, Clayton Godshall and the other men approached a man who was chopping wood on a Sunday afternoon and began to proclaim the Christian message to him. The listener was responsive, and further discussion led to conversion of the man and his wife. The itinerants moved on, but Mr. and Mrs. Godshall returned to the town some time later to encourage this family in their faith, only to learn that they had moved to Hickory. They went there and found him.

Mr. and Mrs. Godshall committed themselves to work in rural Hickory where many people were poor and had no transportation to town for shopping. Moreover, the poorer folks in the community did not feel comfortable in the established churches. So the Godshalls identified a family with musical abilities and added them as partners to go into individual homes with the Christian message. Visitors from Pennsylvania would make weekend round-trips to Hickory to build up the embryonic congregation, and before long the Moyer family with several children moved from there to Hickory, making it possible to offer regular Sunday school starting in 1953.[17] Mountain View Mennonite Church slowly became a reality. At first it provided transportation for worshippers. From an early date, the church was able to send workers to Mennonite Disaster Service projects.

In 1957, with Mountain View a functioning congregation, Clayton Godshall and another couple from the congregation began to develop another Mennonite church, this time in the city of Hickory. This eased the pressure on the Mountain View personnel to transport people to and from the city. As Hickory Mennonite Church developed, its collaboration with Mountain View was intimate. The popular Bible school was given at Mountain View in the morning, and the lessons were repeated in the evenings for those in the city. The two congregations supported each other's Sunday evening services, and for a few years even operated under a single bank account.

Today Mountain View Mennonite Church has about 150 members. Among churches in Mennonite Church USA, this is the oldest in the state. Its purpose continues to be to reach out and form disciples and lead them to Christian maturity. Adults are encouraged to belong to one of the six small groups. A youth program is aimed at children from grades six through twelve.

Today the Hickory area is home to three Mennonite churches, all of which are members of Virginia Mennonite Conference: Mountain View; 3:16 Christian Community Church; and Peace Mennonite Church. These three have extensively cooperated at important times.

The 3:16 Christian Community Church was originally Hickory Mennonite Church. Today it has about fifty members. This congregation and Mountain View Mennonite have felt some influence from the city's many Baptist churches.

Peace Mennonite Church, first known as Hmong Mennonite Church, began in the early 2000s when Laotian Hmong refugees started to settle in Hickory; some of them had been influenced by Mennonite churches in California. A new church began, and the first pastor developed the congregation by teaching the Hmong to read their own language. They have always worshipped in the 3:16 Christian Community Church, and the two congregations occasionally worship together. The evangelistic worship service is animated by lively playing of drums and Hmong traditional instruments.

Employment for many in the Hickory community is in furniture, textiles, and associated trades. The city is also a major supplier of fiber-optic cable.

Triangle and Triad: Durham, Raleigh, Chapel Hill, Greensboro and Graham

Four congregations and a house fellowship constitute the membership of the Eastern Carolina District of the Virginia Mennonite Conference: Durham Mennonite Church, Raleigh Mennonite Church, Chapel Hill Mennonite Fellowship, Greensboro Mennonite Fellowship, and Outlet 10:27, a house fellowship in Graham that takes its name from Luke 10:27. The District representatives meet regularly, and the congregations, especially the three in the Triangle, have significant connections to each other. The district is a member of the North Carolina Council of Churches.

Durham Mennonite Church is the oldest of this group of congregations. It began in 1969 when a pastor was sent by the Virginia Mennonite Mission Board with a vision for church development. At first, they met in the pastor's home, then as their number grew, in meeting rooms nearby in the community. Even before they had a church of their own, they took part in a Mennonite Disaster Service project to repair a needy home in the community.

In 1973, the congregation purchased land for a church and quickly built a log cabin on the site, leaving space for the church building that followed in two stages, finally completed late in 1981. Membership, soon after, reached thirty-seven and regular attendance fifty-six.

During the early 1980s, a trickle of families began regular worship in the congregation, driving some distance to do so. Their common situation was such that it would have been more convenient to be worshipping in Raleigh. The group grew, and the Durham pastor recognized this, encouraging them to establish a church in Raleigh. In early 1986, the Raleigh contingent, having grown to more than thirty people, called a pastor who had just completed seminary studies; the first service, in Raleigh's YWCA, took place in August of that year. On the same Sunday, Durham's founding pastor announced his resignation. The simultaneous loss of pastor and members was difficult to overcome. However, the church retained its commitment to the expansion of Mennonite congregations, drawing up plans in 1987 for a new congregation in Chapel Hill the following year. These plans did not materialize. Later, under new pastoral leadership, the Durham church operated a Montessori preschool for some years. It has always considered itself "a church for all people."

Raleigh Mennonite Church (RMC), having evolved within the Durham church, and consisting mainly of young, ambitious people, made a strong start in 1986. It now includes fifty-four members and has an average attendance that slightly exceeds membership. In the beginning much effort was expended to draft a covenant statement, annually reaffirmed by members, that has served through the years. It declares "Jesus Christ and His gospel of grace and peace" to be the foundation of the congregation's fellowship. It makes few doctrinal points; the primary concern is practical Christian living.

In 1987, the Raleigh and Durham churches sponsored a peace booth at the state fair, which has become a long-term commitment of the Raleigh church. In 1988, and for some years thereafter, RMC hosted a Mennonite Central Committee (MCC) Self-Help sale over an autumn weekend. In 1995, this gave way to a year-round Raleigh store selling goods imported by Ten Thousand Villages, the fair-trade agency that MCC set up for this purpose. That store continues its sale of goods for which artisans in the third world are paid a wage that reflects the value of their work in their own culture. Recently the store moved to Cary.

In 1994, RMC moved from the YWCA to a former elementary school that had become a social-work ministry in an economically troubled neighborhood near public housing. This downtown relocation gave the ministry the benefit of the church's rent, and opened up opportunities for service to the community. In 2000, the public housing was torn down and replaced by housing for mixed-income residents. Neighborhood needs changed and impacted the congregation.

Other RMC ministries have included a relationship to international students at North Carolina State University and a Peace Center that served the immediate neighborhood after 1994. The congregation has also hosted a Service Adventure unit for young people just out of high school, some of them foreign-born, and a Community Development Ministry that aims to teach financial skills to people seeking to improve their lot in the urban world.

Raleigh Mennonite Church believes strongly in the benefits of close fellowship among its members and encourages participation in small groups. One such group consisted of members from Durham and Chapel Hill who were willing to travel to Raleigh for regular worship. But the group also included a roughly equal number of persons who wished to retain their Mennonite ties but were not able to travel to Raleigh. This "small group" grew large enough that hosting became challenging. Rather than split into two groups, the bold step was taken to begin to worship together late in 2001.

Thus, Durham Mennonite Church launched Raleigh Mennonite, which in turn launched Chapel Hill Mennonite Fellowship, though in the latter case the Raleigh church planted the seed of the new congregation without realizing it was doing so.

From the beginning, the Chapel Hill Mennonite Fellowship (CHMF) has benefited greatly from the participation of students in the Duke University Divinity School and the Graduate Program in Religion. No pastor was ever sent to Chapel Hill with the assignment to plant a church. As a result, CHMF grew up by itself and functioned well for the first five years with no designated pastor. Several members participated in a preaching rotation, and others took the responsibilities needed to maintain a simple congregational life. Though CHMF now has a full-time pastor, he preaches approximately half the time, with other Sundays filled by six or seven women and men in the congregation. Faithful adherence to the Revised Common Lectionary is important because, as an early member declared, "it will keep people from preaching on their favorite subjects."

All the preachers hear each other from week to week, which results in some continuity but provides considerable differences in approach and style. Guest preachers are rare. In its first twelve years, CHMF heard sermons from eighty-four preachers.

Because the Duke students are preparing for careers, they come and go, so that CHMF is annually welcoming new members and feeling the loss of some who have finished their studies and moved away. The congregation has to consider itself a "sending congregation" in order to put aside the sense of loss, and instead find satisfaction in seeing its members leave to enter Christian ministry or similar careers. Five of its former members are in university or seminary teaching careers, and at least six are in ministry. There are forty-five members currently active, and an average attendance of fifty, not counting children.

Hymn leaders in CHMF have usually sought hymns that support the sermon topic of the day. As a result, the congregation has sung more than 70 percent of the hymns in *Hymnal: A Worship Book*, jointly published in 1992 by Mennonites and Church of the Brethren.

Greensboro Mennonite Fellowship officially began in September of 1990 after an exploratory group met for two years. The church today has twenty-one members and approximately between thirty-five and forty who regularly attend services. GMF is a diverse congregation representing varying ethnicities, ages, economic levels, and backgrounds. Because of the many talents among members, they attempt to include numerous people in creating Sunday services. The congregation meets for worship in rented space very near the campus of UNC–Greensboro.

A few people from the Greensboro Mennonite Fellowship live in Graham and have developed a group there for fellowship and outreach. It is not clear whether the group will seek membership in a Mennonite conference.

In 2011, the churches of the Eastern Carolina District formed the nucleus of a crew that built a Mennonite Disaster Service house in Cameron, Louisiana, for a man whose home had been destroyed in 2005 by Hurricane Rita. Ten churches, not all Mennonite, contributed to the total crew.

A congregation in Winston-Salem began to form in 1969, first meeting as a Friday evening fellowship in the home of the pastor. The group took the name of Winston-Salem Mennonite Fellowship. Property was purchased and the group met as the Vest Mill Mennonite Church through 1985, at which time the state purchased and cleared the site to build an interstate highway intersection. The congregation moved to another property and took the name Oak Hill Mennonite Church. Membership attrition led to closure in 1999.

Asheville

Asheville Mennonite Church (AMC) began in 1981 as an initiative of three couples who sought membership in the Virginia Mennonite Conference as soon as the nascent group's name was chosen. Membership grew, slowly at first, but by 1987 the congregation moved into its own new building erected with strong cooperation from members on two acres of land.

Today the church's forty members are committed to multiple forms of witness. A widely advertised twice-yearly chicken dinner and bake sale draws many from the community. A meal is prepared in alternate months for over two hundred men with help from AMC, which also collects food items for the needy, and works on the annual fund drive for local pregnancy support services. A care group ministry assists residents in a nursing home. A Spanish-language group rents the church for regular use. These varied activities express a high degree of congregational unity and friendliness toward the people reached in these ways.

Rocky Mount: Fellowship of Christ Church

The congregation was founded in 1977 as Rocky Mount Mennonite Church; the name change occurred in the early 1990s. Originally the congregation was Caucasian, but membership dwindled around 1997 when the neighborhood transitioned to a predominantly African American population. An African American pastor was trained and called. The current ministers are a husband-and-wife team. Their congregation has about one hundred members and is part of the Virginia Mennonite Conference.

The church operates Bethesda House, a transitional living house designed to meet the needs of men who have had problems with substance abuse, domestic conflict, or other difficulties. It provides a safe place where residents receive counseling and training in life skills. The Church also offers a "Graceful Girls" program (ages 8 to 15) to help them develop their identity as Christians and to guide them through adolescent years to wise adulthood in the church. A similar program called "Young Men in Purpose" (ages 12 to 18) seeks to guide boys to pursue a successful and productive Christian lifestyle.

Charlotte: Mara Christian Church

In recent years, thousands of ethnic Chin people have left Myanmar, and many have come to North America. Four congregations, in Baltimore, Indianapolis, and Atlanta, as well as Charlotte, have strong ties to each other and have developed a promising relationship with Mennonite Church USA through its regional conferences. They speak the Mara dialect and identify ethnically with that name.

The church in Charlotte consists of about sixty typically young adults and many children; about 140 persons gather for Sunday afternoon worship in a large Presbyterian church. A lively youth group provides music with a southeast Asian flavor plus times of prayer. At present, there is no ordained leadership.

The Mara men do blue-collar work, some as machinists. A strong work ethic drives them to make their lives succeed in the new country. They believe that their future here depends in part on building solid relationships with other Christian believers. They are aware of other Chin groups and want to establish new congregations among them.

The next two churches are members of Church of God in Christ, Mennonite (Holdeman).

Grifton: Lighthouse Mennonite Church

This congregation of about 140 members started in the mid–1980s; the first people to arrive were from Mississippi. Others have come from Kansas, Ohio, and Ontario. Some members are employed in carpentry (framing), raising livestock, landscape work, or nursing. A school at the same site offers instruction for kindergarten through grade eight and serves about thirty students. The character of the congregation is best summarized by its desire to reach others with the Gospel. The denomination supports a colonization board that identifies attractive sites for new congregations and provides loans to enable young families to relocate and become part of a new witness to the Gospel. The denomination also emphasizes voluntary service for young people.

Morven: Southern Pines Church of God in Christ, Mennonite

The church is in rural Anson County, southeast of Charlotte, just north of the South Carolina line. The nearby town is Morven. Formed in 2001, the church consists of ten families plus six other youths, for a current total of twenty-six members. The families came from Arkansas, Kansas, Georgia, Texas, and Mississippi.

They worship in a double-wide mobile home that also houses a school for grades one through eight. The congregation reaches out to the community by singing in rest homes, Christmas caroling, and sponsoring Easter programs. Employment is varied: farming, raising poultry, home construction, and food service.

Members have health insurance in collaboration with a church conference plan. The church is always pleased to welcome visitors, some of whom come from the surrounding vicinity.

Pantego, Beulaville and Severn

Hope Mennonite Church is in Pantego, approximately forty miles straight east of Greenville. It was founded in 1965 by Mennonites, most of whom relocated from the vicinity of Virginia Beach. A small private school was started in the same year and serves grades one through ten. Some leading characteristics of the congregation are a spirit of love, helpfulness, and even sacrifice for each other. Though a small group, they essentially self-insure to meet needs that are beyond the means of individual members. Logging plus sawmill operation and forestry products are major economic activities, though there are other options.

Currently there are nearly ninety members. This congregation has thus far solved the problem of crowded worship space by relocating members to form congregations in Beulaville and Severn. Home of Cedar Fork Mennonite Church, Beulaville has about thirty-five members and is located between Goldsboro and Jacksonville. Severn Mennonite Church has about fifty members and is just outside of Severn, but has a postal address in nearby Margarettesville. Both towns are northeast of Roanoke Rapids, just below the Virginia state line.

The three congregations affiliate with Nationwide Fellowship Churches, whose members hold various views but share a strong common core. For example, avoidance of too much conformity to the world might mean a stated preference for dark cars, but on the historic Mennonite values, such as nonresistance, there is good uniformity.

Rutherfordton: Pine Ridge Mennonite Church

Pine Ridge Mennonite Church was founded in 1989. It has forty-six members and an average attendance of seventy-eight persons, including many children. The congregation meets the community by distributing literature and aiding families that have suffered disaster or misfortune.

Typical employment is in contracting, logging, cabinetry, and general woodworking. One member operates a butcher shop. Some have taken part in the work of Mennonite Disaster Service. Members highly value their fellowship and the unity that inspires them in Christian living. This congregation also belongs to the Nationwide Fellowship Churches. It is located north of town.

Yanceyville: Caswell Mennonite Church

Caswell Mennonite Church is a congregation of thirteen members located in Yanceyville, Caswell County. It is a satellite of a larger Mennonite church in South Boston, Virginia, and exists in this location as a witness to Mennonite values and lifestyle. It belongs to the Southeastern Mennonite Conference, most of whose seventeen members are in Virginia. The members are engaged in several occupations—writing and publication, carpentry, manufacturing, and health care. In addition to weekly Sunday school followed by a preaching service, there are services on the first Sunday evening and the first and third Wednesday evenings.

The population of Caswell County fell by 2 percent from 2010 to 2013. The population of Yanceyville also fell slightly. During the same period, North Carolina's population grew by about 3 percent.

Etowah Mennonite Church

Etowah is about twenty miles straight south of Asheville on U.S. Highway 64. The Etowah Mennonite Church, started in 1995, has twenty-four members and a typical attendance of thirty-five. The church belongs to Biblical Mennonite Alliance, consisting of some sixty congregations.

The church is a committed group of believers who work well together. They sing from the 1969 *Mennonite Hymnal* and from another book. The church offers a summer Bible school, an important connection to the community. Special services, promoted in the community, are also held at times.

Construction and carpentry are primary occupations of members, some of whom have taken part in Mennonite Disaster Service projects; the congregation also includes a medical doctor and a nurse.

Hiddenite: Dayspring Christian Fellowship

Dayspring Christian Fellowship in Hiddenite, northwest of Statesville, is the only Beachy Amish[18] congregation in the state. It began in 2006 and has about thirty-five members. About half the original members came from Ohio. They currently meet in a community center, but have purchased land and will soon build a place of worship. "Dayspring" comes from Luke 1:78 ("Through the tender mercy of our God; whereby the dayspring from on high hath visited us"), and the congregation sings from the *Christian Hymnary*, compiled by John Overholt.

One member is a paramedic, though most of the men are in construction trades; others do masonry, lawn care, or truck driving. The local economy is stimulated by the presence of orchards and poultry farms, as well as by furniture manufacturing. As North Carolina continues to draw families from other areas, construction work is plentiful. Not surprisingly, the Fellowship has done Habitat work. The congregation also provides a monthly nursing home service. They help the elderly and have an annual widows' supper, which is drawing a growing response.

Members present a clear Christian witness to a mainly religious population. In a moment of levity, the pastor suggested that Alexander County may be the buckle on the Bible belt.

Hiddenite, by the way, is both the town name and the name of an extremely rare green gemstone found in Alexander County and few other places.

Yadkin Valley: Amish

An Amish community was established in the Yadkin Valley west of Winston-Salem in 1985. The group numbers about thirty families. They worship in their own church house; services are in high German, and the Bible is the Martin Luther translation. They sing from a German-language songbook derived from the *Ausbund,* the oldest hymnal in continuous use by Protestants.[19] Travel is by horse and buggy. All families have a plot of land, a cow, and chickens.

These Amish do not belong to any church conference or similar organization. Each congregation is autonomous, but fellowship is close with other Amish settlements that live by the same *Ordnung,* or book of order. They participate in Conservative Mennonite Aid, which springs into action when members suffer a serious loss of property or require costly medical care. Sometimes these Amish also aid when non–Amish neighbors sustain property losses, an occasion to "let our light shine."

The congregation consists of people who are committed to be disciples, to live and work together, and to follow the Sermon on the Mount. The *Ordnung* urges working at home to assure strong family life. If a business becomes too large, it can be split. Thus there are two main crews that construct storage buildings. An Amish store purchases furniture from an Ohio manufacturer and retails it in the area. There are also a greenhouse and a general store with bakery. Hydroponic vegetable growing is done.

An Earlier Amish Settlement[20]

From 1918 to 1944, the Amish occupied reclaimed swampland near Moyock, east of the Great Dismal Swamp State Park, just below the Virginia line, in Currituck County. An Ohio land developer had drained some of the swamp prior to the arrival of the Amish and assisted in the settlement effort.

The rich, highly organic soil supported farming. A nearby rail line made it possible to transport products to an Amish settlement near Norfolk, Virginia. However, the soil also caused a serious problem: hunters (on adjacent lands?) sometimes dropped cigarette butts that would ignite the soil, which would burn until rain came. Mosquitoes were better adapted to the swampy area than the Amish, and pestered them for much of the year. Moreover, the Amish were never able to attract a spiritual leader to the rural community, or produce one. The soil offered no high ground for a cemetery, so that the dead were buried alongside those of the Norfolk settlement. Today there is no trace of the former Amish community. If it had survived it would easily be the second-oldest Mennonite presence in the state, and would be approaching its centennial.

In the entries above are as many North Carolina Mennonite churches as the author has been able to locate. However, the list may grow. Just recently a Bruderhof team from New York state began to explore part of rural North Carolina to seek a suitable site for a new settlement.

The term *Bruderhof* (Society of Brothers) was first used by Hutterites, Anabaptist followers of Jakob Hutter, in lands beyond Switzerland (e.g., Moravia) in the first half of the sixteenth century. Some of them established a Christian communitarian lifestyle. Much later, some migrated to North America; their history is continuous, but not in Germany. The name and the lifestyle were re-established there between the world wars, but the Gestapo interfered sufficiently to drive them out; they scattered to several countries.[21]

Concluding Observations and Questions

How the North Carolina Mennonite Churches Began

In the twentieth century, three starting points for church formation were at work. The first is illustrated in Elk Park, Ashe County, and Hickory, where there were originally no Mennonites; a missionary couple or church planter arrived and began to attract a following, perhaps by service to the local population along with some rudimentary worship. The second genesis of church formation took place where a small group of Mennonites moved to the same rural location in the state more or less simultaneously and began to worship together on arrival. The third, often where people were attracted by educational institutions or employment opportunities, occurred when it was recognized that there might be enough Mennonites in one city to justify finding them and drawing them together. Sometimes they find each other by recognizing ethnic last names, familiar hometowns, or mutual acquaintances. Church development is obviously easiest when people are ready to worship together. What is impressive in the North Carolina experience is that the first churches, all in the western part of the state, slowly grew as a result of bold missionary work.

Acts of the Apostles 1:8 includes this charge to the early Christian believers: "You will be my witnesses ... to the ends of the earth." Suggesting today that any part of North Carolina was ever "the ends of the earth" is a most unwelcome thought. However, the missionary zeal that began in the United States early in the nineteenth century continued well into the twentieth century, and any region where the Gospel, or a particular variety of it, was not being proclaimed was seen by some as a mission field. That spirit seems to have motivated the early work in Elk Park, Ashe County, and Hickory.

Clayton Godshall had previous experience as a church planter. A key step in his method consisted of inviting other Mennonites to join him as a church was beginning to form, then moving on when a leader was identified. Over the course of many years he was responsible for the development of at least ten Mennonite churches, starting in Pennsylvania. He was never ordained.

Membership

Christian churches all need to see their membership increase. Human mortality and the mobility of Americans make finding new members a necessity; new members at more than 5 percent of existing membership per year are needed merely to maintain stability. Broadly speaking, the two ways to achieve this are to attract new believers from the surrounding community and to raise children in a manner that will keep them true to the beliefs of their parents. Where parents have careers and families are small, members' clear expression of the merits and values of their faith will attract others to it, though not usually in great numbers. Where church members, usually very traditional, are tightly bound to the ways that set them apart from the surrounding population, the option is large families with a high expectation that the children will remain in the fold. The Amish are a growing population; there are more Amish in the United States than members of Mennonite Church USA. While transition from a standard American childhood to an Amish adult life is rare, it happens.[22] One example is Marlene C. Miller, author of *Called to Be Amish,* who is "one of fewer than 100 people who have joined the Amish since 1950 and stayed."

Size of Fellowship

Mennonite congregations are generally small, here and across the land, though there are exceptions. In sum, there are many mini-churches but no megachurches. In Mennonite Church USA, 63 percent of the congregations that reported membership numbers in 2015 have fewer than one hundred members. The percentage of congregations with fewer than one hundred is surely higher in North Carolina, but the actual figure is not known.

Population and Population Density

Based on partial data, the population of Mennonites in the state is probably below fourteen hundred members, with congregations typically reporting more attendees than members, a sign of health. The churches are widely scattered over the state, and there appears to be no site where two historically related congregations are close to each other. In contrast, Lancaster County, Pennsylvania, in an area just under one thousand square miles, has Mennonite churches belonging to eighteen conferences, not counting the Old Order Amish, who have made the county a major tourist destination.

"Mennonite" in the Church Name

Is the Mennonite label an asset or a liability? Does it invite people to worship or keep them away? Five of the churches described above do not have the word in the church name. It was a liability in the world wars, when the official pacifist position and the refusal of many Mennonites to enter the armed forces made the Mennonite label unpatriotic. In addition, at all times some people tend to associate Mennonites with Amish. While this has historical validity, and while a nearly continuous gradation or spectrum of cultural adaptations from Amish through Mennonites can be made, the association says almost nothing about today's more progressive Mennonites. Clear identification as Mennonite also attracts some people who are familiar with Anabaptist/Mennonite practices, or who may be drawn to a church that upholds the peace position.

Dropping the denominational label from the name of a congregation, while retaining denominational membership, also occurs in other denominations, such as the Baptists. It is probably less common among Methodists, and unknown among Catholics.

Affiliations

Overall, twenty-nine of the churches described above belong to one of seven conferences, which means an average of just over four churches per conference. This is both misleading and instructive; misleading because the number of Mennonite churches in the state is small, so the number per affiliated conference will be small. However, it also points to a general Mennonite phenomenon—the tendency to deal with differences in the practice of Christian life by breaking apart, whether the differences are large or sometimes small. According to 2010 research by Donald Kraybill, a professor at Elizabethtown College, American Mennonites belong to roughly sixty different organizing bodies, and some of the more traditional groups are growing rapidly because of their high birth rates.[23] The number of organizing bodies is no cause for pride, but neither is it a problem only for Mennonites.

Ease of Highway Access

As a broad generalization, congregations that belong to Mennonite Church USA are the most progressive Mennonites in the state and in the country, though both have quite a range of positions. In North Carolina, all the congregations that belong to MC USA are in cities served by major federal highways. Though there are exceptions, this tends not to be the case for the other Mennonite congregations, many of which are very rural. Whether this means that the MC USA congregations wish to interact more freely with the world, or that the other congregations prefer to be at a remove from the world's traffic and distractions, is conjecture. The cities along major highways offer more career and educational opportunities, but the cost of land for homes and churches is considerably higher. This has to be a serious consideration for some of the congregations whose members have settled in rural counties in recent decades. North Carolina still offers affordable land, but no Mennonite church is within thirty miles of the Outer Banks. It is tempting and true to say that all of the MC USA churches are near Interstate highways, but the Interstate highways were not always built prior to the establishment of the various congregations.

How Much Education Is Good?

Mennonites in this state participate in the full range of educational institutions, from some who come for advanced degrees to others who are enrolled in a local Mennonite school seeking just enough education to be productive members of their community. The state has no Mennonite college, and there is no thought of establishing one. However, there are Mennonite faculty members at Duke University, UNC–Chapel Hill, UNC–Greensboro, and North Carolina State University.

A Simple Lifestyle?

Mennonites have historically claimed a simple lifestyle, and continue to do so, perhaps out of habit. However, the basis of the claim is easily obscured by iPhones and other appurtenances of modern life on one end of the aforementioned spectrum of cultural adaptations. All that can be said today for Mennonites is that they are generally not obsessed with material possessions. No competition is felt with the next person on the church bench.

Are Mennonites Wealthy?

Though no income data are at hand, it is safe to say that very few Mennonites in North Carolina, if any, are destitute, and few would be considered very wealthy. Some are prosperous, but rarely is there an ostentatious car parked near a Mennonite church; the typical car is likely to give the owner years of service.

Is There a Mennonite Glass Ceiling?

The present author has not dealt with any Mennonite congregation that has a woman as pastor, with the exception of the husband-and-wife team that leads the Rocky Mount congregation; and they have worked together for years. Raleigh Mennonite Church also had such a team for quite a few years, but no woman was called to a North Carolina Mennonite pastorate except as an adjunct to her husband until Raleigh Mennonite Church did so in 2016.

Elements of Worship

A highly liturgical Mennonite service is almost an oxymoron. Worship tends to be low-church, in some cases with no prescribed attire for the preacher, and sometimes no raised chancel. At the extreme, one can preach in jeans and sandals, and no one will be bothered. In matters of dress, the "priesthood of all believers" connotes equality in the sight of God.

Singing

Mennonites have a strong tradition of singing four-part harmony, often unaccompanied. Some congregations can sing as well as nonprofessional church choirs. There are also some Mennonites who like to sing to the accompaniment of praise bands. Modernity can be hard to avoid.

Some of the contacted congregations have named the hymnal they currently use. With the exception of the churches in MC USA, the hymnal is seldom the one produced and promoted for use in MC USA congregations. However, most of the other congregations retain the word "Mennonite" in their names. While this is bad for Mennonite hymnal sales, it is clearly good for the historic Mennonite brand.

Mennonites and the Cultures of North Carolina

The impetus for publication of this book comes from the North Caroliniana Society, which deals in literature, history, and culture. It is thus appropriate to ask what contributions, if any, Mennonites have made in these three areas. In literature, nothing significant has been written that shows Mennonites to be Carolinians. Elsewhere, fictional works based on the Amish have become a popular genre, but this movement has not yet drawn attention to the Amish of this state. No historical works other than the occasional doctoral dissertation come to mind.[24]

The reader may be puzzled by the plural word "cultures" above. The author tells friends living elsewhere that if North Carolina must be described in a single word, the word is "diverse." It is appropriate to consider the ways in which various North Carolina Mennonites situate themselves in their local or proximate cultures; the term "resident aliens" probably describes the relationship of most Mennonites to their cultural environment, though to differing degrees.[25] From professors and lawyers in cities, to farmers and carpenters in rural areas, the state makes a home for all of them.

ACKNOWLEDGMENTS

The author thanks the following persons, all of whom either supplied useful information or pointed toward it: Tom Coletti, Jim Duncan, Keith Ensz, Edward Godshall, Kelvin Good, Simone Horst, Harold Huber, Terry Hunt, Rosemary King, Sidney King, Mark Landis, Mary Jo Lehman, Jesse Martin, Ross Mast, Anthony Miller, Lowell Miller,

Vernon Moyer, Wellington Moyer, Marcia Nice, Dave Nickel, Alan Reberg, Rosene Rohrer, Dwight Roth, Kim Schneider, Bill Sommers, Skip Tobin, Mervin Wengerd, Dan Yoder.

NOTES

1. Dyck, Cornelius J. ed., *An Introduction to Mennonite History* (Scottdale, PA: Herald Press, 1967); Estep, William R., *The Anabaptist Story* (Grand Rapids, MI: Eerdmans, 1995); Klaassen, Walter, *Anabaptism In Outline: Selected Primary Sources (Classics of the Radical Reformation)* (Scottdale, PA: Herald Press, 1981; Loewen, Harry, and Steven Nolt, *Through Fire and Water: an overview of Mennonite History* (Scottdale, PA: Herald Press, 1996); Smith, C. Henry, *The Story of the Mennonites*, 4th edition, revised and enlarged by Cornelius Krahn (Newton, KS: Mennonite Publication Office, 1957); Snyder, C. Arnold, *Anabaptist History and Theology: An Introduction* (Pandora Press, 1995); Weaver, J. Denny, *Becoming Anabaptist: The Origin and Significance of Sixteenth-Century Anabaptism* (Scottdale, PA: Herald Press, Second Edition, 2005).

2. Dyck, Cornelius J. ed., *An Introduction to Mennonite History* (Scottdale, PA: Herald Press, 1967), 39.

3. Dyck, Cornelius J. ed., *An Introduction to Mennonite History* (Scottdale, PA: Herald Press, 1967), 33–34.

4. C. Henry Smith, *The Story of the Mennonites*, 4th edition, revised and enlarged by Cornelius Krahn. (Newton, KS: Mennonite Publication Office, 1957), 428ff.

5. http://churchofgodinchristmennonite.net/en/who_we_are, accessed July 20, 2016.

6. http://www.britannica.com/EBchecked/topic/52364/Baptist, accessed July 20, 2016.

7. http://docsouth.unc.edu/nc/graffenried/graffenried.html, accessed on July 20, 2016 © This work is the property of the University of North Carolina at Chapel Hill.

8. "Mennonites in North Carolina," *Mennonite Quarterly Review*, 1, no. 3 (July 1927): 69.

9. Harold S. Bender, Reynold Sawatzky and Richard D. Thiessen, "North Carolina (USA)," *Global Anabaptist Mennonite Encyclopedia Online*. February 2009. Web. April 16, 2015. http://gameo.org/index. php?title=North_Carolina_(USA)&oldid=114435.

10. Ira. D. Landis, "The 1797 North Carolina Land Swindle," *Mennonite Historical Bulletin* VII, no. 1 (March 1946).

11. Conrad Ostwalt and Phoebe Pollitt, "The Salem School and Orphanage; White Missionaries, Black School," in *Appalachians and Race: The Mountain South from Slavery to Segregation*, ed. John C. Inscoe (Lexington, KY: The University Press of Kentucky, 2001), 235–44.

12. http://en.wikipedia.org/wiki/Elk_Park,_North_Carolina.

13. Barrett, Lois. "Wiebe, Elizabeth Pauls (1876–1957) and Wiebe, Henry V. (1871–1943)." *Global Anabaptist Mennonite Encyclopedia Online*. 1989. Web. 5 Mar 2015. http://gameo.org/index.php?title=Wiebe,_ Elizabeth_Pauls_(1876–1957)_and_Wiebe,_Henry_V._(1871–1943)&oldid=122656.

14. This section is based on a personal communication from Pastor Terry Hunt, District Minister for the Mennonite Brethren churches of the area.

15. Heidi Corydell Williams, *Our State* magazine, February 2015. http://www.ourstate.com/junaluska/. Accessed March 10, 2015.

16. Ross Mast, personal communication, April 2015. See also E. Roger Sappington, "The Mennonites in the Carolinas," *Mennonite Quarterly Review* XLI, no. 2 (April 1968): 96–116.

17. Edward Godshall, personal communication, May 11, 2015.

18. Beachy Amish are less strict than the majority of Amish, and accept some technologies such as tractors and telephones.

19. Friedmann, Robert. "Ausbund." Global Anabaptist Mennonite Encyclopedia Online. 1953. Web. May 6, 2015. http://gameo.org/index.php?title=Ausbund&oldid=130415.

20. "The Amish Settlement at Moyock in Currituck County, NC." Web. 11 July 2015. http://amishamerica. com/north-carolina-amish/

21. Arnold, Eberhard C.H. "Rhönbruderhof (Hessen, Germany)." Global Anabaptist Mennonite Encyclopedia Online. 1959. Web. 3 Dec 2015. http://gameo.org/index.php?title=Rh%C3%B6nbruderhof_(Hessen,_ Germany)&oldid=106655.

22. Marlene C. Miller, *Called to Be Amish: My Journey from Head Majorette to the Old Order* (Harrisonburg, VA: Herald Press, 2015.)

23. Green, Emma. 2015. Gay and Mennonite. *The Atlantic*, March 18. Accessed April 25, 2015. http:// www.theatlantic.com/features/archive/2015/03/gay-and-mennonite/388060/.

24. Thomas A. Lehman and Michael T. Lee, *North Carolina State Parks*, 2nd ed. (Amazon, 2013).

25. Stanley Hauerwas and William Willimon, *Resident Aliens: Life in the Christian Colony*. (Nashville, TN: Abingdon Press, 1989).

Methodists

Michael Perdue

> People did not want to become Methodists because they hoped thereby to
> secure social, political, or economic advancement. On the contrary, it was
> unpopular to be a Methodist.... Methodism made progress in America
> because it was not hampered by traditions, by creedal tests, or by racial
> ties. It could work with all classes of people and with all nationalities....
> The Methodists endeavored to spread scriptural holiness rather than the-
> ology over America.[1]

This observation by the eminent twentieth-century Methodist historian and church
leader Paul N. Garber stressed the existence of American Methodism on the eve of the
Unification of 1939, a juncture of social change and religious consciousness. Methodism
was more than an evangelical movement in the annals of American religious history.
Garber expounded upon the premise, which forms one aspect of this survey of North
Carolina Methodism, that these followers of John Wesley and Francis Asbury evolved
from a rural-dominated religious sect into a powerful, national denomination with its
strength and leadership based in the urban areas. Methodism developed from humble
origins in England in the mid-eighteenth century to become the largest religious group
in America a century later. By the dawn of the twentieth century, Methodism represented
a cross section of society, a leading bastion of which was the upper class.

The history of Methodism in North Carolina has too seldom attracted the interest
of professional or novice historians. The church, as one of the last remaining essential
societal links with the past, maintains an important, albeit imperfect, bond within the
American South today. Yet Methodist leaders in the local church and at higher levels
have oftentimes over the decades paid tepid lip service to the cause of historic preservation. Consequently, the denomination has suffered grievous losses in areas of historic
church architecture and records and has yet to reverse this negative trend in a major way.
Unlike Quakers, Moravians, and Presbyterians, for example, Methodists in North Carolina never demonstrated until recent years a true appreciation for—and a desire to preserve—their heritage. This indifferent attitude can be attributed, in part, to the fact that
the early Methodists were not often among the more learned people of the region. The
foundation of this fledgling denomination, steeped in the tradition of the circuit-riding
itinerant pastor and the multi-church circuit system, did not promote a stability, reliability,
or permanence that is essential to maintaining church records and historical data. It is
this unfortunate tradition of Methodism, in spite of limited yet noteworthy recent

achievements in historic preservation and scholarship, that continues to plague the denomination. Likewise, in North Carolina, no comprehensive history of its Methodists of all stripes has been produced.[2]

Not in the nineteenth, twentieth, nor in the twenty-first century, have the Methodists been "one people." There existed then and continue to exist many divisions, sub-groups, and, yes, barriers under the standard of Methodism. However, overcoming those divisions and barriers ultimately promoted growth and achievement in the story of the Tar Heel disciples of Wesley and Asbury. Perhaps this essay about the rise and development of Methodism in North Carolina will inspire a sustained spirit of historical scholarship.

The birth pangs of Methodism have been recorded in many studies and lie beyond this scope; here we focus on how Wesley's subordinates and followers fanned the flames of faith in North Carolina. Arriving somewhat late upon the scene in the Royal Colony of North Carolina, Methodism was not initially perceived as a separate religious denomination. Indeed, nothing could have been further from the mind of Mr. Wesley, who identified the great need for reform and revival within a stagnated Church of England. Wesley saw Methodism as a means of promoting reform and change within an already well-established church system. Traditionally, the origins of Methodism are traced to Wesley's famed, yet ill-fated, attempt to minister to the Native Americans while he was an Anglican missionary in Georgia in the 1730s. To Wesley, his time in Georgia was a dismal failure countered only by his fortuitous association with Moravian missionaries whose strong faith in God made him question his own. Subsequent contact with these brethren led Wesley to his actual conversion at a Moravian meeting on Aldersgate Street in London in May 1738. The so-called "Aldersgate Experience," during which Wesley felt his heart "strangely warmed," brought the troubled cleric to the full realization of the grace of God.

Ultimately, Wesley would disagree with the Moravians on a number of doctrinal issues. For example, the Moravian practice of "stillness," in which the unsaved should in silence refrain from all means of grace until truly converted, was rejected by Wesley, who believed that grace was expressed through the discipline of the means of grace. Wesley contended that good works could be done as the unsaved grew in faith until conversion was achieved, and that God's grace—prevenient grace—would carry the seeker until he responded to the offer of salvation *by faith*. Nevertheless, Wesley did adopt some of the Moravian traditions and practices into his Methodist reform movement.[3] It is ironic that while many Moravians are quite familiar with their ties to and influences upon John Wesley, comparatively few Methodists are.

John Wesley organized several Oxford University leaders into a group of Anglican reformers known derogatorily by critics as "Methodists," due to the group's methodical practices. It has been said that Wesley's beliefs and subsequent policies "differed mainly in emphasis rather than in substance" from the Anglican Church; he wished to reform, not secede from, the Church of England. Methodism stressed the emotional rebirth of the soul as opposed to the deductive reasoning route to salvation that was espoused in the established church. Moreover, this reform movement emphasized a "preaching" aspect that was not only lacking in the formalistic Church of England, but was suspect. Wesley's precepts of freedom of choice, a God abundant in prevenient and redeeming grace, and a society without class distinction appealed to those of the lower "unchurched" classes in England.[4]

As the Wesleyan movement took hold and spread like wildfire in England, plans were made to bring the crusade to America. In 1739, George Whitefield, the noted English

Anglican cleric and associate of Mr. Wesley, arrived in America. During the tremendous wave of revivalism known as the Great Awakening, he began to lay the foundations of Methodism in the colonies. Whitefield would make seven visits to the colonies during his long ministry, and he preached throughout north and south. In North Carolina he preached in several settlements including New Bern, Wilmington, and Bath—where tradition relates that he placed upon the spiritually wayward community a curse to remain a small town—but his success in the colony was greatly limited, as he noted in a January 1740 diary entry: "In North Carolina there is scarcely so much as the form of religion." Clearly, he did not enjoy the achievements he attained in the northern colonies. Yet it must be stated that Whitefield was not a personal representative of Wesley as has been alluded to by earlier historians.[5]

Not until 1769 did the first "official" Wesleyan missionaries arrive in America. In 1772, one of these preachers, Joseph Pilmore, began a southern trip and organized Methodist societies in Virginia, namely in Portsmouth and nearby Norfolk. On September 29 of that year, Pilmore delivered what has been regarded as the first "official" Methodist sermon in North Carolina when he spoke to a congregation at Currituck Courthouse near what is now Coinjock. In December, Pilmore spoke to assemblages at Edenton; New Bern, "the genteelist congregation since leaving Philadelphia"; and Brunswick. A subordinate of Pilmore's, the Rev. Robert Williams, a native of Ireland and an unauthorized publisher of Wesley's hymns, arrived in America just ahead of Pilmore; in company with the noted Anglican priest Devereux Jarratt he extended his preaching into the Roanoke River valley of northeast North Carolina. It has been suggested in recent years that Williams may have beaten Joseph Pilmore, ever so slightly, in preaching the first "official" Methodist sermon in the colony, but this claim cannot be conclusively proven by the surviving fragmentary documentation. Until after the American Revolution, then, the development of Methodism was mostly confined to areas in close proximity to the eastern seaboard, communities where the Anglican Church existed.[6]

In 1773, the first American Conference of Methodists in America convened at Philadelphia; by 1776, growth in North Carolina was encouraging enough for the Methodist Conference to establish the Carolina Circuit. It was the first to lie entirely within the colony, although its precise limits remain unknown. Initially, the circuit contained 683 adherents; by the following year, that number had increased by nearly thirty percent, making it the second largest circuit in the colonies. In 1778, the Carolina Circuit was divided into three smaller circuits from east to west: Roanoke, Tar River, and New Hope; the last of these only extended as far west as approximately present-day Greensboro. During the late 1770s, circuit riders began to traverse the western part of North Carolina, and in 1780 a new circuit, the Yadkin, was added to cover the remainder of the state.

These four circuits were further divided in the 1780s as membership increased. It doubled to a few thousand between 1782 and 1784. More itinerants were needed to travel these circuits as momentum increased. By the fateful year of 1784, nearly one-fifth of the nation's fifteen thousand Methodists lived in North Carolina.[7]

As the American Revolution was drawing to a close, Francis Asbury, Wesley's "General Assistant" in America who remained in the colonies during the war, considered the eventual outcome of the Methodist movement. The Anglican Church in the former colonies was for all intents and purposes dead. Would Methodism die an ignominious death alongside her Anglican mother, or would she have to assert herself as a separate religious entity? Asbury struggled to find within himself the proper answer and course to take. Finally, he concluded that Methodism, in order to survive, must become a separate organized denomination. Mr. Wesley was most reluctant to accept this point of view, but even he realized that without the ordained Anglican clergy to administer the sacraments to Methodists the movement would disintegrate, and an independent denomination, *totally* free from Wesley's influence, would arise in America.[8]

Faced with such alarming possibilities, Mr. Wesley had no other course but to allow for the organization of a "Methodist Church" in America. In September 1784, he ordained fellow Anglican minister Thomas Coke "Superintendent" of the Methodist societies in America. Upon arrival in the States, Coke informed Asbury of Wesley's views concerning the organization of the new church. Asbury would give up his position as Wesley's General Assistant in order to serve as joint superintendent with Coke and also to possess the powers and privileges, if not the title, of bishop. Seeing that Wesley still wanted to maintain control from England and now wanting to distance himself from the leader of the movement, Asbury was apathetic to the plan. He accepted it only on the condition that he be elected to the position of joint superintendent by the unanimous vote of the Methodist preachers in America. Asbury was confident of winning such an election, for the American preachers looked to him, not Wesley, for guidance and final decisions. Obviously, Asbury was letting Wesley know in no uncertain terms that henceforth the directives of the latter "would no longer carry the force of law."[9]

The Christmas Conference of December 1784 in Baltimore organized the "Methodist Episcopal Church" in the United States of America, the first national religious organization in the young republic. Asbury and Coke were elected superintendents for the Methodist societies. On his own initiative, Asbury later assumed the title of "bishop" for the denomination, another indication of his increasing independence from Wesley. The Christmas Conference had also approved the adoption of the Articles of Religion, Wesley's abridgement of the Thirty-Nine Articles of the Church of England. This form of church discipline served as a means of regulating all Methodist societies. The Christmas Conference also gave birth to the General Conference or, in other words, the national association of Methodist ministers in America. In essence, Methodist preachers could now become ordained ministers and administer the sacraments of the church. Methodism had turned a full 180 degrees from its original intended purpose; the reform movement within an established denomination had become an organized and functioning religious entity unto itself.[10]

Following the Christmas Conference in December 1784, the Green Hill House at Louisburg in Franklin County, North Carolina, was selected as the site for the first meeting of an annual conference of the fledgling Methodist Episcopal Church. From April 20 to 24, 1785, twenty preachers from circuits in Virginia and the Carolinas met in the home, which today is a United Methodist Heritage Landmark and is on the National Register of Historic Places.[11]

The name "Methodist Episcopal Church" has often been misunderstood by the laity. The term "Episcopal" referred to the system of church government. Under the episcopal system, bishops were elected to office for life and presided over the conference of preachers on the national or general level, and later the sub-conference or annual conference level. Originally the bishop of the General Conference made the appointments of ministers to their respective circuits. The fact that the Methodist Episcopal Church was controlled solely by ministers would be a bone of contention for the denomination for nearly a century. In 1801, the district concept of church governance was implemented whereby several adjoining circuits were placed into districts presided over by an elder. These "Presiding Elders" served as intermediaries between the circuit minister and the bishop. (In the twentieth century, the title was changed to "District Superintendent" and continues today.) In 1802, the annual conference level was instituted to group together adjoining districts within a certain geographic area or state. The conference met yearly and made pastoral appointments to the districts, circuits, and stations—one church charges.[12]

Much of North Carolina originally fell into the Virginia Annual Conference in two districts. The Salisbury District encompassed the north central portion of the state to the foothills; the New Bern encompassed most of the coastal region. Moreover, the South Carolina Conference reached into south central and southeastern North Carolina, and the Western Conference's Holston District took in some North Carolina territory west of the Blue Ridge Mountains. The Virginia Conference membership would soon be nearly equally divided between the states of Virginia and North Carolina, but it would not be until the 1830s that Methodists in the Old North State would be able to establish themselves into more of a statewide conference largely their own. In the meantime, the Virginia Annual Conference would occasionally meet in North Carolina in such towns as New Bern, Tarboro, Raleigh, and Oxford. As early as the 1810s, the Methodist faith, buoyed by the camp meeting movement now sweeping the region, was quickly becoming an important force in the state.[13]

As the number of members and societies or congregations increased, circuits and districts would be divided and realigned into smaller, more manageable units. Even so, it was not at all uncommon for one rider to have as many as twenty preaching points on a single circuit. For these reasons, worship services were in many cases held during the week and not solely on Sundays.

Still, it was not until 1836 that the General Conference approved a division of the Virginia Conference and consequent establishment of a North Carolina Conference that would include most of the eastern and piedmont regions of the Old North State. The first pastoral appointments to the North Carolina Conference were made at the 1837 session of the Virginia Conference, and the new conference held its first annual session in Greensboro in January 1838. Many pastors in the Virginia Conference with ties to North Carolina transferred to the new conference.[14] The dividing line between the Virginia and North Carolina conferences during some of the antebellum years did not strictly follow state boundaries; there would be from time to time some spillover from one conference into another. The South Carolina Conference continued to extend into southeastern and southwestern North Carolina, including at times towns such as Wilmington and Charlotte, as late as 1869. In 1824, the Holston Conference was created from the Tennessee Conference, and much of the north central mountain region of North Carolina—for example, the Asheville area—remained in the Holston Conference until 1889.[15]

Even with the development of districts and the annual conference system of Methodist church governance, the most important element or structure in these early years was the class meeting. In England and America, each society or congregation was divided into classes, or sub-groups, of some twelve-to-fifteen people each. The leader of each class was to keep watch over the spiritual welfare of the members and collect tithes and offerings that would be handed over to the stewards of the circuit. Members who remained in good moral standing would be issued tickets for admission to the Lovefeasts, services adapted from the Moravians including a simple meal of bread and water, singing, exhorting, and preaching. Eventually, by the mid-nineteenth century, class meetings began to die out partly as a result of the success of the camp meeting movement, the rise of Sunday schools, and the greater tolerance of human frailties. Still, the class meeting helped to fill a great spiritual void that monthly or twice-monthly worship services could not fill.[16]

Local church government was largely invested in the circuit quarterly conference. These quarterly meetings were held on a rotating basis among the numerous churches on the circuit or in relatively fewer station churches. The district presiding elder would moderate meetings with the circuit or station pastor, hear reports from local church officials, transact whatever business was pertinent, collect offerings, and hold preaching services.[17]

The circuit minister possessed the most arduous position of authority in the church. A touchstone of American Methodism, the horseback-riding itinerant preacher made the rounds to visit as many as twenty congregations in some early circuits. Because of such all-consuming duties, preachers were not encouraged to marry nor were arrangements made to house a preacher's family if one did marry. To marry generally meant to retire from the itinerancy and "locate," the term used by the denomination. The travel schedule was so brutal that one historian claimed that during the years prior to 1819, sixty percent of circuit riders who died in active service were under the age of forty.[18]

An institution that advanced Methodism in North Carolina from "backwoods evangelism to respectable town revivalism" was the camp meeting, a concept embraced by Bishop Asbury. The origins of the camp meeting movement in the United States are obscure at best and often the focus of disputes. The Presbyterians, for instance, are often credited with being among the "first movers" of the phenomena. Open air preaching was not unknown to such early Methodists as Wesley, who employed the practice in England, but the great divine would not have approved of the overpowering emotional demonstrations that often accompanied such meetings. Especially in the South, the early campgrounds were largely in cleared areas near the local meetinghouses or just outside the towns and settlements. Services lasted for days, sometimes weeks, with preaching as often as four times a day. Itinerant and local pastors drew hundreds and even thousands from surrounding counties to attend these annual events that led to countless conversions and expanded membership rosters.[19]

It is far beyond the scope of this survey of North Carolina Methodism to ascertain the precise origins of camp meetings, but the earliest known one in the state dates to 1794 when the Rev. Daniel Asbury (no relation to Francis) held such an assembly near the Lincoln-Catawba County line. Thus began what came to be known as Rock Springs Campground at Denver, North Carolina. This site is still active in camp meetings today and is on the National Register of Historic Places. In the ensuing years, camp meetings sprang up all over the state and continued until the Civil War. Thereafter, they were far less numerous and in rural areas only.[20]

Times of Unrest, Schism and Division

It was inevitable that Methodism in the United States would experience times of instability, turmoil, and division. In fact, seeds of unrest were sown within the fertile soils that produced the initial crop of Methodists in America. As representative democracy was developing, so too was the rather exclusive hierarchy of the Methodist Episcopal

Church. In a time when the common man was the foundation of civil authority, the church of the followers of Wesley was under the governance of one man, Francis Asbury, and a rather small lot of like-minded clergy. Asbury controlled all pastoral appointments on the district and local levels. Appointments to a particular charge seldom lasted more than one year in those early days; the famed four-year pastoral appointment was decades in the future. Ministers' annual appointments were unknown to them until simply "read out" at the close of the conference by Bishop Asbury.[21]

That a minister could not appeal an appointment he felt to be detrimental or unsuitable was an issue that rankled deeply a prominent presiding elder in the church from Virginia, James O'Kelly. At the 1792 General Conference, O'Kelly sponsored a resolution calling for the right to appeal an appointment; it was voted down after a long and exhausting debate. O'Kelly and his ministerial supporters and several churches withdrew from the denomination to form one of their own. In it, laymen and ministers were accorded rights not extended to them under the discipline of the Methodist Episcopal Church. The "O'Kellyites," then known as the "Republican Methodist Church," grew in sufficient numbers to reverse membership growth among Episcopal Methodists in both Virginia and North Carolina during the 1790s, and by the dawn of the new century emerged with a new name for their new denomination: the Christian Church.[22]

By the 1820s rising sentiment favored an increase in power of both the laity and the local (or non-itinerant) pastors, all of whom had been absent from the annual and general conferences since the Christmas Conference of 1784. Episcopal Methodism was, in essence, an aristocracy in which "the spirit of democracy worked," a denomination that "faced the curious paradox of gaining phenomenal influence among lay persons with whom it would not share ecclesiastical authority."[23] At the 1824 General Conference, a petition was submitted and rejected for the incorporation of democratic principles into the church government. Consequently, members of the clergy and laity organized to advocate for democratic reform within the Methodist Episcopal Church, and many of these "Union Societies" were organized all over the eastern half of the country, especially in North Carolina. The Roanoke Union Society, organized at Sampson's Meeting House in Halifax County in November 1824, was the first of its kind in the state and the second of its kind in the nation. It must be stated here that the Union Societies desired to reform the Methodist Episcopal Church, not to create a separate denomination.[24]

Yet, weary of failed attempts at reform, advocates called for a meeting at Whitaker's Chapel near present-day Enfield in Halifax County on December 19, 1828. Here was established the North Carolina Conference of the Associated Methodist Church, an entity wholly separate from the Methodist Episcopal Church. With a few exceptions, in which entire congregations withdrew from the Methodist Episcopal Church, local congregations were organized by ministers of the Associated Methodist and later the Methodist Protestant Church. Once the General Conference of the Methodist Protestant Church was organized in 1830, the North Carolina Conference of the Associated Methodist Church became allied with the national body. Technically, the North Carolina Conference predated the General Conference and was older than any other annual conference within the new denomination. During the period between the formation of the North Carolina Conference and its assimilation into the Methodist Protestant Church in 1830, six preaching circuits were created within the eastern half of the state.[25]

The basic democratic principles of the Methodist Protestant Church arose from the enthusiasm for Jeffersonian Democracy that abounded in rural America. The central portion of North Carolina possessed deep commitment to this sentiment, and there the Methodist Protestant Church would always be the strongest. Among the changes initiated in the new denomination, both laity and local pastors were admitted into the annual and general conferences, a marked departure from the Methodist Episcopal Church. Second, the "M.P. Church" refused to have an episcopacy, opting instead for presidents elected from the conference bodies themselves. Third, the district presiding elders were elected by the membership of the annual conference and not appointed by a bishop. Consequently, the Methodist Protestant Church was perhaps American Methodism's most direct and shining attempt at establishing a democratic form of church government.[26]

The next major schism that threatened the stability of the Methodist Episcopal Church was little more than a decade away, but the roots of disunion could be traced back to the denomination's origins. The role of African Americans in early Methodism in North Carolina has been a neglected and largely untold story. For the most part, the early history of African Americans in the denomination was intertwined with the white communicants. A remarkable case in point was in Fayetteville where a free African American local preacher, Henry Evans (c. 1760–1810), brought Methodism to that town and built a meetinghouse for his race. Local whites were mesmerized by this divine man's preaching and selfless ministry. When Evans died, he was buried under the chancel in his church where he rested for a number of years equally loved and mourned by both races in the town he adopted.[27]

Though beautiful, the story of Henry Evans was a rare departure from the normal subordinate arrangement in which African American Methodists found themselves. When the North Carolina Conference of the M.E. Church organized in 1838, there were nearly four thousand African Americans, representing one-fifth of the total membership scattered among the various circuits and stations mostly in the eastern half of the state.[28] The anti-slavery sentiment among early Methodists had decreased considerably in the South, where the institution was an accepted part of society. Accordingly, the region's increasingly affluent Methodists realized that ministering to the slave population had many intrinsic benefits. The paternalistic attitude of master to slave at home continued in the church, where African American members, usually relegated to seating in a gallery or the rear of the main sanctuary floor, were preached to by white ministers and controlled by white leaders of the congregation. In eastern North Carolina, where the greatest concentration of African Americans resided, they often outnumbered the white members in congregations, as recalled by the Rev. John Edwards who was assigned to churches at New Bern and Raleigh in the 1840s:

> When I was pastor at the Methodist Church in Newbern … the colored membership was two or three times as large as the white membership; and we all worshiped in the same house. The negro classes were regularly met—many of their leaders being colored men —and they were as regularly served, by myself, with the Lord's Supper as the whites. They had a weekly leaders' meeting, attended by the pastor, and the colored classes reported their weekly contributions for current expenses as regularly as the whites. This was the condition of things during the two years of my pastorate in Newbern [now Centenary Church]. So it was in Raleigh in 1844–1845, while I was in charge of that station [now Edenton Street Church]. The colored membership, even there, was in excess of the white membership. They occupied the gallery of the church and worshiped with the whites, having no house of worship of their own at that time. In both of these charges there was a Sunday afternoon service, held exclusively for the negroes in addition to the morning and evening services to which they had access. This was the prevailing condition of affairs.[29]

In addition to New Bern and Raleigh, African Americans greatly outnumbered white communicants in the congregations in Fayetteville's Hay Street Church and Wilmington's Front Street Church. However, superiority in numbers did not translate into a like control of the congregation, as would be attempted in Wilmington at the close of the Civil War.

During the late eighteenth and early nineteenth centuries, sessions of the General Conference of the M.E. Church had been disrupted by arguments concerning slaveholding members of the clergy and laity. While Wesley, Asbury, and other Methodist leaders were opposed to the "peculiar institution," the church's leadership in the South had become more tolerant of slavery. So Methodists in North Carolina, as in other areas of the South, attempted to handle the situation with African Americans through two paths: increasingly ministering to the slaves to make them submissive to a white-controlled church; and maintaining an active interest in the American Colonization Society that advocated the relocation of free African Americans from North America to the area of Africa that eventually became the country of Liberia.[30]

Some historians have made the mistaken assumption that the rural, yeoman-dominated Southern Methodists were not overly concerned with the slavery issue. Yet abolition in North Carolina was a deeply troubling issue. As early as October 1835, the Guilford Circuit Quarterly Conference of the M.E. Church, including parts of at least three rural piedmont counties, unanimously adopted a resolution condemning the circulation of "incendiary" publications produced by Northern abolitionists. The quarterly conference also went on record as opposing and condemning the views of all Northern abolitionists as being injurious to the South.[31]

The issue of slavery simmered within the national M.E. Church until the 1844 General Conference when it became a most explosive issue, yielding the "Great Separation." Northern delegates requested that Bishop James O. Andrew of Georgia resign his episcopal position because he had taken a slaveholder as his wife. Church discipline forbade the owning of slaves except in those states where manumission was illegal; Georgia was one such state. Both Northern and Southern delegates were ruled by passions and tempers, and a schism long beneath the surface now developed. The Southern delegates believed that a division of the M.E. Church was the only peaceful remedy. Thus the General Conference adopted a "Plan of Separation" whereby churches in the South would be placed in their own autonomous denomination apart from the M.E. Church. Both factions agreed not to take control of churches that adhered to one or the other branches of Episcopal Methodism. In 1845, the Methodist Episcopal Church, South, the naming of which is attributed to the North Carolina Conference's the Reverend Peter Doub, was organized at Louisville, Kentucky, with the first session of its General Conference convening in Petersburg, Virginia, the following year.[32]

Meanwhile the Methodist Protestants in North Carolina were facing similar situations on the matter of slavery. Like the M.E. Church, South, the M.P. Church promoted mission work among the slaves—especially after their North Carolina Conference granted permission for local churches to admit "colored members" into full membership and govern them in accordance with the church discipline.[33]

While the Southern Methodists initially believed that the separation plan had been accomplished amicably, such would not prove to be the case. The General Conference of the (Northern) M.E. Church in 1848 rejected the "Plan of Separation" to which they had agreed just four years earlier, on the pretext that the annual conferences had not been given the opportunity to debate and vote on the issue. The M.E. Church, South, instituted legal proceedings that carried all the way to the United States Supreme Court, which ruled in favor of the Southern brethren; the "Plan of Separation" was upheld.[34] Other North Carolina M.E. Church members decided on a separation of their own. In southern Guilford County where abolitionist activity was rampant, a number of members of the Guilford Circuit pulled out from the M.E. Church, South, in 1846 and joined the new and anti-slavery Wesleyan Methodist Connection of America. The Methodist Protestants in this same section of the state, in turn, waged war with these "spurious Wesleyan Methodists" and banned their followers from participating in any religious service performed in any of the local M.P. churches.[35]

The basic attitude of both the M.E. Church, South, and M.P. conferences in North Carolina was to consider slavery a political, not a moral, issue and therefore a matter for the civil authorities (and not the church) to decide. Apparently as an afterthought, the 1858 General Conference of the M.E. Church, South, removed the ban on the buying and selling of slaves from the General Rules.[36] The Civil War now loomed on the horizon.

Methodism and Education in North Carolina

Since Methodism was not the denomination of the upper class in early America, many of its adherents would be surprised to know that education was a motivating force among its early leaders in the fledgling nation.

These leaders longed to see an American equivalent to John Wesley's Kingswood School in England, and in 1784 the Christmas Conference voted to establish such an institution in Abingdon, Maryland: the short-lived Cokesbury College, which suffered an unrecoverable fire in 1795. Following an entreaty by Bishop Asbury for "district schools" to be created, a school also named Cokesbury was established by 1793 on the Yadkin River in present-day Davie County, North Carolina. Asbury visited Cokesbury School and described it as being "twenty feet square, two stories high and well set out with doors and windows." The rather isolated location of the school and the perennial problem of securing financial support sounded its death knell within two years.[37] Still, the appetite of early Methodists for educational institutions had been whetted. When in 1820, 1824, and 1828, the General M.E. Conference called upon the various annual conferences to establish "literary institutions" within their provinces, Methodists in North Carolina began to explore ways and means of implementing that directive. Meanwhile the rank-and-file church members continued their journey of social advancement.[38]

It must be noted that in these early days much of North Carolina was still within the bounds of the Virginia Annual Conference, and it would be that entity that established institutions of higher learning. At the 1825 Session of the Virginia Conference, meeting at Oxford in Granville County, a resolution was adopted to establish a "literary institution." This action was fueled by a $10,000 donation made by interested citizens and church members in adjacent Mecklenburg County, Virginia. In February 1830, the Virginia General Assembly approved the chartering of Randolph-Macon College—named, oddly enough, for non–Methodist but politically astute leaders John Randolph of Virginia and Nathaniel Macon of North Carolina. A site, strategically positioned in the small courthouse village of Boydton in Mecklenburg County, close to the common border of Virginia and North Carolina, was secured. The first buildings were soon constructed: in October

1832, Randolph-Macon College, the oldest continuous Methodist College in the United States, opened for classes. An increasing number of the ministers who served in the Virginia—and soon the North Carolina—conferences would receive their advanced education within the massive brick walls of this institution. In 1868, the college was moved to Ashland, Virginia; today, the noble and ghostly ruin of the original campus still graces the southern Virginia countryside—yearning, one imagines, for preservation.[39]

As the division of the Virginia Conference was in the offing in the 1830s, a movement was underway to establish a college for women in Greensboro, as that North Carolina county seat was undergoing an unprecedented religious and educational growth. The catalyst of progress in Greensboro was the Reverend Peter Doub. Of German and English ancestry and largely a self-educated man, Doub had entered the Methodist ministry in 1818 and quickly amassed a widespread reputation throughout the Virginia Conference for his preaching. He was also a popular camp meeting evangelist who could preach for hours. His duties on the Guilford Circuit included a small but persistent congregation at Greensboro, now known as West Market Street Church. Through his encouragement of women's primary education in the area, coupled with support from some of the leading North Carolina pastors in the Virginia Conference, Doub petitioned that Conference in February 1837 to establish a female college at Greensboro.

This matter was taken up by the newly created North Carolina Conference when it met in its inaugural session at Greensboro in January 1838. The Conference successfully petitioned the North Carolina General Assembly to grant a charter for the college. In 1846, Greensboro Female College officially opened, overcoming many obstacles and some attempts to relocate the school, and a campus was created on the west side of the small but growing county seat.[40]

Greensboro College was not the only Methodist institution for higher learning for women in the state. In 1855, a camp meeting of prosperous citizens in Caldwell County to the west raised some $12,000 to establish a school for females in that region. A substantial part of that sum came from aged former legislator and prominent citizen Col. William Davenport. Davenport Women's College thus opened in Lenoir that same year. In 1883, the South Carolina Conference of the M.E. Church, South (the owner of Davenport College) transferred the school to the North Carolina Conference, the area falling into the new Western North Carolina Conference after 1890. Declining enrollment and finances led Davenport College to merge with Greensboro College in the 1930s.[41]

Meanwhile, in northwest Randolph County there arose a movement to establish another institute of higher learning. In early 1838, local pastor and teacher Brantley York began an academy for young men that, by 1841, was incorporated as Union Institute. Its name commemorated the unity of local Methodists and Quakers devoted to this effort. With the departure of York in 1842, leadership of the school was assumed by Braxton Craven, who led it until his death in 1882. Craven became the heart and soul of Union, and under his devoted but polarizing leadership the school slowly grew. In 1851, the North Carolina General Assembly rechartered Union as Normal College with the plan that it would train teachers.[42]

Hoping to attract additional patronage, Craven shrewdly persuaded the North Carolina M.E. South Conference to endorse Normal College if Methodist ministerial students would be admitted tuition-free. While the Conference was still officially committed to the support of Randolph-Macon College in Virginia, this commitment was beginning to erode. In 1855–1856, a great dispute now largely forgotten but with long-lasting effects broke out between Randolph-Macon President W.A. Smith and a former professor at Randolph-Macon, the very popular Reverend Charles F. Deems of the North Carolina Conference. (The interesting, if extremely petty, issue between two overly ambitious, egotistical, and obstinate ministers is beyond the scope of this survey.) Repercussions of their acrimonious war of words led the North Carolina Conference to accept Craven's offer of Normal College in 1856. The following year, all formal North Carolina Conference support of Randolph-Macon was withdrawn.[43] Incidentally, another byproduct of this feud gave rise to a publication for the North Carolina Conference that until that time was still supportive of the Virginia Conference's periodical. Thus, in 1855, the *North Carolina Christian Advocate* with its subsequent various reincarnations and name changes was born.[44] In 1859, Normal College was rechartered as Trinity College under the auspices of the North Carolina Conference. From that day forward, noted Methodist historian Albea Godbold, "Trinity was the most important Methodist college in North Carolina."[45]

During this time, the Methodist Protestants in North Carolina were poised to establish an advanced educational outpost of their own. In 1855, the North Carolina General Assembly chartered Yadkin Institute, a high school for young men, and immediately a two-story building was erected on the Yadkin River in Davidson County between Mocksville and Lexington. Briefly in 1861, and from 1873 to 1883, it served as a college and thereafter as an academy and preparatory school. Financial difficulties led the North Carolina M.P. Conference to seek an annulment of its charter from the legislature in 1895; rechristened Yadkin High School, the former college existed for three more decades. In 1924, the crowning educational achievement of the M.P. Church was realized with the opening of High Point College, now High Point University. By that time, the story of the Methodist Protestants in North Carolina was nearing its end.[46]

Civil War and Reconstruction

At the beginning of the Civil War, the Methodists made up the largest denomination in the United States, but in the South the churches were ill-equipped to endure a war that would be mostly fought in their territory. The history of North Carolina Methodism during the Civil War is one that has eluded the attention of most historians and scholars. The majority of local church records from this period no longer exist, and even the *North Carolina Christian Advocate* suspended publication for half of the war, leaving today's researchers to consult other sources for historical information. During the war, church publications and literature were difficult to obtain and even harder to ship. A ministerial shortage developed when a number of pastors enlisted in the Confederate Army as chaplains (a fascinating story requiring additional research). Camp meetings largely ceased. Annual conferences continued to be held, but due to enemy occupation of much of eastern North Carolina, these sessions were held in areas as far from the field of battle as practical. Southern Methodist bishops, all of whom resided outside of North Carolina, oftentimes had considerable difficulty in reaching the state to preside over the annual conferences.[47]

One of the more interesting, if bizarre, events in North Carolina Methodism during the war concerns the erstwhile, little-known circuit pastor Marble Nash Taylor, who had been assigned by the North Carolina M.E. Church, South, Conference in 1860 to the

Cape Hatteras Mission on the Outer Banks. When Hatteras Island fell to Union Forces in the summer of 1861, the good pastor changed allegiances all in one day and served as a guide to the enemy. Taylor then worked to sway the locals on the Outer Banks to reunite with the Union and to establish a Unionist government for North Carolina in the occupied areas of the coast. In November 1861, Taylor was proclaimed "acting governor" by a small local group of Unionists. He and his associates journeyed north to present their credentials to government leaders in Washington and to solicit financial backing from sympathetic New Yorkers. The Lincoln Administration declined to recognize "Governor" Taylor, so his efforts came to naught. Another man was appointed military governor, and at the 1861 session of the North Carolina Conference Taylor was promptly expelled from that body. He faded into obscurity in the state's Sandhills region.[48]

Churches that fell behind enemy lines of occupation faced an uncertain existence and were cut off from their fellow communicants still under Confederate control. When Wilmington fell to Union forces in February 1865, the Rev. L.S. Burkhead, the recently arrived pastor of Front Street M.E. Church, South, found himself in an unenviable position. The African American members of his congregation, having sworn their loyalty to the pastor, forgot their promise as soon as federal troops occupied the city. Not only did these parishioners, who comprised a majority of the total membership, wish to dispense with the Rev. Burkhead's services and sever connections with the M.E. Church, South, but they also attempted to lay claim to the church building. In a yearlong tempest that drew into the fray the federal army and government, local officials, and the North Carolina Conference of the M.E. Church, South, the white members at Front Street eventually retained their claim to the church property.[49]

Postwar Exodus and Education

By the end of the Civil War, it was becoming clear to white Methodists that the days of biracial congregations were coming to an end. Understandably, once African Americans were emancipated they desired to have someone of their own race to minister to them. White ministers were unwilling to share pulpits with African American clergymen, and consequently the African Americans began to withdraw from the M.E. Church, South, churches to establish their own congregations, usually under the (Northern) M.E. Church, the African Methodist Episcopal Church (A.M.E), or the African Methodist Episcopal Zion Church (A.M.E.Z). These three bodies were often engaged in fierce and bitter competition to win the freedmen who were largely former members of the M.E. Church, South.

The wartime decline of the Methodists and the Union occupation of much of eastern North Carolina created optimal conditions for the Methodist Episcopal Church (or the "Northern Methodists"), the A.M.E., and the A.M.E. Zion Church to send missionaries into the South even before the cessation of hostilities. In 1864, James Walker Hood, an African Methodist Episcopal Zion missionary from New England, arrived in Union-occupied New Bern and Beaufort and successfully persuaded the African American M.E. Church, South, congregants to join the A.M.E. Zion Church. The congregation at New Bern, named St. Peter's, traditionally is viewed as the mother church of all A.M.E. Zion churches in the southern United States. Hood went on to organize a number of A.M.E. Zion congregations in North Carolina and in 1872 became a bishop in his denomination.

Hood was instrumental in the establishment of Livingstone College at Salisbury in Rowan County. This college possessed a graduate-level seminary, the present-day Hood Theological Seminary.[50]

The A.M.E. Church, having made an initial success at Wilmington, organized its North Carolina Conference, formerly and originally part of the South Carolina Conference, in that city in 1868. Freedmen in North Carolina are said to have held their first lawful assembly at St. Paul's Church in Raleigh in 1865. The growth of the denomination permitted the formation of the Western North Carolina Conference branch in 1900. In 1886, the North Carolina Conference had established, in Vance County, Kittrell College, which provided African Americans a higher-education option until 1975.[51]

Regarding the "Northern Methodists," M.E. Church, South, leaders viewed this intrusion as a blatant violation of the spirit, if not the policy, of the 1844 "Plan of Separation." Nevertheless, the Southern Methodists were powerless to prevent encroachment into their territory. In 1867, the Virginia and North Carolina Mission Conference of the M.E. Church was established, and the following year witnessed the creation of a "North Carolina District." Continued growth led to the creation of the North Carolina M.E. Conference in 1869 with approximately three thousand members of both races. In the western end of the state—except that portion under the Holston Conference—the North Carolina Conference largely consisted of white members, while the number of African American members increased as one journeyed east. In 1879, the whites pulled out to organize the Southern Central Conference (renamed the Blue Ridge Conference and later still the Blue Ridge–Atlantic), and for the rest of its existence the Methodist Episcopal Church in North Carolina was a racially separated denomination.[52] The remaining North Carolina Conference of the M.E. Church was thereafter predominantly African American; however, this change was not officially designated until the Discipline of 1904. During the 1880s, at least, white ministers had been occasionally appointed to serve African American charges and African Americans to minister to mostly white charges. This North Carolina Conference spilled over into the tidewater section and the border counties of Southside Virginia.[53]

It was this branch of the church that fostered much support for a small school that local African Americans in Greensboro established in 1873 at Saint Matthews M.E. Church under the auspices of the Freedman's Aid Society. This school was named after a benefactor from New York, Lyman Bennett, and the North Carolina Conference purchased property so that the first buildings could be built for what became Bennett Seminary, now Bennett College. It became a woman's college in 1926, and since then over seven thousand women have graduated from this early leader in historically black colleges nationwide.[54]

As the African American Methodists in the state had largely gone over to the A.M.E., A.M.E. Zion, or the Northern M.E. Church, the leaders in the M.E. Church, South, were already stymied in their efforts to establish a church for their African American brethren remaining tenuously within their fold. Somewhat belatedly with the initial leadership of the M.E. South leaders, the Colored Methodist Episcopal Church (C.M.E.) was organized in 1870 for the African American Methodists who desired to keep many aspects of the M.E. Church, South, but preferred a "separate and distinct Church." In 1873, its North Carolina Conference was established, but in comparison with the A.M.E. Zion or the M.E. Church, the C.M.E. Church always trailed in numbers and grappled with the stigma of its original relationship with the white M.E. Church, South. In 1954, the name of the denomination was changed to the Christian Methodist Episcopal Church.[55]

Societal Issues: Prohibition

Methodists were long noted for their stand on the issue of alcohol. The General Rules of the church forbade the consumption of spirits except in cases of necessity. Whatever was considered "necessity" was loosely and conveniently interpreted. There was no widespread participation by the denomination in North Carolina in any major temperance movement prior to the Civil War. The rigors of battle and gradual resurgence of the "New South," however, brought to the forefront a demand for temperance. One outlet for the Methodist war on alcohol in the postwar period was through the Independent Order of Good Templars, which "stressed the moral and religious phases of temperance." The organization's first North Carolina Chapter was established in 1872, and within a few short years, new chapters dotted the state. As in the case of the Masonic Order, many of the leaders in the Good Templars came from the active membership of Methodist congregations.[56]

The Good Templars Society, in part, during its relatively short duration, helped lay the groundwork for the Methodist participation in the state referendum on Prohibition in 1881. At the 1879 session of the North Carolina Conference of the M.E. Church, South, a resolution was passed to encourage the General Assembly to consider a "general prohibitory liquor law." At the next session the following year, the conference agreed to sponsor a petition calling for direct action by the Assembly. Together with the conference, the Baptist State Convention formed the nucleus of the ecclesiastical assault in North Carolina upon the evils of intemperance. Support for Prohibition came also from Governor Thomas J. Jarvis, an active Methodist from Pitt County. Yet the liquor dealers in the state proved to be a formidable, better organized, and better financed foe. In the August 1881 referendum, the reformers were defeated by a three-to-one vote.[57]

After this brief foray into reform, the Methodists shifted away from controversial issues and focused attention upon church growth, mission work, and support of church-sponsored education. When the next statewide referendum on alcohol was held, in 1908, it prevailed, though the Methodists, while passing resolutions in favor of Prohibition, were less vociferous in their opposition to drink. Gradually, but certainly, Methodists were becoming less associated with temperance. Most communicants today are likely unaware of the church's one-time outspoken opposition to alcohol.[58]

Church Growth, Educational Advancement and Auxiliary Ministries

As the Reconstruction Era progressed, white Methodists in North Carolina began to rebuild their numbers and consequently their financial base. This subsequent revival, which was predominant within the Methodist Episcopal Church, South, was successful for several reasons: the appeal of the "protracted meetings," or revivals, as a latter-day successor to the camp meetings; the maturation of auxiliary ministries within the local church; the urbanization of the local church; Methodism's increasing involvement in higher education and social issues; and, finally, its seeming indifference to theological disputes. The Methodism that had first come to prominence as a rural-based movement had shed its provincial image and was becoming a major part of the religious scene in the towns and cities across North Carolina, as well as the rest of the South. Only the

Methodist Protestants were slow in making inroads in the town and cities, but by the end of the nineteenth century, they, too, began to establish congregations in more urbanized areas. Even then, the Southern Methodists were already well ahead in members and finances and would remain so.[59]

While the Northern Methodists and Methodist Protestants enjoyed modest postwar growth in North Carolina, the Southern Methodists were enjoying a period of expansion they had not witnessed since the antebellum period. Throughout the remainder of the nineteenth century, revived congregations in rural areas were building new frame sanctuaries to replace their decrepit forerunners. In towns and cities, more and more brick churches were being constructed, most of the time including space for Sunday School classes. The "Akron Plan" of church design became popular: essentially, a large sanctuary surrounded by smaller classrooms divided from, yet connected to, the sanctuary by means of folding doors or sliding shutters. Preaching circuits were becoming smaller in the rural areas, and more churches in the small towns were becoming single, or station, charges.[60] By the first decade of the twentieth century, the membership of the branches of Methodism in the state stood as follows:

M.E. Church, South: 151,808
M.E. Church: 20,805
M.P. Church: 18,271
African Methodists (i.e., A.M.E., A.M.E.Z. and C.M.E. churches): 85,512.[61]

The North Carolina Conference of the M.E. Church, South, was also enjoying territorial growth after the Civil War. The South Carolina Conference ceded its last remaining territory in North Carolina during Reconstruction, and the Holston Conference relinquished its western North Carolina land in the late 1880s. This action fueled a decade-long debate that called for the division of the North Carolina Conference into two smaller ones. At the 1890 General Conference, the Western North Carolina Conference was created from the western half of the North Carolina Conference with the eastern boundary lines of Rockingham, Guilford, Randolph, Stanly, and Anson counties serving as the common border. This division remains largely intact today.[62]

While the North Carolina Conference was being divided, another matter was coming to a head that would forever change the course of North Carolina Methodism. Following the 1882 death of its mainstay, Braxton Craven, Trinity College in Randolph County was on the verge of financial collapse despite conscientious and dedicated efforts to keep it afloat. A new young president, a non–Methodist from the North, John F. Crowell, revamped the curriculum and concluded that Trinity could only survive in the increasingly competitive world of higher education by moving to a more urban and prosperous setting in the "New South." The Trinity trustees accepted the idea. With the offer of financial support from Durham tobacco magnate (and Methodist) Washington Duke and land from Col. Julian S. Carr, the college moved to Durham where classes commenced in 1892. A new president, the Rev. John C. Kilgo, later elevated to the episcopacy and destined to become the most controversial leader in the college's history, continued to court the Duke family for support, much to the bitter disgust of many prominent North Carolina Methodists. They did not like Mr. Duke's tobacco money and equated the ambitious efforts of the charismatic, if polarizing, Kilgo to demagoguery, hypocrisy, and sycophancy. Be that as it may, Trinity's path to success was now well assured.[63]

In December 1924, James B. Duke, the wealthiest of Washington Duke's sons, established the Duke Endowment. Essentially, it was a $40 million trust fund, the annual income of which was to be divided among children's homes, hospitals, the M.E. Church, South, and educational institutions, including especially Trinity College. Nineteen million dollars was thus made available to rebuild and expand Trinity, which would be renamed Duke University as a memorial to Washington Duke and his family. Thus began the transformation of Trinity into Duke and into becoming a leading liberal arts institution in the United States. The Duke Endowment has continued to fund rural church development in the state and provide support for retired ministers, among other worthy causes.[64]

The Duke Family had already been responsible for bringing into the Methodist fold a small college northeast of Raleigh at Louisburg, the seat of Franklin County. In the 1890s, Washington Duke acquired struggling Louisburg College, which had long enjoyed unofficial ties with Methodists. After Duke's death in 1905, his family donated the college to the North Carolina Conference of the M.E. Church, South. Soon the school was reorganized into an institution with a junior college rating. Declining enrollment and finances nearly closed the college, but its future brightened when it became co-educational during the depths of the Great Depression. The school survives today as a symbol of Methodist support of higher education, but more importantly as a source of great pride for the people of Franklin County.[65]

Another women's college that was patronized by members of the North Carolina Conference was Littleton College in Warren County, established by the Rev. J.M. Rhodes of that conference. The school opened in 1882 and showed much promise, but fell victim to a great fire in 1919. Lacking an endowment, it was never rebuilt.[66] In the southeastern part of the state, the North Carolina Conference in 1907 chartered Carolina College for women at Maxton in Robeson County. This liberal arts school opened in 1911, and it, too, showed great potential, but the financial woes of the 1920s, coupled with the Conference's preoccupation with the transformation of Trinity College into Duke University, led to the demise of Carolina College in 1926.[67]

Methodist commitment to higher education only accelerated during the twentieth century. In 1903, Miss Emily Pruden, a teacher from Connecticut who had come south in the 1880s to establish a school in the region, donated her institution near Lenoir to the Woman's Home Missionary Society of the M.E. Church. This school, known as the Oberlin Home and School, was renamed the Mitchell Industrial Home and School after a patron of the Missionary Society. In 1909, the school relocated to Misenheimer in Stanly County and received accreditation as a junior college in 1932. The substantial patronage of the school by the Henry Pfeiffer family of New York led to renaming the school Pfeiffer Junior College. Continued support yielded four-year college status in 1953, and six years later it requested affiliation with the Western North Carolina Conference of the Methodist Church. Restructured in 1996 as Pfeiffer University, the school now has satellite campuses for graduate studies in Charlotte and Morrisville.[68]

The economic hardships of the Great Depression had a definite impact on many of North Carolina's Methodist-affiliated schools. Davenport in Lenoir had merged with Greensboro College by 1938, and in 1932 the Western North Carolina Conference of the M.E. Church, South, ordered the consolidation of two other struggling junior colleges, Rutherford in Burke County and Weaver in Buncombe, to form one coeducational college. The result was complex. Weaver College, established in 1873, had been under church ownership since 1883. It was closed in 1934 and merged into the newly founded Brevard

College in Transylvania County. Rutherford College, dating back to the 1850s, had been acquired by the Western North Carolina Conference at the turn of the century and was also absorbed eventually into Brevard College. Brevard College suffered its own battles of declining fortunes after World War II but bounced back and has since enjoyed a brighter future, so much so that in 1995 the junior college adopted a four-year curriculum.[69]

After World War II, the North Carolina Conference further increased support of higher education. In 1956, following a mandate from the General Conference, plans were laid to establish two new four-year schools, North Carolina Wesleyan at Rocky Mount and Methodist College in Fayetteville. In both cases, local support for these institutions, which opened for students in 1960, were major motivators and sustainers. The first chair of Methodist College's trustees was Fayetteville attorney Terry Sanford, later North Carolina Governor, President of Duke University, and United States Senator. In its fortieth anniversary year, 1996, Methodist College was reorganized as Methodist University. These two colleges constituted what many historians regarded as the "most ambitious undertaking in higher education ever attempted by an annual conference" in North Carolina.[70]

Unifications and Growth of Auxiliary Ministries

As the twentieth century progressed, Methodism was experiencing growth, and with that growth came renewed sentiments advocating the unification of the three major branches of American Methodism. In North Carolina, the Methodist Protestants were among the most vocal supporters of unification. Both branches of Episcopal Methodism, the M.E. Church South, especially, had accepted the principle of lay representation, the touchstone doctrine of the Methodist Protestants. J. Elwood Carroll, the North Carolina Methodist Protestants' historian in 1939, commented in 1990 that "the Methodist Protestant Church had basically served its purpose and accomplished its goals" and had also reluctantly come to realize that tighter administrative control over the churches was necessary.[71] The end of slavery and the rise of the "New South" had made those issues that divided the M.E. Church in 1844 now largely irrelevant.

Even under the nomenclature "New South," there were still overwhelming connections with the past that could not be overcome in the proposed unification. Many Southern Methodists opposed erasing the racial divide and granting African Americans total racial equality within the church. As a form of compromise, African Americans would be included within the new Methodist Church, but their annual conferences were to be grouped into one jurisdictional conference, a new administrative level known as the Central Jurisdiction. The white conferences would be placed into jurisdictional conferences based upon geographic proximity. In North Carolina, white Methodists would be placed into the Southeastern Jurisdiction that stretched from Virginia to Mississippi and included Cuba. While whites and African Americans were under the umbrella of the new Methodist Church, the General Conference would be the only forum in which the African Americans could *appear* as equals to the whites, but even then be greatly outnumbered. At the national uniting conference in May 1939, the Methodist Episcopal Church, Methodist Episcopal Church, South, and the Methodist Protestant Church were merged into the Methodist Church. In North Carolina, it was deemed advisable to retain the geographic divisions of the M.E. Church, South, and in so doing the white Methodists fell into either the North Carolina Conference or the Western North Carolina Conference. The African Americans remained in their own North Carolina Conference under the Central Jurisdiction, a contrivance that was vividly separate and unequal. This arrangement was no doubt made because the Methodists of that time were unwilling to deal with the "race issue."[72]

In the years prior to and following the 1939 Unification, Methodists wished to establish a retreat in the South on par with the famous Chautauqua Institution in southwest New York State. In no church leader did that desire burn more brightly than in Bishop James Atkins of the M.E. Church, South. Bishop Atkins and others garnered support to establish a lake resort in Haywood County near Waynesville with an auditorium and pertinent buildings. This "Southern Assembly" was incorporated by the North Carolina General Assembly. The large, manmade lake was named Junaluska in honor of nearby Mount Junaluska, itself named for the respected tribal leader of the Eastern band of Cherokee Indians. In 1929, the Southern Assembly became the Lake Junaluska Methodist Assembly.[73]

During the Great Depression, the Assembly was forced into bankruptcy, but after establishing a more stable financial position, the General Conference of the M.E. Church, South, at its last session before Unification in 1938 finally accepted ownership of Junaluska, which it had refused on previous occasions. In 1948, the General Conference of the Methodist Church transferred ownership of Lake Junaluska Assembly to the Southeastern Jurisdiction of the church. In 1952, the World Methodist Council established its American headquarters at Junaluska, and three years later the World Methodist Building was completed. Church functions, workshops, concerts, and conferences draw over one hundred thousand visitors annually to Junaluska, and since 1957 the Western North Carolina Conference has held its annual sessions there.[74]

The twentieth century also witnessed the advancement of women into leadership roles in the Methodist faith, but this advancement was not without pitfalls and struggles. In 1956, the General Conference of the Methodist Church granted full clergy rights to women, and the first ordination of a woman in North Carolina came three years later.[75] Moreover, women in Methodist congregations have traditionally been very supportive of missionaries in foreign lands: Africa, China, South America, Japan, and Korea are only a few of the mission fields. In time, women, too, began to fill the ranks of missionaries.[76] The women's foreign missionary societies had begun organizing among the North Carolina Methodist churches as early as 1878 when the North Carolina Conference of the M.E. Church, South, organized its forces. One of the mainstays of this body was Mrs. Frances M. Bumpas of Greensboro, the widow of a prominent minister in the conference and the beloved publisher of the religious paper *The Weekly Message*.[77] In 1890, the new Western North Carolina Conference established its own Woman's Foreign Missionary Society. Within the next decade both North Carolina conferences had established Home Missionary societies also.[78] As the term implies, the Home societies were concerned with mission work on the local level. Cases in point are the conference orphanages established at Raleigh by the North Carolina Conference in 1899, and ten years later the Western North Carolina Conference orphanage at Winston (now Winston-Salem).[79] The Foreign and Home Missionary societies in each of those conferences merged in 1912 and thereafter provided much guidance and support for the Epworth Leagues for children, Sunday schools, and Vacation Bible Schools that started to appear on the scene mostly after World War I. The Methodist Protestants in the state had established foreign and home missionary societies in 1900 and 1908, respectively. They merged in 1928 and provided financial support for their conference orphanage at Denton. Later moved to High Point, it was the only orphanage of the Methodist Protestants in the country, a distinction of which the North Carolina Conference was justifiably proud.[80] In 1905, the Home Missionary Society of the North Carolina Conference of the M.E. Church was organized at Winston. Much of its work was focused on the needs of youth in the church and garnering support for Bennett College at Greensboro and the Allen High School in Asheville.[81]

One of the most visible examples of Methodism's auxiliary ministries has been the development of homes for the aged and retired clergy and laity. Methodist Homes were opened in Charlotte (1943), Durham (1957), Asheville (1979), Winston-Salem (1980), Greenville (1987), and Laurinburg (1987). They and their successors with expanded programs have offered dignified and productive residences in a Christian environment to a rapidly growing segment of the population. In 1957, a special facility for retired missionaries and deaconesses of the Methodist Church, now known as the Brooks-Howell Home, was established at Asheville. With the rising costs of senior living, these institutions are increasingly heavily pressed to provide supplemental funding for those residents who have outlived their means.[82]

With the approach of the final third of the twentieth century, American Methodism was undergoing a great change. Much unfinished business still lingered with African Americans who had been herded into a neglected Central Jurisdiction following the 1939 Unification. With the Civil Rights Movement of the 1950s and 1960s, the folly of continuing this segregation became more obvious. Moreover, a merger was planned between the Methodist Church and the Evangelical United Brethren that had no congregations in North Carolina, its strength being to the north and northwest of the state. With the formation of the United Methodist Church at its uniting General Conference in Dallas in April 1968, Methodism had reached a pinnacle of unity and strength never before achieved.[83] The Central Jurisdiction was abolished, and the African American congregations were absorbed into the already established boundaries of the Southeastern Jurisdiction and the formerly white North Carolina Conference and Western North Carolina Conference. Officially, this unification seemed complete, yet there would remain the persistent stigma of racially segregated congregations especially among the conservative-leaning rural areas. The United Methodist Church and three historically black Methodist denominations, the African Methodist Episcopal, African Methodist Episcopal Zion, and Christian Methodist Episcopal churches, have been exploring union since 1985. All four churches share a common heritage in the Methodist movement and have a combined membership of some twelve million.[84]

In the years since the 1968 unification, Methodism, like many of the mainline Protestant denominations, has suffered a decline in membership. It is no coincidence that this decline has happened as the fires of evangelism have ebbed or in many cases have been virtually extinguished.[85] During the late twentieth century the denomination has, on its own admission by church leaders, become bogged down with more bureaucracy, the so-called "corporate culture." While the two United Methodist conferences in North Carolina have tried to trim back their own bureaucracies by realignment, slimming the number of districts and jettisoning non-essential positions among conference staffs, still a gap between the church hierarchy and the rank-and-file laity persists with each passing year. The denominational decline in North Carolina has not been as noticeable as in other states, but a weakening of once fervent Methodist vigor is apparent. As United Methodism nears its half-century mark in 2018, the two conferences in North Carolina claim a little over a half million adherents in some approximately 1900 churches statewide. Collectively, Methodists make up the second largest mainline Protestant denomination in North Carolina.

Methodists in North Carolina do a laudatory job in ministering to the needs of the downtrodden, needy, and penitent, but they have not enjoyed a major revival of faith in decades. Moreover, the General Conference in the spring of 2016 was forced to address issues that denominational leaders have handled ever so gingerly in recent years. On the agenda was how the denomination should address the matter of homosexuality, same-sex unions, and bridging the gap between the races and cultures within the denomination so that diversity does not mean divisiveness.[86] Also facing the denomination in North Carolina are other issues that can no longer be ignored. They include dealing with Methodists determined to maintain traditional worship versus the increasingly popular, if more secularly inspired, contemporary worship movement, the decline of rural churches, and the competition of urban churches with new age, nondenominational megachurches. Will the United Methodist Church be able to stem the tides of extremism from both ends of the spectrum and, unlike the 1844 schism in the Methodist Episcopal Church over slavery, remain solid and open to people from a myriad of cultures, backgrounds, or lifestyles to make manifest, if you will, a diverse faith community? And, if so, how can this miracle be accomplished without a grassroots revival the likes of which the church has not witnessed since before the Civil War?

And what of the past, how relevant is it to the future of the church? Seekers need look no further than to the admonition from a local Methodist pastor from Raleigh, R.H. Whitaker, who penned these words more than a century ago: "It is a sad commentary upon the gratitude of a church and community to say that they do not hold in proper reverence those who planted the trees which are bearing such delicious fruit. They pluck and eat, yet forget that love and sacrifice planted the trees which yield the fruit they so much enjoy."[87]

Whatever path Methodism in North Carolina, and to a greater extent the nation, decides to take, may its adherents not forget the words of the Psalmist who wrote: "My times are in Thy hands."

Notes

1. Paul N. Garber, *The Romance of American Methodism* (Greensboro, NC: The Piedmont Press, 1931), 325–28.

2. The first attempt to provide an in-depth account of the early history of North Carolina Methodism was W. L. Grissom's *History of Methodism in North Carolina from 1772 to the Present Time* (1905), the first of a projected multi–volume account that, due to the author's death and loss of records, never materialized beyond the first volume.

3. William Thomas Smith, "Eighteenth Century Encounters: Methodist–Moravian," *Methodist History*, XXIV, no. 3 (April 1986): 141–156; John Wesley, *John Wesley's Journal*, ed. Nehemiah Curnock, vol. 1 (London: Epworth Press, 1976), 476; Donald W. Haynes, *Methodism* (Salisbury, NC: Hood Theological Seminary, published draft, 2008), 60.

4. William Henry Williams, *The Garden of American Methodism: The Delmarva Peninsula, 1769–1820* (Wilmington, DE: Scholarly Services, 1984), 21.

5. George Whitefield, *George Whitefield's Journals* (Guildford and London: Banner of Truth Trust, Billing and Sons, Ltd., 1960), 373–81; The legend of Whitefield's curse upon the spiritually challenged town of Bath is recalled in Herbert R. Paschal, *A History of Colonial Bath* (Raleigh, NC: Edwards & Broughton Company, 1955), 41.

6. Joseph Pilmore, *The Journal of Joseph Pilmore, Methodist Itinerant for the Years August 1, 1769 to January 2, 1774* (Philadelphia: Historical Society of the Philadelphia Annual Conference of the United Methodist Church, 1969), 156, 170, 174; Other more recent sources give the dates as November and December 1772 when

Pilmore spoke at Currituck, but his diary is quite clear that the actual date is September 29, 1772; John K. Bergland, *The Journeys of Robert Williams: Irish Street Preacher and Methodist Circuit Rider* (Xulon Press, 2010), 11, 15, 23, 81.

7. Larry E. Tise, "North Carolina Methodism from the Revolution to the War of 1812" in *Methodism Alive in North Carolina*, ed. O'Kelly Ingram (Durham, NC: Duke University Divinity School, 1976), 36–37.

8. Williams, 48–49.

9. *Ibid.* 67.

10. Tise, 36–37.

11. James Reed Cox, *Pioneers and Perfecters of Our Faith: A Biography of the Reverend Green Hill, North Carolina Statesman, Revolutionary War Patriot, Zealous Methodist Preacher, Crusader for Liberty* (Nashville, TN: Parthenon Press, 1975), 42–45.

12. Frederick A. Norwood, *The Story of American Methodism* (Nashville, TN: Abingdon Press, 1974) 119–32.

13. Tise, 38, 41.

14. Vivian P. Mitchell, *Pioneer Methodist Preachers: Charter Members of the North Carolina Conference, February 1837* (Raleigh: The Author, 1987), preface. *Raleigh Christian Advocate*, December 13, 1893.

15. Elmer T. Clark, *Methodism in Western North Carolina* (Nashville, TN: Parthenon Press, 1966), 34–36, 67. Clark's account comes as close to being a historical survey of North Carolina Methodism (albeit only the western half of the state) as anything published to date.

16. Hilary T. Hudson, *The Methodist Armor* (Nashville, TN: Southern Methodist Publishing House, 1887), 146–62; "The General Rules of the Methodist Church: The Nature, Design, and General Rules of Our United Societies," The United Methodist Church, accessed December 2, 2014, http://www.umc.org/what-we-believe/general-rules-of-the-methodist-church. The class meeting system was finally discontinued formally soon after the Civil War. Lovefeast services were already on the decline by the Civil War and nearly became extinct, only to enjoy a slight revival in recent years as a Christmas observance.

17. James E. Kirby, Russell E. Richey, Kenneth E. Rowe, *The Methodists* (Westport, CT: Greenwood Press, 1996), 72.

18. Nathan O. Hatch, *The Democratization of American Christianity* (New Haven: Yale University Press, 1989), 55.

19. Charles A. Johnson, *The Frontier Camp Meeting* (Dallas: Southern Methodist University Press, 1955), 25, 40. Michael Perdue, *Center United Methodist Church: A History* (Greensboro, NC: 1998) 14–27.

20. Clark, 30–32.

21. M.H. Moore, *Sketches of the Pioneers of Methodism in North Carolina and Virginia* (Nashville, TN: Southern Methodist Publishing House, 1884), 295–97. Clark, 24–26.

22. Durward T. Stokes, "James O'Kelly," *NCpedia*, accessed December 21, 2014, http://ncpedia.org/biography/okelly-james.

23. Hatch, 11.

24. J. Elwood Carroll, *History of the North Carolina Annual Conference of the Methodist Protestant Church* (Greensboro, NC: McCulloch & Swain, Printers; 1939), 13–14.

25. Carroll, 24; Clark, 69; *Raleigh Register*, December 3, 1829.

26. Carroll, 11–21.

27. Moore, 310–14.

28. *Minutes of the Annual Conferences of the Methodist Episcopal Church for the Years 1829–1839, Volume II* (New York: G. Mason and T. Lane, 1840), 525–26.

29. *Raleigh Christian Advocate*, October 22, 1884. Dr. John E. Edwards (1814–1891) transferred to the Virginia Conference in 1845 and in the following four decades became an influential leader in that conference. From 1882 to 1891, he penned many reminiscent articles for the *Raleigh Christian Advocate*.

30. The role of African Americans in the antebellum Methodist churches in North Carolina is a subject of scant scholarship. Among those active in the American Colonization Society in North Carolina was the Rev. Samuel S. Bryant of the North Carolina Conference who was appointed an "agent" for the society by the conference in 1856. Bryant was expelled from the conference the following year apparently for unrelated reasons. Mitchell, 10.

31. *A Book of Records for the Guilford Circuit 1832–1865*, Minutes of the Quarterly Meeting October 10, 1835 (Box NCC 48), United Methodist Church Records, Rare Book, Manuscript, and Special Collections Library, Duke University.

32. Albert Henry Radford, *History of the Organization of the Methodist Episcopal Church, South* (Nashville, TN: A.H. Radford, Agent for the Methodist Episcopal Church, South, 1875), 159–69, 414–21, 504–10.

33. Carroll, 34–35.

34. John M. Moore, The *Long Road to Methodist Union* (Nashville, TN: Abingdon-Cokesbury Press, 1943), 47–48.

35. Carroll, 34; *Cyclopedia of Methodism. Embracing Sketches of its Rise, Progress and Present Condition, with Biographical Notices and Numerous Illustrations*, 1883 ed., s.v. "Adam Crooks" and "Daniel Worth."

36. *Raleigh Register*, June 9, 1858. *Journal of the General Conference of the Methodist Episcopal Church, South; May 1858* (Nashville, TN: J. B. McFerrin, Agent, 1858), 459–60; *The Quarterly Review of the Methodist Episcopal Church, South; Volume 12* (Nashville, TN: Southern Methodist Publishing House, 1858), 384–86.

37. Clark, 44–45; *Raleigh Christian Advocate*, January 23, 1889; April 10, 1889.

38. John Caknipe, Jr., *Randolph-Macon in the Early Years: Making Preachers, Teachers and Confederate Officers, 1830–1868* (Jefferson, NC: McFarland, 2015), 9.

39. *Ibid.*, 7–17.

40. *North Carolina Christian Advocate*, March 28, 1894; Samuel Bryant Turrentine, *A Romance of Education: A Narrative including recollections and other facts connected with Greensboro College* (Greensboro, NC: Piedmont Press, 1946), 22–34.

41. *Raleigh Christian Advocate*, February 21, 1877; Clark, 97. *Cyclopedia of Methodism*, s.v. "Davenport Female College."

42. Clark, 100. Albea Godbold, "Methodism and Higher Education in North Carolina, 1776–1976" in *Methodism Alive in North Carolina: A Volume Commemorating the Bicentennial of the Carolina Circuit*, ed. O. Kelly Ingram (Durham: The Divinity School of Duke University, 1976), 118–19.

43. *Ibid.* See also *Proceedings of the Virginia Conference in the Trial of W.A. Smith, D.D. on Charges Preferred by C.F. Deems, D.D. at the Session of 1855. Reported from the Authentic Documents, Published by the Order of the Conference.* (Richmond: Charles H. Wynne, Printer, 1856).

44. J.B. Bobbitt, "Raleigh Christian Advocate and Religious Journalism," *North Carolina Christian Advocate*, May 31, 1956, 10–11. *The North Carolina Christian Advocate*, its readership and finances declining and its editorship increasingly out of step with mainline church members, died a slow and lingering death until it ceased operations in November 2014.

45. Clark, 100; Godbold, 119.

46. Virginia Gunn Fick, *Country College on the Yadkin: A Historical Narrative* (Winston-Salem, NC: Hunter Publishing Company, 1984), 36–37.

47. Among the few known eyewitness accounts of North Carolina Methodists during the Civil War is R.H. Whitaker, "[North Carolina] Methodism during the Civil War" in *Southern Methodist Handbook*, 1906 ed., 195–200. Whitaker was a local Methodist preacher who lived in Raleigh and wrote extensively of the city in the nineteenth century. A complete list of Methodist chaplains from North Carolina who served in the Confederate Army seemingly does not exist, but a fair accounting can be found in *Faith in the Fight: Civil War Chaplains*, ed. John W. Brinsfield et al. (Mechanicsburg, PA: Stackpole Books, 2003). Probably the most noted Methodist chaplain in the Confederate Army from North Carolina was the Rev. Alexander D. Betts (1832–1918), author of *Experience of a Confederate Chaplain 1861–1864* (Greenville, SC: W.B. Betts, n. d.). *Mount Olive* (NC) *Tribune*, July 24, 31, 1992.

48. *Daily Dispatch* (Richmond, VA), December 16, 1861; *The New York Herald*, October 28, 1861; *Fayetteville Observer* (Fayetteville, NC), December 12, 1861; Fred M. Mallison, *The Civil War on the Outer Banks: A History of the Late Rebellion along the Coast of North Carolina from Carteret to Currituck, with Comments on Prewar Conditions and an Account of Postwar Recovery* (Jefferson, NC: McFarland, 1998) 57–60.

49. L.S. Burkhead, "History of the Difficulties of the Pastorate of the Front Street Methodist Church, Wilmington, N.C., for the Year 1865," *An Annual Publication of Historical Papers Published by the Historical Society of Trinity College*, Series VIII (1908–1909), 35–118; the Rev. Burkhead continued a successful ministry in the North Carolina Conference until his sudden death at the Annual Session in 1887 in Fayetteville; *Raleigh Christian Advocate*, December 7, 1887.

50. Joseph B. Bethea, "Black Methodists in North Carolina," *Methodism Alive in North Carolina*, 90–93.

51. Bethea, 88–90; Clark, 77. In 2007, the Kittrell College Alumni Association erected a historical marker at the site of the college on U.S. Highway 1 in Kittrell.

52. George W. Bumgarner, *Methodist Episcopal Church in North Carolina, 1865-1939* (Winston-Salem: Hunter Publishing Company, 1990), xi–xiii; Clark 77–79.

53. Linda D. Addo and James H. McCallum, *To Be Faithful to Our Heritage: A History of Black United Methodism in North Carolina* (Commissions on Archives & History of the North Carolina Annual Conference, Western North Carolina Annual Conference, United Methodist Church, 1980, 2011 rpt.), 29–31.

54. Addo and McCallum, 28–29, 70–77.

55. C.H. Phillips, *The History of the Colored Methodist Episcopal Church in America: Comprising Its Organization, Subsequent Development and Present Status* (Jackson, TN: Publishing House of the C.M.E. Church, 1925), 27–38, 57–58, 71; Clark, 76–77. One of the prominent clergy in the M.E. Church, South, behind the establishment of the C.M.E. Church was Bishop Robert Paine (1799–1882), a native of Person County, North Carolina.

56. Daniel Jay Whitener, *Prohibition in North Carolina, 1715–1945* (Chapel Hill: University of North Carolina Press, 1945), 18, 55–57.

57. *News & Observer* (Raleigh, NC), May 26, 1881, August 26, 1881.

58. Whitener, 157.

59. Carroll, 29–32.

60. While the "Akron Plan" of church architecture was northern in origin, many churches in the South constructed around the turn of the twentieth century adopted it. Among the more familiar examples among Methodist churches in North Carolina still in use are West Market Street Church in Greensboro, Jarvis Memorial Church in Greenville, Fifth Street Church in Wilmington, First Church in Murphy, and Hawthorne Lane Church in Charlotte.

61. *Department of Commerce and Labor, Bureau of the Census, Special Reports, Religious Bodies, 1906, Part 1, Summary and General Tables* (Washington: Government Printing Office, 1910) 343.

62. *Raleigh Christian Advocate*, May 28, 1890; June 4, 1890.

63. Nora C. Chaffin, *Trinity College, 1839–1892: The Beginnings of Duke University* (Durham, NC: Duke University Press, 1950), 478–516; Godbold, 120–22. The best detailed, if overly favorable, biography of Bishop Kilgo is still Paul Neff Garber, *John Carlisle Kilgo, President of Trinity College, 1894–1910* (Durham, NC: Duke University Press, 1937).

64. Robert Franklin Durden, *Lasting Legacy to the Carolinas: The Duke Endowment, 1924–1994* (Durham, NC: Duke University Press, 1998), 165–82.

65. "Our History" *Louisburg College: America's Premier Private Two-Year College*, https://www.louisburg.edu (accessed October 28, 2015).

66. Ralph Hardee Rives, "Littleton Female College," *North Carolina Historical Review*, 39, no. 3 (July 1962): 363–377; Grady L. E. Carroll, "Littleton College" NCpedia, http://ncpedia.org/Littleton-college (accessed January 26, 2015).

67. Godbold, 123. *Raleigh Christian Advocate*, May 23, 1912.

68. Godbold, 123–24, 126–27.

69. Clark, 96–97.

70. "History of Methodist University," Methodist University, http://www.methodist.edu/university-history (accessed March 11, 2016); "North Carolina Wesleyan College: Our History," North Carolina Wesleyan College, http://www.ncwc.edu/about/ (accessed March 11, 2016).

71. J. Elwood Carroll, interview by the author, December 15, 1990.

72. Moore, *Long Road*, 231–236; *The Daily Christian Advocate* ("A Record of the Uniting Conference of the Methodist Episcopal Church, the Methodist Episcopal Church, South and the Methodist Protestant Church"), May 8, May 10, May 11, 1939.

73. Bill Lowry, *The Antechamber of Heaven: A History of the Lake Junaluska Assembly* (Franklin, TN: Providence House Publishers, 2010), 189–208; Clark 104–06.

74. *Ibid.*; estimate of annual visits courtesy of the *Mountaineer* (Waynesville, NC), Jan. 18, 2018.

75. Miss Maloie Bogle Lee was received into full connection in the Western North Carolina Conference at its 1959 Session. The Rev. James Pyatt, Archival Associate for the Western North Carolina Archives, email message to the author, February 23, 2016. The North Carolina Conference received its first woman into full connection a little more than a decade later.

76. The first American Methodist missionary to Africa was the former pastor of the Edenton Street Church in Raleigh, the Rev. Melville Cox, who began a mission work in Liberia in 1833 but died after a short stay there. Sue McDowell, *Edenton Street: Edenton Street United Methodist Church, Raleigh, North Carolina, 1811–2011* (Raleigh: Edenton Street United Methodist Church, 2011), 36–37. The first Methodist woman from North Carolina to go into the foreign missionary field was Ellen Morphis Wood, who accompanied her husband, the Rev. M.L. Wood (later President of Trinity College) to China in 1859. Mrs. W.R. (Willie Kelly) Harris, *Fifty Years of Missionary Achievement: Historical Sketch of the Woman's Missionary Society, Western North Carolina Conference* (Woman's Missionary Society, Western North Carolina Conference, 1940), 35. Another noted Methodist missionary with North Carolina connections was Charles Soong, the patriarch of the famous Soong Family of Nationalist China, who was baptized in Fifth Street Church in Wilmington in 1880 and was the first international student at Trinity College. William E. King, "Charles Soong (1863–1918) Trinity College's First International Student." *Duke Dialogue*, January 1998, http://library.duke.edu/rubenstein/uarchives/history/articles/soong (accessed March 23, 2016).

77. Harris, 7.

78. Harris, 9, 16. The North Carolina Conference established its Home Missionary Society in 1891, followed by the Western N.C. Conference a decade later.

79. Perry Lefeavers, *The Children's Home: The First Seventy-Five Years* (Elizabeth City, NC: P. Lefeavers, 1983); "Methodist Orphanage (Raleigh)," *StoppingPoints.com*, https://www.stoppingpoints.com/north-carolina/sights.cgi?marker=Methodist+Orphanage&cnty=wake (accessed March 14, 2015.)

80. Harris, 18. Carroll, 68–73.

81. Addo, 78–84.

82. George William Bumgarner and James Elwood Carroll, *The Flowering of Methodism in Western North Carolina* (Charlotte, NC: Commission on Archives and History of the Western North Carolina Conference of the United Methodist Church, 1984), 95–106.

83. Bumgarner and Carroll, 16. Charles Yrigoyen, Jr., John G. McEllheney, and Kenneth E. Rowe, *United Methodism at Forty; Looking Back, Looking Forward* (Nashville, TN: Abingdon Press, 2008), 27–28.

84. Bumgarner and Carroll, 9–10. "United Methodists at-a-Glance: Ecumenical Relationships," United

Methodist Church, http://www.umc.org/news-and-media/united-methodists-at-a-glance (accessed January 5, 2016).

85. Yrigoyen, McEllheney, and Rowe, 39–41.

86. "General Conference 2016: Major Legislative Issues" United Methodist Church, http://www.umc.org/who-we-are/general-conference-2016-major-legislative-issues (accessed March 1, 2016).

87. R.H. Whitaker, *Whitaker's Reminiscences, Incidents and Anecdotes: Recollections of Other Days and Years: Or, What I Saw and Heard and Thought of People Whom I Knew, and What They Did and Said* (Raleigh: Edwards & Broughton, 1905), 310.

Moravians

C. Riddick Weber

The Moravian Church[1] came to North Carolina in 1753, the first tangible step in the planning of an intentional community that had been years in the making. Founded in an isolated hundred-thousand-acre tract in the backwoods of North Carolina, it was the epitome of decades of theological, political, social, and economic development of a small, worldwide faith community, headquartered in what is now the eastern part of Germany. The story of the Moravian Church in North Carolina is its adaptation to the changes in the religious, political, and socioeconomic climates with which it has interacted.

Before beginning to look in earnest at the influences that created the Moravian Church in North Carolina, it is important to note that for much of their history, Moravians have had substantial connections with Moravians outside of North Carolina, not only in America, but throughout the world. North Carolina Moravians were greatly impacted by the decisions of denominational leaders in Pennsylvania and Germany from the beginnings of the work in 1753 until 1848. Their global connections have continued to grow since then. Therefore, it is hard to speak about the Moravian Church only in North Carolina from an administrative, let alone a spiritual, perspective.

Furthermore, for those who do not know much about the Moravian Church in North Carolina, a visit to Old Salem in Winston-Salem could be historically informative, but very misleading. Old Salem is a historical entity that interprets the lives of members of an eighteenth-century, German-speaking, communally-based religious group set in the middle of the twenty-first-century city of Winston-Salem. Strolling through Old Salem's central grassy square and down the tree-lined streets that lie between centuries-old buildings might give the impression that Moravians have been antiquarians looking for a refuge from the skyscrapers and urbanization that surround them, meaning the moniker "Quiet People of the Land"[2] would be fitting. Nothing could be further from the truth.

Basic Moravian History and Characteristics

When Moravians came to the Wachovia[3] region of North Carolina, they embodied a progressive theological and social life that brought the benefits and safety of European technology and civilization to those living in the wilderness around them. Rather than being a quiet oasis in the midst of skyscrapers that one experiences today, Moravians were building the skyscrapers of their day in the middle of the wilderness. They were able to do this because, unlike many religious groups that developed in North Carolina, Moravians came to this state as a group with well-developed ideas about how religious thought and practice impacted communal life.

Several Moravian historians have written histories of the church in North Carolina for various anniversaries, the most recent and complete being *With Courage for the Future,* written by the Rev. Dr. Daniel Crews and Richard Starbuck for the two-hundred-fiftieth anniversary.[4] With a chronology forty-eight pages long in itself, their book covers not only the history of the Moravian Church in North Carolina, but also its expansion into other southeastern states. Moreover, it was written primarily for Moravians and secondarily for historians and other scholars.[5] Non-Moravian scholars have also written about the early Moravians who settled in the Wachovia region, with various socioeconomic, political, and racial questions providing the foundations for their works.[6] The interested reader who follows up this essay with further reading in these works, particularly *With Courage for the Future,* will find much more detailed information and a more nuanced understanding of the events described and issues discussed in this essay. Even a cursory examination of the existing scholarship will reveal that research has paid a great deal of attention to the first century of Moravians in North Carolina and very little to anything after the Civil War. In short, the Moravians abandoned particular earlier practices and increasingly blended into the North Carolina religious and cultural landscape.

The Moravian Church dates back to 1457 when certain followers of the Czech Catholic priest, educator, and reformer Jan Hus, who had been martyred in 1415, formed a separate church, calling itself the *Unitas Fratrum,* or Unity of the Brothers.[7] After years of persecution and intermittent growth, under Bishop Lukas of Prague the Moravian church engaged in dialog with leaders of the Reformed and Lutheran churches, but remained a separate church. The *Unitas Fratrum* nearly completely died out after the Thirty Years' War (1618–1648). In response, in 1650, Bishop Jan Amos Comenius authored *The Bequest of the Dying Mother,* in which he wrote about the spiritual riches that his church could leave to the remaining Protestant churches. When Comenius died in exile in 1670, he expected that his church would die out.

The *Unitas Fratrum* experienced a profound spiritual renewal as religious refugees from the area of Moravia in what is now the Czech Republic settled on the estate of Nikolaus Ludwig von Zinzendorf, a count of the Holy Roman Empire. Zinzendorf and a close group of family members and followers provided the leadership for this renewal. Beginning with the founding of Herrnhut, a village in the eastern part of Germany near the Polish and Czech borders, in 1722 the Moravians began a series of socioeconomic and theological developments that were essentially a generation in the making.[8] An interest in sharing the gospel led missionaries out of Herrnhut into the Baltic region as early as 1728, though the mission movement has been traditionally dated to 1732 when Moravians first traveled to the Caribbean.

During the critical formative years of this Moravian movement, many affiliated with this renewal were primarily seeking to be a reforming agent within the European state churches. Over time, Moravians did become a separate denomination. They began to devote more energy to missions and to evangelism, not in a competitive way, but by sending missionaries to places where other missionaries were not going. Moravians mostly ministered among indigenous people in non–European settings. By the time Moravians came to North Carolina, developments in Moravian life had led to a unique set of social and theological constructs that emphasized close familial relationship with God and close communal relationships within the church. When Count Zinzendorf died in 1760, the church slowly backed away from the more progressive and experimental approaches it had embraced, more quickly in Europe but in North Carolina as well.

Moravians brought to North Carolina the "choir system" that they had developed in Germany from the late 1720s through the 1740s. Though Moravians did and often still do express their faith in musical ways, this term does not refer to choirs in a musical sense; rather it refers to the division of community and devotional life into groups determined by gender and marital status. The choir system meant that women held official leadership positions within the church, with some being ordained "deaconesses" and a few even becoming "priestesses."[9]

Moravian communities had distinctive economic as well as spiritual practices. In what was called the "General Economy," the church owned all the land and many buildings and made all the local business and economic decisions. Only Moravians lived in Moravian settlements, and they pooled their work and resources in order to focus on their spiritual lives and to offer financial support for the church's mission work. A church board known as the *Aufseher Collegium*[10] consulted about how many of what kinds of craftsmen were needed and where and how to find or train them within the larger Moravian Church. This practice had obvious ramifications for people's careers and financial possibilities. While members knew they would not become personally wealthy, they knew that they and their families would find cradle-to-grave housing, health care, education, and employment, all within the context of the shared values of a religious community. Moravian communities also relied on the Lot, a practice derived from Acts 1, to be used when divine approval was sought to confirm decisions thought to be wise from a human perspective.[11] Finally, many of the earliest Moravian settlers had close personal ties to members of the Zinzendorf family.[12]

The eighteenth-century Moravian Church had unique theological understandings that correlated with its unique practices. Though Moravians have always believed in the Trinity, the Moravians of this period centered their devotion on Jesus Christ and on the Holy Spirit. While Jesus was understood to be Lord and Savior, the relationship between the Divine and the believer was likened to the relationship between earthly spouses, drawing from Biblical imagery of Christ who was seen as the Bridegroom and as the Creating Word. In addition, the side wound of Jesus was seen to be especially important for faith, as it was for the disciple Thomas in John's Gospel. Linking together Jesus' promise to send a Comforter, with Isaiah's words that God comforts God's people as a mother comforts her children, Moravians referred to the Holy Spirit as the Mother.[13] The mutually reinforcing emphases on the feminine in the Divine and female leadership arose at roughly the same time in the 1740s and was still in practice when the Moravians came to North Carolina.

In September 1753, a dozen German-speaking single men, all members of the Moravian Church, left Pennsylvania, journeying south to North Carolina.[14] Although the group began this journey from Christiansbrunn in eastern Pennsylvania, they had come to Christiansbrunn from several different British colonies, several different regions of Germany, and other European countries. Moravian historians have noted three primary reasons for their movement to North Carolina: establishing a new Moravian town, serving their new neighbors, and evangelizing Native Americans.[15] They brought with them the core beliefs and practices outlined above and used them to ground the community they built. This carefully selected group formed the vanguard of a thoroughly planned and organized migration of church members to what became known as the Wachovia Region.[16] Within thirteen years, these original settlers, together with the men, women, and children who were chosen to follow in planned stages of migration, primarily from Pennsylvania, had created what they themselves defined as a complete community.[17]

Multinational, multiracial, pacifist, dedicated to social action and to evangelism, and theologically and liturgically creative, the Moravian Church challenged many of the conventions of the European nations, their colonies, and their state churches. Though there is no direct evidence that Moravian women ever consecrated the elements of the Eucharist or baptized new believers, ordained Moravian women performed sacramental functions, such as distributing the elements of communion and laying hands on those being baptized or ordained. Women also provided pastoral care for which they were trained, work women in other religious groups were not allowed to do. Similarly, though Moravians did not seek to abolish slavery, Moravians offered unique leadership and community opportunities to free and enslaved Africans. Their granting of social status and liturgical authority to women and their initial integration of free and enslaved Africans into the social and worship spheres of these communities were progressive and controversial even in the unsettled, emerging religious landscape of North America. During their first thirty years in Wachovia, Moravians established and organized a series of villages and congregations that stood in stark contrast to the primarily unsettled region around them. Likewise, the members of the congregations differed from most of their neighbors in that region in terms of language,[18] living and working arrangements, and worship.

The initial settlers built Bethabara, the first step toward constructing their grand religious community, Salem, which they eventually built about six miles south.[19] Moravians soon began adapting their plans and practices to deal with the realities of the new contexts in North Carolina. In order to work with the Church of England, the existing state church of the colony, the Moravians formed a separate parish called Dobbs Parish.[20] Though this might appear to be ecclesiological nitpicking, the Moravian Church took legal issues involving church and state quite seriously. Practically, this meant that Moravians were able to offer preaching services, baptisms, and funerals to care for the spiritual needs of their non–Moravian neighbors.[21]

This community served its neighbors in other ways as well, thus laying the groundwork for an important theme in the history of the Moravian Church in North Carolina: serving neighbors both directly and indirectly. Refugees fleeing violence on the frontier during the French and Indian War, for example, arrived in the community of Bethabara.[22] The experiences of communal living and worship impressed many of these refugees who then sought to join the church community, prompting church leaders to create a second community just a few miles away named Bethania in 1759. This interrupted plans for building Salem, which was then begun in 1766.

With three congregations now underway, Moravians formed an administrative body called the *Helfer Conferenz* in 1773.[23] Among its first members were two couples, Frederic William and Hedwig Elizabeth Marshall, and Johann Michael and Getraut Jacke Graff.[24] They provided outstanding and effective leadership for these communities and others soon to follow. The planned migrations, primarily from Moravian settlements in Pennsylvania, led to the flourishing of Bethania and Salem. Difficulties in other Moravian communities in Pennsylvania, Maryland, and Maine,[25] coupled with land development and population pressures in these areas, led to the creation of three additional communities:

Friedberg (1773), Hope (1780), and Friedland (1780). With the founding of these congregations, the total number of Moravians in the Wachovia area reached 573, not counting children in the last three congregations.[26] Evangelists from these congregations traveled widely, and in 1800 began work among the Cherokee in northern Georgia. However, no new congregations in the American South were founded from 1780 until 1822, when a separate church was created for African American Moravians living in Salem.

The years following 1753, when the first members arrived in Wachovia, to the outbreak of the American Civil War, saw vast changes throughout the Moravian Church. Over the course of two generations, many of the theological and communal characteristics that had distinguished the Moravians from their neighbors had almost, if not completely, disappeared. Liturgies were forgotten. Important leadership roles for women were taken away. Pacifism was rejected. Settlement towns opened up to allow non–Moravians to live and work there. Moravians segregated their living and worship spaces. These changes in the Wachovia Region were so critical that, by 1861, Moravians had more in common with the armed combatants with whom they enlisted in the forces of the Confederate States of America than with the pacifist Moravian forebears who had founded their communities.[27]

Since the founding of the first Moravian settlement in North Carolina, Moravians have experienced the tensions of attempting to witness to and serve their neighbors in a variety of ways, while wrestling with how to adapt to religious, social, and political changes, usually questioning whether to adopt new ways of thinking and acting. Within the Moravian Church there have often been conservative voices, who, based on their understandings of certain parts of Moravian traditions, have called, along with socially conservative elements within North Carolina, the church to stay true to its roots and foundations. Other groups, drawing upon their understandings of other parts of Moravian traditions, have called, along with more socially progressive forces within the state, upon the church to change.

General Chronology

In terms of the life of the Moravian Church, the first six decades were times of both consolidation and adaptation. First, through Bethabara and, then, through the central community of Salem, Moravians created for themselves and their neighbors an outpost for hospitality, trade, craftsmanship, medical services, musical entertainment, and education—even running water indoors. Though this will receive more in-depth attention later, for now it is important to note that in April 1772, Elizabeth Oesterlein began teaching three young girls. Her work began the foundation of what is now Salem Academy and College.[28] Many Moravians who had traveled extensively as the church grew and expanded in Europe eventually settled into the Wachovia area. Moravian leadership successfully guided the community through the French and Indian War and through the American Revolution, upholding its commitment to pacifism while serving the wounded on both sides. Slowly Moravian congregations grew as they became more accustomed to being in an American context.

While the accommodations to the American context were generally positive for the white male population, they had a negative impact on women and African Americans. For the first three decades Moravians lived in North Carolina, ordained deaconesses served many parishioners. Ten women had been ordained elsewhere and later served in Wachovia. Ten others were ordained there. Of the six congregations founded in North Carolina, five were served by at least two deaconesses during their early years. Girls in those congregations would have grown up thinking that they might have the opportunity to lead and serve in similar ways.[29] However, after 1786 the Moravians in North Carolina ordained no more women for nearly two centuries—until 1978. Men began exercising more spiritual and administrative authority over the Single Sisters choir. Women no longer were allowed to serve on the highest administrative conferences. Likewise, African Americans who had once been welcomed into the Salem congregation with the kiss of peace from their European brothers and sisters were moved to the back of worship spaces. Eventually a separate congregation was organized for them in 1822.

In addition to these changes, Moravian leadership dealt with the slow transition from the managed General Economy and church control of social and economic life to a more American approach to personal liberties and freedoms, including more freedom in marital, career, and economic decisions. Wachovia Moravians gained administrative independence from European Moravians in 1848 and continued becoming more like their North Carolina neighbors who were even allowed to live among them when Salem ceased to be a closed community of Moravians in 1857.[30]

As Methodist and Baptist congregations grew up around them, Moravians were leery of the Methodists' loud and free-spirited worship and newer sounding songs, but generally managed good relationships with them and other denominations. Moravian ministers had many preaching stations as well as various Sunday school outreaches, some starting as early as the 1820s and reaching as far north as the Virginia mountains. Some of the Sunday schools would eventually grow into congregations. Moravian leaders in the 1840s and 1850s did not have the resources to follow up on various requests to begin new works in Texas, Iowa, and Arkansas where other Moravians had moved. Even work that was begun in Illinois by a Southern Province pastor eventually became part of the work of the Northern Province.[31] Mission interest, focused on the Cherokee to the west and on the potential outreach to slaves on plantations, never produced large numbers, despite devoted efforts by generations of missionaries to the Cherokee. Missions to slaves on plantations never succeeded, primarily due to frustrations with plantation owners and their treatment of slaves.

The Civil War, far more than the French and Indian War or the American Revolution, impacted Moravians in North Carolina. Prior to the war, Moravians expressed mixed sentiments about secession, and of the two local papers, the one that "served as the unofficial newspaper of the Moravian Church" was more Unionist.[32] As early as November 1861, when Jefferson Davis had called for a day of humiliation and prayer, even before the horrors and losses of the war had had time to mount up, at Friedberg, the Rev. Christian Lewis Rights noted: "Praying for the Southern Confederacy is not popular here."[33] Having abandoned their pacifist principles, Moravians enlisted in the Confederate Army, with many of them serving in the 26th Regimental Band. One of the great ironies is that Union Moravians from Bethlehem, Pennsylvania, likely fought Confederate Moravians from Salem on Cemetery Hill during the Battle of Gettysburg.[34]

Scarce goods and rising commodity prices added to the miseries of those who stayed at home receiving or dreading to receive news of the loss of loved ones. Being far from all battlefronts until near the end of the war, Salem Female Academy was seen as a refuge for many daughters in the South; its population doubled between 1861 and 1865.[35] Female academies like Salem played a lead role in the transition, necessitated by the loss of so many men during the war, from teaching being a male-dominated to a female-dominated profession.[36]

As some of the Sunday schools near Salem that had been founded earlier grew into congregations, Moravians began to expand beyond the town of Salem beginning in the 1840s. Even so, it took founding Providence Moravian, just north of Salem and north of the newer town of Winston, in 1880 for the denomination to reach twelve congregations, doubling the number of congregations founded between 1753 and 1780.[37] With Providence, the number of Moravians in North Carolina finally topped two thousand. Christian Lewis Rights (1820–1891) should be noted for his work during this time of growth. Though not officially trained for pastoral work, his ministerial gifts were recognized, and despite his Methodist-influenced services, he was acknowledged as a pastor who brought needed spiritual revival to several different Moravian congregations. He became a member of the highest administrative body in the Province and eventually served as its President.[38]

In 1880, The Moravian Church entered one of its periods of fastest growth. Over the next two decades the church grew by fourteen new congregations and more than doubled its membership to over five thousand. This period of growth and development within the church was paralleled by civic and economic growth and development in and around Salem. Though modest growth in the number of congregations continued for the next twenty years, membership rose steadily from 5272 in 1900 to 7877 in 1920. That year, Winston-Salem was the largest city in the state (Salem had merged with Winston to form one city in 1913). The Roaring Twenties aptly described growth in the Moravian Church, although the moral implications were certainly different. Membership continued its steady rise up to 11,658 in 1930 as the number of congregations grew by another ten during the decade. This expansion carried the Moravian Church outside of the Winston-Salem area in large numbers for the first time. Moravians expanded their work in southern Virginia, moved as far east as Eden in Rockingham County, and reached into Charlotte for the first time.

Amazingly, one man led the denomination through the growth periods of the 1880s and the 1920s, President of the Provincial Elders Conference (PEC),[39] Bishop Edward Rondthaler. Rondthaler was born in Pennsylvania and had served congregations there and in New York before being called to be the pastor at Salem in 1877. He served there until 1908, but continued his service to the province as the President of the PEC, which he had begun in 1890, until 1929. Following the Civil War, tough economic times led the Southern Province to consider merging with the Northern Province, centered in Bethlehem, Pennsylvania. Serious discussions lasted for three years until the Southern Province realized that terms of the merger would only worsen the impact on the struggling congregations in the South. Although he had been active in the discussions, Rondthaler voted against the merger.

Rondthaler's leadership at Salem oversaw not only the vitality of that congregation, but helped with the growing Sunday school movement. Under his leadership, laypersons from Salem started Sunday schools in many of the suburbs springing up around Salem and Winston. Furthermore, the Moravian Church not only continued to spread into new suburbs, but also outside of Forsyth County in a significant way. His deep, collegial friendship and cooperation with the Rev. Henry A. Brown, the pastor of First Baptist Church in Winston, and their ability to work with business leaders were key to creating the atmosphere that allowed Winston-Salem to merge and grow into the state's largest city.[40]

In the eighty-five years following Rondthaler's leadership, the Moravian Church has opened only thirteen new churches in North Carolina. Several reasons, many outside of the church's control, account for this very slow growth. The Great Depression slowed but did not stop or reverse growth. Congregations that had begun expansions during the late 1920s were able to pay off their debts despite the bleak financial times. Even though no new churches were built, membership continued to rise during World War II, despite attendance being down due to the draft, relocation of members due to the war effort, and rationing.

As noted earlier, the Moravians in North Carolina are part of a province that had begun to extend into Virginia in the nineteenth century, and had always been a part of a worldwide church with members on four continents. Being part of a global church began to impact Moravians in North Carolina in a more substantial way in the 1950s and 1960s. Moravians have normally sought to carry on mission work in areas where other churches were not going. Sensing that to be the case in Florida, Moravians started work there in the 1950s. Many people were migrating to the Sunshine State, and it presented lots of opportunities for ministry without competing against churches that were already there. Preliminary investigations beginning in 1956 led to the founding of Coral Ridge Moravian Church near Fort Lauderdale. That was the first of four congregations in Florida to be started by 1975. The Cuban missile crisis overshadowed the development of Moravian plans in Florida, and after the crisis was over, more well-known denominations began working in Florida. The Moravian initiatives did not flourish, and three of the Moravian congregations closed by 1990. Political unrest in Nicaragua and subsequent migration to south Florida led the Moravian Church to look at ministries to those refugees and to consider work among other Moravians from the Caribbean who had immigrated there.

Responsibility for the mission work in the Caribbean shifted from the leadership of the British province to the leadership of American provinces in 1955. The British Province had already begun moving the Caribbean provinces towards self-sufficiency and indigenous leadership, and the North American Moravians continued this process. North American Moravian clergy ministered in this region most actively from the mid–1950s through the early 1970s. Sending significant numbers of missionaries was a big change for the Moravians in North Carolina who, after a long history of ministerial shortages, were now able to send pastors. While these issues might seem outside the scope of this essay, the Moravian work in Florida and the Caribbean impacted the administration and distribution of both human and financial resources of the church centered in North Carolina.

During this period, the Moravian Church also began wrestling with several significant social issues. It did not do this alone, however, as the Moravian Church sent the Rev. J. Kenneth Pfohl and Walser Aller to exploratory and organizational meetings for the North Carolina Council of Churches with which many Moravians have been actively engaged.[41] Moravian synods, comprised of lay and clergy legislative delegates from congregations and agencies that currently meet every four years, dealt with issues related to divorce, the Vietnam War, nuclear weapons, U.S. policy in Central America, the ordination of women, race relations, and human sexuality, especially related to homosexuality.

Within many organizations, approaches to authority have changed since the beginning of the Vietnam War. The Southern Province is no exception. It had just four PEC presidents from 1880 to 1968, yet it has already elected six different presidents in the less than five decades from that time to the present.[42] In 1970, the province reached its high point in membership with a total number of 22,357. The latest membership statistics count 15,600 Moravians in 2015.[43] The forty-six congregations in North Carolina are spread from Mount Airy to Charlotte and from Newton to Wilmington, with the majority clustered around Winston-Salem.

Thematic Considerations Related to the Moravian Church in North Carolina

In addition to having a chronological overview of the development of the Moravian Church in North Carolina, it is also helpful to look at how significantly key principles the Moravians first brought with them in the eighteenth century have continued to impact the church. In doing so we will look not only at the church itself, but roles that key church members played, often influenced by the church's principles, emphases and connections. We will look at education, industry, commerce and civic life, social action, race relations, and the role of women.

Education

Educational opportunities and endeavors probably form the most far-reaching impact of Moravians on the state of North Carolina. Moravians began officially educating young Moravian girls in 1772. Though this was extremely rare, in 1785 Adam Schumacher, a Moravian with a farm near Salem, requested, and apparently received, unquestioned approval that "a Negro girl on his place be permitted to attend the school."[44] Word of the school spread, and soon white, non–Moravian families were asking to send their daughters to Salem. "Outside" students began arriving in 1804, and by 1805 Salem was a boarding school with facilities dedicated to caring for these students.[45] One of the earliest boarding students was Sarah Davie, the daughter of William R. Davie. As a female, Sarah was not allowed to attend the University of North Carolina, which her father helped found.[46] Sarah was later joined by her younger sister Rebecca.[47] News of the school led to a visit from Governor Nathaniel Alexander in 1807.[48] Other notable students included Sarah Childress of Murfreesboro, Tennessee, who arrived in 1817, and later married James K. Polk.[49] By the 1820s, daughters of Cherokee chieftains were studying there.[50]

After thriving through the Civil War, in 1866 the school incorporated, officially earning the ability to grant degrees, even though official baccalaureates were not awarded until 1890. Special celebrations in 1902 brought to campus Gov. Charles B. Aycock, who issued an appeal to raise an endowment for the school.[51] Additional endowments garnered recognition and contributions from national sources such as the Southern Education Board, Andrew Carnegie, and John D. Rockefeller.[52] By 1911, the college had grown to the point that it needed more specialized expertise than the members of the PEC could bring, and people who were not members of the PEC were allowed to serve on the Board of Trustees. In 1931, the overall educational complex was expanded by building facilities for the Academy nearby but distinct from the College.

Moravians did educate their boys as well, but attempts at creating schools for them were not as successful. Educational opportunities already existed for boys in the region, and some Moravian boys from North Carolina, especially those going into the ministry, were educated at Moravian institutions in Pennsylvania. It is also worth noting that in addition to William R. Davie's sending his daughters to Salem, Davie invited Lewis David von Schweinitz, one of the church's lead administrators for the Wachovia region, a botanist, and the first American-born person to earn a Ph.D., to serve as the President of Davies' beloved educational institution at Chapel Hill. Von Schweinitz turned down the honor because he would have had to discontinue his service to the church.[53] He did, however, serve the university as a trustee.[54]

On a far less grand, though more controversial, scale, Moravians for a while educated African American members of the community. In 1827, Sunday school for African Americans in Salem included instruction in spelling and reading. Soon, some African Americans were even employed to assist the teachers. This continued until the practice was made illegal by state law in 1831.[55] Moravians at times still tried to give religious instruction to African Americans; Moravians in Bethania found a way around the law by teaching through storytelling and talks.[56]

Moravian emphasis on education continued to play out in other ways as well. Shortly after the Civil War, Salem Moravians quickly responded to the requests of nearby African Americans for educational opportunities.[57] William A. Blair and Henry E. Fries were early trustees of the Slater Industrial Academy, which grew and developed in scope, eventually becoming Winston-Salem State University.[58] Fries' educational interests also included serving on the Forsyth County School Board, which undertook the building of new schoolhouses for the entire system during his term, and he was instrumental in the founding of the agriculturally and mechanically focused college that eventually became known as North Carolina State University.[59] Initial Moravian educational facilities in Clemmons were eventually leased to the state for the founding of a "farm life school."[60] In 1958, the Charlotte school system opened a junior high school named for a Moravian Bishop, Herbert Spaugh, who started serving on the school board in 1937. Bishop Spaugh's active civic involvement also included playing horn in the Charlotte Symphony and writing a newspaper column, *The Everyday Counselor.*[61]

Industry, Commerce and Civic Life

We noted earlier that Moravians were gifted craftsmen and tradesmen and that Salem became an important commercial center for the western piedmont during the 1760s. Bethabara had a grist mill by the end of 1755.[62] This was of great benefit not only to the Moravian residents, but to many of their neighbors as well. A Moravian paper mill built along a creek near Salem in 1791 likewise benefited both the Moravians and their neighbors.[63]

As the Moravian Church relaxed its control over the General Economy, it began an uneasy relationship, and at times partnership, with individual Moravians who wanted to start various industrial and commercial ventures. The church participated in bringing steam power to the textile industry by not only buying shares in the Salem Cotton Manufacturing Company but also selling the land outright to the company, rather than leasing the land according to previous practice. It sold the company land for firewood to power the steam engines and established a Sunday school for the children of mill workers.[64] Ultimately this cotton factory was not profitable due to the founding of several other cotton companies in North Carolina, a financial panic, and the difficulty of receiving payments in barter rather than currency.[65]

Woolen manufacturing was far more successful. Begun in Salem in 1839 by Moravian leaders Johann Christian Wilhelm Fries and his son Francis L. Fries, by 1842 the mill was dealing with the public and providing the piedmont region of North Carolina with woolen goods. The arrangements worked out by the church and the Fries family regarding their use of slaves point out the complexities inherent in the Moravian Church's responses to race and to slavery.[66] In 1858, Francis Fries built a gas plant so that gas lamps could be used in the factory. By 1860, he was dealing with merchants throughout the South and as far north as New York.[67] Despite having manufactured cloth for Confederate uniforms, the company was trading in northern markets soon after the war.[68]

Perhaps no other scenario could have so succinctly encompassed the massive changes to the Moravian Community of Salem as did the Fries' enterprises. The German-speaking, pacifist founders of the community would have worshipped with slaves, but kept non–Moravians out of the community. Now English-speaking Moravians were using slave labor as they worked alongside their non–Moravian neighbors to support the Confederate War effort.

In addition to offering employment opportunities through its mills, Salem began to develop a reputation as a resort community, especially during summers, when people wanted to "escape the unpleasantness and dangers of the lowlands in summer," arising out of its cultural offerings and connections coming from Salem College.[69] Moravians in industry and commerce, who benefited from increased trade and improved communications brought about by the Fayetteville and Western Plank Road Company chartered in 1849, included Fries, who was one of the directors.[70] Upon its completion, the road ran 129 miles from Fayetteville through Salem to Bethania, reportedly the longest plank road to be constructed.[71]

Other businesses owned by Moravians contributed to the region's economy. In 1834, John P. Nissen, the grandson of Tycho Nissen, who had been a wagon maker[72] before becoming the founding pastor at Friedland, took up his grandfather's trade. The sturdy Nissen wagons allowed area farmers to make the most of the Fayetteville and Western Plank Road. This was especially true as the tobacco markets developed after the Civil War, prompting Nannie M. Tilley to note in *The Bright-Tobacco Industry* that "so essential were the Nissen wagons in marketing tobacco that they have been deemed a decisive factor in the development of the tobacco industry through the entire piedmont area."[73]

At this point it is worth sharing a lengthy quotation of Professor William Powell's description of the citizenry in 1860 from his definitive history of North Carolina:

By 1860, North Carolina was much changed from the state Archibald D. Murphey had known just a generation earlier. On the surface it had become progressive, as demonstrated by its splendid system of public or common schools; its railroads, including one owned largely by the state; its newspapers; its natives holding high national office, among others a president, a vice president, a cabinet member, and an ambassador; and, most important, its many new business enterprises. Yet the people had hardly changed at all. They were still largely rural and dependent on agriculture, very independent, ultraconservative, often superstitious, clannish, seldom aware of events outside their immediate neighborhood, and above all satisfied with these characteristics.[74]

Even though Moravians had changed greatly during the first century they had been in North Carolina, their advanced cultural and technological offerings in their communities meant that they still differed substantially from many of their neighbors, as assessed by Powell. Despite these amenities, their influence, due to sheer numbers, was declining. In 1860, Moravians were tied as seventh most numerous religious group with a population of two thousand members in ten churches, alongside the Quakers who had the same number, but in twenty-two different congregations. The Baptists, the largest group, far outnumbered them with 65,000 members in 780 congregations.[75]

We have already noted the importance of geography for the safety offered the Salem Female Academy during the Civil War, and that was true for the town as well, which suffered little physical war damage.[76] This good fortune set the stage for continued growth and development after the Civil War as the South began to rebuild. Powell notes: "Salem was the first town in the state, and perhaps in the South, to have electric lights in a manufacturing plant when the Salem Woolen Mill and the new plant of the Arista Cotton Mills owned by F.H. Fries acquired them."[77] Winston and Salem were among the first cities in the state to have telephones, electric lights, electric-powered streetcars, and a sewer system.[78]

As industries grew and expanded, the need for labor drew many people to the area. Much of the construction—industrial and commercial, residential, and even some church-related buildings—was done by Fogle Brothers.[79] This company was started in 1870 by members of an active and connected Moravian family at Salem whose members included both civic and religious leaders. Their business partnerships included projects with Henry Fries. Their last major project was building the facilities that housed Salem Academy when it moved into separate quarters, distinct from Salem College.

The Fries family's economic and religious interests also impacted the town of Mayodan in that he built a cotton mill there in 1895, and by 1896 the Moravian Church also started a new congregation there.[80] Likewise Henry Fries started a new cotton mill in the "Southside" area of Salem in 1896. Sunday school work among the mill workers in the area resulted in the founding of the Pine Chapel congregation in 1904.[81]

Earlier we noted the cooperation of the Moravian Bishop Edward Rondthaler and the Baptist Dr. Henry Brown in working together ecumenically and within the business community as Winston and Salem grew and eventually joined together. We described the growth in amenities available to its citizens, brought about to some extent by Moravian industrial and commercial enterprises. It is worth noting also that, as the automobile industry grew, Nissen wagons became obsolete. Upon the sale of the company, Nissen's heirs built the Nissen building, an eighteen-story skyscraper that was the tallest building in North Carolina until it was succeeded by Winston-Salem's Reynolds Building in 1929.[82] Though Winston-Salem had become a more cosmopolitan city, the influence and contributions of Moravians to its thriving at the time were undeniable.

When Moravians and others celebrated the Bicentennial of the founding of Salem, Bishop Kenneth Hamilton noted many ways that Moravians had contributed to the area: "May not the prosperity of this community and the good labor relations which it has generally enjoyed be considered a heritage of the day when hardworking, shrewd, but devout pioneers laid the foundation for this community in the heart of Wachovia?"[83] He further wrote that "some of the leading personalities connected with the Wachovia National Bank … had had a part in the earlier banking ventures in Salem."[84] Writing about philanthropy, Hamilton said: "In view of the ideals which motivated the founders of Salem and dominated life within that community for so long a period, the generous spirit found in this city today can be regarded at least in part as a fruit of commitment to God and concern for the needs of others, needs which the church as such no longer is in a position to supply."[85]

Following up on Hamilton's comments related to Wachovia Bank and Moravian generosity related to the city, it is worth acknowledging the importance that Archie K. Davis played in both the life of Winston-Salem and in the founding of the Research Triangle, which has played a significant role in the economy of the state and in the educational institutions located near it. As David Moltke-Hansen remarked in his obituary for Davis, "No individual did more over the second half of the twentieth century to influence the economic development of his native state."[86] An active member of Home Moravian Church, Davis began his career at Wachovia Bank, eventually becoming its president in 1956. He was active in historical and musical nonprofit organizations. Davis was president of the Research Triangle Foundation from its inception in 1959 until 1981, and he served as chair until retirement in 1997.[87]

Moravians have also made significant contributions to the role of music in the state. Though numerous visitors had commented on the active musical life of the congregations in Wachovia well before 1786, the *Collegium Musicum Salem* dates to that year. It was the fourth of such groups founded in the British colonies or the United States.[88] Comprised of amateur musicians who were ministers or artisans by profession, they continued well into the next century, though their repertoire became increasingly secular.[89] The commencement exercises of the Salem Female Academy, which included musical performances, attracted a great deal of attention, at times unwanted by the town and the young women, from parents and potential suitors.[90]

The mid-twentieth century saw a resurgence of interest in the music of the early Moravians that led to both a series of Moravian Music Festivals and the founding of the Moravian Music Foundation, both of which continue to the present day.[91] Mutual musical interests also led to shared relationships with what is now known as the University of North Carolina School of the Arts.[92] The Moravian Music Foundation achieved national prominence by offering a concert of Moravian Music as part of a series of opening concerts at the Kennedy Center for Performing Arts in 1971.[93] It is worth noting finally that while the Moravian Music Foundation brought Moravian Music to a national audience, Andy Griffith, a Moravian from Mount Airy who had once considered going into the Moravian ministry, brought a good deal of pastoral sensibility and his own musical tastes to a national audience as well.

Social Action

Social action has often been a part of the discourse of Moravians and has affected their relationships with the wider world. As early as 1772, just six years after the founding of Salem, the leadership discussed constructing a brewery, hoping it would lead to less drinking of stronger spirits.[94] While some Moravians became active in temperance movements in the nineteenth century, at least some saw that as youthful enthusiasm against the more moderate approaches of the older generation.[95] Current Moravian teaching advocates moderation in the consumption of alcohol and other areas of life.[96]

Going back to their early days as a persecuted church, Moravians have often been leery of punishment distributed by the state. It is not surprising that when Forsyth County was created in 1849 and neighbors asked Salem to build a courthouse with a jail, gallows, and whipping post, authorities in Salem denied their request. When they did buy land for building a courthouse and jail, it was written into the deed, and made forever binding, that no whipping post might be set up on the lands transferred.[97] Moravians today continue to support a prison ministry through the work of the Rev. Robert Wolfe, a Moravian chaplain on the staff of the Forsyth Jail and Prison Ministries, who has served in that capacity since 1995.

In words that echo eerily today, Bishop Rondthaler noted in the "Memorabilia" of 1900 that the coming century "will be an age of tremendous struggle between capital and labor, or rather between wealth and poverty. Will there come to be an equitable settlement between the two?"[98]

When the Rev. William E. Gramley, pastor of Olivet Moravian Church near Winston-Salem from 1966 to 1969, was actively involved in opposition to the Vietnam War, he found relatively little support from his once-pacifist denomination, and the Provincial Elders Conference, when asked by the National Council of Churches to issue a statement regarding its stance on the war, chose not to do so. In 1969, the PEC, following up on a 1968 Synod resolution, did set up a committee to certify those who were conscientious objectors,[99] and in doing so was in continuity with similar actions taken prior to World War II.[100]

Regarding issues of human sexuality, the 1962 Synod allowed for remarriage of divorced persons, noting the need to act "compassionately and redemptively with human frailty … including failure in the marriage state."[101] The 1995 Synod resolved, "That in the interest of justice, we oppose without reservation all acts of violence, coercion, and intimidation against persons who are homosexual, or who are perceived to be homosexual, and that we affirm certain basic human rights and civil liberties are due all persons." The 2010 and 2014 Synods had additional discussions related to homosexuality. Though these have at times been difficult conversations, Moravians have acknowledged that individual members and the church as a whole maintain a variety of different beliefs. Some congregations have openly homosexual members, though openly homosexual pastors cannot be called to serve congregations in North Carolina. As of 2015, the Southern Province is conducting a series of ongoing meetings for continuing education and discussions related to the Province's stance on these matters.

Race Relations

The Moravian Church in North Carolina has a conflicted history of race relations. Even before coming to North Carolina, eighteenth-century Moravians felt the tension between trying to minister to enslaved people and maintaining good relations with governments and slave owners in order to have the access to slaves they needed to be able to minister to them.[102] Scott Rohrer also addresses the role of African American members as he argues for the creation of a unique German-American subculture that featured powerful ties of African American kinship and spiritual connectivity within it.[103] The Moravian Church in North Carolina did decide to allow slaveholding, with the church itself purchasing slaves at times. Early on, these slaves were full members of the community, attending worship with their European counterparts, with freed slaves remaining members of the community as well. Although the church owned slaves, it remained very restrictive of when and where individual Moravians could own slaves.

Yet the church was also aware of the problems this stance created for slaves and for the church that ministered to them. How could the church ask slaves to be faithful as husband and wife, when it knew that slave families might be broken up through sales?[104]

As noted earlier, Moravian efforts to educate slaves were made illegal by state law, though Moravians attempted to circumvent this code in some cases by educating through storytelling, rather than through reading and writing.[105] Moravians' exemption from military service was terminated by the state legislature in the aftermath of Nat Turner's slave rebellion in 1831.[106] Jacob Siewers, a Moravian missionary from North Carolina to slaves in Florida, was forced to leave his mission when he complained to the slaveholder about his treatment of slaves.[107] Legally, matters worsened when North Carolina law required that manumitted slaves leave the state.[108] This meant that Moravian slaveholders who were concerned about such matters knew that their slaves would no longer be able to worship in the Moravian congregation comprised of African Americans. The complexities of the Moravian stances related to slavery are highlighted by the case of Phebe who, when she died in 1861 around the age of 90, was "a retired slave of the Moravian Church, living on a pension from the church."[109] Despite the fact that Moravians had founded a separate African American congregation to segregate the worship spaces in Salem, large special services involving African Americans, such as baptisms and funerals, were still held in the large Salem (white) church rather than the smaller African American church.[110] After the Civil War, Moravians quickly responded to the request of freed slaves for a school.[111]

At least one Moravian was so repulsed by slavery that he left for Illinois.[112] Even though he had little education and formal theological training, Martin Hauser founded West Salem using some of the communal principles that had grounded the Moravian communities in North Carolina nearly a century earlier. The community grew as other Moravians from North Carolina joined him. It is difficult to tell, however, how many of West Salem's residents came there due to opposition to slavery and how many came due to lure of fertile soil and open space.

Complicated race relations did not end with the Civil War. As the African American community in the eastern side of Winston-Salem grew in the middle portion of the twentieth century, it came into contact with two white Moravian congregations, Fairview and Fries Memorial. Unfortunately, the congregations did not see this as an opportunity for outreach. Instead the following rhetoric can be found in various articles and reports: Fries Memorial contemplated moving due to "encroachment of the negroes" and noted in a report to the *Wachovia Moravian* that "Every white congregation in this section of our city is threatened with extinction."[113]

Officially, Moravians have moved beyond such sentiments. After World War II, Moravian synods expressed interest in outreach to the African American community[114] and support for Supreme Court decisions ending segregation.[115] Despite the fact that the Southern Province has a very small percentage of African Americans, Mae Rodney, an African American woman, has served as the Vice Chair of Synod.[116] The *Wachovia Moravian* published an article that spoke out strongly against the assassination of Martin Luther King, Jr., calling his killer "a cowardly assassin whose sick mind speaks for the cancer of our society."[117] Along these lines, the 1995 Moravian hymnal updated its All Saints Day prayer, based on the Hebrews 11 description of martyrs of the church that have been slain, to include the words "they were killed by an assassin's bullet."[118] The 2006 Synod "apologize[d] to the African-American community for the past participation of the Moravian Church in the institution of slavery" and called for increased efforts in "racial reconciliation, the elimination of institutional racism, and the fostering of diversity in churches of the Southern Province."[119]

Moravians also dealt with race relations in the nineteenth century through their missionary efforts to the Cherokee, towards whom they were very sympathetic. One missionary, Miles Vogler, wanted to accompany the group during their forced removal, but church officials denied his request, fearing that it would appear Moravians were in agreement with such treatment. Instead Vogler, Gottlieb Ruede, and Johann Schmidt traveled ahead to Indian Territory to work with the Cherokee as they began their life in exile.[120]

The Role of Women

Earlier we noted that women had unique and authoritative positions within the Moravian Church. Though Moravians ordained women in the eighteenth century, this practice was either unknown to or ignored by authors who have written about the role of women in the state. Alan Watson highlights the importance of Elizabeth Osterlein, the first teacher at Salem,[121] and notes the particular care given to widows and impoverished women. However, though he includes a picture of Gertraud Graff, he does not mention the power and authority accorded to her in her Moravian context. She was herself ordained and participated in the ordination of other women.

Although the Lot[122] was abandoned, its role in marriage could be seen as more advantageous to women than the prevalent marriage practices in the eighteenth century. Many non–Moravian women had spouses chosen for them in accordance with their parents' financial, social, or political interests. Moravian women could choose not to be married, and many spent their lives as Single Sisters. If they did so, they were respected members of the community who were able to live in communal Single Sisters housing, contribute to the community throughout their lifetime, and be cared for in their old age. If they did wish to marry, community leaders would suggest a match with a man believed capable of supporting a wife and family. That was then submitted to the Lot. Only then was the match suggested to the woman, and she still had the right of refusal, which some women chose.[123]

The Moravians in North Carolina stopped ordaining women in 1786. Synod resolutions nearly two centuries later prepared the way for women to be ordained again. These discussions related to the ordination of women centered more on equal rights and did not address issues of biblical interpretation.[124] Though this approach seemed wise at the time, it has made it difficult for women to serve as pastors in some Moravian settings where members raised objections based on their interpretation of scripture. The Rev. Carol A. Foltz was ordained in 1978, the first Moravian woman to be ordained in North Carolina since 1786. Since then, twenty-six women have been ordained in the Southern Province of the Moravian Church or were ordained in other denominations and have served in the Southern Province. Currently only eight women are serving under call. Two have interim appointments; seven have retired, and four serve in the Northern Province. However, several women who have trained for ministry or have even been ordained currently do not have calls. Four more grew up Moravian, but were ordained in other denominations, at least partly due to their belief that it would be hard for them as women to receive calls. The numbers point out that it is difficult for women to receive calls to congregational ministry. At least partly because the church did not clearly articulate principles for Biblical interpretation when it addressed the ordination of women, not only does it still struggle with Biblical issues related to the ordination of women, but it also struggles with issues of Biblical interpretation as it addresses issues related to homosexuality.

Current Service and Connection to North Carolina

Moravians are probably most well known in North Carolina for their Christmas and Easter traditions, many of which are being adopted by other Christians who find them meaningful. On the day before Easter, Moravians gather in God's Acre, the Moravian graveyard in Salem, to wash the flat headstones and put flowers on the graves in preparation for the Easter Sunrise Service. This day of preparation has received attention on national television news shows. The service itself begins in the darkness outside of Home Moravian Church. Worshippers proceed to God's Acre where they see the sun rise over the decorated graves as those gathered participate in responsive readings and sing songs that celebrate the resurrection of Jesus Christ, accompanied by hundreds of wind musicians in the band. The service draws thousands of worshippers, many of whom are visitors or non–Moravians, each year.

Many others also know about Moravian sugar cake and Christmas cookies that are now sold in many stores and shipped throughout the world. Moravians place multi-pointed stars in their churches and homes during the seasons of Advent, Christmas, and Epiphany. This practice, in particular, is being adopted by many other faith communities, and the largest Moravian Star in the world now sits atop Wake Forest University Baptist Medical Center, shedding its light on Moravians, Baptists, and all who pass by it in the city of Winston-Salem.

Moravians use Lovefeast services to celebrate many special occasions. This simple service, which is not a sacrament, like communion or baptism, dates back to 1727 in Herrnhut, Germany. Worshippers partake in a simple meal, often a bun and coffee. Though there is normally a brief message, the theme of the service is found in the words of the hymns that are sung throughout the service, including while the meal is brought on trays carried by *dieners*.[125] Congregational anniversaries, Thanksgiving services, and special services highlighting mission work, youth ministry, or work with the elderly are often celebrated with a Lovefeast.

The most well known of the Lovefeast services is the Christmas Eve Candlelight Lovefeast. Before this service, congregational bands play Advent and Christmas tunes for a prelude. During the service the Christmas story is read; the congregation sings Christmas carols; choirs offer special music, and worshippers share the meal of a bun and coffee. In addition, at the end of this service, the *dieners* return to give each worshipper a lit, beeswax candle. The candles are trimmed with red crepe paper to keep the wax from dripping on worshipers' fingers. The light of the candle symbolizes the light that the Christ child brings into the world, and worshippers are invited to lift their candles high during a verse of the last hymn to symbolize their desire to share that light with the world.

Finally, a word about the Moravian Archives is in order. The Moravian Archives shares its home in Winston-Salem with the Moravian Music Foundation in the Archie K. Davis Building, situated between God's Acre and Salem College. Though located there for practical purposes, its location is richly symbolic. The Archives contains many of the historical documents that have grounded the writing of this essay. The documents range from the autobiographical *Lebenslauefe*[126] and funeral memoirs written by pastors for those who are buried near the building, to the minutes of congregational boards and the decisions of Provincial Synods. The Archives is rooted in the past, but it makes the past available for study, research, and education. Though its documents are primarily about Moravians, they are valuable for all North Carolinians since they offer many insights into the lives and institutions with which the Moravian Church has interacted over the centuries.

Looking Ahead

It is fitting to close this history with a look toward the future. The Moravian Church faces challenges similar to those faced by other Protestant denominations in the current religious, social, economic, and political climates. Moravians came to North Carolina offering a very different understanding of the intersection of religion and practice than was operative among their neighbors. Today, however, many congregations seem rather like the majority of the Protestant congregations nearby. Most Moravians would argue, however, that the practice of their faith is distinctive due to the value placed on relationships, missions, history, and music more than particular doctrines.

Two of the newest ministries of the Moravian Church are offering fresh perspectives on the more progressive theological and socioeconomic visions that brought their ancestors to North Carolina. Anthony's Plot, named after the slave who gave the Moravians the impetus to begin overseas mission work, is a residential community with this mission:

> As a community, we strive to identify with the poor and disenfranchised through our living and our work, to be intentional about bearing witness to Jesus and the interdependency of Christian community, to provide occasions for people to grow in faith and serve together, and to close the disparities between churches and our struggling communities relationally and tangibly through committed Christ-like actions.[127]

The community lives in the former parsonage of Trinity Moravian Church in a diverse and economically challenged area in Winston-Salem. Their concern for the disenfranchised has led to extensive advocacy work with the homeless of the city.

A second ministry is called Come and Worship. Having been located in several different restaurants and commercial sites in downtown Winston-Salem, it offers an informal worship service blending the Moravian tradition of hymns and liturgies with more contemporary music. It reaches out to people who are looking for a worship experience different from what they find in more traditional Moravian services. It partners with homeless ministries and other ministries, including supporting the growing Moravian Church in Cuba monetarily and assisting short-term missionaries in going to the island.

Over time, Moravians developed and now hold to a three-part essential belief about God and a three-part essential belief about humanity's response. Moravians believe God's love for humanity, effected by the saving work of Christ, is made real by the Holy Spirit in the lives of believers as the Spirit gives gifts to share this Good News with others. At their best, Moravians in turn respond with active faith to share these beliefs with others, hope in the midst of worldly circumstances, and love for God and neighbor. Moravians in North Carolina today attempt to embody these core essentials in twenty-first-century contexts just as their innovative ancestors did when they first arrived over two hundred and fifty years ago.

Notes

1. This essay will use the name "Moravian Church," even though it is anachronistic. The geographical region of Moravia in the Czech Republic is the origin of the church's current name in English-speaking regions: The Moravian Church. The first settlers in North Carolina would have identified as members of the *Brüdergemeine*. This term is closer in line with the *Unitas Fratrum*, the Latin name for the religious group that they saw as their spiritual forebears. For issues related to nomenclature see Peter Vogt's "How Moravian Are the Moravians: The Paradox of Moravian Identity," *The Hinge*, Vol. 3, No. 19, Winter 2013–2014.

2. Hunter James, *Quiet People of the Land: A Story of the North Carolina Moravians in Revolutionary Times* (Chapel Hill: University of North Carolina Press, 1976). This title reflects the state of the church during the Revolution, when Moravians did not want to be drawn into armed conflict. In terms of socioeconomic and theological controversy Moravians were much quieter in the 1780s in America than they were in Germany in the 1730s and 1740s.

3. The name Wachovia, the Latinized version of the German word *Wachau*, was given to the 100,000-acre tract because it was said to resemble the Wachau region of Austria, one of the ancestral lands of Count Zinzendorf, the Moravian's patron and leader. The financial institution later took this name. In this essay, Wachovia will refer to a geographical and administrative region of the Moravian Church, rather than the financial institution, unless specified otherwise.

4. Daniel Crews and Richard Starbuck, *With Courage for the Future: The Story of the Moravian Church, Southern Province* (Winston-Salem, NC: Moravian Church in America, Southern Province, 2002). Dr. Crews was the archivist and Mr. Starbuck was the assistant archivist at the time. Dr. Crews has since retired and been succeeded by Mr. Starbuck. I am greatly indebted to their book and to their ongoing help with research.

5. *Ibid.*, xvi.

6. Daniel Thorp, *The Moravian Community in North Carolina: Pluralism on the Southern Frontier* (Knoxville, TN: The University of Tennessee Press, 1989), studied how religious concerns of the leaders of the Moravian communities in Germany and America informed and managed a variety of social and economic contacts in North Carolina. Elisabeth Sommer, *Serving Two Masters: Moravian Brethren in Germany and North Carolina, 1727–1801* (Lexington: University of Kentucky Press, 2000), compared political and religious changes in light of American freedoms in North Carolina and German Enlightenment notions in Europe. Though both Thorp and Sommer addressed the development of slavery within the Wachovia congregations, Jon Sensbach, *A Separate Canaan: The Making of An African-American World in North Carolina 1763–1840* (Chapel Hill: The University of North Carolina Press, 1998), studied slavery in Wachovia in far greater detail. Scott Rohrer, *Hope's Promise: Religion and Acculturation in the Southern Backcountry* (Tuscaloosa: The University of Alabama Press, 2005), studied changes in language usage and acquisition, patterns of land and property acquisition, and distribution of wealth to argue that the Moravians developed a distinctive Anglo–German culture in the first century of settlement in the Wachovia region. Four unpublished dissertations address changes within the Wachovia congregations. Jerry Surratt, "From Theocracy to Voluntary Church and Secularized Community: A Study of the Moravians in Salem, North Carolina, 1772–1860" (Ph.D. diss., Emory University, Atlanta, GA, 1968), used Max Weber's secularization thesis to address the political and social changes within the Salem Congregation as it moved from a church-controlled village to an open city. Wendy Pfeiffer-Quaile, "Self-Expression in the Personal Writings of the Brethren: A Study of the Diaries, Lebenslaüfe and Poetry of the Moravians in North Carolina from 1752–1859" (Ph.D. diss., Rutgers University, New Brunswick, NJ, 2001), has analyzed the diaries, spiritual autobiographies (*lebenslaüfe*) and poetry of Moravian writers active in Salem during its formative period. Jo-Ellen Patterson, "Church Control and family Structure in a Moravian Community of North Carolina: 1753–1857" (Ph.D. diss., University of North Carolina at Greensboro, Greensboro, NC, 1981), studied the correlations between declining church control over individuals' decisions and changes in family patterns. Moravian theology and practices have been always secondary to the primary concerns of historians. Likewise, scholars addressing theological issues within the eighteenth-century Moravian Church have never considered them primarily in the context of the Wachovia communities. My own dissertation, "Zinzendorfs' Utopia: Discovering the Radical Roots of the Eighteenth Century *Brüdergemeine* in Wachovia" (Ph.D. diss., University of Virginia, 2009), looked at the relationships between the theological beliefs and practices and the socioeconomic structures that the Moravians put in place in North Carolina and how they had changed by 1818.

7. For more information on the *Unitas Fratrum* from its founding until its eighteenth-century renewal see Craig D. Atwood, *The Theology of the Czech Brethren from Hus to Comenius* (University Park: Penn State University Press, 2009), and Daniel Crews, *Faith, Love, Hope: A History of the Unitas Fratrum* (Winston-Salem, NC: Moravian Archives, 2008).

8. J. Taylor Hamilton and Kenneth G. Hamilton, *History of the Moravian Church: The Renewed Unitas Fratrum 1722–1957* (Bethlehem, PA, and Winston-Salem, NC: Interprovincial Board of Christian Education, Moravian Church in America, 1967), is the best history of the Moravian Church in English, though it is very dated in terms of its understandings of Zinzendorf and the trajectories of Moravian theology in the eighteenth century. Arthur J. Freeman, *An Ecumenical Theology of the Heart: The Theology of Count Nicholas Ludwig von Zinzendorf* (Bethlehem, PA, and Winston-Salem, NC: The Moravian Church in America, 1998), offers

the most comprehensive look at Zinzendorf's theology which Craig Atwood, *Community of the Cross: Moravian Piety in Communal Bethlehem* (University Park: Pennsylvania State University Press, 2004), used to look at how this theology was foundational for the founding of Bethlehem, PA in the 1740s. I then applied many of Atwood's questions and methods to look at the Wachovia congregations in my dissertation.

9. For specifics of the choir system see Rosamond Smith, "The Choir System in Salem," *The Three Forks of the Muddy Creek*, Vol. V, 1978, 12–25. For an analysis of the way the choir system and the ordination of women were incorporated in Wachovia see Riddick Weber, "Some of Our Women Amazed Us," 2nd Bethlehem Conference on Moravian History and Music, October 2010. For broader understandings of the ordination of Moravian women, see Peter Vogt, "A Voice for Themselves: Women As Participants in Congregational Discourse in the Eighteenth Century Moravian Movement," in *Women Preachers and Prophets Through Two Millennia of Christianity*, Beverly Mayne Kienzle and Pamela J. Walker, editors (Berkeley: University of California Press, 1998), Vernon Nelson, "Ordination of Women in the Moravian Church in America in the Eighteenth Century," *TMDK* 17 (1999): 14–23; and Ingeborg Baldauf, "Sisters Behind the Liturgical Table: Introduction of the Ordination of Women in the European Continental Unity Province," *TMDK* 17 (1999): 73–96.

10. Crews and Starbuck, *With Courage for the Future*, 83.

11. Using the Lot was the practice of seeking divine guidance, after human reason had been tried and exhausted, by drawing scripture passages, and seeking divine confirmation of important decisions. Decisions were placed in the form of yes/no questions. One scripture passage indicating an affirmative answer and one indicating a negative answer were placed along with a blank sheet into a bowl. The answer that was drawn was understood to express the will of Christ. (August Spangenberg, *The Life of Nicholas Lewis, Count Zinzendorf, Bishop and Ordinary of the Church of the United (or Moravian) Brethren*. Trans. and ed. Samuel Jackson (London: S. Holdsworth, 1838), 92–93. Moravians took the idea from Acts 1:15–22 where Matthias was selected as the apostolic replacement for Judas. In 1732, Moravians used the Lot to confirm a proposed marriage, and soon after it became required to approve all proposed marriages. The Lot was only used to confirm proposed marriages, not to force anyone into marriage.

12. For reasons too complicated to describe in this essay, Moravian historians began distancing themselves from the influence of the Zinzendorfs very early. My dissertation argues that the primary sources bear witness to the Zinzendorfs' broad and long-lasting influence in North Carolina.

13. See Gary Kinkel, *Our Dear Mother the Spirit* (Lanham, MD: The University Press of America, 1990).

14. The next several pages draw heavily, at times verbatim, from the instruction of my dissertation, "Zinzendorfs' Utopia."

15. Crews and Starbuck, *With Courage for the Future*, defends these reasons, giving service to neighbor preeminent position, though the last one in particular has been questioned by secular historians, 3.

16. *Records of the Moravians in North Carolina*, Volume 1: 1752–1771, ed. Adelaide L. Fries (Raleigh, NC: Edwards and Broughton Printing Company, 1922), 73–4.

17. Aaron Fogelman, *Hopeful Journeys: German Immigration, Settlement, and Political Culture in Colonial America, 1717–1775* (Philadelphia: University of Pennsylvania Press, 1996), 124.

18. Moravians spoke exclusively or primarily German, while most of their neighbors were English speakers.

19. Both of these settlements are now within the city limits of Winston-Salem.

20. Crews and Starbuck, *With Courage for the Future*, 22.

21. Daniel Thorp sees the Moravian solution of creating and staffing Dobbs Parish as duplicitous, *The Moravian Community in North Carolina*, 160. The letter calling Jacob Rogers to serve as the pastor of Dobbs Parish gives a very public example in English of many of the theologically distinctive understandings of Zinzendorfian piety. See also *RMNC* Vol. 1, 176.

22. William S. Powell, *North Carolina Through Four Centuries* (Chapel Hill: University of North Carolina Press, 1989), 110. Moravians appear from time to time in Powell's text, and this is their earliest mention.

23. Crews and Starbuck, *With Courage for the Future*, 838. Eventually the *Helfer Conferenz* became known as the Provincial Elder Conference (PEC). Presently the PEC is the elected body that administrates the Province between Provincial Synods, which is the highest governing body of the Southern Province.

24. Both women had been ordained in Europe in the 1740s and provided pastoral care to the women and leadership to all the Moravian communities in North Carolina.

25. Members of the Broadbay settlement in what was then Massachusetts, but now is part of Maine, started the Friedland congregation; *RMNC*, 383.

26. Crews and Starbuck, *With Courage for the Future*, 832.

27. The heavy dependence on the introduction to "Zinzendorfs Utopia" ends here.

28. Frances Griffin, *Less Time for Meddling: A History of Salem Academy and College, 1772–1866* (Winston-Salem: John F. Blair, 1979), offers a history of the first century of this institution.

29. Weber, "Some of Our Women Amazed Us," 5, 14.

30. Crews and Starbuck, *With Courage for the Future*, 324–25.

31. Crews and Starbuck's work devotes a great deal of attention to various financial challenges, often specifically dealing with congregations that could not adequately support pastoral leadership, or were not financially supporting the work of the Province, or both.

32. Crews and Starbuck, *With Courage for the Future*, 330.

33. *Ibid.*, 341.

34. *Ibid.*, 350.

35. David Silkenat, *Driven from Home: North Carolina's Civil War Refugee Crisis* (Athens: University of Georgia Press, 2016), 167.

36. *Ibid.*, 175, 181.

37. For a listing of founding dates for congregations, see Crews and Starbuck, *With Courage for the Future*, 830.

38. For more details, see Crews and Starbuck, *With Courage for the Future*, especially 395–402. This section is one of the rare instances where Crews and Starbuck devote a section of the book to the work of a single person.

39. The Provincial Elder Conference is the current name for the elected body that administrates the Province between Provincial Synods. The PEC was originally named the *Helfers Conferenz* in the eighteenth century and has gone through several name changes. Synods are the highest governing bodies in the Moravian Church.

40. As was the case with Christian Lewis Rights, Crews and Starbuck, *With Courage for the Future*, devotes a special section to the importance of Rondthaler and Brown's friendship, 534–36.

41. Crews and Starbuck, *With Courage for the Future*, 558.

42. *Ibid.*, see list on pages 839–40.

43. http://mcsp.org/?page_id=13 (accessed 10/07/2015). Though these figures are for all of the Southern Province, the vast majority of members are in North Carolina since all of the congregations are in North Carolina with the exception of one in Georgia, three in Virginia, and four congregations and seven fellowships in Florida.

44. Griffin, *Less Time for Meddling*, 27.

45. Crews and Starbuck, *With Courage for the Future*, 178–180.

46. Griffin, *Less Time for Meddling*, 58.

47. *Ibid.*, 65.

48. Crews and Starbuck, *With Courage for the Future*,180.

49. Griffin, *Less Time for Meddling*, 131.

50. Crews and Starbuck, *With Courage for the Future*, 219.

51. *Ibid.*, 467.

52. *Ibid.*, 480.

53. *"Schweinitz, Lewis David von"* in *Appletons' Cyclopædia of American Biography*, James Grant Wilson and John Fiske, editors, New York: D. Appleton (1900). https://en.wikisource.org/wiki/Appletons'_Cyclop%C3%A6dia_of_American_Biography/Schweinitz,_Lewis_David_von (accessed December 3, 2015).

54. Crews and Starbuck, *With Courage for the Future*, 204.

55. *Ibid.*, 248.

56. *Ibid.*, 294.

57. *Ibid.*, 382–83.

58. *Ibid.*, 439.

59. Roger N. Kirkman, "Henry Elias Fries" in *Dictionary of North Carolina Biography*, William S. Powell, editor, The University of North Carolina Press, http://ncpedia.org/biography/fries-henry-elias (Accessed December 3, 2015).

60. Crews and Starbuck, *With Courage for the Future*, 481.

61. *Ibid.*, 645.

62. *Ibid.*, 26.

63. *Ibid.*, 132.

64. Adelaide Fries, "One Hundred Years of Textiles in Salem," *NCHR*, January 1950: 10–11.

65. *Ibid.*,13.

66. *Ibid.*, 15. For additional religious and burial complications of the slave ownership of the Fries family, see Leland Ferguson, *God's Fields: Landscape, Religion, and Race in Moravian Wachovia* (Gainesville: University of Florida Press, 2013).

67. Fries, "One Hundred Years of Textiles in Salem," 16–17.

68. *Ibid.*, 18–19.

69. Douglas L. Rights, "Salem in the War Between the States," *NCHR*, July 1950: 278.

70. Robert B. Starling, "The Plank Road Movement in North Carolina, Part II," *NCHR* April 1939: 151.

71. Powell, *North Carolina Through Four Centuries,* 305.

72. http://ncpedia.org/nissen-wagon-works (accessed 10/16/2015).

73. http://www.learnnc.org/lp/editions/nchist-antebellum/5348 (accessed 10/16/2015).

74. Powell, *North Carolina Through Four Centuries*, 327.

75. *Ibid.*, 326, see Table 17–2.

76. Rights, "Salem in the War Between the States," 286–87.

77. Powell, *North Carolina Through Four Centuries*, 441.

78. *Ibid.*

79. http://ncarchitects.lib.ncsu.edu/people/P000340 (accessed 12/15/2015).

80. Crews and Starbuck, *With Courage for the Future,* 435.

81. *Ibid.,* 465.

82. https://en.wikipedia.org/wiki/Nissen_Building (accessed 10/16/2015). Interestingly, both of these buildings are key elements in the current rejuvenation of downtown Winston-Salem. For more information, see http://cloud.lib.wfu.edu/blog/heardithere/2013/11/26/life-in-the-nissen-building/ (accessed 10/16/2015).

83. Kenneth G. Hamilton, "The Moravians and Wachovia," *North Carolina Historical Review,* Spring 1967: 152.

84. *Ibid.*

85. *Ibid.,* p. 153.

86. David Moltke-Hansen, "Archie Kimbrough Davis" obituary http://www.americanantiquarian.org/proceedings/44525141.pdf (accessed Dec. 3, 2015).

87. http://www.historync.org/laureate%20-%20Archie%20Davis.htm (accessed Dec. 3, 2015).

88. Donald M. McCorkle, "The *Collegium Musicum Salem*: Its Music, Musicians, and Importance" *NCHR,* October 1956: 485. All the previously founded organizations were in Moravian settlements in Pennsylvania.

89. *Ibid.,* 491.

90. Griffin, *Less Time for Meddling,* see Index, page 303, for references to the troubles caused by visitors streaming into town for the musical portions of the final examinations of the young women, and by their desires for musical programs by the town's musicians.

91. Crews and Starbuck, *With Courage for the Future,* 628–31.

92. *Ibid.,* 638.

93. *Ibid.,* 705.

94. Crews and Starbuck, *With Courage for the Future,* 82.

95. *Ibid.,* 255. The spiritual leaders, first of Bethabara, then of other congregations, and eventually of the province, wrote Memorabilia, historical and theological reflections at the end of the year that provided a summation of the past year and looked ahead to the coming one.

96. *Moravian Covenant for Christian Living,* V.C.31. http://www.moravian.org/the-moravian-church/moravian-covenant-for-christian-living/ (accessed 12/3/2015).

97. http://www.forsythnchistory.com/files/joining.pdf (accessed 10/07/2015).

98. Crews and Starbuck, *With Courage for the Future,* 455.

99. *Ibid.,* 672.

100. *Ibid.,* 565.

101. *Resolutions and Elections: Provincial Synod of the Southern Province of the Moravian Church in America, 1962,* p. 31.

102. Jon Sensbach has written two books that address these issues. *A Separate Canaan: The Making of An African-American World in North Carolina 1763–1840* (Chapel Hill: University of North Carolina Press, 1998) deals with the Moravian Church and slave ownership in the Wachovia region. *Rebecca's Revival: Creating Black Christianity in the Atlantic World* (Cambridge, MA: Harvard University Press, 2006), offers a later, more nuanced look at Moravians and slavery in a more global context. Ferguson also addresses these complexities.

103. Rohrer, *Hope's Promise,* studied language and property usage and acquisition to argue that the Moravians developed a distinctive Anglo-German with a significant African American component.

104. Crews and Starbuck, *With Courage for the Future,* 247.

105. *Ibid.,* 248, 294.

106. *Ibid.,* 255.

107. *Ibid.,* 311.

108. *Ibid.,* 313.

109. *Ibid.,* 341. See footnote 1.

110. *Ibid.*

111. *Ibid.,* 383.

112. For this section I am indebted to William Petig of Stanford University for his conference paper on Martin Hauser at Fourth Bethlehem Conference on Moravian History and Music (October 2014).

113. Crews and Starbuck, *With Courage for the Future,* 550.

114. *Ibid.,* 616.

115. *Ibid.,* 619.

116. *Ibid.,* 774.

117. *Ibid.,* 671.

118. *Moravian Book of Worship.* The Moravian Church in America: Bethlehem and Winston-Salem, 1995, 105.

119. 2006 Moravian Church Southern Province Synod, Resolution 24.

120. Crews and Starbuck, *With Courage for the Future,* 272.

121. Alan D. Watson, "Women in Colonial North Carolina: Overlooked and Underestimated," *NCHR*, Winter 1981:12.

122. See above, footnote 11.

123. The most interesting case is that of Rosina Kaske Biefel Bachhoff Schmidt. She was ordained a deaconess when her husband, Ludolph Bachhoff, was ordained a deacon. After he died, the elders suggested that she marry a certain Mr. Schmidt. She at first refused the offer. After she changed her mind and married a year later, the elders realized she might have been right in the first place as it proved not to be a good match. Bishop Graff noted that this was the first refusal of its kind, *RMNC*, Vol. 4, 1522, quoted in Belinda Riggsbee, "Woman of Wachovia," *The Three Forks of the Muddy Creek*, Vol. III (Winston-Salem, NC: Old Salem, Inc., 1976), 35.

124. Riddick Weber and Carol Foltz, "The Reintroduction of the Ordination of Women to the Moravian Ministry in the Southern Province in the 20th Century," 3rd Bethlehem Conference on Moravian History and Music, October 2012: 8, 9.

125. The German word for a servant.

126. This is the plural form of the German word *Lebenslauf*, meaning literally "life's path" or spiritual autobiographical memoir. Writing the *Lebensaluf* was standard practice in the eighteenth century, and many modern Moravians are resuming the practice.

127. http://anthonysplot.org/about/ (accessed 12/04/2015).

Presbyterians

Robert J. Cain

The following essay focuses on a number of topics that the author considers important in the history of North Carolina presbyterianism. The wider story of the Presbyterian Church in the United States is crucial to this effort, and has been included throughout. Due to constraints of space, very little is said about individual churches or ministers. Those wishing a fuller treatment of these matters should consult the forthcoming work by Harold J. Dudley on Presbyterians in North Carolina, and church histories available on the Internet. The only comprehensive history of the Presbyterian Church in North Carolina is Walter H. Conser, Jr., and Robert J. Cain, *Presbyterians in North Carolina: Race, Politics, and Religious Identity in Historical Perspective*. An older work, from 1907, by D.I. Craig, *Development of the Presbyterian Church in North Carolina and of Synodical Home Missions*, treats the general history of North Carolina Presbyterianism in thirty-nine pages. William H. Foote's 1846 *Sketches of North Carolina, Historical and Biographical* contains numerous errors of fact, but is still useful.

It might also be pointed out that there is no recent comprehensive history of Presbyterians in the United States. A serviceable work published in 1864 is E.H. Gillett, *History of the Presbyterian Church in the United States of America*. Also useful are Robert Ellis Thompson, *A History of the Presbyterian Church in the United States*, from 1895, and especially the compact but excellent *A Brief History of the Presbyterians*, from 1996, by James H. Smylie.

* * *

The ethnic roots of Presbyterianism in North Carolina are unmistakable. The seeds of the faith were planted wherever groups of Scots—both those from Scotland and those from the north of Ireland—established settlements. Only a sprinkling of identifiably Scottish names appears in the colony's earliest land grant records.[1] Although some individuals called themselves Presbyterian as early as 1704, and the "Father of American Presbyterianism," Francis Mackemie, visited North Carolina in 1683 and '84,[2] people of that faith were a decided rarity before the first sizable body of 350 Scots landed in two vessels at the mouth of the Cape Fear River in September 1739—the Argyll Colony. Over the following decades, many others followed seeking land, settling upriver from the ports of Brunswick and Wilmington, and establishing farms.[3]

The Scots who had settled first in Ireland came mostly by land rather than by water. From a trickle beginning around 1718, by mid-century thousands of their countrymen had disembarked at the port of Philadelphia and trekked westward toward an ever-expanding frontier. The supply of affordable land was not inexhaustible, and beginning in the 1730s the Great Wagon Road from Philadelphia through the Valley of Virginia to Salisbury and beyond funneled cascades of Scotch Irish and Germans into the upland piedmont region of North Carolina.[4]

Although they professed the same beliefs and employed the same presbyterian system of church governance (rule by elders, or "presbyters"), there were important differences between the pre–American experiences of the Scots and the Scotch Irish. The former were members of a state-sanctioned, state-supported, "established" church, the Church of Scotland, and would have had no impediments put on the free exercise of their faith. By contrast, the church of the Scotch Irish was "dissenter," the established church in Ireland being Anglican, or Church of Ireland. This meant that communicants of the Scottish church suffered no "disabilities" such as not being allowed to hold civil office or a military commission, or having restrictions placed on landholding, or marriages performed by their clergy being declared invalid, and a number of others. Scotch Irish Presbyterians, on the other hand, were so afflicted, and in addition were taxed to support the Church of Ireland, a faith not their own.[5] These differences can at least in part explain the fact that during the American Revolution the more recent immigrants from Scotland notoriously supported the established civil authority, the crown, and those from northern Ireland equally notoriously supported the cause of independence. It is also worth noting that during the Regulator unrest of the 1760s and early 1770s, many of the insurgents were Scotch Irish, and their most vocal Presbyterian opponent and supporter of the government was the prominent Presbyterian minister and Scottish immigrant Henry Pattillo.[6]

The theology espoused by these Presbyterian immigrants was Calvinist, embodied in the Westminster Confession of 1646 with its strong emphasis on the primacy of scripture and subordination of tradition, the sovereignty of God, and the predetermined fate of individual souls to salvation or damnation. The system of governance as it evolved was multi-layered, starting with the congregation, presided over by the session, composed of a minister and lay leaders (elders). The next layer, the presbytery, was territorially defined and composed of all ministers within its boundaries, along with a number of elders. The synod comprised a group of presbyteries; and the general assembly, established in 1789 in America, meeting annually and composed of ministers and elders, was the supreme judicature for the denomination in America. A presbytery and synod were erected in Philadelphia (1706, 1717) at first for all the American colonies; Hanover Presbytery was formed in 1755, mainly for Virginia. In 1770, Orange Presbytery was constituted for North Carolina.[7]

One consequence of this tardiness was that despite the significant and growing numbers of Presbyterians in the colony, North Carolina's needs were not adequately represented in the denomination's centers of power (Philadelphia and New York) during most of the colonial period. As a result, the colony experienced chronic difficulty in securing an adequate supply of ordained ministers, the most serious impediment to the growth of presbyterianism within its borders. The first recorded cleric in the colony was the scandalous Mr. Clemens, who was in Bath in 1726. Of better repute was Hugh McAden, who itinerated in 1756 and '57 before settling in the colony. John Thomson settled among the Scotch Irish in 1751, and the Gaelic-speaking James Campbell began his ministry to the Cape Fear Scots in 1758.[8] However, in 1753 the Synod of New York had rightly noted that "in the whole colony of North Carolina, where numerous congregations of Presbyterians are forming, … there is not one Presbyterian minister settled."[9] Only ordained ministers could baptize and conduct a communion service,[10] the two most solemn rituals of the faith. Beyond administering these sacraments, a resident minister provided a focus for congregational life that could only partially be filled by clusters of Presbyterians meeting informally for worship. Ordination could take place only at a meeting of presbytery, and no aspiring candidates from North Carolina undertook the expensive and difficult trip to Philadelphia in order to achieve this goal. Presbyterians in the colony sometimes sent petitions to Scotland for ministers—usually with indifferent results—but as a practical matter had to look north to fill their needs. Repeated plaintive requests sometimes resulted in northern clergy being sent to itinerate for brief periods in the backcountry. The first of a number of such requests is recorded in 1744, when "a representation from many people in North Carolina, was laid before the Synod, showing their desolate condition,"[11] but such sporadic exercises did not make for thriving religious communities. The erection of Orange Presbytery and the consequent capacity to ordain locally was a major landmark in the growth of presbyterianism in North Carolina. By 1860, three presbyteries (Orange, Fayetteville, and Concord) had been erected in the state, and 124 ministers and ministers-in-training were serving 18,000 adult communicants gathered into 170 congregations.[12]

The establishment of presbyteries was not the sole reason for the increased number of ordained clergy. Another was the founding of classical schools and institutions of higher learning. The well-known and longstanding emphasis of presbyterianism on education, and especially a learned clergy, was the basis for the ordination requirement that ministers of the Gospel in most instances be graduates of a college or university. A demonstrated proficiency in Greek and Hebrew, and in the earlier years Latin, as well as theology, history, geography, and other subjects of a liberal and classical education, could only be obtained in an institution of higher learning,[13] and as these became more accessible, more ministers became available to fill pulpits. Most early North Carolina ministers had studied either in Scotland or at the College of New Jersey (later Princeton), founded in 1746. When Hampden-Sydney College, the first non–Anglican college in the South, was established in Virginia under Presbyterian auspices in 1775, and Virginia's Union Theological Seminary in 1812, North Carolina presbyterianism was reasonably well served by denominational institutions of higher learning.[14] Although Presbyterians were prominent in the chartering (1789) and administration of the state university, North Carolina's first Presbyterian college, Davidson, was founded in 1837 as an all-male academic and manual school with an emphasis on training for ordination.[15] The rigorous educational requirements for ordination were occasionally challenged, usually as the result of revivalist fervor,[16] but they have largely persisted to the present day.

In the divided church of the post–Civil War era, the northern Presbyterian Church in 1867 founded Biddle Memorial Institute (later University, renamed Johnson C. Smith University in 1923) in Charlotte for the education of black men, especially for the ordained ministry.[17] The northern church also established, after several changes of name, what became Warren Wilson College, at Swannanoa in 1942.[18] The Synod of North Carolina of the southern church founded several colleges for women in the antebellum period and after: Floral College near present Maxton (1841–1878); Warrenton Female Academy (1841–1866, 1870–1873); Peace Institute (later College, now William Peace University) in 1872 in Raleigh; Flora Macdonald College (after several changes of name), in Red Springs

(1896–1961); Presbyterian Female College (later Queens College, now University), 1896. In 1867, Scotia Seminary (later Barber-Scotia College) for black women was founded in Concord by the Rev. Luke Dorland of the northern church, for the training of social workers and teachers.[19]

The preeminent place of education was not confined to the higher realms. Churches often had modest day schools attached to them, with the minister serving as schoolmaster. In the colonial and antebellum periods, a number of notable academies were founded in North Carolina under Presbyterian auspices, including Samuel McCorkle's Zion-Parnassus Academy at Thyatira Church (Rowan County, late eighteenth century); David Caldwell's Log College (Guilford County, 1767, which trained a number of ministers); Queen's Museum (1771, Charlotte); and James Tate's academy (Wilmington, 1760), among others.[20] The remarkable John Chavis (ca. 1763–1838), a free black, Revolutionary War veteran, and Presbyterian licentiate, in 1808 opened a highly-regarded academy in Raleigh whose students included a number of prominent whites.[21]

Periodic conflicts—some apparently trivial by today's standards, but provoking lively debate at the time, as well as some of more lasting significance—helped define and shape the denomination. One such battle was over the type of music to be allowed in church services. When the first Presbyterians arrived in North Carolina their musical tradition permitted no instruments, and vocal music was confined to psalms sung in strict meter. The publication of Isaac Watts's psalms and hymns in the early eighteenth century led to fierce debates within the Church about their appropriateness for use in worship. Over the course of the century, the psalms became more and more accepted, although the matter was still being discussed in the General Assembly in the 1850s.[22] Throughout the nineteenth century and into the next, heated debates arose over such questions as ministers wearing robes to conduct worship services; the substitution of grape juice for wine in communion; the use of individual communion cups rather than the traditional common cup; strict observance of the Sabbath; and attitudes toward dancing, card-playing, and other "worldly amusements."[23] Of more profound and lasting significance were questions relating to theological understandings; the relationship of faith and science; slavery; attitudes toward the poor; involvement of the church in politics—questions that occasionally led to schisms. These clashes can perhaps best be viewed as manifestations of the recurring tensions between, broadly, traditionalism and modernity.

One such encounter, the Great Awakening, a revivalist movement that swept England and the mainland American colonies in the late 1730s and 1740s, was ignited in America by the Church of England itinerant preacher George Whitefield, who visited North Carolina on several occasions.[24] As revivalism—characterized by an emphasis on repentance, personal salvation, and emotional worship services--gained strength throughout the colonies, conservative Presbyterians mounted a stout defense of traditional theology and modes of worship.[25] In 1741, the conservatives succeeded in expelling the revivalists from the synod, and the opposing parties divided into two synods: the conservative (Old Side or Old Light) Synod of Philadelphia and the revivalist (New Side or New Light) Synod of New York. North Carolina was little affected by the schism, and both synods sent itinerant missionaries into the colony's back country.[26]

In 1764, the Synod of New York and Philadelphia (the two synods papered over their differences in 1758) betrayed some anxiety about the direction presbyterianism was taking in North Carolina, and for the first time issued specific instructions to the two missionaries being sent there. The synod "considering the state of many congregations to the southward, and particularly North Carolina, and the great importance of having those congregations properly organized," ordered the missionaries to "form societies, help them in adjusting their bounds, ordain elders, administer sealing ordinances, instruct the people in discipline, and finally direct them in their after conduct...."[27]

Precursors of another revivalist movement, the Great Revival of 1800, had begun to appear in the late 1780s in Virginia, New England, western Pennsylvania, and elsewhere. The most famous manifestation of the phenomenon took place in Logan County, Kentucky, in 1800. Sparked by a Presbyterian minister from North Carolina, James McGready, the revivalist torrent swept across much of the nation, especially the south and west, before subsiding. As with the Great Awakening, the Revival of 1800 led to a sharp divergence of views within the body of presbyterianism, with passions running high on each side—even to the point of McGready's being threatened with death on several occasions.[28] Revivals and camp meetings followed in the wake of the Revival of 1800, lasting for the remainder of the antebellum period and beyond in North Carolina.[29] The New School/Old School schism of 1837 to 1869 divided along the same innovator-versus-traditionalist fault line, with rival synods again emerging in Philadelphia (Old School) and New York (New School). This time North Carolina was more directly involved, when New School missionaries from east Tennessee provoked an ideological battle with the existing Old School churches in Morganton Presbytery (erected 1835, dissolved 1841), thereby weakening both schools so much that Presbyterian influence in the mountains of North Carolina was dealt a near-fatal blow.[30]

The next division in the denomination, one deeper and more long-lasting, came in 1861, with the formation of the Presbyterian Church in the Confederacy. This time the split was not over doctrine or modes of worship, but over the issue of slavery and the related question of continuation in a federal union increasingly hostile to that peculiar institution. The Synod of North Carolina voted with the rest of the southern synods of the Old School Presbyterians to establish a new denomination.[31] After the calamity of defeat, North Carolina joined its sister synods in the former Confederacy in declining to heal the breach with the "northern church." Instead, in 1865 they continued the schism by forming the Presbyterian Church in the United States (PCUS), with the northern body retaining the name Presbyterian Church in the United States of America (PCUSA). In general, the southern PCUS was the more conservative of the two on questions of church governance and social issues, although any substantive differences in the doctrinal essentials of the faith and moral standards were by and large inconsequential. Over the succeeding 118 years, halting attempts were made, especially by the northern PCUSA, to heal the breach, but only in 1983 was this finally effected with the formation of the PC (USA), the new name representing a merger of northern and southern.[32]

Although in the present essay the main body or bodies of Presbyterians are the ones considered, other manifestations of presbyterianism arose in America, including North Carolina. The church in Scotland and Northern Ireland had from time to time been convulsed by groups separating from the main body over questions of belief or practice.[33] Some of these independent presbyteries coalesced in the colonies to become the Associate Reformed Presbyterian Church, which founded a number of churches in western North Carolina.[34] Periodic disruptions in the American church also led to the splintering off of smaller bodies professing essentially the same core beliefs and organized in the same way as the larger body of Presbyterians, but differing enough to feel alienated from them.

Such was the case with the Cumberland Presbyterian Church, formed in Tennessee in 1810 as a consequence of the Great Revival of 1800.[35]

The largest schismatic denominations currently, both of which have a number of congregations in North Carolina, are the Presbyterian Church in America, organized in 1973,[36] and the Evangelical Presbyterian Church, erected in 1981,[37] both viewing themselves as conservative alternatives to what they consider an increasingly liberal PC(USA). The main issues fueling the division are the seemingly intractable ones of abortion, the position of homosexuals in the church, the ordination of women, the authority of scripture, and the Westminster Confession. Revivalism, the root cause of the acrimonious separations of the Great Awakening and Great Revival, played no direct part in the divisions of the 1970s and after, even as it had not in the fracture of 1861.

Although the once-potent question of race cannot be blamed for recent fissures in the denomination, it was an underlying issue in the separation of 1861 and the continuing separation thereafter. From their earliest appearance in America, Presbyterians had owned slaves. Nothing in scripture or the Westminster standards forbade the practice, and Old School general assemblies did not condemn it outright until the very eve of the Civil War. Only occasionally did individuals in the southern states publicly express reservations about the morality of owning and trading in human beings, and such persons could easily be dismissed as deluded fanatics. Although a few ministers and elders in North Carolina had professed open opposition to slavery, or at least to the law prohibiting the teaching of slaves to read,[38] most either remained silent or defended it.

Paradoxically, there was no barrier to keep a person of color, slave or free, from becoming a full, communing member of a Presbyterian congregation if he or she were accepted by a church's session. Indeed, Scripture sanctioned, even encouraged, the reception of slaves into Christian congregations. Fortunately, relevant statistical data exist from antebellum Presbyterian congregations throughout the slaveholding states, and they tell a somewhat surprising story. Beginning in 1847, the annual statistical survey of Presbyterian congregations adhering to the Old School (Philadelphia) assembly, to which almost all southern congregations (including North Carolina's) belonged, included returns of the numbers of "colored communicants."[39] The practice continued in the southern church during the war years (1861–1865), and ceased thereafter. For the denomination as a whole, a significant proportion of southern church members were reported as "colored." For example, in North Carolina in 1849 the churches submitting returns reported 780 "colored," or 7.5 percent of all communing members in the synod, with the highest concentration being in the Piedmont area of the state.[40] Several congregations in Fayetteville Presbytery consistently reported higher numbers of blacks than of whites.[41] During the Civil War numbers increased sharply in the state, to 2,622 in 1863, or almost 14 percent of the total communing membership.[42]

Unfortunately, historians have only fleeting and indistinct glimpses of the participation of nonwhite communicants in the congregational life of the antebellum church, but it is safe to say that any activities implying social equality with whites would not have been tolerated. As a practical matter, males would not have been eligible for election as elders, and females would not have taken part in women's organizations. It is likely that in churches having a "slave gallery," all blacks, slave and free, would have been seated there for services. If the church did not have this amenity, blacks would have sat in the body of the church, presumably in a designated section. The 1858 general assembly reported optimistically that throughout the slave states "provision at once special and liberal is made for the accommodation of the coloured people, so that they may enjoy the privileges of the sanctuary in common with the whites," and that in addition "nearly all our ministers hold a service in the afternoon of the Sabbath, in which the exercises are particularly adapted to their capacities and wants."[43] The Lord's Supper was at least symbolically a meal, partaken of by all communing members regardless of race. However, the social implications of breaking bread together would have stood as an insurmountable barrier to full integration of the communion service; blacks sat at tables separate from whites, and partook of a common communion cup only among themselves.[44]

Old School general assemblies very rarely, and southern synods never, questioned the right of slaveholders to their property. The assembly justified this position as "winning the confidence of masters, in our freedom from fanaticism," and asserted that "the position taken by our Church ... secures to us unlimited opportunities of access to master and slave, and lays us under heavy responsibilities ... not to neglect our duty to either."[45] Both assembly and synod regularly took notice of the spiritual needs of the human chattels in their midst. Reports on their condition were invariably roseate, with one noting "many remarkable examples on the part of master and mistresses and members in our churches, who have given themselves to a zeal and devotion" for the religious instruction of slaves. In addition, the "largest and most promising Sunday-schools in several of the Southern towns, [are] filled with coloured children."[46]

Much less time was devoted by either assembly or synod to addressing the physical condition of slaves, as opposed to the moral and spiritual, although the Synod of North Carolina was at pains to denounce any hint that they were treated unfeelingly, stating on one occasion that it was "a gross slander, to charge Southern Christians, as they have been often charged, with regarding and treating their slaves as beasts of burden; or, at best as mere hewers of wood and drawers of water."[47]

The end of slavery brought profound changes to presbyterianism in the South. The sounds of war had scarcely faded when "the General Assembly of the Presbyterian Church in the (late) Confederate States of America" convened in Macon, Georgia, in December 1865. In response to an overture inquiring about the Church's attitude toward the former slaves, the assembly, avoiding any hint of advocating social equality or brotherhood outside the confines of a church building, somewhat disingenuously responded that "our churches, pastors, and people have always recognized [blacks'] claim to Christian equality and brotherhood, and have rejoiced to have them associated in Christian union and communion in the public services and precious sacraments of the sanctuary." The resolution went on to maintain that "the abolition of slavery ... has not altered" the relationship, and that the assembly wished it to continue—albeit with whites continuing to exercise a guiding and stabilizing hand. Nevertheless, it recognized the new reality: "Should our colored friends think it best to separate from us and form their own congregations under white pastors and elders for the present, or under colored elders and pastors as soon as God ... shall raise up men suitably qualified for those offices, this Church will do all in its power to encourage, foster, and assist them."[48]

Few of the recent slaves took the assembly up on its offer to continue a relationship. The Synod of North Carolina in 1883 noted ruefully that no presbytery reported any "special efforts for the spiritual instruction of the colored race." An attitude of fatalism is evident when it went on to observe that blacks had "their own churches, which they prefer," that "they do not seek our aid," and that "few come to hear when the opportunity for instruction is given." Still, North Carolina Presbyterians had "a great responsibility" toward blacks: "let it not be said we have been found wanting in interest or zeal in their behalf."[49] These observations could form a virtual template for the attitudes of most Presbyterians in the state, down to the 1983 reunion.

Although a tiny scattering of black communicants would continue to attend their old churches, most who remained within the Presbyterian fold joined one of the new congregations being formed by the northern church. The PCUSA quickly established its most significant southern presence in North Carolina,[50] sending missionaries both as teachers and ministers, with numbers of women included among the former. The missionaries did not always confine their efforts to blacks; an assembly report of 1881 noted that there were four teachers "among the poor whites of North Carolina."[51] The new PCUSA congregations—numbering forty in North Carolina by 1870, eighty-six ten years later, and one hundred thirty-three in 1902[52]—were gathered into new presbyteries and synods throughout the south. The Synod of Atlantic and its constituent presbyteries of Cape Fear, Yadkin, and Catawba were in North Carolina, and were entirely separate from the PCUS's Synod of North Carolina with its presbyteries of Concord, Orange, Fayetteville, and Wilmington.[53] Although there was little or no overt hostility between the two denominations, neither was there any notable warmth or sustained cooperation. Predictably, the PCUSA congregations in the south were almost entirely nonwhite, and except for a handful of black churches affiliated with it, the PCUS was white. White ministers were the norm in the northern church at the beginning, with ordained black men gradually replacing them as theological training became more available at schools such as Biddle University.

The southern church periodically made pious gestures toward the idea of "colored evangelization," with a permanent committee dedicated to that end annually soliciting denomination-wide contributions. The fundraising was invariably disappointing, and there were scant results from the committee's work.[54] The scenario was paralleled in North Carolina. Here too were expressions of concern for the spiritual welfare of blacks, and of the pressing need for Presbyterians in the state to assume responsibility for that welfare. Committees were appointed, funds were solicited from the presbyteries, but only small sums were ever raised and inevitably the committee's hopes were dashed. In 1920, a special report of the synod's Colored Evangelization Committee summed up the dismal results of over half a century of labor: a total of two ministers (one of whom was J.S. Morrow in North Wilkesboro and the other "[a] much respected old colored preacher"), six churches, and 113 communicants. The committee contrasted this with the northern church's accomplishments in its three North Carolina presbyteries: ninety ordained ministers, 138 churches, and 10,116 communicants, with the churches being well-organized, "fairly strong," and with resident pastors in most of the larger urban areas. The committee spoke plainly and accurately in its analysis of the basic reason for the absence of success by the Synod of North Carolina:

> Our greatest lack in this work is that we are not in living helpful touch with these people, without which we can do nothing. We have them in our kitchens and in our fields and factories, but religiously we are strangers to their conditions and to the efforts they themselves are making for their own betterment.

The report recommended that no new programs be undertaken, but rather that congregations begin to "study and know the religious conditions and needs of the colored people in their own communities" and to act upon that knowledge. It also recommended close cooperation with the PCUSA in the work of evangelization of blacks.[55]

Both denominations made efforts to educate blacks. For the southern church this was a revolutionary change from antebellum times, when the slave codes of most southern states, including North Carolina, forbade the teaching of slaves even to read and write. The northern church with its superior resources in funding and personnel greatly outshone its southern brethren in this endeavor. Within a few years after the end of the war, its Committee on Freedmen had established numerous schools and placed in them a sizable number of teachers, most of them white women.[56] The PCUS General Assembly urged its churches to undertake Sunday schools for blacks, and in higher education the southern church established Tuscaloosa Institute in Alabama in 1875 (renamed Stillman Institute in 1895) "for the education of coloured preachers."[57] The institute received only lukewarm support from the southern church, despite the assembly's repeated calls for generous contributions from synods and presbyteries. In 1910, Stillman had only fifty students, thirty of whom were studying for the ministry.[58] The northern church's previously-mentioned Biddle Institute was more generously supported, and over the decades after its founding went from strength to strength.

The end of the century saw the inauguration of Jim Crow legislation throughout the southern states. *De facto* racial separation became *de jure*, and the hardening of attitudes and practices did not spare churches, including the Presbyterian. The few nonwhite churches in the PCUS were an anomalous presence, a circumstance addressed sporadically by various judicatories. Separate ecclesial structures were tried: the Afro-American Synod (1916, renamed Snedecor Synod, dissolved in 1951); the presbyteries of Ethel (Mississippi, 1891); Central Alabama (1896); Central Louisiana, North and South Carolina (1917)—none of which survived for more than a few years.[59] At intervals the denomination's General Assembly, as well as the Synod of North Carolina, would earnestly declare an imperative need to advance the cause of "colored evangelization," coupling it with a plea for financial contributions.[60] Such attempts proved embarrassingly unsuccessful. The paucity of interest in the work of evangelization of blacks mirrors the fact that the minutes of the first meeting of the Synod of North Carolina taking place subsequent to the so-called "race riot" in Wilmington in 1898 were devoid of any reference to the event, despite the fact that it had been discussed extensively in the local and national press. However, the synod's official organ, the Presbyterian Standard, under the editorship of the redoubtable A.J. McKelway, did take notice—but by viewing the "revolution" by Wilmington's whites as a good thing, demonstrating as it did that "the negro race has never been capable of governing itself through all the centuries of its history" and that "the Anglo-Saxon is the dominant race in the world today," sentiments undoubtedly applauded by a sizable majority of North Carolina Presbyterians.[61]

Over the course of the next half-century, however, the southern church's General Assembly began to make at first timorous, then increasingly forthright statements about Christianity and race. The first of these came in 1920 when, against the backdrop of a resurgent Ku Klux Klan and race riots in Chicago and elsewhere, it urged cooperation with the newly-formed Southern Inter-Racial Committee.[62] In the Second World War, the assembly expressed sympathy for the persecuted Jews of Europe and Japanese American internees, and closer to home enjoined Presbyterians to take to heart the observation that "It is constantly flung at us when we condemn the Nazi persecution of non–Aryans that we are ourselves guilty of racial prejudice and injustice … in our own land." Some of the denomination's young people had blazed a trail toward racial justice when, beginning in the 1930s, those attending youth leadership conferences at Montreat, the PCUS's retreat in the Blue Ridge mountains, began to insist that black youth of Snedecor Synod be allowed to attend the conferences, and that they be accorded equal treatment in accommodations.[63]

A corner was turned decisively by the General Assembly and white southern presbyterianism in 1954. In June of that year, only a few weeks after the Supreme Court handed down its *Brown v. Board of Education* ruling that ended mandated segregation in public schools, the assembly condemned "enforced segregation of the races" as being "out of harmony with Christian theology and ethics." In addition, it urged local churches to ignore race when admitting members, and for good measure announced that the few institutions under its direct control would be desegregated. With its vote on the question of school segregation, the southern assembly effectively abandoned the Presbyterian doctrine of the "spirituality" of the Church—the idea that the political and the spiritual realms were entirely separate, and that consequently churches should not meddle in matters relating to the state. Implicitly recognizing that acquiescing in the status quo is actually taking a political stance, the general assembly asserted that "the Church, in its relationship to cultural patterns, should lead rather than follow"—a principle that would be applied subsequently to other social questions, and one that would usually provoke heated discussion within the denomination. Southern assemblies down to reunion in 1983 periodically reaffirmed this position on race.[64]

The Synod of North Carolina, meeting in Charlotte in July 1954, heard the outgoing moderator and general secretary, Harold J. Dudley, call for an "offensive religion ... unafraid to invade the moral, social, economic and political areas of life and society." Dudley's sermon left little doubt about its reference, nor was there much to doubt about his exhortation that "These are not times for ministers of the Gospel to remain quiet on great issues."[65] The general assembly's statements were received with coldness or outright hostility by the majority of southern Presbyterians, including those in North Carolina. The state's synod, however, succeeded in maintaining an essentially non-confrontational position that was able both to calm a potentially explosive situation, and also to keep the great majority of congregations from leaving the denomination. The synod studied the matter for a year, then with marked caution and without actually taking a position on the issue concluded that the assembly's action should be accepted "as a legitimate expression dealing with a complicated issue," and further that "the efforts of earnest individuals seeking worship opportunities should be recognized."[66] By the time of the merging of the PCUS and PCUSA in 1983, race seems largely to have disappeared as a cause for maintaining the separation, nor had it been overtly apparent in the birth of the largely southern Presbyterian Church in America (PCA) in 1973.[67]

In 1956, Margaret Towner, a thirty-one-year-old Pennsylvanian, was ordained a minister in the PCUSA, the denomination having already permitted women elders in 1930. A few years later, in 1964, the General Assembly of the PCUS made it mandatory for women to be considered for all offices in the southern church.[68] The following year Rachel Henderlite, daughter of a Presbyterian minister in Henderson, North Carolina, became the first female ordained in the PCUS. The first black woman in either denomination to receive ordination was another North Carolinian, Katy G. Cannon, born in Kannapolis and ordained in 1974 by the PCUSA's Catawba Presbytery. In 1979, the PCUS ordained the first female Hispanic in either church, Rebecca Reyes, who had received a master's degree in social work at UNC–Chapel Hill and had worked in the Triangle area. Seemingly impenetrable barriers had at last been breached in both the northern and southern churches.[69]

The role of women in the life of the church evolved at a leisurely pace over the years from the first appearance of presbyterianism in colonial America to the middle of the twentieth century. One constant, however, was the lack of access by women to the formal levers of power at any level, from congregation to general assembly. In both the northern and southern churches not only were women denied access to the pulpit, they were barred from speaking publicly in any religious assemblies where men were present—the reason presumably being that women should not give the appearance of instructing men in matters of religion. The general assemblies of both the PCUSA and the PCUS, along with most of Christendom, based the strict prohibition on women speaking in church on the words of the Apostle Paul in I Corinthians 14:34: "Let your women keep silence in the churches, for it is not permitted unto them to speak...." This exclusionary policy, coupled with an injunction that women be obedient to their husbands, was reiterated a number of times over the years, usually when a synod, presbytery, or individual church would seek clarification concerning it. The formulation that stood as definitive for decades was a pastoral letter from the assembly to all churches in 1832: "To teach and exhort, or lead in prayer in public and promiscuous [i.e., mixed] assemblies is clearly forbidden to women in the Holy Oracles."[70] The southern church's assembly (1880) was even more pointed in its response to a similar query: Preaching by women was opposed to the advancement of true piety and to the promotion of the peace of the Church, and this to such an extent as to make the introduction of women into our pulpits for the purpose of publicly expounding God's Word an irregularity not to be tolerated.[71]

The Synod of North Carolina also addressed the question. Meeting in 1879, it declared that some in the synod had been "disturbed by 'Woman-Preaching'" and wanted guidance on the matter. The body reassured them that such activity was contrary to the Word of God and was to be given "no countenance" by the faithful.[72]

The general assembly's deliverance of 1832 was not entirely negative. The body strongly encouraged "[m]eetings of pious women by themselves for conversation and prayer...." In fact, a pathway to meaningful service in the Presbyterian Church, in the form of women's societies, was already an established feature of congregational life in increasing numbers of churches. Earlier in the nineteenth century, women had begun to organize locally in order to collect funds for worthy causes, such as providing assistance to needy theological students, teaching literacy to adults, "supplying the pressing wants and alleviating the bodily diseases of the indigent sufferer."[73] Importantly, like the ones in Great Britain on which they were modeled, the societies were largely independent of ecclesiastical control, thereby affording women an opportunity to develop and hone skills in organization and governance. In these and other benevolent endeavors, women were joining and putting their own stamp on a movement that over the coming decades would see the establishment of associations and societies throughout American protestant Christianity for such things as the distribution of Bibles, the publication of religious tracts, the education of slaves, and the establishment of Sunday schools, as well as purely local projects such as the construction of church buildings.[74] In the Synod of Virginia around 1816, a "Female Mite Society for the Education of Heathen Children in India" came into existence, while at the same time in Mecklenburg County, North Carolina, a minister noted with pride that "Charitable institutions have multiplied exceedingly. There is a Sunday School at almost every Church, in which black people are taught to read. Tract Societies are very numerous," and funds for the Bible society and missionary society "are respectable and increasing."[75] Although the minister neglected to note the fact, women formed the backbone of the charitable activities. One example of many in the state is the "Female Scholarship of Orange Presbytery," funded by women for the benefit of divinity students at Princeton University.[76]

As the century progressed, women's organizations in both the PCUS and the PCUSA proved ever more crucial to the success of enterprises that necessitated the raising of funds, which is to say virtually all of them. Minutes of general assembly meetings of both denominations illustrate this fact abundantly in reports on charitable activities of various kinds, such as foreign and domestic missionary societies, temperance societies, and educational societies.[77] By 1875, a scant decade into the existence of the PCUS, women's missionary associations, along with Sunday schools, were providing one-third of the foreign missions budget of the denomination.[78] In time, the associations became the main source of missions funding, and remained so during the life of the denomination. Women's associations flourished in the Synod of North Carolina as well. By 1890, 125 missionary societies (of a total of 578 in the entire denomination) were contributing a quarter of the revenue for mission work. However, many women in the synod were becoming decidedly restive because of the perceived lack of appreciation of their work by the men in charge of missions, and these latter now noted with unease a "danger now impending of a diversion of the zeal of our women to other and extra-ecclesiastical channels"—which could well have included the nascent women's suffrage movement, a decidedly distasteful prospect for the synod's males.[79] Fortunately the crisis passed. Presbyterian women's societies in North Carolina continued their growth in numbers and fundraising, and subsequent meetings of synod were at pains to express deep appreciation for women and their work. By 1920, 328 societies across the state, with over 8,000 members, were still raising substantial funds for the denomination's foreign and home missions, as well as for local causes such as the synod's orphanage at Barium Springs.[80] Women were also becoming an indispensable source of personnel for foreign missions. Although their presence on the mission field was considered definitely subordinate to that of their ordained male colleagues, and their work was largely confined to teaching, catechizing, and domestic duties, they endured the same challenging conditions as the men at mission posts scattered across the globe.[81]

The preparation of women for responsible positions in the church took another step forward in 1915, when the general assembly established a "training school" for laity in Richmond, Virginia, later named the Presbyterian School of Christian Education. Many of the students were women, and within a few years of its founding women were being appointed to its board of trustees—the first such appointment to a governing body in the history of the PCUS.[82] In 1922, the southern general assembly decreed that women could officially "aid the deacons" in ministering to the sick and needy, the assembly having some years before this (1907) decided not to permit the creation of the position of "deaconess" to perform this function—without doubt because it would be perceived as giving women an independent (if unordained) place in the ecclesiastical structure.[83]

Regardless of the fact that women had for a century or more been a vitally important part of the work of the church, in the opening years of the twentieth century they were still barred from all positions of leadership outside the limited sphere of their own organizations. And even here, the permanent committees of assembly and synod with oversight of "women's work" were composed of men, with women not being permitted even to speak about their own activities on the floor at meetings of general assembly, synod, or presbytery. The long era of total male domination in the PCUS and the other Presbyterian bodies was, however, beginning to draw to a close—although it would still be some while before the process was complete, with women being eligible for all offices in the church and their voices fully heard. A milestone was reached in 1912, when a remarkable woman, Hallie Paxson Winsborough[84] of Kansas City, persuaded the General Assembly to centralize its several departments concerned with women's work into one agency, of which Winsborough became the first superintendent. Although the Department of Woman's Work remained under male supervision and budgetary control, and conservative opposition grumbled about "the cloven hoof of woman's suffrage behind the petticoats," the innovation held out the promise of a louder and more coherent voice for women in the governance of the church. Winsborough was also the guiding force in the establishment (1916) of Colored Women's Conferences throughout the PCUS, and was a leader in the anti-lynching movement and other activities opposing the oppression of African Americans. The general esteem in which she was held was demonstrated in her appointment in 1924 to an interdenominational Christian conference in Stockholm, Sweden, which marked "the first time that a woman represented the whole constituency of the church."[85] Another long-standing barrier crumbled in 1927, when Winsborough read to the general assembly her department's annual report, thereby becoming the first female ever permitted unreservedly to address that body.[86] Winsborough's exceptional accomplishments in expanding the role for women in southern presbyterianism lived on after her death in 1940.

North Carolina's Presbyterians saw parallel changes within their own synod. One thing that did not change was that women continued to provide much or most of the funds for the major programs of the denomination in North Carolina. This fact did not escape the satirical notice of the Statesville *Landmark* newspaper when it reported on a meeting of Concord Presbytery in April 1900. A suggestion that women's missionary societies form a union was sat upon, albeit by a very narrow majority. This was a little hard on the sisters. If it weren't for their efforts in raising money, three-fourths of the churches would be bankrupt; notwithstanding their good work, they must keep quiet and let the men do the talking.

The committee vote was close, fifteen to twelve, with the majority feeling that such an innovation "took woman out of her sphere and made her too prominent in the public eye."[87] A typical example of women's undiminished importance would be the 1919 report of synod's Committee on Woman's Work, which saw an annual total of $98,739 raised by women for home and foreign missions, schools and colleges, and an orphans' home, among other benevolences.[88] Meetings of synod continued to heap fulsome praise on women for their contributions,[89] and even to express admiration for the auxiliary's "excellent form of organization and business methods"—high praise indeed from a body composed exclusively of males, many of whom were businessmen.[90] Such innovations as the institution of a woman's page—with a woman editor—in the denominational newspaper,[91] and the spread of "business women's circles" in Presbyterian churches around the state[92] indicated both an increasing appreciation of the work of women in the synod, and a recognition of their changing roles in society. The appointment in 1921 of an equal number of men and women to the board of regents of the Barium Springs orphanage signaled a change of historic significance, a "new departure" as the minutes expressed it.[93] The path was clear, if lengthy, for the 1964 PCUS General Assembly's decision that all offices in the church must be open to women.[94]

Serious challenges to both orthodoxy (accepted doctrine) and orthopraxy (accepted behavior) confronted American presbyterianism in the waning decades of the nineteenth century and into the twentieth. Doctrinal challenges concerned mainly doubts about the literal truth of the Bible, and the associated question of whether or not humans had emerged from lower life-forms. The challenges to accepted norms of Christian moral behavior revolved chiefly around questions relating to recreation (drinking, dancing, card-playing, Sabbath observance) and the life of the family, such as divorce and birth control.

The so-called "higher criticism" of the Bible, the close, objective examination of scripture mainly through the lenses of linguistic analysis and the discoveries of archaeology, was not a new phenomenon in the later nineteenth century. It was, however, one that was coming increasingly to the notice of both educated laity and clergy throughout the church, both north and south. Dr. William M. McPheeters, Professor of Old Testament at Columbia Seminary in Georgia and a highly respected voice for conservative Presbyterians in the PCUS, noted in 1892 that "The views of the 'Higher Critics' are being rapidly popularized and propagated among all the more intelligent people of our churches." Although this might at the moment, he suggested, be true more of the northern church than the southern, he urged that "we will make a sad, possibly fatal mistake, if we flatter ourselves that we do not have to face these issues."[95] In the PCUS generally, any suggestion that the Bible was anything other than literally true in every detail undoubtedly would have met a storm of hostility from almost every pulpit where the matter might be raised. There is little reason to believe, however, that the question was directly confronted over the following years, or that the faithful in the pews felt significantly less secure in their beliefs.[96]

The related matter of Darwinism was taken more seriously. Charles Darwin (1809–1882) in his *On the Origin of Species* (1859) posited the discomforting idea that humankind had come into being as part of an evolutionary process rather than as a unique creation of God. A southern Presbyterian minister and professor at Columbia Seminary, James Woodrow, uncle of President Woodrow Wilson, sparked intense debate within the PCUS when in 1884 he declared his belief in Darwin's theory. Woodrow's views carried special force because of his training as a scientist at Harvard and his doctorate, summa cum laude, from the University of Heidelberg. The 1886 General Assembly declared by a 137 to thirteen vote—and after hearing Woodrow defend his views for two hours—that "Adam's body was directly fashioned by Almighty God, without any natural animal parentage of any kind, out of matter previously created from nothing." The decision was reaffirmed several times, including once in 1924 on an overture from Mecklenburg Presbytery, a hotbed of Presbyterian opposition to the teaching of evolution in the public schools.[97] Surprisingly, the question of the church and evolution was not considered again by the national body until 1969, when the assembly declared the previous deliverances on the subject to be "in error," and "no longer represent[ing] the mind of our Church."[98] During the turmoil of the Scopes "monkey trial" in 1925, the question of evolution roiled North Carolina Presbyterians as no other controversy involving their faith had ever done. The synod wrestled with the question that year, and to no one's surprise came down firmly on the side of the anti-evolutionists.[99]

The controversy over evolution well demonstrated that the PCUS did not live in a sealed environment. The wider world made periodic incursions, which became more pronounced and frequent with the quickening pace of communications, and which often necessitated some kind of response. Such was the case with the southern church's relationship with other denominations and faiths. While still garbed in Confederate gray, it merged with the United Synod of the South (the New School's southern incarnation) and the eleven congregations of the Independent Presbyterian Church, and after the war it absorbed a scattering of synods and presbyteries in the border states. One union was that of 1895 between the PCUS and the Waldensian Church. Calvinists who emigrated from their home in the Italian Alps to the North Carolina mountains in 1893, the Waldensians traced their protestant lineage to Peter Waldo in the twelfth century.[100]

Periodic negotiations between the two largest Presbyterian bodies in the nation, the PCUS and PCUSA, sometimes reached the brink of an agreement to unite, but the goal proved elusive until 1983. In 1870, the first proposal for organic union was considered by both bodies. The southern church's reply was a curt refusal, and taking its stand with the doctrine of the spirituality of the church, it delivered a stinging rebuke to their "former associates" for "fatally complicating [*sic*] themselves with the State in political [i.e., prounion] utterances, deliberately pronounced year after year." Additionally, "the ear of the whole world has been filled" with charges amounting to "heresy and blasphemy" against the former Confederate church. The charges "could not be quietly ignored," and must be "openly and squarely withdrawn. So long as they remain upon record they are an impassable barrier to official intercourse."[101] The following years saw numerous efforts to negotiate amicably. By 1882, tempers had cooled enough for serious negotiations to be resumed. Several plans of union were presented to both assemblies, including a union of most of the presbyterian and reformed bodies in the nation, but the PCUS consistently rejected all suggestions of organic union. A positive, substantial move by the southern church came in 1937 with its appointment of a Permanent Committee on Cooperation and Union, and the two denominations slowly but steadily drifted toward eventual merger.[102] Among North Carolina Presbyterians, as throughout the southern church, the question of reunion enjoyed a mixed reception over the years.[103]

The southern church approached with caution proposals to join ecumenical bodies, most notably the Federal Council of Churches, founded in 1908. The PCUS's relationship with the council was stormy throughout the years of its membership (1912–1931, 1941–1950), as it frequently took left-of-center positions on such questions as race relations, poverty, and industrial relations, thereby incurring the vehement opposition of numerous presbyteries, including several in North Carolina.[104] In 1950, the FCC was absorbed by the National Council of Churches of Christ in America. The World Council of Churches included at its founding (1948) both the PCUS and PCUSA, as well as most other protestant and Orthodox bodies throughout the world. Although the council has been under sustained attack by Presbyterian conservatives for its perceived liberal bias, the contemporary PC(USA) continues its membership in the body.[105]

The spirit of ecumenism was not notably in evidence when it came to consideration of a number of other Christian faiths. The southern Presbyterian church, along with most protestant denominations until relatively recent times, had a deep and long-standing loathing of Roman Catholicism. Perceiving the Catholic Church as a "menace to liberty," a 1911 general assembly resolution referred to that body as a "politico-religious organization" and "so-called church" that "is, and always has been, a menace or a blight to the civil and religious liberty of every kind where it has obtained a foothold." The resolution expressed alarm at the silence of "public men," the federal government's alleged granting of "special favors" to the church, and the "ominous silence" of the press in reporting anything detrimental to it. In later years, the assembly counseled against intermarriage with

Catholics, and repeatedly objected to any kind of diplomatic relations with the Vatican.[106] The Synod of North Carolina, as well as its presbyteries, were fully in accord with such sentiments. Regardless of the fact that the Roman Catholic presence in the state was minuscule, the Synod of North Carolina in 1867, fearing immigration, had issued its own dire warning about "the man of sin," the Roman pontiff, having "his eye on our broad lands—our blue mountains and green valleys." North Carolina Presbyterians were earnestly exhorted not to give any kind of encouragement to "this unchristian, unscriptural, self-righteous, unholy, idolatrous, blasphemous, deceitful, soul-torturing, enslaving, persecuting and doomed synagogue of Satan."[107] The synod's newspaper, the *North Carolina Presbyterian*, in the mid–1880s ran a series of articles and editorials on the danger to the south posed by the Jesuit order and its plan to encourage immigration. Concord Presbytery heartily thanked the newspaper for alerting the state to the danger of "the colonization among us of a class of citizens who owe first allegiance to a foreign power."[108] Remarkably, as late as 1952, Orange Presbytery asked the General Assembly to substitute "Holy Christian Church" for "Holy Catholic Church" in the Apostles Creed, lest the unwary be ensnared by the phrase.[109] The present official attitude of the PC(USA) toward the Roman Catholic Church has undergone a complete transformation to one of comity, and on occasion cooperation—a dramatic change well symbolized by the visit to Pope John Paul II by the stated clerk and other prominent Presbyterians in 2001. The Synod of North Carolina's minutes begin to reflect a positive attitude toward the Roman Catholic Church from the mid–1960s, following the deliberations of Vatican II in Rome and the election and assassination of the nation's first Roman Catholic president.[110]

Roman Catholicism was not alone in receiving unfavorable notice from southern Presbyterians. Unitarians, Universalists, Quakers, Swedenborgians, Campbellites (Christian Church), Christian Scientists—all were deemed by the General Assembly to have fallen short in some particular, sometimes involving their form of baptism.[111] These alien faiths were, however, usually looked upon more with disdain than with the detestation and fear accorded the Romanists. Mormonism, a *bête noire* for many orthodox believers ever since its founding by Joseph Smith in the 1820s, was roundly blasted by the PCUSA General Assembly in 1879 and several times thereafter.[112] Strangely, the General Assembly of the PCUS apparently never took official notice of it. Some North Carolina Presbyterians, however, felt themselves on the front line of what they perceived to be a Mormon onslaught on their state. In 1898, the *North Carolina Presbyterian* claimed that more Mormon elders were proselytizing in North Carolina than there were Presbyterian ministers. "[At] the present rate of increase it will not be long before the Mormons will have more churches and more communicants in the state than the Presbyterians."[113] In time, and especially after polygamy was renounced by Mormon leaders (1890) and gradually ceased to be the hallmark of the faith, the feeling of alarm on the part of mainline denominations began to fade.[114]

Views on moral behavior in southern Presbyterian judicatories shifted dramatically in the years following the Second World War, as they did in other mainline protestant denominations. Dancing and other "fashionable" or "worldly" or "dissipated and lascivious" amusements, mainly card-playing and attending theater performances, were dealt with repeatedly by both northern and southern assemblies, and in North Carolina they were a perennial concern of both synod and presbytery.[115] The 1893 PCUS General Assembly had held that under certain circumstances dancing could be punished by excommunication, whereas in 1945 the assembly refused to condemn it, and in 1946 Orange

Presbytery permitted students at the colleges of Flora Macdonald, Davidson, and Peace to dance on campus.[116] In the era of films, television, and video games—contemporary variants of theater—the assembly of the PC(USA) continues to grapple with questions of appropriate entertainment, but must do so in an age of graphic and pervasive depictions of sex and violence, coupled with a steady decline in the ability of organized Christianity to influence events in the secular world.[117] Sabbath observance, which throughout the nineteenth century and most of the twentieth had been a matter of utmost concern to Presbyterians, by the dawn of the new millennium was essentially a nostalgic memory, as a result of the encroachment of the worlds of commerce and sport.[118]

Until 1959, the only recognized grounds for divorce in the PCUS were adultery and willful desertion, and only the innocent party could legitimately remarry.[119] The question of homosexuality, not addressed by any general assembly prior to the late twentieth century, was the cause of prolonged, intense, often rancorous controversy in general assemblies and congregations for several decades prior to 2011, when the required number of presbyteries voted to allow the ordination of gay people. This was followed in 2015 by the approval of same-sex marriages.[120] Abortion was another issue provoking a bitter division between traditionalists and liberals. The northern general assembly in 1869 had declared induced abortion "a crime against God and against nature," and as late as 1965 it had stated that "the fetus is a human life to be protected by the criminal law from the moment when the ovum is fertilized." Five years later, the assembly reversed its position, stating that "women should have full freedom of personal choice concerning the completion or termination of their pregnancies." Repeated subsequent campaigns by abortion opponents to have the position reversed or modified have met with no success.[121] By the time of the reuniting of the two denominations in 1983, the southern church had also embraced a pro-choice position, although the two largest breakaway denominations (PCA and EPC) continue to teach that abortion is a sin.[122]

Although a bedrock tenet of strict Calvinism is that good works play no part in personal salvation—only faith through grace can accomplish that mystery—American Presbyterians have nevertheless involved themselves in a variety of causes or "social questions" over the centuries. Slavery, the most consuming social question of the nineteenth century, has been mentioned, as have the efforts of the church to deal with the monumental problems coming in the wake of its abolition.

The temperance/abstinence/prohibition movement was a social cause embraced with enthusiasm by many Presbyterians. As early as 1766, the church had condemned the evils of alcohol—including especially "the too great use of spirituous liquors at funerals"—and throughout the nineteenth century both the northern and southern churches kept up a drumbeat against the evils of alcohol, from pulpits and in general assembly pronouncements. Women's organizations such as the Women's Christian Temperance Union were vehicles for women's empowerment.[123] In the post–Civil War period, the general assembly of the northern church went so far as to recommend to sessions the expulsion from their congregations of manufacturers and sellers of beverage alcohol, and advocated the lobbying of legislatures on behalf of the cause—thus severing the frayed bonds holding it to the doctrine of non-involvement in secular politics.[124] The 1910 PCUS General Assembly also sidestepped the doctrine of the spirituality of the church when it approved an attempt to influence legislation on alcohol. More usually, however, it held up the ideal of personal abstinence and education to combat the evils of alcohol, and later of "narcotism."[125] The last deliverance of the PCUS General Assembly on the subject came in 1958, when it "reaffirm[ed] voluntary total abstinence as the Christian ideal toward which church members should aspire." Presbyterians in North Carolina also played their part in the fight against intemperance,[126] but with the failure of prohibition the long battle against alcohol went the way of Sunday observance.

The growth of manufacturing industry in the south opened new fields of concern for Presbyterians in the region. In a few of North Carolina's mill villages, Presbyterian mission schools and Sunday schools were opened and ministers conducted services.[127] However, Baptists and Methodists could more rapidly produce the needed evangelists for this work. The visible urban poverty following in the wake of the establishment of textile mills, cigarette factories, and other manufacturing enterprises led the southern church gradually to become more aware of and voluble about what in the late nineteenth and early twentieth centuries became known as "social reform," or less threateningly, "social service." General assemblies, synods, and presbyteries began slowly to emerge from the mold of what had been essentially an introverted concern with the life of the denomination—such things as doctrine, raising funds, adding to membership rolls, organizing and building new churches, founding church schools, educating ministers, establishing denominational outposts overseas—and became increasingly mindful of the world beyond the elect. Not coincidentally, this process began with the advent of "progressivism," a national phenomenon that sought to curb the excesses of big business and machine politics in the waning years of the nineteenth century and opening years of the twentieth. The ecclesiastical analogue of the progressive movement was the "social gospel," American Christianity's affirmation that the physical welfare of society at large was a legitimate concern of the Church.[128]

Regulation was the watchword of progressivism, a concept seized upon by a North Carolina minister and editor of the synod's newspaper, the *Presbyterian Standard,* Alexander J. McKelway (1866–1918), who spearheaded the struggle for enactment of child labor laws in the state.[129] In 1899, McKelway in his newspaper called for public opinion to be brought to bear on legislators to convince them that "life is more sacred than luxury, and the convenience of the few shall not be purchased by the sufferings of the many."[130] In 1906 the Synod of North Carolina, largely because of McKelway's influence, strongly denounced the exploitation of children in factories and mills:

> ... the Synod of North Carolina believing that the employment of young children in factories tends to dwarf the body, darken the mind, and deaden the soul, and that the system of child labor now in vogue comes therefore under the condemnation of the Lord Jesus Christ ... calls upon Christian employers, parents and citizens to exert all legitimate influence to remove this offence from the path of the children of our land.[131]

The statement is notable not only because the textile industry, a notorious employer of child labor, was of great importance in the state's economy, but also because a sizable proportion of textile mill owners were Presbyterians. It was also noteworthy because heretofore the only references to children in synod minutes had been anodyne ones relating to their instruction in Scripture and catechism so that they might be "raised in the nurture and admonition of the Lord."[132] The following year the synod also appointed a committee to oversee mission work among factory workers.[133]

The action of the synod reflected stirrings within American Presbyterianism toward addressing social questions in an organized, sustained way. Remarkably, the general assemblies of both PCUS and PCUSA, along with several other Presbyterian bodies, issued a joint declaration in 1914, as Europe and America were on the brink of massive social and political upheavals. The document was lengthy, blunt in its condemnation of economic disparities and capitalist greed, and gave unmistakable hints that social concerns would continue to be a prominent feature of denominational activity by both northern and southern churches. The statement no doubt shocked many sensibilities when it declared that advances in science and technology had brought into being "... [a] vast increase in wealth, [with] its unequal and, often, unjust distribution, and the consequent increase of the power of the privileged few to exploit their fellowmen for private and selfish ends."

The development of huge corporations had weakened "the sense of individual responsibility for social wrongs," which Christians had a duty to address. It was therefore incumbent on Presbyterians to ensure that "every man do his full share of the world's work" and that there be a "fair return for labor, sufficient to support the man and his family against illness and old age." Children should enjoy a life free from "forced labor," and women should not be exposed to "conditions degrading womanhood."[134]

Although the pace of change would be too slow for some Presbyterians, and much too rapid for many others, the direction of the change was unmistakable and would continue into the twenty-first century. Rigid orthodoxy of belief in predestination and the inefficacy of works, coupled with an inflexible neutrality in matters relating to the state and politics, were coming to be viewed by many mainline Presbyterian clergy and laity alike as less important to the Christian life in the contemporary world than working to increase peace and economic justice.

FURTHER READING

Walter H. Conser, Jr., and Robert J. Cain, *Presbyterians in North Carolina: Race, Politics, and Religious Identity in Historical Perspective* (Nashville: University of Tennessee Press, 2011).

D. I. Craig, *Development of the Presbyterian Church in North Carolina and of Synodical Home Missions* (Richmond, VA: William Black, 1907).

William H. Foote, *Sketches of North Carolina, Historical and Biographical* (New York: R. Carter, 1846).

E.H. Gillett, *History of the Presbyterian Church in the United States of America* (Philadelphia: Presbyterian Publication Committee, 2 vols., 1864).

Robert Ellis Thompson, *A History of the Presbyterian Church in the United States* (New York: The Christian Literature Co., 1895).

James H. Smylie, *A Brief History of the Presbyterians* (Louisville, KY: Geneva Press, 1996).

NOTES

1. Caroline B. Whitley and Susan M. Trimble, *North Carolina Headrights, A List of Names* (Raleigh: North Carolina Department of Cultural Resources, 2001).

2. Robert J. Cain, ed., *North Carolina Higher-Court Minutes, 1724–1730*, vol. VI of *The Colonial Records of North Carolina* [Second Series] (Raleigh: North Carolina Division of Archives and History [projected multivolume series, 1963–] 1981), xxxv; Ernest Trice Thompson, *Presbyterians in the South*, 3 vols. (Richmond, VA: John Knox Press, 1963–73), I, 21, hereinafter cited as Thompson, *Presbyterians in the South*.

3. Duane Meyer, *The Highland Scots of North Carolina, 1732–1776* (Chapel Hill: University of North Carolina Press, 1961), 59, 72.

4. Harry Roy Merrens, *North Carolina in the Eighteenth Century: A Study in Historical Geography* (Chapel Hill: University of North Carolina Press, 1964) 53–55, 63, 68–73; Robert W. Ramsey, *Carolina Cradle: Settlement of the Northwest Carolina Frontier, 1747–1762* (Chapel Hill: University of North Carolina Press, 1964), *passim*; Tyler Blethen and Curtis Wood, *From Ulster to Carolina: the Migration of the Scotch-Irish to Southwestern North Carolina* (Cullowhee, NC: Western Carolina University, Mountain Heritage Center, 1983), *passim*. In addition, a number came directly from Ireland, some of whom were sponsored by a compatriot, Governor Arthur Dobbs (1754–65). Robert J. Cain, ed., *Records of the Executive Council, 1735–1754*, vol. VIII of *The Colonial Records of North Carolina* [Second Series] (Raleigh: North Carolina Division of Archives and History [projected multivolume series, 1963–] 1988), xxi, hereinafter cited as Cain, *Colonial Records*, VIII; Desmond Clarke, *Arthur Dobbs, Esquire, 1689–1765* (Chapel Hill: University of North Carolina Press, 1957), 73–74, 95–97, 120.

5. Jonathan Bardon, *A History of Ulster* (Belfast: Blackstaff Press, 1992), 170–75. A wide-ranging and

penetrating treatment of Ulster Scots in America; *see* Patrick Griffin, *The People with No Name: Ireland's Ulster Scots, America's Scots-Irish, and the Creation of a British Atlantic World, 1689–1764* (Princeton and Oxford: Princeton University Press, 2001). *See also* Kenneth W. Keller, "The Origins of Ulster Scots Emigration to America: A Survey of Recent Research," *America Presbyterians*, vol. 70, no. 2 (Summer 1992), 71–80.

6. Walter Conser and Robert J. Cain, *Presbyterians in North Carolina: Race, Politics, and Religious Identity in Historical Perspective* (Nashville: University of Tennessee Press, 2011), 42–44, hereinafter cited as Conser and Cain, *Presbyterians in North Carolina.* This work also notes that Pattillo's punctiliousness in observing the Presbyterian doctrine of the duty of obedience to legitimately constituted authority in the case of the Regulators, was abandoned entirely when he became an ardent supporter of American independence. See also Durward Stokes, "Henry Pattillo in North Carolina," *The North Carolina Historical Review*, vol. 44, no. 4 (October 1967), *passim.* The key role of Presbyterians in the Regulator movement may be gleaned from William S. Powell et al., *Regulators in North Carolina: A Documentary History, 1759–1776* (Raleigh, NC: Department of Archives and History, 1971). The role of the Scotch Irish in the American Revolution is analyzed in James G. Leyburn, "Presbyterian Immigrants and the American Revolution," *Journal of Presbyterian History*, vol. 54, no. 1 (Spring 1976), 9–32.

7. Thompson, *Presbyterians in the South*, I, 1–66; Robert Hamlin Stone, *A History of Orange Presbytery, 1770–1970* (Greensboro, NC: Orange Presbytery, 1970), hereinafter cited as Stone, *Orange Presbytery*; James H. Smylie, *A Brief History of the Presbyterians* (Louisville, KY: Geneva Press, 1996), hereinafter cited as Smylie, *Brief History.*

8. Conser and Cain, *Presbyterians in North Carolina*, 7–8, 10.

9. *Records of the Presbyterian Church in the United States of America* (Philadelphia: Presbyterian Board of Publication, 1841, 256n, cited hereafter as PCUSA *Records*, 1841. A later edition of this source (Guy S. Klett, *Minutes of the Presbyterian Church in America, 1706–1788* [Philadelphia, Presbyterian Historical Society, 1977]) is incompletely indexed, and has not been used in the present essay. Conser and Cain, *Presbyterians in North Carolina*, 49–51; Durward T. Stokes, "North Carolina and the Great Revival of 1800," *The North Carolina Historical Review*, vol. 43, no. 4 (Oct. 1966, 401–12).

10. For a description of communion services in the eighteenth century *see* David A. Ramsey and R. Craig Koedel, "The Communion Season—an 18th Century Model," vol. 54, no. 2 (Summer 1976), 203–16.

11. *Records*, 1841, 173.

12. General Assembly of the Presbyterian Church in the United States of America, *Minutes* (Philadelphia: Presbyterian Board of Publication, 1860), 219–24, hereinafter cited as PCUSA *Minutes.*

13. Thompson, *Presbyterians in the South*, I, 274–285. See generally "Colonial Education among Presbyterians," *The Journal of Presbyterian History*, vol. 76, no. 1 (Spring 1998) 17–29.

14. Conser and Cain, *Presbyterians in North Carolina*, 66–67; Thomas J. Wertenbaker, "The College of New Jersey and the Presbyterians," *The Journal of Presbyterian History*, vol. 36, no. 4 (December 1958), 209–16. A strong Presbyterian influence is evident in the founding and launching of the University of North Carolina, especially in the composition of its administrators, faculty, and benefactors. *See* Kemp Plummer Battle, *History of the University of North Carolina* (n.p., the author, 2 vols., 1907), vol. I, *passim.*

15. William D. Snider, *Light on the Hill: A History of the University of North Carolina at Chapel Hill* (Chapel Hill: University of North Carolina Press, 1992); Mary D. Beaty, *A History of Davidson College* (Davidson, NC: Briarpatch Press, 1988).

16. Conser and Cain, *Presbyterians in North Carolina*, 19; *A Digest of Acts and Proceedings of the General Assembly of the Presbyterian Church in the United States, 1861–1965* (Atlanta: Office of the General Assembly, 1966), 211, hereinafter cited as PCUS *Digest*, notes that "Despite a number of efforts to lower the educational standards required for a minister, the General Assembly [of the southern church] has consistently maintained the examination for licensure and ordination at their high level." The southern church, for example, required the candidate's thesis to be written in Latin until 1913.

17. Inez Moore Parker, *The Biddle-Johnson C. Smith Story* (Charlotte, NC: Charlotte Publishing, 1975).

18. Conser and Cain, *Presbyterians in North Carolina*, 152, 169.

19. Conser and Cain, *Presbyterians in North Carolina*, 152, 167; Mark Banker, "Warren Wilson College: From Mountain Mission to Multicultural Community," *American Presbyterians*, vol. 73, no. 2 (Summer 1995), 111–23.

20. Margaret Burr Deschamps, "Presbyterians and Southern Education," *Journal of the Presbyterian Historical Society*, vol. 31, no. 2 (June 1953), 113–24; Thomas T. Taylor, "Samuel McCorkle and a Christian Republic, 1792–1802," *American Presbyterians*, vol. 63, no. 4 (Winter 1985), 375–85. Charles L. Coon's *North Carolina Schools and Academies, 1790–1840* (Raleigh, NC: North Carolina Historical Commission, 1915), xvii and *passim*, notes that it was usual for Presbyterian ministers to teach school, in addition to their other responsibilities.

21. Edgar W. Knight, "Notes on John Chavis," *The North Carolina Historical Review*, vol. 7, no. 3 (July 1930), 326–45. See also "John Chavis, 1763–1838: A Social-Psychological Study," *The Journal of Negro History*, vol. 64, no. 2 (Spring 1979), 142–56.

22. Conser and Cain, *Presbyterians in North Carolina*, 208; William E. Moore, *The Presbyterian Digest of 1886* (Philadelphia: Presbyterian Board of Publication, 1886), 775–82, hereinafter cited as Moore, *Digest of*

1886. It should be noted that the "deliverances" (advisory pronouncements) of the general assembly were the same for the entire church, north and south, until 1861, when the denomination divided. Therefore the "digests" (deliverances arranged topically) for the PCUSA (northern) church record deliverances that were valid for what became the PCUS (southern) church until that year, and thereafter the PCUS compiled its own digest of deliverances of the southern general assembly.

23. Conser and Cain, *Presbyterians in North Carolina*, 206.

24. Hugh T. Lefler and William S. Powell, *Colonial North Carolina, A History* (New York: Charles Scribner's Sons, 1973), 205.

25. Smylie, *Brief History*, 48–50. See Maurice W. Armstrong and others, *The Presbyterian Enterprise: Sources of American Presbyterian History* (Philadelphia: The Westminster Press, 1956), 33–61, for a flavor of the inflamed passions on both sides. See also Anthony L. Blair, "Shattered and Divided: Itinerancy, Ecclesiology, and Revivalism in the Presbyterian Awakening," *The Journal of Presbyterian History*, vol. 81, no. 1 (Spring 2003), 18–34.

26. *Records*, 1841, 209, 214, 219, 225. New Light clergy in North Carolina and Virginia were viewed by some conservatives as seditious, even traitorous; *see* Alice M. Baldwin "Sowers of Sedition: The Political Theories of Some New Light Presbyterian Clergy of Virginia and North Carolina," *The William and Mary Quarterly*, vol. 5, no. 1 (January 1948), 52–76. See also Marilyn Westerkamp, "Division, Dissension, and Compromise: The Presbyterian Church during the Great Awakening," *The Journal of Presbyterian History*, vol. 78, no. 1 (Spring 2000), 3–18, and John Fea, "In Search of Unity: Presbyterians in the Wake of the First Great Awakening," *The Journal of Presbyterian History*, vol. 86, no. 2 (Fall/Winter, 2008), 53–60.

27. *Records*, 1841, 339.

28. Conser and Cain, *Presbyterians in North Carolina*, 49–51; Durward T. Stokes, "North Carolina and the Great Revival of 1800," *The North Carolina Historical Review*, vol. 43, no. 4 (Oct. 1966), 401–12; John Thomas Scott, "James McGready: Son of Thunder, Father of the Great Revival," *American Presbyterians*, vol. 72, no. 2 (Summer 1994), 87–95.

29. Guion Griffis Johnson, "The Camp Meeting in Ante-Bellum North Carolina," *The North Carolina Historical Review*, vol. 10, no. 2 (April 1933), 95–110. For a thoughtful analysis of the phenomenon and its wide-ranging influence *see* John B. Boles, *The Great Revival, 1787–1805: The Origins of the Southern Evangelical Mind* (Lexington: University Press of Kentucky, 1972). The Presbyterian contribution to the phenomenon in the antebellum South is treated in Anne C. Loveland's "Presbyterians and Revivalism in the Old South," *Journal of Presbyterian History*, vol. 57, no. 1 (Spring 1979), which contends p. 39 that Presbyterians in the Carolinas "made sparing use of camp meetings in the 1820s, 1830s, and 1840s." The North Carolinian and Presbyterian missionary to Siam, Daniel McGilvray (1828–1911), wrote a detailed account of a four-day camp meeting at the "Fall Communion" of his home church, Buffalo, in present Lee County, in the 1830s. Numerous sermons, hymn-singing, tents erected by pew-holders in order to offer hospitality to all comers, and a communion of wine and bread served at long tables characterized the event. Daniel J. McGilvary, *A Half Century Among the Siamese and the Lao* (New York: Fleming H. Revell Company, 1912), 22–23.

30. Such at least is the thesis of Harold Parker, "New School Presbyterian Disruption in North Carolina (1835–1846)," Iliff Review, 32 no. 2 (Spring 1975), 51–63. *See also* the very useful article by S. Donald Fortson, III, "New School Calvinism and the Presbyterian Creed," *The Journal of Presbyterian History*, vol. 42, no. 4 (Winter, 2004), 221–43, and James H. Moorhead, "The 'Restless Spirit of Radicalism': Old School Fears and the Schism of 1837," *The Journal of Presbyterian History*, vol. 78, no. 1 (Spring 2000), 19–33. The standard history of the New School, written from an Old School perspective, is Samuel J. Baird, *A History of the New School…* (Philadelphia: Claxton, Remsen & Haffelfinger, 1868).

31. Minutes of the General Assembly of the Presbyterian Church in the Confederate States of America (Augusta, GA: Steam Power Press Chronicle and Sentinel, 1861), hereinafter cited as PCCSA *Minutes*; W. Harrison Daniel, "Southern Presbyterians in the Confederacy," *The North Carolina Historical Review*, vol. 44, no. 3 (July 1967), 241–55. A useful discussion of Presbyterians and slavery in the eighteenth century is J. Earl Thompson, Jr., "Slavery and Presbyterianism in the Revolutionary Era," *Journal of Presbyterian History*, vol. 54, no. 1 (Spring 1976), 121–41.

32. PCUS *Digest*, 1965, 389–432, traces in detail the tortuous path to eventual reunion, beginning in 1870. See also J. Treadwell Davis, "Obstacles to Reunion of the Presbyterian Church, 1868–1888," *Virginia Magazine of History and Biography*, vol. 63, no. 1 (January 1955), 28–39.

33. Finlay Holmes, *Our Presbyterian Heritage* (Belfast: Publications Committee of the Presbyterian Church in Ireland, 1985), 55–94; J.D. Mackie, *A History of Scotland*, 2d ed. (New York: Dorset Press, 1978), 331–32.

34. *The Centennial History of the Associate Reformed Presbyterian Church, 1803–1903* (Charleston, SC: The Associate Reformed Synod, 1905), 15, 46, 56, 70, 73, and *passim*.

35. A.C. Biddle, comp., *Cumberland Presbyterian Digest, 1810–1919* (Nashville, TN: General Assembly of the Cumberland Presbyterian Church, 1920).

36. Frank Joseph Smith, *The History of the Presbyterian Church in America* (Lawrenceville, GA: Presbyterian Scholars Press, 1998). Rick Nutt, "The Tie That No Longer Binds: The Origins of the Presbyterian Church in America," in Milton J. Coalter, John M. Mulder, and Louis B. Weeks, eds., *The Confessional Mosaic: Presbyterians and Twentieth-Century Theology* (Louisville, KY: Westminster/John Knox Press, 1990).

37. Russell E. Hall, "American Presbyterian Churches—A Genealogy, 1706–1982," *The Journal of Presbyterian History*, vol. 60, no. 2 (summer, 1982), 116; *The Book of Order of the Evangelical Presbyterian Church* (Detroit: Office of the General Assembly of the Evangelical Presbyterian Church, 1987).

38. Notably, the Rev. Matthew Grier, minister of First Church, Wilmington, and the Rev. P.A. McMartin of Hillsborough Presbyterian Church; Calvin H. Wiley, an elder and superintendent of public schools; the Rev. James Stafford at Thyatira Church. The Rev. Eli Caruthers (1793–1865), longtime minister of Alamance Church, famously prayed that the soldiers in his congregation might be "blessed of the Lord and returned in safety, although engaged in a bad cause," Conser and Cain, *Presbyterians in North Carolina*,127, 132–33; George Troxler, "Eli Caruthers: A Silent Dissenter in the Old South," *The Journal of Presbyterian History*, vol. 45, no. 2 (June 1967), 95–111.

39. PCUSA *Minutes*, 1847, 432 ff.

40. PCUSA *Minutes*, 1849, 354–59.

41. Synod of North Carolina, *Minutes*, 1844, 21, hereinafter cited as Synod of North Carolina *Minutes*.

42. PCCSA *Minutes*, 1863, 206–12.

43. PCUSA *Minutes*, 1858, 184.

44. Undoubtedly typical of such services would be the ones reported in J.B. Alexander, "By-gone Modes of Worship," *Charlotte Observer*, July 16, 1905; same author, "Church Privilege of Slaves," *Charlotte Observer*, July 22, 1906; Robert Milton Winter, "American Presbyterians, the Directory for Worship, and Changing Patterns of Sacramental Practice," *American Presbyterians*, vol. 71, no. 3 (Fall 1993), *n.* 24; Thompson, *Presbyterians in the South*, I, 434. See also John L. Bell, Jr., "The Presbyterian Church and the Negro in North Carolina During Reconstruction," *The North Carolina Historical Review*, vol. 40, no. 1 (January 1963), 16, hereinafter cited as Bell, "The Presbyterian Church and the Negro." A report to Fayetteville Presbytery in 1845 decried the fact that in a typical communion service hundreds of whites assemble, along with a "mighty concourse of coloured people"; of the latter, however, "only four or five come to the table." Fayetteville Presbytery *Minutes*, 1845, p. 292.

45. PCUSA *Minutes*, 1849, 254; 1858, 184.

46. PCUSA *Minutes*, 1853, 600; Synod of North Carolina *Minutes*, 1844, 21.

47. Synod of North Carolina *Minutes*, 1847, 14.

48. PCUS *Minutes*, 1865, 375.

49. Synod of North Carolina *Minutes*, 1883, 408. At this same meeting it was reported that only two of five presbyteries (Orange and Concord) had contributed to a General Assembly fund for its Tuscaloosa Institute for the training of black ministers. The total sum was a paltry $174.02.

50. PCUSA *Minutes*, statistical reports, 1865–1875, *passim*.

51. PCUSA *Minutes*, 1881, 532.

52. PCUSA *Minutes*, 1870, 218–20; 1880, 202–07; 1902, 378–84.

53. *See* general assembly minutes for both denominations. Over the years both the PCUS and the PCUSA made adjustments to boundaries and erected new synods and presbyteries, all of which are chronicled in the minutes.

54. W.A. Alexander, ed., *A Digest of the Acts and Proceedings of the General Assembly of the Presbyterian Church in the United States* (Richmond, VA: Presbyterian Committee of Publication, 1888, 163, 165–66, 242; same editor, *Supplement to the Digest...* (Richmond, VA: Presbyterian Committee of Publication, 1898, 113–14; PCUS *Digest*, 1965, 171–72. Bell, "The Presbyterian Church and the Negro," *passim* is a very useful source.

55. Synod of North Carolina, *Minutes* 1920, 420–23.

56. The steady progress of the PCUSA's efforts can be followed in the committee's lengthy reports, included in the minutes of annual meetings of the general assembly.

57. PCUS *Minutes*, 1876, 208; University of Alabama, Bureau of Educational Research, *A Study of Stillman Institute, a Junior College for Negroes* (Tuscaloosa: University of Alabama Press, 1947); Ernest Trice Thompson's "Black Presbyterians Education, and Evangelism after the Civil War," *The Journal of Presbyterian History*, vol. 51, no. 2 (Summer 1972), 174–98, is the best treatment of the subject, and includes an appreciation of the work of the Rev. C.A. Stillman, who prodded the PCUS into establishing the Tuscaloosa Institute. *See also* Roberta Alexander, *North Carolina Faces the Freedmen: Race Relations During Presidential Reconstruction, 1865–67* (Durham, NC: Duke University Press, 1985).

58. PCUS *Minutes*, 1910, 103.

59. Conser and Cain, *Presbyterians in North Carolina*, 151; PCUS *Digest*, 1965, 104–05; Darius L. Swann and James F. Reese, "Perspectives on the Development of the Black Presbyterian Church in the South," *The Journal of Presbyterian History*, vol. 85, no. 1 (Spring/Summer 2007), 48–56.

60. For example, PCUS *Minutes*, 1890, 53–54, 73; Synod of North Carolina *Minutes*, 1900, 320.

61. *The Presbyterian Standard* (Charlotte, NC), May 18, 1899, 10.

62. PCUS *Minutes*, 1920, 45.

63. PCUS *Digest*, 1965, 173; Mary-Ruth Marshall, "Handling Dynamite: Young People, Race, and Montreat, *American Presbyterians*, vol. 74, no. 2 (Summer 1996), 141–54.

64. PCUS *Digest*, 1965, 171–77; Joel L. Alvis Jr., *Religion and Race: Southern Presbyterians, 1946–1983* (Tuscaloosa and London: University of Alabama Press, 1994), hereinafter cited as Alvis, *Religion and Race*.

On the spirituality of the church see Joe L. Coker, "The Sinnott Case of 1910: The Changing Views of Southern Presbyterians on Temperance, Prohibition, and the Spirituality of the Church," *The Journal of Presbyterian History*, vol. 77, no. 4 (Winter 1999) 247–62, hereinafter cited as Coker, "The Sinnott Case," where the author analyses the principle and argues that the PCUS General Assembly in 1910 abandoned it in a case involving the issue of prohibition. The complexities of the doctrine are well presented in Jack P. Maddex, "From Theology to Spirituality: the Southern Presbyterian Reversal on Church and State," *The Journal of Presbyterian History*, vol. 54, no. 4 (Winter 1976), 438–57.

65. *The Robinsonian* (newspaper), July 14, 1954, 4.

66. Alvis, *Religion and Race*, 65, 100–01, 104, 110, 120, 138.

67. Cf. Conser & Cain, *Presbyterians in North Carolina*, 215. Alvis, 132–39, argues that since racial liberals were very often liberal in their theology and politics as well, the two tended to merge in the minds of many conservatives. For a treatment of the Presbyterian Church, north and south, and people of color, *see* Andrew Murray's *Presbyterians and the Negro: A History* (Philadelphia: Presbyterian Historical Society, 1966).

68. PCUS *Digest*, 1965, 215–16.

69. Conser and Cain, *Presbyterians in North* Carolina, 203; Margaret Lamberts Bendroth, "An Understated Tale of Epic Social Change: Women's Ordination 50 Years Ago and Now," *The Journal of Presbyterian History*, vol. 83, no. 2 (Fall/Winter 2005), 105–17; Carol Lakey Hess et al., "A Life Lived in Response: Rachel Henderlite: Christian Educator, Advocate for Justice, Ecumenist, and First Woman Ordained in the PCUS," *American Presbyterians*, vol. 69, no. 2 (Summer 1991), 133–44; PCUS *Digest*, 215–16. Also useful is Harriet Harbison Penfield, "Women in the Presbyterian Church—an Historical Overview," *The Journal of Presbyterian History*, vol. 55, no. 2 (Summer 1977), 107–23. The standard work on the history of women in the Presbyterian Church is Lois A. Boyd and R. Douglas Brackenridge, *Presbyterian Women in America: Two Centuries of a Quest for Status* (Westport, CT: Greenwood Press, 2d. ed., 1983). *See also* Gertrude J. Howell, *History of the Women of the Church: Synod of North Carolina, Presbyterian Church in the United States, 1912–1962* (Raleigh, NC: Edwards and Broughton, 1962).

70. PCUSA *Digest*, 1907, p. 79.

71. Conser and Cain, *Presbyterians in North Carolina*, 203; PCUS *Digest*, 1911, 54.

72. Synod of North Carolina *Minutes*, 1879, 84. A compelling reason for the numerous reiterations of the rule was the growing demand by women of various denominations that ordination to the ministry be opened to them. See, for example, Mary Kavanagh Oldham Eagle, ed., *The Congress of Women Held in the Woman's Building, World's Columbian Exposition…* (Philadelphia and Chicago: Board of Lady Managers, 1894) 46, 609, 795; *The Literary Digest*, February 5, 1921, 31.

73. PCUSA, *Extracts from the Minutes of the General Assembly* (Philadelphia: Jane Aitkin, 1815), 237.

74. Conser and Cain, *Presbyterians in North Carolina*, 25, 45, 59, 67, 68, 70, 161, 178–80, 202, and *passim*. The numerous facets of benevolent activities undertaken by Presbyterians are presented in Lois W. Banner "Presbyterians and Voluntarism in the Early Republic," *The Journal of Presbyterian History*, vol. 50, no. 3 (Fall 1972), 187–205.

75. Thompson, *Presbyterians in the South*, I, 286–88.

76. PCUSA *Minutes*, 1849, 405.

77. Conser and Cain, *Presbyterians in North Carolina*, 25, 26, 67, 68, 179, and *passim*.

78. Thompson, *Presbyterians in the South* II, 305. A useful overview of the foreign mission program is G. Thompson Brown, "Overseas Mission Program and Policies of the Presbyterian Church in the U.S. 1861–1983," *American Presbyterians*, vol. 65, no. 2 (Summer 1987), 157–70. An early and long-serving missionary from North Carolina to Siam is the subject of Cornelia Kneedler Hudson's "Daniel MacGilvary in Siam: Foreign Missions, the Civil War, and Presbyterian Unity," *American Presbyterians*, vol. 69, no. 4 (Winter 1991), 283–93.

79. Synod of North Carolina *Minutes*, 1890, 477–78.

80. Synod of North Carolina *Minutes*, 1920, 448.

81. The "Foreign Mission Statistical Table" for 1915 lists a total of 339 missionaries for all mission fields (Africa, Brazil, China, Cuba, Japan, Korea, and Mexico), well over half (199) of them being women—most of whom were teachers, and two of whom were physicians. PCUS *Minutes*, 1915, 282–85. Annual contributions for foreign missions almost invariably exceeded those for the various domestic missions. *See* financial reports included in the general assembly minutes of both the PCUS and PCUSA. *See also* Sophie Montgomery Crane, "A Century of PCUS Medical Mission, 1881–1983," *Journal of Presbyterian History*, vol. 65, no. 2 (Summer 1987), 135–46.

82. PCUS Minutes, 1921, 155–56.

83. PCUS *Digest*, 1965, 67.

84. Julie Durway, "'The Field Is Endless': Hallie Paxson Winsborough and Interracial Work in the PCUS Women's Auxiliary, 1912–1940," *Journal of Presbyterian History*, vol. 78, no. 3 (Fall 2000), 207–19, hereinafter cited as Durway, "Winsborough."

85. Durway, "Winsborough," 214.

86. Durway, "Winsborough," 214. Cf. Conser and Cain, *Presbyterians in North Carolina*, 202.

87. *The Landmark* (Statesville), April 24, 1900.

88. Synod of North Carolina *Minutes*, 1919, 301.

89. Synod of North Carolina *Minutes*, 1920, 448.

90. Synod of North Carolina *Minutes*, 1922, 39.

91. Synod of North Carolina *Minutes*, 1921, 613.

92. *See*, e.g., *The Charlotte News*, May 2, 1915, 6; *Asheville Gazette-News*, June 9, 1915, 6; *Durham Morning Herald*, February 15, 1921, 6.

93. Synod of North Carolina *Minutes*, 1921, 598.

94. PCUS *Digest*, 1965, 215.

95. Quoted in Thompson, *Presbyterians in the South*, III, 212. For a full treatment of McPheeters's views see "'Our Church Will Be on Trial': W.M. McPheeters and the Beginnings of Conservative Dissent in the Presbyterian Church in the United States," *The Journal of Presbyterian History*, vol. 84, no. 1 (Spring/Summer 2006), 52–66.

96. Beginning in 1883, the state's press, especially the religious but also the secular, began to direct its fire at "the devil in the church," in the words of the state's main Baptist organ. *The Biblical Recorder* (Raleigh), February 20, 1884, 2.

97. PCUS *Digest*, 1965, 6–8; Conser and Cain, *Presbyterians in North Carolina*, 181–82.

98. PC(USA), Office of Theology and Worship, ca. 2013, "Evolution Statement."

99. Synod of North Carolina, *Minutes*, 1925, 491, 503; The definitive work on this topic is Willard B. Gatewood, Jr., *Preachers, Pedagogues, and Politicians: the Evolution Controversy in North Carolina, 1920–1927* (Chapel Hill: University of North Carolina Press, 1966).

100. Conser and Cain, 175–76; George B. Watts, *The Waldenses of Valdese* (Charlotte, NC: Heritage Printers, 1965).

101. PCUS *Minutes*, 1870, 530.

102. The labyrinthine negotiations to 1965 are presented in the PCUS *Digest*, 1965, 389–432; *see also* Ernest Trice Thompson, "Presbyterians North and South—Efforts Toward Reunion," *Journal of Presbyterian History*, vol. 43, no. 1 (March 1965), 1–15. *See* Thompson, *Presbyterians in the South*, III, 559–82 for a detailed account of later negotiations, down to 1972.

103. Orange Presbytery considered the matter periodically (Stone, *Orange Presbytery*, 224–31), as did Concord Presbytery (Neill Roderick McGeachy, *Confronted by Challenge: A History of the Presbytery of Concord, 1795–1973* (n.p., The Presbytery, 1985), 266–71, hereinafter cited as McGeachy, *Confronted by Challenge*), and Wilmington Presbytery (John Roscoe Dail, comp., *A History of Wilmington Presbytery and Its Predecessors* (n.p., ca. 1984), 155–242, *passim*, hereinafter cited as Dail, *Wilmington Presbytery*; Conser and Cain, *Presbyterians in North Carolina*, 213–15, 219).

104. In 1950, the general assembly accused the federal council of "tending toward political socialism in this country ... contrary to our time-honored principles of free enterprise and representative democracy." PCUS *Digest*, 1965, 455–66. Mecklenburg Presbytery in 1930 blasted the council's leadership as being theologically liberal, and also in sympathy with Communism and "Russian Soviet propaganda." Mecklenburg Presbytery *Minutes*, 1930, 29; Stone, *Orange* Presbytery, 232–35; Dail, *History*, 143. See also Robert A. Schneider, "The Federal Council of Churches and American Presbyterians, 1900–1950," *The Journal of Presbyterian History*, vol. 84, no. 2 (Fall/Winter 2006), 103–22.

105. PCUS *Digest*, 1965, 473–77; Theodore A. Gill, Jr., "Journey of the WCC and PC(USA): 'A Drama with a Cast of Thousands,'" *The Journal of the Presbyterian History*, vol. 84, no. 2 (Fall/Winter 2006), 139–51.

106. PCUS *Digest*, 1965, 177–80.

107. Synod of North Carolina *Minutes*, 1867, 18–19; Conser and Cain, *Presbyterians in North Carolina*, 177.

108. McGeachy, *Confronted by Challenge*, 400.

109. Stone, *Orange Presbytery*, 251. Presbyterian reaction to the Kennedy-Nixon campaign of 1960 is chronicled in James S. Wolfe, "The Religious Issue Revisited: Presbyterian Responses to Kennedy's Presidential Campaign," *Journal of Presbyterian History*, vol. 57, no. 1 (Spring 1979), 1–18.

110. Clifton Kirkpatrick, "Presentation to His Holiness, John Paul II, on behalf of the Delegation from the Presbyterian Church (U.S.A.)," *The Journal of Presbyterian History*, vol. 80, no. 2 (Summer 2002), 103–04. *See also* the rest of this special number on Presbyterian and Roman Catholic relations, from which this article is taken. Synod of North Carolina *Minutes*, 1967, 180, 183; 1968, 179, 180; 1969, 203.

111. PCUS *Digest*, 1965, 20, 23, 24, 45, 55.

112. William E. Moore, *Presbyterian Digest of 1898*, 94; James H. Moorhead and Frederick J. Heuser, Jr., "Presbyterians and Mormons: An Introduction," *The Journal of Presbyterian History*, vol. 80, no. 4 (Winter 2002), 203–04.

113. Quoted in *Public Opinion*, vol. XXIV (January–June 1898), 434.

114. The Mormon faith is still outside the pale of true Christianity in the opinion of the anonymous author of "Mormon Beliefs: A Presbyterian View," *The Journal of Presbyterian History*, vol. 80, no. 4 (Winter 2002), 247–53.

115. PCUS *Digest*, 1965, 14–15.

116. William E. Moore, *The Presbyterian Digest of 1898* [PCUSA] (Philadelphia: Presbyterian Board of

Publication, 1905), 607–08; PCUS *Digest*, 1965, 192–99; Synod of North Carolina *Minutes*, 1866, 15; 1897, 205; 1910, 278; 1915, 314; 1920, 156; Stone, *Orange Presbytery*, 82.

117. PCUS *Digest,* 1965, 195, 197; Stone, *Orange Presbytery*, 82–83.

118. PC(USA) *Minutes*, 2012, 688, 1354.

119. Assemblies of both the PCUSA and PCUS repeatedly urged a strict observance of the Sabbath by society in general, as well as by church members. Moore, PCUSA *Digest,* 1886, 585, 761–67; PCUS *Digest,* 1965, 136, 237–59. The decline in an emphasis on Sabbath observance in the southern church is highlighted by the fact that the assembly's Permanent Committee on the Sabbath, created in 1878, was abolished in 1949. PCUS *Digest*, 1965, 237, 239.

120. Jack Rogers, "Biblical Interpretation regarding Homosexuality in the Recent History of the Presbyterian Church (U.S.A.)," *Review of Religious Research*, vol. 41, no. 2 (Dec. 1999), 223–38; "PC(USA) relaxes constitutional prohibition of gay and lesbian ordination," Presbyterian News Service, May 11, 2011; "Presbyterian Church (U.S.A.) approves marriage amendment," Presbyterian News Service, March 17, 2015; Fred W. Beuttler, "Making Theology Matter: Power, Polity, and the Theological Debate over Ordination of Homosexuals in the Presbyterian Church (U.S.A.)," *The Journal of Presbyterian History*, vol. 79, no. 1 (Spring 2001), 5–23.

121. PCUSA *Minutes,* 1869, 937; Presbyterians Pro-Life, "A Short History…" n.d., n.p.; PC(USA) *Minutes*, 2014, pp. 624–25; R. Frame, "Presbyterians Consider Four Views of Abortion," *Christianity Today*, 33, December 15, 1989, 52–55.

122. Presbyterian Church in America, "Position Papers, 1973–1998, Abortion," 2014; Evangelical Presbyterian Church, "Abortion," 2013.

123. PCUSA *Records*, 1841, 359; PCUSA *Digest*, 1898, 618–30; PCUS *Digest*, 1965, 142–45.

124. PCUSA *Minutes*, 1877, 558; 1898, 104; 1902, 102; 1903, 159; 1905, 180.

125. PCUS *Digest*, 1965, 144; Coker, "The Sinnott Case," *passim.*

126. PCUS *Digest*, 1965, 145; Daniel J. Whitener, "North Carolina Prohibition Election of 1881 and its Aftermath," *The North Carolina Historical Review*, vol. 11, no. 2 (April 1934) 71–93; Minutes of meetings, Synod of North Carolina, *passim*; Stone, *Orange Presbytery*, 83–85; McGeachy, *Confronted by Challenge*, 372–73.

127. Synod of North Carolina *Minutes*, 1894, 299; 1896, 60.

128. For the contribution of a North Carolinian to the development of the social gospel *see* Peter H. Hobbie, "Walter L. Lingle, Presbyterians, and the Enigma of the Social Gospel in the South," *American Presbyterians*, vol. 69, no. 3 (Fall 1991), 191–202.

129. William S. Powell, comp. and ed., *Dictionary of North Carolina Biography*, 6 vols. (Chapel Hill: University of North Carolina Press, 1979–96) 4: 157–58; see also Herbert J. Doherty, Jr., "Alexander J. McKelway: Preacher to Progressive," *The Journal of Southern History*, vol. 24 no. 2 (May 1958), 177–90.

130. Quoted in Elizabeth Hoey Davidson, "The Child-Labor Problem in North Carolina, 1883–1903," *The North Carolina Historical Review*, vol. 13, no. 2 (April 1936), 105–21. *See also* the same author, "Child-Labor Reforms in North Carolina since 1903," *The North Carolina Historical Review*, vol. 114, no. 2 (April 1937), 109–34. An influential critic of industrial society generally, both north and south, was the southern theologian and polemicist Robert Lewis Dabney, whose incisive arguments resonate even today. See David H. Overy, "When the Wicked Beareth Rule: A Southern Critique of Industrial America," *The Journal of Presbyterian History*, vol. 48 no. 2 (Summer 1970), 130–42.

131. Synod of North Carolina, *Minutes,* 1906, 398. This was the first time that the evils of child labor had been considered by the synod, although the question had been gaining national attention since at least the 1880s.

132. *See* Synod of North Carolina, *Minutes*, 1905, 277, for one example (of hundreds) of the use of the formula, still in use today.

133. Synod of North Carolina *Minutes*, 1907, 603.

134. PCUS *Digest*, 1965, 137–40. For a survey of Presbyterian social awareness and activity see Dale T. Irvin, "Social Witness Policies—an Historical Overview," *The Journal of Presbyterian History*, vol. 57, no. 3 (Fall 1979), 353–403.

Quakers

MAX L. CARTER

Quakers Emerge in the Carolina Backcountry

Conditions were right in the seventeenth-century Carolina backcountry for religious dissenters and nonconformists such as the people "vulgarly known as Quakers." Unlike in other colonies where the established church held sway, the Church of England had little influence on the frontier. The grant given in 1663 by King Charles II allowed religious toleration, a condition that the proprietors hoped would attract settlers. John Locke, the Enlightenment philosopher, served as secretary to the Lords Proprietors of the Carolinas, and his influence can be seen in provisos for a diversity of opinions in the colony.

To this liberal attitude towards dissent was added the physical reality of the back-country. It was an undeveloped area, one that would not be attractive to an ordained clergy trained at university, accustomed to the amenities of the manse and a cultivated congregation. This would make it naturally attractive to those nonconformists who eschewed an ordained clergy and all the trappings of established religion. The Carolinas were tailor-made for Quakers.

What became officially known as the Religious Society of Friends began as a mid-seventeenth-century movement in England to restore "primitive Christianity." Influenced by themes of anti-authoritarianism and the rights of the common citizenry in the English Civil War, Quakerism grew among a populace tired of war, disgusted by the hypocrisy they witnessed among professing Christians, and emboldened by other movements seeking a leveling of opportunity in a class-ridden society. The word *Quaker* was initially given to the group as a pejorative term. It derided their claims to the direct inspiration of God and the Holy Spirit's moving men and women alike, not only to minister out of the silence of their "waiting on the Lord" in worship, but also at times to tremble and quake as the Spirit came over them.

Among the first Quakers was George Fox (1624–1691) who, after a time of spiritual seeking, had an "opening" in 1647, an epiphany that what he had been searching for in others' religious experience or in sacred texts was available to him directly from Christ, unmediated by Church or religious hierarchy. This "Inward Light of Christ" was believed to be universal, available to all who would turn to the inner promptings of the Light. Because it was from God, it took precedence over the doctrines of the Church, the Bible, and the decrees of "professors" of religion. It was sufficient salvation for all who were empowered by that Light to overcome their darkness and seek a more perfected life. This

Light, experienced as an Inward Teacher, Redeemer, and Prophet, led Quakers to oppose war as inconsistent with the teachings of Christ, acknowledge the spiritual equality of men and women, demand absolute integrity in all matters, and lead lives of plainness.

As Fox and other "convinced" Quakers shared their message and their experience, the movement grew in great numbers in the 1650s, spreading throughout England and into the English colonies. Quaker "Publishers of Truth" visited Virginia in 1656 and were in New England in such numbers by 1659 that it was made a capital offense for a Quaker to return to Massachusetts a third time following banishment. The Puritans did not want a large population of nonconformists who refused to serve in the militia, did not recognize the authority of the ordained clergy, and would not pay tithes to the established church. In 1659 and 1660, William Robinson, William Leddra, Marmaduke Stevenson, and Mary Dyer were hanged on Boston Common for being Quaker. Many others were severely tortured and banished.

Probably to escape such persecution in New England, in 1665 the Henry Phillips (Phelps) family settled in Perquimans County near where the town of Hertford is now located. They are the first known Quakers to reside in the Carolinas. It was seven years before they saw another Friend, that being William Edmundson, a noted Irish Quaker who traveled widely to share the Quaker message. Shortly after Edmundson's visit in 1672, the leader of the Quaker movement, George Fox, came to the Carolinas. The two gathered the first "convincements" of local residents, thus beginning the growth of Quakerism in the area.

Fox's visit occurred after an extended journey through Virginia. In what is now Suffolk County, just across the North Carolina state line, he preached to a gathering at "Summers' Towne," which resulted in the establishment of Somerton Friends Meeting, a congregation that has been in continuous existence since then and is now a part of North Carolina Yearly Meeting (Friends United Meeting). After crossing into the Carolinas, Fox had other public gatherings and disputations with local officials. An entry in his journal gives some sense of the mixed reception he received:

> And from thence, we passed on the 25th of the 9th month down the River Maratick [now the Roanoke River] ... and came to the governor's house [Peter Carteret in Edonton].... And there was a doctor that did dispute with us, which was of great service and occasion of opening much to the people concerning the Light and the Spirit. And he so opposed it in every one, that I called an Indian ... and asked him [if there were that in him which reproved him when he did wrong].... And he said there was such a thing in him....[1]

Thus began a rapid growth of Quaker influence in the Carolinas. Many in the local population were convinced by the Quaker message, and not always for deeply religious reasons: Not paying church tithes, not having to support an ordained clergy, and not serving in the militia were attractive elements to some. Others found that Quakerism "spoke to their spiritual condition" and were satisfied with a simple faith that did not require a divinity school–educated leadership, outward ordinances, or elaborate edifices for worship.

By the 1680s, the Carolinas had a Quaker governor, John Archdale, who served two terms through the 1690s. Eventually the colonial Assembly was largely Quaker, and when North Carolina Yearly Meeting was established in 1698, it was the first organized European religious body in the colony, leading to the popular joke among twenty-first-century Friends that "we're hardly organized now!" In 1705, Friends in Pasquotank County established the Symon(d)'s Creek School, the first public school in the Carolinas.

Such a rapid growth of Quakerism in the colony did not amuse some in England, and missionaries from the Church of England were dispatched to try to convert the dissenters back to orthodoxy. The new Friends proved to be incorrigible, and the representatives of the Society for the Propagation of Christian Knowledge and the Society for the Propagation of the Gospel reported that the colony was "under a dark cloud of Quakerism." Resorting to other means to save the Carolinas from this "dark cloud," laws were implemented to require loyalty oaths of all colonists. Their testimony of integrity not allowing them to swear an oath, and taking seriously Jesus's commandment in the Gospels not to, Quakers were dispensed from government.

Banished from government, Quakers continued nonetheless to flourish in the backcountry, eventually establishing twelve meetings in Perquimans and Pasquotank counties, with others dotting the eastern part of North Carolina down the coast and inland as far along as tributaries of the Neuse River. The future of Quakerism in the Old North State, however, was not to be along the Atlantic Ocean but rather in the Piedmont.

Quaker Migration into Piedmont North Carolina

During the 1740s and 1750s in southeastern Pennsylvania, population growth, land costs, and frontier violence encouraged large numbers of Quakers to take the Philadelphia Wagon Road through the Shenandoah Valley into central North Carolina. Soon Friends meetings were being established in present-day Alamance and Guilford counties. By the mid-eighteenth century, a sectarian group rather than missionary-minded Quaker growth in the Piedmont came by way of this immigration. Cane Creek Friends Meeting was established in 1751 near today's Snow Camp. New Garden Friends Meeting was organized in 1754 in western Guilford County, more than fifty years before Greensboro came into existence. Both continue to be vital Friends Meetings today. Providence, Deep River, Centre, and other meetings were settled in rapid succession through the 1750s, each also continuing to be vital congregations.

The next wave of Quaker immigration came from the island of Nantucket. Like southeastern Pennsylvania, the island was becoming overcrowded, and whaling was moving farther and farther offshore. Scores of Nantucket families with the names of Coffin, Starbuck, Macy, Folger, and Gardner joined their fellow religionists in the Piedmont, with the flood of emigration from the island peaking in 1772.

Escaping the frontier wars in Pennsylvania and the British battleships encircling Nantucket, Quakers who settled in the Piedmont soon found themselves confronted by violence in North Carolina. The Regulator Movement (1765–1771) tempted some Friends to take up arms, but overwhelmingly the testimony against preparing for or participating in war held firm among the Quaker population. A greater test was coming, though.

With the outbreak of the Revolutionary War and its southern campaign, Quakers were faced again with demands to take up arms, swear oaths of allegiance, and provide support for the war effort. The advice to Friends from the leadership of the Yearly Meeting was unwavering: "Thus we may with Christian firmness withstand and refuse to submit to the arbitrary injunctions and ordinances of men who assume to themselves the power of compelling others ... to join in carrying on war, and of prescribing modes of determining our religious principles...."[2]

Friends suffered greatly for their neutrality. Fines were levied, and their farms and households were looted by foraging armies. The impact was especially felt as the British and American forces faced each other in the consequential Battle of Guilford Court House in March 1781. Skirmishes prior to the major battle were fought in the New Garden Quaker community the morning of March 15, with scores left dead and dying for the Quaker community to tend to. In the New Garden Friends graveyard is a mass grave of both Tory and Revolutionary soldiers. Estimates are that between 125 and 150 men are buried there together. Some Friends contracted camp fever and smallpox from tending to the soldiers. Richard Williams, who sold the land for the New Garden graveyard and meetinghouse, was one of those, dying from smallpox contracted from a British officer he and his wife tended in their farm house.

The battles resulted in interesting stories of resistance to and participation in the violence. A story handed down through generations of the Mendenhall family tells of the foraging British army, camped out at the Deep River Friends Meeting in western Guilford County, taking all the provisions of James and Judith Mendenhall's mill on the Deep River and then making off with their last milk cow. With a family to feed, Judith, of sturdy Nantucket Gardner stock, marched up the hill to the headquarters of the British army, demanded her cow back, and returned home, leading the cow.[3]

On the morning of the major battle, William Armfield, whose farm had also been overrun, walked out the door with his hunting rifle, telling his wife he was "going hunting." Returning that evening after participating in the fighting, he responded to his wife's query about whether he had secured any game by saying, "I didn't shoot anything worth keeping."[4] By contrast, when one of the manufacturers of those famous Quaker hunting rifles, Matthew Osborne, learned that a gun he had sold to a neighbor had been used in the fighting, he bought the gun back and broke it so that it would never again be used in violation of Quaker testimony.[5]

Antislavery Work and the Beginnings of Migration to the North

Revolutionary War battles were not the only challenges facing Friends in the latter part of the century. A growing conviction among Quakers that slavery was inconsistent with the will of God and in clear opposition to the Golden Rule had them wrestling with their consciences and with prevailing culture and law. Quakers in the plantation area of eastern North Carolina owned slaves, while the Friends who settled the Piedmont had come from areas where opposition to slavery had grown in strength. Soon, even those who owned slaves were feeling compelled to free them. The influential abolitionist Quaker John Woolman (1720–1772) visited Friends in the Carolinas in 1757 to convince them to end slaveholding. In a letter to Friends ahead of his visit, he located the desire for slaveholding in greed as well as violence and noted the effects it had not only on the enslaved but also the slave owner:

> Where people let loose their minds after the love of outward things and are more engaged in pursuing the profits and seeking the friendships of this world than to be inwardly acquainted with the way of true peace,...[t]heir examples are often hurtful to others, and their treasures thus collected do many times prove dangerous snares to their children."[6]

By the late 1770s, the combined efforts of Friends' opposition to slavery from within and outside North Carolina led North Carolina Yearly Meeting to adopt an antislavery position. One could not remain a Friend in good standing while involved in slavery. Given laws preventing the freeing of slaves, Quakers were faced with a dilemma. At first, they advocated for sending the enslaved to Africa or the Caribbean. That proved to be unacceptable. By 1808, the solution was to turn title of slaves over to the Yearly Meeting, thus observing the letter of the law but allowing the formerly enslaved to live freely, becoming known as "Quaker free Negroes." (At the height of the plan, the Yearly Meeting was one of the largest slave owners in the state.)

Merely freeing their own slaves was not enough for some Friends, however. The sin of slavery was too egregious to be satisfied merely with excising it from among the Religious Society of Friends. In 1816, the state's first Manumission Society was formed in the Centre Friends Meeting community, and Quakers such as Vestal Coffin of New Garden were actively involved beyond Quaker circles in advocating legally for the end of slavery and using legal means to manumit the enslaved. In one famous case, Coffin and fellow Friends George Swain and Enoch Macy used the courts to attain the freedom of Benjamin Benson, a free black who had been kidnapped and sold back into slavery. Benson's release in 1820 is believed to be the first case in the United States of a black person's use of the courts to gain freedom from slavery.

Other Friends were not satisfied with the slow processes of the law in gaining enslaved persons their freedom. Already by the early 1800s, fugitives from slavery were finding their way to Quaker communities to seek refuge from oppression. Levi Coffin (1798–1877) of the New Garden community recalled his own encounter with these fugitives when he was a young boy:

> Runaway slaves used frequently to conceal themselves in the woods and thickets in the vicinity of New Garden, waiting opportunities to make their escape to the North.... My father, in common with other farmers in that part of the country, allowed his hogs to run in the woods, and I often went out to feed them. My sack of corn generally contained supplies of bacon and corn bread for the slaves, and many a time I sat in the thickets with them ... and listened to the stories they told of hard masters and cruel treatment....[7]

In 1819, the first known incident in the state of what became known as the Underground Railroad occurred when a free black named John Dimrey was kidnapped in the New Garden community, and his daughter ran to get the help of Vestal Coffin. Coffin interceded, distracting the kidnappers long enough for Dimrey to escape; later that night he met with Dimrey and provided instructions on how to get to freedom in Richmond, Indiana, a town established by North Carolina Quakers a decade before. Until his death in 1826, Coffin worked with his cousin Levi and other abolitionists in the community to funnel hundreds of fugitives along the Underground Railroad to free states.

The route that fugitives took to freedom in the North was the same route (over the Blue Ridge Mountains to Charleston, West Virginia, along the Kanawha River to the Ohio River, and by boat or foot to Cincinnati and then northward) that Quakers themselves were taking in greater and greater numbers to leave the slave culture of the South. Already in the 1790s, some Friends from New Garden had removed to eastern Tennessee, where there was less impact of slavery, and founded the community of Friendsville. In 1803, a traveling Friends minister named Zachariah Dicks prophesied in the Bush River, South Carolina, meetinghouse, "O Bush River! Bush River! How hath thy beauty faded away and gloomy darkness eclipsed thy day."[8] Dicks foresaw the coming of war because of slavery, and the large and prosperous Bush River Quaker community took his warning seriously, completely abandoning the settlement within years, ending the Quaker presence in the Palmetto State. Some of those Friends settled in Bush Hill (now Archdale), North Carolina; most went to Indiana Territory.

Quaker migration to free states reached flood tide in the 1820s. Levi Coffin and his family left in 1826, the last of the Coffin family to reside in North Carolina. By 1831, so few Quakers remained in North Carolina that few teachers or students populated the Quaker schools that were said to provide a "guarded and religious education" to Friends children. The Yearly Meeting committee on education recommended that a boarding school be established so there would be at least one place in the state for families to send their children for proper Quaker formation. In 1834, a charter was received for a school for such purposes, and in 1837, New Garden Boarding School opened in western Guilford County, serving twenty-five boys and twenty-five girls, the first co-educational school in the South. It was the predecessor to Guilford College.

Quaker migration not only led to the establishment of a noted educational institution, it also led to a lessening of abolitionist fervor among Friends. Activist Friends left the state, leaving behind those who were less willing to take the risks of breaking the law, even while some quietly assisted escaping slaves. In the 1830s, the Yearly Meeting officially began discouraging Friends from breaking the law, even in the cause of liberty for the enslaved.

As the Civil War approached, the Carolina Quaker population continued to dwindle with emigration, not only owing to antislavery sentiments and the dark clouds of war, but also for economic reasons. A primarily agricultural people, Friends were seeing the hard clay soil produce fewer bountiful crops, and the deep loam of the Midwest beckoned. By some historical estimates, a population of some twenty thousand Quakers in the South around 1800 was reduced to fewer than two thousand members by the end of the Civil War.

Effects of the Civil War

The reduction in numbers threatened even the boarding school that had been established to provide an education for the remnant community's children. At the dawn of the 1860s, the school's board of trustees decided to sell the property, pay off the growing indebtedness, and be done with the attempt to maintain a Quaker educational presence in North Carolina. Two families, however, deeply committed to keeping the school open, took New Garden Boarding School on their own shoulders—Jonathan and Elizabeth Cox and Nereus and Orianna Mendenhall. Their decision meant that they would remain through the devastation of the Civil War. Such commitment deserves some expansion of the story.

Nereus Mendenhall, Principal of New Garden, had determined that he should remove his family to the North and join his brother Richard, a prosperous businessman, and cousin Samuel Hill, a prosperous lawyer, in Minnesota. Mendenhall himself was well positioned to thrive in the North. Haverford College–educated, he was not only a teacher but also a trained physician and engineer. He and Orianna had sold most of their belongings, packed up personal items, and had their boxes waiting at the railroad station near the boarding school. On the day of departure, however, Nereus took one last walk through the school building and could not bring himself to leave, knowing it would mean its closing. He told his wife about his decision, and she fully supported him. They unpacked their belongings, borrowed household furnishings, and remained.

New Garden Boarding School remained open throughout the war as a result not only of the Mendenhalls' and Coxes' decision to stay, but also because the young men did not march off to war, often hiding in the New Garden woods to avoid conscription while Nereus himself refused induction into the Confederate army and held Confederate draft officers at bay. Challenged themselves to provide food for their own families and the students (school histories tell of times when all there was to eat was green corn foraged from surrounding fields), Orianna and Elizabeth hung baskets of food in the woods for any who might be hiding there, whether students or fugitives from the war or slavery.

Meanwhile, Friends elsewhere in the state were faced with their own challenges. As with the Revolutionary War, Quaker pacifism was not met with great sympathy, although the Yearly Meeting appealed to the Confederate Congress for understanding:

> Your petitioners respectfully show that it is one of our fundamental religious principles to bear a faithful testimony against all wars and fightings, and that in consequence we cannot aid in carrying on any war.... This is no new principle of our Society, but one which was adopted at its rise, as the doctrine taught by our Saviour ... and has ever been and is now held as one of our fundamental and vital principles, and one we cannot yield or compromise in any degree whatsover....[9]

Such petitions were not received favorably. Some Friends "paid a substitute"—in reality, a substantial fine of hundreds of dollars; some worked in shoe factories or salt works as "alternative service"; some were imprisoned and tortured; a few were executed. Addison Boren and John Woody were among Friends from the New Garden community who walked to Indiana to evade the draft, while another New Garden Friend, John Van Lindley, went to Missouri and joined the Union cavalry. A few Quakers engaged in the first known instance of cross-dressing: A Randolph County Quaker, going "bushwhacking" in the woods to escape the draft, kept a close eye on his family as they kept the farm going. During planting and harvesting, he would don women's clothing and, in such disguise, help his wife and children with the work, then escape back into hiding.

Some Quakers were forced to march with the army into the North, threatened with execution frequently for refusing to carry a weapon. One such person was Thomas Hinshaw, who with other Quakers was marched to Gettysburg, where, after the disastrous defeat of the Confederate army, they were arrested and thrown in a Union jail. Abraham Lincoln himself interceded and ordered their release. The freed men found their way to Indiana, where they remained through the duration of the war. Hinshaw's young wife learned of her husband's safety; packing up a wagon and a nursing child, she traveled through both Confederate and Union lines to reunite with her husband. After the war, they returned to North Carolina.

Learning of the war's impact on the Quaker community in the South, a committee of Friends from Baltimore, led by prominent businessman Francis T. King (1817–1891), organized relief supplies, and King, provided with a pass across Union lines by Abraham Lincoln, delivered them to Friends in North Carolina. Returning to Baltimore, he brought letters and packages to Confederate soldiers in Federal prisons.

War's end brought little relief to the devastated Quaker community. Migration to the North increased, whole trains being booked with Friends desperate to find a better life. All but one of the Friends meetings in Pasquotank and Perquimans counties, once the center of North Carolina Quakerism, disappeared with the migrations. The new center of Friends in the state was the Piedmont. Francis T. King continued his relief work through the Baltimore Association to Advise and Assist Friends in the Southern States and dedicated the remaining years of his life to rebuild the remnant community of Friends in North Carolina. Through his efforts the equivalent of several million dollars was raised to address the pressing needs of Quakers in the South.

The Baltimore Association of Friends and the Beginning of Great Change

To stem the tide of emigration, King knew that the agricultural economy had to be improved. The Baltimore Association thus bought an old Quaker farm near High Point in 1867 and turned it into a model of modern, scientific agriculture. A farm house, mills, barns, and other outbuildings were constructed; a farm manager from Maine was brought to oversee the work; newsletters and workshops spread the knowledge of new methods of animal husbandry, rotation and manuring of crops, and other methods of improving the soil and crop and herd yields. The enterprise was a huge success during the two decades of the model farm's operation.

Apart from the Baltimore Association's work, other Friends from the North responded to needs created by the Civil War and its aftermath. Philadelphia Friend Yardley Warner (1815–1885) purchased land in Greensboro to create a planned community for those freed from slavery; the community became known as Warnersville. Similar efforts were made by other Friends, resulting in black communities in otherwise "white sides of town." Many Quaker teachers headed into the state, establishing schools for "freedmen," some through the Freedmen's Aid Society and others independently. One such school in Asheboro eventually moved to High Point, where it became the William Penn School, lasting until integration in the late 1960s. Quaker involvement in the origins of Winston-Salem State University and North Carolina A & T State University was also significant.

But it wasn't only the devastated rural economy and the needs of the emancipated that had to be addressed. The Quaker community was spiritually depleted, and the once thriving Quaker educational system was reduced to the bare-bones boarding school at New Garden. King and his committee addressed those needs, too. Dilapidated meetinghouses were repaired and new ones built. Literary societies were started, and other programs of self-improvement were initiated by the Baltimore Association's first superintendent, Joseph Moore (1832–1905), a Friends minister from Indiana who left his position as a professor of biology at Earlham College to oversee the work in North Carolina. The story is told of one elderly Quaker woman who, after attending one of Moore's lectures, commented, "Why, I can't believe he has a college education, I could understand everything he said!"

One of the singular achievements of the Baltimore Association's work was in rebuilding the Friends school system. New Garden Boarding School was renovated and re-equipped with new instruments, furnishings, and curricula. New schools were built using the same architectural plans as developed for new meetinghouses. Textbooks were published; "normal schools" trained teachers; a superintendent of instruction oversaw the system. Soon there was a Quaker school system numbering more than seventy schools, serving Quaker communities and communities of the recently emancipated, several years before North Carolina's public-school system. It must be noted, however, that the schools were segregated. (More about that to come.)

The sum effect of these efforts was that the tide of emigration was, indeed, stopped. But a new problem surfaced, one that threatened the whole project. After successfully serving as Superintendent of the Baltimore Association's work, Joseph Moore was called back to Earlham as president. In his place came another Hoosier, Allen Jay (1831–1910). He continued the work started by King and Moore, including extensive fund-raising. In 1870, upon returning from a trip to solicit funds in New York, Jay's wife met him at the train station with news that "…the Methodists were holding a revival meeting at Trinity College, some three miles from Springfield [the site of the model farm and the head-quarters of the association's work], and that some of our young Friends had gone to the mourners bench and professed conversion, and that some of the parents had forbidden their children to go, but that the young people and some who were older had gone in spite of the counsels of the older people."[10]

At the time, Friends in the South were still in what historians of Quakersim call "Quietism." Defined by carefully constructed social boundary markers of plain speech (thee, thou, and thy), plain dress, renunciation of the outward forms of Protestantism, testimonies against war and oaths, and a deep suspicion of "the world," Quietist Friends avoided assemblies with "the world's people," worldly entertainments, "enthusiastic" religion, and even marrying non–Friends. The Methodist revivals were a direct affront to such Quietist Quaker culture. Friends' worship was based on a deep silence and "expectant waiting" on God's Spirit to move. There was no programmed message; no liturgy except the silence; no outward sacraments; no music. After some 150 years of the development of this culture, only a few men and women in each meeting were "recorded" as having gifts of ministry, and only they were expected to give ministry out of the silence. Even they were hesitant to speak, lest they "outrun the Guide" and preach out of their own will and "flesh." Sometimes, meetings for worship would be held for weeks and months on end without anyone's assurance that they had a message from God. This meant that the worship, often much longer than an hour's length, would proceed in absolute silence.

Imagine, then, young Friends who had endured the hardships of the recent war, were denied the "entertainments of the world," and who sat through months of silent worship without ever hearing music, vocal prayer, or invigorating preaching. And then the Methodist revivals came to town. It was the social event of the year; everyone was going, it was exciting; it was literally the only show in town. No wonder the young people were heading to the Trinity Revivals and coming under "conviction." No wonder the Quietist elders were convinced that their children should refrain from such worldly activity.

This was Allen Jay's dilemma. The work of the Baltimore Association to revive the Southern Friends community would come to naught if they lost the next generation, but the culture was such that he could not force "new measures" on them. If the elders persisted in their opposition, the young people would flee Friends. If Jay didn't do something about the young people's "apostasy," he would lose the confidence of the Quaker community, and his work would be compromised.

Jay's decision was to go to the elders in the community and explain the problem, get their permission to allow the young people to attend the revivals if they promised to remain Friends, and accompany the attendees of the revivals himself to assure that they felt the support of the community—and keep an eye on the young people personally.

Fortunately, in his time as Superintendent, Jay had won the deep trust and devotion of Friends, and his plan was accepted.

In the ensuing revival meetings, many more young Friends experienced conversion, but all remained Friends, as they had promised their beloved Allen Jay. This, however, had a ripple effect even on the Quietist elders and the young people's families. It moved Jay to believe it would be good to hold a series of special meetings for worship in the Quaker community. Again, Jay approached the leaders at Springfield to get their permission, promising not to force new measures on anyone but remaining open to the Spirit's leading should anyone call for a hymn, be moved to preach themselves, or come forward to a "mourners bench."

Permission was granted, and Jay led a series of meetings in the Springfield meetinghouse. Jay describes the sequence of events:

> … a meeting was announced for that night. It was largely attended, and a deep feeling came over all. The next night, a young man came up and knelt down by me, and in deep contrition asked me to pray for him. The next night three came forward without any invitation, thus establishing an altar of prayer without any action on my part. But the climax was reached on the third or fourth night, when someone broke out singing. My wife came to me and asked me to stop it. My reply was, "I did not start it and I shall not stop it."[11]

Subsequently, Jay (who, incidentally, was born with a hare lip and cleft palate, but witnesses to his preaching maintained that he was so moving they barely noticed his lisp) was asked by religious leaders in neighboring High Point to lead a community revival. He agreed to on the Quietist conditions that he would not prepare a sermon; he would not be given any instructions on scripture to use or topics to address; and that all would be dependent on the Spirit's leading. The conditions were agreed to, and Jay successfully preached nightly for nearly four weeks, with the result of many coming to conversion.

The revival spread, and soon the Quaker community grew by thousands, almost all coming into Quakerism from outside the closed confines of the culture. The impact was inevitable. Unused to peculiar Quaker ways, new converts began questioning the peculiar testimonies of Friends, and as their numbers overwhelmed the Quietist Friends (and Quietist Friends, themselves, "converted"), ancient Quaker prohibitions vanished almost overnight. Music and prepared sermons were accepted; plain speech and dress disappeared as "outward forms" and were associated with "works righteousness"; visiting evangelists were pressed to stay beyond the duration of revivals to instruct new converts, inevitably leading to a "settled" pastorate. Combined with the effects of changes in the broader society (railroads, national journals, a changing economy, the decline in isolation of rural communities), the influx of new members proved to be a hinge in Quaker history.

Added to these factors, there was also an influx of preachers from "outside," in some cases, women from other denominations who were denied opportunity to have authority in the church, whereas Friends welcomed women in the ministry. In other cases, the congregational polity of Friends, minus bishops or other forms of a leadership hierarchy, attracted preachers from other denominations who wanted to assert their own authority. And where evangelical fervor led to the establishment of new meetings—as "church plants," outreach to mill villages, or in the mountains—there were no residual Quietist cultural tendencies to mitigate against a full embrace of mainstream Protestantism. The overall effect was that Friends in the South would never be the same again.

Such enormous change brought about inevitable tensions in the Quaker community. Friends such as Joseph Moore, who returned to North Carolina in the 1880s to help New Garden Boarding School transition to Guilford College, Nereus Mendenhall, his daughter Mary Mendenhall Hobbs and her husband Lewis Lyndon Hobbs, and Allen Jay himself favored "renewal" among Friends but were wary of the excesses of revivalism. Others embraced the growing Holiness revival and wanted to see its emphases expressed among Friends: entire sanctification, rejection of any forms of works righteousness, and new measures for bringing people to salvation, including the techniques developed by revival preachers such as Charles Finney. A few, such as Holiness Quaker preacher David B. Updegraff and his supporter, North Carolina–born-and-bred Friend Dougan Clark, Jr., advocated for "liberty" in the use of the outward ordinances of water baptism and the Lord's Supper.

In 1887, a conference was called of Friends who adhered to the branch of Quakerism that had embraced an evangelical theology as articulated by English Quaker Joseph John Gurney (1788–1847). This included Friends in North Carolina, whether "renewal" or "revival" Quakers. Through the influence of such patriarchs as Nathan Hunt (1758–1853), Quakers in North Carolina had avoided the various separations that had wracked Friends in the wider North American Friends community in the nineteenth century. They remained firmly "Orthodox" and Gurneyite through the century, while meetings accepted or rejected the new measures on their own.

These Gurneyite Friends gathered in Richmond, Indiana, in the fall of 1887 to determine how to define their Quaker faith in light of the enormous changes that had occurred. The conference embraced a thoroughly evangelical statement of faith while affirming traditional Friends testimonies against war and the taking of oaths. The doctrine of entire sanctification was rejected, as were allowances for the practice of the outward ordinances. On the whole, the resulting Richmond Declaration of Faith looked very much like standard Protestantism, minus the Lord's Supper and baptism. Friends of the Gurneyite variety had turned from being a sect to being a denomination. As representatives from North Carolina returned home and reported on the results of the conference, North Carolina Yearly Meeting approved the Declaration as its own.

As a result of the Richmond conference, a denominational structure began to develop, including a central office in Richmond, Indiana, and the creation of a uniform "discipline" to be observed by constituent meetings. In 1902, that structure was named the Five Years Meeting of Friends (indicative of its frequency). Remaining Quietist Friends and meetings balked. They had accommodated the great changes in the Friends community in North Carolina by maintaining their own observance of traditional Quakerism while other meetings embraced a settled pastorate, music, programmed worship, and evangelical mission work. "Live and let live" was their approach, even though some refused to provide funding for Yearly Meeting projects that went against their Quietist tendencies.

Separation and Growing Assimilation

A first separation among Friends in North Carolina occurred as the Five Years Meeting sent down the Uniform Discipline in 1904. That was not Quietist polity. Theirs was "bottom up," not "top down." Whole meetings left the main body, and others split over the different emphases in their membership. It was a sad rending in some cases of families. The "Conservative" Friends, as they came to be called, were in the distinct minority, but there was strength enough that several Conservative meetinghouses were built, along with the few entire meetings that remained Quietist. For a time, an intentional community of Conservative Friends supported its own boarding school in the eastern part of Randolph County.

Inevitably, such a separation leads to each remaining group developing an identity around the extremes of the previous spectrum of faith and practice. Without the ameliorating influence of "the other," the larger body of Friends appeared more and more Protestant, while the smaller body retained separatist peculiarities, including a long retention of plainness in dress, speech, meetinghouse architecture, and silent, waiting worship. The larger body, on the other hand, continued to assimilate into the Christian mainstream, its worship reflecting the Methodists and Baptists around them, their new meetinghouses looking more like the architectural style of other Protestant bodies. In essence, as some have described it, Quakers in North Carolina were like tofu: possessing substance, but absorbing flavor from the culture in which they were simmering at the time.

This basic assimilation meant that in social terms, Friends remained segregated as segregation became the law of the state. Meetings had no black members, and even black Friends meetings were discouraged. Sadly, Friends expressed the same racism as the wider society, their antislavery history notwithstanding. Guilford College remained segregated until 1962. In the main body of Friends, Quaker "peculiarities" of dress and speech disappeared, the "thees" and "thys" remaining only as endearments in some families. When the United States entered World War I, many young men joined the military.

An example of this development can be seen in the experience of George Levering, an evangelical Friends pastor who served Asheboro Street Friends Meeting in Greensboro (now First Friends) during the war. A committed Christian pacifist himself, Levering preached against buying war bonds. He was pilloried in the Greensboro press, and even members of his congregation opposed him. Experiencing extreme stress from the situation, he took a leave from his pastorate and retreated with his wife and children to an orchard operated by his brother. There he died, it is reported by family, of a stress heart attack.[12] The meeting provided no insurance or pension for the widow and children. Emily Levering eventually found employment as matron of a women's residence hall at Guilford College.

World War II saw a similar mixed response from the Quaker community. Many young men performed alternative service as conscientious objectors in Civilian Public Service camps in the Blue Ridge Mountains, one of which was supervised by Raymond Binford, a former president of Guilford College. William Edgerton, a Winston-Salem Friend and Guilford College graduate, served as a non-combatant in Europe and was one of the people who discovered the Germans' use of youth hostels for experimentation in eugenics. Many more, however, entered direct military service. One person of note, Greensboro Friend Mary Nicholson, joined the Air Transport Auxiliary of the Royal Air Force and died in a plane crash in England in 1943 while ferrying a war plane from the factory.

Into the middle of the twentieth century, the main body of Friends in North Carolina continued its assimilation, hastened in many instances by more and more non–Friends ministers coming into Quaker pastorates, often from Fundamentalist or Pentecostal backgrounds. Meanwhile, in urban areas, especially closer to colleges such as Guilford, more liberal influences were being felt. Tensions began growing under the surface in the Five Years Meeting (FYM) body of Friends in the state, even while strong leadership sought to hold things together. Inevitably, though, broader social forces, often masking as theology, began rending the fabric of the community.

Race Issues

One of the first issues to take prominence was the issue of race. At the annual sessions of North Carolina Yearly Meeting of Friends (FYM) in August of 1949, a young lawyer named James Mattocks rose during a business session to alert Friends to an impending court case that would certainly lead to the desegregation of public schools in the United States. That case would later be known as the 1954 Supreme Court ruling in *Brown vs. Board of Education*. Friends should be at the forefront of assuring that desegregation occurred appropriately and peacefully, Mattocks urged.[13]

Most rural areas remained averse to any change in the culture, as did many in urban areas. The "minority/majority" split mirrored the "gradualist/abolitionist" split among Friends in the early nineteenth century, as some favored immediacy while others didn't want to get ahead of the culture. Greensboro, and particularly the community around Guilford College, was the center of attempts at change. In 1953, J. Floyd Moore, a professor of religion at Guilford College and native North Carolina Quaker, wrote a letter to the Guilford Board of Trustees urging desegregation of the college. It never had a chance. The Board consisted entirely of white Quakers, many of them conservative businessmen, the most influential of whom served as mayor of Greensboro, believed in so-called "separate but equal" (he was simultaneously chair of the Guilford Board and of the board of the historically black institution now known as North Carolina A&T State University), and had a reputation as a landlord of sub-standard housing for minorities.

Meanwhile, Friends primarily in the New Garden community were working with the American Friends Service Committee (AFSC), a Quaker peace and relief organization headquartered in Philadelphia, to bring about the desegregation of public schools as mandated by the 1954 Supreme Court ruling. In 1955, the AFSC brought Eleanor Roosevelt to Greensboro to speak on civil rights. Her address was held in the meetinghouse of North Carolina Yearly Meeting (FYM), adjacent to the Guilford College campus, and featured a mixed audience of blacks and whites seated together. It was described by some as a "promiscuous mingling of the races."

That same year, three dozen people, mostly Guilford College employees and members of the New Garden Friends Meeting, signed an open letter that was published in the Greensboro paper calling for desegregation. Some of the signers of that letter with non–Guilford employment lost their jobs. Mackie Furniture next to campus lost customers and ultimately went out of business because the Mackies were signees. Homes of other signees that night were surrounded by armed men. But in 1957, through the efforts and training of the AFSC, Josephine Boyd Bradley (1940–2015) became the first black student to enter Greensboro Senior High School.

Elsewhere in the state, individual Quakers played significant roles in the integration of schools such as in High Point and Goldsboro. In the latter, Nathaniel Shope, Superintendent of Schools, oversaw the process of integration in 1965. On the eve of the first blacks entering the previously all-white schools, Shope received a call from the National Guard, offering to be present the next day. He said their services were not needed, and integration proceeded peacefully.[14]

During the civil-rights struggles of the 1960s, Friends continued to be conflicted about "mixing" with those of another race. Most congregations remained segregated. One Sunday at worship, Willie Frye, pastor of the Winston-Salem Friends Meeting, introduced the African American director of a Head Start program using the Meeting's facilities. It caused such a stir that the incident contributed to the Meeting's splitting. Students at Guilford College were not encouraged by the administration to participate in the pivotal Woolworth lunch-counter sit-ins in 1960, but some did. Faculty continued to work towards integrating the college. There was not a uniform response from Friends, other than unease in bucking the dominant culture.

Guilford College did finally integrate in 1962 by bringing two Quaker students from the Kenyan mission field. When that passed without incident, African American students were soon enrolled. The scheme to integrate came in response to the desire of the college to host the 1967 World Gathering of Friends, an every-fifteen-years event of major Quaker importance. With fully half of worldwide Friends being people of color, there would be no way the planning body for the Gathering would accept an invitation to a segregated campus. The college and Greensboro Quaker community did host the 1967 event, with the major speaker being United Nations Secretary-General U Thant.

The Quaker Community Continues to Experience Division

Great cultural shifts in the 1960s impacted the Quaker community in North Carolina as it did most other groups. Debates over race continued. There were divisions over the American war in Vietnam, with one result being some Friends meetings placing American flags in the worship room while other Friends participated in weekly protests, and Quaker House, a military counseling center, was established in Fayetteville near military installations. Political loyalties began shifting from the Democratic Party to the Republican Party, especially in conservative, rural areas. A focus for growing differences in the larger Yearly Meeting developed around Guilford College, as its campus ethos changed swiftly from the tightly controlled student behavior that had been the norm to the freewheeling campus culture of the late '60s. This was also mirrored in growing tensions within the Yearly Meeting between rural and urban Friends. Liberal and evangelical movements in the wider culture impacted Quaker attitudes as social issues such as abortion, feminism, and homosexuality became topics of conversation.

Through the 1970s and '80s, the differences widened. A strong evangelical influence came into the larger Yearly Meeting through pastoral leadership and the growth of evangelical programs and media in the wider Christian culture. Meetings with more liberal leadership and a reputation for diversity became more and more marginalized. By the early 1990s in the larger Yearly Meeting, there were active attempts by a group of conservative pastors to expel the liberal meetings they dubbed "Stonecutters of Satan." Attempts were made to rebuke ministers who supported more liberal theology and the rights of homosexuals. Annual business sessions became tense affairs, exacerbated by an inability through a "consensus process" to make decisions one way or the other. There was a great deal of political maneuvering and bickering. Some members left in disgust; a few meetings did the same. Finally, something like a truce was declared, and a "listening project" was undertaken based on the work of Herb Walters, a Quaker peace & justice activist. Volunteers attended willing Friends meetings and listened to their concerns, reporting back to the Yearly Meeting Committee on Ministry and Counsel. As this project proceeded, Friends entered into a period of putting the issues to rest and focused on projects of common interest.

One of those was the North Carolina Friends Disaster Service (FDS) initiated in the late 1980s. Open to all and committed to "just building houses" rather than concern over the orthodoxy or heterodoxy of participants, FDS attracted a wide array of people on its work projects and made a special outreach to college students on their fall and spring breaks. It became a model of cooperation across the "divides" in the larger Yearly Meeting.

Meanwhile, the smaller North Carolina Yearly Meeting Conservative added a few meetings, lost a few of the original ones, experienced growth in urban areas such as Durham and Greensboro, but saw dwindling numbers in the rural areas of its early strength. It remained unprogrammed, preserving many of the traditions of old Quietist Quaker culture. With fewer than ten meetings in the Yearly Meeting, people knew each other well, and even when divisive issues were raised, meetings trusted each other to make decisions appropriate to their own understanding. The Yearly Meeting's embrace of "bottom-up" decision making served it well through the tempests of the late twentieth century.

Other associations of Friends emerged during the century, some by way of evangelical meetings leaving the larger Yearly Meeting and joining the Evangelical Friends International and others by way of the creation of liberal unprogrammed meetings around university campuses. These typically joined the Friends General Conference, a primarily northeastern U.S. gathering of more liberal Quakers. The diversity of Friends in North Carolina by the early 2000s was such that two young graduates of Guilford College, one liberal and one evangelical, developed an instructional video called "Can We All Be Friends?" that detailed the differences among four congregations of Friends in Greensboro, one associated with Friends United Meeting (formerly Five Years Meeting), one with Friends General Conference, one with the Conservative Yearly Meeting, one with Evangelical Friends International.[15]

At the turn of the twenty-first century, all the same elements challenging other religious groups were impacting Friends in North Carolina. But through it all, meetings appeared to be maintaining strength. An article in the Greensboro News & Record in 2002, however, indicated that perhaps appearances were deceiving. Citing a national study of denominations by the Glenmary Research Center, the article was headlined "Catholics Soar; Quakers Decline" and reported a 37 percent loss in Quaker membership in Guilford County.

The article piqued the interest of two Guilford College professors whose sociology class and Quaker studies class combined efforts to study local meetings and test the reported findings. Their research, subsequently published in Quaker Life magazine,[16] indicated that rumors of the death of Quaker meetings in the county were exaggerated. Two-thirds of the fourteen meetings in the county reported an increase in attendance over the previous five years, while only two reported a decrease. Other results of the study, however, foreshadowed issues to come. Half of the people surveyed said they did not know Quaker history; fifty-five percent said they read the Bible regularly, while 39 percent said they seldom or never read it. Several meetings had the American and Christian flags in their worship rooms and allowed for only a minute or two of silent waiting during worship, while others did not have flags and incorporated between fifteen minutes and a full hour of silence in worship.

North Carolina Yearly Meeting (FUM) Dissolves

Unfortunately, the "truce" among Friends in the larger Yearly Meeting that maintained a tentative *Waffenstillstand* through the 1990s and into the early 2010s did not hold. Political and cultural issues in the wider culture manifested themselves in demands by certain meetings and individuals that North Carolina Yearly Meeting (FUM) "purge" liberal meetings. Quaker decision-making processes required "unity" in going forward; with no unity possible, and strident voices increasing, a rapid dissolution of the Yearly Meeting began to take place. First individuals resigned positions and memberships, and then a steady flow of meetings began departing. A Yearly Meeting that encompassed more than seventy meetings in 2010 had forty-six in 2017, a membership drop from more than seven thousand to less than five thousand. Finances were accordingly affected, and drastic measures had to be taken.

At the annual sessions of North Carolina Yearly Meeting (FUM) in August of 2016, a plan for reorganizing the 319-year-old body was approved. The Yearly Meeting was to remain only as a fiduciary "umbrella" organization to care for the substantial property and endowments of the organization, while individual meetings would decide to which of two associations under that umbrella they would belong. The two groups would be defined by their choices of institutional authority ("top down" or "bottom up"). Essentially, they were "more or less conservative" and "more or less liberal."

The reason for the decision was explained, in part, in an introduction to the plan:

> Over the past 319 years, the North Carolina Yearly Meeting has never been without a time when we debated who we were as Christians and as Quakers and the steps that we should take to fulfill the missions of Christ on earth. As the years have become decades and the decades have become centuries, the multiple views and competing positions in this discussion have moved farther apart. The challenge of bridging our differences has become an increasingly daunting task. In recent years, the chorus of voices concerned about our differences has risen, and we have labored diligently to find a way to maintain our unity of purpose, our unity of worship and the unity of our corporate body.[17]

Conclusion

"My friends that are gone, and are going over to plant, and make outward plantations in America, keep your own plantations in your hearts, with the spirit and power of God, that your own vines and lilies be not hurt."[18]

This was the entreaty from George Fox to Friends in the latter part of the seventeenth century. Already by then the enthusiasm of the first generation of Quakers was waning through death, legal toleration, and the onset of 150 years of Quietism. The advice was heeded, however, and firm social boundary markers were erected around the "outward plantations" of Friends to maintain the "inward spiritual plantations" of a sectarian people. Such discipline enabled Quakers in North Carolina to accomplish many great things and leave a lasting legacy in areas of civil rights, education, peace, and spirituality.

However, factors in the middle of the nineteenth century that were affecting others began impacting the Quaker community, the most significant being war, innovations in transportation and communication, and revivalism. As the social boundary markers maintaining a "peculiar people" disappeared, Friends assimilated rapidly into the Protestant mainstream. When other factors challenging Friends meetings in the twentieth and twenty-first centuries surfaced, little distinctive Quaker identity remained in many of them to help stem the tide of those leaving. Loss of attendance and membership in both liberal and evangelical meetings accelerated in the first part of the twenty-first century, leaving only a few strong meetings in the larger Yearly Meeting. Membership in the Conservative Yearly Meeting declined in rural areas but grew in urban settings. Meetings in the liberal Friends General Conference fold held steady or grew, with a new yearly meeting—the Piedmont Friends Yearly Meeting—emerging as a combination of progressive pastoral and unprogrammed meetings.

Today, Friends meetings can still be found "from Murphy to Manteo" (except in those two cities), with a concentration in the Piedmont. The architecture of the faith has changed a great deal over the 350 years that Quakers have been in the state. A great example of both the diversity and change in North Carolina Quakerism may be witnessed in the physical architecture of Friends meetings. Step inside a Quaker meetinghouse and witness blank walls, benches in a hollow square or "in the round," with clear windows and no visible focus for authority, and one will be in a traditional ("Conservative") or a liberal Quaker setting. If the building has all the trappings of a standard Protestant house of worship—pews facing forward towards a focal point of choir loft and pulpit, with stained glass windows, flags, and a painting of Jesus behind the altar—then one will be in a more evangelical meeting.

Essentially, Quakers in North Carolina now reflect the same polarizations present in other denominations and in the American body politic. It is "red state" Quakerism and "blue state" Quakerism, states being replaced by counties. Randolph County Quakers are, by and large, not like Guilford County Quakers. Urban Friends are typically quite different from rural Friends. Theological differences often are but masks for the real political and cultural norms underneath.

By what standard, then, do they call themselves Quaker? Some actually prefer not to be, identifying as Christian rather than Quaker. But there certainly is no uniform adherence to the historical Quaker testimonies of simplicity, unprogrammed worship, nonviolence, equality, and integrity. If anything, there is a general avoidance of following a set liturgy in worship, with an openness to the possibility of the Spirit's leading in a different direction than expected. But that's about it for commonality.

As the old Quaker joke goes, if there are four Friends in town, there will be five meetinghouses.

Notes

1. George Fox, *Journal,* Nickalls edition (London Yearly Meeting, reprinted 1952), 642.
2. Minutes of North Carolina Yearly Meeting, 1776, cited in Seth B. Hinshaw, *The Carolina Quaker Experience* (North Carolina Yearly Meeting, 1984), 49–50.
3. Mary Mendenhall Hobbs papers, Friends Historical Collection, Guilford College.
4. Oral tradition in the New Garden community.
5. Kay Coltrane, *Centre Friends Meeting: The Legacy of the Meeting on the Hill* (Centre Friends Meeting, 2008), 116.

6. John Woolman, *Journal,* Moulton Edition (Richmond, VA: Friends United Press, 1971), 68.

7. Levi Coffin, *Reminiscences of Levi Coffin, the Reputed President of the Underground Railroad* (Cincinnati, OH: Robert Clarke & Co., 1880), 20.

8. Stephen B. Weeks, *Southern Quakers and Slavery* (Baltimore, MD: Johns Hopkins Press, 1896), 307.

9. Hinshaw, *The Carolina Quaker Experience,* 154.

10. Allen Jay, *Autobiography* (Richmond, VA: Friends United Press, 2010 edition), 173.

11. Jay, *Autobiography,* 175.

12. Author interview with Levering descendant George White, October 2016.

13. Minutes of North Carolina Yearly Meeting of Friends (FYM), August 1949. Friends Historical Collection, Guilford College.

14. Author interview with Patricia Shope Sebens, daughter of Nathaniel Shope, October 2016.

15. Betsy Blake and Coleman Watts, "Can We All Be Friends?" (privately produced video, 2005).

16. Max L. Carter, "Catholics Soar; Quakers Decline," *Quaker Life,* October 2003.

17. Minutes of the Reorganization of the Religious Society of Friends in North Carolina, August 13, 2016.

18. George Fox, *Epistles* (London: E. Marsh, 1848).

Roman Catholics

Daniel Hutchinson

The story of Roman Catholicism's growth within North Carolina is as dramatic a story as any of the religious traditions of the American South. For much of its history, North Carolina was the least Catholic state in the nation's least Catholic region. For well after a century after the state's first parish was founded, less than one percent of the state's population claimed membership in the world's largest Christian denomination. The legacies of the Reformation, the dynamics of colonial settlement, and a hostile political environment all contributed to Catholicism's diminutive presence for much of the state's history. Yet a tenacious laity and a determined church hierarchy labored for generations to establish their church in the Old North State. These labors bore remarkable fruit. By the beginning of the twenty-first century, Catholicism was expanding spectacularly and becoming among the state's most influential faith communities. This essay explores the remarkable expansion in Carolina Catholicism over three centuries, particularly focusing on the Catholic Church's institutional development and the men and women who helped lay the denomination's foundations in the state.[1]

The history of Roman Catholicism in North Carolina stands apart from other southern states, a divergence originating in the colonial period. While Protestantism became a bedrock of southern identity in the eighteenth century, recent scholarship has persuasively argued that Catholicism was the region's most dynamic creed during much of the colonial era.[2] Supported by the Spanish and French colonial regimes, the Catholic Church established a network of churches, missions, schools, and convents serving a population extending from the Texas plains to Florida's Atlantic coast. Europeans, Native Americans, and Africans alike established a diverse and distinct form of Catholicism in a region itself experiencing rapid transformation.[3] Small, but nonetheless prominent, Catholic communities likewise developed in the Chesapeake colonies of Maryland and Virginia, although in a nakedly hostile climate resulting from the conflicts of the English Reformation.[4] Historians have utilized a documentary record produced by ecclesiastical authorities, prominent lay families, and colonial administrators on both sides of the Atlantic to vividly reconstruct the origins of southern Catholicism. Unfortunately, historians of Catholicism in North Carolina labor under what historian Maura Jane Farrelly describes as "the exaggerated version of a perennial problem in the field of colonial American history: the scarcity of sources."[5] This scarcity is due to the reality that for two centuries Tar Heel Catholics were a minuscule and scattered minority dwelling in an overwhelmingly Protestant region.

The dynamics of North Carolina's colonial history played an important role in the inhospitable conditions for Catholic settlement. The *Fundamental Constitutions of Carolina* (1669), the colony's founding charter written by John Locke, initially recognized the civil liberties of any freedman acknowledging God. "Jews, heathens, and other dissenters from the purity of the Christian religion" could freely immigrate to the colony, as could presumably Catholics.[6] But the initial liberties granted in the *Fundamental Constitutions* proved short lived. As in other English colonies, Catholics were perceived as a particularly dangerous source of religious and political dissension. By 1682, the charter was amended to welcome Christian ministers of every Protestant denomination to the colony, with the notable exception of Catholic clergy. Further laws restricted the celebration of the mass in 1704 and denied voting rights to Catholics by 1717.[7] While some Catholics doubtlessly dwelled in the colony, the communal structures required to maintain and perpetuate the faith were difficult to establish in such a climate. Indeed, no organized Catholic parish would emerge in North Carolina for over a century.

If a hostile political climate impeded Catholic settlement, so too did the dynamics of colonial immigration. North Carolina did not attract a colonial proprietor like Baron Cecil Calvert, who promoted Catholic migration to Maryland, or William Penn, whose commitment to religious freedom in Pennsylvania ensured that Catholics could openly practice their creed. The Irish, the largest Catholic ethnicity immigrating to colonial America, largely avoided North Carolina. As late as 1860, the Irish were a negligible presence, representing less than one-tenth of a percent of North Carolina's overall population.[8] Non-English immigrants hailed largely from regions of Protestant Europe scarred by the simmering religious conflicts of the eighteenth century. Highland Scots, Ulster Scots Irish, German Lutherans, and Czech Moravians arriving by sea or along the Great Wagon Road all hailed from homelands divided along sectarian lines.[9] There is currently little evidence suggesting the presence of Catholics among Africans arriving to North Carolina via the Atlantic slave trade, although the possibility is not out of the question. Suggestive evidence indicates the presence of Catholic Africans brought to South Carolina from regions of west and central Africa proselytized by Portuguese missionaries in the sixteenth century.[10]

Given the region's religious climate and immigration patterns, Catholicism's scant presence in the colony's historical record is unsurprising. Those few Catholics who do appear seem to have concentrated near North Carolina's port communities on the Atlantic coast. An Anglican missionary writing from Bath, the colony's first incorporated town, observed in 1741 the presence of a dozen Catholics in the community. Another Anglican cleric in New Bern recorded in 1760 a similar observation in his community: "As for papists, I cannot learn there are above 9 or 10 in the whole County." William Tryon, North Carolina's royal governor, wrote in 1765 that "every sect of religion abounds here except the Roman Catholic."[11] Little evidence has survived documenting the experience of these lay Catholics disconnected from the larger church. The early history of Catholicism in North Carolina must largely be told through the travails of circuit-riding missionary priests and the beleaguered bishops overseeing them.

Yet the presence of the clergy was a rare occurrence. North Carolina's first permanent priest, Fr. Patrick Cleary of Ireland, arrived in 1784. Initially arriving in New Bern to settle a probate dispute involving his late brother's estate, the Gaelic-speaking priest remained in the community and served the scattered pockets of Catholic faithful until his death six years later. No permanent clergy would replace him for thirty years. Infrequent visits by priests from Norfolk, Virginia, and the neighboring diocese of Richmond filled the interim. Yet despite irregular pastoral attention, Catholic communities nonetheless managed to survive, and even fitfully grow, due to natural increase and the scant Catholic immigration that did occur. As the early nineteenth century progressed, small Catholic congregations emerged in Washington, Wilmington, Fayetteville, and Raleigh. They held religious services at local courthouses, academies, and in the churches of other denominations. But the absence of the sacramental rites central to Catholic life, and of the priests who performed them, continued to be a source of difficulty. As Fr. Stephen Worsley, the principal historian of this era, notes: "More than anything else, [priests'] infrequent visits sharpened the desire in these small Catholic communities for more regular pastoral attention. Petitions by these groups for a resident priest went unfilled."[12] North Carolina's plight was shared by other Catholic congregations across the young nation. The Catholic Church's growth required priests, as well as the bishops who would ordain them. The foundations of the nation's institutional church were established following John Carroll's ordination as bishop of the Diocese of Baltimore in 1790, the United States' first independent diocese, later raised to an archdiocese. In 1791, Bishop Carroll established Georgetown University, America's first Catholic seminary and institution of higher learning.[13]

Remarkably, Georgetown shaped the life of North Carolina's arguably most prominent Catholic, William Gaston. Hailing from New Bern, William was the oldest child of Alexander and Margaret Gaston, born in 1778. Alexander was an accomplished physician serving in the Royal Navy until his immigration to New Bern after the Seven Years' War. Alexander Gaston wed Margaret Sharpe in 1775, another recent immigrant to New Bern and a devout English Catholic educated in a French convent. The Gastons established a sizeable plantation near New Bern and numbered among the town's most notable families. Alexander also became an early supporter of the Patriot cause during the American Revolution, resulting in his death at the hands of a Tory raiding party in 1781. The widowed Margaret, now tasked with raising two children while also managing the family plantation, determined that her young son would receive a Catholic education despite the lack of options within North Carolina. At age twelve, young William was enrolled at Georgetown University as its very first student. The college's president, Robert Plunkett, wrote William's mother that "he is the best scholar & most exemplary youth in Geo-Town." Unfortunately, ill-health forced young William to withdraw from Georgetown, and he concluded his education at Princeton University in 1796. But the theological and spiritual formation Gaston received from his mother's fierce devotion and at Georgetown University shaped the rest of his remarkable life.[14]

Gaston pursued a career in law and politics in his native Craven County with singular success. In 1798, at age twenty, Gaston was admitted to the state bar after studying under Francois-Xavier Martin, a prominent North Carolina jurist and future chief justice of the Louisiana Supreme Court. Two years later, Gaston won election to North Carolina's General Assembly, aligning himself with the Federalist Party. Gaston's election marked the beginning of a lengthy political career spanning the next three decades, taking him from the speakership of the General Assembly, to the halls of Congress, and onwards to national prominence.[15]

Gaston's political rise was all the more remarkable given the existence of a foreboding provision in North Carolina's 1776 state constitution: "That no person, who shall deny the being of God or the truth of the Protestant religion ... or who shall hold religious principles incompatible with the freedom and safety of the State, shall be capable of holding any office or place of trust or profit in the civil department within this State."[16] Gaston's swift political ascent reflects the statute's rare enforcement, being a legacy of a colonial-era animus towards Catholicism. But anxieties about Catholic loyalties remained potent within early America for decades ahead. This perennial concern questioned whether Catholics could reconcile their religious loyalties to Rome with their political allegiance to Washington. North Carolina's constitutional drafters were not alone in this apprehension. Vermont, New Jersey, Georgia, and South Carolina's state constitutions adopted similar restrictions. As Maura Jane Farrelly notes, "The men who drafted the constitutions … did not believe that Catholics could overcome their faith's hierarchical orientation and develop the sense of virtue and individual responsibility that were essential to republicanism."[17] This constitutional provision remained a controversy among the state's Catholics in the years ahead.

Nonetheless, William Gaston's political fortunes continued to rise, as did his efforts to foster the growth of Catholicism in his native New Bern. He quickly emerged as the leader of the state's nascent Catholic community and wrote repeatedly to Archbishop John Carroll of Baltimore requesting a permanently assigned priest to serve North Carolina. Dissatisfied with the infrequent visits of clergy from distant parishes, Gaston offered to pay for the relocation of a priest to New Bern and even opened his own home to house the potential priest. "I am solicitous for others of the Church … who long for an opportunity for practising [*sic*] the duties of their religion." Carroll could not accommodate Gaston's requests, bereft as he was of sufficient clergy within his own diocese. Nonetheless, Gaston soon found another effective partner in championing the growth of Catholicism in North Carolina.[18]

Arriving on New Year's Eve, 1820, in the newly established Diocese of Charleston was a thirty-three-year-old prelate from Ireland, Bishop John England. The bishop's ecclesiastical domain was as vast as the challenges facing his young ministry. Extending from Charleston to include both Carolinas as well as Georgia, the diocese possessed a scattered population and two established parishes. England could rely upon few parishioners, fewer benefactors, and just two priests for assistance. His diocese, England wrote to his superiors in Rome, "is one of the largest, and perhaps it is the poorest, in all Christendom. Comprising a vast territory, it covers a measureless extent of insalubrious swamps in a warm climate, where every summer and autumn deadly fevers prevail."[19] Given these conditions, securing the support of a prominent local Catholic such as William Gaston was essential for his ministry's success. England wrote a letter of introduction to the noted legislator shortly after his arrival to Charleston. "From the statements which have been made to me of your zeal for Religion, & the very dreadful situation of North Carolina, totally destitute of every opportunity of attending the holy sacrifice or receiving the Sacraments, I take the liberty of addressing you upon the subject." This correspondence began what would become an important relationship that would lay the foundations for the first flourishing of Catholicism in North Carolina.[20]

Bishop England soon visited the scattered flock of his oversized diocese, arriving to North Carolina's eastern shores in May 1821 and recording his experiences in a diary. England traveled first to Wilmington, meeting some twenty-two Catholics, many of whom were expatriates of Portugal, Ireland, France, and Cuba. England lamented the consequences of an absent Catholic clergy: "The Catholics who lived here … were in the habit of going to the other places of worship (Episcopal Protestant, Methodist & Presbyterian), and had nearly lost all idea of Catholicity."[21] Yet England earnestly worked to revive local zeal. In the following days the bishop celebrated mass, heard confessions, baptized infants, performed weddings, spoke to curious Protestant congregations on Catholic theology, and above all attempted to organize the scattered Catholics of the region into what would become the state's first parishes. England soon made his way from Wilmington to Washington, and then on to New Bern, celebrating mass in the home of William Gaston. An analysis of the Catholic Carolinians mentioned in England's diary by Fr. Stephen Worsley reveals that "Catholics were much better represented among the merchant and professional groups in 1821 than would have been statistically expected." Some of this number pledged substantial funds for the construction of a parish church in New Bern during the bishop's visit.[22]

England then traveled onwards towards North Carolina's interior on a taxing circuit ride lasting two months, visiting Edenton, Elizabeth City, Murfreesboro, Halifax, Warrenton, Louisburg, Raleigh, and finally Fayetteville. Falling ill amid his lengthy journey, he recorded frustrating setbacks. His entry for July 14, 1821, notes: "Arrived in Halifax—no Catholic. In the Evening arrived at Warrenton—no Catholic here, nor in its vicinity. Still feeling very ill." Nonetheless, England's mere presence provided opportunities for promoting Catholicism even in the absence of Catholic faithful. No powerful prelate of the Roman Catholic Church had ever before toured the state. England's presence represented both a novelty and a reflection of the state's growing stature. In Raleigh, a group of Protestant citizens invited the bishop to address residents at the local Presbyterian Church. England characterized the audience as "a very large and respectable congregation amongst whom were the Governor of the State [Jesse Franklin] and the Judges of the Supreme Court." England's tour extended for four more months, taking him to Philadelphia, Baltimore, and Washington, D.C., where he was granted an audience with President James Monroe and Secretary of State John Quincy Adams. England concluded his eight-month tour with an untimely return visit to eastern North Carolina, which was in the grips of a yellow fever epidemic.[23]

Bishop England's first tour of his parish made him fully aware of the daunting obstacles confronting his ministry. Priest shortages remained the greatest challenge. England actively recruited priests from other dioceses and from abroad, especially his native Ireland. Unfortunately, even the most zealous clergy could not be enticed to make lengthy circuit rides to scattered, diminutive, and often impoverished parishes. "I find it exceedingly difficult to procure a priest to undertake any of [the] missions of North Carolina," England lamented in a letter to William Gaston. Those few priests who did arrive were often of variable ability. "Never again to be received into this Diocese [is] a priest who was permitted easily to leave of Diocese of his birth," England fumed in another letter. Training local clergy was essential, and the bishop successfully raised funds to establish a seminary in Charleston in 1824. The establishment of North Carolina's first parishes followed in due course over the next two decades, due to the persistent efforts of the local laity and England's energetic governance.[24]

A critical part of England's ministry focused on promoting the standing of the Roman Catholic Church within the overwhelmingly Protestant region. Especially important was emphasizing Catholicism's compatibility with America's republican ideals. Conscious of the mistrust directed towards Catholics and shaped by his own experiences of religious conflict in his native Ireland, England vocally supported the American ideal of separation of church and state (a concept that remained controversial in Rome). England

Table 1—First Catholic Parishes of North Carolina

Parish Name and Location	Date of Church Construction
St. John the Evangelist, Washington, NC	1823
St. Patrick, Fayetteville, NC	1829
St. John the Baptist, Raleigh, NC	1835
St. Paul's, New Bern, NC	1841
Saints Mary and Joseph, Gaston County, NC	1844
St. Thomas, Wilmington, NC	1847
St. Peter, Prince of the Apostles, Charlotte, NC	1851
St. Anne, Edenton, NC	1858

Source: Stephen C. Worsley, "Catholicism in Antebellum North Carolina." North Carolina Historical Review 60, no. 4 (1983), 426.

advocated this issue at length in a diocesan publication that became the nation's first Catholic newspaper, the influential *United States Catholic Miscellany*. From his pulpit and his printing press, England became a well-known and respected clerical leader within North and South Carolina. While his mitre and crosier marked him as a novelty to many, England successfully established social ties with prominent figures from the region's Protestant elite.[25]

England's boosterism paid unexpected dividends. For example, David Swain, a young lawyer from Buncombe County, was struck by the charismatic homily and distinctive liturgical elements of a marriage ceremony officiated by England in 1823. "For the first time in my life," Swain recorded in a letter to his father, "I have seen a miter [*sic*], a stole, & witnessed the 1000 peculiarities which distinguish the Catholic from the Protestant in the performance of this interesting ceremony."[26] Twelve years later in 1835, Swain was governor of the state and overseeing a convention revising North Carolina's 1776 state constitution. Held amid the populist tumult of the Jacksonian era, delegates debated amendments regarding federal representation, suffrage among African American freedmen, and, notably, the constitutional amendment barring Catholics from public office.[27] Swain numbered among the power brokers of the convention. So too did William Gaston. Following his speakership of the state's General Assembly, Gaston rose to the ranks of the U.S. House of Representatives, serving two terms from 1813–1816 and gaining national attention for his oratory during the War of 1812. In the 1820s, Gaston returned to the State Assembly as a member of the Whig Party and pioneered efforts to establish vital infrastructure for the state's growth, as well as the regional banks that might finance the construction of roads, canals, and railroads. In 1833, Gaston was appointed a judge of North Carolina's Supreme Court, his political and legal influence at its apogee. He employed that influence in confronting the anti–Catholic amendment during the state constitutional convention.

Intense debate centered on the issue. As described by the principal historian of the convention: "Little was left unsaid as delegate after delegate rose to say he would not long detain the convention, then rambled on for hours. Other delegates came from their sickbeds to address the convention.... Such was the excitement generated by this issue."[28] Defenders of the prohibition against Catholic officeholders argued the amendment stood as a preventive measure against the influence of an extra-territorial and anti-democratic institution, the Papacy. Delegate Jesse Cooper of Martin County conceded that "there were some honest men among the Catholics," but warned "we know the doctrine is a dangerous one, we ought to exclude them," proclaiming that "the Roman Catholic is the very offspring of a despot." Less vituperative defenders adopted subtler justifications. Emanuel Shober of Stokes County asserted that faithful Catholics, such as Gaston, could in fact hold the truth of the Protestant faith without theological contradiction. After reviewing the historical causes of the Reformation, Shober argued that "a sincere Catholic, therefore, may in conscience and truth say, that he believes in the truth of the Protestant Religion—because the principles on which it is founded, tended to raise and elevate his own Church to its true character." Others argued that Gaston's singular prominence indicated that the amendment was merely a general endorsement of religiosity among office-holders, and not a religious test prohibited by the U.S. Constitution.[29]

Gaston offered an impassioned rebuttal. Condemning the overheated rhetoric relitigating the conflicts of the Reformation and depictions of Catholics as thralls to a foreign power, Gaston asked:

> But why is this humiliating and disgusting subject raked up, and exhibited? Is it for the purpose of awakening ancient animosities, of creating bad feelings, of blowing into a flame the sleeping embers of wrath, malice and uncharitableness? This does not seem a very humane, wise or liberal purpose. Alas! I fear that even now we are deserving of the reproach of the cynical [Jonathan] Swift: we have just enough religion to hate, and not enough to love each other.

Addressing arguments that the amendment had no practical effect in barring Catholics from office, Gaston retorted:

> [B]ut it does not thence follow that no practical evil has arisen from it. If it has impaired the attachment of any citizen to the institutions of his country, by causing him to feel that a stigma was cast, or attempted to be cast, upon him, in its fundamental law; if it has swelled the arrogance or embittered the malice of sectarian bigotry by bidding it hold up its head on high above the suspected castes of the community; if it has checked the fair expression of honest opinion, or operated as a bribe to hypocrisy and dissimulation; if it has drawn down upon the Constitution of North Carolina, the double reproach of manifesting at once the *will* to persecute, and the *inability* to execute, its purpose— then, vast indeed, has already been its practical mischief.[30]

"Gentlemen have had too much pride, too much sense of character, to undertake before this enlightened Assembly, to *vindicate* this proscriptive Article of our constitution," Gaston also noted. "They have argued about and around the true question, and have suggested different considerations for declining to act on the subject; but they have not ventured to come out openly, and insist that the Article is a wise and salutary provision. The cause of Intolerance has been undefended, because it is indefensible." Gaston's oratory during the debate was well received by fellow delegates, and national newspapers hailed the eloquence of his arguments. Members of the constitutional convention finally moved to substitute "Christian" for "Protestant" in the text of the amendment, voting seventy-one to fifty-four (joining Gaston in the affirmative was Governor David Swain). While this substitution reflected an imperfect victory for the ideal of religious freedom, to Gaston the change represented an important advance and was arguably the high point of his political career.[31]

William Gaston's historic legacy was further enhanced by his stance on the institution of slavery. Gaston emerged as a distinctive voice in the increasingly tense climate following Nat Turner's insurrection in 1831. While delivering a lecture at the University of North Carolina in 1832, Gaston condemned slavery as an immoral institution to the students in his audience, urging them to move North Carolina beyond:

> On you too, will devolve the duty which has been long neglected, but which cannot with impunity be neglected much longer, or providing for the mitigation, and (is it too much to hope for in North Car-

olina?) for the ultimate extirpation of the worst evil that afflicts the Southern part of our Confederacy.... Disguise the truth as we may, and throw the blame where we will, it is Slavery which, more
than any cause, keeps us back in the career of improvement. It stifles industry and represses enterprise—it is fatal to economy and providence—it discourages skill—impairs our strength as a community, and poisons morals at the fountain head.[32]

Gaston's contrarian views concerning slavery were reinforced in his interpretation of the
law. As a judge on North Carolina's Supreme Court, Gaston had written an important
legal opinion in 1834 affirming the rights of slaves to protect themselves from physical
assaults by their masters. Gaston's legal conclusion was cited in the critical dissent to the
infamous *Dred Scott v. Sanford* decision denying citizenship to African Americans.[33] Gaston likewise argued against stripping away the voting rights of African American freedmen during the 1835 constitutional convention, a cause that ultimately failed.[34]

Yet William Gaston's moral clarity concerning slavery was complicated by the great
paradox of American history. As described most famously by historian Edmund Morgan,
men like Gaston helped forge a society "dedicated to human liberty and freedom" while
simultaneously profiting from "a system of labor that denied human dignity and liberty
every hour of the day."[35] Gaston's success in public life was enabled by the profits derived
from his family's plantation and the toil of the 163 slaves who resided there.[36] Gaston's
complicity in America's original sin was shared by other southern Catholics. Bishop John
England privately condemned slavery as "the greatest moral evil that can desolate any
part of the civilized world." Yet his Charleston-based *Catholic Miscellany* publicly
endorsed the institution, a concession to a city ardently supportive of what their senator,
John C. Calhoun, described as a "positive good."[37] Despite their distinctive religious tradition, historians have found that most southern Catholics resembled their Protestant
neighbors in attitudes towards and participation in slavery.[38] Indeed, Catholic priests,
parishes, religious orders, and even Georgetown University itself owned slaves. The challenging legacies of this reality remain a source of debate and introspection into the
twenty-first century.[39]

The contradictions arising from American slavery were further complicated by
Catholic theology, which long tolerated the institution of slavery but emphasized the
humanity of the enslaved. Slaves were not merely to be treated humanely, but were to be
baptized, receive access to the sacraments, permitted religious instruction, and to worship
in the same churches as white parishioners.[40] These theological edicts led to the spread
of Catholicism to African Americans, who came in time to represent a significant percentage of all Catholics in North Carolina in the antebellum period. Yet if sources on
Catholic Carolinians in general are scarce, evidence relating the experience of African
American Catholics is elusive indeed. For example, Bishop John England's 1822 diary
repeatedly records the baptism and religious instruction of numerous slaves held by
Catholic slaveholders, including William Gaston.[41] "The soul of the most humble slave
is as dear to the Catholic church, as is that of the most powerful monarch," England
would later write in his *Catholic Miscellany*. This sentiment reflected real zeal, and
England successfully convinced Protestant as well as Catholic slaveowners to allow him
and other priests to preach among their slaves. The bishop estimated at least one thousand
African American Catholics dwelled in his diocese.[42] Unfortunately, the identities of
these individual slaves remain obscure, as do their own perspectives of Catholicism. The
comparative experience of African American Catholics in other southern states offers
possible insights. Among many slaves, the religious instruction sanctioned by their

masters, whether Catholic or Protestant, was suspect, as merely a spiritual means of supporting their earthly subordination. Yet, as historians such as Randall Miller and Cyprian Davis have shown, numerous African Americans genuinely embraced the faith, adapting Catholic spirituality to reflect their own experience and "enlist[ing] Catholic beliefs and resources for their social security."[43]

William Gaston and Bishop John England both died in the 1840s. Both left notable legacies, and arguably these partners in establishing Catholicism in North Carolina number among two of the most influential figures in the state's religious history. Gaston's stature as a national political figure was commemorated in 1846, two years after his death, by the founders of the newly christened Gaston County (a site of future importance to Catholicism in the state).[44] Bishop England's pioneering efforts created an organized leadership for the scattered Catholic communities for much of the southeast, and beyond. England's pastoral responsibilities had expanded to include east Florida and Haiti, added burdens credited for the exhaustion that contributed to his death in 1844. Even Charleston's Protestant community noted his passing with respect: "Bishop England, although but an adopted citizen, loved our Union and our Sunny South with truly filial affection," wrote one Charleston newspaper.[45] Yet the foundations England laid paved the course for future evangelization. The seminary England founded trained priests that continued his work, and his *Catholic Miscellany* remained one of the nation's most prominent religious publications under England's successors, Bishops Ignatius Reynolds and Patrick Lynch.

While Gaston and England had done much to raise Catholicism's profile within North Carolina, new challenges emerged after their death as the larger American Catholic Church underwent transformation and the nation experienced increasingly dangerous division. The arrival of tens of thousands of German and Irish immigrants in the 1840s to cities such as New York, Philadelphia, and Boston made Catholicism the nation's fastest growing creed. A subsequent nativist backlash resulted in religious violence and ethnic tension across the nation, even the emergence of a nakedly anti-immigrant political party, the American Party, better known to history as the "Know-Nothings."[46] North Carolina was not removed from these larger debates. Isolated, yet heated, theological controversies flared between Protestant and Catholic clergy, especially following the conversion of a prominent Episcopal bishop to Catholicism in 1852. Some sources even note a few reported outbreaks of religious violence. The tensions, while sharp, ultimately proved short-lived, and far from universal. In 1855, students at the University of North Carolina invited Archbishop John Hughes of New York City to speak at their commencement ceremonies. To Catholics, particularly the Irish, Archbishop Hughes was a fierce champion for the advancement of their church. To Protestants, Hughes was better known as "Dagger John," a provocative and feared figure often placed at the center of lurid conspiracies to topple the American Republic. Hughes declined the initial invitation due to scheduling conflicts, but he accepted a subsequent offer and addressed Chapel Hill's graduates during the 1860 commencement exercises.[47]

Whatever the tenor of religious tensions within the state, the threat of the Civil War eclipsed all other concerns. As with slavery, southern Catholics largely shared the same attitudes towards secession as their Protestant neighbors, and likewise participated in the Confederate war effort. Irish immigrants in southern cities particularly heeded the call to military service, often in units organized along ethnicity.[48] Yet sources on Catholic Carolinians serving in the Confederacy are scarce, as only an estimated six hundred

Catholics dwelled in North Carolina at the start of the war.[49] Yet clearly some North Carolina Catholics fought for their state, such as Isaac Peale of Northampton County. Peale joined Company H of the 2nd North Carolina Calvary Regiment as a private in July 1861. His unit participated in the Battle of New Bern in 1862, a Confederate defeat that left the city, and the state's oldest Catholic parish, in Union hands for the remainder of the war. The regiment would fight on in battles throughout the war, and remnants of the battered unit were present at Robert E. Lee's surrender at Appomattox. Yet Peale did not live to see the war's end. During the prelude to the Gettysburg Campaign, Peale participated in a cavalry raid led by Major General J.E.B. Stuart on Hanover, Pennsylvania, on June 30, 1863. Peale was thrown from his horse amid the chaos of battle and fractured his skull. As he was treated by Union surgeons, Peale called out for a priest, and before his death Peale received last rites from a northern cleric.[50]

While ascertaining the experiences of ordinary Catholic supporters of the Confederacy is challenging, the views of the Catholic Church's regional leadership are far clearer. The South's Catholic bishops all supported the Confederate cause, particularly Charleston's Bishop Patrick Lynch, a native South Carolinian. Lynch ordered the *Te Deum*, a Catholic hymn of praise, sung in the city's cathedral following the surrender of Fort Sumter in 1861. He later represented the Confederacy at the Vatican, in a futile effort to realize Jefferson Davis's hopes of winning official diplomatic recognition in Europe. Bishop Lynch even considered splitting North Carolina into a separate diocese because of the state's initial ambivalence towards secession.[51] America's northern bishops supported the Union, and political disagreements between regional church leaders were aired publicly throughout the conflict. Yet the hierarchical structures of the Catholic Church provided a measure of cohesion that other denominations did not enjoy. American Catholicism largely avoided the controversies concerning slavery that had ruptured the national Baptist and Methodist denominations into distinct regional congregations during the 1840s. Roman Catholicism's international structure ensured continued union between southern and northern dioceses during the Civil War, despite the significant tensions that existed within the American conference of bishops.[52]

The enduring union of southern bishops with the larger Catholic Church proved crucial for the challenging years following the Civil War. Numerous parishes and schools were destroyed in South Carolina, putting the diocese under severe financial strain. Catholic communities in North Carolina fared little better. Washington's parish, one of the oldest in the state, had been destroyed following the arrival of Union troops, along with much of the town. The sacramental objects used for the celebration of the mass had been plundered by Union troops in Edenton's small church. No priests were present to celebrate mass, in any case. The absence of clergy, compounded by the exigencies of war, had left the state's Catholics without access to sacraments for extended periods. In 1866, an Edenton laywoman implored Bishop Patrick Lynch for a priest to serve their "little abandoned flock." Likewise, a Catholic community in Charlotte collected five hundred dollars to induce the assignment of a permanent priest to their area, no small sum during the turbulence of Reconstruction. Lynch, himself, managed to raise thirteen hundred dollars to aid North Carolina communities, Catholic and Protestant alike. Yet Lynch could do little more, given the precarious state of the diocese.[53]

Bishop Lynch concluded it was time for North Carolina to chart its own course under independent leadership. Lynch took his concerns to the Second Plenary Council of Baltimore in 1866, the first major conference of American bishops after the Civil War.

Lynch succeeded in convincing his peers of the necessity to split North Carolina from the Diocese of Charleston. But the state still required substantial missionary work before it could support its own diocese. After approval from Rome, North Carolina was designated an apostolic vicariate in 1868, a proto-diocese theoretically under the direct supervision of the Vatican's Congregation for the Propagation of the Faith but in practice governed by a vicar empowered with the ecclesiastical authority of a bishop. This first vicar responsible for North Carolina's Catholic faithful was James Gibbons, a thirty-four-year-old priest who became America's youngest bishop and one of the American church's most influential figures.[54]

Born in Baltimore in 1834 to a family of Irish immigrants, Gibbons was ordained a priest in 1861. The young priest quickly made an impression on his superiors within the Archdiocese of Baltimore for his zeal ministering to immigrant parishes and as a military chaplain at nearby Fort McHenry. Archbishop Martin John Spalding, the leader of Baltimore's diocese and first among equals in American bishops, promoted Gibbons as his cathedral secretary in 1865. Gibbons also served as the assistant chancellor responsible for coordinating the Second Plenary Council of Baltimore, the church conference that determined North Carolina's status as an apostolic vicariate. Spalding's support, as well as Gibbons' favorable impression on the other church notables assembled in Baltimore, secured his appointment as vicar apostolic over other local candidates from the Diocese of Charleston.[55] The sermon delivered by a colleague at Gibbons' installation in 1868 carried a revealing, if hopeful, note on the precariousness of Catholicism's status within North Carolina.

> You, Right Reverend Sir, are to go to the large state of North Carolina. It appalls one to think of that State of more than a million inhabitants, with but a few [Catholic] altars and one or two priests to minister to them....Again I say to you, that I cannot congratulate you on going to North Carolina ... which in a religious sense, may be called a desert. It will not be long, I predict, before that desert will be made to bloom and produce much fruit.[56]

Gibbons arrived to his see in 1868, making St. Thomas Church in Wilmington the seat of his vicariate. The city was still recovering from the destructive battle that had damaged the city's port in 1865, and the presence of federal soldiers occupying the city only added to the disorder. The estimated eight hundred Catholics in North Carolina, scattered in distant communities across the state, demanded immediate pastoral care. Gibbons soon made his first tour of the state, spanning four weeks and some 925 miles by coach, rail, and steamboat. For his efforts, Gibbons confirmed sixteen converts into the Church and provided the sacraments to four hundred more, including an Irish woman in the tiny village of Chinquapin who claimed she had not seen a priest in forty-five years.[57] But providing a sustainable ministry for this far-flung flock would require additional priests as well as substantial funding, both resources in great scarcity. As Gibbons would later recall, the challenges of the vicariate were daunting. "I at once painfully experienced the poverty and isolation of the charge. Humanly speaking, I felt myself sent out alone to a strange country among strangers where few Catholics were to be found.... I could only say to myself: '*Deus providebit*' [God will provide]."[58]

Despite these trials, Gibbons proved to be an energetic and effective prelate. The vicar recognized that Catholic education was central to the church's growth in the state. Gibbons successfully recruited members of the Sisters of Our Lady of Mercy who established the first Catholic schools in the state. The religious order knew Wilmington well, as some of their nurses had served in the city during an 1862 outbreak of yellow fever that had claimed over ten percent of the city's population.[59] From Wilmington, the Sisters opened new schools and hospitals in the western half of the state: Sacred Heart Academy in Gaston County in 1892, St. Joseph's Sanatorium for treatment of tuberculosis in Asheville in 1900, and Charlotte's Mercy General Hospital in 1906. Gibbons also enjoyed success in recruiting new priests and new benefactors for his vicariate, helping raise critical funds from northern dioceses and abroad. As predicted, his toil in the "desert" of North Carolina quickly yielded spiritual fruit. Within four years of his arrival, the number of Catholics in the state had grown to fourteen hundred souls, ministered to by eight priests, the largest number yet in North Carolina's history. Amid this activity, Gibbons traveled to Rome to participate in the First Vatican Council, making a significant impression among the bishops and cardinals gathered there to debate the theology of papal infallibility. Gibbons' remarkable success in the vicariate inevitably made him a candidate for promotion to full bishop. After the death of Richmond's bishop in 1872, the Vatican named Gibbons the new bishop of the diocese, taking him from the vicariate. From Richmond, Gibbons' star rose further. In 1878, Gibbons was appointed Archbishop of Baltimore, the nation's preeminent see, and in 1886 he became only the second American inducted into the College of Cardinals. While Gibbons' departure benefited the entire American church, the vacuum left behind in the apostolic vicariate created uncertainty for some years.[60]

The void was filled by an unlikely source: a community of Pennsylvania monks led by a pair of imposing abbots wielding almost medieval authority. Among the leaders of nineteenth-century Catholic America, few could claim the distinctive influence of Abbot Boniface Wimmer. A professed Benedictine monk of St. Michael's Abbey at Metten in Bavaria, Wimmer organized an exodus of monks to serve the spiritual needs of America's growing German immigrant communities, founding St. Vincent's Abbey outside of Pittsburgh in 1846. Under Wimmer's energetic direction, by 1891, St. Vincent's served as the spiritual center of a far-flung network of twelve Benedictine communities with 350 monks responsible for the care of seventy parishes and five schools extending from New Hampshire to Washington.[61] Bishop Patrick Lynch and other prelates had repeatedly attempted to draw Wimmer's expansionist zeal southwards. But the region's few Germans, fewer Catholics, and severe economic climate initially inspired little enthusiasm.[62]

Paradoxically, the state's poor economy was precisely what brought the Pennsylvania Benedictines to North Carolina. The western half of the Diocese of Charleston had long been served by Fathers Jeremiah and Lawrence O'Connell, two Irish brothers who traveled the Piedmont as itinerant priests. After decades of lengthy circuit rides and increasingly delicate health, Lawrence O'Connell retired as the permanently assigned priest of St. Peter's Church in Charlotte. Jeremiah O'Connell sought similar repose near his brother, especially after the Catholic school he founded in Columbia, South Carolina, was destroyed by Union forces in 1865. As the careers of the O'Connell brothers ebbed, Jeremiah sought to recruit a religious order to western Carolina to establish a Catholic school and continue his life's work. The land needed for such an endeavor was affordable amid the hard times of postwar Reconstruction. In 1871, O'Connell purchased at auction in Gaston County a five-hundred-acre plantation for ten dollars near the Garibaldi train stop along the Richmond & Danville Railroad.[63] But even a free grant of land failed to entice the interest of prospective religious communities. O'Connell then turned his attentions to Abbot Wimmer, who had recently established yet another abbey in Richmond.

At the urging of the recently promoted Bishop James Gibbons, Boniface Wimmer reluctantly agreed to accept the gift of land. On April 21, 1876, a monk and two students from Richmond arrived to take possession of the property and establish Wimmer's newest Benedictine priory, Mary Help of Christians, or Maryhelp, and start the first day of classes for what became St. Mary's College. Despite his initial reluctance, Wimmer later perceived the geographic advantages offered by his newest monastic community. Maryhelp priory could be a springboard for Wimmer's growing ambitions to plant new abbeys in Savannah, Florida, and Alabama. Yet the monks of Maryhelp struggled in those first years, and St. Mary's enrollment was meager. Ever dependent on distant St. Vincent's for leadership, personnel, and funding, Wimmer perceived that Maryhelp would never prosper without the firm direction of a local abbot.[64]

In 1885, Wimmer dispatched to Maryhelp a new group of monks and a newly elected abbot, Leo Haid, a thirty-five-year-old Pennsylvanian apprehensive of his new responsibilities. Yet Haid quickly became a formidable abbot in his own right. Despite Maryhelp Abbey's small size, its priests represented the greatest concentration of Catholic clergy in a state eager for pastoral care and local leadership. The apostolic vicariate had been held temporarily by the bishops of Richmond and Charleston following Bishop James Gibbons' departure in 1872. Yet Gibbons continued to express concerns for the welfare of his former see, and he believed the leader of a permanent monastic community made an appealing choice as the next vicar. Haid expressed concerns whether his monks could honor their Benedictine vows of stability while serving scattered missions across the state. He also doubted his own capacities to reconcile what he feared were the incompatible duties of abbot and vicar. In a letter to Boniface Wimmer, Haid lamented: "One mitre has thorns enough. Two would be too much."[65] Despite his misgivings, North Carolina's needs and Bishop Gibbons' sizeable influence secured Haid's appointment as vicar apostolic in 1887.[66]

Over the next four decades, Leo Haid oversaw a remarkable expansion of Catholicism within the state, though not without difficulty. The abbot-bishop frequently toured the state's Catholic communities, just as Bishops England and Gibbons had done decades before. Haid also succeeded in raising badly needed funds from northern dioceses. The abbot enjoyed particular success in cultivating the generosity of Katharine Drexel, the Philadelphia-born heiress (and future saint) who donated her family's fortune for the ministry of Native American and African American Catholics. Drexel pledged substantial sums for the construction of Maryhelp Abbey's church and the purchase of St. Thomas Catholic Church in Wilmington. Haid also negotiated the move of the Sisters of Mercy's motherhouse from Wilmington to Gaston County in 1892, on land neighboring the monastery in a town newly rechristened as Belmont (Garibaldi possessing problematic connotations with Giuseppe Garibaldi's recent war against the Vatican). Soon the monastery and the college it sponsored would be better known as Belmont Abbey. Meanwhile, the monastery's monks began their work as mission priests. Sadly, Haid's initial apprehensions upon becoming vicar were soon realized. The abbot's lengthy departures coincided with an internal division among the monks over the monastery's Benedictine identity as a contemplative order. In an effort to balance his dual responsibilities, in 1891 Haid successfully petitioned Rome to cede nine western North Carolina counties as a personal fiefdom of Belmont Abbey, a diocese within a diocese that could be staffed exclusively by Benedictines and avoid the circuit-riding duties of generations past. Yet this inevitably caused tensions with the secular, or non-monastic, priests of the vicariate, who maintained their lengthy circuits and sometimes chafed under Haid's singular authority.[67] That authority only increased in 1912 when Haid won from the Vatican a distinctive status for his monastery as an *abbatia nullius dioecesis* ("abbey of no diocese"). This jurisdictional innovation, more common in medieval times, was without precedent in North America. The decree effectively gave the monastery independence from future episcopal authority, and theoretically made the abbot of Belmont Abbey the perpetual vicar of North Carolina, forestalling the creation of an independent diocese. North Carolina's secular priests vocally complained to Rome and requested the immediate establishment of a separate diocese based in Wilmington, but to little effect.[68]

Abbot Leo Haid's efforts to endure the thorns of two distinct mitres might have caused dissension, but during his four decades of leadership Catholicism took deeper root within the state than in any previous period. Catholics remained a tiny minority in an overwhelmingly Protestant state, with priests and funds in short supply, yet the work of generations of laypeople, religious orders, and clergy yielded a remarkable harvest. From 1890 to 1926, the Catholic population in North Carolina had nearly tripled in size, with the densest concentrations of Catholic faithful located in New Hanover, Gaston, Mecklenburg, Buncombe, and Craven counties.[69] The state's Catholic Church now numbered twenty-four parishes, each with its own resident priest, as well as forty mission churches. The monks of Belmont Abbey and the Sisters of Mercy each provided Catholic institutions of higher education, and numerous parochial schools soon followed. Catholicism's growth during Abbot Haid's reign was in many ways the realization of William Gaston's dream, despite the criticism sometimes directed towards North Carolina's abbot–bishop. Following Haid's death in 1924, Rome finally determined that North Carolina now possessed sufficient resources to support its own diocese.[70]

Table 2: Reported Number of Catholics Based on the U.S. Census of Religious Bodies[71]

Census Year	Reported Number of Catholics in North Carolina
1890	2,640
1906	3,981
1916	4,989
1926	6,900
1936	10,219

Sources : *Bureau of the Census, Religious Bodies, 1906, pt. 2 (Washington, D.C.: Government Printing Office, 1910), 609; Bureau of the Census, Religious Bodies, 1916, pt. 1 (Washington, D.C.: Government Printing Office, 1919), 204, 206; Bureau of the Census, Religious Bodies: 1926, vol. 2 (Washington, D.C.: Government Printing Office, 1929) 1256; Bureau of the Census, Religious Bodies: 1936, vol. 2, pt. 2 (Washington, D.C.: Government Printing Office, 1941), 1531.*

This growth would accelerate under the leadership of the state's first diocesan bishops. In the aftermath of Haid's death, the presiding Archbishop of Baltimore, Michael Curley, helped guide North Carolina's foundation as a diocese. Fearful of the intrigues that had divided the monastic and secular priests of the state, Curley secured the nomination of a trusted outsider as North Carolina's first bishop, William Hafey, the Archdiocese's chancellor secretary. While Wilmington and Belmont had respectively served as the two historic centers of Catholicism in the state, the Vatican choose Raleigh as the seat of the diocese due to its status as state capital.[72] Belmont Abbey initially retained its independence as an *abbatia nullius* and kept the nine western counties attached to it, although the monastery's domain would be repeatedly partitioned by Rome and subsequent bishops (the abbey's distinctive status ended in 1977).[73] Bishop Hafey was installed in June 1925 in the newly constructed Cathedral of the Sacred Heart, the nation's smallest cathedral. Hafey replicated the efforts of his predecessors with extensive travel across the state and determined recruitment of new vocations for the priesthood. The perpetual need for fundraising was made even more challenging by the burdens of the Great Depression. Nonetheless, under Hafey's leadership the diocese thrived, with two new parishes established annually on average. By 1937 and the end of Hafey's tenure, the diocese claimed ten thousand Catholics within the state. Succeeding him was Eugene McGuinness, a Pennsylvania-born bishop who like his predecessor was an outsider to the state. Administering the diocese amidst the tumult of World War II, McGuinness oversaw the church's continued growth to eighty-six parishes and a marked increase in the number of priests until his departure for another diocese in 1945.[74]

Raleigh's next bishop, Vincent Waters, took charge as leader of the diocese at a moment equally prosperous and tumultuous. America's postwar boom provided the South a welcome escape from the legacies of poverty from the Reconstruction era, yet the legacy of Jim Crow proved far more divisive. Since emancipation, the leaders of southern dioceses had directed substantial resources for the spiritual care and education of their African American parishioners. Yet these same leaders nonetheless acceded to the growing power of segregation that increasingly divided southern society. In parishes across the region separate pews were reserved for black faithful in the rear of the church, and communion offered to them last.[75] Soon, distinct black parishes and schools were established across the region—twenty-four churches and thirteen schools in North Carolina's case.[76] These institutions were staffed largely by members of religious orders dedicated to serving African Americans, such as the Society of St. Joseph of the Sacred Heart (Josephites).[77]

Bishop Waters seemed an unlikely candidate to challenge the status quo. A native of Roanoke, Virginia, and educated at Belmont Abbey College during the final years of Leo Haid's abbacy, Waters served as a priest in the Diocese of Richmond. However, Waters had experienced several personal encounters with racism that made him adamantly opposed to Jim Crow. Following Waters' installation in 1945, the bishop began a cautious and unpublicized integration of the diocese's lay organizations. By 1950, Waters hinted at the future desegregation of the diocese's parochial schools. "It will be some time in North Carolina before we can open our schools to both colored and whites," Waters wrote in a diocesan report, "but that time is not as distant as it seemed five years ago."[78] By 1951, the bishop issued a pastoral letter condemning racism as heresy and ordering the end of segregated pews and communion service.

Bishop Waters soon put words into action. In April 1953, Waters took the fateful step of merging two segregated parishes in rural Newton Grove, a remote but historically significant Catholic community established during the vicariate of Joseph Gibbons.[79] The merger of the black St. Benedict's Church with the white parish of Our Holy Redeemer sparked considerable resentment and national notoriety. "I would not be at all surprised that there will be a murder committed at the church next Sunday if your order is carried out," threatened one white congregant in a letter to Bishop Waters. Indeed, the garage of the parish priest's rectory was burnt to the ground, an extreme but not isolated example of vandalism. The African American congregants held their own objections, not least the sudden closure of their beloved parish with no prior consultation. Undeterred, Waters and the diocesan chancellor confronted angry crowds outside of Our Holy Redeemer on

May 31, 1953, the first Sunday of integrated masses. A riotous holy day unfolded, all witnessed by newspaper reporters. Over the next few weeks the parish lost half its congregation. The experience proved a searing one for the bishop, yet he persisted on the path towards integration. The *Brown v. Board of Education* decision in 1954 struck down "separate but equal" public education, but private schools remained exempt. Waters nonetheless carefully inched towards the integration of the diocese's parochial schools. Cautiously starting first at the high school level and then proceeding towards elementary schools, Waters' careful desegregation of diocesan schools moved far more quickly than the deliberately glacial pace set by state authorities. Bishop Waters continued to guide his diocese towards equality as the civil rights movement unfolded in North Carolina. Criticized both as a gradualist and as a radical, Waters sought a difficult middle ground towards the theological vision of the Church as a united, mystical body of Christ, overcoming sin's earthly divisions of humanity.[80] Waters died in 1974 after twenty-nine years as bishop of Raleigh, and is buried at the site of his most intense spiritual battle, in the parish cemetery of Newton Grove.[81]

A further testament to Waters' leadership of the state was the sustained growth of North Carolina's Catholic community. At his installation in 1945, North Carolina's diocese numbered some fifteen thousand Catholics. By 1970 there were sixty-seven thousand. Wondrously, this growth triggered an event scarcely imaginable fifty years previously: the establishment of a second diocese within the state. In 1970 Waters initiated the process to split the state's diocese into two, with a new bishop installed in a diocesan seat of Charlotte. Charlotte's dramatic transition into a banking capital and regional economic engine had attracted hundreds of thousands of migrants, including numerous Catholics from northern and midwestern dioceses.[82] The candidate Waters recommended to Rome for Charlotte's diocese had traveled a unique path to the episcopacy. Michael Begley was a Massachusetts-born priest who had arrived in North Carolina in 1934, serving first as a missionary priest in Wilmington before service as the head of the diocese's branch of Catholic Charities. Over time Begley developed a vocation for social work, helping to establish new parishes in the growing Charlotte area while earning a graduate degree from the University of North Carolina–Charlotte. Begley was widely esteemed for his pastoral care, and Waters considered him the natural choice as Charlotte's first bishop. So did Rome, and Begley was installed as the first bishop of Charlotte in 1972.[83] In the decades since Begley's installation, three subsequent bishops have served the rapidly expanding diocese: John F. Donoghue (1984–1993), William G. Curlin (1994–2002), and Peter J. Jugis (2003–present). After Waters' death, Raleigh's diocese was faithfully served by Francis J. Gossman (1975–2006), Michael F. Burbidge (2006–2016), and Luis R. Zarama (2017–present).

Catholicism's future in North Carolina appears to be continuing a trajectory of dramatic expansion. The dynamism of economic centers like Charlotte and the Research Triangle have drawn remarkable demographic growth to the state, much of it drawn from heavily Catholic regions of the northeast and the midwest. According to data collected by the Association of Religion Data Archives, over the last thirty years the growth of the Catholic population in the state has far outpaced nearly every other religious denomination. From 1980 to 2010, North Carolina's overall population increased by eighteen percent. But survey data taken from Catholic congregations indicates an increase of over 300,000 adherents over the same period, a 315 percent increase. Much of this demographic growth is particularly concentrated in the state's largest metropolitan areas.[84]

Yet even rural North Carolina has been impacted by this influx. Sustained immigration has contributed to the growth of Carolina Catholicism for the first time since the colonial era. By far the most significant source of immigration to North Carolina and the entire South comes from Mexico and Central America, drawn by work in the state's agribusiness sector. By 2006, some 160,000 Latinos called North Carolina home, a swift migration coming from nations with strong Catholic identities.[85] According to a 2015 Pew Research Center study conducted on contemporary religious trends, "the geographic center of Catholicism is shifting gradually from the Northeast and Midwest toward the South and West." The study further notes another remarkable shift: "Today a slim majority of Catholics live in the South and West. This shift is being driven by the continuing growth of Hispanics as a share of the U.S. Catholic population; three-quarters of Hispanic Catholics reside in the South or West."[86] North Carolina, once hailed in the nineteenth century as the heart of the "New South," has recently been described as a twenty-first century "*Nuevo* South."[87]

Table 3: Growth of Catholic Adherents in Selected North Carolina Metropolitan Statistical Areas, 1980–2010

Metropolitan Statistical Area	Total Increase in Adherents	Percentage Change
Charlotte-Concord-Gastonia	94,830	410%
Asheville	9,870	197%
Durham–Chapel Hill	19,505	319%
Elizabeth City	773	100%
Fayetteville	4,485	86.8%
Brevard	1,963	421.2%
Burlington	1,415	85.6%
Forest City	379	135%
Goldsboro	1,530	120%
Greensboro	11,095	133%
Greenville	4,674	573%
New Bern	3,881	144%
Raleigh	91,595	744%
Rocky Mount	921	98%
Winston-Salem	11,041	150%

Source : *Metropolitan statistical reports taken from 2010 U.S. Religion Census: Religious Congregations & Membership Study. Collected by the Association of Statisticians of American Religious Bodies (ASARB) and distributed by the Association of Religion Data. Reports can be found in the Association of Religion Data Archives.*

A concrete manifestation of Catholicism's growth is Raleigh's Cathedral of the Sacred Heart. Constructed in 1924 for the ordination of the state's first bishop, William Hafey, the entire state's congregation at the time numbered a little over six thousand. The Gothic Revival structure boasted considerable architectural grace, but modest seating space for 320 congregants. Only the cathedral serving Juneau, Alaska, stood smaller among American dioceses. By 2014, three thousand households flocked weekly to Sacred Heart. To accommodate this dynamic growth, the cathedral held eleven Sunday masses weekly, with spillover services in the cathedral's parochial school, a neighboring hotel, and sometimes even outdoors. To accommodate a parish bursting at the seams, in July 2017 the diocese completed construction of a new cathedral, Holy Name of Jesus, with a capacity for two thousand worshippers, on par with two of America's most historic cathedrals in Baltimore and Philadelphia.[88]

As construction concluded on Raleigh's new cathedral, a parish in a bustling Charlotte neighborhood claimed a distinctive superlative: the largest parish in the nation.

When St. Matthew's Catholic Church was founded in 1986, some 237 families attended the neighborhood parish located on the sparsely populated southern edge of the metropolis's suburban frontier. But the frontier receded quickly. Over the next two decades the area became a hub of development following the completion of the city's interstate highway loop and the establishment of Ballantyne, a planned housing community for the metropolis's affluent. St. Matthew's parish enjoyed the same exponential growth as the surrounding suburbs. By 2017, over 10,300 families had registered with the church, requiring ten masses every weekend to accommodate this multitude. Other superlatives abound: some seven thousand lay volunteers participate in over one hundred ministries; a second parish campus offers additional masses and religious education; and an off-site warehouse stores food, clothing, and other charitable donations (along with a parish-owned forklift). Local leaders have actively studied Evangelical megachurches, such as Saddleback Church in Orange County, California, for inspiration in structuring the management of their own mega-parishes for the years ahead.[89]

Based on the 2010 U.S. Religion Census estimates, nearly four hundred thousand Catholics dwell in the state.[90] While Carolina Catholics remain a religious minority, the denomination's current status is a far cry from William Gaston's era when Catholicism itself was considered an alien creed within the state. The Catholic Church's expansion in the state since 1980 has been buoyed by the larger economic and demographic transformations that have benefited the entire Sunbelt South. But impersonal forces alone cannot account for Catholicism's dramatic growth in North Carolina. Generations of laity, monks, sisters, priests, and bishops sacrificed in the uncertain hope that Catholicism might one day flourish in the state. In 1886 Abbot Leo Haid gave a prayer of dedication for the cornerstone of a new building at his growing college in Belmont. His prayer of hope was as applicable to his congregations as it was his monastery. The works and prayers of those dedicated to Catholicism, Haid prayed, "shall spread God's blessing over this beautiful country in the years to come, when perhaps few of you who are listening to me now shall be among the living."[91] Like the miracle of the fishes and the loaves, the blessings of previous generations have yielded an unimaginable abundance today.

Notes

1. For an inclusive examination of Catholicism's history in North Carolina, see William F. Powers, *Tar Heel Catholics: A History of Catholicism in North Carolina* (Lanham, MD: University Press of America, 2003).

2. Jon F. Sensbach, "Religion and the Early South in an Age of Atlantic Empire." *Journal of Southern History* 73, no. 3 (2007): 631–42; Maura Jane Farrelly, "Catholicism in the Early South." *Journal of Southern Religion* 14 (2012). Enduring URL: http://jsr.fsu.edu/issues/vol14/farrelly.html. Accessed September 1, 2017.

3. For an overview, see Allan Greer and Kenneth Mills, "A Catholic Atlantic," in *The Atlantic in Global History*, eds. Jorge Cañizares-Esguerra and Erik R. Seeman (Upper Saddle River, NJ: Pearson Prentice Hall, 2007), 3–19.

4. On the development of Catholicism in England's southern colonies, see: Robert Emmett Curran, *Papist Devils: Catholics in British America* (Washington, DC: Catholic University of America Press, 2014).

5. Maura Jane Farrelly, "Catholicism in the Early South."

6. William McDonald, ed., "Fundamental Constitutions of Carolina," in *Select Charters and Other Documents Illustrative of American History, 1606–1775* (New York: Macmillan, 1904), 165.

7. James M. Woods, *A History of the Catholic Church in the American South, 1513–1900* (Gainesville: University Press of Florida, 2011), 120.

8. David T. Gleeson, *The Irish in the South, 1815–1877* (Chapel Hill: University of North Carolina Press, 2002), 26.

9. On Protestant immigration to colonial North Carolina, see Tyler H. Blethen and Curtis W. Wood Jr., *From Ulster to Carolina: The Migration of the Scotch-Irish to Southwestern North Carolina* (Raleigh: North Carolina Department of Cultural Resources and Offices of Archives and History, 1998); Daniel Thorp, *The*

Moravian Community in Colonial North Carolina: Pluralism on the Southern Frontier (Knoxville: University of Tennessee Press, 1989).

10. On the problems of establishing the ethnic origins and religious practices of Africans in colonial North Carolina, see Marvin L. Michael Kay and Lorin Lee Cary, *Slavery in North Carolina, 1748–1775* (Chapel Hill: University of North Carolina Press, 1995). On African Catholicism in South Carolina, see John K. Thornton, "African Dimensions of the Stono Rebellion," *American Historical Review* 96, no. 4 (1991): 1101–03.

11. Stephen C. Worsley, "Catholicism in Antebellum North Carolina," *North Carolina Historical Review* 60, no. 4 (1983): 400.

12. *Ibid.*, 400–01.

13. Jay Dolan, *The American Catholic Experience* (New York: Doubleday & Company, 1984), 104–07.

14. J. Herman Schauinger, *William Gaston: Carolinian* (Milwaukee, WI: Bruce Publishing Company, 1948), 1–10; Robert Emmett Curran, *The Bicentennial History of Georgetown University: From Academy to University* (Washington, DC: Georgetown University Press, 1993), 34–35.

15. On Gaston's political career, see: Schauinger, *William Gaston: Carolinian*; John L. Sanders, *William Gaston as a Public Man* (Chapel Hill: North Caroliniana Society, 1997).

16. Francis Newton Thorpe, ed., "The Constitution of North Carolina—1776" in *The Federal and State Constitutions, Colonial Charters, and Other Organic Laws of the States, Territories, and Colonies Now or Heretofore Forming the United States of America*, vol. 5 (Washington, DC: Government Printing Office, 1909), 2793, amendment 32.

17. Maura Jane Farrelly, *Papist Patriots: The Making of an American Catholic Identity* (Oxford: Oxford University Press, 2012), 253–54.

18. Schauinger, *William Gaston: Carolinian*, 200–02.

19. Michael O'Brien, *Conjectures of Order: Intellectual Life and the American South, 1810–1860*, vol. 2 (Chapel Hill: University of North Carolina Press, 2004), 1084.

20. Worsley, "Catholicism in Antebellum North Carolina," 402.

21. John England, *Diurnal of the Right Rev. John England, D.D.: First Bishop of Charleston, S.C. from 1820 to 1823* (Philadelphia: American Catholic Historical Society, 1895), 18.

22. Worsley, "Catholicism in Antebellum North Carolina," 403–04.

23. England, *Diurnal of the Right Rev. John England*, 17–28; Schauinger, *William Gaston: Carolinian*, 203; Worsley, "Catholicism in Antebellum North Carolina," 402–04.

24. Worsley, "Catholicism in Antebellum North Carolina," 416, 418.

25. For more on England's ministry and political outlook, see: Joseph Lawrence O'Brien, *John England, Bishop of Charleston: The Apostle to Democracy* (New York: Edward O'Toole, 1934); Patrick W. Carey, *An Immigrant Bishop: John England's Adaption of Irish Catholicism to American Republicanism* (Yonkers, NY: U.S. Catholic Historical Society, 1979); Peter Clarke, *A Free Church in a Free Society: The Ecclesiology of John England, Bishop of Charleston* (Hartsville, SC: Center for John England Studies, 1982); Lou F. McNeil, *Recovering American Catholic Inculturation: John England's Jacksonian Populism and Romanticist Adaption* (Lanham, MD: Lexington Books, 2008).

26. O'Brien, *Conjectures of Order*, 1091.

27. For an overview of the constitutional convention, see: Harold J. Counihan, "The North Carolina Constitutional Convention of 1835: A Study in Jacksonian Democracy," *North Carolina Historical Review* 46, no. 4 (Oct. 1969): 335–64.

28. Counihan, "The North Carolina Constitutional Convention of 1835: A Study in Jacksonian Democracy," 351.

29. *Proceedings and Debates of the Convention of North Carolina Called to Amend the Constitution of the State* (Raleigh, NC: Joseph Gales & Son, 1836), 242, 253–54.

30. *Proceedings and Debates of the Convention of North Carolina*, 279–80 (emphasis added); Counihan, "The North Carolina Constitutional Convention of 1835: A Study in Jacksonian Democracy," 352.

31. *Proceedings and Debates of the Convention of North Carolina*, 302, 331; Counihan, "The North Carolina Constitutional Convention of 1835: A Study in Jacksonian Democracy," 353; Schauinger, *William Gaston: Carolinian*, 193–94.

32. William Gaston, *Address Delivered Before the Philanthropic and Dialectic Societies at Chapel-Hill, June 20, 1832* (Raleigh, NC: Joseph Gales & Son, 1832), 14; Schauinger, *William Gaston: Carolinian*, 165.

33. Patrick S. Brady, "Slavery, Race, and the Criminal Law in Antebellum North Carolina: A Reconsideration of the Thomas Ruffin Court," *North Carolina Central Law Journal* 10 (1978–79): 248–60; Thomas D. Morris, *Southern Slavery and the Law, 1619–1860* (Chapel Hill: University of North Carolina Press, 2004), 279–81.

34. *Proceedings and Debates of the Convention of North Carolina*, 79–80.

35. Edmund S. Morgan, "Slavery and Freedom: The American Paradox," *Journal of American History* 59, no. 1 (June 1972), 6.

36. John Wertheimer, *Law and Society in the South: A History of North Carolina Court Cases* (Lexington: University Press of Kentucky, 2009), 197, fn. 19.

37. Andrew H.M. Stern, *Southern Crucifix, Southern Cross: Catholic–Protestant Relations in the Old South* (Tuscaloosa: University of Alabama Press, 2012), 161.

38. On Catholic attitudes and participation in slave ownership see: Maura Jane Farrelly, "American Slavery, American Freedom, American Catholicism," *Early American Studies* 10, no. 1 (Winter 2012): 69–100.

39. Julie Zauzmer, "Grappling with its history of slavery, Georgetown gathers descendants for a day of repentance." *Washington Post*, April 18, 2017. In an effort to engage with the legacies of slavery, Georgetown University has organized an archive documenting the lives of those enslaved by the institution, the Georgetown Slavery Archive. Enduring URL: http://slaveryarchive.georgetown.edu/

40. On Catholic theology concerning slavery in the 19th century, see: Kenneth J. Zanca, ed., *American Catholics and Slavery, 1789–1866: An Anthology of Primary Documents* (Lanham, MD: University Press of America, 1994).

41. England, *Diurnal of the Right Rev. John England,* 10, 14, 24, 28, 29.

42. Stern, *Southern Crucifix, Southern Cross,* 163, 167.

43. On the experience of African American Catholics, see: Randall M. Miller, "Slaves and Southern Catholicism," in *Masters and Slaves in the House of the Lord: Race and Religion in the American South, 1740–1870,* John B. Boles, ed. (Lexington: University Press of Kentucky, 2015): 127–52; Fr. Cyprian Davis, O.S.B., *History of Black Catholics in the United States* (New York: Crossroad Books, 1992).

44. David Leroy Corbitt, *The Formation of North Carolina Counties, 1663–1943* (Raleigh: Division of Archives and History, North Carolina Department of Cultural Resources, 1950), 103–04.

45. Gleeson, *The Irish in the South,* 77–79.

46. On nativism and the response to Catholic immigration in the pre–Civil War era, see Jay P. Dolan, *The Immigrant Church: New York's Irish and German Catholics* (Baltimore, MD: John Hopkins University Press, 1975).

47. Worsley, "Catholicism in Antebellum North Carolina," 423–30. On Protestant perceptions of Archbishop John Hughes, and his influence on American Catholicism, see Richard Shaw, *Dagger John: The Unquiet Life and Times of Archbishop John Hughes of New York* (New York: Paulist Press, 1977).

48. David T. Gleeson, *The Green and the Gray: The Irish in the Confederate States of America* (Chapel Hill: University of North Carolina Press, 2013.)

49. David C. R. Heiser, *Patrick N. Lynch, 1817–1882: Third Catholic Bishop of Charleston* (Columbia: University of South Carolina Press, 2015), 70.

50. Roger H. Harrell, *The Second North Carolina Calvary* (Jefferson, NC: McFarland), 157; John W. Moore, *Roster of North Carolina Troops in the War Between the States,* vol. 2 (Raleigh, NC: Ashe & Gatling, State Printers and Binders, 1892), 147.

51. Heiser, *Patrick N. Lynch,* 73–78, 94–113.

52. David T. Gleeson, "'No Disruption of Union': The Catholic Church in the South and Reconstruction." Edward J. Blum and W. Scott Poole, eds. *Vale of Tears: New Essays on Religion and Reconstruction* (Macon, GA: Mercer University of Press, 2005), 164–86.

53. Heiser, *Patrick N. Lynch,* 130, 143; Powers, *Tar Heel Catholics,* 173.

54. *Ibid.,* 146–47.

55. John Tracey Ellis, *The Life of James Cardinal Gibbons,* abridged by Francis L. Broderick (Milwaukee, WI: Bruce Publishing Company, 1962), 1–16.

56. Allen Sinclair Will, *Life of James, Cardinal Gibbons* (London: John Murphy Company, 1911), 30–31.

57. *Ibid.,* 35–42.

58. Cardinal James Gibbons, *Reminiscences of Catholicity in North Carolina* (Unknown publisher, 1891), 2. University of North Carolina Wilson Special Collections Library, North Carolina Collection.

59. Walter H. Conser, *A Coat of Many Colors: Religion and Society Along the Cape Fear River of North Carolina* (Lexington: University Press of Kentucky, 2006), 210; Powers, *Tar Heel Catholics,* 352–53.

60. Powers, *Tar Heel Catholics,* 353–60; Will, *Life of James, Cardinal Gibbons,* 43–44; Ellis, *The Life of James Cardinal Gibbons,* 29.

61. Jerome Oetgen, *An American Abbot: Boniface Wimmer, O.S.B., 1809–1887* (Washington, DC: Catholic University of America Press, 1997), 258.

62. Heiser, *Patrick N. Lynch,* 158.

63. Fr. Jeremiah O'Connell, *Catholicity in the Carolinas and Georgia: Leaves of Its History* (Westminster, MD: Ars Sacra, 1964), 477–79.

64. Fr. Paschal Baumstein, O.S.B., *My Lord of Belmont: A Biography of Leo Haid* (Charlotte, NC: Laney-Smith & the Archives of Belmont Abbey, 1995), 26–36.

65. Baumstein, *My Lord of Belmont,* 88.

66. Fr. Paschal Baumstein, O.S.B., "An Abbatial Diocese in the United States," *Catholic Historical Review* 79, no. 2 (April 1993), 217–20.

67. Baumstein, *My Lord of Belmont,* 103–08, 119–21; Conser, *A Coat of Many Colors,* 214; Powers, *Tar Heel Catholics,* 210–11. The nine counties ceded to Maryhelp Abbey were Mecklenburg, Lincoln, Cleveland, Cabarrus, Rowan, Davidson, Guilford, Forsythe, and Gaston.

68. Baumstein, "An Abbatial Diocese in the United States," 224–27.

69. Henry K. Carroll, *Report on Statistics of Churches in the United States at the Eleventh Census, 1890* (Washington, DC: Government Printing Office, 1894), 38, 231, 243.

70. Powers, *Tar Heel Catholics*, 237–38.

71. On the utility of the U.S. Census's surveys of religious bodies, see: Kevin J. Christiano, *Religious Diversity and Social Change: American Cities, 1890–1906* (Cambridge, MA: Cambridge University Press, 1987), 32–41.

72. Powers, *Tar Heel Catholics*, 235–46; Baumstein, *My Lord of Belmont*, 265.

73. Baumstein, "An Abbatial Diocese in the United States," 227–45.

74. Powers, *Tar Heel Catholics*, 247–64.

75. On the impact of segregation within southern Catholicism, see Davis, *The History of Black Catholics in the United States;* John T. Gillard, *The Catholic Church and the American Negro* (Baltimore, MD: St. Joseph's Society Press, 1929); James B. Bennett. *Religion and the Rise of Jim Crow in New Orleans* (Princeton, NJ: Princeton University Press, 2005); Danny D. Collum, *Black and Catholic in the Jim Crow South* (New York: Paulist Press, 2006).

76. Mark Newman, "Towards 'Blessings of Liberty and Justice': The Catholic Church in North Carolina and Desegregation, 1945–1974." *North Carolina Historical Review* 85, no. 3 (July 2008), 322.

77. Stephen Ochs, *Desegregating the Altar: The Josephites and the Struggle for Black Priests, 1871–1960* (Baton Rouge: Louisiana State University Press, 1990).

78. Newman, "Towards 'Blessings of Liberty and Justice,'" 322.

79. Powers, *Tar Heel Catholics*, 161–66.

80. Newman, "Towards 'Blessings of Liberty and Justice,'" 326–33.

81. Powers, *Tar Heel Catholics*, 311–19.

82. On Charlotte's growth as a banking center: William Graves and Jonathan Kozar, "Blending Southern Culture and International Finance: The Construction of a Global Money Center," in *Charlotte, NC: The Global Evolution of a New South City*, William Graves and Heather Smith, eds. (Athens: University of Georgia Press, 2012), 87–101.

83. Powers, *Tar Heel Catholics*, 27.

84. Association of Religion Data Archives, "North Carolina Religious Traditions Report, 1980–2010 Change." Enduring URL: http://www.thearda.com/rcms2010/r/s/37/rcms2010_37_state_name_1980_ON.asp. Accessed September 1, 2017.

85. Hannah E. Gill, *The Latino Migration Experience in North Carolina: New Roots in the Old North State* (Chapel Hill: University of North Carolina Press, 2010), 3.

86. Pew Research Center, "America's Changing Religious Landscape" (May 12, 2015), 67, 146. Enduring URL: http://assets.pewresearch.org/wp-content/uploads/sites/11/2015/05/RLS-08–26-full-report.pdf. Accessed September 1, 2017.

87. Heather A. Smith and Owen Furuseth, "The 'Nuevo South': Latino Place Making and Community Building in the Middle Ring Suburbs of Charlotte," in *Twenty-First Century Gateways: Immigrant Incorporation in Suburban America*, Audrey Singer and Susan W. Hardwick, eds. (Washington, DC: Brookings Institution Press, 2009), 281–307.

88. Rebecca Martinez and Eric Hodge, "Raleigh's Catholic Congregation has outgrown America's Second-Smallest Cathedral," *WUNC*, December 19, 2014. Enduring URL: http://wunc.org/post/raleighs-catholic-congregation-has-outgrown-americas-second-smallest-cathedral#stream/0; Martha Quillan, "2,000 gather in Raleigh for 'a once-in-a-lifetime experience'" *The News & Observer* (Raleigh), July 26, 2017.

89. Jeff Parrott, "Where 20,000 or 30,000 are gathered: life in a Catholic Megaparish," *U.S. Catholic* 77, no. 4 (April 2012); Tim Funk, "NC now has country's biggest Catholic parish—in Charlotte," *Charlotte Observer,* April 25, 2017; Leah Libresco, "The Largest Parish in America," *America: The Jesuit Review,* 216, no. 10 (May 2017).

90. Clifford Grammich, et al., eds., *2010 Religion Census: Religious Congregations and Membership Study* (Fairfield, OH: Glenmary Research Center & Association of Statisticians of American Religious Bodies, 2012), 37.

91. Fr. Paschal Baumstein, O.S.B., and Debra Estes, *Blessings the Years to Come: Belmont Abbey, a Pictorial Perspective* (Belmont, NC: Archives of Belmont Abbey, 1997), iii.

World Religions

GEORGE W. BRASWELL, JR.,
and LISA STOVER GRISSOM

Religions with origins in Asia and the Middle East, such as Hinduism, Buddhism, Sikhism, Islam, and Baha'i have found their expressions in North Carolina. For generations, followers of these religions have come to the state to attend its universities, to find employment in educational and business and research institutions, and to become citizens. They have brought extended families from their homelands and raised their children in communities across the state.

Desiring to practice their native religious traditions, they have built temples and mosques and religious schools and employed priests and nuns and imams and other personnel to be leaders in worship and schools.

Religions with their roots in Christianity, yet with distinct variations from it, have also been formed in America. The Church of Jesus Christ of Latter-day Saints, popularly known as Mormons, and the Jehovah's Witnesses are two primary examples of indigenous American religions in North Carolina. Mormons have built their churches, called wards, and placed one of only 148 temples worldwide in Apex, North Carolina. Jehovah's Witnesses have built their kingdom halls across the state. Mormons and Jehovah's Witnesses are two of the fastest growing religious communities in the region.

The select religious communities of Hinduism, Buddhism, Zen Buddhism, Islam, Sikhism, Baha'i, Church of Jesus Christ of Latter-day Saints, and Jehovah's Witnesses in North Carolina will be highlighted in this essay.

Hinduism in North Carolina

Introduction

Hinduism, a term assigned to religious traditions in India, originated in India several thousand years ago. Its belief system and worship patterns include a diversity of expressions centering on the adoration of deities and the dictates of morality in individual and community life. There are more than nine hundred million Hindus in India. Several thousand North Carolinians practice Hinduism.

Expressions of Hinduism may include various temples dedicated to multiple deities. Vedanta societies emphasize various philosophies from the Vedic scriptures, and

287

Transcendental Meditation includes various forms of Yoga. Yoga schools are led by North Carolina teachers or masters of different techniques of meditation exercises.

Hinduism may be one of the most inclusive and eclectic religious traditions with its variety and diversity of philosophies and methods; Jainism may be closely associated with Hindu practices. Examples of Hinduism in North Carolina may be seen in three primary communities: The Hindu Society of North Carolina (HSNC) in Morrisville, the Sri Venkateswara Temple in Cary, and The International Society of Krishna Consciousness in Hillsborough.

Hindu Society of North Carolina

The Hindu Society of North Carolina (HSNC) was begun in Raleigh in 1976. With a growing community of Asian Indians, there was a need to provide worship and cultural experiences for them. The founding priest was Dr. Ganga Sharma. He and Mrs. Sharma were born, raised, and married in India. His father was a Hindu priest, and Dr. Sharma was trained as a priest by him. Dr. Sharma had served as a scientist with the United Nations until his retirement when he relocated in Raleigh to teach at North Carolina State University.

Dr. and Mrs. Sharma led their community to purchase some eighteen acres on Aviation Parkway in Morrisville. There, a temple and a social hall have been built. The temple contains multiple icons of marble deities transported from India. The social hall, known as one of the largest in North America, seats some 1500, hosting family and wedding occasions as well as cultural and training events. The temple is served by several priests trained in the Sanskrit language who live on the property.

Among the deities are Ganesh, known as the elephant deity, who provides success and wisdom; Hanuman, known as the monkey deity, who gives strength and devotion; Shiva, the deity of death and destruction; Rama, known for his chivalry and virtue; Lakshmi, the female deity of good luck and fortune; and Krishna, the deity of love and devotion who is the most complete expression of Vishnu.

Worshippers remove their shoes upon entering the temple where the altar's thirty marble deities are clothed in colorful attire. The temple is open daily for members to enter and offer prayers and gifts before the deities. Membership is composed of some 1100 families and single members who celebrate major Hindu festivals there and in the social hall.

The literature of Hinduism presents a way of life based on eternal Dharma, the universal nature of religion, duty, and righteousness.

The Sri Venkateswara Temple

Plans for the Sri Venkateswara Temple were envisioned in 1998 when a local couple bought a 2.5 acre plot in Cary, North Carolina. They used temporary quarters for gatherings. In time, they raised money to build a temple. Fourteen artisans from southern India along with local workers built the elaborate cement moldings. The temple was dedicated in May 2009 at a cost of some 3.5 million dollars.

Modeled after a temple with the same name in the south of India, the new structure featured a nine-foot, two-ton statue of Sri Venkateswara on the altar. Sri Venkateswara is a representation of the supreme deity, Vishnu, who is the preserver and protector of the world. Eight other deities are located in the temple complex, for Hindus believe that the supreme deity can take many forms.

Following the Hindu calendar, many festivals are celebrated in the temple. Followers also drop by during the course of the day to offer prayers, to meditate, and bring offerings. Since many residents in the area are from south India, the temple offers them traditions from their native region. The intricate structure is intended to suggest the human body. The entrance represents the feet. The two sides of the temple represent the hands. The top of the temple portrays the head.

Membership of this temple has grown such that more than six priests are needed. They run a Sunday school that meets in a local elementary school. More than fifteen thousand members are on the email roster. There are other Sri Venkateswara temples in Bridgewater, NJ, in Pittsburgh, and in Chicago.

The International Society of Krishna Consciousness

The New Goloka Temple (ISKCON of North Carolina) was founded in 1982 as a communal retreat in the forests off Dimmocks Mill Road in Hillsborough, North Carolina. Soon residents built an octagonal temple on the seventeen acres purchased with the aid of the local Asian Indian community. Swami Bir Krishna das Goswami, born in America and a convert to the Hare Krishna movement in the 1970s, became the leader. The temple operates under the international movement known as The International Society of Krishna Consciousness, which is a branch of Hinduism.

The altar of the temple includes statues of the deity Krishna and his consort Radha. The Hare Krishna are followers of the singular deity Krishna and give their devotion exclusively to him. Daily worship services begin at 4:30 a.m. with the chanting of Krishna's holy names. There are other services throughout the day. A Sunday program at 5:00 p.m. includes chanting, a lecture, and a meal. Daily programs attract the local residents who are in full-time service. The Sunday program attracts numerous members and visitors, especially Asian Indians, from across the area.

A life-size figure seated in a throne chair in the temple is that of A.C. Bhaktivedanta, affectionately called Pravhupada. He is the founder of the Hare Krishna community. Born in India, he left his wife and family in India and came to the United States as an adult to launch his missionary movement in the late 1970s. It became known worldwide as the International Society of Krishna Consciousness, with its *Bhagavad Gita* in the English language.

Those who attend the temple programs are approximately 12 percent Western devotees (North and South American, European), one to two percent East Asian and African devotees, and the remainder Asian Indians. At major festivals, the Asian Indian attendees constitute 90 percent of the crowd.

Distributing food to students and handing out literature, the devotees are active on university campuses. There are approximately two thousand people on the temple's membership list. New Goloka has become a thriving suburban community serving thousands of Hindu Asian Indian devotees of the god Krishna and over one hundred western Hare Krishna. The young Anglo-American converts who joined the movement in the '70s have matured, married, and had children.

Relationship of Hinduism to Wider Society

A sacred religious holiday for all Hindus, including Sikhs and Jains, is Diwali, a five-day festival that represents the start of the New Year. Often called the festival of lights, it is considered one of the most important observations in Hindu tradition and culture. It is a time for families to connect with long-held Asian Indian traditions and share them with the general public.

Temples are decorated with lights, traditional dances and other rituals are performed, and temple members and families and guests enjoy the delicacies of Asian Indian foods. Often public spaces are rented for Diwali festivities, and the general public is invited.

Islam in North Carolina

Introduction

Islam had its beginnings with its prophet Muhammad (570–622 CE) in the the city of Mecca on the Arabian peninsula. After gaining a following, he moved to the city of Medina where he established the religion Islam. Later, the Qur'an, based on messages he received from the angel Gabriel sent from Allah, became the foundation for Muslims.

Islam rapidly expanded to become a global religion: It presently has 1.6 billion followers and composes some 25 percent of the world's population. Sunni and Shia are the two major divisions of Islam, based on differences of their understanding of the successor to the prophet. The Sunni, who compose some 85 percent of Islam, believe in a caliph. The Shia, who compose some 15 percent of Islam, believe in an Imam. Saudi Arabia is predominantly Sunni; Iran is Shia.

Muslims have been attracted to North Carolina to study at universities. Some have married non–Muslim women and become American citizens. Others have moved to the state to join the professions of education, medicine, and other vocations. They have sought to follow their religion by building mosques and educational facilities to nurture their families in the teachings of the Qur'an and its prescriptions for living the strictly Muslim life.

The Islamic Association of Raleigh provides a primary example of a Muslim community engaged in the essential beliefs and practices of Islam. Worship, prayer rituals, educational programs centered on the Qur'an, and outreach activities are basically similar in all Muslim communities both globally and in North Carolina.

Islamic Association of Raleigh (IAR)

In 1981, Muslim students, along with others in the area, formed the Islamic Association of North Carolina and held prayers at NC State University Student Center. With the increase of Muslim immigrants to the area, the Muslim Student Association (MSA) together with others during 1984–85 raised money to build a mosque on Atwater Street in Raleigh. This mosque, the Islamic Association of Raleigh (IAR), has given the mosque community a constitution and bylaws.

A full-time Imam was brought from Jordan to head up the activities of IAR in 1985. Soon, the Al-Furqan Weekend Sunday Islamic School for children was begun, along with the organization of a youth group. In 1992, the Al-Iman Islamic School opened, meeting all the accreditation requirements for pre–K through 8th grade of the state of North Carolina. Its mission statement is to "be guided by the Qur'an and Sunnah according to the methodology of the people of Sunnah and Jama'ah." Its facilities include classrooms, computer labs, science lab, cafeteria, full-size gym, and playground.

The school "shall through the teaching of Islamic and scholastic courses prepare students to: achieve excellence in education and a strong Muslim identity, meet or exceed the goals of the NC standard course of study and the National Educational goals, exhibit high morals and exemplary citizenship."

Land was also purchased in 1995 in Wake County for a Muslim cemetery.

The building of a three-story mosque was completed in 2008 with a large prayer hall, multipurpose rooms, library, sisters' area, a kitchen and cafe, and administrative offices for two Imams. The prayer hall is used daily for the five stated prayers described in the Qur'an, in addition to individual prayers. Muslims not only come to pray in the prayer hall but also to quietly sit and read the Qur'an. In Morrisville, future development will take place on a twelve-acre plot.

Friday is the "Sabbath" for Muslims. Besides the stated prayers, a sermon is given by the Imam. To accommodate the increasing Muslim population and to alleviate the challenge of parking, three shifts of Friday prayers are offered.

Besides the Sunday school for Muslim children and the Al-Iman school (pre–K through the 8th grade), there is the Al Bayan School for Qur'an memorization and learning. Regular activities are held for youth, and there are many classes held for adults including Qur'anic study. Social services include alms (*zakat*) and charity (*sadaqa*) for distribution to the needy and for refugees. Hajj group services are offered each year for those making the pilgrimage to Mecca. Personnel of IAR offer funeral and burial services in the mosque and at the private Muslim cemetery in Zebulon. IAR plans various community events including annual picnics, a health fair offering free medical services, and observances related to the Islamic calendar. The Al-Maidah Kitchen and Café is open for lunch and dinner and provides catering services. IAR has two Imams who lead the activities with the services of many volunteers and under the guidance of the Board of Directors, the Shura, and the Executive Committee.

Beliefs and Practices of Islam in Relationship to the Public Square

Because of certain specific Islamic teachings found in the Qur'an and the traditions of their prophet Muhammad, Muslims in North Carolina (as well as globally) relate to society in special ways. The call to prayer required five times daily may necessitate some Muslims to request special places in the workplace or in a school environment to perform the prayers. The direction to Mecca must be established. Many Muslims go to the mosque, especially to perform the noonday prayers, and may request time off from work. Muslims often request that food services in public spaces be sensitive to their religious mandate; the eating of pork, very common to North Carolina culture, is prohibited in Islamic dietary regulations. The attire of Muslim women includes wearing a head covering in public and may involve clothing that covers the entire body from head to feet.

The Church of Jesus Christ of Latter-Day Saints

Introduction

The Church of Jesus Christ of Latter-day Saints was founded in 1830 in upstate New York by Prophet Joseph Smith. Its members are known as Mormons, or Latter-day Saints. The *Book of Mormon* contains the visions that came to Smith; it was published in 1830. Conflicts between Mormons and non–Mormons characterized the church's journeys westward through several states. In fact, Joseph Smith and his brother were killed by mob gunfire in 1844. By that time, church administration included a prophet and twelve apostles. Brigham Young arose from the apostles to become the second prophet of the church. Young led the Mormons to Salt Lake City where eventually the famous temple was built. Smith proclaimed that his church was a restoration of the true Gospel, the true church, and the true priesthood. The organization of the church included the offices of the prophet, his two counselors, the twelve apostles, and various levels of leadership known as quorums.

The local church is called a ward, and an association of wards is called a stake. Worship services, Sunday schools, priesthood meetings for men, a women's Relief Society, and seminary classes for high school youth compose the major programs on the local level. Select churches have an office for genealogy/ancestor research and are open to interested visitors. The temple is a very special place in the life of Mormons. A Mormon must qualify to enter the temple by meeting certain standards of tithing and morality. Temple ceremonies include purification rites, a service of marriage for eternity, and baptism for the dead.

The church has become a global missionary movement. Its ideal is to send young men and women on a two-year assignment. Some eighty-five thousand missionaries are active today. The church is nearing seven million members in the United States and eight million members in multiple countries. It is the fourth largest religious community in the United States and one of the fastest growing religions in the world. Churches are present in 176 nations, with greater than twenty-nine thousand congregations. And the church has grown to 148 temples worldwide—including Apex, North Carolina.

The Church of Jesus Christ of Latter-Day Saints in North Carolina

Mormons became associated with North Carolina when their headquarters in Salt Lake City created the Southern States Mission in 1896. As churches grew over time, it was renamed the North Carolina–Virginia Mission, in 1970. This state is now divided into two missions: The Charlotte Mission is assigned its own missionaries for the western part of the state, and the Raleigh Mission, which includes a few churches on the Virginia border, also has its own missionaries; some five hundred missionaries are assigned to the two missions. Across North Carolina are fifteen stakes with multiple wards and a membership of some seventy-five thousand Mormons. A temple dedicated in Apex in 1999 is the only one between Washington, D.C., and Atlanta.

The programs in wards, stakes, and temples across the world are quite uniform. On the local level, unpaid volunteers serve; the church has no paid clergy. A bishop, similar to the role of a pastor, serves the ward. A stake president supervises the functions of several wards. These leaders work at their regular jobs as medical doctors, lawyers, professors, business executives, and other vocations. They may volunteer between twenty and thirty hours of work per week during evenings and weekends. Various classes are held during the week and Sundays for men, women, youth, and families. The Bible, *The Book of Mormon, Doctrines and Covenants,* and *Pearl of Great Price* are mainstays of their literature.

Family Home Evening is a special time for each Mormon family to eat together, pray together, discuss important matters together, and play games. Monday evening is a favorite time that is set aside for no outside disturbances. A youth for his or her high school years attends a class known as seminary, held weekdays in the church before school. Many churches also sponsor Scout troops. Select churches have a Mormon Family History Center open to the public for the tracing of family genealogies. Also open to non–Mormons are church employment centers that assist with résumé writing, interviews, and advice for job-hunting. There are Mormon storehouses in select areas that gather food, clothing, and other essentials for distribution to the needy. Each of the 148 temples around the world is different in size and architecture. However, each is consistent with the gold-plated Angel Moroni atop the spire with a bugle in hand. And each consistently offers the same major functions. Every temple is open for the public to tour just before its dedication, but once dedicated, the temple is open only to Mormons who have qualified for a "temple recommend."

The temple in Apex is located on Bryan Drive, next to the church. Designed by Dan Dills, it features a classic, modern, single-spire design; at 10,700 square feet, and seventy-one feet high, the temple sits on twelve acres. Groundbreaking occurred February 6, 1999; open house for the public was December 13 to 18, 1999; and the temple was dedicated by Prophet President Gordon B. Hinckley on December 18, 1999. In order to gain entrance inside the temple and to participate in its three major ceremonies, a Mormon must obtain a permission card called a temple recommend. To obtain the card, one must observe and obey the "Words of Wisdom" found in *Doctrines and Covenants.* These include tithing, no alcohol and drug consumption, and a pure family life. One satisfies these requirements by examination by the bishop of the ward; temple recommends must be renewed yearly.

The three major ceremonies are ordinances of purification, marriage for eternity (also called celestial marriage), and baptism for the dead. The administration of the temple is led by the temple president, appointed by the Salt Lake City headquarters of the church. The staff consists of volunteers only. Ordinances of purification include ceremonies for spouses to be productive in having children. Ceremonies for marriage for eternity seal a husband and wife and their children to live forever in their own kingdom in eternity. Ceremonies for baptism for the dead occur in a pool of water surrounded by twelve oxen representing the tribes of Israel. Temple Mormons may be baptized vicariously for a deceased family member or other individual in the temple pool. The Church of Jesus Christ of Latter-day Saints has gathered genealogical records of several billion deceased people, stored in vaults in Utah.

Jehovah's Witnesses

Introduction

Charles Taze Russell (1852–1916) founded the Zion's Watchtower Tract Society. Its headquarters are located in Brooklyn, NY. His followers were labeled "Russellites," and by 1931 his organization was officially titled Jehovah's Witnesses. A governing board, known as the "Theocratic Society," assumed leadership of the organization and operated in headquarters known as "Bethel" in Brooklyn. The board is composed of fifteen to eighteen men who preside over all matters of Jehovah's Witnesses.

Russell had a background in Presbyterian and Congregational churches. He reacted against certain teachings of traditional Christianity. Among his teachings he denied the existence of hell, the doctrine of the Trinity, the physical return of Jesus Christ, mankind's possession of a soul, and the validity of the churches.

He was a voluminous writer, and his major writings included *Studies in the Scriptures*. His teachings were focused on prophesies and dates including Armageddon, the millennium, and the elect. He is well known for his teaching on the 144,000 elect from his studies of the book of Revelation in the New Testament. The major scripture of Jehovah's Witnesses is the *New World Translation of the Holy Scriptures*. Russell's interpretations are woven throughout this Bible. Among many other publications are two of the widest-distributed magazines globally, *The Watchtower* and *The Awake*.

The governing board, the "Theocratic Society," initiates decisions and programs that affect all members. The local congregation of Witnesses meets in a Kingdom Hall. Members known as "Publishers" study the board literature and prepare to go out two-by-two to outlying communities to knock on doors and share their testimonies and magazines. Witnesses are basically a layperson and non-clergy organization divided into zones both nationally and globally with leaders who administer the work under supervision of Bethel headquarters. The church maintains publishing houses throughout the world. The latest self-reported statistics indicate that 8,201,545 Jehovah's Witnesses are located in 239 lands, with 115,416 Kingdom Halls, 9,499,933 free home Bible studies conducted, and 19,950,019 witnesses attending the annual Memorial of Christ's Death, held in select settings globally.

Jehovah's Witnesses in North Carolina

Jehovah's Witnesses compose less than one percent of the population of North Carolina (.08 percent, to be precise). Their Kingdom Halls are located across North Carolina from Wilmington to Boone. Each one is built to a basic plan, housing roughly two hundred members, constructed primarily by their members who come from various states over a long weekend to complete it.

The beliefs and practices of the Witnesses are quite uniform in every Kingdom Hall. It is the place for Witnesses to worship, to study materials sent from Bethel headquarters, to train for door-to-door visitation, and to receive literature to place in homes that they visit. The Kingdom Hall is simple in décor with a main auditorium for worship and study sessions and with a small library where members receive the literature to carry on visitations. The care of the building and grounds is provided by volunteers. Routinely there are five meetings held weekly for the continual process of training members: Four are held in the Kingdom Hall and one in a home. The four meetings held weekly in the Kingdom Hall for one hour each are the Public Talk, The Watchtower Study, The Kingdom Ministry School, and The Service Meeting. Both old and young prepare for door-to-door visitation through memorizing scriptures, developing skills to communicate with people, and supplying their briefcases with literature to distribute. The fifth meeting is held in a private home with a study of a Watchtower Society book.

The organizational framework of Jehovah's Witnesses is founded upon Jehovah and His chief minister Jesus Christ. The governing board, or Theocratic Society, is led by the president and some fifteen to eighteen men. Appointments are made by the Board of Leaders with various titles as Servants, Elders, and Overseers who supervise zones, regions, and circuits from global to national to local areas. On the local level, a Witness is expected to voluntarily become a Publisher to spend multiple hours in visitation and distribution of literature. Precise records are kept of every hour of service, of every piece of literature distributed, and of attendance at meetings on every level. Special conferences are held in major cities emphasizing various teachings of Jehovah's Witnesses. Recently, a three-day conference was held at the convention center in Raleigh with the theme "Remain Close to Jehovah." It was free and open to the public; some twenty thousand were in attendance. More than 120 congregations from eastern and central North Carolina were represented. Sessions focused on enhancing family communication, protecting spirituality, and keeping a close relationship with God. Each year, a Memorial Service of Christ's Death is held in select settings around the globe including North Carolina, with a reported total of twenty million global attendees.

Buddhism in North Carolina

Introduction

In the latter part of the sixth century BC, a young prince by the name of Siddhartha was born into the Gautama clan in the land of India, in what is now known as Nepal, and was raised in the Hindu tradition.[1] His father, Suddhodana, the king and ruler of the Sakya people, wanted Siddhartha to one day be king. So he raised Siddhartha with all the privileges and amenities that that life could offer. In order to protect the young prince from the evils and dangers of life, the king confined Siddhartha to the palace and forbade him from venturing outside its walls.[2]

Growing more and more restless about the deeper meanings of life, Siddhartha, against his father's wishes, secretly left the palace one night to discover for himself the outside world.[3]

Shocked and disturbed by what he encountered, Siddhartha earnestly sought the answers to the sufferings of life. He turned first to his religion of Hinduism. Finding no solace there, Siddhartha, at the age of twenty-nine, escaped from the palace, leaving behind his former life along with his wife and young son to seek answers to the questions of the meaning of life and its suffering.[4] In his quest for understanding of life and suffering, Siddhartha sought the company of the Hindu holy men, *sannyasi,*[5] and became their student. He meditated on Hindu philosophy and followed the strict discipline of an ascetic life. But in all this Siddhartha found no satisfaction.

Buddhist tradition says that Siddhartha sat under the bodhi tree for forty-nine days, at which time he experienced enlightenment and took on the name of Buddha, which means "enlightened one" or "awakened one."[6] Siddhartha, now known as the Buddha, developed the teachings of Buddhism that are still observed today. In Buddhism, anyone who follows the Four Noble Truths and the Eightfold Path can become a Buddha and achieve Buddhahood. There is no reliance on gods, prayers to gods, or priests. It is only dependent on the work and effort of the individual. In the original tradition of Buddhism,

Buddha was not worshipped but highly respected as the inspiration and a model for a spiritual practice as a way of life. Buddha is believed to have found and shown this path to others to follow in achieving ultimate enlightenment, or Nirvana.

Presently, there are approximately 488 million Buddhists worldwide. Half of the world's Buddhists live in one country, China. The largest Buddhist populations outside China are in Thailand (13 percent), Japan (9 percent), Burma (Myanmar) (8 percent), Sri Lanka (3 percent), Vietnam (3 percent), Cambodia (3 percent), South Korea (2 percent), India (2 percent) and Malaysia (1 percent). An estimated 2.45 million to 4 million Buddhists reside in the U.S.[7]

It is difficult to determine the exact number of Buddhists who live in the state of North Carolina; Buddhists do comprise a portion of the 3 percent of the total Eastern religious groups that reside here.[8] The city of Raleigh is listed as one of the top ten cities in the United States with the largest Buddhist populations.[9]

Fo Guang Shan Temple

One expression of Buddhism that came to the United States is Fo Guang Shan, from China and Taiwan. In Chinese, "Fo" means Buddha, "Guang" means Light, and "Shan" means Mountain. The idea originated from Venerable Master Hsing Yun.[10] Born Li Guoshen on August 19, 1927, in a small rural village in the Jiangdu region of Jiangsu Province in China, Venerable Master Hsing Yun would be ordained in 1941 as a Buddhist monk in the Linji lineage of the Chan School of Buddhism.[11]

In 1948, communism in China was gaining power, and civil unrest was growing as millions of Chinese, including the Buddhist monastics, left mainland China and sought refuge on the island of Taiwan. Venerable Master Hsing Yun was included in that number.[12] It was during this time in Taiwan that Venerable Master Hsing Yun put into practice the idea of putting people first. He showed people that Buddhism was "about our world right now" and "not only about the next life." He felt that Buddhism should benefit society and bring people joy. Additionally, Venerable Master Hsing Yun felt that "Buddhism should adapt itself to modern times and the needs of individuals." This was the foundational thinking of what Venerable Master Hsing Yun would call "Humanistic Buddhism."[13]

In 1967, Venerable Master Hsing Yun brought this vision of Humanistic Buddhism to life by beginning the construction of the first Fo Guang Shan Monastery in Kaohsiung, Taiwan. This would be the first of two hundred temples that would be built worldwide, spanning six continents. Presently, there are more than twenty Fo Guang Shan Temples in the United States. Only one is in the state of North Carolina.[14] As Fo Guang Shan flourished over the decades it would come to include not only monasteries but colleges, hospitals, and other civic-minded organizations worldwide. Venerable Master Hsing Yun cast another vision for the Fo Guang Shan Buddhist movement. He wanted to propagate Buddhism by bringing it to the west. So, in 1988, Venerable Master Hsing Yun built the Hsi Lai Temple, which means "coming to the west" in Chinese, in Los Angeles, California. This would become the global headquarters for Fo Guang Shan and the first footprint of Fo Guang Shan in the United States.

In 1992, North Carolina members of the laity organization of Fo Guang Shan, Buddhist Light International Association (BLIA), traveled to Los Angeles, California, to attend the dedication of the Hsi Lai Temple. While there, these BLIA members had a vision to build a Fo Guang Shan Temple in North Carolina. In 1998, Venerable Master Hsing Yun came to North Carolina, specifically to the Research Triangle Park (RTP) area, and determined that "the conditions were right" to build a Fo Guang Shan Temple in RTP. Venerable Master Hsing Yun appointed Venerable Chueh Chuan to stay and supervise and oversee the eventual construction of the Fo Guang Temple that is currently located on Prince Drive in Raleigh.

The Fo Guang Shan Temple of Raleigh was dedicated in 2010. The monastic order of Fo Guang Shan, International Buddhist Progress Society, directs and superintends the temple and all activities that are open to the public. The BLIA members volunteer a significant number of hours and copious resources in the work of aiding and assisting the monastic nuns in the daily maintenance and operation of the temple. The Fo Guang Shan Temple houses in its shrine a fourteen-ton statue of Buddha. Hewn from a single piece of white jade from Taiwan, the statue is elevated atop an expansive platform and is the centerpiece in the Fo Guang Shan weekly dharma services.

In keeping with the vision of the propagation of Humanistic Buddhism to the west, the Fo Guang Shan Temple in Raleigh opens its doors to the public for weekly Sunday "dharma" or teaching services, meditation classes, classes in Buddhism, special events, special celebrations such as the Chinese New Year and the Buddha's birthday. Fo Guang Shan in Raleigh estimates that approximately two to three thousand people visit their temple annually. Theirs is not a proselytizing mission, but an effort in seeking ways to integrate into their immediate communities by way of the teachings of Buddhism, The Four Noble Truths, and the Eightfold Path. Through their Buddhist beliefs, Fo Guang Shan monastics and laity wish to be positive contributors to their community. Fo Guang Shan in Raleigh share in the task of community assistance efforts through blood drives, disaster relief, and visiting local nursing homes.

Accompanying a larger-than-life rendering of Venerable Master Hsing Yun that can be seen immediately upon entering the temple, the words stating the objectives of Fo Guang Shan are printed:

> Give confidence to others.
> Give hope to others.
> Give joy to others.
> Make things convenient for others.

Corresponding are the humanistic Buddhist teachings of Venerable Master Hsing Yun:

> To propagate Buddhist teachings through cultural activities.
> To foster talent through education.
> To benefit society through charitable programs.
> To purify human hearts and minds through Buddhist practice.[15]

Fo Guang Shan teaches that people do not have to abandon their own belief systems to participate in and be a part of the Buddhist community. Humanistic Buddhism can help to enrich all faith traditions through the practices of meditation, silence, and chanting. To the Christian community, Fo Guang Shan believes that their practice of the teachings of Humanistic Buddhism compliments and somewhat emulates the teachings of Jesus to "love thy neighbor."

Zen Buddhism

Introduction

Over time, two major schools of Buddhism developed: Theravada, also known as Hinayana, and Mahayana.

Hinayana Buddhism, literally translated from Sanskrit (the classical language of India, the birthplace of Hinduism and Buddhism), means the "Lesser Vehicle." Hinayana Buddhism is considered the more traditional form of Buddhism highlighting the teachings and writings of Buddha and views Buddha as more of a teacher and instructor.[16] Because branch affiliations of Buddhism are not measured by most censuses or surveys, it is believed that Hinayana Buddhist practitioners comprise a small number within the Buddhist community worldwide, with populations primarily in Cambodia, Sri Lanka, Laos, Myanmar, and Thailand.[17]

Mahayana Buddhism—which, literally translated, means the "Greater Vehicle"—developed as Buddhism moved toward more eastern countries such as China, Japan, Mongolia, Korea, and Taiwan.[18] Mahayana adherents are believed to be much larger in number within the Buddhist diaspora.[19] Mahayana Buddhism focuses more on the mystical or spiritual aspect of Buddhism. Buddha became more a savior and less a teacher.

As Mahayana traveled into countries like China and Japan, another expression of Buddhism developed. Around AD 520, Buddhism moved from India into China and became known as Ch'an Buddhism.[20] During the twelfth century it migrated to Japan where it became known as Zen.[21] In Chinese, Ch'an means meditation, and equivocally in Japanese, Zen means meditation. This form of Buddhism focused primarily on the practice of meditation.

The practice of *zazen,* or seated meditation, is the core of Zen Buddhism. It is "a way of vigilance and self discovery."[22] It is "the experience of living from moment to moment" and "living in the here and now."[23] It is thought in the Zen Buddhist tradition that *zazen* was the method by which the original Buddha, Siddhartha Gautama, achieved enlightenment while seated under the bodhi tree. Therefore, in Zen Buddhism, *zazen* is the path to spiritual awakening for those who practice meditation with the ultimate purpose of achieving *satori,* or enlightenment. Zen Buddhists do not view Zen Buddhism as a piece of knowledge or a religion or a belief. It is not something to be intellectually grasped. Zen Buddhism does not tell people what to believe, but to think—or in this case, not to think. Zen Buddhism is a mindful practice of focusing on the spiritual path through meditation. There are no scriptures to study or rituals to observe, only quiet and seated meditation.[24]

Zen Buddhism became widely known across America after the 1950s through the writings, lectures, and students of the noted Zen Buddhist in America, D.T. Suzuki of Japan.[25] Because Suzuki's writings and teachings in America attracted followers, Zen meditation centers, beginning in San Francisco and Los Angeles, began to spring up across the country. In 1961, the San Francisco Zen Center opened, and as its membership grew it would acquire more land and expand its facilities—eventually establishing a Zen Mountain Retreat in 1972. In 1966, the Zen Meditation Center of Rochester was established, influenced by the teachings of Suzuki. This was to be the beginning of the growth of Zen meditation centers across America.

Two schools or traditions have developed in Zen Buddhism. The older tradition is

Rinzai, and the younger but more prominent tradition in America is Soto. The two differ particularly on the practices toward attaining enlightenment, or *satori*. The Rinzai may stress the attempt to solve intellectual puzzles called *koans*, while the Soto may emphasize "just sitting."[26]

Because the Zen Buddhist population is so embedded within the Buddhist population, estimated between 2.45 to 4 million, it is difficult to know the exact number of Zen practitioners in the United States. The same could be said of the Zen Buddhist adherents in North Carolina. They do share in the 3 percent of Eastern religion practitioners in North Carolina. To accommodate these Zen practitioners, North Carolina contains approximately a dozen Zen centers or meditation halls.

The North Carolina Zen Center

Located on fifteen acres of wooded land and rolling hills is the Brooks Branch Zendo of The North Carolina Zen Center (NCZC) in Pittsboro, North Carolina.[27] Also known by its temple as the Sosen-ji, the North Carolina Zen Center practices the Rinzai tradition of Zen Buddhism. It offers a place of quiet and meditation for practicing Zen Buddhists, Buddhists, or other people looking for a place of respite from their busy lives. With a meditation hall that seats up to twenty-four participants, a full kitchen, five dormitories, and full shower facilities for both men and women, the NCZC is equipped to handle up to twenty-two guests, with future plans for expansion.[28] The roots of the NCZC began modestly in the north Pittsboro home of Susanna Stewart where she led meditation groups. Desiring to provide a place of *dai-sesshin,* or intensive meditations, for the east coast, Stewart built a meditation hall near her home. Incorporated in 1977, the Squirrel Mountain Zendo of the North Carolina Zen Center was born. In 1977, Susanna married Sandy Stewart, a fellow student of Zen Buddhism. Sandy had a vision for not only a meditation center but a residential center with a full retreat experience in meditation. In 1995, a student of Sandy's donated fifteen acres of nearby land to the Squirrel Mountain Zen Center, and in 1998 the Brooks Branch Zendo of The North Carolina Zen Center meditation center was completed. A kitchen was added in 2001, dormitories in 2003, and shower facilities in 2005.

The NCZC was dedicated in 2007 by the spiritual mentor of Susanna and Sandy, Joshu Sasaki Roshi, who was ninety-nine years old at the time. It was at this dedication that the NCZC officially received its temple name of Sosen-ji. Sandy Stewart went on to be the Abbott and teacher of the NCZC for 35 years and retired in April 2015. The NCZC continues to independently operate as a Rinzai Zen center and does not align itself with any particular Zen lineage in America. Currently, the NCZC estimates that it welcomes some one hundred visitors annually to practice sitting in the zendo or meditation hall or walking meditation on the wooded grounds. The private donations of between twenty-five and thirty committed members provide for the maintenance and operation of the NCZC.

Chapel Hill Zen Center

The Chapel Hill Zen (CHZC) Center located in Hillsborough, North Carolina, is founded on the Soto school of Zen Buddhism, established in the thirteenth century in Japan by Zen Master Eihei Dogen. The CHZC follows the religious practice of seated meditation. Following the teachings of Buddha in which Zen Buddhism has its roots, it is because of ignorance created by greed, hate, and delusion that one is unable to achieve enlightenment or Nirvana. The *zazen,* or seated meditation practice, of Zen Buddhism helps guide one to realize his or her Buddha nature and subsequent enlightenment.[29]

In 1981, the CHZC was formed by a small group of friends who "took turns meditating in each other's homes in the Durham–Chapel Hill area in North Carolina."[30] In response to its growing membership, in 1997, the CHZC was formally and legally named and headed by a board of directors.[31] Because several of the members of the CHZC originally practiced at the San Francisco Zen Center (SFZC), the CHZC is formally affiliated with SFZC.

In 1991, at the request of the CHZC membership to the SFZC, Josho (Teacher) Pat Phelon came to CHZC to lead the Center. In 2000, Josho Phelon was installed as the Abbess of the CHZC.

Like the North Carolina Zen Center (NCZC) in Pittsboro, the CHZC is located in a heavily wooded area immediately off of Highway 86. Although not as expansive as the NCZC, the CHZC offers a relatively quiet and meditative atmosphere for its members and visitors. Its meditation hall and adjoining kitchen and social hall are CHZC's singular facility feature. Although the CHZC does offer weeklong intensive meditation retreats throughout the year, unlike the NCZC it does not provide for overnight retreats, and no residential accommodations are on the grounds.

The CHZC is open to the public for the more than eight morning and evening scheduled *zazen* services offered each week. The CHZC also offers special lectures or ceremonies such as burning ceremonies and memorial services to the general public. The CHZC has proven to be quite convenient for those located near the center to come early in the morning and experience quiet guided meditation before work. It is estimated that the CHZC welcomes between fifty and sixty people per week.

The CHZC teaches that "Zen realization shows us that we are directly connected to and dependent on, all living beings and everything that exists" and that "compassionate concern for the welfare of others and for the environment flow naturally from this insight."[32] With this in mind, the CHZC reaches out to its immediate community not to proselytize but to be a part of the concerns of its community.

The Chapel Hill Zen Center:

- Engages in local environmental efforts.
- Participates in the local Interfaith Council.
- Visits the Orange County Corrections Department four times a month and provides a meal there once a month.
- Visits four NC state prisons and two federal prisons each month and has officiated at two weddings in the prison; upon request, it has offered hospice care there as well.
- Offers Buddhist-oriented substance abuse recovery programs.
- Volunteers at local shelters.
- Offers children's services.
- Offers chaplaincy services at UNC Hospitals.
- Has participated for the last twelve years in an annual interfaith Thanksgiving meal.
- Gives talks at public schools, colleges, and universities on Zen Buddhism.

Currently, the CHZC has approximately fifty members with a small percentage, approximately 8 percent, of Asian origin. Membership and visitors cross all socioeconomic lines. Given the local university populations, college students and professors are proportionally represented in this number. It was also noted that most members of the CHZC are over the age of forty.

The CHZC partners with eight other Zen Centers in North Carolina. They are located throughout the state, in Asheville, Charlotte, Greensboro, Durham, and Raleigh.

Baha'i in North Carolina

Introduction

The Baha'i religion arose in the middle of the nineteenth century in the land of Persia, present-day Iran.[33] It developed from the Iranian Shi'ite doctrine of the coming of the Twelfth Imam, a messiah type that would return "to bring justice and righteousness to the world."[34]

In May of 1844, in the city of Shiraz, Iran, Siyyid 'Alí-Muhammad (1819–1850) declared that he was the Twelfth Imam, as foretold, and proclaimed "that a greater prophet was to follow who would bring a new age of peace for all peoples."[35] Siyyid 'Alí-Muhammad, now called the *Bab* (Arabic for "the gate"), was persecuted for his teachings by the Islamic officials in Iran. In 1850, the Bab would be imprisoned and later executed in Tabriz by the Islamic government.[36]

Born in Tehran, Iran, a young protégé of the Bab was Mirza Husayn Ali (1817–1892). In 1852, during his incarceration in an Iranian prison in Tehran, Ali came to believe that he was the long-awaited manifestation of God as prophesied by the Bab.

Baha'i publications describe the moment: "In April of 1863, he declared to some of his followers that he was the messenger that was prophesied by the Bab."[37] Ali would come to be known as the Baha'ullah, which means "Glory of God" in Baha, the universal language of the Baha'i. "Throughout His ministry, Baha'ullah revealed thousands of personal prayers and meditations, explanations of religious principles, and a wealth of spiritual and social guidance that form the core of the Baha'i sacred scriptures."[38]

The teachings of the Baha'i are universal and all-inclusive. Their central theme is oneness:

> The oneness of God and religion, the oneness of humanity and freedom from prejudice, the inherent nobility of the human being, the progressive revelation of religious truth, the development of spiritual qualities, the integration of worship and service, the fundamental equality of the sexes, the harmony between religion and science, the centrality of justice to all human endeavors, the importance of education, and the dynamics of the relationships that are to bind together individuals, communities, and institutions as humanity advances towards its collective maturity.[39]

The Baha'i operate on three administrative levels: the Local Spiritual Assembly, the National Assembly, and the Universal House of Justice. The Local Spiritual Assembly is made up of nine members that serve on the council. They oversee the administration of the local Baha'i Faith Center. The National Spiritual Assembly is made up of nine members as well; they oversee the administration of the Baha'i Faith Centers in the United States. Its headquarters are in Wilmette, Illinois, and was "initiated by the visit of Abdul Baha in 1912."[40]

The Universal House of Justice is also comprised of nine members. It is located at the Baha'i world center on Mount Carmel in Haifa, Israel. "It functions as the supreme governing body, applying the laws taught by Baha'ullah and ruling on matters not included in the sacred texts."[41]

Despite historical and contemporary persecutions of the followers of the Baha'i faith in Iran and other Arab countries, it is estimated that there are six million Baha'i followers worldwide including countries in Africa, Asia, the Americas, and Europe. Baha'i literature reports that:

> [T]he Baha'i have established significant communities in more countries and territories than any other independent religion except Christianity.[42]
>
> In just over 150 years, the Baha'i Faith has grown from an obscure movement in the Middle East to the second-most widespread of the independent world religions. Embracing people from more than 2,100 ethnic, racial, and tribal groups, it is quite likely the most diverse organized body of people on the planet. Its unity challenges prevailing theories about human nature and the prospects for our common future.[43]

Currently, because of the restrictions by the United States census with regard to questions of religious affiliations, it is difficult to calculate the exact number of Baha'i adherents nationally and in North Carolina. However, in 2012, the Association of Statisticians of Religious Bodies reported that in a 2010 census, there were an estimated 1,136 Baha'i communities in the United States with an estimated 171,449 Baha'i nationally.[44] The percentage of Baha'i in North Carolina is estimated to be less than 1 percent of the total statewide population.

There are an estimated twenty-five communities within 568 localities in North Carolina, and the numbers can vary as to size and number of each community from one person to three- or four-hundred people.[45] In the Durham area, for example, a group of 150 comprise the local Baha'i community, with a demographic representation of 35 percent black, 35 percent white, and 30 percent Persian or Latino.[46]

The Raleigh Baha'i Center

Another example of a local Baha'i community is The Raleigh Baha'i Center (RBC) located in downtown Raleigh.[47] What began in cities like San Diego and Atlanta in the 1930s and 1940s, moved into North Carolina by the 1950s, creating Baha'i communities. By 1996, an old church in Raleigh had been purchased to house the first Raleigh Baha'i Center where it stands today.

Because the Baha'i believe that God sent messengers or prophets to speak to mankind throughout human history, they also believe that the writings of these prophets are all equally sacred, so it is commonplace to hear readings and devotions from the Qur'an or the Holy Bible, as well as Baha'ullah. Sunday services include prayers, readings, and music and conclude with a time of informal group discussion. There are no clergy, so membership participation is encouraged.

Each Baha'i community forms adult spiritual study circles to promote spiritual growth within the Baha'i faith. They are encouraged to meet weekly in each other's homes to foster a sense of community and connectedness. The RBC currently has more than forty adult spiritual study circles.

Baha'i communities also place great importance in the care and the spiritual nurturing of their children and youth. Like all Baha'i local assemblies, the RBC offers children's classes to help "develop their moral capacities" for "not only their future happiness, but to the service and advancement of our entire society."[48]

The Baha'i community provides spiritual guidance and growth through their Junior Youth Spiritual Empowerment Programs (JYSEP). The JYSEP membership is youth ages twelve to fourteen and helps youth "navigate through crucial stages in their lives," as denominational literature explains. "The program helps them form a strong moral identity and empowers them to contribute to the well-being of their communities and the world at large."[49] The RBC currently enrolls approximately 198 members in their JYSEP, with 175 of the members not of the Baha'i faith.

Both of these groups meet weekly and are open to anyone of any or no faith. Parents are encouraged to participate as well.

To reflect their sense of unity and equality, a group of approximately fifteen Baha'i men of color met in Greensboro, North Carolina, in 1987. This group would later be known as The Black Men's Gathering. Dr. Harvey McMurray shares his memory of the events: "The Black Men's Gathering … was an individual initiative that was inspired by two realities, the plight of the men of African descent in the United States and an unyielding faith in the redemptive power of the healing message of Baha'ullah, the Prophet Founder of the Baha'i Faith."[50]

Supported by the Baha'i Universal House of Justice, Dr. William "Billy" Roberts called these men to meet and to pray in order "to spiritual(ly) uplift and empower men of African descent to play their part in helping to build the 'new world order'[51] foretold by Baha'ullah" and to "consult on pathways to their spiritual transformation and service to the Baha'i faith."[52] It is worth noting that not all Baha'i members supported this initiative.

With much celebration and lauding, the Universal House of Justice brought the Black Men's Gathering to its conclusion in 2011. The initiative was never meant to be a permanent fixture within the Baha'i tradition but gratefully "acknowledged its unique experience of men of color in the US."[53]

Sikhism

Introduction

In AD 1469, Nanak, the founder of the Sikh religion, was born in the Punjab region in the north of India, present-day Pakistan, in a small village called Talwandi, west of Lahore. Nanak was born to Hindu parents and lived in a Muslim-controlled province. He was fluent in both Arabic and Persian. It was said that Nanak demonstrated a particular intelligence and insight at an early age.[54]

Following a deeply spiritual experience in 1499, Nanak declared, "There is no Hindu, no Muslim." And further,

> There is but One God, His name is Truth, He is the Creator, He fears none,
>   He is without hate, He never dies, He is beyond the cycle of births and death,
>   He is self illuminated, He is realized by the kindness of the True Guru.
>   He was True in the beginning, He was True when the ages commenced
>   and has ever been True, He is also True now.[55]

Now referred to as *guru,* a reverential term in Punjabi (the native language spoken by Sikhs) for "teacher" or "messenger," Nanak traveled extensively throughout India and beyond into countries like Sri Lanka, Persia, and Tibet to spread his newfound message.

Believing his message would be more easily understood via music, Guru Nanak chose to share his message through the medium of hymns. He would sing them in the local language wherever he went.

Guru Nanak set up local cells called *manjis,* derived from the Sanskrit word for stage, where his followers could gather to meditate and recite the hymns. Followers of this message were called Sikhs, Punjabi for "disciple." The Sikh is a disciple of the One God.

After the death of Guru Nanak in 1539, nine other gurus were to follow him, each guru contributing to the Sikh religion.[56] Some would add to the collection of hymns of Guru Nanak. Some would introduce the written language of Punjabi, in which the Sikh scripture would later be written. Some would strengthen the Sikh tradition of the *langar,* the communal kitchen. The fourth guru, Guru Ram Das (guru from 1574 to 1581) founded the Sikh holy city of Amristar and started the construction of the Golden Temple that first housed the Sikh Holy Scriptures, *Adi Granth,* in 1604, which was codified by the fifth guru, Guru Arjen Dev.

The tenth guru, Guru Gobind Singh (1675–1708) was the last of the Sikh gurus. Guru Gobind Singh contributed greatly to the Sikh tradition. "During his lifetime, Guru Gobind Singh established the Khalsa order (meaning "The Pure"), soldier saints. The Khalsa uphold the highest Sikh virtues of commitment, dedication, and social conscious [sic]."[57] The Khalsa order includes both men and women "who have undergone the Sikh baptism ceremony and who strictly follow the Sikh Code of Conduct and Conventions and wear the prescribed physical articles of the faith."[58]

The prescribed articles that easily identify a Sikh follower are called the five "K"s.

- Kangha is the comb to hold the hair in place and denotes spirituality.
- Kara is the steel bracelet worn on the right arm to denote unity.
- Kesa is uncut hair, which is the sign of a holy man.
- Kirpan is a doubled-edge sword to symbolize the warrior's protection of the weak.
- Kach is knee-length trousers worn to express modesty and oral restraint.[59]

Because of these "physical articles of the faith," Sikhs are often mistaken for Arabs or Muslims.[60] As a further effort to distinguish them from the Hindu or Islamic faith, and to demonstrate equality of all men and women and a rejection of the caste system, Guru Gobind Singh gave all Sikh men the last name of "Singh." In Punjabi, it means lion. All Sikh women were given the last name of "Kaur," meaning princess.

Before his death in 1708, Guru Gobind Singh declared that there would no longer be any human gurus. The Holy Scriptures, *Adi Granth,* which means "first book" in Punjabi, would be the final guru or messenger for the Sikh warriors. Now called Guru Granth Sahib, the final and eleventh guru, it is considered the Sikh supreme authority and contains words of all the human gurus as well as the writings of people of other faiths. It is universal in nature and scope, containing the revelation of the One God to his messengers:

Sikhs arrived in North America in 1897 and played a pivotal role in the opening of the West and construction of the Panama Canal in 1904. In 1906, Sikhs established their first *gurudwara,* or place of worship, in the United States; today 700,000 Americans and Canadians are Sikh, and nearly every major city has a Sikh place of worship and community center.[61]

Doctoral students coming from India were the first Sikhs to arrive in North Carolina in the 1960s. The 1970s brought the arrival of approximately eight Sikhs to North Carolina who were medical professionals. They lived in Smithfield, Asheboro, Kernersville, and Fayetteville. Trained in London, they moved to the United States to set up medical offices. There was no particular strategy to their relocation to North Carolina, just coincidental opportunities.[62]

Estimates range from twenty to twenty-five million in the Sikh global population, making it the fifth largest religion in the world.[63] According to the 2010 U.S. Census, there are about 57,000 Indians in North Carolina.[64] To estimate the number of Sikh adherents within that number would be difficult. There are, however, three major cities in North Carolina that accommodate a Sikh population: Charlotte, High Point, and Durham all have *gurudwaras* (meaning, "the gateway"), or places of worship, for their respective Sikh communities.

Formed in 1969, The Atlantic Coast Sikh Association (ACSA) was the first Sikh organization that served Sikhs from Virginia to South Carolina. Since then, the ACSA, The Sikh Gurudwara of North Carolina, and several others have been organized to serve their local communities. Currently, there are an estimated forty Sikh gurudwaras in the United States.[65]

The Sikh Gurudwara of North Carolina, Inc.

One such gurudwara is The Sikh Gurudwara of North Carolina, Inc. (SGNC) located in Durham.[66] Initially meeting in homes in the Durham area, a group of Sikh families realized a need for a gurudwara to accommodate their growing numbers. The SGNC was established in 1983 as a result. What started with a membership of approximately fifty has grown to upwards of seven hundred to eight hundred people.

The SGNC has a primarily (99.98%) Indian population, explains Mr. Kulpreet Singh of Durham. "Members of our community are professionals in many fields including medicine, engineering, information technology, and education, among others. [The] children attend various local universities, technical colleges, and grade schools."

The SGNC welcomes anyone who wishes to come and learn more about the Sikh faith. The SGNC Sunday services are offered beginning at 10:00 a.m. and ending with a *langar,* or community meal, at 1:30 p.m.

With their religious belief that all mankind are equal, and their commitment to community service and living a virtuous and truthful life, the SGNC have a tremendous "love thy neighbor" attitude, a desire to connect to their community, and a strong sense of obligation to help and care for their North Carolina neighbors and friends. The SGNC calls the Tar Heel State home and wants to be a vital and contributing partner to its well-being.

Conclusion

For North Carolinians, the display of the rich and multi-colored tapestry of these world religions and their communities is easily visible in our schools, workplaces, and neighborhoods. Adding to North Carolina's many ethnic textures, these religions, whether born at home or abroad, bring with them theological and cultural overlays that extend across the state's geographical and societal landscapes. Their presence can be seen in the changing skylines of cities and towns throughout North Carolina by the temples, halls, and mosques that silhouette the horizons. They are neighbors, co-workers, and fellow North Carolinians desiring to be contributing partners in their respective communities while remaining faithful to their own beliefs and traditions.

FURTHER READING

Publications

Chapel Hill Zen Center News, November & December 2015.
Chapel Hill Zen Center: A Soto Zen Meditation Group pamphlet.
"Hindu Society of North Carolina," pamphlet, self-printed by Society. n.d.
Yun, Venerable Master Hsing. *The Wheel of Rebirth*. Hacienda Heights, CA: Buddha's Light Publishing, 2012.
_____. *The Four Noble Truths: The Essence of Buddhism*. Hacienda Heights, CA: Buddha's Light Publishing, 2011.

Websites

www.buddhapadipa.org/buddhism/buddhism-today
www.hsilai.org
www.sfzc.org
www.bahai.us
www.bahaiteachings.org/bahai-principles-a-universal-language
www.sikh-history.com/sikhhist/gurus/nanak
www.realsikhism.com
www.americansikhcouncil.org/history
www.acsagurdwara.tripod.com
www.gurdwara.us
www.pewresearch.org/2012/08/06/ask-the-expert-how-many-us-sikhs
http://raleighmasjid.org/
http://www.iccharlotte.org/about-ice
http://www.newgoloka.com/
http://www.bkgowami.com/
www.hsncweb.org
www.svtemple/mission.jsp

NOTES

1. George W. Braswell, Jr., *Understanding World Religions* (Nashville, TN: Broadman & Holman Publishers, 1994), 45.

2. "Buddhist Pilgrimage," Buddhist Studies: Buddha Dharma Education Association & Dharma.net, Accessed March 20, 2016, http://www.buddhanet.net/e-learning/buddhistworld/buddha.htm; George W. Braswell, Jr., *Understanding Sectarian Groups in America* (Nashville, TN: Broadman & Holman Publishers, 1994), 241.

3. Buddhist Studies: Buddha Dharma Education Association & Dharma.net, "Buddhist Pilgrimage."

4. *Ibid.*

5. George W. Braswell, Jr., *From Iran to America: Encounter with Many Faiths* (Maitland, FL: Xulon Press Inc., 2014), 177.

6. Braswell, *From Iran to American: Encounters with Many Faiths,* 174.

7. "The Global Religious Landscape: Buddhists," Pew Research Center: Religion & Public Life, Last Modified December 18, 2012, Accessed March 20, 2016, http://www.pewforum.org/2012/12/18/global-religious-landscape-buddhist/.

8. "Religious Landscape Study: Adults in North Carolina," Pew Research Center: Religions & Public Life, Accessed March 20, 2016, http://www.pewforum.org/religious-landscape-study/state/north-carolina/

9. "Are these 'the most Buddhist cities in America?,'" Lions Roar: Buddhist Wisdom for Our Time, Last Modified November 13, 2012, accessed March 20, 2016, http://www.lionsroar.com/the-most-buddhist-cities-in-america/.

10. Jill Chen, President of the Buddhist Light International Association of Raleigh, Interviewed by Author, at Fo Guang Shan Temple, Raleigh, NC, September 19, 2015.

11. Nathan Michon and John Gill, *The Life of Master Hsing Yun* (Hacienda Heights, CA: Buddha's Light Publishing, 2012), 3; Venerable Master Hsing Yun, *The Fundamentals of Humanistic Buddhism* (Hacienda Heights, CA: Buddha's Light Publishing, 2012), Inside Cover.

12. Michon and Gill, *The Life of Master Hsing Yun,* 15.

13. Michon and Gill, *The Life of Master Hsing Yun,* 21.

14. Except where footnoted, remaining information was drawn from personal interviews by author Grissom with Jill Chen and Monastic director Venerable Chueh Shang of the International Buddhist Progress Society on September 19, 2015, and November 15, 2016, at the Fo Guang Shan Temple in Raleigh, North Carolina.

15. "Objectives," Fo Guang Shan Monastery, Accessed March 20, 2016, https://www.fgs.org.tw/en/ Organizations/Objectives/

16. Braswell, *Understanding World Religions,* 56–57.

17. "The Global Religious Landscape: Buddhists," Pew Research Center: Religion & Public Life, Last Modified December 18, 2012, Accessed March 21, 2016, http://www.pewforum.org/2012/12/18/global-religious-landscape-buddhist/.

18. Braswell, *Understanding World Religions,* 56–57.

19. "The Global Religious Landscape: Buddhists," Pew Research Center: Religion & Public Life.

20. Braswell, *Understanding Sectarian Groups in America,* 249.

21. *Ibid.,* 249.

22. "What Is Zen Buddhism?," Zen Buddhism, Accessed March 21, 2016, http://www.zen-buddhism.net/

23. *Ibid.*

24. "What Is Zen Buddhism?," Zen Buddhism, Accessed March 21, 2016, http://www.zen-buddhism.net/

25. Braswell, *Understanding Sectarian Groups in America,* 250.

26. Braswell, *Understanding Sectarian Groups in America,* 249, 251.

27. The North Carolina Zen Center, Accessed March 21, 2016, http://www.nczencenter.org/about-the-center/

28. Except where footnoted, all remaining information was drawn from personal interviews by author Grissom with Jason Dowdle, President of the Board of the North Carolina Zen Center, and Daniel McKinnon, member and resident of the North Carolina Zen Center, at the North Carolina Zen Center in Pittsboro, NC, on November 30, 2015.

29. Chapel Hill Zen Center, Accessed March 21, 2016, http://www.chzc.org/

30. The Rev. Pat Phelon, Abbess of the Chapel Hill Zen Center, interview with author Grissom in Chapel Hill, NC, on November 30, 2015.

31. Except where footnoted, all remaining information was drawn from personal interviews by author Grissom with the Rev. Pat Phelon at the Chapel Hill Zen Center in Chapel Hill, NC, on November 30, 2015.

32. Chapel Hill Zen Center, Accessed March 21, 2016, http://www.chzc.org/

33. Braswell, *Understanding World Religions,* 148.

34. *Ibid.*

35. *Ibid.*

36. Braswell, *Understanding Sectarian Groups in America,* 295.

37. Braswell, *Understanding Sectarian Groups in America,* 295.

38. *The Baha'i Faith: An Introduction* (A Publication by the National Spiritual Assembly of the Baha'is of the United States, Evanston, IL, 2011), Inside Panel.

39. "What Baha'i Believe," Baha'i.org, Accessed March 25, 2016, http://www.bahai.org/beliefs/.

40. Braswell, Understanding Sectarian Groups in America, 298.

41. *Ibid.*

42. *The Baha'i's: A Profile of the Baha'i Faith and its Worldwide Community* (a publication of the Office of Public Information of the Baha'i International Community, Haifa, Israel, 2005), 6.

43. *The Baha'i's: A Profile of the Baha'i Faith and its Worldwide Community,* Front Cover.

44. U.S. Membership Reports: Religious Bodies 2010, Accessed March 25, 2016, http://www.thearda.com/rcms2010/r/u/rcms2010_99_U.S._name_2010.asp.

45. Corrine Perry, Secretary of the Regional Baha'i Council of the Atlantic States, telephone interview with author Grissom, on December 7, 2015.

46. Dr. Harvey McMurray, member of the Baha'i community in Durham, co-author of the book, *The Story of the Baha'i Black Men's Gathering: Celebrating Twenty-Five Years, 1897–2011,* and Associate Professor in the Criminal Justice Department of North Carolina Central University, telephone interview with author Grissom, on December 18, 2015.

47. Except where footnoted, all remaining information was drawn from personal and telephone interviews by Grissom with Corrine Perry and Eric Johnson, Chair of the Baha'i Local Spiritual Raleigh Assembly, Raleigh Baha'i Center on December 7, 2015, December 18, 2015, January 5, 2016, and January 13, 2016.

48. The Raleigh Baha'i Center, Accessed March 25, 2016. www.raleighbahai.org

49. *Ibid.*

50. Fredrick Landry, Harvey McMurray and Richard W. Thomas, *The Story of the Baha'i Black Men's Gathering: Celebrating Twenty-Five Years, 1987–2011* (Wilmette, IL: Baha'i Publishing Trust, 2011), 1.

51. *Ibid.* Back Cover.

52. *Ibid.*

53. Dr. Harvey McMurray, telephone interview by author Grissom, December 18, 2015.

54. "The First Master Guru Nanak (1469–1539)," Sikhs.org, Accessed April 5, 2016, http://www.sikhs.org/gurul.htm.

55. "The First Master Guru Nanak (1469–1539)," Sikhs.org, Accessed April 5, 2016.

56. Braswell, *Understanding World Religions,* 139.

57. "Introduction into Sikhism," Sikhs.org, Accessed April 5, 2016, http://www.sikhs.org/summary.htm.

58. *Ibid.*

59. Braswell, *Understanding World Religions,* 140.

60. "Who Are Sikhs? What Is Sikhism?" Sikh Net: Sharing the Sikh Experience, Accessed April 5, 2016, http://www.sikhnet.com/pages/who-are-sikhs-what-is-sikhism.

61. *Ibid.*

62. Mr. Kulpreet Singh, member of the Board of Trustees for the Sikh Gurudwara of North Carolina, Inc., interviewed by author Grissom, Durham, NC, January 2, 2016.

63. "Who Are Sikhs? What Is Sikhism?," Sikh Net: Sharing the Sikh Experience.

64. "North Carolina Gurudwaras," NCIndia.US, Accessed April 5, 2016, http://www.ncindia.us/.

65. Mr. Kulpreet Singh, interviewed by author Grissom, Durham, NC, January 2, 2016.

66. All remaining information provided by Mr. Kulpreet Singh, interviewed by author Grissom, Durham, NC; January 2, 2016, in person; January 20, 2016, by telephone.

About the Contributors

Jeff **Bach** is an associate professor of religious studies and Director of the Young Center at Elizabethtown College in Pennsylvania. He focuses his teaching and research on Anabaptists and Pietists, religious minorities that form their identities at society's margins. Ephrata Cloister's colonial history is an example. He earned his Ph.D. at Duke.

George W. **Braswell**, Jr., Ph.D., joined Southeastern Baptist Theological Seminary in 1974, retiring in 2004 as a distinguished professor emeritus. He was a senior professor of world religions at Campbell University and Founding Director of the George and Joan Braswell World Religions and Global Cultures Center. He served as a missionary and professor in Iran from 1967 to 1974.

Robert J. **Cain**, a Presbyterian elder, earned a Ph.D. in history from Duke and taught at Wake Forest and Acadia University. He was a researcher in London for the Colonial Records Project of the NC Department of Archives and History and retired as editor of *The Colonial Records of North Carolina* [Second Series]. He is a coauthor of *Presbyterians in North Carolina.*

Max L. **Carter** taught for forty-five years in Quaker secondary and college institutions, retiring in 2015 from Guilford College as the William R. Rogers Director of Friends Center and Quaker Studies. A recorded Friends minister, his seminary education was at Earlham School of Religion. He earned a Ph.D. in American religious history at Temple University.

Gary R. **Freeze** earned his Ph.D. at UNC–Chapel Hill. He is the William R. Weaver Professor of Humanities at Catawba College and periodically serves on the Historical Works Committee of the Evangelical Lutheran Church in America. He wrote *North Carolina: Land of Contrasts*, a middle school social studies textbook.

N. Brooks **Graebner** is rector emeritus of St. Matthew's Episcopal Church in Hillsborough and the historiographer of the Episcopal Diocese of North Carolina. He holds a Ph.D. from Duke and is a former Director and Officer of the Historical Society of the Episcopal Church. He has contributed to *Our State* as well as *27 Views of Hillsborough.*

Lisa Stover **Grissom** received her MDiv in biblical languages and preaching from Campbell University Divinity School, where, for three years, she served as the visiting scholar to the George W. and Joan O. Braswell World Religions and Global Cultures Center. Presently, she is pursuing her ThM in philosophy of religion at Southeastern Baptist Theological Seminary.

Lydia Huffman **Hoyle** is an associate professor of church history and Baptist heritage in the Campbell University Divinity School and an ordained minister. She holds a MDiv from Southwestern Baptist Theological Seminary and a Ph.D. from UNC–Chapel Hill. Her research interests include women in missions and ministry and children and mission education.

Daniel **Hutchinson** is an associate professor and chair of the History Department of Belmont Abbey College. He researches the history of the American South during the 20th century, focusing on World War II, the Civil Rights Movement, and Southern Catholicism. His essay is dedicated to the monks of Belmont Abbey and the Sisters of Mercy of Belmont.

W. Glenn **Jonas**, Jr., is the Charles Howard Professor of Religion and associate dean of the College of Arts and Sciences at Campbell University. He earned his Ph.D. at Baylor and has authored, co-authored, or edited six books, most recently *Nurturing the Vision: First Baptist Church, Raleigh (1812–2012)* and *A Cloud of Witnesses from the Heart of the City: First Presbyterian Church, Raleigh, 1816–2016.*

Thomas A. **Lehman**, a retired liberal arts college professor and assistant editor of journals, has lived among Mennonites on three continents and engaged in several kinds of Mennonite service and church life. Though North Carolina is a Mennonite backwater, he found a longer, richer Mennonite story in this state than he anticipated.

James Ingram **Martin**, Sr., is a professor of history at Campbell University with a Ph.D. from Emory. His research interests include social studies teaching and ethno-history, particularly the Jewish community of North Carolina. He serves as secretary-treasurer of the North Carolina Association of Historians and is actively involved with Phi Alpha Theta History Honor Society.

Sandy Dwayne **Martin** holds a Ph.D. in religion from Columbia University/Union Theological Seminary in New York. He is professor and head of Religion at the University of Georgia and has taught at the Interdenominational Theological Center, Spelman College, and the University of North Carolina at Wilmington. He writes on black religious history and is an associate pastor.

Michael **Perdue** researches Methodist history in his native Rockingham County. He earned degrees from Elon College and UNC–Greensboro. After teaching history in the NC Community College System, he joined the staff of the NC General Assembly and is secretary of the Historical Society of North Carolina. He has authored several church histories.

C. Riddick **Weber** teaches at Moravian Theological Seminary in Bethlehem, Pennsylvania. He studied North Carolina's 18th century Moravians at the University of Virginia. After leading college-age Moravians as a layperson, he served Moravian congregations in Winston-Salem and King and taught as an adjunct professor at Salem College.

H. Stanley **York** of Charlotte, North Carolina, is an ordained minister in the International Pentecostal Holiness Church and Director of the Cornerstone Conference Archives. He is a graduate of East Carolina University and holds a Ph.D. from Regent University in renewal church history. He published *George Floyd Taylor: The Life of an Early Southern Pentecostal Leader* in 2013.

Index